JDBC Recipes

A Problem-Solution Approach

Mahmoud Parsian

Apress®

JDBC Recipes: A Problem-Solution Approach

Copyright © 2005 by Mahmoud Parsian

ISBN: 1-4302-1199-7

Lead Editor: Steve Anglin
Development Editor: Jim Sumser
Technical Reviewer: Sumit Pal
Editorial Board: Steve Anglin, Dan Appleman, Ewan Buckingham, Gary Cornell, Tony Davis, Jason Gilmore, Jonathan Hassell, Chris Mills, Dominic Shakeshaft, Jim Sumser
Associate Publisher: Grace Wong
Project Manager: Beckie Stones
Copy Edit Manager: Nicole LeClerc
Copy Editor: Kim Wimpsett
Assistant Production Director: Kari Brooks-Copony
Production Editor: Katie Stence
Compositor and Artist: Kinetic Publishing Services, LLC
Proofreaders: Liz Welch and Lori Bring
Indexer: Tim Tate

Manufacturing Director: Tom Debolski

Distributed to the book trade worldwide by Springer-Verlag New York, Inc., 233 Spring Street, 6th Floor, New York, NY 10013. Phone 1-800-SPRINGER, fax 201-348-4505, e-mail orders-ny@springer-sbm.com, or visit http://www.springeronline.com.

For information on translations, please contact Apress directly at 2560 Ninth Street, Suite 219, Berkeley, CA 94710. Phone 510-549-5930, fax 510-549-5939, e-mail info@apress.com, or visit http://www.apress.com.

The source code for this book is available to readers at http://www.apress.com in the Source Code section.

This book is dedicated to
my love, Behnaz;
my gozal daughter, Maral;
my gibldiz son, Yaseen;
my mother, Monireh, and the memory of my father, Bagher.

Contents at a Glance

Contents

■CHAPTER 3 **Making Database Connections** 87

About the Author

DR. MAHMOUD PARSIAN is a Sun-certified Java programmer and a senior lead software engineer at Ask Jeeves (`http://www.ask.com`). He received his doctorate degree in computer science from Iowa State University and has been working in the software industry for more than 20 years. Mahmoud's expertise is in Java technology, JDBC, database design/development, and server-side Java programming. Mahmoud's current project is MyJeeves (`http://myjeeves.ask.com`).

Mahmoud's honors include the following:

- Ask Jeeves Bright Star Award, Ask Jeeves; November 2004

- Octopus Award, Octopus.com; July 2001

- Cisco Systems Leadership Award, Cisco Systems; June 2000

- Individual Achievement Award, Cisco Systems; July 2000

- Winner of the Circle of Excellence Award; Digital Equipment Corporation, 1991

- Five-time winner of the Specialist of the Quarter Award; Digital Equipment Corporation, 1990–94

You can contact Mahmoud at `admin@jdbccookbook.com`.

About the Technical Reviewer

 **SUMIT PAL** is a Java and J2EE technical architect. He has more than 12 years of experience in software development and has worked for Microsoft and Oracle as a full-time employee. He has a master's degree in computer science.

Sumit loves to swim and play badminton and now loves to crawl with his baby daughter.

Acknowledgments

I'd like to thank my wife, Behnaz; my daughter, Maral; and my son, Yaseen. They all have had to put up with many lost family evenings and weekends. Without their love and support I could never have finished this book.

I'd also like to thank my dear friend and teacher, Dr. Ramachandran Krishnaswamy. He taught me the fundamentals of computer science and showed me how to be a "good" teacher.

In addition, I'd like to thank a few special individuals at Apress:

- First, I owe a huge debt of gratitude to Steve Anglin, the lead editor of this book. Steve believed in my book project and provided tremendous support for writing this book. Thank you, Steve.

- Jim Sumser, development editor, provided great support and help for writing this book, and when things were not rosy, he gave me moral support and encouragement, which I appreciate a lot. Jim's input on structuring this book was great. Thank you, Jim.

- I thank my technical reviewer, Sumit Pal, for his great job in reviewing the whole book. Sumit's critical questioning kept me on the right path. I value his input and objectivity. Sumit's atten-

- I deeply thank Beckie Stones, project manager, for this book. Beckie's outstanding work and caring attitude were always refreshing and rejuvenating. She was well organized and helped me tremendously in many ways. I owe you a hearty thanks!

- I thank Kim Wimpsett, copy editor, for her outstanding editing skills and her understanding of my JDBC code. Her contributions have greatly improved the accuracy, readability, and value of this book.

- I'll also take this opportunity to thank many other fine people at Apress: Dan Appleman, Ewan Buckingham, Gary Cornell, Tony Davis, Jason Gilmore, Jonathan Hassell, Chris Mills, Dominic Shakeshaft, Grace Wong, Nicole LeClerc, Kari Brooks-Copony, Katie Stence, Tim Tate, Kurt Krames, and Tom Debolski.

I'd also like to thank my "octopus" colleagues: Tuoc Luong, Tony Xue, Chih-Ming Shih, Nick Tran, Peter Zhang, and Annette Truong.

Last, but not least, I thank my sister, Nayer Azam Parsian, and my brother, Dr. Ahmad Parsian, for their support and just being there for me.

Introduction

This book provides complete and working solutions for performing database tasks using JDBC. You can cut and paste solutions from this book to build your own JDBC database applications. All the solutions have been compiled and tested against two leading databases: MySQL and Oracle. This book is ideal for anyone who knows some Java (can read/write basic Java programs) and a little JDBC (can read/write basic queries using JDBC and SQL) and wants to learn more about JDBC. Each section of this book is a complete recipe (including the database setup, the solution, and the MySQL and Oracle solutions), so you can use the code directly in your projects (although sometimes you may need to cut and paste the sections you need).

What Is in This Book?

This book provides solid guidelines for using JDBC to solve tough problems, such as how to load your pictures (binary data) into an Oracle/MySQL database and how to retrieve your pictures from the database as a URL. Most of the solutions presented in this book have been used and tested in real-world database applications. In fact, I have designed and developed all the JDBC code for MyJeeves

What Is the Focus of This Book?

According to Sun (http://java.sun.com/jdbc), the creator of JDBC, the JDBC API contains two major sets of interfaces:

- The first is the JDBC API for application writers.

- The second is the lower-level JDBC driver API for driver writers.

This book focuses on the JDBC API for application writers.

What This Book Is Not

This is not a book to learn Java programming language and the basics of object-oriented programming. I am assuming you know the basics of Java, SQL, and object-oriented programming.

What Is the Structure of This Book?

This book is filled with recipes: it asks real questions and provides real, compiled working answers. You can use Java/JDBC to access many kinds of relational (and possibly nonrelational) database management systems (such as Oracle, MySQL, DB2, SQL Server, and Access, to mention a few).

The goal of this book is to provide step-by-step instructions for using JDBC with two popular relational databases: Oracle and MySQL. I selected these two databases for the following reasons:

- Oracle is the de facto standard for commercial database applications of major companies.

- MySQL is a high-speed, open-source relational database (you can even use a debugger to debug your JDBC method calls).

For every problem raised, you'll see two solutions: one expressed using the Oracle database and the other one using MySQL.

What Does JDBC Do?

In a nutshell, JDBC is a Java API for executing SQL statements (such as querying a database, inserting new records, creating a table, and so on). JDBC makes it possible to perform three tasks:

- Establish a connection with a relational database.

- Using the database connection, send SQL statements (such as a select, insert, update, metadata request, and so on) and result sets.

- Process the result sets (retrieved from database).

JDBC allows Java programs (applets and applications) to communicate with relational databases (so-called SQL databases) easily and efficiently. JDBC consists of classes in the package java.sql and some JDBC extensions in the package javax.sql. Both of these packages are included in the Java 2 Standard Edition (J2SE) version 1.5 (which covers JDBC 3.0).

This book is for software engineers and database application developers who know the basics of Java and JDBC. I also assume you know the basics of the Java programming language (writing a class, defining a new class from an existing class, using basic control structures such as while-loop, if-then-else, and so on). Also, I assume you have a basic understanding of relational database concepts and SQL. Like in any Apress problem-solution book, you are encouraged to use the solutions for your own database applications and as a launching pad for discovering new database solutions using Java/JDBC technology. You can also customize these solutions/recipes as you apply them to a particular problem.

What Software Is Used in This Book?

When developing solutions and examples for this book, I used the following software and programming environments:

- Relational databases:

  - Oracle 8*i* Enterprise Edition Release 8.1.7.0.0 (from http://www.oracle.com)

  - Oracle 9*i* Enterprise Edition Release 9.2.0.1.0 (from http://www.oracle.com)

  - Oracle 10*g* Release 10.1.0.2.0 (from http://www.oracle.com)

  - MySQL 4.0 (from http://www.mysql.com)

  - MySQL 4.1.7 (from http://www.mysql.com)

- Programming languages:

    - Java programming language, J2SE 1.4.2 (from http://java.sun.com)

    - Java programming language, J2SE 5.0 (from http://java.sun.com)

- Operating systems:

    - Linux Enterprise Edition (from http://www.redhat.com)

    - Windows XP Professional (from http://www.microsoft.com)

- Web servers:

    - Tomcat (http://jakarta.apache.org/tomcat/)

All programs in this book were tested with J2SE 1.4.2 and J2SE 5.0 (from http://java.sun.com/). Examples are given in mixed operating system environments (Linux and Windows XP Professional). For all examples and solutions, I developed them using basic text editors (such as Notepad from Microsoft, TextPad from http://www.textpad.com, and vi in Linux) and compiled them using the Java command-line compiler (javac).

Comments and Questions for This Book?

I am always interested in your feedback and comments regarding the problems and solutions described in this book. Please e-mail comments and questions for this book to admin@jdbccookbook.com. You

Mahmoud Parsian

CHAPTER 1

■ ■ ■

Introducing JDBC

This chapter defines some key terms for the remaining chapters. JDBC is a platform-independent interface between relational databases and Java. In today's Java world, JDBC is a standard application programming interface (API) for accessing enterprise data in relational databases (such as Oracle, MySQL, Sybase, and DB2) using Structured Query Language (SQL).

In this chapter, I will introduce all aspects of JDBC, and then you will learn about the more specific ins and outs of JDBC in the following chapters. Data (or information) is at the heart of most business applications, and JDBC deals with data stored and manipulated in relational database systems.

This book takes an examples-based approach to describing the features and functionalities available in JDBC. Whether you are a new or an experienced database/JDBC developer, you should find the examples and accompanying text a valuable and accessible knowledge base for creating your own database solutions.

to Sun Microsystems, JDBC is *not* an acronym (but most Java engineers believe JDBC stands for Java Database Connectivity).

In this book, I will use some basic Java/JDBC utility classes (such as the `DatabaseUtil` class), which are available for download from the book's Web site. The `DatabaseUtil` class provides methods for closing JDBC objects (such as `Connection`, `ResultSet`, `Statement`, and `PreparedStatement`). `VeryBasicConnectionManager` is a simple class that provides `Connection` objects for Oracle and MySQL by using `getConnection(dbVendor)`. In real production applications, the `VeryBasicConnectionManager` class is not an acceptable solution and should be replaced by a *connection pool manager* (such as the `commons-dbcp` package from `http://jakarta.apache.org/commons/dbcp/` or Excalibur from `http://excalibur.apache.org/`). I will use these classes to demonstrate JDBC concepts for different vendors such as Oracle and MySQL. (*Connection pooling* is a technique used for reusing and sharing `Connection` objects among requesting clients.)

1-1. What Is JDBC?

JDBC is a set of programming APIs that allows easy connection to a wide range of databases (especially relational databases) through Java programs. In Java 2 Platform, Standard Edition (J2SE) 5.0, the JDBC API is defined by two packages:

> `java.sql` provides the API for accessing and processing data stored in a data source (usually a relational database) using the Java programming language. This package provides the foundation and most commonly used objects (such as `Connection`, `ResultSet`, `Statement`, and `PreparedStatement`). This package may be used in J2SE and Java 2 Platform, Enterprise Edition (J2EE) environments.

`javax.sql` provides the API for server-side data source access and processing from the Java programming language. According to the Java Development Kit (JDK) documentation, "this package supplements the `java.sql` package and, as of the version 1.4 release, is included in the JDK. It remains an essential part of [J2EE]." This package provides services for J2EE (such as `DataSource` and `RowSet`).

JDBC (`http://java.sun.com/products/jdbc/`) is Sun Microsystems' attempt to create a platform-neutral interface between relational databases and Java. According to Sun Microsystems, "JDBC technology is an API that lets you access virtually any tabular data source from the Java programming language. It provides cross-DBMS connectivity to a wide range of SQL databases, and now, with the new JDBC API, it also provides access to other tabular data sources, such as spreadsheets or flat files."

More specifically, JDBC is a low-level, simple (has a well-defined API), and portable (since Java is portable across platforms) SQL call-level interface (CLI) written in Java. JDBC is an industry-standard SQL database access interface, providing consistent and uniform access to a wide range of relational databases (such as Oracle, MySQL, DB2, Sybase, Microsoft SQL Server 2000, Microsoft Access, and so on). It also provides a common base on which higher-level tools and interfaces can be built. JDBC has a support mechanism for the *ODBC bridge*. The ODBC bridge is a library that implements JDBC in terms of the ODBC-standard C API.

In today's programming world, JDBC is *the* standard for communication between a Java application and a relational database. The JDBC API is released in two versions, JDBC version 1.2 (released with JDK 1.1.*x* in the package `java.sql`) and version 2.0 (released with Java platform 2 in the packages `java.sql` and `javax.sql`—now both of these packages are included in J2SE 1.4). JDBC is simple and powerful because it is a database-independent way of manipulating data from any relational database. JDBC version 1.3 is the latest from Sun Microsystems and is included in JDK 1.5.

objects (such as `ResultSet`) that represent the results of your query. JDBC is designed in a simple way, so most database programmers need to learn only a few methods to do most of what database programmers need to do to accomplish database programming tasks.

Figure 1-1 shows how a database application uses JDBC to interact with one or more databases.

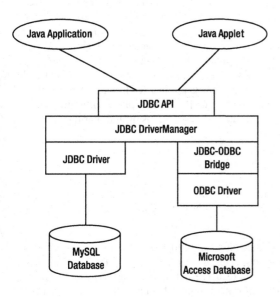

Figure 1-1. *Java database application using JDBC*

In this section, I presented the basic outline of the JDBC architecture. JDBC's DriverManager class provides the basic service for managing a set of JDBC drivers. I will talk about these classes and interfaces in detail in section 1-10.

1-2. What Is JDBC's High-Level Architecture?

Figure 1-2 illustrates a high-level architecture of JDBC. You can use JDBC from your Java programs (applications, applets, servlets, and JavaServer Pages).

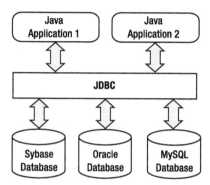

Figure 1-2. *JDBC's high-level architecture*

(such as employee records) from databases and to write data (such as inserting new employee records) back to the databases. With JDBC, though, you can do more than reading/writing records. You can even read the metadata about tables, views, and other useful objects (such as stored procedures and indexes) in databases. For example, using JDBC's DatabaseMetadata, you can find out the name and number of columns for a given table and their associated data types. This information is useful in developing graphical user interface (GUI)–based applications.

According to Sun Microsystems, the JDBC API contains two major sets of interfaces:

- The first is the JDBC API for application writers.

- The second is the lower-level JDBC driver API for driver writers. (For details on JDBC technology drivers, please visit http://java.sun.com/products/jdbc/overview.html.)

The focus in this book is on the JDBC API for application writers.

1-3. What Is JDBC's Detailed Architecture?

Figure 1-3 illustrates a detailed architecture of JDBC.

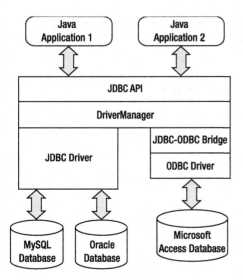

Figure 1-3. *JDBC's detailed architecture*

The JDBC API does most of the things through the DriverManager class (java.sql.DriverManager). What is DriverManager? It is a connection factory class. In fact, DriverManager is the only class that

as Oracle, MySQL, and Sybase) provides a set of drivers.

If you refer to JDBC's architecture (Figure 1-3), you can observe the following facts:

- Java code calls a JDBC library (using the java.sql and javx.sql packages).

- JDBC loads a driver; for example, an Oracle driver is loaded using the following code snippet:

  ```
  Class.forName("oracle.jdbc.driver.OracleDriver")
  ```

- Calling Class.forName() automatically creates an instance of the driver and registers the driver with the DriverManager class.

- The driver talks to a particular database such as Oracle or MySQL.

Note that you can have more than one driver and therefore more than one database.

Figure 1-4 illustrates how a Java application uses JDBC to interact with one or more relational databases (such as Oracle and MySQL) without knowing about the underlying JDBC driver implementations. Figure 1-4 exposes the core JDBC classes/interfaces that interact with Java/JDBC applications.

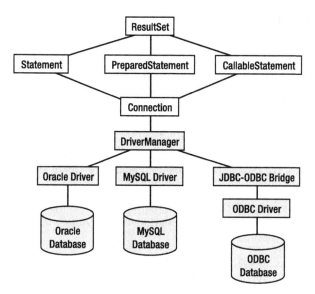

Figure 1-4. *Java application using JDBC components*

Who provides these JDBC drivers? Usually, a database vendor (such as MySQL, Oracle, Sybase,

Following the JDBC architecture, a Java database application uses the DriverManager class to get the java.sql.Connection object, which represents a database connection. Then, using a Connection object, you can create Statement/PreparedStatement/CallableStatement, which can execute SQL queries and stored procedures and return results as ResultSet objects. (ResultSet is a table of data representing a database result set, which is usually generated by executing a statement that queries the database.)

The JDBC API is comprised of two Java packages: java.sql and javax.sql. The following are core JDBC classes, interfaces, and exceptions in the java.sql package:

- DriverManager: This class loads JDBC drivers in memory. You can also use it to create java.sql. Connection objects to data sources (such as Oracle, MySQL, and so on).

- Connection: This interface represents a connection with a data source. You can use the Connection object for creating Statement, PreparedStatement, and CallableStatement objects.

- Statement: This interface represents a static SQL statement. You can use it to retrieve ResultSet objects.

- PreparedStatement: This interface extends Statement and represents a precompiled SQL statement. You can use it to retrieve ResultSet objects.

- CallableStatement: This interface represents a database stored procedure. You can use it to execute stored procedures in a database server.

- ResultSet: This interface represents a database result set generated by using SQL's SELECT statement.

- SQLException: This class is an exception class that provides information on a database access error or other errors.

1-4. What Is a Relational Database?

What is a database? What is a relational database? A *database* is a system to store, retrieve, and organize information. A telephone yellow pages is a database, which stores names and business names and their associated phone numbers. A *database management system* (DBMS) is a computer application that enables a user to store, manage, and retrieve data. If you store your addresses and phone numbers online, you can consider the file where you store the information a database.

Dr. E. F. Codd invented the relational database at IBM in 1970. (Codd passed away on April 18, 2003.) The term *relational database* has many definitions. I will mention two of them here:

- A relational database is a finite set of data items organized as a set of formally described tables from which data can be accessed or reassembled in many different ways without having to reorganize the database tables.

- A relational database management system (RDBMS) is a persistent system that organizes data into related rows and columns as specified by the relational model. MySQL, Oracle, and Microsoft SQL Server are examples of RDBMSs.

Examples of relational databases are Oracle, MySQL, Sybase, Microsoft SQL Server 2000, Microsoft Access, DB2, and so on. The major purpose of JDBC is to access/update relational databases. The standard user and application program interface to a relational database is SQL. SQL statements are used both for retrieving information from a relational database by using interactive queries and for retrieving data for reports.

You can assume the following for a relational database:

- A database is essentially a container/repository for tables, views, and stored procedures.

- A *row*/*record* is a container comprised of columns.

- A *column* is a single data item having a name, type, and value.

- A database stores all its data inside tables, with nothing else. All operations on data take place on the tables themselves or produce additional tables as the result.

1-5. What Is ODBC?

Open Database Connectivity (ODBC) is a programming interface from Microsoft that provides a common language for Windows applications to access databases on a network. ODBC is a C-based interface to SQL-based database systems. It provides a consistent interface for communicating with a database and for accessing database metadata (information about the database system vendor and how the tables, views, and data are stored).

A client can connect to a database and manipulate it in a standard way. ODBC began as a PC standard, and it has nearly become an industry standard. Vendors provide specific drivers or *bridges* (the so-called ODBC bridge) to their particular database management system. For example, to access an ODBC-based database from a Java client, you may use a JDBC-ODBC bridge developed by Sun Microsystems and Merant (now Serena Software). (For details, see http://java.sun.com/j2se/1.5.0/docs/guide/jdbc/getstart/bridge.doc.html.) Therefore, you can use the JDBC-ODBC bridge to access databases that support ODBC; for example, you can use the JDBC-ODBC bridge to access Microsoft Access databases.

According to Microsoft's ODBC Programmer's Reference (http://msdn.microsoft.com/library/), the ODBC architecture has four components:

- *Application*: Performs processing and calls ODBC functions to submit SQL statements and retrieve results.

- *Driver manager*: Loads and unloads drivers on behalf of an application. Processes ODBC function calls or passes them to a driver.

- *Driver*: Processes ODBC function calls, submits SQL requests to a specific data source, and returns results to the application. If necessary, the driver modifies an application's request so that the request conforms to syntax supported by the associated DBMS.

- *Data source*: Consists of the data the user wants to access and its associated operating system, DBMS, and network platform (if any) used to access the DBMS.

Figure 1-5 shows an ODBC architecture and the relationship between these four components.

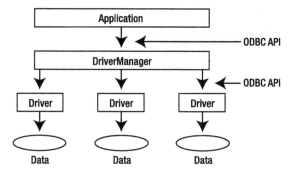

Figure 1-5. *ODBC architecture*

ODBC is a set of function calls based on the SQL Access Group (SAG) function set for utilizing a SQL database system (back-end system). The SAG set implements the basic functionality of Dynamic SQL. Embedded SQL commands can be translated to call ODBC. With ODBC, Microsoft extended the basic SAG function set to include functions for accessing the database catalog and for controlling and determining the capabilities of ODBC drivers and their data sources (back ends). Microsoft also has refined and fleshed out the SAG proposal. Microsoft supplies the ODBC driver manager for its operating systems (Windows, Windows 95, and Windows NT). The ODBC driver manager coordinates access to ODBC drivers and their associated data sources.

Although SQL is well suited for manipulating databases, it was not designed to be a general application language; rather, it was intended to be used only as a means of communicating with databases. Unfortunately, you cannot easily write a program that will run on multiple platforms, even though the database connectivity standardization issue has been largely resolved. For example, if you wrote a database client in C++, you might have to totally rewrite the client for another platform; that is, your PC version would not run on a Macintosh. There are two reasons for this. First, C++ as a language is not portable because C++ is not completely specified (for example, how many bits does an "int" data type hold?). Second, and more important, support libraries such as network access and GUI frameworks are different on each platform. Another problem with ODBC is that its interface is complicated and takes time to learn to use well. JDBC eliminated these problems and introduced a platform-independent solution to relational database access.

Because of its poor performance and lack of transaction support, the JDBC-ODBC bridge driver is recommended only for experimental use or when no other alternative is available.

1-6. What Is a JDBC-ODBC Bridge?

In a nutshell, the JDBC-ODBC bridge provides JDBC access via most ODBC drivers. The JDBC-ODBC bridge package is the interface between JDBC and ODBC. The JDBC-ODBC bridge—a joint development of Merant (now Serena Software) and Sun Microsystems—is a JDBC driver that implements JDBC operations by translating them into ODBC operations. (ODBC operations are implemented in C-based libraries—the ODBC functionality remains in binary code libraries; if your database or hardware platform changes, you will need to replace the ODBC libraries.) The JDBC-ODBC bridge implements JDBC for any database for which an ODBC driver is available. The bridge is implemented as the sun.jdbc.odbc Java package and contains a native library used to access ODBC. The sun.jdbc.odbc package is defined in the <jdk1.4-installation-directory>/jre/lib/rt.jar file, which contains the sun.jdbc.odbc.JdbcOdbcDriver class (which is a required class for loading the JDBC driver).

Not that the JDBC-ODBC bridge is a "one-size-fits-all" approach. Since it is designed to work with any database that supports ODBC, it may be slower than other JDBC drivers that are designed to take advantage of protocols specific to an individual database. The JDBC-ODBC bridge implements a "level-one" type of JDBC driver that links to a driver manager (the libodbc.so.1 and libodbcinst.so.1 files) to communicate with a database-specific ODBC driver. The JDBC-ODBC bridge is comprised of two packages (that list the classes and interfaces):

- sun.jdbc.odbc provides JdbcOdbcDriver for loading the JDBC-ODBC bridge driver.

- sun.jdbc.odbc.ee provides implementations of javax.sql.DataSource and javax.sql.ConnectionPoolDataSource.

For details on these packages, refer to http://java.sun.com/j2se/1.5.0/docs/guide/jdbc/bridge.html.

Figure 1-6 shows a JDBC-ODBC bridge architecture.

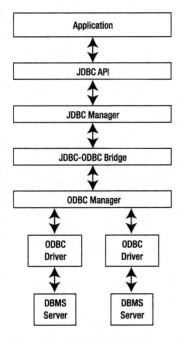

Figure 1-6. *JDBC-ODBC bridge architecture*

The JDBC-ODBC bridge currently targets straightforward, simple applications. It is not meant for complex applications with many threads and functional components and with complex program logic during execution.

Is the JDBC-ODBC bridge driver recommended for commercial applications? According to Sun Microsystems, "the JDBC-ODBC bridge driver is recommended only for experimental use or when no other alternative is available." (For details, see http://java.sun.com/j2se/1.3/docs/guide/jdbc/getstart/bridge.doc.html.)

Where can you get the JDBC-ODBC bridge? The JDBC-ODBC bridge is bundled with the Java 2 SDK, Standard Edition, so there is no need to download it separately. (The JDBC-ODBC driver class sun.jdbc.odbc.JdbcOdbcDriver is included in the Java 2 SDK.)

How fast is the JDBC-ODBC bridge? The JDBC-ODBC bridge is not as fast as commercial JDBC drivers (such as Oracle and MySQL).

Is the JDBC-ODBC bridge multithreaded? No. The JDBC-ODBC bridge does not support concurrent access from different threads. The JDBC-ODBC bridge uses synchronized methods to serialize all the calls it makes to the ODBC layer (written in the C programming language). Multithreaded Java programs may use the JDBC-ODBC bridge, but they will not get the advantages of multithreading.

Does the JDBC-ODBC bridge support multiple concurrent open statements per database connection? No. You can open only one Statement object per Connection object when you are using the JDBC-ODBC bridge.

Does the JDBC-ODBC bridge support all data types? No. It does not support all data types. (For Blob and Clob

Using the JDBC-ODBC Bridge

You can use the JDBC-ODBC bridge by opening a JDBC connection using a database uniform resource locator (URL) with the odbc subprotocol. The subprotocol odbc is a special case that has been reserved for database URLs that specify ODBC-style data source names and has the special feature of allowing any number of attribute values to be specified after the subname (the data source name). The full syntax for the odbc subprotocol is as follows:

```
jdbc:odbc:<data-source-name>[;<attribute-name>=<attribute-value>]*
```

The following are valid jdbc:odbc names:

- Valid URL without username/password: jdbc:odbc:employees

- Valid URL without username/password and additional attributes:
  jdbc:odbc:caspian;CacheSize=10;ExtensionCase=LOWER

- Valid URL with username/password: jdbc:odbc:payroll;UID=alex;PWD=mypassword

Before you can establish a connection, you must load the bridge driver class, sun.jdbc.odbc.JdbcOdbcDriver. You can load a class in two ways.

First, you can add the class name to the java.lang.System property named jdbc.drivers:

```
String JDBC_DRIVERS_KEY = "jdbc.drivers";
String existingDrivers = System.getProperty(JDBC_DRIVERS_KEY);
if (existingDrivers == null) {
  // sets the system property indicated by the specified key.
  System.setProperty(JDBC_DRIVERS_KEY, "sun.jdbc.odbc.JdbcOdbcDriver");
}
```

```
else {
    String newDrivers = existingDrivers + ":" +
                        "sun.jdbc.odbc.JdbcOdbcDriver";
    System.setProperty(JDBC_DRIVERS_KEY, newDrivers);
}
```

Alternatively, the class must be explicitly loaded using the Java class loader. You can perform explicit class loading using the following code:

```
Class.forName("sun.jdbc.odbc.JdbcOdbcDriver");
```

When a class is loaded, the ODBC driver creates an instance of itself and registers this with the JDBC driver manager.

Example of Using the sun.jdbc.odbc Package

To use a JDBC-ODBC bridge to access a database, you need to follow these steps:

1. Create a database, or use an existing database.

2. Register the database.

3. Create a simple JDBC program.

4. Run the simple JDBC program.

After I cover these steps in the following sections, I will discuss the JDBC program in detail.

northwind in a Windows XP environment.

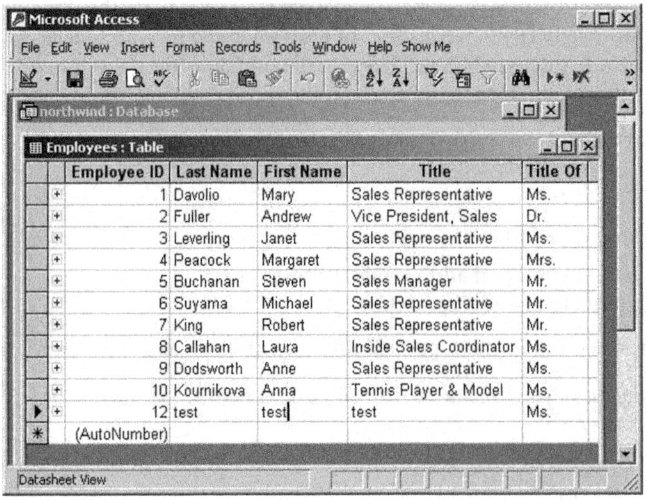

Figure 1-7. *Data source definition in a Windows XP environment*

Step 2: Registering the Database

Use the Microsoft ODBC Data Source Administrator to register your database, as shown in Figure 1-8. (For details, please see http://www.simongibson.com/intranet/odbc/ or http://www.cicorp.com/data/odbc/.)

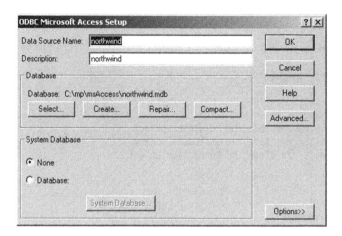

Figure 1-8. *Using the Microsoft ODBC Data Source Administrator*

The following listing shows a simple JDBC program; I have added line numbers for discussion purposes.

```
1.import java.sql.DriverManager;
2.import java.sql.Connection;
3.import java.sql.Statement;
4.import java.sql.ResultSet;
5.import jcb.util.DatabaseUtil;
6.
7. public class Test_JDBC_ODBC {
8.    public static Connection getConnection() throws Exception {
9.        String driver = "sun.jdbc.odbc.JdbcOdbcDriver";
10.       String url = "jdbc:odbc:northwind";
11.       String username = "";
12.       String password = "";
13.       Class.forName(driver);    // load JDBC-ODBC driver
14.       return DriverManager.getConnection(url, username, password);
15.  }
16.
17.   public static void main(String args[]) {
18.       Connection conn = null;
19.       Statement stmt = null;
20.       ResultSet rs = null;
21        try {
22.           conn = getConnection();
23.           stmt = conn.createStatement();
24            String query =
```

```
25              "select EmployeeID, LastName, FirstName from Employees";
26.             rs = stmt.executeQuery(query);.
27.             while(rs.next()){
28.                System.out.println(rs.getString("EmployeeID")+
29.                     "-"+ rs.getString("LastName")+
30.                     "-"+ rs.getString("FirstName"));
31.             }
32.          }
33.          catch (Exception e){
34.             // handle the exception
35.             e.printStackTrace();
36.             System.err.println(e.getMessage());
37.          }
38.          finally {
39.             // release database resources
40.             DatabaseUtil.close(rs);      // close the ResultSet object
41.             DatabaseUtil.close(stmt);    // close the Statement object
42.             DatabaseUtil.close(conn);    // close the Connection object
43.          }
44.    }
```

Step 4: Running the Simple JDBC Program

The next step is to run the simple program:

```
$ javac Test_JDBC_ODBC.java$ java Test_JDBC_ODBC
1.-Davolio-Mary


4.-Peacock-Margaret
5.-Buchanan-Steven
6.-Suyama-Michael
7.-King-Robert
8.-Callahan-Laura
9.-Dodsworth-Anne
10.-Kournikova-Anna
11.-test-test
```

Breaking the Simple JDBC Program Down

I will now break this program down and discuss the importance of each line:

Lines 1–5: These lines import the required classes and interfaces from the java.sql package.

Lines 8–15: The getConnection() method loads the proper driver for the database I intend to use. In this case, I used Microsoft Access to create the database, which uses ODBC. To handle ODBC databases, a JDBC-ODBC bridge acts as the driver. I am using the method Class.forName() to load the driver. This method gets a Connection object from the DriverManager class. All interactions with the database happen through this Connection object.

Lines 22–26: These lines generate a SQL query and retrieve data from the database. First, I get a Connection object and then get a Statement object from the Connection object. A Statement object is basically used to perform a single SQL statement. In this case, I used the executeQuery() method to execute the simple SELECT statement shown.

Lines 27–30: The ResultSet object contains the retrieved data from the database. A ResultSet is a container that holds the results of the query. A ResultSet works as an iterator, as shown in the code.

Lines 33–37: This is the place to catch the JDBC errors and handle them properly.

Lines 38–43: These lines close all the database resources. In most cases, if you close a database resource, all of its dependent resources will close with it. (For example, closing a connection will close any statements issued from it, which will close any ResultSet objects obtained from them.) From a good software engineering point of view, you should put close() statements in a finally clause, because the Java virtual machine (JVM) guarantees that the statements in the finally clause will be executed as the last step regardless of whether an exception has happened.

Debugging Supported by the Bridge

The bridge provides extensive tracing when DriverManager tracing is enabled. The following line of code enables tracing and sends it to standard out:

```
java.sql.DriverManager.setLogStream(java.lang.System.out);
```

When using the DriverManager.setLogStream() method, you may direct the tracing output to any java.io.PrintStream object.

New JDBC 2.0 API Features Supported by the Bridge

According to Sun Microsystems (http://java.sun.com/j2se/1.4.2/docs/guide/jdbc/getstart/bridge.doc.html), the JDBC-ODBC bridge driver supports the following new features in the JDBC 2.0 API: batch updates; updatable result sets; scrollable result sets; the new BigDecimal methods; the new Date, Time, and Timestamp methods, and multithreaded ODBC drivers.

As noted, the JDBC-ODBC bridge allows Java applications to use the JDBC API with many existing ODBC drivers. The bridge is itself a driver based on JDBC technology (a *JDBC driver*) that is defined in the class sun.jdbc.odbc.JdbcOdbcDriver. The bridge defines the JDBC subprotocol odbc. For details, refer to http://java.sun.com/j2se/1.5.0/docs/guide/jdbc/getstart/bridge.html.

1-7. What Is SQL?

SQL (pronounced "sea-quill") is a standardized database language for creating, manipulating, examining, and managing relational databases (such as Oracle, Sybase, DB2, and MySQL). This book will not extensively explain SQL, although it will provide basic SQL concepts. Specifically, SQL is a keyword-based language. Each statement begins with a unique keyword. SQL statements consist of clauses, which begin with a keyword. SQL syntax is not case-sensitive.

IBM (and Dr. E. F. Codd) originally created SQL in the mid-1970s, but many vendors have since developed dialects of SQL. In the 1980s, the American National Standards Institute (ANSI) started developing a relational database language standard. ANSI and the International Organization for Standardization (ISO) published SQL standards in 1986 and 1987, respectively. ANSI and ISO jointly worked on an extension to the standard called SQL2 (or SQL-92 or SQL/92). A SQL3 effort is underway to enhance relational capabilities and add support for object-oriented features. The SQL3 standard provides new features, such as allowing you to define new data types (so a column can reference a record type by itself).

SQL is a Data Manipulation Language (DML—the set of SQL commands affecting the content of database objects) and a Data Definition Language (DDL—the set of SQL commands affecting the structure of database objects). SQL also provides commands for controlling transactions (such as commit and rollback). Table 1-1 shows some DML commands, Table 1-2 shows some DDL commands, and Table 1-3 shows some transaction commands.

Table 1-1. *Partial Data Manipulation Language Commands*

SQL Command	Semantics
SELECT	Retrieves data from the database
INSERT	Inserts new rows into a table
UPDATE	Updates existing rows in a table
DELETE	Deletes existing rows from a table

Table 1-2. *Partial Data Definition Language Commands*

SQL Command	Semantics
CREATE	Creates a new database object
DROP	Drops an existing database object
ALTER	Modifies the structure of a database object
GRANT	Grants privileges on tables and views to other users
REVOKE	Revokes privileges on tables and views from other users

Table 1-3. *Partial Transaction Commands*

ROLLBACK statement	Rolls back the current transaction

SQL *statements* perform tasks such as reading data from a database, updating data on a database, or deleting data from a database. A relational database system (such as Oracle or MySQL) contains one or more objects called *tables* (a table is a two-dimensional table with rows and columns). The data for the database is stored in these tables. Tables are uniquely identified by their names and are comprised of columns and rows. Columns contain the column name, data type, and any other attributes for the column (such as security and privileges). Rows contain the records or data for the columns. Table 1-4 shows a sample table called MyEmployees.

Table 1-4. MyEmployees *Table*

Id	firstName	lastName	title	salary
60	Bill	Russel	CTO	980000
70	Alex	Baldwin	Software Engineer	88000
40	Alex	Taylor	Hardware Engineer	90000
50	Jane	Shakian	Manager	88000
30	Mary	Keys	CEO	100000
10	Alex	Smith	Software Engineer	78000
20	Bob	Sundance	Manager	85000

As you may observe, Table 1-4 has five columns (Id, firstName, lastName, title, and salary) and seven rows/records.

The following code listings show how to use SQL to do common tasks. Specifically, the following code shows how to create a table using SQL:

```
CREATE TABLE employees (
    badgeNumber  varchar(10),
    lastName  varchar(32),
    firstName  varchar(32),
    dept  varchar(10)
);
```

The following code shows how to retrieve data:

```
SELECT badgeNumber, lastName FROM employees;
```

The following code shows how to insert data:

```
INSERT INTO employees(badgeNumber, lastName, firstName)
    VALUES ('12345', 'Smith', 'Alex');
```

The following code shows how to update data:

```
UPDATE employees SET firstName='Alex Jr'
    WHERE badgeNumber='12345';
```

1-8. What Is JDBC Programming?

1. Import the required packages.

2. Register the JDBC drivers.

3. Open a connection to a database.

4. Create a Statement object.

5. Execute a query and return a ResultSet object.

6. Process the ResultSet object.

7. Close the ResultSet and Statement objects.

8. Close the connection.

The first hands-on experience with JDBC in this book involves a basic example to illustrate the overall concepts related to creating and accessing data in a database. The following sections describe in detail the steps involved in writing a database application.

Step 1: Creating a Database

Database creation is DBMS-specific. This means each vendor has a specific set of commands for creating a database. For this obvious reason, database creation commands are not portable. (This is the main reason JDBC has stayed away from creating database commands.)

You can create a database using the command line or tools supplied by the database vendor or using SQL statements fed to the database from a Java program; this task is normally carried out by a database administrator (or someone with database administrator privileges). Typically, you will use a CREATE DATABASE statement, but each vendor has its own way of creating databases. (Be sure to review your vendor-specific SQL reference, as it is not part of the SQL standard but is DBMS-dependent.) Not all JDBC drivers support database creation through DDL.

The following listing shows a shell script (create_kitty.sh) in Unix (Sun/Solaris) that creates an Oracle database called kitty. It is assumed that the Oracle database is installed on /home/oracle (the value of the ORACLE_BASE environment variable) directory. In the example, ORACLE_HOME has the value /home/oracle/product817.

```
$ chmod 775 create_kitty.sh
$ cat create_kitty.sh
#!/bin/sh
ORACLE_SID=kitty
export ORACLE_SID
/home/oracle/product817/bin/svrmgrl << EOF
spool /home/oracle/admin/kitty/create/crdb1.log
connect internal  startup nomount pfile =
  "/home/oracle/admin/kitty/pfile/initkitty.ora"

CREATE DATABASE "kitty"
        maxdatafiles 254
        maxinstances 8
        maxlogfiles 32
        character set UTF8
        national character set UTF8
        DATAFILE '/u01/oradata/kitty/system01.dbf'
        SIZE 260M AUTOEXTEND ON NEXT 10240K
        logfile
            '/u01/oradata/kitty/redo01.log' SIZE 500K,
            '/u01/oradata/kitty/redo02.log' SIZE 500K,


spool off
exit
EOF

$ ./create_db.sh
```

Creating and dropping databases in MySQL is easy; just create a database called kitty and then drop the database as shown in the following code listing:

```
mysql> show databases;
    +----------+
    | Database |
    +----------+
    | mysql    |
    | test     |
    | tiger    |
    +----------+
    3 rows in set (0.00 sec)

mysql> create database kitty;
Query OK, 1 row affected (0.01 sec)
```

```
mysql> show databases;
+-----------+
| Database  |
+-----------+
| kitty     |
| mysql     |
| test      |
| tiger     |
+-----------+
4 rows in set (0.00 sec)

mysql> drop database kitty;
Query OK, 0 rows affected (0.00 sec)

mysql> show databases;
+-----------+
| Database  |
+-----------+
| mysql     |
| test      |
| tiger     |
+-----------+
3 rows in set (0.00 sec)
```

Step 2: Connecting to an Existing Database

a database username (a valid username in the database), and a database password (the associated password for the database user). Depending on the type of driver, many other arguments, attributes, or properties may be available.

The java.sql package contains mostly interfaces. So, which classes implement JDBC's interfaces? The implementation of these interfaces is all part of the JDBC driver. A JDBC driver allows a Java application to communicate with a SQL database. A JDBC driver is a set of database-specific implementations for the interfaces defined by the JDBC. These driver classes come into being through a bootstrap process. This is best shown by stepping through the process of using JDBC to connect to a database, using Oracle's type 4 JDBC driver as an example.

First, the main driver class must be loaded into the Java VM:

```
Class.forName("oracle.jdbc.driver.OracleDriver");
```

The specified driver (that is, the oracle.jdbc.driver.OracleDriver class) must implement the java.sql.Driver interface. A class initializer (static code block) within the oracle.jdbc.driver. OracleDriver class registers the driver with the java.sql.DriverManager class.

Next, you need to obtain a connection to the database:

```
String dbURL = "jdbc:oracle:thin:@localhost:1521:kitty";
String dbUsername = "system";
String dbPassword = "manager";
java.sql.Connection connection =
    java.sql.DriverManager.getConnection(dbURL, dbUsername, dbPassword);
```

DriverManager determines which registered driver to use by invoking the acceptsURL(String url) method of each driver, passing each the JDBC URL. The first driver to return "true" in response will be used for this connection. In this example, OracleDriver will return "true," so DriverManager then invokes the connect() method of OracleDriver to obtain an instance of OracleConnection. It is this database-specific connection instance implementing the java.sql.Connection interface that is passed back from the java.sql.DriverManager.getConnection() call.

You can also use an alternate method for creating a database connection: you can first get a SQL driver and then use the SQL driver to get a connection, like so:

```
String dbURL = "jdbc:oracle:thin:@localhost:1521:kitty";
String dbUsername = "system";
String dbPassword = "manager";
java.util.Properties dbProps = new java.util.Properties();
java.sql.Driver sqlDriver =
        getSqlDriver("oracle.jdbc.driver.OracleDriver");
dbProps.put("user", dbUsername);
dbProps.put("password", dbPassword);
java.sql.Connection connection = sqlDriver.connect(databaseURL, dbProps);
```

The getSqlDriver method is as follows:

```
/**
 * Get a sql driver
 * @param driver the name of JDBC driver
 * @return a JDBC driver based on a given driver name
 */
public static java.sql.Driver getSqlDriver(String driver)


        IllegalAccessException {
    java.sql.Driver sqlDriver = null;
    sqlDriver = (java.sql.Driver) Class.forName(driver).newInstance();
    System.out.println("getSqlDriver() is OK. sqlDriver=" + sqlDriver);
    return sqlDriver;
}
```

The bootstrap process continues when you create a statement:

```
java.sql.Connection connection = <get-a-valid-Connection-object>;
java.sql.Statement statement = connection.createStatement();
```

The connection reference points to an instance of OracleConnection. This database-specific implementation of Connection returns a database-specific implementation of Statement, namely, OracleStatement.

Invoking the execute() method of this Statement object will execute the database-specific code necessary to issue a SQL statement against the Oracle database and retrieve the results (as a table):

```
String query = "SELECT id, lastName FROM MyEmployees";
java.sql.ResultSet result = statement.executeQuery(query);
```

The result is a table returned by executing the SELECT statement. Again, what is actually returned is an instance of OracleResultSet, which is an Oracle-specific implementation of the java.sql.ResultSet interface. By iterating the result, you can get all the selected records.

So, the purpose of a JDBC driver is to provide these implementations that hide all the database-specific details behind standard Java interfaces.

Step 3: Creating a Table

The database is a set of tables (plus other data structures to manage these tables, privileges, and roles); the tables are the actual components that contain data, in the form of rows/records and columns. You can create tables using the CREATE TABLE (DDL) statement. This statement has many options, with some differing from vendor to vendor. For details on creating tables, refer to your DBMS SQL reference for specifics. The following code shows the syntax for creating a table in Oracle and MySQL:

```
create table MyEmployees (
    id INT PRIMARY KEY,
    firstName VARCHAR(20),
    lastName VARCHAR(20),
    title VARCHAR(20),
    salary INT
);
```

To create a table using the mysql prompt, use the following code:

```
mysql>          create table MyEmployees (
    -               id INT PRIMARY KEY,
                    firstName VARCHAR(20),
                    lastName VARCHAR(20),
                    title VARCHAR(20),
                    salary INT
                );
Query OK, 0 rows affected (0.04 sec)

mysql> describe MyEmployees;
```

```
+-----------+-------------+------+-----+---------+-------+
| id        | int(11)     |      | PRI | 0       |       |
| firstName | varchar(20) | YES  |     | NULL    |       |
| lastName  | varchar(20) | YES  |     | NULL    |       |
| title     | varchar(20) | YES  |     | NULL    |       |
| salary    | int(11)     | YES  |     | NULL    |       |
+-----------+-------------+------+-----+---------+-------+
5 rows in set (0.02 sec)
```

With Oracle, use the following code at the sqlplus prompt:

```
$ sqlplus octopus/octopus
SQL*Plus: Release 8.1.7.0.0 - Production on Thu Jun 6 18:35:52 2002
SQL>            create table MyEmployees (
  2                 id INT PRIMARY KEY,
  3                 firstName VARCHAR(20),
  4                 lastName VARCHAR(20),
  5                 title VARCHAR(20),
  6                 salary INT
  7             );

Table created.
SQL> describe MyEmployees;
Name            Null?     Type
----------      --------  -------------
 ID             NOT NULL  NUMBER(38)
 FIRSTNAME                VARCHAR2(20)
 LASTNAME                 VARCHAR2(20)
 TITLE                    VARCHAR2(20)
 SALARY                   NUMBER(38)
```

In general, in real project development, you define a SQL script that defines all the tables, views, and indexes. But it is also possible to create a table with a Java program. I will provide solutions in MySQL and Oracle. The following code shows the solution for MySQL:

```
$ javac CreateEmployeeTable.java
$ java CreateEmployeeTable mysql
---CreateEmployeeTable begin---
---CreateEmployeeTable: table created---

$ mysql --user=root --password=root --default-character-set=utf8
mysql> use octopus;
Database changed
mysql> desc MyEmployees3;
+-----------+-------------+------+-----+---------+-------+
| Field     | Type        | Null | Key | Default | Extra |
+-----------+-------------+------+-----+---------+-------+
| id        | int(11)     |      | PRI | 0       |       |
| firstName | varchar(20) | YES  |     | NULL    |       |
| lastName  | varchar(20) | YES  |     | NULL    |       |
| title     | varchar(20) | YES  |     | NULL    |       |
| salary    | int(11)     | YES  |     | NULL    |       |
+-----------+-------------+------+-----+---------+-------+
5 rows in set (0.01 sec)

mysql> select * from MyEmployees3;
+-----+-----------+----------+-------+--------+
| id  | firstName | lastName | title | salary |
+-----+-----------+----------+-------+--------+
| 200 | Mary      | NULL     | NULL  | NULL   |
+-----+-----------+----------+-------+--------+
2 rows in set (0.02 sec)
```

To run CreateEmployeeTable.java, use the following code:

```java
import java.sql.Connection;
import java.sql.Statement;
import java.sql.DriverManager;
import java.sql.SQLException;

import jcb.util.DatabaseUtil;
import jcb.db.VeryBasicConnectionManager;

public class CreateEmployeeTable {

    private static final String EMPLOYEE_TABLE =
        "create table MyEmployees3 ( " +
        "    id INT PRIMARY KEY, " +
        "    firstName VARCHAR(20), " +
        "    lastName VARCHAR(20), " +
        "    title VARCHAR(20), " +
        "    salary INT " +
        ")";

    public static void main(String args[]) {
        Connection conn = null;
        Statement stmt = null;
        System.out.println("---CreateEmployeeTable begin---");
```

```java
String dbVendor = args[0];  // database vendor
try {
    conn = VeryBasicConnectionManager.getConnection(dbVendor);
    stmt = conn.createStatement();
    stmt.executeUpdate(EMPLOYEE_TABLE);
    stmt.executeUpdate("insert into MyEmployees3(id, firstName) "+
        "values(100, 'Alex')");
    stmt.executeUpdate("insert into MyEmployees3(id, firstName) "+
        "values(200, 'Mary')");
    System.out.println("---CreateEmployeeTable: table created---");
}
catch(ClassNotFoundException ce) {
    System.out.println("error: failed to load JDBC driver.");
    ce.printStackTrace();
}
catch(SQLException se) {
    System.out.println("JDBC error:" +se.getMessage());
    se.printStackTrace();
}
catch(Exception e) {
    System.out.println("other error:"+e.getMessage());
    e.printStackTrace();
}
finally {
    // close JDBC/database resources
    DatabaseUtil.close(stmt);
}


    }

}
```

The following code shows the solution for Oracle:

```
$ javac CreateEmployeeTable.java
$ java CreateEmployeeTable oracle
---CreateEmployeeTable begin---
---CreateEmployeeTable: table created---

$ sqlplus scott/tiger
SQL*Plus: Release 10.1.0.2.0 - Production on Thu Oct 28 10:50:58 2004
SQL> desc MyEmployees3;
 Name              Null?    Type
 ----------------- -------- ------------
 ID                NOT NULL NUMBER(38)
 FIRSTNAME                  VARCHAR2(20)
 LASTNAME                   VARCHAR2(20)
 TITLE                      VARCHAR2(20)
 SALARY                     NUMBER(38)

SQL> select * from MyEmployees3;

   ID FIRSTNAME  LASTNAME  TITLE  SALARY
 ----- ---------- -------- ----- ------
   100 Alex
   200 Mary
```

Step 4: Populating a Database (Inserting Rows/Records into a Database)

Again, you can enter and maintain data using database-specific tools (GUI tools, SQL*Plus, and so on) or using SQL statements sent with JDBC programs.

To insert records using SQL, use this code:

```
insert into MyEmployees(id, firstName, lastName, title, salary)
    values(60, 'Bill', 'Russel', 'CTO', 980000);

insert into MyEmployees(id, firstName, lastName, title, salary)
    values(70, 'Alex', 'Baldwin', 'Software Engineer', 88000);
```

To insert records using JDBC, I will provide a Java program that accomplishes this. The interface is as follows:

```
java InsertEmployeeRecord <db-vendor> <id> <firstName>
    <lastName> <title> <salary>
```

The InsertEmployeeRecord.main() method will accept six arguments, and then it will insert that record into the database.

Now, to insert the following records, use this code:

```
60  Bill  Russel  CTO  980000
70  Alex  Baldwin  Software Engineer  88000
```

and do the following from the command line:

```
$ java InsertEmployeeRecord oracle 60  Bill Russel  CTO  980000
$ java InsertEmployeeRecord oracle 70  Alex Baldwin "Software Engineer" 88000
```

Note that "Software Engineer" has double quotes to represent a single string.

Step 5: Retrieving Table Records

I will now show how to write a program to accept an ID and to selectively retrieve all related information (such as firstName, lastName, and so on) for that ID. I will show how to do this by using JDBC to get results in variables. The interface is as follows:

```
java GetEmployee <db-vendor>  <id>
```

For example, the following is the code to retrieve table records from MySQL:

```
$ java GetEmployeeRecord mysql 60
ok: loaded MySql driver.
GetEmployeeRecord: main(): record retrieved.
GetEmployeeRecord: main(): firstName=Bill
GetEmployeeRecord: main(): lastName=Russel
GetEmployeeRecord: main(): title=CTO
GetEmployeeRecord: main(): salary=980000
```

For example, the following is the code to retrieve table records from Oracle:

```
$java GetEmployeeRecord oracle 70
ok: loaded Oracle driver.    GetEmployeeRecord: main(): record retrieved.
GetEmployeeRecord: main(): firstName=Alex
GetEmployeeRecord: main(): lastName=Baldwin
GetEmployeeRecord: main(): title=Software Engineer
GetEmployeeRecord: main(): salary=88000
```

To review the discussion so far, you can use any JDBC program to load a JDBC driver with this:

```
Class.forName(driver);
```

Then, you may use the DriverManager class to get a database connection:

```
Connection conn = null;
conn = DriverManager.getConnection(url, username, password);
```

The connection (java.sql.Connection) is the most important interface in JDBC. Without a connection, you cannot do much.

Step 6: Processing the Result Set

ResultSet.next() returns a boolean; it returns "true" if there is a next row and "false" if not (meaning the end of the data/set has been reached). Conceptually, a pointer/cursor is positioned just before the first row when the ResultSet is obtained. Invoking the next() method moves to the first row, then the second, and so on.

Once positioned at a row, the application can get the data on a column-by-column basis using the appropriate ResultSet.getXXX method. Here are the methods used in the example to collect the data:

```
if (rs.next()) {
    String firstName = rs.getString(1);
    String lastName = rs.getString(2);
    String title = rs.getString(3);
    int salary = rs.getInt(4);
```

```
if (rs.next()) {
    String firstName = rs.getString("firstName");
    String lastName = rs.getString("lastName");
    String title = rs.getString("title");
    int salary = rs.getInt("salary");
}
```

Step 7: Closing JDBC Objects

Releasing/closing JDBC resources (such as the ResultSet, Statement, PreparedStatement, and Connection objects) immediately instead of waiting for this to happen can improve the overall performance of your application. From a good software engineering point of view, you should put close() statements in a finally clause; this guarantees the statements in the finally clause will be executed as the last step regardless of whether an exception has taken place.

Step 8: Closing ResultSet

ResultSet has a close() method that releases the ResultSet object's database and JDBC resources immediately instead of waiting for this to happen when it is automatically closed. The following code shows some sample code for closing a ResultSet object; it is always a good idea to have utility classes close these JDBC resources:

```
/**
 * Close the ResultSet object. Releases the
 * ResultSet object's database and JDBC resources
 * immediately instead of waiting for them to be
 * automatically released.
 * @param rs a ResultSet object.
 */
```

```java
public static  void close(java.sql.ResultSet rs) {
    if (rs == null) {
        return;
    }

    try {
        rs.close();
        // result set is closed now
    }
    catch(Exception ignore) {
        // ignore the exception
        // could not close the result set
        // cannot do much here
    }
}
```

Step 9: Closing Statement

Statement has a close() method that releases this Statement object's database and JDBC resources immediately instead of waiting for this to happen when it is automatically closed. The following code shows some sample code for closing a Statement object; it is always a good idea to have utility classes close these JDBC resources:

```java
/**
 * Close the Statement object. Releases the Statement
 * object's database and JDBC resources immediately instead


 */
public static  void close(java.sql.Statement stmt) {
    if (stmt == null) {
        return;
    }

    try {
        stmt.close();
        // result set is closed now
    }
    catch(Exception ignore) {
        // ignore the exception
        // could not close the statement
        // cannot do much here
    }
}
```

Step 10: Closing PreparedStatement

PreparedStatement does not have a direct close() method, but since PreparedStatement extends Statement, then you may use Statement.close() for the PreparedStatement objects; it is always a good idea to have utility classes close these JDBC resources. The following code shows you how to close a PreparedStatement object:

```java
/**
 * Close the PreparedStatement object. Releases the
 * PreparedStatement object's database and JDBC
 * resources immediately instead of waiting for them
```

```
 * to be automatically released.
 * @param pstmt a PreparedStatement object.
 */
public static  void close(java.sql.PreparedStatement pstmt) {
    if (pstmt == null) {
       return;
    }

    try {
       pstmt.close();
       // PreparedStatement object is closed now
    }
    catch(Exception ignore) {
       // ignore the exception
       // could not close the PreparedStatement
       // cannot do much here
    }
}
```

Step 11: Closing the Connection

If you are using a connection pool manager (to manage a set of database Connection objects), then you need to release (this is called a *soft close*) the Connection object to the connection pool manager; otherwise, you can use the close() method, which releases this Connection object's database and JDBC resources immediately instead of waiting for them to be automatically released. The following Connection

```
/**
 * Close the Connection object. Releases the Connection
 * object's database and JDBC resources immediately instead
 * of waiting for them to be automatically released.
 * @param conn a Connection object.
 */
public static  void close(java.sql.Connection conn) {
    if (conn == null) {
       return;
    }

    try {
       if (!conn.isClosed()) {
          // close the Connection object
          conn.close();
       }
       // Connection object is closed now
    }
    catch(Exception ignore) {
       // ignore the exception
       // could not close the Connection object
       // cannot do much here
    }
}
```

1-9. What Is the JDBC API (in a Nutshell)?

The JDBC API is comprised of two Java packages (both are included in JDK 1.4):

- `java.sql`: This is the initial package that provides the API for accessing and processing data stored in a data source (usually a relational database) using the Java programming language. For details, please refer to the official documentation at `http://java.sun.com/j2se/1.5.0/docs/api/java/sql/package-summary.html`.

- `javax.sql`: This is an extended package that provides the API for server-side data source access and processing from the Java programming language. For details, please refer to the official documentation at `http://java.sun.com/j2se/1.5.0/docs/api/javax/sql/package-summary.html`.

As mentioned, the `java.sql` package provides the API for accessing and processing data stored in a data source (usually a relational database) using the Java programming language. This JDBC API includes a framework and architecture whereby different drivers (implemented by different database vendors) can be installed dynamically to access different data sources (see Figure 1-9). Although the JDBC API is mainly geared to passing SQL statements to a database, it provides for reading and writing data from any data source with a tabular format. The reader/writer facility, available through the `javax.sql.RowSet` group of interfaces, can be customized to use and update data from a spreadsheet, flat file, or any other tabular data source.

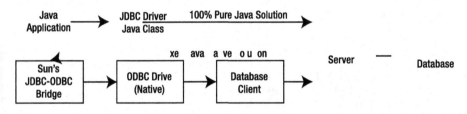

Figure 1-9. *JDBC architecture in a nutshell*

The `javax.sql` package supports the following concepts:

- The `DataSource` interface as an alternative to `DriverManager` for establishing a connection with a data source. Chapter 2 discusses `DataSource` in detail.

- Connection pooling

- Distributed transactions

- Row sets

1-10. What Are the Core JDBC Classes/Interfaces?

Figure 1-10 shows the core JDBC classes/interfaces used to access a database.

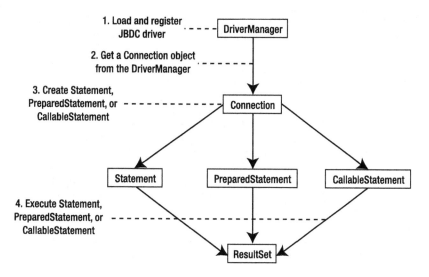

Figure 1-10. *Core JDBC classes/interfaces*

The core JDBC classes/interfaces are as follows:

- java.sql.DriverManager: The major task of the DriverManager class is to access the JDBC

- java.sql.Connection: This interface represents a database connection. This is the key for accessing most of the database objects (such as tables, columns, and so on).

- java.sql.Statement: The Connection object creates Statement objects. You can use the Statement object to execute SQL statements and queries, which produce ResultSet objects (the result of executing SQL statements and queries).

- java.sql.PreparedStatement: The Connection object creates PreparedStatement (parameterized statement) objects. You can use the PreparedStatement object to execute SQL statements and queries, which produce ResultSet objects (the result of executing SQL statements and queries).

- java.sql.CallableStatement: The Connection object creates CallableStatement (statements used to execute stored procedures) objects. You can use the PreparedStatement object to execute SQL statements and queries, which produce ResultSet objects (the result of executing SQL statements and queries).

- java.sql.ResultSet: The result of a SQL query is returned via a ResultSet object (a table of data representing a database result set, which is usually generated by executing a statement that queries the database).

1-11. What Is a JDBC Driver?

A *JDBC driver* allows a Java application/client to communicate with a SQL database. A JDBC driver is a Java class that implements the JDBC's java.sql.Driver interface and understands how to convert program (and typically SQL) requests for a particular database. The JDK provides a JDBC-ODBC bridge driver. A Java program that uses the JDBC API loads the specified driver for a particular DBMS before it actually connects to a database. The JDBC DriverManager class then sends all JDBC API calls to the loaded driver.

Therefore, in order to connect to a relational database, your Java application/client requires a driver. This is a piece of software (that is, a Java class) that connects programs to databases in a standard way (JDBC). This is the Java version of ODBC.

Installing a JDBC driver is simply a matter of configuring the Java CLASSPATH (an operating system environment variable) to ensure that the required JDBC classes and interfaces are available. Consult the documentation for the database you are using to find out where to obtain the JDBC driver, or consult the list of available JDBC drivers. Drivers are typically packaged as either .zip or .jar archives.

To use Oracle's JDBC driver in an application, you must set your CLASSPATH environment variable to point to the driver files. The CLASSPATH environment variable tells the JVM and other applications where to find the Java class libraries used in a Java program. You have two ways of setting your CLASSPATH environment variable.

You can find Oracle's implementation of the java.sql package and other supporting classes found in a file called classes12.zip. For convenience, rename this file to classes12.jar. (Plus, in a Unix environment, Apache Tomcat expects .jar files from the lib directories.) Add the full pathname of the classes12.jar file (this file is from Oracle and contains the implementation of all interfaces defined in the java.sql package) to the CLASSPATH environment variable, as shown in the following examples.

The following apply to Oracle 8.1.7:

- Unix, C shell:

```
setenv CLASSPATH /home/oracle/product817/jdbc/lib/classes12.jar:$CLASSPATH
```

- Unix, bash:

- Windows 2000:

```
set CLASSPATH=c:\home\oracle\product817\jdbc\lib\classes12.jar;%CLASSPATH%
```

The following apply to Oracle 9*i*:

- Unix, C shell:

```
setenv CLASSPATH /home/oracle/oracle9/jdbc/lib/ojdbc.jar:$CLASSPATH
```

- Unix, bash:

```
CLASSPATH=/home/oracle/oracle9/jdbc/lib/ojdbc.jar:$CLASSPATH
export CLASSPATH
```

- Windows 2000:

```
set CLASSPATH=c:\home\oracle\oracle9\jdbc\lib\ojdbc.jar;%CLASSPATH%
```

The following apply to MySQL:

- Unix, C shell:

```
setenv CLASSPATH /home/mysql/jars/mysql.jar:$CLASSPATH
```

- Unix, bash:

```
CLASSPATH=/home/mysql/jars/mysql.jar:$CLASSPATH
export CLASSPATH
```

- Windows 2000:

```
set CLASSPATH=c:\home\mysql\jars\mysql.jar;%CLASSPATH%
```

1-12. How Do You Load a JDBC Driver?

Before you can connect to the database, you have to load/register the JDBC driver. A JDBC driver is a Java class that implements JDBC's java.sql.Driver interface. JDK provides the JDBC-ODBC bridge driver. (The driver name is the sun.jdbc.odbc.JdbcOdbcDriver class, which you can connect to data sources registered by the Microsoft ODBC Data Source Administrator.) Note that the driver name will be different for each database vendor. The JDBC-ODBC bridge driver (provided by Sun Microsystems as part of JDK) is sun.jdbc.odbc.JdbcOdbcDriver, the JDBC driver for MySQL database is org.gjt. mm.mysql.Driver (or you can use com.mysql.jdbc.Driver), and the JDBC driver for Oracle database is oracle.jdbc.driver.OracleDriver. Each database vendor might have more than one driver for the same database (with different efficiency and price/performance features).

The class you are loading must be locatable in the CLASSPATH environment variable. This means you need to properly add your JAR file, which contains the driver class and supporting classes (when adding a JAR file to your CLASSPATH, use the absolute path name to the JAR file), to the CLASSPATH environment variable. (Java will extract class information from the CLASSPATH environment variable.)

You can load a JDBC driver in six ways:

- *Method 1*: You can use Class.forName().

- *Method 2*: You can use DriverManager.registerDriver().

- *Method 3*: You can create an instance of a Driver class.

- *Method 4*: You can use System.properties() inside a program.

- *Method 5*: You can use System.properties() from a command line.

- *Method 6*: You can use a Thread class.

Method 1: Using Class.forName()

In Java, every object has a corresponding class object. This class object instance is shared among all instances of that class type. Class.forName() loads and returns the class/interface object for the given class name. So, for example, if you write the following:

```
String className = "org.gjt.mm.mysql.Driver";
Class driverObject = Class.forName(className);
```

the JVM will load and return the class object for the org.gjt.mm.mysql.Driver class. Using JDBC, Class.forName() loads the JDBC driver into the JVM. Therefore, a call to Class.forName("X") causes the class named X to be initialized.

Method 2: Using DriverManager.registerDriver()

java.sql.DriverManager provides basic services for managing a set of JDBC drivers. The DriverManager class is the management layer of JDBC, working between the user and the JDBC drivers. It keeps track of the JDBC drivers that are available and handles establishing a connection between a database and the appropriate driver.

DriverManager.registerDriver(driverObject) registers the given driverObject with the DriverManager class. A newly loaded driver class should call the method registerDriver to make itself known to the DriverManager class, which is shown in the following code using MySQL:

```
//String className = "org.gjt.mm.mysql.Driver";
try {
    // Registers the given driver with the DriverManager.
    // A newly loaded driver class should call the method
    // registerDriver to make itself known to the DriverManager.
    DriverManager.registerDriver(new org.gjt.mm.mysql.Driver());
    // here the class is loaded
```

```
}
catch (SQLException e) {
    // database access error
    // driver not loaded; handle the exception
    e.printStackTrace();
}
```

Method 3: Creating an Instance of a Driver Class

You can load the JDBC drivers by creating an object using the vendor's JDBC Driver class. For example, the following example loads two JDBC drivers:

```
public class LoadJDBCDrivers {
    // load Oracle driver:
    oracle.jdbc.driver.OracleDriver oracleDriver =
            new oracle.jdbc.driver.OracleDriver();

    // load MySQL driver:
    org.gjt.mm.mysql.Driver mysqlDriver =
            new org.gjt.mm.mysql.Driver();
}
}
```

Method 4: Using System.properties() Inside a Program

You can provide a Java System property, jdbc.drivers, whose value is a list of driver class names.

```
import java.util.*;
import java.io.*;
import java.sql.*;

public class TestSystemProperty {

    // Create an JDBC/ODBC connection...
    public static Connection getJdbcOdbcConnection() throws Exception {
        //String driver = "sun.jdbc.odbc.JdbcOdbcDriver";
        // note: northwind data source must be defined
        // using the ODBC Data Source Administrator
        String url = "jdbc:odbc:northwind";
        String username = "";
        String password = "";
        //Class.forName(driver);  // load JDBC-ODBC driver
        return DriverManager.getConnection(url, username, password);
    }

    // Create an Oracle connection...
    public static Connection getOracleConnection() throws Exception {
        //String driver = "oracle.jdbc.driver.OracleDriver";
        String url = "jdbc:oracle:thin:@localhost:1521:scorpian";
        String username = "octopus";
        String password = "octopus";
        //Class.forName(driver);    // load Oracle driver
        return DriverManager.getConnection(url, username, password);
    }
```

```
    // Create an MySQL connection...
    public static Connection getMySqlConnection() throws Exception {
        //String driver = "org.gjt.mm.mysql.Driver";
        String url = "jdbc:mysql://localhost/tiger";
        String username = "root";
        String password = "root";
        //Class.forName(driver);    // load MySQL driver
        return DriverManager.getConnection(url, username, password);
    }

    public static void main(String[] args) {
        System.out.println("-- TestSystemProperty begin --");
        Connection oracleConn = null;
        Connection mysqlConn = null;
        Connection odbcConn = null;

        System.out.println("System.getProperty(\"jdbc.drivers\")="+
        System.getProperty("jdbc.drivers"));

        // try getting a MySQL connection
        try {
            mysqlConn = getMySqlConnection();
            System.out.println("mysqlConn="+mysqlConn);
        }
        catch(Exception e) {
            System.out.println("error 1111="+e.getMessage());
        }


        // try getting an ODBC connection again
        try {
            odbcConn = getJdbcOdbcConnection();
            System.out.println("mysqlConn="+odbcConn);
        }
        catch(Exception e) {
            System.out.println("error 2222="+e.getMessage());
        }
        System.out.println("-- TestSystemProperty end --");
    }
}
```

The following code shows how to run the TestSystemProperty program:

```
$ javac TestSystemProperty.java

$ java TestSystemProperty
-- TestSystemProperty begin --
System.getProperty("jdbc.drivers")=null
error 1111=No suitable driver
error 2222=No suitable driver

$java -Djdbc.drivers=org.gjt.mm.mysql.Driver:
    sun.jdbc.odbc.JdbcOdbcDriver TestSystemProperty
-- TestSystemProperty begin --
System.getProperty("jdbc.drivers")=
    org.gjt.mm.mysql.Driver:sun.jdbc.odbc.JdbcOdbcDriver
```

```
mysqlConn=com.mysql.jdbc.Connection@efd552
mysqlConn=sun.jdbc.odbc.JdbcOdbcConnection@fd54d6
-- TestSystemProperty end --
```

$

You should put the specified classes (following option -D) in the CLASSPATH environment variable; then the DriverManager class automatically loads the JDBC drivers into your program. The sun.jdbc.odbc.JdbcOdbcDriver is part of the JDK distribution, so there is no need to add it directly to the CLASSPATH environment variable.

Method 5: Using System.properties() from a Command Line

You can also pass the driver names to jdbc.drivers (as a System property), whose value is a list of driver class names (class names are separated by a colon), like so:

```
java -Djdbc.drivers=org.gjt.mm.mysql.Driver:sun.jdbc.odbc.JdbcOdbcDriver
    <jdbc-application-program>
```

Method 6: Using a Thread Class

Another method to load a JDBC driver is to use a Thread class, like so:

```
String className = "sun.jdbc.odbc.JdbcOdbcDriver";
Class theClass = null;
try {
    Thread currentThread = Thread.currentThread();


}
catch (ClassNotFoundException e) {
    // your class not found in CLASSPATH
    // driver not loaded
    // handle the exception
    e.printStackTrace();
    // ...
}
```

Sun Microsystems maintains a list of JDBC drivers for all major database systems. You can find this list at http://java.sun.com/products/jdbc/jdbc.drivers.html.

1-13. How Do You Test a JDBC Driver Installation?

How do you test to see if a certain JDBC driver is installed properly? The simplest way is to try to load the desired JDBC driver; if it loads successfully, then it means your JDBC driver is installed properly. Otherwise, either the JDBC driver is not properly added to your CLASSPATH environment variable or there might be some other problem.

MySQL

To test a JDBC driver installation using MySQL, use the following code:

```
public class TestJDBCDriverInstallation_MySQL {
    public static void main(String[] args) {
        System.out.println("-- TestJDBCDriverInstallation_MySQL begin --");

        // Test a JDBC driver installation
```

```
        try {
            String className = "org.gjt.mm.mysql.Driver";
            Class driverObject = Class.forName(className);
            System.out.println("driverObject="+driverObject);
            System.out.println("your installation of JDBC Driver OK.");
        }
        catch(Exception e) {
            // your installation of JDBC driver failed
            System.out.println("Failed: JDBC Driver Error: "+e.getMessage());
        }

        System.out.println("-- TestJDBCDriverInstallation_MySQL end --");
    }
}
```

Next, set PATH and CLASSPATH, but do not add the Driver JAR:

```
$ set PATH=.;C:\java\j2sdk15\bin
$ set CLASSPATH=.;c:\jdk\lib\dt.jar;c:\jdk\lib\tools.jar
$ set CLASSPATH
CLASSPATH=.;c:\jdk\lib\dt.jar;c:\jdk\lib\tools.jar
```

Then, compile and run the test program:

```
$ javac TestJDBCDriverInstallation_MySQL.java
$ java TestJDBCDriverInstallation_MySQL
-- TestJDBCDriverInstallation_MySQL begin --
JDBC Driver Error: org.gjt.mm.mysql.Driver
```

Next, add the MySQL Connector/J driver to your CLASSPATH:

```
$ set CLASSPATH
CLASSPATH=.;c:\jdk\lib\dt.jar;c:\jdk\lib\tools.jar
$ set CLASSPATH=%CLASSPATH%;c:\j\mysql-connector-java-3.1.1-alpha-bin.jar
$ set CLASSPATH
CLASSPATH=.;c:\jdk\lib\dt.jar;c:\jdk\lib\tools.jar;c:\j\
        mysql-connector-java-3.1.1-alpha-bin.jar
```

Finally, run the test program, and the program should succeed:

```
$ java TestJDBCDriverInstallation_MySQL
-- TestJDBCDriverInstallation_MySQL begin --
driverObject=class org.gjt.mm.mysql.Driver
your installation of JDBC Driver OK.
-- TestJDBCDriverInstallation_MySQL end --
```

Oracle

To test a JDBC driver installation using Oracle, use the following:

```
public class TestJDBCDriverInstallation_Oracle {
    public static void main(String[] args) {
        System.out.println("-- TestJDBCDriverInstallation_Oracle begin --");

        // Test a JDBC Driver Installation
        try {
            String className = "oracle.jdbc.driver.OracleDriver";
            Class driverObject = Class.forName(className);
            System.out.println("driverObject="+driverObject);
            System.out.println("your installation of JDBC Driver OK.");
        }
```

```
    catch(Exception e) {
        // your installation of JDBC Driver Failed
        System.out.println("Failed: JDBC Driver Error: "+e.getMessage());
    }

    System.out.println("-- TestJDBCDriverInstallation_Oracle end --");
  }
}
```

Next, set PATH and CLASSPATH, but do not add the Driver JAR:

```
$ set PATH=.;C:\java\j2sdk15\bin
$ set CLASSPATH=.;c:\jdk\lib\dt.jar;c:\jdk\lib\tools.jar
$ set CLASSPATH
CLASSPATH=.;c:\jdk\lib\dt.jar;c:\jdk\lib\tools.jar
```

Then, compile and run the test program:

```
$ javac TestJDBCDriverInstallation_Oracle.java
$ java TestJDBCDriverInstallation_Oracle
-- TestJDBCDriverInstallation_Oracle begin --
JDBC Driver Error: oracle.jdbc.driver.OracleDriver
-- TestJDBCDriverInstallation_Oracle end --
```

Next, add the Oracle Thin driver to your CLASSPATH:

```
$ set CLASSPATH
CLASSPATH=.;c:\jdk\lib\dt.jar;c:\jdk\lib\tools.jar
$ set CLASSPATH=%CLASSPATH%;c:\j\ojdbc14.jar
```

Finally, run the test program, and the program should succeed:

```
$ java TestJDBCDriverInstallation_Oracle
-- TestJDBCDriverInstallation_Oracle begin --
driverObject=class oracle.jdbc.driver.OracleDriver
your installation of JDBC Driver OK.
-- TestJDBCDriverInstallation_Oracle end --
```

1-14. Where Can You Obtain a JDBC Driver for Your Database System?

You can find a JDBC driver for your database system in several places:

- Check the vendor of the database system; for example, Oracle (http://www.oracle.com) and MySQL (http://www.mysql.com) provide their own JDBC drivers for their database systems.

- Sun Microsystems maintains a list of JDBC drivers for all major database systems. You can find this list at http://servlet.java.sun.com/products/jdbc/drivers; this database currently has 219 JDBC drivers.

- The last resort is to search for a JDBC driver using an engine such as Ask.com or Google.com.

1-15. What Is a JDBC Driver Type?

According to Sun Microsystems (http://java.sun.com/products/jdbc/driverdesc.html), JDBC technology drivers fit into one of four categories:

A JDBC-ODBC bridge provides JDBC API access via one or more ODBC drivers. Note that some ODBC native code (and, in many cases, native database client code) must be loaded on each client machine that uses this type of driver. Hence, this kind of driver is generally most appropriate when automatically installing and downloading a Java technology application is not important.

A native-API and partly Java technology–enabled driver converts JDBC calls into calls on the client API for Oracle, Sybase, Informix, DB2, or other DBMSs. Note that, like the bridge driver, this style of driver requires that some binary code be loaded on each client machine.

A network-protocol fully Java technology–enabled driver translates JDBC API calls into a DBMS-independent net protocol that is then translated to a DBMS protocol by a server. This net server middleware is able to connect all its Java technology-based clients to many different databases. The specific protocol used depends on the vendor. In general, this is the most flexible JDBC API alternative. It is likely that all vendors of this solution will provide products suitable for intranet use. For these products to also support Internet access, they must handle the additional requirements for security, access through firewalls, and so on, that the Web imposes. Several vendors are adding JDBC technology–based drivers to their existing database middleware products.

A native-protocol fully Java technology–enabled driver converts JDBC technology calls into the network protocol used by DBMSs directly. This allows a direct call from the client machine to the DBMS server and is a practical solution for intranet access. Since many of these protocols are proprietary, the database vendors will be the primary source for this style of driver. Several database vendors have these in progress.

The *type 1 driver* translates its calls into ODBC calls (see Figure 1-11). ODBC then interacts with the desired database. It is the most available but slowest type, and it works only on Microsoft Windows and Sun Solaris. There is only one driver in existence, `sun.jdbc.odbc.JdbcOdbcDriver`. You may use this driver to access the Microsoft Access personal database.

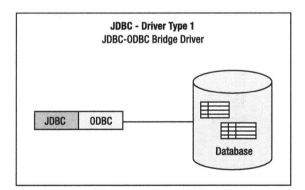

Figure 1-11. *JDBC driver type 1*

The *type 2 driver* translates its calls to the native (C, C++, Pascal, and so on) API calls of the desired database, which then call the desired database (see Figure 1-12). For example, Oracle Call Interface (OCI) calls are used in developing Oracle's type 2 drivers. (The Oracle OCI is a set of low-level proprietary APIs used to interact with Oracle databases. It allows you to use operations such as logon, execute, parse, fetch, and so on. OCI programs are normally written in C or C++, although they can be written in almost any programming language; for details, see http://www.orafaq.com/faqoci.htm.) You will need a driver for each database and operating system combination. Performance is faster than type 4 drivers.

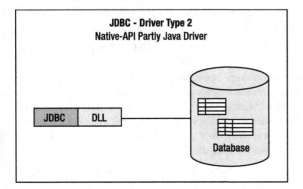

Figure 1-12. *JDBC driver type 2*

The *type 3 driver* is a multitier (*n*-tier) driver (see Figure 1-13). It is database-independent unlike

the type 3 driver's class name and a data source name to connect to; there is no need to change the client code when the back-end database changes.

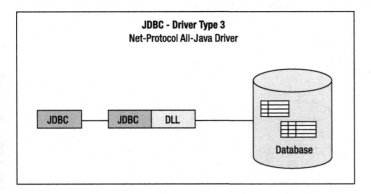

Figure 1-13. *JDBC driver type 3*

The *type 4 driver* is for databases that have written their APIs in Java, not C or C++ (see Figure 1-14). So, no translation is needed at runtime by the driver; it calls the database using its Java API. MySQL's Connector/J driver and Oracle's Thin driver are both type 4. Note that type 1, 2, and 4 are two-tier (client-server) drivers. In other words, there is no application server in the middle. You can use these drivers in typical client-server environments.

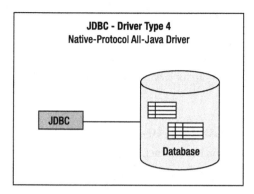

Figure 1-14. *JDBC driver type 4*

Figure 1-15 illustrates relationships of drivers with databases.

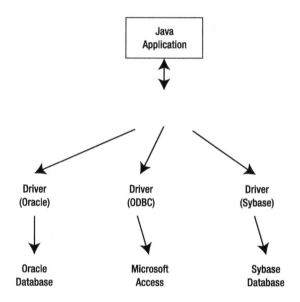

Figure 1-15. *JDBC drivers and databases*

1-17. What Are the Selection Criteria for JDBC Drivers?

When you are selecting a driver for an application, you need to consider the following factors:

- *Features and ease of use*: Does it support the features you need?
- *Speed/performance*: Does it handle the operations as fast as possible?
- *Reliability*: Does it pass a set of standard tests?
- *Security*: Does it handle privileges properly?
- *Portability*: Can you use the driver in another platform?

- *Support*: Can the selling company help you when you need some help?
- *Price*: Can you afford the price with respect to your project requirements?
- *Open source*: Will the license allow you to add/modify features?
- *Compatibility*: Is the JDBC driver on the client side compatible with the one on the application server?

1-18. What Is the URL Syntax for Connecting to a Database?

The database URL syntax is based on the premise of URLs on the Internet. The format is as follows:

jdbc:<subprotocol>:<subname>

The subprotocol just shown represents where you would put the particular type of database mechanism, and the subname is used to actually connect to a database. The database URL tells JDBC where your database is located. You can even specify a port in the subname where the database should connect. Table 1-5 shows some examples of what a JDBC URL looks like.

Table 1-5. *Examples of JDBC URL*

Database URL	Database	Vendor
jdbc:db2:MYDB2	DB2	IBM
jdbc:mysql://localhost/octopus	MySQL	MySQL
jdbc:oracle:thin:@calistoga:1521:wooster	Oracle 8*i*	Oracle
jdbc:odbc:msAccess	Access	Microsoft
jdbc:inetdae7://mparsian/northwind	SWL Server 2000	Microsoft

In general, the structure of the database URL depends on the type and brand of JDBC driver being used. In the case of Oracle's JDBC drivers, the URL structure is as follows:

driver_name:@driver_specific_information

where driver_name specifies the name of the Oracle JDBC driver you want to use. This may be any one of the names listed in Table 1-6.

Table 1-6. *Oracle JDBC Driver Names*

Driver Name	Description
jdbc:oracle:thin	Oracle JDBC Thin driver (for Oracle 7 and above)
jdbc:oracle:oci	Oracle JDBC OCI driver (for Oracle 9*i* and above)
jdbc:oracle:oci8	Oracle JDBC OCI8 driver (for Oracle 8*i* and Oracle 8)
jdbc:oracle:oci7	Oracle JDBC OCI7 driver (for Oracle 7)

driver_specific_information specifies any driver-specific information required to connect to the database. This depends on the driver being used. In the case of the Oracle JDBC Thin driver (type 4 driver), you can specify the driver-specific information in the following format:

hostName:portNumber:DATABASE_SID

For all the Oracle JDBC drivers, you can specify the driver-specific information using an Oracle Net8 (or above) keyword-value pair in the following format:

```
(description=(address=
                (host=HOST_NAME)
                (protocol=tcp)
                (port=PORT_NUMBER)
            )
            (connect_data=(sid=DATABASE_SID)
            )
)
```

The syntax elements are as follows:

- HOST_NAME: Specifies the name of the machine on which the database is running.

- PORT_NUMBER: Specifies the port number on which the Net8 database listener waits for requests. 1521 is the default port number.

- DATABASE_SID: Specifies the system identifier (SID) of the database instance to which you want to connect. Your DBA will be able to provide you with the correct database SID to use.

You may also use an Oracle Net8's TNSNAMES string. (For more information on this, refer to your Oracle installation directory, $ORACLE_HOME/network/ADMIN/tnsnames.ora, and consult the Oracle documentation. The tnsnames.ora file is a configuration file used to define Oracle database instances to Oracle tools on other services that use Oracle databases.) The following example shows the connect() method being used to connect to a database using the Oracle Thin driver (note that, in this example, the database SID is wooster, the database user is scott, and the database password is tiger):

```
"jdbc:oracle:thin:@(description=(address=(host=localhost)" +
"(protocol=tcp)(port=1521))(connect_data=(sid=wooster)))",
"scott",
"tiger"
);
```

The Oracle JDBC Thin driver is the most widely used driver since it has the least amount of system resource requirements and is generally used in lightweight, client-based programs such as Java applets. You can use the Oracle JDBC Thin driver to access Oracle 7 databases and above.

1-19. What Is the Mapping Between Java to JDBC SQL Types?

Table 1-7 shows how the JDBC SQL types translate to their equivalent Java types.

Table 1-7. *JDBC Types Mapped to Java Types*

JDBC Type	Java Type
CHAR	java.lang.String
VARCHAR	java.lang.String
LONGVARCHAR	java.lang.String
NUMERIC	java.math.BigDecimal
DECIMAL	java.math.BigDecimal
BIT	boolean
TINYINT	byte

Continued

Table 1-7. *Continued*

JDBC Type	Java Type
SMALLINT	short
INTEGER	int
BIGINT	long
REAL	float
FLOAT	double
DOUBLE	double
BINARY	byte[]
VARBINARY	byte[]
LONGVARBINARY	byte[]
DATE	java.sql.Date
TIME	java.sql.Time
TIMESTAMP	java.sql.Timestamp
CLOB	java.sql.Clob
BLOB	java.sql.Blob
ARRAY	java.sql.Array
DISTINCT	Mapping of underlying type
STRUCT	java.sql.Struct

Table 1-8 has two purposes. First, it illustrates the general correspondence between types in the Java programming language and the JDBC types. Second, it shows the mapping used by CallableStatement.getXXX methods and SQLInput.readXXX methods.

Table 1-8. *Java Types Mapped to JDBC Types*

Java Type	JDBC Type
java.lang.String	CHAR, VARCHAR, or LONGVARCHAR
java.math.BigDecimal	NUMERIC
boolean	BIT
byte	TINYINT
short	SMALLINT
int	INTEGER
long	BIGINT
float	REAL
double	DOUBLE
byte[]	BINARY, VARBINARY or LONGVARBINARY
java.sql.Date	DATE
java.sql.Time	TIME
java.sql.Timestamp	TIMESTAMP
java.sql.Clob	CLOB
java.sql.Blob	BLOB

Java Type	JDBC Type
java.sql.Array	ARRAY
java.sql.Struct	STRUCT
java.sql.Ref	REF
Java class	JAVA_OBJECT

Table 1-9 shows the conversions used for IN parameters before they are sent to the DBMS and used by the PreparedStatement.setXXX and RowSet.setXXX methods. These same conversions are also used by ResultSet.updateXXX methods and SQLOutput.writeXXX methods. The mapping for String will normally be VARCHAR but will turn into LONGVARCHAR if the given value exceeds the driver's limit on VARCHAR values. The same is true for byte[], which may be mapped to either VARBINARY or LONGVARBINARY values, depending on the driver's limit on VARBINARY values. In most cases, the choice between CHAR and VARCHAR is not significant. In any case, drivers will just make the right choice. The same is true for the choice between BINARY and VARBINARY.

Table 1-9. *JDBC Types Mapped to Java Object Types*

JDBC Type	Java Object Type
CHAR	java.lang.String
VARCHAR	java.lang.String
LONGVARCHAR	java.lang.String
BIT	java.lang.Boolean
TINYINT	java.lang.Integer
SMALLINT	java.lang.Integer
INTEGER	java.lang.Integer
BIGINT	java.lang.Long
REAL	java.lang.Float
FLOAT	java.lang.Double
DOUBLE	java.lang.Double
BINARY	byte[]
VARBINARY	byte[]
LONGVARBINARY	byte[]
DATE	java.sql.Date
TIME	java.sql.Time
TIMESTAMP	java.sql.Timestamp
DISTINCT	Object type of underlying type
CLOB	java.lang.Clob
BLOB	java.lang.Blob
ARRAY	java.lang.Array
STRUCT	java.lang.Struct or java.lang.SQLData
REF	java.lang.Ref
JAVA_OBJECT	Underlying Java class

Table 1-10 shows the mapping from Java object types to JDBC types that is used by the ResultSet.getObject and CallableStatement.getObject methods.

Table 1-10. *Java Object Types Mapped to JDBC Types*

Java Object Type	JDBC Type
java.lang.String	CHAR, VARCHAR, or LONGVARCHAR
java.math.BigDecimal	NUMERIC
java.lang.Boolean	BIT
java.lang.Integer	INTEGER
java.lang.Long	BIGINT
java.lang.Float	REAL
java.lang.Double	DOUBLE
byte[]	BINARY, VARBINARY, or LONGVARBINARY
java.sql.Date	DATE
java.sql.Time	TIME
java.sql.Timestamp	TIMESTAMP
java.sql.Clob	CLOB
java.sql.Blob	BLOB
java.sql.Array	ARRAY
java.sql.Struct	STRUCT
Java class	JAVA_OBJECT

1-20. How Do You Handle JDBC Errors/Exceptions?

In JDBC, errors/exceptions are identified by the java.sql.SQLException class (which extends the java.lang.Exception class). SQLException is a "checked" exception. Java has two types of exceptions: checked and unchecked (called *runtime*). A checked exception is a subclass of java.lang.Throwable (the Throwable class is the superclass of all errors and exceptions in the Java language) but not of RunTimeException (RuntimeException is the superclass of those exceptions that can be thrown during the normal operation of the JVM). Checked exceptions have to be caught (and handled properly) or appear in a method that specifies in its signature that it throws that kind of exception.

When a JDBC object (such as Connection, Statement, ResultSet, and so on) encounters a serious error, it throws a SQLException. For example, invalid database URLs, invalid database usernames/ passwords, database connection errors, malformed SQL statements, nonexistent table/views, and insufficient database privileges all throw SQLException objects.

The client (database application program) accessing a database server needs to be aware of any errors returned from the server. JDBC gives access to such information by providing several levels of error conditions:

SQLException: SQLException is a Java exception that, if not handled, will terminate the client application. SQLException is an exception that provides information on a database access error or other type of error.

SQLWarning: SQLWarning is a subclass of SQLException, but it represents nonfatal errors or unexpected conditions and, as such, can be ignored. SQLWarning is an exception that provides information on database access warnings. Warnings are silently chained to the object whose method caused it to be reported.

BatchUpdateException: BatchUpdateException is an exception thrown when an error occurs during a batch update operation. In addition to the information provided by SQLException, a BatchUpdateException provides the update counts for all commands that were executed successfully during the batch update, that is, all commands that were executed before the error occurred. The order of elements in an array of update counts corresponds to the order in which commands were added to the batch.

DataTruncation: DataTruncation is an exception that reports a DataTruncation warning (on reads) or throws a DataTruncation exception (on writes) when JDBC unexpectedly truncates a data value.

The SQLException class extends the java.lang.Exception class and defines an additional method called getNextException(). This allows JDBC classes to chain a series of SQLException objects together. In addition, the SQLException class defines the getMessage(), getSQLState(), and getErrorCode() methods to provide additional information about an error/exception.

I will discuss the SQLException class in Chapter 11.

In general, a JDBC client application might have a catch block that looks something like the following:

```
String dbURL = ...;
String dbUser = ...;
String dbPassword = ...;
Connection conn = null;
try {
    conn = DriverManager.getConnection(dbURL, dbUser, dbPassword);
    //


    // (i.e., conn) to do something useful with the database
    ...
}
catch (SQLException e) {
    // something went wrong: maybe dbUser/dbPassword is not defined
    // maybe the dbURL is malformed, and other possible reasons.
    // now handle the exception, maybe print the error code
    // and maybe log the error, ...
    while(e != null) {
        System.out.println("SQL Exception/Error:");
        System.out.println("error message=" + e.getMessage());
        System.out.println("SQL State= " + e.getSQLState());
        System.out.println("Vendor Error Code= " + e.getErrorCode());
        // it is possible to chain the errors and find the most
        // detailed errors about the exception
        e = e.getNextException(  );
    }
}
```

To understand transaction management, you need to understand the Connection.setAutoCommit() method. Its signature is as follows:

```
void setAutoCommit(boolean autoCommit) throws SQLException
```

According to J2SE 1.5, setAutoCommit() sets this connection's autocommit mode to the given state. If a connection is in autocommit mode, then all its SQL statements will be executed and committed as individual transactions. Otherwise, its SQL statements are grouped into transactions that are terminated by a call to either the method commit or the method rollback. By default, new connections are in autocommit mode.

The following code shows how to handle commit() and rollback() when an exception happens:

```java
String dbURL = ...;
String dbUser = ...;
String dbPassword = ...;
Connection conn = null;
try {
    conn = DriverManager.getConnection(dbURL, dbUser, dbPassword);
    conn.setAutoCommit(false);  // begin transaction
    stmt.executeUpdate("CREATE TABLE cats_tricks(" +
        "name VARCHAR(30), trick VARHAR(30))") ;
    stmt.executeUpdate("INSERT INTO cats_tricks(name, trick) " +
        "VALUES('mono', 'rollover')") ;
    conn.commit() ;  // commit/end transaction
    conn.setAutoCommit(true) ;
}
catch(SQLException e) {
    // print some useful error messages
    System.out.println("SQL Exception/Error:");
    System.out.println("error message=" + e.getMessage());
    System.out.println("SQL State= " + e.getSQLState());
    System.out.println("Vendor Error Code= " + e.getErrorCode());
    // roll back the transaction
    conn.rollback();
    // optionally, you may set the auto commit to "true"
    conn.setAutoCommit(true) ;
}
```

cats_tricks table), you can type VARZCHAR. (The database server will not understand VARZCHAR, and therefore it will throw an exception.)

```java
String dbURL = ...;
String dbUser = ...;
String dbPassword = ...;
Connection conn = null;
try {
    conn = DriverManager.getConnection(dbURL, dbUser, dbPassword);
    conn.setAutoCommit(false);
    stmt.executeUpdate("CREATE TABLE cats_tricks("+
        "name VARZCHAR(30), trick VARHAR(30))") ;
    stmt.executeUpdate("INSERT INTO cats_tricks(name, trick) "+
        "VALUES('mono', 'rollover')") ;
    conn.commit() ;
    conn.setAutoCommit(true) ;
}
catch(SQLException e) {
    // print some useful error messages
    System.out.println("SQL Exception/Error:");
    System.out.println("error message=" + e.getMessage());
    System.out.println("SQL State= " + e.getSQLState());
    System.out.println("Vendor Error Code= " + e.getErrorCode());
    // rollback the transaction
    conn.rollback();
    // optionally, you may set AutoCommit to "true"
    conn.setAutoCommit(true) ;
}
```

CHAPTER 2

■ ■ ■

Exploring JDBC's Novel Features

This chapter further defines some key JDBC terms for the remaining chapters. Topics defined in this chapter are as follows:

- Database metadata
- Transaction management
- Connection pool management
- Steps for improving JDBC applications
- Two-tier and three-tier models for JDBC

2-1. What Is Database Metadata?

data, or information, about a database; the database in turn provides structured, descriptive information about other data. You can use JDBC to obtain information about the structure of a database and its tables, views, and stored procedures. For example, you can get a list of tables in a particular database and the column names for any table. This information is useful when programming for any database because the structure of a database may not be known to the programmer but can be obtained by using database metadata and result set metadata.

JDBC provides four interfaces that deal with database metadata:

java.sql.DatabaseMetaData: Provides comprehensive information about the database as a whole: table names, table indexes, database product name and version, and actions the database supports. Most of the solutions in this chapter are extracted from the solution class DatabaseMetaDataTool.

java.sql.ResultSetMetaData: Gets information about the types and properties of the columns in a ResultSet object.

java.sql.ParameterMetaData: Gets information about the types and properties of the parameters in a PreparedStatement object. ParameterMetaData, introduced in JDBC 3.0, retrieves information such as the number of parameters in PreparedStatement, the type of data that can be assigned to the parameter, and whether the parameter value can be set to null.

javax.sql.RowSetMetaData: This interface extends the ResultSetMetaData object, which contains information about the columns in a RowSet object. This interface has methods for setting the values in a RowSetMetaData object. When a RowSetReader object reads data into a RowSet object, it creates a RowSetMetaData object and initializes it using the methods in the RowSetMetaData interface. Then the reader passes the RowSetMetaData object to the row set. The methods in this interface are invoked internally when an application calls the method RowSet.execute; an application programmer would not use them directly.

For example, to get the name of tables, you can write the following code:

```
String databaseID = "payroll";
// get a valid database Connection object
Connection conn = getConnection(databaseID);
DatabaseMetaData dbmd = conn.getMetaData();
ResultSet rs = null;
if (dbmd == null) {
    System.out.println("vendor does not support database metadata");
}
else {
    rs = dbmd.getTables( null, null, null, new String[] {"TABLE"});
    // iterate result set object and get table information
    while (rs.next()) {
        ...
    }
}
```

In general, using database metadata (DatabaseMetaData) is expensive and not good on performance; therefore, you should make sure to use it effectively. For example, when you know the catalog/schema name, you should pass it to DatabaseMetaData.getTables() and other methods that require such data. (Explicitly passing values rather than null will improve performance.) Since schema information does not change frequently, you can cache this database metadata information.

2-2. What Is a Transaction?

- Something transacted, especially an exchange or transfer of goods, services, or funds
- Plural: the often published record of the meeting of a society or association
- An act, process, or instance of transacting
- A communicative action or activity involving two parties or things that reciprocally affect or influence each other

The word *transaction* has a special meaning in database technology. A transaction defines an *atomic* scope of work performed by a database server. From the begin/start transaction command until the commit/rollback command, *all* requests to manipulate (modify/update/insert/delete) database tables will either succeed (commit) or fail (roll back) together.

To simulate a real business transaction, a program may need to perform several steps. A financial program (such as automatic teller machines—ATMs), for example, might give/transfer cash from a checking account to the account holder (user of the ATM) with the steps listed in the following pseudocode:

```
begin transaction
    Step 1: debit checking account
    Step 2: deliver cache to ATM placeholder (to the ATM user)
    Step 3: update history log
commit transaction
```

Either all three of these steps must complete or all must fail. Otherwise, data integrity is lost. Because the steps within a transaction are a unified whole, a transaction is often defined as an indivisible unit of work.

If step 1, step 2, and step 3 finish completely and successfully (that is, with no errors/exceptions), then the transaction will be committed; if, for any reason, one of the steps is not completed, then the transaction will terminate/end. In general, a transaction can end in two ways: with a commit or with a rollback. When a transaction commits (all the steps finish successfully), the data modifications made by its statements are saved. If a step within a transaction fails, the transaction rolls back, undoing the effects of all steps in the transaction. In the pseudocode, for example, if sufficient funds do not appear in the user's checking account (or a disk drive crashed during the update history log step), then the transaction will roll back and undo the data modifications made by the debit statement to the checking account.

According to http://en.wikipedia.org/wiki/ACID, atomicity, consistency, isolation, and durability (ACID) are considered to be the key transaction processing features of a DBMS. Without the ACID characteristics, the integrity of the database cannot be guaranteed. The following section discusses ACID in more depth.

Understanding Transactions in Database Systems

From what you have seen already, you can conclude that a transaction is a set of logically related actions/steps. From a relational database point of view, a transaction is a set of one or more SQL statements that make up a logical unit of work that you can either commit or roll back and that will be recovered in the event of a system failure. All the statements in the transaction are atomic. In addition, a transaction is associated with a single java.sql.Connection object.

JDBC allows SQL statements to be grouped into a single transaction. Thus, you can ensure the ACID properties using JDBC transactional features. Table 2-1 further explains the ACID characteristics.

ACID Property	Description
Atomic	A transaction's changes to the database are atomic: either all happen or none happen.
Consistent	A transaction is a correct transformation of the state. The actions taken as a group do not violate any of the integrity constraints associated with the state.
Isolated	Even though transactions can execute concurrently, it appears to each transaction that others executed either before or after it.
Durable	Once a transaction completes successfully (for example, commit() returns success), then its changes to the state of the database survive any later failures.

* *This information comes from* http://www.hk8.org/old_web/linux/dbi/ch06_03.htm.

According to TheFreeDictionary.com (http://encyclopedia.thefreedictionary.com/ database%20transaction), a *database transaction* is a unit of interaction with a DBMS or similar system that is treated in a coherent and reliable way independent of other transactions. Ideally, a database system will guarantee all the ACID characteristics in databases.

Understanding How JDBC Performs Transactions

In JDBC, the java.sql.Connection object performs the transaction control. When a connection is created, by default it is in autocommit mode (which means that each SQL statement is treated as a transaction by itself—which might not be efficient or might not match business requirements) and will be committed as soon as its execution finishes.

2-3. How Do You Turn On Autocommit Mode?

You can turn on autocommit mode for an active Connection object with this code:

```
java.sql.Connection conn = ...;
...
conn.setAutoCommit(true);
```

2-4. How Do You Turn Off Autocommit Mode?

You can turn off autocommit mode for an active Connection object with this code:

```
java.sql.Connection conn = ...;
...
conn.setAutoCommit(false);
```

2-5. How Do You Roll Back a Transaction?

At any point before committing a transaction, you may invoke rollback() (a method of a Connection object) to roll back the transaction and restore values to the last commit point (before the attempted updates). The following example shows rollback() and commit() together:

```
java.sql.Connection conn = getConnection();
conn.setAutoCommit(false); // start a transaction
java.sql.Statement stmt = conn.createStatement();
stmt.executeUpdate("INSERT INTO emp_table(id, name) VALUES('11', 'alex')");
stmt.executeUpdate("INSERT INTO emp_table(id, name) VALUES('22', 'mary')");

conn.commit(); // end the transaction
```

Let's walk through the preceding example to understand the effects of the rollback() and commit() methods:

1. You first set autocommit off, indicating that the following JDBC statements need to be considered as a unit.

2. You attempt to insert two new records into the emp_table table; however, this change has not been finalized (committed) yet.

3. When you invoke rollback(), you cancel the two insert statements and in effect remove any intention of inserting tuples for 'alex' and 'mary'.

4. Note that emp_table now is still as it was before you attempted the two insert statements.

5. You then attempt another insert, and this time, you commit the transaction. It is only now that emp_table is permanently affected and has the new tuple (with a value of 'jeff') in it.

2-6. How Do You Start and End a Transaction in JDBC?

JDBC's default behavior is to consider every operation as atomic; this means for every single statement, a transaction begins, and if execution of the statement is successful, then it is committed; otherwise, an exception will be thrown (the transaction is rolled back automatically). Therefore, by default in the JDBC model, a connection is in autocommit mode, and its autocommit flag is set to true; this means each statement executed in this connection has its own transaction that is committed and rolled back when the call to executeQuery, for instance, is returning.

Using Explicit Transactions: Model 1

Using JDBC, you can use explicit transactions by following this model:

```
Connection conn = <get-a-valid-connection-object>;
// set the connection in explicit transaction mode
// begin a new transaction
conn.setAutoCommit(false);
    conn.executeQuery(sqlQuery1); // step-1
    conn.executeQuery(sqlQuery2); // step-2
    conn.executeQuery(sqlQuery3); // step-3
// commits all the transactions
conn.commit();
```

or by following this:

```
// cancel (roll back) all the transactions
conn.rollback();
```

Using Explicit Transactions: Model 2

Using JDBC, you can also use explicit transactions by following this model:

```
Connection conn = <get-a-valid-connection-object>
// set the connection in explicit transaction mode
// begin a new transaction
conn.setAutoCommit(false);
try {


    conn.executeQuery(sqlQuery3); // step 3
    // commits all the transactions
    conn.commit();
}
catch (Exception e){
    //cancel (roll back) all the transactions
    conn.rollback();
    // to see what went wrong
    e.printStackTrace();
}
```

Model 2 is the preferred way of doing transactions in JDBC.

Instead, you can set the transaction to the autocommit mode by using this:

```
conn.setAutoCommit(true);
```

2-7. What Is Connection Pool Management?

Some JDBC objects (such as java.sql.Connection) are expensive. It might take up to two to three seconds to create these objects. If you have a lot of clients that are all interested in database services, you do not need to create a single connection per client and then close/discard it after usage. Instead, you can define a *pool of connections* and, when a client needs a connection, lend a connection to a client. When the client is done with that borrowed connection, the client simply returns the connection to the pool of connections. (Returning the Connection object to the pool is called a *soft close.*) This way you can improve your application's performance.

To manage a pool of connections, you need a pool manager. A *pool manager* is a control structure (a class with some useful methods for checking in and checking out Connection objects) that manages Connection objects by requiring them to be checked in and out of a finite pool. The number of

Connection objects available at any given time will vary. A database client can check out a Connection object, use it, and then return it to the pool manager so some other client can use it. Sometimes, the connection pool will run dry (which means all Connection objects are checked out by clients); if no Connection objects are in the pool when a client makes a request, the client will have to wait until one is checked back in.

This sharing of Connection objects has at least two benefits:

Limited connections: The number of connections allowed to a particular database may be limited because of server capacity or database licensing restrictions. Hence, you need to limit the number of connections created. (You can best handle this with a pool of connections and pool manager infrastructure.)

Performance: Database connections are costly in terms of the amount (two to three seconds) of time needed for connecting and disconnecting to the database. Reusing and managing the connections (by the pool manager), rather than discarding and re-creating them every time one is needed, means that each Connection object will be connected to the database for its entire lifetime. (If a connection goes bad—because of a network problem, for example—then the pool manager will have to replace bad/defected/stalled connections with new good Connection objects.) This reuse of Connection objects results in a drastic increase in performance, as the connection is already live when the client acquires it.

Connection Pool Manager Minimal Functionality

The database connection pool manager should provide the following methods to database clients:

•

• *Release*: Release/free all resources, and close all connections at shutdown.

Also, for management purposes, a pool manager should provide the following methods:

• Get the pool status.
• Get the connections status (how many have been checked out, and so on).
• Enable/disable the pool manager.

Connection Pool Requirements

To define a connection pool, you need to provide the following:

• Database URL
• JDBC driver class
• Username (database user)
• Password (database user's password)
• Pool minimum (minimum number of connection to be created)
• Pool maximum (maximum number of connection to be created)
• Pool grow amount (how much the pool will be increased by)
• Timeout (timeout for Connection objects)
• Vendor parameters (that help you use vendor-specific features)
• Read-only/write (whether connections will update database)

Connection Pool Implementations

Many commercial/open-source implementations of connection pools are available.
The javax.sql package provides two public interfaces for managing a pool of Connection objects:

- ConnectionPoolDataSource: This is a factory for PooledConnection objects. An object that implements this interface will typically be registered with a naming service that is based on the Java Naming and Directory Interface (JNDI).

- PooledConnection: This is an object that provides hooks for connection pool management. A PooledConnection object represents a physical connection to a data source. The connection can be recycled rather than being closed when an application is finished with it, thus reducing the number of connections that need to be made.

The following are sample implementations of connection pools:

- The open-source Apache Avalon/Excalibur (org.apache.avalon.excalibur.pool)
- Oracle's package (oracle.jdbc.pool)
- Apache's open-source Commons Pool project
- Apache's open-source DBCP component and the package org.apache.commons.dbcp (which relies on code in the commons-pool package to provide the underlying object pool mechanisms it utilizes)
- WebLogic's connection pool (weblogic.jdbc.connectionPool)

A program that does not perform acceptably is not functional. Every program must satisfy a set of users, sometimes a large and diverse set. If the performance of the program is truly unacceptable to a significant number of those users, it will not be used. A program that is not being used is not performing its intended function.

From the Performance Management Guide at http://publib.boulder.ibm.com/infocenter/
pseries/index.jsp?topic=/com.ibm.aix.doc/aixbman/prftungd/perfplanning.htm

What is performance? And what is a performance problem? According to Merriam-Webster's dictionary, *performance* means the following:

- The execution of an action/something accomplished
- The fulfillment of a claim, promise, or request

When a software problem is reported, it can be either a functional problem or a performance problem. When a software application (such as a JDBC application) is not behaving correctly, this is referred to as a *functional problem*. For example, if a SQL query does not return the desired number of records for a table, this is a functional problem.

Sometimes functional problems lead to *performance problems*; for example, this happens when functions are working correctly but the speed of the functions is slow. In these cases, rather than tune the system, it is more important to determine the root cause of the problem and fix it.

In addition, if you make lots of unnecessary metadata calls to the database server, then your whole application will run slowly. Another example is when you create a database Connection object per client request and then discard it after the user request finishes. (Creating database Connection objects is expensive, so you should use a pool mechanism for sharing database Connection objects.) Experience indicates that performance advice usually depends on the specifics and type of your database application, server, and environment. This means there's no single silver bullet for performance problems.

The following sections contain tips to improve JDBC performance. The performance of your JDBC application depends on many factors, including the network speed, the Web server, the application server, the database server environment, and the way you have written your application. I'll focus on the JDBC component only.

To improve the performance of your JDBC applications, you should consider the following guidelines and use them when necessary.

Improving Performance: Selecting the Right JDBC Driver

The JDBC driver is the key player in any JDBC application; it acts as a mediator between the database application (written in Java) and the database server. When you are selecting a driver for an application, you need to consider the following factors:

- *Driver type*: JDBC defines four types of drivers to use.
  - Type 1 (JDBC-ODBC driver)
  - Type 2 (native-API, partly Java driver)
  - Type 3 (JDBC-net, all-Java driver)
  - Type 4 (native-protocol, all-Java driver)

---

drivers are faster than other drivers; type 3 has a facility for optimization techniques (such as connection pooling and caching database objects) provided by an application server, and type 4 drivers do not need to translate database calls to ODBC or a native connectivity interface. Type 2 drivers give better performance than type 1 drivers.

- *Speed/performance*: The driver must meet the project requirements.
- *Reliability*: The driver should perform for many hours in a production environment.
- *Security*: The driver should support access control lists for managing different users and resources.
- *Portability*: The driver should move from one platform to another.
- *Support*: The driver should be able to get help in case of a problem.
- *Price*: The driver should be affordable.
- *Open-source*: The driver should add/modify features in a timely manner.

Improving Performance: Simplifying SQL Queries

Evaluating complex SQL queries on a database server is slow and will reduce concurrency. Complex SQL queries will take more time to be parsed.

Improving Performance: Minimizing the Use of Database Metadata Methods

In general, database metadata methods take longer than other JDBC methods to execute. Compared to other JDBC methods, database metadata methods that generate java.sql.ResultSet objects are relatively slow. Database applications should cache information returned from result sets that generate database metadata methods so that multiple executions are not needed.

Improving Performance: Managing Database Connection Objects

This is one of the most important factors in JDBC application optimizations. Properly using Connection objects can improve the response time of your applications drastically. Lack of attention to connection management can bring your system to its knees in a heavy load (a large number of clients at the same time).

The java.sql.Connection interface encapsulates database connection functionality. Using the Connection interface, you can fine-tune the following operations, which we'll look at one by one in the following sections:

- Setting optimal connection properties
- Using a connection pool
- Controlling a transaction
- Choosing the optimal transaction isolation level
- Closing the connection when finished

Setting Optimal Connection Properties

A JDBC driver provides settings for connection properties. Each of these properties affects the performance. Some of the connection property names are different per driver. For example, Oracle and MySQL drivers have some common connection properties, but each of them also provides a unique set of connection properties for their driver implementations.

You can set connection properties in at least two ways and then create a new Connection object:

- Driver.connect(String url, java.util.Properties props)

where props (the second argument) represents the connection properties. For example, MySQL Connector/J has a property called autoReconnect, which can have true and false values. When autoReconnect=true, the driver tries to reestablish bad connections. (If a connection has become defunct/stale, then the driver reestablishes the connection.)

Setting an Optimal Row Prefetch Value

You can pass connection properties (that is, database-specific information to the database server by passing properties) using the java.util.Properties object to improve performance. For example, when you use the Oracle database, you can pass the default number of rows that must be prefetched from the database server and the default batch value that triggers an execution request. Oracle has the default value of 10 for both properties. By increasing the value of these properties, you can reduce the number of database calls, which in turn improves performance. The following code illustrates this approach. It sets defaultRowPrefetch to 40 and defaultBatchValue to 15. (Depending on your database application requirements, you should set these values accordingly.) DriverManager will use these properties to create Connection objects that satisfy these new property values. Some of these property names are the same among all vendors, but most of them will be different. You should consult the vendor's specific driver properties.

```
To set a prefetch value://import packages, and register the driver
import java.sql.Connection;
import java.sql.DriverManger;
import java.util.Properties;
import oracle.jdbc.OracleDriver;
...
// register the driver
DriverManager.registerDriver (new OracleDriver());
```

```
// define database user/password
String dbUser = "mp";
String dbPassword = "mp2";
String dbURL = "jdbc:oracle:thin:@myserver:1521:scorpian";
// specify the Properties object
Properties props = new Properties();
props.put("user", dbUser);
props.put("password", dbPassword);
props.put("defaultRowPrefetch","40");
props.put("defaultBatchValue","15");

// create a new Connection object with desired properties
Connection conn = DriverManager.getConnection(dbURL, props);
```

Using a Connection Pool

Among JDBC objects, creating a Connection object (java.sql.Connection) to the database server is expensive. It is even more expensive if the database server is located on a remote machine. A database application can easily spend several seconds every time it needs to establish a connection. *Connection pooling* is a technique used for sharing server resources (such as connections) among requesting clients.

Each time a resource (such as a Statement or PreparedStatement object) attempts to access a database, it must connect to that database. And to connect to a database, you need a database Connection object (that is, a java.sql.Connection object). A database connection incurs overhead—it requires resources to create the connection, maintain it, and then release it when it is no longer

applications because of the surfing nature of Internet users.

In a nutshell, a *connection pool* is a set of available connections that can be reused. It is the container (that can be represented as a Java object) of a finite set of Connection objects in which a defined amount of active database connections are waiting to be used and reused; when a client needs a database connection, it checks out a connection from a pool and then uses it (to do something useful such as querying a table), and then the client checks in the Connection object to the pool (after using the connection). All this takes place without physically opening or closing a connection on the database server, which alone will boost your database application's performance.

A connection pool contains a finite number of open database connections with a minimum and maximum number of connections (you need a maximum, because some databases limit the number of active connections), which means the connection pool has open connections between minimum and maximum numbers that you specify. The pool expands and shrinks between the minimum and maximum sizes depending on the incremental capacity. You need to give minimum, maximum, and incremental sizes (which is called a *grow amount*) as properties to the pool in order to maintain this functionality. You get the connection from the pool rather than directly from the database. For example, you can set up your connection pool using the following properties:

- *JDBC driver*: oracle.jdbc.driver.OracleDriver
- *Database URL*: jdbc:oracle:thin:@myserver:1521:maui
- *Database user*: mp
- *User's password*: mp2
- *Minimum*: 6
- *Maximum*: 30
- *Grow amount*: 3

Connection management is important to database application performance. Optimize your database application by connecting once and using multiple statement objects, instead of performing multiple connections. Several connection management tools are available, so you do not need to start from scratch. Refer to the next section, "Evaluating Choices for Connection Pools."

Evaluating Choices for Connection Pools

You have several choices when selecting a connection pool management tool:

- *Use a third-party connection pool management tool*: For this you need to license software from a vendor so you can understand the requirements and restrictions.

- *Use Apache Avalon Excalibur's pool*: You can find Avalon Excalibur's pool implementations in the org.apache.avalon.excalibur.pool package. Many implementations are thread-safe, and one is not. You have the option of not limiting used resources at all or limiting the used resources based on specific rules.

- *Use Apache Avalon Excalibur's* DataSource: Avalon Excalibur's DataSource package in org.apache.avalon.excalibur.datasource allows you to manage pooled connections in one of two ways. You can have the package handle it for you, or you can use a J2EE server's DataSource management. It provides the same kind of access regardless of which method you choose—since you obtain them through Avalon's Component Manager infrastructure.

- *Use Oracle's package*: This is oracle.jdbc.pool.

- *Use Apache's Commons Pool project*: You can find this at http://jakarta.apache.org/commons/pool.

package to provide the underlying object pool mechanisms it utilizes.

- *Use WebLogic's connection pool*: This is weblogic.jdbc.connectionPool.

- *Use connection pools supported by an application server (such as BEA's WebLogic and IBM's WebSphere)*: Most application servers support connection pooling, which you need to configure. (You need to give properties such as the minimum, maximum, and growth amount to the application server.)

- *You can use JDBC interfaces*: Use javax.sql.ConnectionPoolDataSource and javax.sql. PooledConnection if your driver implements these interfaces.

- *Use custom connection pools*: You can create your own connection pool if you are not using any application server or JDBC 2.0–compatible driver. In general, this is error-prone; you need to test your solution before releasing it to the production environment.

Controlling a Transaction

In database terminology, a *transaction* represents one atomic unit of work or a bunch of code in the program that executes in its entirety or not at all. To be precise, it is all or no work. In JDBC, a transaction is a set of one or more Statement objects that execute as a single unit. The java.sql.Connection interface provides the following methods to control a transaction in JDBC:

```
boolean  getAutoCommit();
void  setAutoCommit(boolean autoCommit);
void  commit();
void  rollback();
```

In JDBC, by default, the autocommit mode is true. This means a transaction starts and commits after each statement's execution on a connection. If a connection is in autocommit mode, then all its SQL statements will be executed and committed as individual transactions. (In this case, you do not need to write a commit() method explicitly after each statement.) When the autocommit mode is true, your database application gives poor performance (since beginning and ending/committing a transaction will cost some time). Therefore, to improve the performance of your application, it is better to group logically related JDBC statements and then execute all of them under the umbrella of a transaction.

This batch transaction gives good performance by reducing commit calls after each statement's execution. The batch transaction approach is as follows:

```
Connection conn = null;
Statement stmt = null;
PreparedStatement pstmt = null;
PreparedStatement pstmt2 = null;
try{
    conn = getConnection();
    // start transaction explicitly
    conn.setAutoCommit(false);
    String updateBookTable =
        "update books_table set author=? where isbn=?";
    pstmt = conn.prepareStatement(updateBookTable);
    pstmt.setString(1, "Don Knuth");
    pstmt.setString(2, "1234567890");
    pstmt.executeUpdate();


    pstmt2 = conn.prepareStatement(createBook);
    pstmt2.setString(1, "Mahmoud Parsian");
    pstmt2.setString(2, "1122334455");
    pstmt2.executeUpdate();

    //
    // end transaction explicitly
    //
    conn.commit();
}
catch(SQLException e){
    // handle the exception
    // undo all of the operations
    connection.rollback();
}
finally{
    // close the JDBC resources
    DatabaseUtil.close(pstmt);
    DatabaseUtil.close(pstmt2);
    DatabaseUtil.close(conn);
}
```

Choosing the Optimal Transaction Isolation Level

According to http://www.javaperformancetuning.com/tips/jdbctransaction.shtml, you should do the following:

If you are not using stored procedures or triggers, turn off autocommit. All transaction levels operate faster with autocommit turned off, and doing this means you must code commits. Coding commits while leaving auto-commit on will result in extra commits being done for every db operation. Use the appropriate transaction level. Increasing performance costs for transaction levels are TRANSACTION_NONE, TRANSACTION_READ_UNCOMMITTED, TRANSACTION_READ_COMMITTED, TRANSACTION_REPEATABLE_READ, TRANSACTION_ SERIALIZABLE. Note that TRANSACTION_NONE, with autocommit set to true gives access to triggers, stored procedures, and large object columns.

Data accessibility is controlled through the transaction isolation level mechanism. Transaction isolation level determines the degree to which multiple interleaved transactions are prevented from interfering with each other in a multiuser database system. How do you achieve transaction isolation? You achieve it by locking mechanisms that guide the reading and writing of transaction data.

The java.sql.Connection interface provides methods and constants to set and get transaction isolation levels. For example:

```
public interface Connection {
    public static final int   TRANSACTION_NONE                = 0
    public static final int   TRANSACTION_READ_COMMITTED      = 2
    public static final int   TRANSACTION_READ_UNCOMMITTED    = 1
    public static final int   TRANSACTION_REPEATABLE_READ      = 4
    public static final int   TRANSACTION_SERIALIZABLE         = 8
    int  getTransactionIsolation();
    void  setTransactionIsolation(int transactionIsolationLevel);
}
```

passing the previous constants (TRANSACTION_XXX) to this method. You can also get the existing transaction isolation level with the getTransactionIsolation() method.

Improving Performance: Avoiding Using Generic Search Patterns

DatabaseMetaData and ResultSetMetaData have methods that you can use to issue generic search patterns to the database server by passing the null values. Using null arguments or search patterns in database metadata methods results in generating time-consuming queries. (In a production environment, you might cache these metadata values in order to improve the performance.) In addition, network traffic potentially increases because of unwanted results. Always supply as many non-null arguments to result sets that generate database metadata methods as possible.

Because DatabaseMetaData methods are slow, database applications should invoke them as efficiently as possible. Many applications pass the fewest non-null arguments necessary for the function to return success.

The non-efficient method call is as follows:

```
Connection conn = ...;
DatabaseMetaData meta = conn.getMetaData();
ResultSet rs = meta.getTables (null, null, "EmpTable", null);
```

```
  The efficient method call is:Connection conn = ...;
DatabaseMetaData meta = conn.getMetaData();
String[] tableTypes = { "TABLE" };
ResultSet rs =
    meta.getTables ("empCatalog", "empSchema", "EmpTable", tableTypes);
```

Improving Performance: Retrieving Only Required Data

Retrieving only the required data can reduce the size of data retrieved. For example, do not issue the following:

```
select * from emp_table where ...
```

If you just need the id and name, then issue the following:

```
select id, name from emp_table where ...
```

You should return only the rows you need. If you return ten columns when you need only two columns, you will get decreased performance, especially if the unnecessary rows include long data.

Another way to reduce network traffic and improve your application performance is to reduce the size of any data being retrieved to some manageable limit by calling driver-specific methods:

- Statement.setMaxRows(int max): Sets the limit for the maximum number of rows that any ResultSet object can contain to the given number. If the limit is exceeded, the excess rows are silently dropped.

- Statement.setMaxFieldSize(): Sets the limit for the maximum number of bytes in a ResultSet column storing character or binary values to the given number of bytes. This limit applies only to BINARY, VARBINARY, LONGVARBINARY, CHAR, VARCHAR, and LONGVARCHAR fields. If the limit is exceeded, the excess data is silently discarded. For maximum portability, use values greater than 256.

- ResultSet.setFetchSize(int max): Gives the JDBC driver a hint as to the number of rows that should be fetched from the database when more rows are needed for this ResultSet

- Statement.setFetchSize(int max): Gives the JDBC driver a hint as to the number of rows that should be fetched from the database.

Another method of reducing the size of the data being retrieved is to decrease the column size. You can accomplish this by defining an optimized schema. For example, if the driver allows you to define the packet size, use the smallest packet size that will meet your needs.

The Statement Object vs. the PreparedStatement Object

Generally, use the Statement object instead of the PreparedStatement object. If you plan to execute a SQL query many times with different input parameter values, then you should use the PreparedStatement object. JDBC drivers are optimized based on the perceived use of the functions being executed. Choose between the PreparedStatement object and the Statement object depending on the planned use. The Statement object is optimized for a single execution of a SQL statement. In contrast, the PreparedStatement object is optimized for SQL statements that will be executed two or more times. You should note that the overhead for the initial execution of a PreparedStatement object is high. The advantage comes with subsequent executions of the SQL statement.

How to Choose the Right Cursor

Choosing the appropriate type of cursor (that is, the ResultSet object) allows maximum application flexibility. Three types of cursors exist and can impact the performance of your JDBC application:

ResultSet.TYPE_FORWARD_ONLY: The constant indicating the type for a ResultSet object whose cursor can move only forward. A forward-only cursor provides excellent performance for sequential reads of all the rows in a table.

ResultSet.TYPE_SCROLL_INSENSITIVE: The constant indicating the type for a ResultSet object that is scrollable but generally not sensitive to changes made by others. Insensitive cursors are ideal for database applications that require high levels of concurrency on the database server and require the ability to scroll forward and backward through result sets. The first request to an insensitive cursor fetches all the rows and stores them on the client. Therefore, the first request is very slow when long data is retrieved. Note that subsequent requests do not require any network traffic and are processed quickly.

ResultSet.TYPE_SCROLL_SENSITIVE: The constant indicating the type for a ResultSet object that is scrollable and generally sensitive to changes made by others. Using sensitive cursors, each request generates network traffic; therefore, performance can be very slow.

Batch Multiple Update Statements

A *batch update* is a set of multiple update statements (such as SQL's UPDATE and INSERT statements) submitted to the database for processing as one. Sending multiple update statements to the database together as a unit can, in some situations, be much more efficient than sending each update statement separately. You can use the java.sql.Statement, java.sql.PreparedStatement, and java.sql. CallableStatement objects to submit batch updates.

The Oracle and MySQL JDBC drivers allow you to accumulate SQL INSERT, SQL DELETE, and SQL UPDATE operations of Statement and PreparedStatement objects at the client and send them to the database server in batches. This feature reduces round-trips to the database server; therefore, this can improve the performance of database applications.

```
Connection conn = null;
Statement stmt = null;
try {
    // get a valid Connection object
    conn = ...
    // turn off autocommit
    // and start a new transaction
    conn.setAutoCommit(false);

    stmt = conn.createStatement();
    stmt.addBatch(
        "INSERT INTO books_table(isbn, author) VALUES ('11223344', 'Donald Knuth')");
    stmt.addBatch(
        "INSERT INTO books_table(isbn, author) VALUES ('11223355', 'Donald Knuth')");
    stmt.addBatch(
        "INSERT INTO dept_table(name, city) VALUES ('software', 'New York')");
    stmt.addBatch(
        "INSERT INTO dept_table(name, city) VALUES ('marketing', 'Los Gatos')");
    stmt.addBatch("delete from dept_table where name = 'hardware'");

    // submit a batch of update commands for execution
    int[] updateCounts = stmt.executeBatch();

    // commit the transaction
    conn.commit();
}
catch(Exception e) {
    // handle the exception
```

```
        e.printStackTrace();
        conn.rollback();
}
```

Batch Multiple Update Statements Using java.sql.PreparedStatement

The following code illustrates batch updates using the java.sql.PreparedStatement object:

```
Connection conn = null;
PreparedStatement pstmt = null;
try {
    // get a valid Connection object
    conn = ...
    // turn off autocommit
    // and start a new transaction
    conn.setAutoCommit(false);

    pstmt = conn.prepareStatement("insert into dept_table values (?, ?)");

    pstmt.setString (1, "sales");
    pstmt.setString (2, "Troy");
    pstmt.addBatch();   //JDBC queues this for later execution

    pstmt.setString (1, "business");
    pstmt.setString (2, "Los Angeles");
    pstmt.addBatch();   //JDBC queues this for later execution


    pstmt.addBatch();   //JDBC queues this for later execution

    // now, the queue size equals the batch value of 3
    // submit a batch of update commands for execution
    // submit the updates to the DBMS; calling the
    // PreparedStatement.executeBatch() clears the statement's
    // associated list of batch elements.
    int[] updateCounts = pstmt.executeBatch();

    // commit the transaction
    conn.commit();
}
catch(Exception e) {
    // handle the exception
    e.printStackTrace();
    conn.rollback();
}
```

Batch Multiple Update Statements Using java.sql.CallableStatement

The batch update facility works the same with CallableStatement objects as it does with PreparedStatement objects. You can use the CallableStatement (which extends PreparedStatement) to execute SQL *stored procedures* (methods/procedures defined inside the database server).

Multiple sets of input parameter values may be associated with a callable statement and sent to the DBMS together. Stored procedures invoked using the batch update facility with a callable statement must return an update count and may not have IN or INOUT parameters. The CallableStatement. executeBatch() method should throw an exception if this restriction is violated.

To call a stored procedure, you invoke methods in the `CallableStatement` interface. The basic steps are as follows:

1. Invoke the `Connection.prepareCall` method to create a `CallableStatement` object.

2. Invoke the `CallableStatement.setXXX` methods to pass values to the input (IN) parameters.

3. Invoke the `CallableStatement.registerOutParameter` method to indicate which parameters are output-only (OUT) parameters or input and output (INOUT) parameters.

4. Invoke the `CallableStatement.executeUpdate` method to call the stored procedure.

5. If the stored procedure returns result sets, retrieve the result sets.

6. Invoke the `CallableStatement.getXXX` methods to retrieve values from the OUT parameters or INOUT parameters.

Please note that for batch updates steps 3, 5, and 6 are not required.

The following code snippet illustrates calling a stored procedure that has two input parameters, no output parameters, and no returned `ResultSet` objects:

```
Connection conn = null;
CallableStatement cstmt = null;
...
// Create a CallableStatement object
cstmt = con.prepareCall("CALL insert_book_stored_procedure(?, ?)");

// prepare the first batch
cstmt.setString (1, "11223344");



// prepare the second batch
cstmt.setString (1, "11223377");
cstmt.setString (2, "Donald E. Knuth");
cstmt.addBatch(); // queue the stored procedure call

// call the stored procedures
cstmt.executeBatch();
```

Improving Performance: Caching PreparedStatement Objects

Caching prepared statements is another mechanism (introduced in JDBC 3.0) through which you can improve a JDBC application's response time. Use `PreparedStatement` object pooling only with SQL queries that rarely change. You should not use this in queries that have dynamically generated SQL or queries with frequently changing variables.

Improving Performance: Avoiding Memory Leaks

If you receive messages that you are "running out of cursors" or that you are "running out of memory," make sure all your `Statement`, `PreparedStatement`, `CallableStatement`, `Connection`, and `ResultSet` objects are explicitly closed. To close these objects, use the `close()` method. From a software engineering point of view, you should put `close()` statements in a `finally` clause because this guarantees that the statements in the `finally` clause will be executed as the last step regardless of whether an exception has taken place.

The following code provides a sample code template to do this:

```java
Connection conn = null;
Statement stmt = null;
PreparedStatement pstmt = null;
ResultSet rs = null;
try {
    // get a valid Connection object
    conn = ...
    // turn off autocommit, and start a new transaction
    conn.setAutoCommit(false);

    stmt = conn.createStatement();
    stmt.executeUpdate("create table dept_table(...)");

    String insert = "insert into dept_table values (?, ?)";
    pstmt = conn.prepareStatement(insert);

    pstmt.setString (1, "sales");
    pstmt.setString (2, "Troy");
    pstmt.addBatch();   //JDBC queues this for later execution

    pstmt.setString (1, "business");
    pstmt.setString (2, "Los Angeles");
    pstmt.addBatch();   //JDBC queues this for later execution

    // now, the queue size equals the batch value of 3
    // submit a batch of update commands for execution


    // associated list of batch elements.
    int[] updateCounts = pstmt.executeBatch();

    rs = stmt.executeQuery("select * from dept_table");
    while (rs.next()) {
        ...
    }

    // commit the transaction
    conn.commit();
}
catch(Exception e) {
    // handle the exception
    e.printStackTrace();
    conn.rollback();
}
finally {
    // close JDBC resources
    DatabaseUtil.close(rs);
    DatabaseUtil.close(stmt);
    DatabaseUtil.close(pstmt);
    DatabaseUtil.close(conn);
}
```

The following is according to Oracle documentation:

The Oracle JDBC drivers do not have finalizer methods. They perform cleanup routines by using the close() method of the ResultSet and Statement classes. If you do not explicitly close your result set and statement objects, significant memory leaks can occur. You could also run out of cursors in the database. Closing a result set or statement releases the corresponding cursor in the database. Similarly, you must explicitly close Connection objects to avoid leaking and running out of cursors on the server side. When you close the connection, the JDBC driver closes any open statement objects associated with it, thus releasing the cursor objects on the server side.

For properly closing JDBC resources such as `Connection`, `ResultSet`, and `Statement`, refer to Chapter 14.

2-9. What Are Oracle's JDBC Drivers?

Oracle's JDBC drivers, releases 7.3.4, 8.0, 9.0, and 10g (and their higher versions), implement the standard JDBC interface as defined at `http://java.sun.com/jdbc`. These drivers comply with JDBC versions 1, 2, and 3. In addition to the standard JDBC API, Oracle drivers provide properties, type, and performance extensions. In most situations, as much as possible, you should stay away from using the extensions (otherwise your programs will not be portable to other JDBC drivers).

Introducing the Oracle JDBC Thin Driver

The Thin driver does not require Oracle software on the client side. It connects to any Oracle database

Registering the Oracle JDBC Thin Driver

There are several ways to register the driver:

```
//
//  this approach uses the Class.forName() method
//
try {
   Class.forName("oracle.jdbc.driver.OracleDriver");
}
catch(ClassNotFoundException e) {
   // handle the exception properly
   System.out.println("cannot find  oracle.jdbc.driver.OracleDriver");
   System.exit(1);
}
```

```
//
// this approach uses the DriverManager.registerDriver() method
//
try {
   DriverManager.registerDrive( new oracle.jdbc.driver.OracleDriver());
}
catch(SQLException e) {
   // handle the exception properly
   System.out.println("cannot register oracle.jdbc.driver.OracleDriver");
   System.exit(1);
}
```

Introducing the Oracle JDBC OCI Driver

What is the OCI? The OCI is a set of low-level APIs to perform Oracle database operations (for example, logon, execute, parse, fetch records). OCI programs are normally written in C/C++, although they can be written in almost any programming language. OCI programs are not precompiled. To use the OCI driver, you must also download the appropriate shared library or DLL files.

Oracle's JDBC OCI drivers are type 2 JDBC drivers. They provide an implementation of the JDBC interfaces, and the implementation uses the OCI to interact with an Oracle database. This driver can access Oracle 7.x and higher servers. Because they use native methods, they are platform-specific. The JDBC OCI driver requires an Oracle client installation including SQL*Net and all other dependent files. The supported platforms are as follows:

- *Solaris*: Version 2.5 and above

- *Windows*: Windows 95 and NT 3.51 and above

- *Linux*: Red Hat 9

2-10. How Do You Connect with Oracle's JDBC Thin Driver?

The JDBC Thin driver provides the only way to access Oracle from the Web (applets). It is smaller and faster than the OCI drivers, and it does not require a preinstalled version of the JDBC drivers. The following code shows how to connect with the Thin driver:

```java
import java.sql.*;
import jcb.util.DatabaseUtil;



        String driver = "oracle.jdbc.driver.OracleDriver";
        String url = "jdbc:oracle:thin:@localhost:1521:scorpian";
        String username = "octopus";
        String password = "octopus";
        Class.forName(driver);     // load Oracle driver
        return DriverManager.getConnection(url, username, password);
    }

    public static void main (String args []) throws Exception {
        Connection conn = null;
        Statement stmt = null;
        ResultSet rs = null;
        try {
            conn = getConnection();
            stmt = conn.createStatement();
            rs = stmt.executeQuery ("select object_name from user_objects");

            while (rs.next()) {
                    // print object_name
                    System.out.println (rs.getString(1));
            }
        }
        catch(Exception e) {
            // handle exception
            System.out.println(e.getMessage());
        }
        finally {
            DatabaseUtil.close(rs);
            DatabaseUtil.close(stmt);
```

```
            DatabaseUtil.close(conn);
        }
    }
}
```

2-11. How Do You Connect with Oracle's JDBC OCI Driver?

To use OCI drivers, you must have Net8 (SQL*Net) installed and working before attempting to use one of the OCI drivers. The solution is almost identical to the Thin driver with the exception of the getConnection() method:

```
public static Connection getConnection() throws Exception {
    String driver = "oracle.jdbc.driver.OracleDriver";
    String url = "jdbc:oracle:oci9:@scorpian";
    String username = "octopus";
    String password = "octopus";
    Class.forName(driver);     // load Oracle driver
    return DriverManager.getConnection(url, username, password);
}
```

2-12. How Do You Connect with Oracle's KPRB Driver?

You can obtain a handle to the default or current connection (KPRB driver) by calling the OracleDriver. defaultConnection() method. You should note that you do not need to specify a database URL, username, or password, as you are already connected to a database session.

exception of the getConnection() method:

```
public static Connection getConnection() throws Exception {
    oracle.jdbc.driver.OracleDriver oracleDriver =
                    new oracle.jdbc.driver.OracleDriver();
    return oracleDriver.defaultConnection();
}
```

Please note that if you use Oracle's KPRB driver, do not close the default connection (otherwise the database will shut down).

2-13. What Are MySQL's JDBC Drivers?

MySQL Connector/J is the official JDBC driver for MySQL. The following is according to the MySQL documentation (http://www.mysql.com/products/connector-j/index.html):

MySQL Connector/J is a native Java driver that converts JDBC calls into the network protocol used by the MySQL database. It lets developers working with the Java programming language easily build programs and applets that interact with MySQL and connect all corporate data, even in a heterogeneous environment. MySQL Connector/J is a type 4 JDBC driver and has a complete JDBC feature set that supports the capabilities of MySQL.

MySQL Connector/J is an implementation of Sun's JDBC 3.0 API for the MySQL relational database server. It strives to conform as much as possible to the JDBC API as specified at http://java. sun.com/jdbc. It is known to work with many third-party products, including Apache Tomcat, JBoss, BEA WebLogic, IBM WebSphere, Eclipse, and Borland JBuilder.

What Is MySQL's Driver Class Name?

The name of the class that implements java.sql.Driver in MySQL Connector/J is com.mysql.jdbc.
Driver. The org.gjt.mm.mysql.Driver class name is also usable to remain backward-compatible
with MM.MySQL. You should use this class name when registering the driver or when otherwise
configuring software to use MySQL Connector/J.

What Is the JDBC URL Format for MySQL Connector/J?

The JDBC URL format for MySQL Connector/J is as follows, with the items in square brackets ([ ])
being optional:

```
jdbc:mysql://[host][,failoverhost...][:port]/[database][?propertyName1]
[=propertyValue1][&propertyName2][=propertyValue2]...
```

If the hostname is not specified, it defaults to 127.0.0.1. If the port is not specified, it defaults
to 3306, the default port number for MySQL servers. For connection properties, please refer to
http://www.mysql.com/documentation/connector-j/index.html.

2-14. How Do You Register the MySQL Driver with the Driver Manager?

The following code shows how to register the MySQL driver with the driver manager:

```
public class LoadMySQLDriver {
    public static void main(String[] args) {


        }
        catch (ClassNotFoundException ce) {
            // handle the exception
        }
        catch (Exception e) {
            // handle the exception
        }
    }
}
```

2-15. How Do You Get a MySQL Connection from the Driver Manager?

The following example shows how you can get a Connection object from the driver manager. There
are a few different signatures for the getConnection() method. You should consult the JDK API
documentation for the proper methods to use.

The following are the methods you can use to create a MySQL Connection object:

- *Method 1*: Use only the database URL.

- *Method 2*: Use the database URL and pass "user" and "password" as parameters.

- *Method 3*: Pass the "user" and "password" parameters as a java.util.Properties object.

Method 1: Using Only the Database URL

The following code shows the first method:

```java
import java.sql.Connection;
import java.sql.DriverManager;
import java.sql.SQLException;

class TestGetMySQLConnection_1
    public static Connection
        getConnection(String dbURL, String user, String password)
        throws SQLException, ClassNotFoundException {
        //load a driver
        Class.forName("com.mysql.jdbc.Driver");
        // form a connection string acceptable to MySQL driver
        String connString =
            dbURL + "?user=" + user + "&password=" + password;
        return DriverManager.getConnection(connString);
    }

    public static void main(String[] args) {
        Connection conn = null;
        try {
            conn = getConnection("jdbc:mysql://localhost/empDB",
                                    "root", "root2");
            // do something useful with the Connection object
        }
        catch (ClassNotFoundException ce) {
            // there was problem in loading a driver
            // handle the exception


            // handle any database exceptions
            System.out.println("SQLException: " + ex.getMessage());
            System.out.println("SQLState: " + ex.getSQLState());
            System.out.println("VendorError: " + ex.getErrorCode());
        }
    }
}
```

Method 2: Using the Database URL and Passing "user" and "password" As Parameters

The following code shows the second method:

```java
import java.sql.Connection;
import java.sql.DriverManager;
import java.sql.SQLException;

class TestGetMySQLConnection_2
    public static Connection
        getConnection(String dbURL, String user, String password)
        throws SQLException, ClassNotFoundException {
        //load a driver
        Class.forName("com.mysql.jdbc.Driver");
        return DriverManager.getConnection(dbURL, user, password);
    }

    public static void main(String[] args) {
        Connection conn = null;
```

```
    try {
        conn = getConnection("jdbc:mysql://localhost/empDB",
                             "root", "root2");
        // do something useful with the Connection object
    }
    catch (ClassNotFoundException ce) {
        // there was problem in loading a driver
        // handle the exception
    }
    catch (SQLException e) {
        // handle any exceptions
        System.out.println("SQLException: " + ex.getMessage());
        System.out.println("SQLState: " + ex.getSQLState());
        System.out.println("VendorError: " + ex.getErrorCode());
    }
  }
}
```

Method 3: Passing "user" and "password" Parameters As a java.util.Properties Object

The following code shows the third method:

```
import java.sql.Connection;
import java.sql.DriverManager;
import java.sql.SQLException;
import java.util.Properties;




                                String user,
                                String password)
        throws SQLException, ClassNotFoundException {
        //load a driver
        Class.forName("com.mysql.jdbc.Driver");
        // create a Properties object and put the "user" and "password"
        // information; you may add additional properties to the driver
        // by invoking props.put(key, value) method.
        Properties props = new Properties();
        props.put("user", user);
        props.put("password", password);
        // add additional connection properties
        // Should the driver try to reestablish bad connections?
        // the default value is false; here we set it to true.
        // not that these are driver-specific keys.
        props.put("autoReconnect", "true");

        return DriverManager.getConnection(dbURL, props);
    }

    public static void main(String[] args) {
        Connection conn = null;
        try {
            conn = getConnection("jdbc:mysql://localhost/empDB",
                                 "root", "root2");

            // do something useful with the Connection object
        }
```

```
        catch (ClassNotFoundException ce) {
            // there was problem in loading a driver
            // handle the exception
        }
        catch (SQLException e) {
            // handle any exceptions
            System.out.println("SQLException: " + ex.getMessage());
            System.out.println("SQLState: " + ex.getSQLState());
            System.out.println("VendorError: " + ex.getErrorCode());
        }
    }
}
```

2-16. What Are the Key JDBC Concepts for an Oracle Database?

The following code illustrates JDBC concepts for an Oracle database. I will show you some sample output and discuss it line by line after presenting the full code here:

```
1 import java.sql.*;
2 import jcb.util.DatabaseUtil;
3
4 public class SimpleProgramToAccessOracleDatabase {
5     public static Connection getConnection()
6         throws SQLException {
7         String driver = "oracle.jdbc.driver.OracleDriver";
8         // load the Oracle JDBC Driver


11         String dbURL = "jdbc:oracle:thin:@localhost:1521:scorpian";
12         String dbUser = "octopus";
13         String dbPassword = "octopus";
14         // get a database Connection object: A connection (session)
15         // with a specific database. SQL statements are executed, and
16         // results are returned within the context of a connection.
17         return DriverManager.getConnection(dbURL, dbUser, dbPassword);
18     }
19
20     public static void main(String[] args)
21         throws SQLException {
22         Connection conn = null ; // Connection object
23         Statement stmt = null;    // statement object
24         ResultSet rs = null;      // result set object
25         try {
26             conn = getConnection(); // without Connection, can not do much
27             // create a statement: This object will be used for executing
28             // a static SQL statement and returning the results it produces.
29             stmt = conn.createStatement();
30
31             // start a transaction
32             conn.setAutoCommit(false);
33
34             // create a table called cats_tricks
35             stmt.executeUpdate("CREATE TABLE cats_tricks " +
36                 "(name VARCHAR2(30), trick VARCHAR2(30))");
37             // insert two new records to the cats_tricks table
38             stmt.executeUpdate(
```

```
39                "INSERT INTO cats_tricks VALUES('mono', 'rollover')" );
40            stmt.executeUpdate(
41                "INSERT INTO cats_tricks VALUES('mono', 'jump')" );
42
43            // commit the transaction
44            conn.commit();
45
46            // set autocommit to true (from now on every single
47            // statement will be treated as a single transaction
48            conn.setAutoCommit(true) ;
49
50            // get all the records from the cats_tricks table
51            rs = stmt.executeQuery(
52                "SELECT name, trick FROM cats_tricks");
53
54            // iterate the result set, and get one row at a time
55            while( rs.next() ) {
56                String name = rs.getString(1);  // 1st column in query
57                String trick = rs.getString(2); // 2nd column in query
58                System.out.println("name="+name);
59                System.out.println("trick="+trick);
60                System.out.println("==========");
61            }
62        }
63        catch(ClassNotFoundException ce){
64            // if the driver class not found, then we will be here


67        catch(SQLException e){
68            // something went wrong, we are handling the exception here
69            if ( conn != null ){
70                conn.rollback();
71                conn.setAutoCommit(true);
72            }
73
74            System.out.println("--- SQLException caught ---");
75            // iterate and get all of the errors as much as possible.
76            while ( e != null ){
77                System.out.println("Message     : " + e.getMessage());
78                System.out.println("SQLState    : " + e.getSQLState());
79                System.out.println("ErrorCode : " + e.getErrorCode());
80                System.out.println("---");
81                e = e.getNextException();
82            }
83        }
84        finally { // close db resources
85            DatabaseUtil.close(rs);
86            DatabaseUtil.close(stmt);
87            DatabaseUtil.close(conn);
88        }
89    }
90 }
```

Running the Simple Program

This code shows how to run the program:

```
$ javac SimpleProgramToAccessOracleDatabase.java
$ java SimpleProgramToAccessOracleDatabase
name=mono
trick=rollover
==========
name=mono
trick=jump
==========

$ sqlplus octopus/octopus
SQL*Plus: Release 9.2.0.1.0 - Production on Sun Feb 22 23:23:10 2004
SQL> desc cats_tricks;
 Name                   Null?    Type
 ------------------ -------- --------------
 NAME                            VARCHAR2(30)
 TRICK                           VARCHAR2(30)

SQL> select * from cats_tricks;

NAME        TRICK
---------- ----------
mono        rollover
mono        jump

SQL>
```

The following list breaks down and explains the program line by line:

- *Lines 1–2*: Import the required classes and interfaces from the java.sql package.
- *Lines 5–18*: Define the Oracle Connection object (use the driver manager to create a Connection object).
- *Lines 29–29*: Using the Connection object (called conn), create a generic Statement object, which can execute SQL statements and queries.
- *Lines 32–32*: Start a transaction by setting the autocommit mode to false.
- *Lines 35–40*: Issue a set of SQL statements (none of these will be committed until you execute conn.commit(), which will commit all the SQL statements to your desired database).
- *Lines 44–44*: Commit the transaction by executing conn.commit(). Either all the SQL statements will be executed successfully or none of them will execute (if there is a problem).
- *Lines 48–48*: Set the autocommit mode to true (from now on every single SQL statement will be treated as a single transaction).
- *Lines 51–51*: Get all the records from the cats_tricks table (by using the Statement. executeQuery() method, which returns a ResultSet object and holds the result of the SQL query).
- *Lines 55–61*: Iterate the result set (the ResultSet object called rs), and get one row at a time.
- *Lines 67–83*: Deal with exception handling. If the driver class not found, then you will be inside lines 69–70; if there is a database exception (identified by SQLException), then the program logic will take you to lines 73–87.
- *Lines 84–88*: Close the database resources.

2-17. What Are the Key JDBC Concepts for a MySQL Database?

The solution to this problem is the same as the previous solution—you will merely replace the getConnection() method with the following (which is specific to the MySQL database):

```
public static Connection getConnection()
     throws SQLException {
     String driver = " com.mysql.jdbc.Driver ";
     // load the MySQL JDBC driver
     Class.forName(driver);
     // define database connection parameters
     String dbURL = " jdbc:mysql://localhost/tiger ";
     String dbUser = "root";
     String dbPassword = "root";
     // get a database Connection object: A connection (session)
     // with a specific database. SQL statements are executed, and
     // results are returned within the context of a connection.
     return DriverManager.getConnection(dbURL, dbUser, dbPassword);
}
```

To run this simple program, use this code:

```
$ javac SimpleProgramToAccessMySQLDatabase.java
$ java SimpleProgramToAccessMySQLDatabase
name=mono
trick=rollover
==========
name=mono

==========

$ mysql
Welcome to the MySQL monitor.  Commands end with ; or \g.
Your MySQL connection id is 4 to server version: 4.0.15-nt

mysql> show databases;
+----------+
| Database |
+----------+
| empdb    |
| javatest |
| mysql    |
| test     |
| tiger    |
+----------+
5 rows in set (0.02 sec)

mysql> use tiger;
Database changed
mysql> desc cats_tricks;
+-------+-------------+------+-----+---------+-------+
| Field | Type        | Null | Key | Default | Extra |
+-------+-------------+------+-----+---------+-------+
| name  | varchar(30) | YES  |     | NULL    |       |
| trick | varchar(30) | YES  |     | NULL    |       |
+-------+-------------+------+-----+---------+-------+
2 rows in set (0.00 sec)
```

```
mysql> select * from cats_tricks;
+------+----------+
| name | trick    |
+------+----------+
| mono | rollover |
| mono | jump     |
+------+----------+
2 rows in set (0.00 sec)
```

2-18. How Do You Set Your Environment for JDBC?

To enable the JDBC APIs, you must set your CLASSPATH environmental variable to indicate to the Java virtual machine and Java-based applications where to find the class libraries, including user-defined class libraries. To view the content of a CLASSPATH on Windows, use the following code:

```
$ set CLASSPATH
CLASSPATH=.;c:\jdk142\lib\dt.jar;c:\jdk142\lib\tools.jar;
c:\mp\book\src;c:\j\httpclient.jar
```

To view the content of a CLASSPATH on Unix/Linux, use the following code:

```
$ echo $CLASSPATH
.:/usr/java/j2sdk1.4.2_03/lib/dt.jar:
/usr/java/j2sdk1.4.2_03/lib/tools.jar:
/usr/java/j2sdk1.4.2_03/lib/htmlconverter.jar
```

For example, if you want to add the Oracle driver to your CLASSPATH, then you must do the fol-

---

■**Note** C:\oracle\product\10.1.0\Db_1\jdbc\lib\ojdbc14.jar is an Oracle JDBC driver for the Oracle 10*g* database in a Windows environment, and /export/oracle/product/10.1.0/Db_1/jdbc/lib/ojdbc14.jar is an Oracle JDBC driver for the Oracle 10*g* database in a Linux environment.

Do the following for Windows:

```
$ set   CLASSPATH=%CLASSPATH%;
c:\oracle\product\10.1.0\Db_1\jdbc\lib\ojdbc14.jar
$ set CLASSPATH
CLASSPATH=.;c:\jdk142\lib\dt.jar;c:\jdk142\lib\tools.jar;
c:\mp\book\src;c:\j\httpclient.jar;
c:\oracle\product\10.1.0\Db_1\jdbc\lib\ojdbc14.jar
```

Do the following for Unix/Linux:

```
$ export CLASSPATH=$CLASSPATH:\
/export/oracle/product/10.1.0/Db_1/jdbc/lib/ojdbc14.jar
$ echo $CLASSPATH
.:/usr/java/j2sdk1.4.2_03/lib/dt.jar:
/usr/java/j2sdk1.4.2_03/lib/tools.jar:
/usr/java/j2sdk1.4.2_03/lib/htmlconverter.jar:
/export/oracle/product/10.1.0/Db_1/jdbc/lib/ojdbc14.jar
```

Each time you want to use JDBC, you will have to set your CLASSPATH properly. You can place these settings in script/batch files (.bat in a Windows environment and .sh files a Unix/Linux environment). To avoid typing these settings (when you need the CLASSPATH), you may invoke the scripts.

2-19. What Are Some JDBC Resources?

Plenty of JDBC resources are available; I'll mention some of the books, tools, and Web sites devoted to JDBC.

JDBC Books

These are useful and practical books about JDBC topics:

- *JDBC API Tutorial and Reference, Third Edition* by Maydene Fisher, Jon Ellis, and Jonathan Bruce (Addison Wesley, 2003)
- *Database Programming with JDBC and Java, Second Edition* by George Reese (O'Reilly, 2000)
- *Java Persistence for Relational Databases* by Richard Sperko (Apress, 2003)
- *Java Programming with Oracle JDBC* by Donald Bales (O'Reilly, 2001)
- *Oracle 9i Java Programming: Solutions for Developers Using PL/SQL and Java* by Bjarki Holm et al. (Wrox, 2001)
- *MySQL Cookbook* by Paul DuBois (O'Reilly, 2002)

JDBC Web Sites

For links to information about JDBC technology, see the JDBC technology home page at `http://java.sun.com/products/jdbc/index.jsp`. The following are additional helpful links:

-

- *MySQL database*: `http://www.mysql.com`
- *JDBC documentation*: `http://dev.mysql.com/doc/connector/j/en/index.html`
- *Aids for learning to use the JDBC API*: `http://java.sun.com/products/jdbc/learning.html`
- *JDBC tutorial*: `http://java.sun.com/docs/books/tutorial/jdbc/`
- *JDBC API interface in a nutshell*: `http://www.cs.unc.edu/Courses/wwwp-s98/members/thornett/jdbc/183.html`
- *Tutorial on using JDBC under Windows*: `http://www.npac.syr.edu/users/gcf/uccjdbcaccess97/`
- *JDBC, explained*: `http://www-106.ibm.com/developerworks/db2/library/techarticle/norton/0102_norton.html`
- *Online courses about database access*: `http://java.sun.com/developer/onlineTraining/Database`
- *Free JDBC books:* `http://www.javaolympus.com/freebooks/FreeJDBCBooks.jsp`
- *JDBC Frequently Asked Questions (FAQs)*:
  - `http://java.sun.com/products/jdbc/faq.html#1`
  - `http://www.jguru.com/faq/JDBC`
  - `http://www.oracle.com/technology/tech/java/sqlj_jdbc/htdocs/jdbc_faq.htm`
  - `http://www.fankhausers.com/postgresql/jdbc/`
  - `http://www.white-mountain.org/jdbc/FAQ.html`
  - `http://e-docs.bea.com/wls/docs81/faq/jdbc.html`

2-20. How Do You Debug Problems Related to the JDBC API?

You have several ways to debug your JDBC programs. One simple way is to use lots of System.out. println() statements so you can see what is retrieved and printed. Another good way is to trace your JDBC calls (that is, enable JDBC tracing). The JDBC trace contains a detailed listing of the activity occurring in the system that is related to JDBC method calls.

You can enable tracing of JDBC operations by using DriverManager. You can use the DriverManager. setLogWriter() method to enable tracing of JDBC operations. The DriverManager.setLogWriter() method sets the logging/tracing PrintWriter object that is used by DriverManager and all drivers. If you use a DataSource object to get a connection, you use the DataSource.setLogWriter() method to enable tracing. And for connections that can participate in distributed transactions, you can use the XADataSource.setLogWriter() method.

■**Note** The key to tracing JDBC operations is to pass a java.io.PrintWriter object to the DriverManager. setLogWriter() method.

Creating a Simple Program to Illustrate Tracing of JDBC Operations

The following code shows a simple program to illustrate the tracing of JDBC operations:

```
import java.util.*;
import java.io.*;
import java.sql.*;
```

```
// simple program to illustrate the tracing of JDBC operations
public class TestDebug_MySQL {
    public static Connection getConnection() throws Exception {
        String driver = "org.gjt.mm.mysql.Driver";
        String url = "jdbc:mysql://localhost/octopus";
        String username = "root";
        String password = "root";
        Class.forName(driver);    // load MySQL driver
        return DriverManager.getConnection(url, username, password);
    }

    public static int countRows(Connection conn, String tableName)
        throws SQLException {
        // select the number of rows in the table
        Statement stmt = null;
        ResultSet rs = null;
        int rowCount = -1;
        try {
            stmt = conn.createStatement();
            rs = stmt.executeQuery("SELECT COUNT(*) FROM "+ tableName);
            // get the number of rows from the result set
            rs.next();
            rowCount = rs.getInt(1);
        }
        finally {
            DatabaseUtil.close(rs);
            DatabaseUtil.close(stmt);
        }
```

```
        return rowCount;
    }

    public static void main(String[] args) {
        Connection conn = null;
        try {
            System.out.println("------TestDebug_MySQL begin---------");
            PrintWriter pw =
                new PrintWriter(new FileOutputStream("mysql_debug.txt"));
            DriverManager.setLogWriter(pw);
            conn = getConnection();
            String tableName = args[0];
            System.out.println("tableName="+tableName);
            System.out.println("conn="+conn);
            System.out.println("rowCount="+countRows(conn, tableName));
            System.out.println("------TestDebug_MySQL end---------");
        }
        catch(Exception e){
            e.printStackTrace();
            System.exit(1);
        }
        finally {
            // release database resources
            DatabaseUtil.close(conn);
        }
    }
}
```

Running the Simple Tracing Program

This code shows how to run the simple program:

```
$ javac TestDebug_MySQL.java
$ java TestDebug_MySQL dsns
------TestDebug_MySQL begin---------
tableName=dsns
conn=com.mysql.jdbc.Connection@1546e25
rowCount=30
------TestDebug_MySQL end---------

$ cat  mysql_debug.txt
DriverManager.initialize: jdbc.drivers = null
JDBC DriverManager initialized
registerDriver: driver[className=com.mysql.jdbc.Driver,com.mysql.jdbc.Driver@b8df17]
DriverManager.getConnection("jdbc:mysql://localhost/octopus")
    trying driver[className=com.mysql.jdbc.Driver,com.mysql.jdbc.Driver@b8df17]

getConnection returning driver[className=com.mysql.jdbc.Driver,
com.mysql.jdbc.Driver@b8df17]
```

2-21. Does MySQL Support Transactions?

The short answer is "yes" and "no" (depending on the table type at the time of table creation). The MySQL database system supports several storage engines that act as handlers for different table types. MySQL storage engines include both those that handle transaction-safe tables and those that handle non-transaction-safe tables.

MySQL has the following table types (note that, among these table types, only InnoDB and BDB support transactions):

MyISAM: This is the default table type and does not support transactions.

ISAM: According to the MySQL manual, "the original storage engine was ISAM, which managed nontransactional tables. This engine has been replaced by MyISAM and should no longer be used. It is deprecated in MySQL 4.1 and will be removed in MySQL 5.0."

InnoDB: The InnoDB storage engine that handles transaction-safe tables was introduced in later versions of MySQL 3.23. It is available in source distributions as of MySQL 3.23.34a. InnoDB also is included in MySQL-Max binary distributions for MySQL 3.23. Beginning with MySQL 4.0, InnoDB is included by default in all MySQL binary distributions. In source distributions, you can enable or disable either engine by configuring MySQL as you like. See http://www.innodb.com for more information.

BDB: The BDB storage engine that handles transaction-safe tables was introduced in later versions of MySQL 3.23. It is available in source distributions as of MySQL 3.23.34a. BDB is included in MySQL-Max binary distributions on those operating systems that support it. See http://www.sleepycat.com for more information.

Heap: According to the MySQL manual, "the MEMORY (heap) storage engine creates tables with contents that are stored in memory. Before MySQL 4.1, MEMORY tables were called HEAP tables. As of 4.1, HEAP is a synonym for MEMORY, and MEMORY is the preferred term. Each MEMORY table is associated with one disk file. The filename begins with the table name and has an extension of .frm to indicate that it stores the table definition." To specify explicitly that you want a MEMORY table, indicate that with an ENGINE or TYPE table option:

```
CREATE TABLE t (i INT) TYPE = HEAP;
```

MEMORY tables are stored in memory and use hash indexes. This makes them fast and useful for creating temporary tables! However, when the server shuts down, all data stored in MEMORY tables is lost.

According to the MySQL online manual, "when you create a new table, you can tell MySQL what type of table to create by adding an ENGINE or TYPE table option to the CREATE TABLE statement." For example:

```
CREATE TABLE t (i INT) ENGINE = INNODB;
CREATE TABLE t (i INT) TYPE = MEMORY;
```

ENGINE is the preferred term but cannot be used before MySQL 4.0.18. TYPE is available beginning with MySQL 3.23.0, the first version of MySQL for which multiple storage engines were available. If you omit the ENGINE or TYPE option, the default table type is usually MyISAM. You can change this by setting the table_type system variable. To convert a table from one type to another, use an ALTER TABLE statement that indicates the new type:

```
ALTER TABLE t ENGINE = MYISAM;
ALTER TABLE t TYPE = BDB;
```

MySQL does not support distributed transactions. The latest version (mysql-connector-java-3.1.4-beta) of MySQL Connector/J (the JDBC driver) does not implement the javax.sql.XAConnection interface. (It is an object that provides support for distributed transactions.)

2-22. Does Oracle Support Transactions?

The answer is "yes." Oracle supports transactions and distributed transactions (a single transaction that can apply to multiple heterogeneous databases that may reside on separate servers).

Using Oracle, by default, DML operations (INSERT, UPDATE, DELETE) are committed automatically as soon as they are executed. This is known as *autocommit mode*. You can, however, disable auto-commit mode with the following method call on the Connection object:

```
java.sql.Connection conn = ...;
conn.setAutoCommit(false);
```

If you disable autocommit mode, then you must manually commit changes with the appropriate method call on the Connection object, like so:

```
conn.commit();
```

or roll them back, like so:

```
conn.rollback();
```

Oracle's Support for a Distributed Transaction

According to Oracle, a distributed transaction, sometimes referred to as a *global transaction*, is a set of two or more related transactions that must be managed in a coordinated way.

The transactions that constitute a distributed transaction might be in the same database but more typically are in different databases and often in different locations. Each transaction of a distributed transaction is referred to as a *transaction branch*.

Oracle provides a JDBC implementation of distributed transactions. In Oracle, distributed transactions are supported through the standard javax.sql package.

Distributed transactions are multiphased transactions, often using multiple databases, that must

is a database connection that can be used in a distributed transaction, and XADataSource is a data source that can be used in a distributed transaction.

Oracle supplies the following three packages that have classes to implement distributed transaction functionality according to the XA standard:

- oracle.jdbc.xa (the OracleXid and OracleXAException classes)

- oracle.jdbc.xa.client

- oracle.jdbc.xa.server

For more details on these APIs, please see Oracle's JDBC documentation. Distributed transactions require the JDBC 2.0 Optional Package (JDBC 2.0 Standard Extension API) in the javax.sql package. This is available under either JDK 1.2.*x* or 1.1.*x*.

Oracle Distributed Transactions Code Sample

Code sample is provided in Oracle 9*i* JDBC Developer's Guide and Reference (http://ocpdba.net/9idoc/java.920/a96654.pdf). The example uses a two-phase distributed transaction with two transaction branches, each to a separate database (both databases are Oracle 9*i*).

2-23. What Do the Different Versions of JDBC Offer?

Sun Microsystems' Java group (http://java.sun.com) prepares and maintains the JDBC specification (http://java.sun.com/products/jdbc). Since JDBC is just a specification (suggestions for writing and using JDBC drivers), third-party vendors (such as Oracle, MySQL, IBM, and so on) develop JDBC drivers adhering to this specification. JDBC developers then use these drivers to access data sources. To be JDBC-compliant, the driver has to pass a suite of tests developed by Sun Microsystems.

JDBC has gone through several major releases; for more details, please refer to `http://java.sun.com/products/jdbc/index.jsp`:

JDBC 1.0: The first version provides basic functionality; it focuses on ease of use.

JDBC 2.0: The second version offers more advanced features and server-side capabilities. For details on JDBC 2.0, refer to `http://java.sun.com/developer/onlineTraining/Database/JDBC20Intro/`.

JDBC 3.0: This version provides performance optimizations. It adds features in the areas of connection pooling and statement pooling, and it provides a migration path to Sun Microsystems' connector architecture. The JDBC 3.0 API is the latest update of the JDBC API. It contains many features, including scrollable result sets and the SQL:1999 data types. The JDBC 3.0 API is comprised of two packages: the `java.sql` package (standard package, foundation API) and the `javax.sql` package (which adds server-side capabilities). You automatically get both packages when you download J2SE 1.4.2 or J2SE 5.0. You can get the JDBC 3.0 specification from the following site: `http://java.sun.com/products/jdbc/download.html`.

JDBC 4.0: Refer to `http://www.jcp.org/en/jsr/detail?id=221`.

2-24. What Is the Core Functionality of a JDBC Driver?

As mentioned in Chapter 1, a *JDBC driver* is a Java class that implements the JDBC driver interface (`java.sql.Driver`) and is loaded into the JDBC driver manager. The `java.sql.Driver` interface is one that every driver class must implement. The Oracle and MySQL products come with JDBC drivers, and the JDBC driver enables a Java application to communicate with a relational/SQL database.

1. Create a database `Connection` object (`java.sql.Connection` object).

2. Send SQL queries to the database using the `Connection` object.

3. Process the results (as `java.sql.ResultSet`) returned from the database.

4. Close the `ResultSet` and other objects.

5. Close the `Connection` object.

The following test program demonstrates the steps outlined previously. I offer a MySQL and an Oracle version to suit your environment.

Creating a Core JDBC Functionality Test Program (MySQL Version): SmallTestMySQL.java

The following program creates a table (called `employees_table`). If the table creation is successful, then it inserts two new records into that table; finally, it reads all the existing records (the two inserted records) using a `ResultSet` object via the `Statement.executeQuery()` method.

```
import java.sql.*;
import jcb.util.DatabaseUtil;

public class SmallTestMySQL {

    private static final String EMPLOYEE_TABLE =
        "create table employees_table ( " +
        "  id INT PRIMARY KEY, " +
        "  name VARCHAR(20))";
```

```java
    public static Connection getConnection() throws Exception {
        String driver = "org.gjt.mm.mysql.Driver";
        String url = "jdbc:mysql://localhost/octopus";
        String username = "root";
        String password = "root";
        Class.forName(driver); // load MySQL driver
        return DriverManager.getConnection(url, username, password);
    }

    public static void main(String args[]) throws Exception {
        Connection conn = null;
        Statement stmt = null;
        ResultSet rs = null;
        try {
            // get a database connection
            conn = getConnection();
            // create table
            stmt = conn.createStatement();
            stmt.executeUpdate(EMPLOYEE_TABLE);
            System.out.println("SampleTestMySQL: main(): table created.");
            // insert couple of records
            stmt.executeUpdate("insert into employees_table(id, name)"+
                values('100', 'alex')");
            stmt.executeUpdate("insert into employees_table(id, name)"+
                values('200', 'mary')");



            while (rs.next()) {
                int id = rs.getInt(1);
                String name = rs.getString(2);
                System.out.println("id = "+id+"\t name = "+ name);
            }
        }
        catch( Exception e ) {
            // handle the exception
            e.printStackTrace();
        }
        finally {
            // close database resource not needed
            DatabaseUtil.close(rs);
            DatabaseUtil.close(stmt);
            DatabaseUtil.close(conn);
        }
    }
}
```

Testing the SampleTestMySQL Program

Use this code to test the program:

```
$ javac SmallTestMySQL.java
$ java SmallTestMySQL
SampleTestMySQL: main(): table created.
id = 100          name = alex
id = 200          name = mary
```

Viewing the Output of MySQL Database

This is the output from SmallTestMySQL.java:

```
C:\mysql\bin>mysql --user=root --password=root
Welcome to the MySQL monitor.  Commands end with ; or \g.
Your MySQL connection id is 2 to server version: 4.0.18-nt

mysql> use octopus;
Database changed
mysql> desc employees_table;
+-------+-------------+------+-----+---------+-------+
| Field | Type        | Null | Key | Default | Extra |
+-------+-------------+------+-----+---------+-------+
| id    | int(11)     |      | PRI | 0       |       |
| name  | varchar(20) | YES  |     | NULL    |       |
+-------+-------------+------+-----+---------+-------+
2 rows in set (0.00 sec)

mysql> select * from employees_table;
+-----+------+
| id  | name |
+-----+------+
| 100 | alex |
| 200 | mary |
+-----+------+
```

Creating a Core JDBC Functionality Test Program (Oracle Version): SmallTestOracle.java

The SmallTestOracle.java program is identical to the previous SmallTestMySQL.java program, except for the getConnection() method:

```java
import java.sql.*;
import jcb.util.DatabaseUtil;

public class SmallTestOracle {

    public static Connection getConnection() throws Exception {
        String driver = "oracle.jdbc.driver.OracleDriver";
        String url = "jdbc:oracle:thin:@localhost:1521:caspian";
        String username = "scott";
        String password = "tiger";
        Class.forName(driver);  // load Oracle driver
        Return DriverManager.getConnection(url, username, password);
    }

    public static void main(String args[]) throws Exception {
        // same as the main() method of SmallTestMySQL class.
    }
}
```

Testing the SampleTestOracle Program

Use this code to test the program:

```
$ javac SmallTestOracle.java
$ java SmallTestOracle
```

```
SmallTestOracle: main(): table created.
id = 100          name = alex
id = 200          name = mary
```

Viewing the Output of Oracle Database

This is the output from SmallTestOracle.java:

```
$ sqlplus scott/tiger
SQL> desc employees_table;
 Name                                   Null?    Type
 -------------------------------------- -------- -------------
 ID                                     NOT NULL NUMBER(38)
 NAME                                            VARCHAR2(20)

SQL> select * from employees_table;

       ID NAME
---------- --------------------
      100 alex
      200 mary
```

2-25. Where Can You Find Information and Pointers for Writing a JDBC Driver?

Microsystems (http://java.sun.com/products/jdbc/driverdevs.html). This document specifies the minimum that a JDBC driver must implement to be compliant with the JDBC API. Several drivers are available:

- *SimpleText database*: http://www.thoughtinc.com/simpletext.html

- *MySQL Connector/J*: http://dev.mysql.com/downloads/connector/j/3.0.html

- *FreeTDS*: http://www.freetds.org

- *RmiJdbc*: http://rmijdbc.objectweb.org/index.html

- *jxDBCon open-source JDBC driver framework*: http://jxdbcon.sourceforge.net

2-26. What Is the JDBC Driver Certification Program?

Sun Microsystems offers a JDBC Driver Certification Program, which helps end users find out if a specific JDBC driver has passed a suite of well-defined tests (to determine whether it satisfies JDBC driver requirements). For more details on this program, refer to http://java.sun.com/products/jdbc/certification.html.

The intent of JDBC driver certification program is to give a tool to organizations to make the right selection of JDBC drivers:

> Today driver vendors offer a number of drivers based on JDBC technology ("JDBC drivers") that support various databases. However, not all JDBC drivers implement all the functionality required for working with J2EE-compatible products. The new JDBC certification program will help J2EE-compatible product vendors and applications developers pick the appropriate JDBC drivers for their needs with the confidence that the driver has been certified to work with J2EE compatible products.

Sun Microsystems maintains a searchable database of JDBC drivers at `http://industry.java.sun.com/products/jdbc/drivers`. Figure 2-1 shows this database's Web interface.

Figure 2-1. *JDBC driver database*

Any database vendor (that has JDBC drivers) can add entries to this database. This database contains all JDBC driver entries sent to Sun Microsystems by JDBC driver vendors requesting to be listed in this database. Using the Web interface to this database, you can select a list of JDBC drivers based on your particular needs (for example, database support and features required). Also, you can check the Certified for J2EE check box to list only those drivers that have been certified for use with J2EE-compatible products.

2-27. What Is a Two-Tier Model for JDBC?

Typically, a *two-tier* model refers to a client-server model. A two-tier model for JDBC refers to client-server architectures in which the user interface (Java/JDBC application) runs on the client machine and the database management system (that is, a database server) is stored on the server machine. Figure 2-2 represents a two-tier model for JDBC.

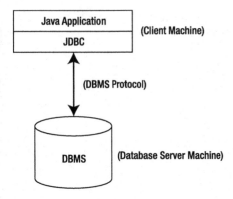

Figure 2-2. *Two-tier model for JDBC*

In a two-tier model for JDBC, the actual application logic can run on either the client or the server. In two-tier architectures, the application code (Java/JDBC application) resides on the *fat client*, which is used to process data.

The major problem with two-tier database applications is that they become complex and hard to support as the user base increases in size. For example, your database application might run fine for 20 concurrent users, but it might be problematic for 100 concurrent users. By using proper design/ programming and configuration techniques, you can avoid these problems.

JDBC connections.

2-28. What Is a Three-Tier Model for JDBC?

Typically, a *three-tier* model is an extension of a two-tier (so-called client-server) model. Instead of having a fat client, you move most of the business logic to the middle tier (application server level). J2EE is an example of a three-tier model. A three-tier model for JDBC has three tiers:

Client tier: The client tier is responsible for presenting data, receiving user inputs and events, and controlling and managing the user interface.

Middle tier (so-called application server tier): This tier is responsible for implementing the business rules (which create business objects) that are available to the client tier. IBM WebSphere (http://www.ibm.com/), BEA WebLogic Server (http://www.bea.com/), and Oracle Application Server (http://www.oracle.com/) are examples of middle tier and Web servers.

Data-server tier: This tier is responsible for data storage and manages the persistence of application data. It is usually composed of one/more relational database servers (such as Oracle or MySQL) and may contain the following:

- Database tables/views/triggers (used primarily for storing data)
- Stored procedures (used to execute database on the server-side)
- File servers (for storing huge files such as images, PDF files, and text)

Figure 2-3 presents a three-tier model for JDBC.

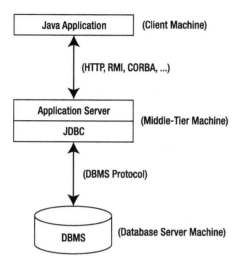

Figure 2-3. *Three-tier model for JDBC*

In a three-tier model for JDBC, the actual application logic runs on the middle tier. In general, tree-tier models are more scalable than two-tier models, because it is easy to add middle-tier and data-server tiers easily. For some JDBC applications, three-tier architecture can be slow because of

performance.

Typical Internet Application Architecture

Figure 2-4 represents a typical three-tier model. In this model, a client application (for example, a browser) communicates with a Java servlet/JSP in a Web server (such as Tomcat from the Apache Software Foundation) using Hypertext Transfer Protocol (HTTP) or HTTP Over SSL (HTTPS). (Tomcat is the servlet container that is used in the official reference implementation for the Java servlet and JSP technologies. For details, see the official Web site at http://jakarta.apache.org/tomcat/index.html.)

The Java code (servlet/JSP) in the Web server uses the JDBC API to access the relational database server.

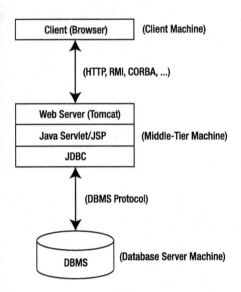

Figure 2-4. *Typical JDBC Internet architecture*

The Advantages of a Three-Tier Architecture for JDBC

as the interfaces among tiers are well defined).

Changes in the data-server tier (such as adding new tables and adding/modifying columns to existing tables) will not impact the clients because clients do not access the data-server tier directly.

Dynamic load balancing is another advantage of a three-tier architecture for JDBC. You can tackle performance problems easier than two-tier models: if a performance problem happens, you can add additional middle-tier servers or move the server process to other servers at runtime.

CHAPTER 3

■ ■ ■

Making Database Connections

Relativity teaches us the connection between the different descriptions of one and the same reality.

—Albert Einstein

In this chapter, you will examine all aspects of database connections using JDBC. You will then learn about the ins and outs of the java.sql.Connection object (which denotes a connection or a session with a specific database); this is one of the most important interfaces defined in JDBC. You can create a java.sql.Connection object in a couple of ways, and you will look at all the specific solutions in this chapter.

The purpose of this chapter is to provide snippets and reusable code samples and methods

This chapter's focus will be on answering the following question: how do you obtain a java.sql.Connection object from the java.sql and javax.sql packages? I can present this question in another way: what are the connection options? This chapter will answer these questions in detail and provide you with working code.

To select data from tables/views, update columns in tables, create a new table in the database, or do anything useful with any database, you need a database connection. (In JDBC, this is called java.sql.Connection.) Typically, database access in any environment starts with the connection.

To illustrate the importance of the java.sql.Connection object, I will list the basic steps for using JDBC:

1. Load the JDBC driver.

2. Define the connection URL.

3. Establish the JDBC connection (that is, create a java.sql.Connection object).

4. Create the JDBC Statement object.

5. Execute a query or update.

6. Process the results.

7. Close the connection.

8. Commit (or roll back) as appropriate.

Without the Connection object, you cannot accomplish many database operations. Steps 4–8 depend on the Connection object created in step 3. Most of the important JDBC API depends on the Connection object. Java.sql.Connection is a factory for the Statement, PreparedStatement, and CallableStatement objects.

3-1. What Is a Connection Object?

The java.sql.Connection object represents a single logical database connection. You use the Connection object for sending a set of SQL statements to the database server and managing the committing or aborting (rollback) of those SQL statements. Without the Connection object, you cannot do much.

The Connection object has the following capabilities:

- Creates SQL statements

- Executes SQL queries, inserts, updates, and deletes

- Handles commits and rollbacks

- Provides metadata regarding the database connection

It is important to note that a Connection object is thread-safe and can be shared between threads without the need for additional synchronization. On the other hand, a Statement object (created from a Connection object) is not thread-safe, and unexpected results can occur if multiple threads access the same Statement object. Therefore, multiple threads can share the same Connection object but should each create their own Statement objects.

According to JDK 1.4, a java.sql.Connection object is a connection (session) with a specific database. SQL statements are executed and results are returned within the context of a connection. A Connection object's database is able to provide information describing its tables, its supported SQL grammar, its stored procedures, the capabilities of this connection, and so on. This information is obtained with the getMetaData() method.

---

itly in order to commit changes; otherwise, database changes will not be saved.

3-2. What Is the Relationship of Connection to Other Objects?

To illustrate the importance of the Connection object, Figure 3-1 shows how Connection objects are created.

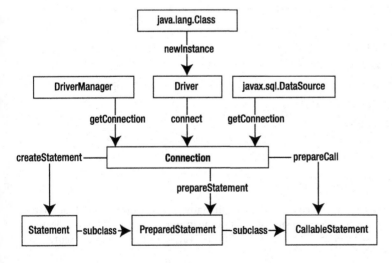

Figure 3-1. *Relationship of* Connection *to other objects*

Also, to illustrate the importance of the Connection object in the java.sql package, Figure 3-2 shows the interactions and relationships between the key classes and interfaces in the java.sql package. It also shows the methods involved in creating statements, setting parameters, and retrieving results; for details, please see the final release of the JDBC 3.0 specification, published by Sun Microsystems.

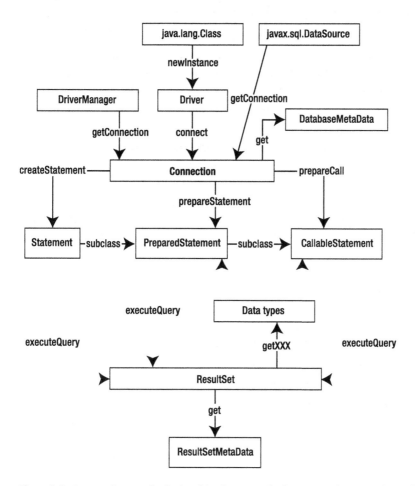

Figure 3-2. *Interactions and relationships between the key JDBC classes and interfaces*

3-3. What Are the Connection Creation Options?

From the JDBC API (the java.sql and javax.sql packages), you can conclude that there are only five ways to create JDBC Connection objects:

- java.sql.DriverManager: This class is the basic service for managing a set of JDBC drivers.

- java.sql.Driver: This is the interface that every driver class must implement. Each driver should supply a class that implements the Driver interface.

- javax.sql.DataSource: This interface is new in the JDBC 2.0 API, and according to JDK 1.4, using a DataSource object is the preferred means of connecting to a data source; you can create more portable code by using DataSource and JNDI.

- `javax.sql.PooledConnection`: This object provides hooks for connection pool management. A `PooledConnection` object represents a physical connection to a data source.

- *Connection cache*: This is an optional extension but not standard.

3-4. What Is the Function of the DriverManager Class?

In a nutshell, the `DriverManager` class manages connections to databases. According to JDK 1.4, the `DriverManager` provides a basic service for managing a set of JDBC drivers. As part of its initialization, the `DriverManager` class will attempt to load the driver classes referenced in the `jdbc.drivers` system property. This allows a user to customize the JDBC drivers used by their applications.

In your `~/.hotjava/properties` file, you might, for example, specify the following:

```
jdbc.drivers=org.gjt.mm.mysql.Driver:oracle.jdbc.driver.OracleDriver
```

Note that drivers are separated by a colon here. A program can also explicitly load JDBC drivers at any time. For example, the following example loads MySQL and Oracle drivers:

```
Class.forName("org.gjt.mm.mysql.Driver");
Class.forName("jdbc.driver.OracleDriver");
```

When `getConnection()` is called, the `DriverManager` will attempt to locate a suitable driver from among those loaded at initialization and those loaded explicitly using the same class loader as the current applet or application. Figure 3-3 illustrates the function of the `DriverManager` class.

Application

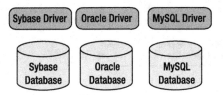

DriverManager manages connections to DBs

Figure 3-3. *Function of the* DriverManager *class*

The `DriverManager` class manages the JDBC drivers in the system. It maintains a registry of drivers and locates the appropriate driver to handle a JDBC database URL.

On startup, `DriverManager` loads all the managers specified by the system property `jdbc.drivers`. The value of this property should be a colon-separated list of fully qualified driver class names. You can load additional drivers at any time by simply loading the driver class with `Class.forName(String driverClassname)`. The driver should automatically register itself in a static initializer.

3-5. How Do You Create Connection(s) Using the DriverManager Class?

The DriverManager class (defined in the java.sql package) provides services for managing a set of JDBC drivers. In a nutshell, because JDBC can work with many drivers (the Oracle driver, MySQL driver, Sybase driver, and so on), the DriverManager class loads and configures your database driver on your client. As part of its initialization, the DriverManager class will attempt to load the driver classes referenced in the jdbc.drivers system property.

How It Works

The DriverManager class provides three static (class-level) methods for getting connections, as explained in Table 3-1.

Table 3-1. *Getting the* Connection *Object*

Method	Summary
static Connection getConnection (String url)	Attempts to establish a connection to the given database URL.
static Connection getConnection (String url, Properties info)	Attempts to establish a connection to the given database URL; the info parameter is a list of arbitrary string key-value pairs as connection arguments. Normally here at least a user and password property should be included. Each
(String url, String user, String password)	database URL.

You must first establish a connection with the relational DBMS you want to use. This involves two steps:

1. Loading the driver

2. Making the connection

Solution

Loading the driver or drivers you want to use is simple. For example, if you want to use the JDBC-ODBC bridge driver, use the following code, which will load the driver:

```
java.lang.String driverName = "sun.jdbc.odbc.JdbcOdbcDriver";
java.lang.Class driverClass = java.lang.Class.forName(driverName);
```

Alternatively, you can write the following (ignoring the return of the forName() method):

```
java.lang.String driverName = "sun.jdbc.odbc.JdbcOdbcDriver";
java.lang.Class.forName(driverName);
```

A call to forName("X") causes the class named X to be initialized. Your driver documentation will give you the class name to use. For instance, if the class name is org.gjt.mm.mysql.Driver (this driver is for the MySQL database), you would load the driver with the following line of code:

```
java.lang.String driverName = "org.gjt.mm.mysql.Driver";
java.lang.Class.forName(driverName);
```

Please note that you do not need to create an instance of a driver and register it with the DriverManager class, because calling Class.forName() will do that for you automatically. (This is a singleton class, and therefore it doesn't have any public constructors.)

If you were to create your own instance, you would be creating an unnecessary duplicate, but it would do no harm. When you have loaded a driver, it is available for making a connection with a relational DBMS. For the driver to be successfully loaded, the driver class must be in the CLASSPATH environment variable; otherwise, these code fragments will throw an exception.

For example, if you want to use the Oracle 9i (Oracle 8i) database, then you need to include the ojdbc.jar file in classes12.zip (provided by Oracle) in the CLASSPATH environment variable. If you want to access more than one database, then you need to include all the required JAR files in your CLASSPATH. These JAR files include classes and interfaces that support the implementation of interfaces and classes in the java.sql and javax.sql packages defined by the JDK.

You can load the driver in another way: just use the following code. When you have loaded a driver, it is available for making a connection with the relational database.

```
String  driverName = "org.gjt.mm.mysql.Driver";
Class driverClass = Class.forName(driverName);
    DriverManager.registerDriver((Driver) driverClass.newInstance());
```

How do you make sure your desired drivers are loaded? Use the DriverManager.getDrivers() method, and then enumerate all the loaded JDBC drivers:

```
// Print out all loaded JDBC drivers.
java.util.Enumeration e = java.sql.DriverManager.getDrivers();
while (e.hasMoreElements()) {
   Object driverAsObject = e.nextElement();
```

As I mentioned, the second step in establishing your connection is to have the appropriate driver connect to the DBMS. You have several ways to specify connection information in the DriverManager.getConnection() method. The following sections describe three methods.

Method 1: Making the Connection

The simplest method is to use a database URL that includes the database name, hostname, and port number of the database server, as well as two additional parameters to specify the database username and password. The following is the general idea:

```
/**
 * Attempts to establish a connection to the given database
 * URL. The DriverManager attempts to select an appropriate
 * driver from the set of registered JDBC drivers.
 */
String dbURL = ...;          // a database URL of the form
                             // jdbc:subprotocol:subname
String dbUsername = ...;      // the database user on whose behalf
                             // the connection is being made
String dbPassword = ...;      // the user's password
Connection conn = null;
try {
    conn = DriverManager.getConnection(dbURL,
                              dbUsername,
                              dbPassword);
}
catch(SQLException e) {
   // if a database access error occurs
   // handle the exception here.
```

```
      e.printStackTrace();
      ...
  }
  finally {
    // close the db resources such as Connection object
    DatabaseUtil.close(conn);
  }
```

DatabaseUtil is a utility class, which has a set of close() methods for closing database/JDBC resources (such as Connection, Statement, and ResultSet objects). Therefore, to connect to a relational database, you need the parameters described in Table 3-2.

Table 3-2. *Connection Object Requirements*

Parameter	Description
driverName	JDBC driver
dbURL	Database URL (uniquely identifies a database)
dbUsername	Database username
dbPassword	Database user password

If you are using the JDBC-ODBC bridge driver, the JDBC URL will start with jdbc:odbc:. The rest of the URL is generally your data source name or database system.

So, if you are using ODBC to access an ODBC data source called Payroll, for example, your JDBC URL could be jdbc:odbc:Payroll. In place of dbUsername, you put the name you use to log into

shown will establish a connection:

```
/** * Attempts to establish a connection to the given database
 * URL. The DriverManager attempts to select an appropriate
 * driver from the set of registered JDBC drivers.
 */
String dbURL = "jdbc:odbc:Payroll";
String dbUsername = "scott";
String dbPassword = "tiger";
Connection conn = null;
try {
    //
    // when the method getConnection is called, the
    // DriverManager will attempt to locate a suitable
    // driver from amongst those loaded at initialization
    // and those loaded explicitly using the same class loader
    // as the current applet or application.
    //
    conn = DriverManager.getConnection(dbURL,
                            dbUsername,
                            dbPassword);
    // use the Connection object
}
catch(SQLException e) {
    // if a database access error occurs
    // handle the exception here.
    e.printStackTrace();
    ...
}
```

```
finally {
  // close the db resources such as Connection object
  DatabaseUtil.close(conn);
}
```

Each vendor has a special format for the database URL. For example, Table 3-3 shows sample database driver names and sample database URLs. (In Table 3-3, the server name is localhost, and the database name is scorpian.)

Table 3-3. *Vendor URL Formats*

Vendor	Driver Name	URL Sample
Oracle 8*i*	oracle.jdbc.driver.OracleDriver	jdbc:oracle:thin:@localhost:1521:scorpian
Oracle 9*i*	oracle.jdbc.driver.OracleDriver	jdbc:oracle:thin:@localhost:1521:scorpian
MySQL	org.gjt.mm.mysql.Driver	jdbc:mysql://localhost/scorpian
Microsoft Access	sun.jdbc.odbc.JdbcOdbcDriver	jdbc:odbc:scorpian
Sybase (jConnect 4.2)	com.sybase.jdbc.SybDriver	jdbc:sybase:Tds:scorpian:2638
Sybase (jConnect 5.2)	com.sybase.jdbc2.jdbc.SybDriver	jdbc:sybase:Tds:scorpian:2638
MS SQL	com.microsoft.jdbc.	jdbc:microsoft:sqlserver://
Server 2000		localhost:port
IBM DB2	COM.ibm.db2.jdbc.net.DB2Connection	jdbc:db2://localhost:6789/scorpian

If you are using a JDBC driver developed by a third party, the documentation will tell you what to use for the driver name and the database URL format.

Method 2: Making the Connection

In this method, you add connection options to the end of the database URL. In using getConnection(String url), the dbUsername and dbPassword values are appended to the database URL. For example, one way of connecting to a database is through the JDBC driver manager using the method DriverManager.getConnection.

This method uses a string containing a URL. The following is an example of using the JDBC driver manager to connect to Microsoft SQL Server 2000 while passing the username and password (as appended to the end of the URL):

```
Class.forName("com.microsoft.jdbc.sqlserver.SQLServerDriver");
String dbURL =
    "jdbc:microsoft:sqlserver://localhost:1433;User=sa;Password=admin";
Connection conn = DriverManager.getConnection(dbURL);
```

For Microsoft SQL Server, the complete connection URL format used with the driver manager is as follows:

```
jdbc:microsoft:sqlserver://hostname:port[;property=value...]
```

where the following is true:

- hostname: Specifies the TCP/IP address or TCP/IP hostname (the assumption is that your network resolves hostnames to IP addresses) of the server to which you are connecting.
- port: Specifies the database server port
- property=value: Specifies connection properties

Appending dbUsername and dbPassword values to the end of the database URL might cause unnecessary errors because of the creation of long strings. (For example, you might forget to separate the fields with a semicolon.)

Method 3: Making the Connection

In this third and final method that I will explain, you can set connection information in a java.util.Properties object and pass this information to the DriverManager.getConnection() method.

With this approach, you do not need to append dbUsername and dbPassword values to the end of the dbURL. Instead of appending values to the end of the dbURL, you put these values as a set of (key,value) into an instance of the java.util.Properties object. The following example specifies the server, user, and password in a Properties object:

```
public static final String DATABASE_USER = "user";
public static final String DATABASE_PASSWORD = "password";

String oracleDriver = "oracle.jdbc.driver.OracleDriver";
Class.forName(oracleDriver);


String dbPassword = "tiger";
// these are properties that get passed
// to DriverManager.getConnection(...)
java.util.Properties dbProperties = new java.util.Properties();
jdbcProperties.put(DATABASE_USER, dbUsername);
jdbcProperties.put(DATABASE_PASSWORD, dbPassword);
Connection conn = DriverManager.getConnection(dbURL, dbProperties);
```

Using the getConnection(String url, Properties info), you can pass additional parameters (such as Character Encoding Scheme) to the database as a set of (key,value) pairs.

3-6. How Do You Get a List of Loaded Drivers?

To make sure your desired drivers are loaded, use the DriverManager.getDrivers() method and then enumerate all loaded JDBC drivers:

```
import java.sql.Driver;
import java.sql.DriverManager;
import java.util.Enumeration;
...
// Retrieves an Enumeration with all of the currently
// loaded JDBC drivers to which the current caller has access.
Enumeration<Driver> e = DriverManager.getDrivers();
while (e.hasMoreElements()) {
    Driver driver = e.nextElement();
    String className = driver.getClass().getName();
    System.out.println("Driver class name="+className);
}
```

Solution

To get a list of currently loaded drivers, use this solution:

```java
package jcb.util;

import java.util.*;
import java.io.*;
import java.sql.*;

/**
 * This class provides methods to support
 * JDBC driver-related functions.
 */
public class DriverManagerTool {

    /**
     * Retrieves an XML with all of the currently loaded
     * JDBC drivers to which the current caller has access.
     * @return all loaded JDBC drivers as an XML (serialized
     * as a String object).
     */
    public static String getLoadedDrivers() {
        java.util.Enumeration e = java.sql.DriverManager.getDrivers();
        StringBuffer sb = new StringBuffer("<?xml version='1.0'>");
        sb.append("<loaded_drivers>");
        while (e.hasMoreElements()) {


        }
        sb.append("</loaded_drivers>");
        return sb.toString();
    }

    private static void appendXMLTag(StringBuffer buffer,
                                     String tagName,
                                     String value) {
        buffer.append("<");
        buffer.append(tagName);
        buffer.append(">");
        buffer.append(value);
        buffer.append("</");
        buffer.append(tagName);
        buffer.append(">");
    }
}
```

And here is how you can get a list of loaded client drivers:

```java
// Print out all loaded JDBC drivers.
public static void main(String[] args) throws Exception {
    try {
        // register two drivers
        Class.forName("org.gjt.mm.mysql.Driver");
        Class.forName("oracle.jdbc.driver.OracleDriver");
        // get loaded drivers
        System.out.println(getLoadedDrivers());
    }
    catch(Exception e) {
```

```
        e.printStackTrace();
    }
}
```

Here is some output from the solution:

```
<?xml version='1.0'>
<loaded_drivers>
    <loadedDriver>com.mysql.jdbc.Driver@affc70</loadedDriver>
    <loadedDriver>oracle.jdbc.driver.OracleDriver@1fc4bec</loadedDriver>
</loaded_drivers>
```

3-7. How Do You Connect to an Oracle Database?

To connect to an Oracle database, you need to create an instance of the java.sql.Connection object.

■**Note** The java.sql.Connection object is an interface, and you need an implementing class for it. Please remember that you do not need to implement this interface, because Oracle's JDBC driver provides such an implementation.

The following example uses an Oracle JDBC driver to connect to an Oracle database instance located at server TIGER and port number 1521 with an SID (Oracle database ID) called scorpian. To

The following shows a portion of the tnsnames.ora file for an Oracle 9i installation. As you can observe, tiger is the server name, tiger.usa.com is the full server name, and scorpian is an SID.

```
...
SCORPIAN.USA.COM =
  (DESCRIPTION =
    (ADDRESS_LIST =
      (ADDRESS = (PROTOCOL = TCP)(HOST = TIGER)(PORT = 1521))
    )
    (CONNECT_DATA =
      (SERVER = DEDICATED)
      (SERVICE_NAME = scorpian.tiger.usa.com)
    )
  )
...
```

Solution (Fragment)

In this solution, I will present the most important code, and then I will expand this fragment to a class and some client code so you can see it really working.

```
Connection conn = null;
try {
    // Load the JDBC driver
    String driverName = "oracle.jdbc.driver.OracleDriver";
    Class.forName(driverName);

    //
    // Create a connection to the database
    //
```

```java
        String serverName = "TIGER";
        String portNumber = "1521";
        String sid = "scorpian";
        String url = "jdbc:oracle:thin:@" + serverName + ":" +
            portNumber + ":" + sid;
        String username = "octopus";
        String password = "octopus";
        conn = DriverManager.getConnection(url, username, password);
        // here the Connection object is ready to be used.
    }
catch (ClassNotFoundException e) {
        // Could not find the database driver
        // When you are here, it means that your .jar file (which contains
        // the Driver class) has not been added to the CLASSPATH properly
        // You have to fix this problem before you
        // can establish a connection to an Oracle database.
        // deal with the exception...
    }
catch (SQLException e) {
        // Could not connect to the database.
        // Either database server is down, or one/more of
        // your parameters is/are not specified correctly.
        // deal with the exception...
    }
finally {
        // close the Connection object
```

Solution: BasicConnectionManager Class

You can rewrite the previous code as a class with a couple of methods, as shown here:

```java
import java.sql.*;
import java.util.*;
import jcb.util.DatabaseUtil;
/**
 * This class provides three basic methods:
 * 1) how to create a connection for a given (url, username, password)
 * 2) how to create a connection for a given (url, databaseProperties)
 * 3) how to load a driver
 */
public class BasicConnectionManager {

    public static final String DATABASE_USER = "user";
    public static final String DATABASE_PASSWORD = "password";

    /**
     * Load the JDBC driver.
     * @param driverName the driver name.
     * @throws ClassNotFoundException Failed to load the driver.
     */
    public static void loadDriver(String driverName)
        throws ClassNotFoundException {
        java.lang.Class.forName(driverName);
    }
}
```

```java
/**
 * Get the connection from a given (url, user, password).
 * @param url database URL.
 * @param username database user.
 * @param user's password.
 * @return Connection object.
 * @throws SQLException Failed to create a Connection object.
 */
public static Connection getConnection(String url,
                                       String username,
                                       String password)
    throws SQLException {
    return DriverManager.getConnection(url, username, password);
}

/**
 * Get the connection from a given (url, user, password).
 * @param url database URL.
 * @param dbProperties database properties (includes database
 * username, password, and other database attributes).
 * @return Connection object.
 * @throws SQLException Failed to create a Connection object.
 */
public static Connection getConnection(String url,
                                       Properties dbProperties)
    throws SQLException {
```

Client Code: Using the BasicConnectionManager Class

The following code shows some client code to work the BasicConnectionManager class just created.
I will provide an output sample later.

```java
import java.sql.*;

public class TestOracleConnectionManager {

    /**
     * Client program to create two connections.
     */
    public static void main(String[] args) {
        try {
            // Step 1: Load the JDBC driver
            String driverName = "oracle.jdbc.driver.OracleDriver";
            BasicConnectionManager.loadDriver(driverName);
        }
        catch (ClassNotFoundException e) {
            // Could not find the database driver; when you are
            // here, it means that your .jar file (which contains
            // the Driver class) has not been added to the CLASSPATH
            // properly; you have to fix this problem before you
            // can establish a connection to an Oracle database.
            // deal with the exception...
            e.printStackTrace();
        }
```

```
        Connection conn1 = null;
        Connection conn2 = null;
        String serverName = "TIGER";
        String portNumber = "1521";
        String sid = "scorpian";
        String url = "jdbc:oracle:thin:@" + serverName + ":" + portNumber + ":" + sid;
        String username = "octopus";
        String password = "octopus";
        try {
            // Step 2: Create a connection to the database
            conn1 = BasicConnectionManager.getConnection(url, username, password);
            System.out.println("conn1="+conn1);
            System.out.println("----------------------");

            // Step 3: Create another connection to the database
            conn2 = BasicConnectionManager.getConnection(url, username, password);
            System.out.println("conn2="+conn2);
            System.out.println("----------------------");
        }
        catch (SQLException e) {
            // Could not connect to the database.
            // Either database server is down or one/more of
            // your parameters is/are not specified correctly.
            // deal with the exception...
            e.printStackTrace();
        }


            BasicConnectionManager.close(conn2);
        }
    }
}
```

The client output is as follows:

```
conn1=oracle.jdbc.driver.OracleConnection@66e815
----------------------
conn2=oracle.jdbc.driver.OracleConnection@a37368
----------------------
```

3-8. How Do You Connect to a MySQL Database?

To connect to a MySQL database, you need to create an instance of the java.sql.Connection object. (Note that java.sql.Connection is an interface, and you need an implementing class for it.)

The following example uses a MySQL JDBC driver to connect to a MySQL database instance located at server localhost and port number 3306 with a database called empDB. To make sure you have the right values for the database name and port, you may view the database names by using interactive mysql, as shown here:

```
C:\mysql\bin>mysql
Welcome to the MySQL monitor.  Commands end with ; or \g.
Your MySQL connection id is 4 to server version: 4.0.2-alpha-nt

mysql> show databases;
```

```
+----------+
| Database |
+----------+
| empdb    |
| mysql    |
| test     |
| tiger    |
+----------+
4 rows in set (0.00 sec)
```

Solution As a Code Fragment

In this solution, I will present the most important code, and then I will expand this fragment to a class and some client code so you can see it really working. As you can observe, empDB is one of the databases in MySQL.

```
Connection conn = null;
try {
    // Load the JDBC driver
    String driverName = "org.gjt.mm.mysql.Driver";
    Class.forName(driverName);

    // Create a connection to the database
        String url = "jdbc:mysql://localhost/empDB";
        String username = "root";
        String password = "root";


catch (ClassNotFoundException e) {
    // Could not find the database driver
    // When you are here, it means that your
    // .jar file (which contains the Driver class)
    // has not been added to the CLASSPATH properly
    // You have to fix this problem before you
    // can establish a connection to an Oracle database.
    // deal with the exception...
}
catch (SQLException e) {
    // Could not connect to the database.
    // Either database server is down or one/more of
    // your parameters is/are not specified correctly
    // deal with the exception...
}
finally {
    DatabaseUtil.close(conn);
}
```

Solution As a Class and Methods: BasicConnectionManager Class

I will use the same BasicConnectionManager class as I presented in section 3-7 previously, since it is generic enough to apply to the current recipe context.

Client Using the BasicConnectionManager Class: MySQL Database

The following code shows the client code to work with the BasicConnectionManager class in the context of a MySQL database:

```java
import java.sql.*;
import jcb.util.DatabaseUtil;

public class TestMySqlConnectionManager {

    /**
     * Client program to create two connections.
     */
    public static void main(String[] args) {
        try {
            // Step 1: Load the JDBC driver
            String driverName = "org.gjt.mm.mysql.Driver";
            BasicConnectionManager.loadDriver(driverName);
        }
        catch (ClassNotFoundException e) {
            // Could not find the database driver;
            // deal with the exception...
            e.printStackTrace();
        }

        Connection conn1 = null;
        Connection conn2 = null;
        String url = "jdbc:mysql://localhost/empDB";
        String username = "root";
        String password = "root";
        try {


            System.out.println("conn1="+conn1);
            System.out.println("-----------------------");

            // Step 3: Create another connection
            conn2 = BasicConnectionManager.getConnection(url, username, password);
            System.out.println("conn2="+conn2);
            System.out.println("-----------------------");
        }
        catch (SQLException e) {
            // Could not connect to the database.
            // Either database server is down or one/more of
            // your parameters is/are not specified correctly.
            // deal with the exception...
            e.printStackTrace();
        }
        finally {
            DatabaseUtil.close(conn1);
            DatabaseUtil.close(conn2);
        }
    }
}
```

The client output is as follows:

```
conn1=com.mysql.jdbc.Connection@19616c7
-----------------------
conn2=com.mysql.jdbc.Connection@b166b5
-----------------------
```

3-9. How Do You Get a List of All Available Parameters for Creating a JDBC Connection?

Interactive development environments (such as NetBeans, VisualCafe, and Borland JBuilder) might need to discover all the available parameters for creating a JDBC connection. JDBC provides methods for discovering such information.

To get a list of all the available parameters for creating a JDBC connection, you need to provide two pieces of information: a driver class name and a database URL. This code fragment shows how to get such information:

```
String driverName = ...
String dbURL = ...
Class.forName(driverName);
Driver driver = DriverManager.getDriver(url);
// Get available properties
DriverPropertyInfo[] info = driver.getPropertyInfo(url, null);
```

The result is returned as an array of `DriverPropertyInfo` objects, which provides driver properties for making a connection. According to the JDK 1.4 documentation, the `DriverPropertyInfo` class is of interest only to advanced programmers who need to interact with a driver via the method `getDriverProperties` to discover and supply properties for connections. You can use the `DriverPropertyInfo` objects for building GUI tools (to discover the required properties and let the user fill/select values for those properties).

Most of the JDBC drivers need to know the database username and password of the user connecting to the database. The properties the driver needs in order to connect to the database will be

's

Solution

This solution, which I'll present in the following sections in richer context than just the code fragment, returns the result as XML (serialized as a `String` object), which can be useful for all types of clients. Let's look at that XML output format, and then I will present the solution.

XML Output Format

The XML returned has the following format:

```
<?xml version='1.0'>
<DriverPropertyInformation
     driver="driver-class-name"
     url="database-url">
     <DriverProperty>
         <name>driver-property-name</name>
         <required>true/false</required>
         <value>driver-property-value</value>
         <description>driver-property-description</description>
         <choices>driver-property-choices</choices>
     </DriverProperty>
     <DriverProperty>
         ...
     </DriverProperty>
     ...
</DriverPropertyInformation>
```

Solution: Java Class

The following code shows how to take the code fragment and implement it within a Java class:

```java
import java.util.*;
import java.sql.*;
import javax.sql.*;

public  class  DriverTool {
    /**
     * Listing All Available Parameters for Creating a JDBC
     * Connection.  Driver.getPropertyInfo() returns a list
     * of all available properties that can be supplied when
     * using the driver to create a JDBC connection. This list
     * can be displayed to the user.
     *
     * @param driverName the driver name.
     * @param url the database url.
     * @return returns the result as an XML (serialized as a String)
     * @throws ClassNotFoundException Failed to find the database driver.
     * @throws SQLException Failed to get available parameters for
     *  Creating a JDBC Connection.
     */
    public static String getDriverPropertyInformaton(String driverName,
                                                     String url)
        throws ClassNotFoundException,  SQLException {
        // Load the driver


        Driver driver = DriverManager.getDriver(url);

        // Get available properties
        DriverPropertyInfo[] info = driver.getPropertyInfo(url, null);
        StringBuffer sb = new StringBuffer("<?xml version='1.0'>");
        sb.append("<DriverPropertyInformation driver=\"");
        sb.append(driverName);
        sb.append("\" url=\"");
        sb.append(url);
        sb.append("\">");
        for (int i=0; i<info.length; i++) {
            appendProperty(sb, info[i]);
        }
        sb.append("</DriverPropertyInformation>");
        return sb.toString();
    }

    private static void appendProperty(StringBuffer sb,
                                       DriverPropertyInfo info) {
        sb.append("<DriverProperty>");
        // Get name of property
        appendXMLTag(sb, "name", info.name);
        // Is property value required?
        appendXMLTag(sb, "required", info.required);
        // Get current value
        appendXMLTag(sb, "value", info.value);
        // Get description of property
        appendXMLTag(sb, "description", info.description);
```

```java
        // Get possible choices for property;
        // if null, value can be any string
        String[] choices = info.choices;
        sb.append("<choices>");
        if (choices != null) {
            for (int c=0; c < choices.length; c++) {
                appendXMLTag(sb, "choice", choices[c]);
            }
        }
        sb.append("</choices>");
        sb.append("</DriverProperty>");
    }

    private static void appendXMLTag(StringBuffer buffer,
                                     String tagName,
                                     String value) {
        buffer.append("<");
        buffer.append(tagName);
        buffer.append(">");
        buffer.append(value);
        buffer.append("</");
        buffer.append(tagName);
        buffer.append(">");
    }

public static void main(String[] args) {
    try {
        String driverName = "org.gjt.mm.mysql.Driver";
        String dbURL = "jdbc:mysql://localhost/empDB";
        String driverPropertyInformaton =
        getDriverPropertyInformaton(driverName, dbURL);
        System.out.println("--- driverPropertyInformaton ---");
        System.out.println(driverPropertyInformaton);
        System.out.println("--------------------------------");
    }
    catch (ClassNotFoundException e) {
        // Could not find the database driver; when you are
        // here, it means that your .jar file (which contains
        // the Driver class) has not been added to the CLASSPATH
        // properly; you have to fix this problem before you
        // can establish a connection to an Oracle database.
        // deal with the exception...
        e.printStackTrace();
    }
    catch (SQLException e) {
        // Could not connect to the database.
        // Either database server is down or one/more of
        // your parameters is/are not specified correctly.
        // deal with the exception...
        e.printStackTrace();
    }
}
```

Output for the MySQL Database

The following is the partial XML output. For the complete output (about three pages), either run the program or visit this book's Web site at http://www.apress.com (the filename is DriverTool.out).

```xml
<?xml version='1.0'>
<DriverPropertyInformation driver="org.gjt.mm.mysql.Driver"
                           url="jdbc:mysql://localhost/empDB">
    <DriverProperty>
        <name>HOST</name>
        <required>true</required>
        <value>localhost</value>
        <description>Hostname of MySQL Server</description>
        <choices></choices>
    </DriverProperty>

    <DriverProperty>
        <name>PORT</name>
        <required>false</required>
        <value>3306</value>
        <description>Port number of MySQL Server</description>
        <choices></choices>
    </DriverProperty>

    <DriverProperty>
        <name>DBNAME</name>


        <description>Database name</description>
        <choices></choices>
    </DriverProperty>
    ...
</DriverPropertyInformation>
```

3-10. How Do You Create Connection(s) Using the Driver Interface?

The Driver interface supports the creation of a database connection. This is the interface that every driver class must implement. Therefore, each driver should supply a class that implements the Driver interface. You can use the Driver interface's connect() method to create new database connections.

JDK 1.4 defines the connect() method:

```
public Connection connect(String url, Properties info)
                 throws SQLException
```

This attempts to make a database connection to the given URL. The driver should return null if it realizes it is the wrong kind of driver to connect to the given URL. This will be common, because when the JDBC driver manager is asked to connect to a given URL, it passes the URL to each loaded driver in turn. The driver should throw a SQLException if it is the right driver to connect to the given URL but has trouble connecting to the database.

You can use the java.util.Properties argument to pass arbitrary string tag-value pairs as connection arguments. Normally, at least user and password properties should be included in the Properties object.

These are the parameters:

- url: The URL of the database to which to connect.

- info: A list of arbitrary string key/value pairs as connection arguments. Normally at least a user or password property should be included.

This returns a Connection object that represents a connection to the URL. And it throws a SQLException if a database access error occurs.

Creating an Instance of java.sql.Driver

To create an instance of a Driver, you can use the following method:

```
public static java.sql.Driver getDriver(String driverClassName)
    throws InstantiationException,
           ClassNotFoundException,
           IllegalAccessException {
    Class driverClass = Class.forName(driverClassName);
    java.sql.Driver driver = (java.sql.Driver) driverClass.newInstance();
    System.out.println("getDriver: driver is OK. driver=" + driver);
    return driver;
}
```

Once you have an instance of java.sql.Driver, then you can use the connect() method to create a new database connection. Here is the code for creating a new database connection:

```
/**



 * @param driver the JDBC driver.
 * @param url a database URL.
 * @param props the database properties.
 * @return a new database Connection object.
 * @throws SQLException Failed to create a new database connection.
 */
public static java.sql.Connection getConnection(java.sql.Driver driver,
                                    String url,
                                    java.util.Properties props)

    throws SQLException {
    if (driver == null) {
        return null;
    }
    else {
        return driver.connect(url, props);
    }
}
```

Creating a New Connection Object from a Driver

Here is the code to create a new Connection object from a driver (I will present the output of this section after the code):

```
public static void main(String[] args) {
    try {
        java.sql.Driver mysqlDriver = getDriver("org.gjt.mm.mysql.Driver");
        String url = "jdbc:mysql://localhost/empDB";
        String username = "root";
        String password = "root";
```

```
      java.util.Properties props = new java.util.Properties();
      props.put("user", username);
      props.put("password", password);
      java.sql.Connection conn = getConnection(mysqlDriver, url, props);
      System.out.println("conn="+conn);
    }
    catch(Exception e) {
      e.printStackTrace();
    }
}
```

The output is as follows:

```
getDriver: driver is OK. driver=org.gjt.mm.mysql.Driver@1e63e3d
conn=com.mysql.jdbc.Connection@19616c7
```

3-11. What Is Basic Connection Management?

Sometimes you may want to connect to multiple data sources and view the results of different queries in a single page (such as a Web-based application); for example, you might be getting historic stock market data for comparing two companies, and each set of data might reside in a different database. In some database applications, it is not uncommon to access more than one data source.

I have developed a "basic" Java package called Basic Connection Management (BCM) that enables you to get connections from multiple data sources. For details, please see the jcb.bcm package, as shown in Figure 3-4. Please note that, for saving space, I will show only portions of the BCM

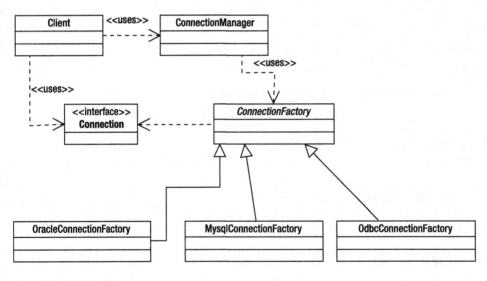

Figure 3-4. *BCM architecture*

Client programs use only the java.sql.Connection interface and a manager class called ConnectionManager. The ConnectionManager class uses ConnectionFactory (an abstract class), which is extended by three specific classes:

- OracleConnectionFactory (creates Oracle Connection objects)
- MysqlConnectionFactory (creates Oracle Connection objects)
- OdbcConnectionFactory (creates JDBC-ODBC Connection objects)

ConnectionManager is a singleton class, which makes sure that only one instance of an object exists at any one time. (*Singleton* is a design pattern; for details, please refer to the *Design Patterns* book by the Gang of Four.) Therefore, clients will not instantiate objects of a singleton class but retrieve/get a reference to the single object created inside singleton class.

Using BCM with Your Values: User, Password, Database Name

To use the BCM package with your own values, you need to modify the following values in the specific connection factory class. For example, to supply your own values for an Oracle database connection, update the following in the OracleConnectionFactory class:

```
public static final String ORACLE_DRIVER =
    "oracle.jdbc.driver.OracleDriver";
public static final String ORACLE_URL_PREFIX =
    "jdbc:oracle:thin:@localhost:1521:";

public static final String DEFAULT_USER = "scott";
public static final String DEFAULT_PASSWORD = "tiger";
public static final String DEFAULT_DATABASE = "scorpian";
```

Method 1: BCM Access Using the Data Source Name

For this method, just use the data source name (the Connection object will be obtained using the default user, password, and database name). The sample client code is as follows:

```
package jcb.bcm;

import java.sql.*;
import jcb.util.DatabaseUtil;

/**
 * This client demonstrates the Basic Connection Management
 * (BCM package) using the data source name.
 */
public class TestConnectionFactory2 {

    // the only reference to the ConnectionManager
    static  ConnectionManager cm = null;

    // driver method
    public static void main(String[] args) {
        Connection conn1 = null;
        Connection conn2 = null;
        Connection conn3 = null;
        try {
            // get the only instance of ConnectionManager
            cm = cm.getInstance();
```

```
        // use default values for user, password, database
        conn1 = cm.getConnection(ConnectionManager.DATA_SOURCE_ORACLE);
        System.out.println("oracle connection="+conn1);

        // get a connection to MySQL database
        conn2 = cm.getConnection(ConnectionManager.DATA_SOURCE_MYSQL);
        System.out.println("mysql connection="+conn2);

        // get a connection to a JDBC-ODBC registered database
        // NOTE: the odbc data source is registered by
        // Microsoft's ODBC Data Source Administrator
        conn3 = cm.getConnection(ConnectionManager.DATA_SOURCE_ODBC);
        System.out.println("odbc connection="+conn3);
    }
    catch(Exception e){
        //handle the exception
        e.printStackTrace();
    }
    finally {
        // close all connections
        DatabaseUtil.close(cm);
        DatabaseUtil.close(conn1);
        DatabaseUtil.close(conn2);
        DatabaseUtil.close(conn3);
    }
}
```

Output from the Client Program

The following is the output:

```
$ javac TestConnectionFactory2.java
$ java jcb.bcm.TestConnectionFactory2
Connection not created. Opening connection phase...
Connecting to 1 database...
Connection successful..
oracle connection=oracle.jdbc.driver.OracleConnection@106082
Connection not created. Opening connection phase...
Connecting to 2 database...
Connection successful..
mysql connection=com.mysql.jdbc.Connection@11121f6
Connection not created. Opening connection phase...
Connecting to 3 database...
Connection successful..
odbc connection=sun.jdbc.odbc.JdbcOdbcConnection@95c083
Closing connection
```

Method 2: BCM Access Using the Data Source Name

For the second method, use the data source name, user, password, and database name. This code shows a sample client using this method:

```java
package jcb.bcm;

import java.sql.*;

/**
 * This client demonstrates the Basic Connection Management
 * (BCM package) using the data source name, user, password,
 * and database name. These values override the default values.
 */
public class TestConnectionFactory3 {

    // the only reference to the ConnectionManager
    static ConnectionManager cm = null;

    public static void main(String[] args){
        Connection conn1 = null;
        Connection conn2 = null;
        Connection conn3 = null;
        try{
            // get the only instance of ConnectionManager
            cm = cm.getInstance();

            // get Oracle connection and override the default values
            conn1 = cm.getConnection(ConnectionManager.DATA_SOURCE_ORACLE,
                "scott", "tiger", "scorpian");
            System.out.println("oracle connection="+conn1);


            // NOTE: the odbc data source is registered by
            // Microsoft's ODBC Data Source Administrator
            conn2 = cm.getConnection(ConnectionManager.DATA_SOURCE_ODBC,
                null, null, "northwind");
            System.out.println("odbc connection="+conn2);

            // get a connection to MySQL database
            conn3 = cm.getConnection(ConnectionManager.DATA_SOURCE_MYSQL,
                "root", "root", "snipit");
            System.out.println("odbc connection="+conn3);
        }
        catch(Exception e){
            // handle the exceptions
            e.printStackTrace();
        }
        finally{
            // close all connections
            DatabaseUtil.close(cm);
            DatabaseUtil.close(conn1);
            DatabaseUtil.close(conn2);
            DatabaseUtil.close(conn3);
        }
    }
}
```

Output from the Client Program

This is the output:

```
$ javac TestConnectionFactory3.java
$ java jcb.bcm.TestConnectionFactory3
Connection not created. Opening connection phase...
Connecting to 1 database...
Connection successful..
oracle connection=oracle.jdbc.driver.OracleConnection@106082
Connection not created. Opening connection phase...
Connecting to 3 database...
Connection successful..
odbc connection=sun.jdbc.odbc.JdbcOdbcConnection@1006d75
Connection not created. Opening connection phase...
Connecting to 2 database...
Connection successful..
odbc connection=com.mysql.jdbc.Connection@95c083
Closing connection
```

BCM Package Features

The BCM package has the following features:

- The ConnectionManager is implemented as a singleton pattern.
- The ConnectionFactory is an abstract class, and it is implemented as a singleton pattern.

  - Database user
  - Database user's password
  - Database name

- The BCM package has three specific factory classes that provide connections (note that each specific connection factory will create one connection, at most, and it will reuse connections as needed):

  - OracleConnectionFactory (creates Oracle Connection objects)
  - MysqlConnectionFactory (creates Oracle Connection objects)
  - OdbcConnectionFactory (creates JDBC-ODBC Connection objects)

BCM's ConnectionManager

The purpose of ConnectionManager is to manage connections supplied by the ConnectionFactory class. The ConnectionManager is extensible, and you may add data sources. The ConnectionFactory is responsible for delivering connections to the ConnectionManager class (the ConnectionManager class manages only those connection created by the ConnectionFactory class).

```
package jcb.bcm;

import java.sql.*;

/**
 * This class manages database connections.
 * This is a "singleton" class.  A singleton
 * class is a class with only one object for
```

```
 * a given class and this object should be
 * easily accessible to clients.
 */
class ConnectionManager {
   ...
}
```

BCM's Connection Factories

The BCM has three factories: OracleConnectionFactory, MySqlConnectionFactory, and OdbcConnectionFactory. The main job of these factories is to produce Connection objects for clients.

OracleConnectionFactory

The purpose of OracleConnectionFactory is to pass the right parameters to ConnectionFactory for creating Oracle connections. This class provides a default driver class and also provides a database URL prefix. (You need just to append the name of Oracle SID to it.)

```
package jcb.bcm;

import java.sql.*;


/**
 * This class extends the abstract ConnectionFactory
 * for connecting to an Oracle database.
 *


   ...
}
```

MySQLConnectionFactory

The purpose of MysqlConnectionFactory is to pass the right parameters to ConnectionFactory for creating connections. This class provides a default driver class and also provides a database URL prefix. (You need just to append the name of the MySQL database to it.)

```
package jcb.bcm;

import java.sql.*;


/**
 * This class extends the abstract ConnectionFactory
 * for connecting to a MySQL database.
 *
 */
class MysqlConnectionFactory extends ConnectionFactory {
   ...
}
```

3-12. How Do You Determine If a Database Supports Transactions?

The Connection interface has a method that provides information about supporting the transactions for the database engine. The Oracle and MySQL databases (and some other databases such as Sybase) support transactions; meanwhile, the Microsoft Access database does not support transactions.

General Solution

The following code presents the general solution, and then I will show how to test the solution against Oracle and MySQL databases.

```java
import java.sql.Connection;
import java.sql.DatabaseMetaData;
import jcb.util.DatabaseUtil;
...
Connection conn = null;
try {
    conn = <get-a-database-connection>;
    DatabaseMetaData dbMetaData = conn.getMetaData();
    if (dbMetaData.supportsTransactions()) {
        // Transactions are supported
    }
    else {
        // Transactions are not supported
    }
}
catch (SQLException e) {
    // handle the exception:
    // could not determine if database
    // server supports transactions
}
finally {
    DatabaseUtil.close(conn);
```

Practical Solution

This code shows a practical implementation of the previous general solution, which you will then be able to test against Oracle and MySQL databases:

```java
import java.sql.Connection;
import java.sql.SQLException;
import java.sql.DatabaseMetaData;

import jcb.util.DatabaseUtil;
import jcb.db.VeryBasicConnectionManager;

public class TestSupportsTransactions {

    public static boolean supportsTransactions(Connection conn)
        throws SQLException {

        if (conn == null) {
            return false;
        }

        DatabaseMetaData dbMetaData = conn.getMetaData();
        if (dbMetaData == null) {
            // metadata is not supported
            return false;
        }

        return dbMetaData.supportsTransactions();
    }
```

```
    public static void main(String[] args) {
        Connection conn = null;
        try {
            String dbVendor = args[0];
            conn = VeryBasicConnectionManager.getConnection(dbVendor);
            System.out.println("--- begin Test ---");
            System.out.println("dbVendor="+dbVendor);
            System.out.println("conn="+conn);
            System.out.println("Transaction Support:"+
                supportsTransactions(conn));
            System.out.println("--- end of Test ---");
        }
    catch(Exception e){
        e.printStackTrace();
        System.exit(1);
    }
    finally {
        DatabaseUtil.close(conn);
        }
    }
}
```

Running Solution for an Oracle Database

This shows how to test the solution for Oracle:

```
--- begin Test ---
dbVendor=oracle
conn=oracle.jdbc.driver.T4CConnection@341960
Transaction Support:true
--- end of Test ---
```

Running Solution for a MySQL Database

This shows how to test the solution for MySQL:

```
$ javac TestSupportsTransactions.java
$ java TestSupportsTransactions  mysql
--- begin Test ---
dbVendor=mysql
conn=com.mysql.jdbc.Connection@8fce95
Transaction Support:true
--- end of Test ---
```

3-13. How Do You Limit the Number of Rows Returned from a SQL Query?

A JDBC client program to a database can limit the number of rows returned. When a SQL query is executed, the number of rows of data that a driver physically copies from the database server to the client is called the *fetch size*. You can control the fetch size (by "setting" and "getting" the fetch size).

To improve the performance of a specific query, you can adjust the fetch size to better match the use of the query. You can set the fetch size on an instance of java.sql.Statement, in which case, all rows (result sets) created from that statement will use that fetch size.

You can also set the fetch size on a result set at any time. In this case, the next time data needs to be fetched from the database server, the driver will copy over as many rows as specified by the current fetch size.

Solution: Getting the Fetch Size

This code shows how to get the fetch size:

```java
import java.sql.ResultSet;
import java.sql.Statement;
import java.sql.Connection;
import java.sql.SQLException;
import jcb.util.DatabaseUtil;
...
ResultSet rs = null;
Statement stmt = null;
Connection conn = null;
try {
    conn = <get-a-database-connection>;

    // Get the fetch size of a statement
    stmt = conn.createStatement ();
    int fetchSize = stmt.getFetchSize();

    // Get the fetch size of a result set
    rs = stmt.executeQuery("select author from books_table");


catch (SQLException e) {
    // handle the exception
}
finally {
    DatabaseUtil.close(rs);
    DatabaseUtil.close(stmt);
    DatabaseUtil.close(conn);
}
```

Solution: Setting the Fetch Size

This code shows how to set the fetch size:

```java
import java.sql.ResultSet;
import java.sql.Statement;
import java.sql.Connection;
import java.sql.SQLException;
import jcb.util.DatabaseUtil;
...
ResultSet rs = null;
Statement stmt = null;
Connection conn = null;
try {
    conn = <get-a-database-connection>;

    // Set the fetch size of a statement
    stmt = conn.createStatement();
    stmt.setFetchSize(20);
```

```
    // Create a result set, which will return only 20 rows
    rs = stmt.executeQuery("SELECT author FROM books_table");
    // Change the fetch size on the result set
    //
    rs.setFetchSize(40);
}
catch (SQLException e) {
    // handle the exception
}
finally {
    DatabaseUtil.close(rs);
    DatabaseUtil.close(stmt);
    DatabaseUtil.close(conn);
}
```

3-14. How Do You Get the Driver of a Connection?

Given a connection, it is *not* possible to determine the driver that created the connection. Although the connection can return a driver name, the returned name cannot be used to find the driver.

```
import java.sql.DatabaseMetaData;
import java.sql.Connection;
import java.sql.SQLException;
import jcb.util.DatabaseUtil;
   ...
Connection conn = null;


    if (dbmd == null) {
        System.out.println("vendor does not support metadata");
    }
    else {
        String driverName = dbmd.getDriverName();
    }
}
catch (SQLException e) {
        // handle the exception
}
finally {
        DatabaseUtil.close(conn);
}
```

The best you can do is to use the same database URL that was used to create the Connection object:

```
import java.sql.Driver;
import java.sql.DriverManager;
import java.sql.Connection;
import java.sql.SQLException;
import jcb.util.DatabaseUtil;
...
Connection conn = null;
try {
    // create connection from database URL
    conn = DriverManager.getConnection(url, username, password);
    // Get driver from database URL
    Driver driver = DriverManager.getDriver(url);
}
```

```
catch (SQLException e) {
    // handle the exception
}
finally {
    DatabaseUtil.close(conn);
}
```

3-15. How Do You Commit and Roll Back Updates to a Database?

The Connection interface has several methods that control the commit and rollback updates to a database. These methods are as follows:

- void commit(): Makes all changes permanent that were made since the previous commit/rollback and releases any database locks currently held by this Connection object.

- boolean getAutoCommit(): Retrieves the current autocommit mode for this Connection object.

- boolean isReadOnly(): Retrieves whether this Connection object is in read-only mode.

- void setReadOnly(boolean readOnly): Puts this connection in read-only mode as a hint to the driver to enable database optimizations.

- void rollback(): Undoes all changes made in the current transaction and releases any database locks currently held by this Connection object.

- void rollback(Savepoint savepoint): Undoes all changes made after the given Savepoint object was set.

  given state.

- Savepoint setSavepoint(): Creates an unnamed savepoint in the current transaction and returns the new Savepoint object that represents it.

- Savepoint setSavepoint(String name): Creates a savepoint with the given name in the current transaction and returns the new Savepoint object that represents it.

- void setTransactionIsolation(int level): Attempts to change the transaction isolation level for this Connection object to the one given.

By default, a database connection commits all updates to the database immediately and automatically. For example, executing an UPDATE SQL query immediately commits the change. The following code shows how to disable autocommits and explicitly commit:

```
import java.sql.Connection;
import java.sql.SQLException;
import jcb.util.DatabaseUtil;
...
Connection conn = null;
try {
    conn = <get-a-database-connection>;
    //
    // disable autocommit
    //
    conn.setAutoCommit(false);

    // execute any number of SQL updates...

    //
    // commit updates
```

```
    //
    conn.commit();
}
catch (SQLException e) {
    //
    // Roll back update
    //
    conn.rollback();
}
finally {
    DatabaseUtil.close(conn);
}
```

3-16. How Do You Determine If a SQL Warning Occurs?

Some database operations (such as truncation errors) can cause a warning (such as a SQLWarning) that is not handled by an exception (such as a SQLException). You must explicitly check for these database warnings. An example of a warning is a data truncation error during a read operation (see the DataTruncation class).

You have three places to check for a warning; the following code recipes check for each of these in turn:

- Connection object

- Statement object

-

Check for Warnings Using the Connection Object

The following code shows how to check for warnings using the Connection object:

```
import java.sql.Connection;
import java.sql.SQLException;
import java.sql.SQLWarning;
import jcb.util.DatabaseUtil;
...
Connection conn = null;
try {
    conn = <get-a-database-connection>;
    //
    // do some operations with the Connection object
    //

    //
    // get warnings on Connection object
    //
    SQLWarning warning = conn.getWarnings();
    while (warning != null) {
        //
        // handle connection warning
        //
        String message = warning.getMessage();
        String sqlState = warning.getSQLState();
        int errorCode = warning.getErrorCode();
        warning = warning.getNextWarning();
    }
}
```

```
catch (SQLException e) {
    // exception happened while getting the warnings;
    // you may handle it or ignore it
}
finally {
    DatabaseUtil.close(conn);
}
```

Check for Warnings Using the Statement Object

This code shows how to check for warnings using the Statement object:

```
import java.sql.Connection;
import java.sql.SQLException;
import java.sql.SQLWarning;
import java.sql.Statement;
import jcb.util.DatabaseUtil;
...
Statement stmt = null;
Connection conn = null;
try {
    conn = <get-a-database-connection>;
    // do some operations with the Connection object
    //
    // Get warnings on Statement object
    //


    // use the statement...

    // get warnings on Statement object
    SQLWarning warning = stmt.getWarnings();
    while (warning != null) {
        //
        // handle connection warning
        //
        String message = warning.getMessage();
        String sqlState = warning.getSQLState();
        int errorCode = warning.getErrorCode();
        warning = warning.getNextWarning();
    }
catch (SQLException e) {
    // exception happened while getting the warnings;
    // you may handle it or ignore it
}
finally {
    DatabaseUtil.close(stmt);
    DatabaseUtil.close(conn);
}
```

Check for Warnings Using the ResultSet Object

This code shows how to check for warnings using the ResultSet object:

```
import java.sql.Connection;
import java.sql.SQLException;
import java.sql.ResultSet;
```

```
import java.sql.SQLWarning;
import java.sql.Statement;
import jcb.util.DatabaseUtil;
...
ResultSet rs = null;
Statement stmt = null;
Connection conn = null;
try {
    conn = <get-a-database-connection>;
    // do some operations with the Connection object
    // create a statement
    stmt = conn.createStatement();

    // use the statement...

    // get a result set
    rs = stmt.executeQuery("SELECT author FROM books_table");
    while (resultSet.next()) {
        // Use result set
        // and process columns retrieved

        // get warnings on the current row of the ResultSet object
        SQLWarning warning = resultSet.getWarnings();
        while (warning != null) {
            // Process result set warnings...
            //


            String message = warning.getMessage();
            String sqlState = warning.getSQLState();
            int errorCode = warning.getErrorCode();
            warning = warning.getNextWarning();
        }
    }
}
catch (SQLException e) {
    // exception happened while getting the warnings;
// you may handle it or ignore it
}
finally {
    DatabaseUtil.close(rs);
    DatabaseUtil.close(stmt);
    DatabaseUtil.close(conn);
}
```

3-17. What Are the MySQL Connection Properties?

You can specify additional properties to the JDBC driver, either by placing them in a java.util.
Properties instance and passing that instance to the DriverManager when you connect or by adding
them to the end of your JDBC URL as name-value pairs. The first connection property needs to be
preceded with ?; separate additional key-value pair properties with &.

In the following examples, I provide three recipes for passing additional properties to the JDBC driver.

Example 1: Passing Additional Properties Using java.util.Properties

The following code shows how to pass additional properties using java.util.Properties:

```java
import java.sql.DriverManager;
import java.sql.Connection;
import java.util.Properties;
...
//
// define and set connection properties
//
Properties properties = new java.util.Properties();
properties.put("user", "root");
properties.put("password","rootp");
properties.put("useUnicode","true");
properties.put("characterEncoding","utf8");
String databaseURL = "jdbc:mysql://localhost/snipit";


//
// create Connection object
//
Connection conn =
    DriverManager.getConnection(databaseURL, properties);
```

Example 2: Passing Additional Properties Using a Database URL

This code shows how to pass additional properties using a database URL:

```java
import java.sql.DriverManager;
import java.sql.Connection;
...

// define and set connection properties using a database URL
//
String databaseURL = "jdbc:mysql://localhost/snipit?user=root"+
     "&password=rootp&useUnicode=true&characterEncoding=utf8";

//
// create Connection object
//
Connection conn = DriverManager.getConnection(databaseURL);
```

Example 3: Passing Additional Properties Using java.util.Properties and a Database URL

You can also pass connection properties by using java.util.Properties and a database URL, as
shown here:

```java
import java.util.Properties;
import java.sql.DriverManager;
import java.sql.Connection;
...
//
// define and set connection properties
//
Properties props = new Properties();
props.put("user", "root");
props.put("password","rootp");

// add additional connection properties to the database URL
String databaseURL = "jdbc:mysql://localhost/snipit?" +
    "useUnicode=true&characterEncoding=utf8";
```

```
//
// create Connection object
//
Connection conn = DriverManager.getConnection(databaseURL, props);
```

For more information about the java.sql.Connection properties, their definitions, and their default values, refer to http://dev.mysql.com/doc/connector/j/en/cj-driver-classname. html#id2624462.

3-18. What Are the Oracle Connection Properties?

In general, to get a database Connection object (that is, a java.sql.Connection) object, you need to provide three values: a database URL, the database user, and the database user's password. Some vendors (such as Oracle) provide additional properties (such as defaultRowPrefetch and defaultBatchValue) for their drivers. Also, I will show how to use Oracle *roles* for user logon (such as SYS).

You can use the DriverManager's getConnection() method to pass additional properties; its signature is as follows:

```
import java.sql.Connection;
import java.util.Properties;
...
public static Connection getConnection(String url,
                                       Properties info)
```

Specifying a Database URL and Properties Object

```
getConnection(String URL, Properties info);
```

where the URL is of this form:

```
jdbc:oracle:<drivertype>:@<database>
```

In addition to the URL, use an object of the standard Java Properties class as input. For example:

```
java.util.Properties info = new java.util.Properties();
info.put ("user", "scott");
info.put ("password","tiger");
info.put ("defaultRowPrefetch","15");
Connection conn = DriverManager.getConnection("jdbc:oracle:oci:@", info);
```

Oracle 10's JDBC drivers recognize an additional driver properties; see http://www.oracle.com/ technology/tech/java/sqlj_jdbc/htdocs/jdbc_faq.htm for more information.

How to Use Roles for Oracle's SYS Logon

Oracle has two prebuilt database users (SYS and SYSTEM) that have a lot of privileges for managing database resources. To specify the role (mode) for the SYS logon, use the internal_logon connection property.

The following example illustrates how to use the internal_logon and sysdba arguments to specify the SYS logon:

```
import java.sql.*;
import java.math.*;
...
// register driver
DriverManager.registerDriver (new oracle.jdbc.OracleDriver());
```

```java
//specify the Properties object
java.util.Properties info = new java.util.Properties();
info.put ("user", "sys");
info.put ("password", "change_on_install");
info.put ("internal_logon","sysdba");

//specify the Connection object
String dbURL = "jdbc:oracle:thin:@mydatabase"
Connection conn = DriverManager.getConnection(dbURL,info);
```

3-19. Can a JDBC Application Connect to More Than One Database?

The answer is "yes." A JDBC application can connect to any number of databases. For each database, you need to create a proper connection before accessing the database.

Solution: Connecting to More Than One Database

The following code shows a code snippet that connects to two databases:

```java
import java.util.*;
import java.io.*;
import java.sql.*;

import jcb.db.*;
import jcb.meta.*;



  /**
   * Create an Oracle connection...
   */
  public static Connection getOracleConnection() throws Exception {
    String driver = "oracle.jdbc.driver.OracleDriver";
    String url = "jdbc:oracle:thin:@localhost:1521:scorpian";
    String username = "octopus";
    String password = "octopus";
    Class.forName(driver);               // load Oracle driver
    return DriverManager.getConnection(url, username, password);
  }

  /**
   * Create a MySQL connection...
   */
  public static Connection getMySqlConnection() throws Exception {
    String driver = "org.gjt.mm.mysql.Driver";
    String url = "jdbc:mysql://localhost/tiger";
    String username = "root";
    String password = "root";
    Class.forName(driver);               // load MySQL driver
    return DriverManager.getConnection(url, username, password);
  }

  public static void main(String[] args) {
    Connection oracleConn = null;
    Connection mysqlConn = null;
```

```
try {
   System.out.println("-- TestConnectToMoreThanOneDatabase begin --");
   // get connection to an Oracle database
   oracleConn = getOracleConnection();

   // get connection to a MySQL database
   mysqlConn = getMySqlConnection();

   System.out.println("oracleConn="+oracleConn);
   System.out.println("mysqlConn="+mysqlConn);

   // now, you may use oracleConn to access an Oracle database
   // and use mysqlConn to access a MySQL database

   //
   // use oracleConn and mysqlConn
   //
   System.out.println("-- TestConnectToMoreThanOneDatabase end --");
}
catch(Exception e){
   // handle the exception
   e.printStackTrace();
   System.exit(1);
}
finally {
   // release database resources


}
  }
}
```

Testing Connection to More Than One Database

To test more than one database, use this code:

```
$ javac TestConnectToMoreThanOneDatabase.java
$ java TestConnectToMoreThanOneDatabase
-- TestConnectToMoreThanOneDatabase begin --
oracleConn=oracle.jdbc.driver.OracleConnection@16f0472
mysqlConn=com.mysql.jdbc.Connection@18d107f
-- TestConnectToMoreThanOneDatabase end --
```

3-20. How Do You Test to See If Your Connection Is Alive?

Among java.sql objects, the JDBC Connection object (java.sql.Connection) is the most important object in the java.sql package. When you get a Connection object, with some simple tests you can figure it out to see if the connection is a valid connection. The following scenarios show how a connection can go bad:

- If you hold a Connection object for a while and then the database server goes down (for any reason), then that connection is no longer a valid connection.

- If you hold a Connection object for a while and then the connection times out (closes itself), then that connection is no longer a valid connection.

- If you hold a Connection object for a while and then the network connection dies, then that connection is no longer a valid connection.

- There might be other situations where you might think you are holding a valid connection but the reality is that the connection cannot do much (which is an obsolete connection).

Now, the real question is this: once you have a connection, how do you determine if that connection is a valid/useful connection and you can get/set data from/to a database? In the following recipes, I have developed a method that accepts a connection and its vendor and then returns true if the connection is a valid connection; otherwise, it returns false. If a connection's validation fails, it must be destroyed, and a new Connection object must be created and returned.

Solution: Testing Validity of Connection

The following code is quite lengthy, but it shows a full creation-and-test sequence so that you can see the validation technique at work. I've put plenty of comments in the code so you can easily see what it's doing. I provide some sample output immediately after this listing.

```
import java.util.*;
import java.io.*;
import java.sql.*;

import jcb.db.*;
import jcb.meta.*;

public class TestValidityOfConnection {


    * Create an Oracle connection...
    */
    public static Connection getOracleConnection() throws Exception {
        String driver = "oracle.jdbc.driver.OracleDriver";
        String url = "jdbc:oracle:thin:@localhost:1521:scorpian";
        String username = "octopus";
        String password = "octopus";
        Class.forName(driver);              // load Oracle driver
        return DriverManager.getConnection(url, username, password);
    }

    /**
    * Create a MySQL connection...
    */
    public static Connection getMySqlConnection() throws Exception {
        String driver = "org.gjt.mm.mysql.Driver";
        String url = "jdbc:mysql://localhost/tiger";
        String username = "root";
        String password = "root";
        Class.forName(driver);          // load MySQL driver
        return DriverManager.getConnection(url, username, password);
    }

    /**
    * Test validity of a connection
    * @param conn a JDBC Connection object
    * @param vendor a database vendor: { "oracle", "mysql", ...}
    * @return true if a given Connection object is a valid one;
    *   otherwise return false.
```

```
 * @throws Exception Failed to determine if a given connection is valid.
 */
public static boolean isValidConnection(Connection conn,
                                        String vendor)
    throws Exception {
    if (conn == null) {
        // null Connection object is not valid
        return false;
    }

    if (conn.isClosed()) {
        // closed Connection object is not valid
        return false;
    }

    // here you have a Connection object that is not null and
    // that is not closed, but it might be a defunct object
    // in order to determine whether it is a valid connection,
    // depends on the vendor of the database:
    //
    // for Oracle database:
    //       you may use the Connection object
    //       with query of "select 1 from dual";
    //       if the query returns the result, then
    //       it is a valid Connection object.
    //


    //       with query of "select 1"; if the
    //       query returns the result, then it
    //       is a valid Connection object.

    if (vendor.equalsIgnoreCase("mysql")) {
        //  if you need to determine if the connection
        //  is still valid, you should issue a simple
        //  query, such as "SELECT 1". The driver will
        //  throw an exception if the connection is
        //  no longer valid.
        return testConnection(conn, "select 1");
    }
    else if (vendor.equalsIgnoreCase("oracle")) {
        //  if you need to determine if the connection
        //  is still valid, you should issue a simple
        //  query, such as "SELECT 1 from dual". The driver
        //  will throw an exception if the connection is
        //  no longer valid.
        return testConnection(conn, "select 1 from dual");
    }
    else {
        // you may add additional vendors here.
        return false;
    }
}

/**
 * Test validity of a connection
 * @param conn a JDBC Connection object
```

```java
    * @param query a sql query to test against database connection
    * @return true if a given Connection object is a valid one;
    *   otherwise return false.
    */
   public static boolean testConnection(Connection conn,
                                        String query) {
       ResultSet rs = null;
       Statement stmt = null;
       try {
           stmt = conn.createStatement();
           if (stmt == null) {
               return false;
           }

           rs = stmt.executeQuery(query);
           if (rs == null) {
               return false;
           }

           if (rs.next()) {
               // Connection object is valid: you were able to
               // connect to the database and return something useful.
               return true;
           }

           // there is no hope any more for the validity



       }
       catch(Exception e) {
           // something went wrong: connection is bad
           return false;
       }
       finally {
           DatabaseUtil.close(rs);
           DatabaseUtil.close(stmt);
       }
   }

   public static void main(String[] args) {
       Connection oracleConn = null;
       Connection mysqlConn = null;
       try {
           System.out.println("-- TestValidityOfConnection begin --");

           // get connection to an Oracle database
           oracleConn = getOracleConnection();
           System.out.println("oracleConn="+oracleConn);
           System.out.println(isValidConnection(oracleConn, "oracle"));

           // get connection to a MySQL database
           mysqlConn = getMySqlConnection();
           System.out.println("mysqlConn="+mysqlConn);
           System.out.println(isValidConnection(mysqlConn, "mysql"));
```

```
            System.out.println("databases are shutting down...");

            // sleep for 30 seconds (enough time to shut down
            // both Oracle and MySQL databases) and during this
            // time shut down both Oracle and MySQL databases:
            Thread.sleep(30000);

            // wake up after 30 seconds
            // test to see if the Oracle connection is valid?
            System.out.println("oracleConn="+oracleConn);
            System.out.println(isValidConnection(oracleConn, "oracle"));

            // test to see if the MySQL connection is valid?
            System.out.println("mysqlConn="+mysqlConn);
            System.out.println(isValidConnection(mysqlConn, "mysql"));

            System.out.println("-- TestValidityOfConnection end --");
        }
        catch(Exception e){
            // handle the exception
            e.printStackTrace();
            System.exit(1);
        }
        finally {
            // release database resources
            DatabaseUtil.close(oracleConn);


    }
}
```

Running Program: Testing Validity of Connection

Use this code to test the validity of the connection:

```
$ javac TestValidityOfConnection.java

$ java TestValidityOfConnection
-- TestValidityOfConnection begin --
oracleConn=oracle.jdbc.driver.OracleConnection@1a125f0
true
mysqlConn=com.mysql.jdbc.Connection@1372a1a
true
databases are shutting down...
oracleConn=oracle.jdbc.driver.OracleConnection@1a125f0
false
mysqlConn=com.mysql.jdbc.Connection@1372a1a
false
-- TestValidityOfConnection end --
java.sql.SQLException: Io exception: Connection reset by peer: socket write error
at oracle.jdbc.dbaccess.DBError.throwSqlException(DBError.java:134)
at oracle.jdbc.dbaccess.DBError.throwSqlException(DBError.java:179)
at oracle.jdbc.dbaccess.DBError.throwSqlException(DBError.java:333)
at oracle.jdbc.driver.OracleConnection.close(OracleConnection.java:1442)
at jcb.db.DatabaseUtil.close(DatabaseUtil.java:67)
at TestValidityOfConnection.main(TestValidityOfConnection.java:176)
```

3-21. How Do You Keep the Connection Alive in a Production Environment?

Maybe you have heard the following from a software/database engineer: "I have a database application that works fine for a day and then stops working overnight...."

This can happen to many database applications. In general, when you get a Connection object from database server, there is a timeout property associated with the Connection object; when this time expires, then the Connection object becomes stale/defunct (becoming a dead, useless Connection object). For example, the MySQL database closes connections after eight hours of inactivity. So, you either need to use a connection pool that handles stale connections or use the autoReconnect parameter.

Using the MySQL database, automatic reconnection is available. Because the Connection object has to "ping" the database before each query, this is turned off by default. To use it, you need to pass autoReconnect=true in the connection URL. You may also change the number of reconnect tries and the initial timeout value via the parameters maxReconnects=n (the default is 3) and initialTimeout=n (the default is two seconds). The timeout is an exponential back-off timeout; in other words, if you have initial timeout of two seconds and a maxReconnects of three seconds, then the driver will time-out for two seconds, four seconds, and then sixteen seconds between each reconnection attempt.

Solution: Creating Connection with Properties (MySQL)

The following code shows how to keep connections alive in a production environment:

```java
import java.sql.*;
import java.util.*;


public class TestCreateConnectionWithProperties_MySQL {

    public static final String DATABASE_USER = "user";
    public static final String DATABASE_PASSWORD = "password";
    public static final String MYSQL_AUTO_RECONNECT = "autoReconnect";
    public static final String MYSQL_MAX_RECONNECTS = "maxReconnects";

    /**
     * Create MySQL connection...which will live for a long time
     */
    public static Connection getConnection() throws Exception {
        String driver = "org.gjt.mm.mysql.Driver";
        // load the driver
        Class.forName(driver);
        String dbURL = "jdbc:mysql://localhost/tiger";
        String dbUsername = "root";
        String dbPassword = "root";

        // these are properties that get passed
        // to DriverManager.getConnection(...)
        java.util.Properties connProperties = new java.util.Properties();
        connProperties.put(DATABASE_USER, dbUsername);
        connProperties.put(DATABASE_PASSWORD, dbPassword);

        // set additional connection properties:
        // if connection stales, then make automatically
        // reconnect; make it alive again;
        // if connection stales, then try for reconnection;
        connProperties.put(MYSQL_AUTO_RECONNECT, "true");
```

```
            connProperties.put(MYSQL_MAX_RECONNECTS, "4");
            return DriverManager.getConnection(dbURL, connProperties);
        }

    public static void main(String[] args) {
        Connection conn = null;
        try {
            System.out.println("-- TestCreateConnection_MySQL begin --");
            // get connection to an Oracle database
            conn = getConnection();
            System.out.println("conn="+conn);
            // use connection ...
            System.out.println("-- TestCreateConnection_MySQL end --");
        }
        catch(Exception e){
            // handle the exception
            e.printStackTrace();
            System.exit(1);
        }
        finally {
            // release database resources
            DatabaseUtil.close(conn);
        }
    }
}
```

To test, use this code:

```
$ javac TestCreateConnectionWithProperties_MySQL.java
$ java TestCreateConnectionWithProperties_MySQL
-- TestCreateConnection_MySQL begin --
conn=com.mysql.jdbc.Connection@14ed9ff
-- TestCreateConnection_MySQL end --
```

3-22. How Do You Disconnect from a Database?

To do something useful with a database, you need a Connection (java.sql.Connection interface) object. When you are done with your database task, you need to close the Connection object. (Closing a Connection object is referred to as disconnecting from a database.) If you have borrowed your Connection object from a connection pool manager, then you have to return it to the connection pool manager; otherwise, you need to close it properly.

Case 1: Borrowing a Connection Object from a Connection Pool Manager

Assume that there is a connection pool manager identified by a singleton class ConnectionPoolManager, which manages a pool of connections for several data sources. Further assume that this class has two static methods:

```
getConnection(String dataSourceName)
releaseConnection(Connection conn)
```

Then you can write the following snippet for getting a connection and then a disconnection from the database. Note that the connection pool manager does a soft close (rather than a hard close) on the connections, which means it just returns the connection to the pool to be used by other clients.

```
Connection conn = null;
try {
    // get Connection object from the pool
    String dataSourceName = "myDataSource";
    conn = ConnectionPoolManager.getConnection(dataSourceName);
    System.out.println("conn="+conn);

    // use connection    do something useful with it.
}
catch(Exception e){
    // handle the exception
    e.printStackTrace();
    // do more handling
}
finally {
    // disconnect from the database
    // release Connection object: this is a soft close
    if (conn != null) {
        ConnectionPoolManager.releaseConnection(conn);
    }
}
```

Case 2: Not Borrowing a Connection Object from a Connection Pool Manager

Assume that there is static method (getConnection()) that returns a new Connection object. Then you can write the following:

```
...
Connection conn = null;
try {
    // get Connection object from the pool
    String dataSourceName = "myDataSource";
    conn = getConnection(dataSourceName);
    System.out.println("conn="+conn);

    // use connection    do something useful with it.
}
catch(Exception e){
    // handle the exception
    e.printStackTrace();
    // do more handling
}
finally {
    // disconnect from the database
    // release Connection object: this is a soft close
        Databaseutil.close(conn);
}
```

3-23. What Are the Rules for Connection's Autocommit?

The java.sql.Connection interface has several methods that control the commit and rollback updates to a database. The void setAutoCommit(boolean autoCommit) method directly deals with the Connection object's autocommit mode; it sets this connection's autocommit mode to the given state.

According to the JDBC specification, by default a database connection commits all updates to the database immediately and automatically. By default, new connections are in autocommit mode. For example, executing an UPDATE SQL query immediately commits the change.

Solution: Disabling Autocommits

The following example shows how to disable autocommits and explicitly commit:

```java
import java.sql.*;
import jcb.util.DatabaseUtil;
...
Connection conn = null;
try {
    conn = <get-a-database-connection>;

    // disable autocommit
    conn.setAutoCommit(false);

    // execute any number of SQL updates...

    // commit updates
    conn.commit();
}
catch (SQLException e) {
    // Roll back update
    conn.rollback();


    DatabaseUtil.close(conn);
}
```

Enabling Autocommits

The following example shows how to enable autocommits:

```java
import java.sql.*;
import jcb.util.DatabaseUtil;
...
Connection conn = null;
try {
    conn = <get-a-database-connection>;

    // enable autocommit
    conn.setAutoCommit(true);

    // execute any number of SQL updates...
    // NOTE: from now on, every statement will commit
}
catch (SQLException e) {
    // handle the exception
}
finally {
    // disconnect from the database: release Connection object
    DatabaseUtil.close(conn);
}
```

What Are the Rules for Autocommit?

The rules for autocommit are as follows: if autocommit is true, then commit happens automatically after every SQL query/statement; if autocommit is false, then it does not. You can get the autocommit value by invoking the `Connection.getAutoCommit()` method.

You can turn off autocommit mode for an active database connection with the following:

```
java.sql.Connection conn = valid-database-connection-object;
conn.setAutoCommit(false) ;
```

and turn it back on again with this:

```
conn.setAutoCommit(true);
```

Once autocommit is off (that is, false), no SQL statements will be committed (that is, the database will not be permanently updated) until you have explicitly told it to commit by invoking the `Connection.commit()` method:

```
conn.commit();
```

Detailed Autocommit Rules

In general, autocommit rules are complex:

- If autocommit is true and the method is `executeUpdate()`, then the commit happens when the method completes.

- If autocommit is true and the method is `executeQuery()`, then the commit happens when the

  statement/query passed to the `execute()` method.

- If autocommit is false and the method is `execute()` or `executeUpdate()` and the SQL statement is `CREATE/ALTER/DROP`, then the commit happens upon statement completion.

- If autocommit is false and the SQL statement is not `CREATE/ALTER/DROP`, then nothing happens. (The commit will take place by the explicit `commit()` method.)

3-24. How Do You Create a New Type Map?

In JDBC, *type mapping* enables user-defined types (UDTs). What is a UDT? It is a data type comprised of other types (such as `VARCHAR`, `INTEGER`, and so on).

Using Oracle database, a data type is a UDT that encapsulates a data structure along with the methods (functions and procedures) needed to manipulate the data. The data is referred to as *attributes*, and the set of operations specified on the data are called the *methods* of the object type.

In relational databases, UDTs enable users to create object-relational databases. To create (write a UDT to a database) and retrieve (read a UDT from a database) UDTs, you can manipulate them as SQL structs and SQL arrays, or you can define Java classes that are mapped to the SQL UDTs, which you then use to materialize the UDTs in your Java program. JDBC provides interfaces (such as `java.sql.SQLData`, `java.sql.SQLInput`, and `java.sql.SQLOutput`) to enable read/write operations of UDTs. In this chapter, we will look at `SQLInput` and `SQLOutput` in detail with the sample running programs (using Oracle 10g).

Oracle enables users to define UDTs. The MySQL database does not offer to define a UDT and therefore does not support `SQLData`, `SQLInput`, and `SQLOutput`.

What Is Type Mapping?

Before you look at UDTs, you need to understand type mapping. According to the J2SE documentation, a user may create a new type map, which is a java.util.Map object, make an entry in it, and pass it to the java.sql methods that can perform custom mapping. In this case, the method will use the given type map instead of the one associated with the connection.

For example, the following code fragment specifies that the SQL type BOOK will be mapped to the class Book in the Java programming language. The code fragment retrieves the type map for the Connection object conn, inserts the entry into it, and then sets the type map with the new entry as the connection's type map.

```
java.sql.Connection conn = a-valid-connection-object;
java.util.Map map = conn.getTypeMap();
map.put("mySchemaName.BOOK", Class.forName("Book"));
conn.setTypeMap(map);
```

3-25. How Do You Create a SQL to Java Type Map Entry?

You can create a SQL to Java type map entry as follows:

```
map.put (<SQL Type Name>,
          <Java class which implements java.sql.SQLData interface>);
```

java.sql.SQLData is the interface used for the custom mapping of a SQL UDT to a class in the Java programming language. The Class object for a class implementing the SQLData interface will be entered in the appropriate Connection object's type map along with the SQL name of the UDT for

java.sql.Connection support for Java Type Map

The Connection interface has two methods for supporting Java type maps, as shown here:

getTypeMap
```
        Signature:
            Map getTypeMap() throws SQLException
        Description:
            Retrieves the Map object associated with this
            Connection object. Unless the application has added
            an entry, the type map returned will be empty.
        Returns:
            the java.util.Map object associated with this Connection object
        Throws:
            SQLException - if a database access error occurs
```

setTypeMap
```
        Signature:
            void setTypeMap(Map map) throws SQLException
        Description:
            Installs the given TypeMap object as the type map for
            this Connection object. The type map will be used for the
            custom mapping of SQL structured types and distinct types.
        Parameters:
            map - the java.util.Map object to install as the replacement
            for this Connection object's default type map
        Throws:
            SQLException - if a database access error occurs or the given
            parameter is not a java.util.Map object
```

Example: Using Custom Mapping

I will provide a complete example on using custom mapping. To fully understand the concept, you need to understand the SQLData interface. This is according to the JDK documentation:

> *The interface, SQLData, used for the custom mapping of an SQL user-defined type (UDT) to a class in the Java programming language. The class object for a class implementing the SQLData interface will be entered in the appropriate Connection object's type map along with the SQL name of the UDT for which it is a custom mapping.*

For details of SQLData interface, please refer to the JDK documentation.

Example: Using Custom Mapping: Oracle Database Preparation

This code shows how to prepare the Oracle database:

```
$ sqlplus scott/tiger
SQL*Plus: Release 10.1.0.2.0 - Production on Tue Oct 12 09:48:48 2004
SQL> create or replace type BOOK as object(
  2  isbn varchar2(10),
  3  title varchar2(20),
  4  author varchar2(20),
  5  edition integer
  6  );
  7  /
```

```
SQL> describe scott.BOOK;
 Name                                    Null?    Type
 ---------------------------------------- -------- ------------
 ISBN                                              VARCHAR2(10)
 TITLE                                             VARCHAR2(20)
 AUTHOR                                            VARCHAR2(20)
 EDITION                                           NUMBER(38)

SQL> create table book_table(
  2  id varchar2(5),
  3  book_object BOOK
  4  );

Table created.

SQL> desc book_table;
 Name                                    Null?    Type
 ---------------------------------------- -------- ------------
 ID                                               VARCHAR2(5)
 BOOK_OBJECT                                      BOOK

SQL> insert into book_table
values('11111', BOOK('1111111111', 'MyTitle', 'Me', 12));
1 row created.

SQL> insert into book_table
values('22222', BOOK('2222222222', 'YourTitle', 'You', 10));
1 row created.
```

```
SQL> select * from book_table;

ID          BOOK_OBJECT(ISBN, TITLE, AUTHOR, EDITION)
---------   ------------------------------------------------
11111       BOOK('1111111111', 'MyTitle', 'Me', 12)
22222       BOOK('2222222222', 'YourTitle', 'You', 10)
```

Example: Using Custom Mapping: Implementing SQLData

Suppose you have decided to use a custom mapping for the structured type BOOK so you can simply make changes to the Java class that maps BOOK. The Java class will have a field for each attribute of BOOK, and you can name the class and the fields whatever you want. The first thing required for a custom mapping is to create a Java class that implements the interface SQLData. (Note that you can use tools to create your required Java class.)

To use the SQLData interface, the implementing Java class must have a member for each element in the named row but can have additional members other than these. The members need not be public and can be in any order. The class must implement the writeSQL(), readSQL(), and getSQLTypeName() methods as defined in the SQLData interface but can provide additional methods.

The Book class implements the java.sql.SQLData interface for the custom mapping of the BOOK type, as shown here:

```
1     import java.sql.SQLData;
2     import java.sql.SQLInput;
3     import java.sql.SQLOutput;
4     import java.sql.SQLException;
5     import java.io.Serializable;


8        * A class to hold a copy of "SCOTT.BOOK" data type
9        */
10       public class Book implements SQLData, Serializable {
11
12           public static final String SQL_TYPE_NAME = "SCOTT.BOOK";
13           public String isbn;
14           public String title;
15           public String author;
16           public int edition;
17
18       // this constructor is required by Oracle's JDBC driver.
19       // if you exclude this constructor, then you will get a
20       // SQLException: "Inconsistent java and sql object types:
21       // InstantiationException: Book"
22       public Book() {
23       }
24
25       public Book (String isbn,
26                       String title,
27                       String author,
28                       int edition) {
29           this.isbn = isbn;
30           this.title = title;
31           this.author = author;
32           this.edition = edition;
33       }
34
35       // retrieves the fully qualified name of the SQL
```

```
36        // user-defined type that this object represents.
37        public String getSQLTypeName() {
38            return SQL_TYPE_NAME;
39        }
40
41        // populates this object with data it reads from stream
42        public void readSQL(SQLInput stream, String sqlType)
43                throws SQLException {
44            this.isbn = stream.readString();
45            this.title = stream.readString();
46            this.author = stream.readString();
47            this.edition = stream.readInt();
48        }
49
50        // writes this object to stream
51        public void writeSQL(SQLOutput stream)
52                throws SQLException {
53            stream.writeString(this.isbn);
54            stream.writeString(this.title);
55            stream.writeString(this.author);
56            stream.writeInt(this.edition);
57        }
58
59        /**
60         * For debugging: prints the raw data obtained from db.
61         */


64            System.out.println("isbn="+isbn);
65            System.out.println("title="+title);
66            System.out.println("author="+author);
67            System.out.println("edition="+edition);
68            System.out.println("--- Book print() raw data end ---");
69        }
70  }
```

Example: Using Custom Mapping: Using a Connection's Type Map

After writing a Java class that implements the interface java.sql.SQLData, the only other thing you have to do to set up a custom mapping is to make an entry in a type map. For this example, that means entering the fully qualified SQL name for BOOK and the Class object for the class Book.

A type map, an instance of java.util.Map, is associated with every new connection when it is created, so you can just use that one. Assuming that conn is the active connection, the following code fragment adds an entry for the UDT BOOK to the type map associated with conn (the Connection object):

```
java.util.Map map = conn.getTypeMap();
map.put("SCOTT.BOOK", Class.forName("Book"));
```

Note that whenever you call the ResultSet.getObject() method to retrieve an instance of BOOK, the JDBC driver will check the type map associated with the connection and see that it has an entry for the custom type BOOK. The JDBC driver will note the Class object for Book, create an instance of it, and then map the custom type BOOK to the Java object Book.

Example: Using Custom Mapping: Writing a New Record

You can insert UDTs into a database in two ways:

- *Method 1*: You can use a typical insert statement. For example, you can use the following SQL insert statement to create a new UDT in the database:

```
insert into book_table values(?, BOOK(?, ?, ?, ?))
```

- *Method 2*: You can use a typical insert statement with setObject(). You can use the following SQL insert statement to create a new UDT in the database where the second argument is a UDT:

```
insert into book_table values(?, ?)
```

Method 1 Solution: Using Custom Mapping: Writing a New Record

This code shows how to write a new record:

```
1   import java.util.*;
2   import java.io.*;
3   import java.sql.*;
4
5   import jcb.db.*;
6   import jcb.meta.*;
7
8   public class InsertCustomType_Oracle {
9
10      public static Connection getConnection() throws Exception {
11          String driver = "oracle.jdbc.driver.OracleDriver";
12          String url = "jdbc:oracle:thin:@localhost:1521:caspian";
13          String username = "scott";


16          return DriverManager.getConnection(url, username, password);
17      }
18
19      public static void main(String[] args) {
20          System.out.println("--- InsertCustomType_Oracle begin ---");
21          if (args.length != 5) {
22              System.out.println("usage: java InsertCustomType_Oracle "+
23                  "<id> <isbn> <title> <author> <edition>");
24              System.exit(1);
25          }
26
27          String id = args[0];
28          String isbn = args[1];
29          String title = args[2];
30          String author = args[3];
31          int edition = Integer.parseInt(args[4]);
32
33          Connection conn = null;
34          PreparedStatement pstmt = null;
35          try {
36              conn = getConnection();
37              String insert =
38                  "insert into book_table values(?, BOOK(?, ?, ?, ?))";
39              pstmt = conn.prepareStatement(insert);
40              pstmt.setString(1, id);
41              pstmt.setString(2, isbn);
42              pstmt.setString(3, title);
43              pstmt.setString(4, author);
```

```
44              pstmt.setInt(5, edition);
45              pstmt.executeUpdate();
46              System.out.println("--- InsertCustomType_Oracle end ---");
47          }
48          catch(Exception e){
49              e.printStackTrace();
50              System.exit(1);
51          }
52          finally {
53              DatabaseUtil.close(pstmt);
54              DatabaseUtil.close(conn);
55          }
56      }
}
```

Running Example: Using Custom Mapping: Writing a New Record

To run the example, use this code:

```
$ javac InsertCustomType_Oracle.java
$ java InsertCustomType_Oracle 77777 1122334455 "Strong Tigers" "Bob Smith" 3
--- InsertCustomType_Oracle begin ---
--- InsertCustomType_Oracle end ---

SQL> select id, book_object from book_table;

ID      BOOK_OBJECT(ISBN, TITLE, AUTHOR, EDITION)


22222   BOOK('2222222222', 'YourTitle', 'You', 10)
77777   BOOK('1122334455', 'Strong Tigers', 'Bob Smith', 3)
```

Method 2 Solution: Using Custom Mapping: Writing a New Record

This example presents a solution that writes a UDT into a database by using the setObject()
method.

This is the code before running the program:

```
SQL> select * from book_table;

ID   BOOK_OBJECT(ISBN, TITLE, AUTHOR, EDITION)
---  --------------------------------------------------------
22   BOOK('2222222222', 'YourTitle', 'You', 10)
11   BOOK('1111111111', 'MyTitle', 'Me', 12)
```

Compare the database before and after this solution to see how the custom mapping code is
working.

```
1   import java.util.*;
2   import java.io.*;
3   import java.sql.*;
4
5   import jcb.db.*;
6   import jcb.meta.*;
7
8   public class InsertCustomType2_Oracle {
9       public static Connection getConnection() throws Exception {
10          String driver = "oracle.jdbc.driver.OracleDriver";
```

```
11              String url = "jdbc:oracle:thin:@localhost:1521:caspian";
12              String username = "scott";
13              String password = "tiger";
14              Class.forName(driver);    // load Oracle driver
15              return DriverManager.getConnection(url, username, password);
16          }
17
18      public static void main(String[] args) {
19          System.out.println("--- InsertCustomType2_Oracle begin ---");
20          if (args.length != 5) {
21              System.out.println("usage: java InsertCustomType2_Oracle "+
22                  "<id> <isbn> <title> <author> <edition>");
23              System.exit(1);
24          }
25
26          String id = args[0];
27          String isbn = args[1];
28          String title = args[2];
29          String author = args[3];
30          int edition = Integer.parseInt(args[4]);
31
32          // create the Book object
33          Book book = new Book(isbn, title, author, edition);
34          book.printNoConversion();
35
36          Connection conn = null;


39              conn = getConnection();
40              // create type map
41              java.util.Map map = conn.getTypeMap();
42              System.out.println("map="+map);
43              map.put("SCOTT.BOOK", Class.forName("Book"));
44              System.out.println("map="+map);
45
46              String insert =
47                  "insert into book_table(ID, BOOK_OBJECT) values(?, ?)";
48              pstmt = conn.prepareStatement(insert);
49              pstmt.setString(1, id);
50              pstmt.setObject(2, book);
51              pstmt.executeUpdate();
52              System.out.println("--- InsertCustomType2_Oracle end ---");
53          }
54          catch(Exception e){
55              e.printStackTrace();
56              System.exit(1);
57          }
58          finally {
59              DatabaseUtil.close(pstmt);
60              DatabaseUtil.close(conn);
61          }
62      }
63  }
```

To run the sample program, use this code:

```
$ javac InsertCustomType2_Oracle.java
$ java InsertCustomType2_Oracle 44 5556668888 "How to play tennis" "Borg" 3
```

```
--- InsertCustomType2_Oracle begin ---
--- Book print() raw data begin ---
isbn=5556668888
title=How to play tennis
author=Borg
edition=3
--- Book print() raw data end ---
map={} map={SCOTT.BOOK=class Book}
--- InsertCustomType2_Oracle end ---
```

Here's the database after running the program:

```
SQL> select * from book_table;

ID   BOOK_OBJECT(ISBN, TITLE, AUTHOR, EDITION)
---  --------------------------------------------------------
22   BOOK('2222222222', 'YourTitle', 'You', 10)
11   BOOK('1111111111', 'MyTitle', 'Me', 12)
44   BOOK('5556668888', 'How to play tennis', 'Borg', 3)
```

This solution shows how to read an existing record using custom mapping.
Here's how to prepare the Oracle database:

```
$ sqlplus scott/tiger
SQL*Plus: Release 10.1.0.2.0 - Production on Thu Oct 14 10:52:20 2004

SQL> desc scott.book;
 Name                                     Null?    Type



 TITLE                                             VARCHAR2(20)
 AUTHOR                                            VARCHAR2(20)
 EDITION                                           NUMBER(38)

SQL> desc book_table;
 Name                                     Null?    Type
 ---------------------------------------- -------- ------------------
 ID                                                VARCHAR2(5)
 BOOK_OBJECT                                       BOOK

SQL> select * from book_table;

ID    BOOK_OBJECT(ISBN, TITLE, AUTHOR, EDITION)
----- ------------------------------------------------------------------
22    BOOK('2222222222', 'YourTitle', 'You', 10)
11    BOOK('1111111111', 'MyTitle', 'Me', 12)
```

For the following solution, I will present a line-by-line discussion of the sample program code after the code and explain how it uses custom mapping and how it changes the database:

```
1   import java.util.*;
2   import java.io.*;
3   import java.sql.*;
4
5   import jcb.db.*;
6   import jcb.meta.*;
7
8   public class ReadCustomType_Oracle {
9
10      public static Connection getConnection() throws Exception {
```

```
11          String driver = "oracle.jdbc.driver.OracleDriver";
12          String url = "jdbc:oracle:thin:@localhost:1521:caspian";
13          String username = "scott";
14          String password = "tiger";
15          Class.forName(driver);  // load Oracle driver
16          return DriverManager.getConnection(url, username, password);
17      }
18
19      public static void main(String[] args) {
20          System.out.println("--- ReadCustomType_Oracle begin ---");
21
22          if (args.length != 1) {
23              System.out.println("usage: java ReadCustomType_Oracle <id>");
24              System.exit(1);
25          }
26
27          String id = args[0];
28          System.out.println("input id="+id);
29
30          Connection conn = null;
31          ResultSet rs = null;
32          PreparedStatement pstmt = null;
33          try {
34              conn = getConnection();
35              System.out.println("conn="+conn);
36              java.util.Map map = conn.getTypeMap();


39              System.out.println("map="+map);
40
41              String query =
42                "SELECT id, book_object FROM book_table where id=?";
43              pstmt = conn.prepareStatement(query);
44              pstmt.setString(1, id);
45              rs = pstmt.executeQuery();
46              while(rs.next()) {
47                  String ID = rs.getString(1);
48                  System.out.println("ID="+ID);
49                  Object bookObject = rs.getObject(2);
50                  System.out.println("bookObject="+bookObject);
51                  Book book = (Book) bookObject;
52                  book.print();
53                  System.out.println("=======================");
54              }
55              System.out.println("--- ReadCustomType_Oracle end ---");
56          }
57          catch(Exception e){
58              e.printStackTrace();
59              System.exit(1);
60          }
61          finally {
62              DatabaseUtil.close(rs);
63              DatabaseUtil.close(pstmt);
64              DatabaseUtil.close(conn);
65          }
66      }
67  }
```

Here's how to run the sample program using ReadCustomType_Oracle:

```
$ java ReadCustomType_Oracle 11111
--- ReadCustomType_Oracle begin ---
input id=11111
conn=oracle.jdbc.driver.T4CConnection@ce5b1c
map={}
map={SCOTT.BOOK=class Book}
ID=11111
bookObject=Book@1d64c37
--- Book print() raw data begin ---
isbn=1111111111
title=MyTitle
author=Me
edition=12
--- Book print() raw data end ---
========================
--- ReadCustomType_Oracle end ---

$ java ReadCustomType_Oracle 22222
--- ReadCustomType_Oracle begin ---
input id=22222
conn=oracle.jdbc.driver.T4CConnection@ce5b1c
map={}
map={SCOTT.BOOK=class Book}
ID=22222
bookObject=Book@1d64c37


title=YourTitle
author=You
edition=10
--- Book print() raw data end ---
========================
--- ReadCustomType_Oracle end ---
```

This breaks down the program:

Lines 1–6: Import required Java packages.

Lines 10–18: The getConnection() method returns a new database Connection object.

Lines 37–40: Here, you provide mapping information to the JDBC driver to map SCOTT.BOOK (the SQL data type) to the Java data type as the Book class. Note that when a java.sql.Connection object is first established, the default type map is empty; you must populate it to use any SQL to Java mapping functionality. When using Oracle database, SQL type names in the type map must be all uppercase, because that is how the Oracle database stores SQL names.

Lines 46–54: The variable bookObject is now an instance of the class Book, with each attribute value being the current value of one of the fields of Book. Note that you have to cast the object retrieved by getObject() to a Book object before assigning it to bookObject. When you retrieve data from Oracle 10g, it is in hexadecimal form. The method Book.print() converts data from hexadecimal to regular string and Book.printNoConversion() prints the raw data (in hexadecimal format).

Lines 58–61: Handle database exceptions (such as SQLException) and other possible exceptions (such as Exception).

Lines 62–66: Release database resources such as Connection and Statement objects.

3-26. Is There Any Limit on the Number of Connections for JDBC?

JDBC API has not set any restrictions on the maximum number of database connections; also, you could say that JDBC drivers don't have any scalability restrictions by themselves. JDBC provides a method (DatabaseMetaData.getMaxConnections()) that retrieves the maximum possible number of concurrent connections to this database. The following code shows a snippet for using the DatabaseMetaData.getMaxConnections() method:

```
import jcb.util.DatabaseUtil;
...
Connection conn = null;
try {
    // get connection to an Oracle database
    conn = getConnection();
    System.out.println("conn="+conn);

    // use connection ...
    DatabaseMetaData metadata = conn.getMetaData();
    if (metadata == null) {
        System.out.println("vendor does not support metadata");
    }
    else {
        int maxConnections = metadata.getMaxConnections();
        System.out.println("maxConnections="+maxConnections);
    }


    // handle the exception
    e.printStackTrace();
}
finally {
    // release database resources
    DatabaseUtil.close(conn);
}
```

DatabaseMetaData.getMaxConnections() returns the maximum number of active connections possible at one time; a result of zero means that there is no limit or the limit is not known.

You can limit the maximum number of connections created by a database server by using the following methods:

- You can set control parameters, which will be read by database servers.

- You can limit the number of connections opened by the connection pool manager.

The following sections discuss how to set control parameters, which will be read by database servers such as Oracle and MySQL.

Limiting Max Connections: Oracle

Using Oracle database, the maximum number of connections may be restricted by the number of processes (in the init.ora file) on the server. For example, the init.ora file has a section for defining processes and sessions:

```
########################
# Processes and Sessions
########################
processes=150
```

In general, a JDBC connection can consume anywhere from one to four file descriptors. The solution is to increase the per-process file descriptor limit.

To increase/decrease the maximum connections for Oracle, you need to do the following steps:

1. Stop the Oracle database server.

2. Edit the init.ora configuration file with processes=200.

3. Start the Oracle database server.

In Linux/Unix environments, if the Oracle database fails to restart properly, then it could be that the processes number exceeds the Linux/Unix system parameter. You may need to update the semaphores of the database server machine. Please refer to Oracle database installation and administration references for the system parameter requirements.

Limiting Max Connections: MySQL

The MySQL database controls the number of simultaneous client connections allowed by the max_connections variable. To see all system variables, issue the following command:

```
mysql> SHOW VARIABLES;
+-------------------------+--------------------+
| Variable_name           | Value              |
+-------------------------+--------------------+
| back_log                | 50                 |
| basedir                 | C:\mysql\          |
| ...                     | + ...              |

| version                 | 4.0.18-nt          |
| wait_timeout            | 28800              |
+-------------------------+--------------------+
126 rows in set (0.01 sec)
```

You can view system variables and their values by using the SHOW VARIABLES statement:

```
mysql> SHOW VARIABLES LIKE 'max_conn%';
+--------------------+-------+
| Variable_name      | Value |
+--------------------+-------+
| max_connections    | 100   |
| max_connect_errors | 10    |
+--------------------+-------+
2 rows in set (0.00 sec)
```

As you can see, the default value for the max_connections system variable is 100. Increasing this value increases the number of file descriptors that mysqld requires.

To increase/decrease the max_connections variable for mysql, you need to follow these steps:

1. Stop the MySQL database server.

2. Edit the MySQL database server configuration file (my.ini file in Windows and my.cnf in Linux), and set the following entries:

   ```
   [mysqld]
   set-variable = max_connections=300
   ```

3. Start the MySQL database server.

4. Check the max_connections variable by executing the following:

```
mysql> SHOW VARIABLES LIKE 'max_connections%';
+--------------------+-------+
| Variable_name      | Value |
+--------------------+-------+
| max_connections    | 300   |
+--------------------+-------+
1 rows in set (0.00 sec)
```

Also, you can set these variables (such as max_connections) at runtime by using the set command. MySQL's set sets different types of variables that affect the operation of the server or your client. You can use it to assign values to user variables or system variables.

```
mysql> set global max_connections=200;
Query OK, 0 rows affected (0.00 sec)

mysql> SHOW VARIABLES LIKE 'max_connections%';
+-----------------+-------+
| Variable_name   | Value |
+-----------------+-------+
| max_connections | 200   |
+-----------------+-------+
1 row in set (0.00 sec)
```

3-27. How Do You Connect As SYSDBA or SYSOPER to an Oracle Database?

startup and shutdown.

According to Oracle's JDBC documentation, the only way to do this is to use the java.util. Properties object when connecting, rather than specifying the username and password as strings. Put the username into the user property and the password into the password property. Then, put the mode into the internal_logon property. For example:

```
String databaseURL = "jdbc:oracle:thin:@localhost:1521:scorpian";
java.util.Properties props = new java.util.Properties();
props.put("user", "scott");
props.put("password", "tiger");
props.put("internal_logon", "sysoper");
java.sql.Connection conn = null;
try {
        conn = java.sql.DriverManager.getConnection(databaseURL, props);
        // success: you got the Connection object.
   // use the Connection object for performing some useful tasks.
}
catch(SQLException e) {
        // failure: handle the exception
        // could not get a Connection object.
        e.printStackTrace();
}
finally {
   // close Connection object...
}
```

Please note that when connecting as SYSDBA or SYSOPER using the Thin driver, the Oracle RDBMS must be configured to use a password file. See "Creating and Maintaining a Password File" in the Oracle Database Administrator's Guide.

3-28. How Do You Check MySQL's/Oracle's JDBC Installation?

After you install the database and JDBC, it is time to check the JDBC installation. This means you should be able to connect to the database and then select/retrieve some information.

Solution

You can use the following sample JDBC program to check the MySQL or Oracle JDBC installation. You can also modify the code to support other databases.

I present this code with line numbers and offer a discussion of its lines immediately afterward.

```
1 import java.sql.*;
2
3 import jcb.util.DatabaseUtil;
4 import jcb.db.VeryBasicConnectionManager;
5
6 public class CheckJDBCInstallation {
7     /**
8      * Test Validity of JDBC Installation
9      * @param conn a JDBC Connection object
10     * @param dbVendor db vendor {"oracle", "mysql" }
11     * @return true if a given Connection object is
12     * a valid one; otherwise return false.
13     * @throws Exception Failed to determine if a given
14     * connection is valid.
15     */


18          throws Exception {
19
20          if (conn == null) {
21              // null Connection object is not valid
22              return false;
23          }
24
25          if (conn.isClosed()) {
26              // closed Connection object is not valid
27              return false;
28          }
29
30          // here you have a Connection object which is not null and
31          // which is not closed, but it might be a defunct object
32          // in order to determine whether it is a valid connection,
33          // depends on the vendor of the database:
34          //
35          // for MySQL database:
36          //      you may use the Connection object
37          //      with query of "select 1"; if the
38          //      query returns the result, then it
39          //      is a valid Connection object.
40          //
41          // for Oracle database:
42          //      you may use the Connection object
43          //      with query of "select 1 from dual"; if
44          //      the query returns the result, then it
45          //      is a valid Connection object.
```

```
46              if (dbVendor.equalsIgnoreCase("mysql")) {
47                  return testConnection(conn, "select 1");
48              }
49              else if (dbVendor.equalsIgnoreCase("oracle")) {
50                  return testConnection(conn, "select 1 from dual");
51              }
52              else {
53                  return false;
54              }
55
56      }
57
58      /**
59       * Test Validity of a Connection
60       * @param conn a JDBC Connection object
61       * @param query a sql query to test against db connection
62       * @return true if a given Connection object is a valid one;
63       *  otherwise return false.
64       */
65      public static boolean testConnection(Connection conn,
66                                      String query) {
67          ResultSet rs = null;
68          Statement stmt = null;
69          try {
70              stmt = conn.createStatement();
71              if (stmt == null) {


74
75              rs = stmt.executeQuery(query);
76              if (rs == null) {
77                  return false;
78              }
79
80              // Connection object is valid: you were able to
81              // connect to the database and return something useful.
82              if (rs.next()) {
83                  return true;
84              }
85
86              // there is no hope any more for the validity
87              // of the Connection object
88              return false;
89          }
90          catch(Exception e) {
91              // something went wrong: connection is bad
92              return false;
93          }
94          finally {
95              // close database resources
96              DatabaseUtil.close(rs);
97              DatabaseUtil.close(stmt);
98          }
99      }
100
101     public static void main(String[] args) {
102         Connection conn = null;
```

```
103          try {
104              System.out.println("-- CheckJDBCInstallation begin --");
105              String dbVendor = args[0];
106              // get connection to a database
107              System.out.println("dbVendor="+dbVendor);
108              conn = VeryBasicConnectionManager.getConnection(dbVendor);
109              System.out.println("conn="+conn);
110              System.out.println("valid connection = "+
111                  isValidConnection(conn, dbVendor));
112              System.out.println("-- CheckJDBCInstallation end --");
113          }
114          catch(Exception e){
115              // handle the exception
116              e.printStackTrace();
117              System.exit(1);
118          }
119          finally {
120              // release database resources
121              DatabaseUtil.close(conn);
122          }
123      }
124 }
```

Discussing CheckJDBCInstallation

The following discussion breaks down the program:

> *Lines 16–56*: isValidConnection() accepts a Connection object and determines whether it is a valid Connection object. After making sure that the connection is not closed, it invokes the testConnection() method, which retrieves the minimum information after connecting to the database.

> *Lines 65–99*: The testConnection() method tests the validity of a Connection object by executing a minimal SELECT statement. The validity check statement for MySQL is select 1 (no need to mention a table name). The validity check statement may differ from vendor to vendor. The validity check statement for Oracle is select 1 from dual. (In Oracle databases, dual is a table that is created by Oracle along with the data dictionary. It consists of exactly one column whose name is dummy and one record. The value of that record is X. The owner of dual is SYS, but the dual table can be accessed by every user.)

Running CheckJDBCInstallation for the MySQL Database

To run the program, use this code for MySQL:

```
$ mysql --user=root --password=root --default-character-set=utf8
Welcome to the MySQL monitor.  Commands end with ; or \g.
Your MySQL connection id is 3 to server version: 4.1.7-nt

mysql> exit
Bye

$ javac CheckJDBCInstallation.java
$ java CheckJDBCInstallation  mysql
-- CheckJDBCInstallation begin --
dbVendor=mysql
```

```
conn=com.mysql.jdbc.Connection@8fce95
valid connection = true
-- CheckJDBCInstallation end --
```

Running CheckJDBCInstallation for the Oracle Database

To run the program, use this code for Oracle:

```
$ sqlplus scott/tiger
SQL*Plus: Release 10.1.0.2.0 - Production on Wed Oct 27 17:11:41 2004

SQL> exit
Disconnected from Oracle Database 10g Enterprise Edition Release 10.1.0.2.0 -

$ javac CheckJDBCInstallation.java
$ java CheckJDBCInstallation  oracle
-- CheckJDBCInstallation begin --
dbVendor=oracle
conn=oracle.jdbc.driver.T4CConnection@341960
valid connection = true
-- CheckJDBCInstallation end --
```

CHAPTER 4

■ ■ ■

Making Database Connections Using DataSource

Relativity teaches us the connection between the different descriptions of one and the same reality.

—Albert Einstein

In this chapter, you will learn how to make database connections using JDBC's DataSource object. The purpose of this chapter is to provide snippets, reusable code samples, and methods that deal with the Connection objects using the javax.sql.DataSource interface. When writing this chapter, I relied on JDK 1.4 and the final release of the JDBC 3.0 specification.

This chapter's focus will be on answering the following question: how do you obtain

each case I will provide working code.

To select data from tables/views, update columns in tables, create a new table in a database, or do anything useful with any database, you need a database connection (in JDBC, this is called java.sql.Connection). Typically, database access in any environment starts with the connection.

4-1. How Do You Create Connection Using a DataSource Object?

DataSource (defined in the javax.sql package) is an abstraction layer for Java database applications. Database applications may use a JNDI context to find DataSource attributes that are configured on the deployment server. You can obtain a DataSource object in two ways:

- *Using JNDI*

- *Without using JNDI*

JNDI is an API for accessing different kinds of naming and directory services. JNDI is not specific to a particular naming or directory service; it can be used to access many different kinds of systems including file systems, Common Object Request Broker Architecture (CORBA), Java Remote Method Invocation (RMI), and Enterprise JavaBeans (EJB), as well as directory services such as Lightweight Directory Access Protocol (LDAP) and Network Information Service (NIS). Although you can use JDBC to access a set of relational databases, you can use JNDI to access a set of naming and directory services.

You will look at both of these options in this chapter. From a portability point of view, obtaining a DataSource interface using JNDI is more portable than not using JNDI, according to http://java.sun.com/products/jdbc/articles/package2.html:

The DataSource interface provides an alternative to the DriverManager class for making a connection to a data source. Using a DataSource implementation is better for two important reasons: it makes code more portable, and it makes code easier to maintain. A DataSource object represents a real-world data source. Depending on how it is implemented, the data source can be anything from a relational database to a spreadsheet or a file in tabular format. When a DataSource object has been registered with a JNDI naming service, an application can retrieve it from the naming service and use it to make a connection to the data source it represents.

The following snippet shows how to retrieve the DataSource object associated with the logical name jdbc/InventoryDB and then use it to get a connection. The first two lines use the JNDI API to get the DataSource object; the third line uses JDBC API to get the connection.

```
Context ctx = new InitialContext();
DataSource ds = (DataSource) ctx.lookup("jdbc/InventoryDB");
Connection con = ds.getConnection("myUserName", "myPassword");
```

The JDK 1.4 documentation defines javax.sql.DataSource as follows:

A factory for connections to the physical data source that this DataSource object represents. An alternative to the DriverManager facility, a DataSource object is the preferred means of getting a connection. An object that implements the DataSource interface will typically be registered with a naming service based on the JNDI API.

- *Basic implementation*: Produces a standard Connection object.

- *Connection pooling implementation*: Produces a Connection object that will automatically participate in connection pooling. This implementation works with a middle-tier connection pooling manager.

- *Distributed transaction implementation*: Produces a Connection object that may be used for distributed transactions and almost always participates in connection pooling. This implementation works with a middle-tier transaction manager and almost always with a connection pooling manager.

A DataSource object has properties that you can modify when necessary. For example, if the data source moves to a different server, you can change the property for the server. The benefit is that because the data source's properties can be changed, any code accessing that data source does not need to be changed.

A driver that is accessed via a DataSource object does not register itself with the DriverManager facility. Rather, a DataSource object is retrieved through a lookup operation and then used to create a Connection object. With a basic implementation, the connection obtained through a DataSource object is identical to a connection obtained through the DriverManager facility.

This is according to Struts (http://struts.apache.org/faqs/database.html):

As a rule, you should always use a connection pool to access a database. The DataSource interface is the preferred way to implement a connection pool today. Many containers and database systems now bundle a DataSource implementation that you can use. Most often, the DataSource is made available through JNDI. The JNDI approach makes it easy for your business classes to access the DataSource without worrying about who set it up.

When connecting to a data source (a relational database such as MySQL or Oracle) using a DataSource object registered with a JNDI naming service rather than using the DriverManager facility, you get three benefits:

- It makes code more portable.

- It makes code much easier to maintain.

- You get the benefit of connection pooling.

For details on these benefits, refer to *JDBC API Tutorial and Reference, Third Edition* (Addison-Wesley, 2003) by Maydene Fisher, Jon Ellis, and Jonathan Bruce.

JDBC 2.0 introduced a DataSource interface that eliminates connection URLs and driver names in your Java applications. DataSource enables you to register (using JNDI API) instances of DataSource with a unique name; then, other applications can retrieve the registered DataSource using the unique name. A DataSource object provides a new method for JDBC clients to obtain a DBMS connection (represented as java.sql.Connection). A DataSource object is usually created, deployed (that is, registered), located (lookup operation), and managed separately from the Java applications that use it.

Figure 4-1 shows the life cycle of a DataSource object.

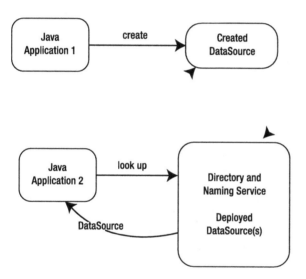

Figure 4-1. *Life cycle of a* DataSource *object*

In this figure, note that the Directory and Naming Service item is JNDI-enabled and can bind/register and hold any number of DataSource objects. Most databases can use CORBA-based naming and directory services, but in order not to tie yourself into a specific implementation of JNDI, in this chapter you will see how to use a file system–based reference implementation of a JNDI SPI driver from JavaSoft. In real production applications, you should select a commercially available naming and directory service product (such as Sun's Directory Server, Novell's Directory Server, and so on).

One Java application (Java Application 1) can create a data source (using some data source configuration from an XML file, a relational database, or a file-based system). Also, Java Application 1 can register (or bind) and manage the created data source. In registering a data source, you have to associate the data source with a unique key. Once the data source is registered, it is accessible to other applications (such as Java Application 2). Java Application 2 can get registered data sources using a lookup method by providing the unique key. Some vendors (such as BEA's WebLogic and IBM's WebSphere) provide tools for deploying DataSource objects and then provide browsing/lookup operations to get the DataSource objects.

4-2. How Do You Create a DataSource Object?

To create a DataSource object, you define it with a vendor-specific Java class, which implements the DataSource interface. For the sake of this discussion, assume that DBVendorDataSource (which is a vendor-specific Java class) implements the DataSource interface. Then you can create a DataSource object by writing the following code:

```
//
// generic solution
//
DBVendorDataSource vendorDataSource = new DBVendorDataSource();
vendorDataSource.setServerName("saratoga");
vendorDataSource.setDatabaseName("payrollDatabase");
vendorDataSource.setDescription("the data source for payroll");
//
// you can set other attributes by using vendorDataSource.setXXX(...)
//

// now cast it to DataSource
DataSource payrollDS = (DataSource) vendorDataSource;
```

To create a DataSource object using the Oracle database, you should use the (vendor-specific) OracleDataSource class (defined in the oracle.jdbc.pool package and available from Oracle). You can create a DataSource object by writing the following code:

```
import oracle.jdbc.pool.OracleDataSource;
import javax.sql.DataSource;
...
OracleDataSource oracleDataSource = new OracleDataSource();
oracleDataSource.setServerName("saratoga");
oracleDataSource.setDatabaseName("payrollDatabase");
oracleDataSource.setDescription("the data source for payroll");
//
// you can set other attributes by
// invoking oracleDataSource.setXXX(...)
//

// now cast it to DataSource
DataSource payrollDS = (DataSource) oracleDataSource;
```

4-4. How Do You Create a DataSource Object Using MySQL?

To create a DataSource object using the MySQL database, you should use the (vendor-specific) MySQLDataSource class. You can create a DataSource object by writing the following code:

```
import com.mysql.jdbc.jdbc2.optional.MysqlDataSource;
import javax.sql.DataSource;
...
MysqlDataSource mysqlDataSource = new MysqlDataSource();
mysqlDataSource.setServerName("saratoga");
```

```
mysqlDataSource.setDatabaseName("payrollDatabase");
mysqlDataSource.setDescription("the data source for payroll");
//
// NOTE: you can set other attributes by
// invoking mysqlDataSource.setXXX(   )
//

// now cast it to DataSource
DataSource payrollDS = (DataSource) mysqlDataSource;
```

4-5. How Do You Create a DataSource Object Using a Relational Database (Oracle/MySQL)?

To create a DataSource object using an Oracle, MySQL, Sybase, or DB2 database, you introduce a vendor parameter. (The vendor parameter uniquely identifies a specific database such as Oracle, MySQL, or Sybase.) Depending on the vendor parameter, you apply a different implementation class for creating a DataSource object. For example, if vendor equals oracle, then you select the OracleDataSource class, and if vendor equals mysql, then you select the MysqlDataSource class; otherwise, you return null. (In addition, you can modify this to support more than two vendors.)

Invoking getDataSource() with a Specific User/Password

This shows how to invoke getDataSource() with a specific user/password:

```
/**


 * is not specified, then it returns null.
 *
 * @param vendor the vendor parameter: "oracle", "mysql",
 *
 */
public static javax.sql.DataSource getDataSource
  (String vendor,
   String user,
   String password,
   String databaseName,
   String driverType,
   String networkProtocol,
   int portNumber,
   String serverName) throws SQLException {

  if (vendor.equals("oracle")) {
     // create Oracle's DataSource
     OracleDataSource ods = new OracleDataSource();      ods.setUser(user);
     ods.setPassword(password);
     ods.setDatabaseName(databaseName);
     ods.setDriverType(driverType);
     ods.setNetworkProtocol(networkProtocol);
     ods.setPortNumber(portNumber);
     ods.setServerName(serverName);
     return ods;
  }
  else if (vendor.equals("mysql")) {
     // create MySQL's DataSource
```

```
      MysqlDataSource mds = new MysqlDataSource();
      mds.setUser(user);
      mds.setPassword(password);
      mds.setDatabaseName(databaseName);
      //mds.setDriverType(driverType);
      //mds.setNetworkProtocol(networkProtocol);
      mds.setPortNumber(portNumber);
      mds.setServerName(serverName);
      return mds;
   }
   else {
      return null;
   }
}
```

Viewing the getDataSource() Results with a Specific User/Password

This code shows the result:

```
public static void main(String[] args)
   throws SQLException, javax.naming.NamingException {
   // create an Oracle DataSource with
   // specific username/password
   DataSource ods = getDataSource("oracle",
      "system", "gozal", "scorpian", "thin",
      "tcp", 1521, "localhost");
   Connection oraConn = ods.getConnection();


   // create a MySQL DataSource with
   // specific username/password
   DataSource mds = getDataSource("mysql",
      "root", "root", "tiger",
      "", "", 3306, "localhost");
   Connection myConn = mds.getConnection();
   System.out.println("myConn="+myConn);
}
```

Invoking getDataSource() Without a Specific User/Password

This shows how to invoke getDataSource() without a specific user/password:

```
/**
 * This method creates a DataSource object without a
 * specific username/password. If the vendor parameter
 * is not specified, then it returns null.  When client
 * uses this DataSource, it has to pass username/password.
 *
 * @param vendor the vendor parameter: "oracle", "mysql",
 *
 */
public static DataSource getDataSource
   (String vendor,
    String databaseName,
```

```
      String driverType,
      String networkProtocol,
      int portNumber,
      String serverName) throws SQLException {

   if (vendor.equals("oracle")) {
      // create Oracle's DataSource
      OracleDataSource ods = new OracleDataSource();
      ods.setDatabaseName(databaseName);
      ods.setDriverType(driverType);
      ods.setNetworkProtocol(networkProtocol);
      ods.setPortNumber(portNumber);
      ods.setServerName(serverName);
      return ods;
   }
   else if (vendor.equals("mysql")) {
      // create MySQL's DataSource
      MysqlDataSource mds = new MysqlDataSource();
      mds.setDatabaseName(databaseName);
      //mds.setDriverType(driverType);
      //mds.setNetworkProtocol(networkProtocol);
      mds.setPortNumber(portNumber);
      mds.setServerName(serverName);
      return mds;
   }
   else {


}
```

Viewing the getDataSource() Results Without a Specific User/Password

This code shows the result:

```
public static void main(String[] args)
   throws SQLException, javax.naming.NamingException {
   // create an Oracle DataSource with
   // specific username/password
   DataSource ods = getDataSource("oracle",
     "scorpian", "thin", "tcp", 1521, "localhost");
   String user = "system";
   String password = "gozal";
   Connection oraConn = ods.getConnection(user, password);
   System.out.println("oraConn="+oraConn);

   // create a MySQL DataSource with
   // specific username/password
   DataSource mds = getDataSource("mysql",
     "root", "root", "tiger", "", "", 3306, "localhost");
   String user2 = "root";
   String password2 = "root";
   Connection myConn = mds.getConnection(user2, password2);
   System.out.println("myConn="+myConn);
}
```

4-6. How Do You Create a DataSource Object Using a DataSource Factory?

You can create DataSource objects by using a data source factory (DSF) object.

First, you create a DSF object; second, you use the DSF object to create DataSource objects. To create a DSF object, you have at least two options: you can write your own custom code or use a third-party package. In this section, I will show how to use the package org.apache.torque.dsfactory from Apache. (For details about this package, please see http://db.apache.org/torque-32/.) This package has a DataSourceFactory interface implemented by several classes (JndiDataSourceFactory, PerUserPoolDataSourceFactory, and SharedPoolDataSourceFactory). You may provide your own implementation class as well for DataSourceFactory. DataSourceFactory is defined as follows:

```
package org.apache.torque.dsfactory;
import org.apache.commons.configuration.Configuration;

//A factory that returns a DataSource.
public interface DataSourceFactory {
    // returns the DataSource configured by the factory.
    public javax.sql.DataSource getDataSource()
        throws TorqueException;
    // initialize the factory.
    public void initialize(Configuration configuration)
        throws TorqueException;
}
```

You can use one of the implementation classes to create a DataSourceFactory and then use the

```
// create a DataSource configuration object
Configuration config = getConfiguration(<your-datasource-properties>);
// first you need to initialize
jndiDSF.initialize(config);
...
// get a DataSource object:
DataSource ds = jndiDSF.getDataSource();
...
// now use the DataSource object to create Connection objects:
Connection conn = ds.getConnection();
```

4-7. What Are the DataSource Properties?

A DataSource object has several properties that identify and describe the real-world data source (such as an Oracle database, a MySQL database, and so on) that the object represents. These properties include information such as the driver type, the URL of the database server, the name of the database, the network protocol to use to communicate with the database server, and so on.

DataSource properties follow the JavaBeans design pattern and are usually set when a DataSource object is created and deployed. The JDBC API specifies a standard set of properties and a standard name for each property. Table 4-1 describes the standard name, the data type, and a description for each of the standard properties. According to the JDBC specification, a DataSource implementation does not have to support all of these properties.

Table 4-1. *Standard* DataSource *Properties*

Property Name	Type	Description
databaseName	String	The name of a particular database on a server
dataSourceName	String	The logical name for the underlying XADataSource or ConnectionPoolDataSource object; used only when pooling of connections or distributed transactions are implemented
description	String	A description of this data source
networkProtocol	String	The network protocol used to communicate with the server
password	String	The user's database password
portNumber	Int	The port number where a server is listening for requests
roleName	String	The initial SQL role name
serverName	String	The database server name
user	String	The user's account name

If a DataSource object supports a property, it must supply getter (get<PropertyName>) and setter (set<PropertyName>) methods for it. The following code fragment illustrates the methods that a DataSource object, ds, would need to include if it supports, for example, the property description:

```
DataSource ds = <get-a-DataSource object>;
ds.setDescription("This db server is for payroll processing.");
String description = ds.getDescription();
```

Assume that you have created a DataSource object and you want to deploy/register it as jdbc/PayrollDataSource. Using JNDI naming services, you can bind/register a data source with a JNDI naming service.

The naming service provides distributed naming support and can be implemented in many different ways:

- File-based systems
    - java.naming.factory.initial (for example, com.sun.jndi.fscontext.RefFSContextFactory)
    - java.naming.provider.url (for example, file:c:\\jdbcDataSource)
- Directory-based systems (such as LDAP)
    - java.naming.factory.initial (for example, com.ibm.websphere.naming. WsnInitialContextFactory)
    - java.naming.provider.url (for example, java:comp/env/jdbc/SampleDB)
- CORBA-based systems
- NIS-based systems
- DNS-based systems
- RMI-based systems
    - java.naming.factory.initial (for example, com.sun.jndi.rmi.registry. RegistryContextFactory)
    - java.naming.provider.url (for example, rmi://localhost:1099)

4-9. How Do You Use a File-Based System for Registering a DataSource Object?

To use the file system–based JNDI, you need to do the following:

1. Download fscontext1_*.zip from http://java.sun.com/products/jndi. (The asterisk refers to a version number of the software bundle.)

2. Extract providerutil.jar and fscontext.jar.

3. Include in your CLASSPATH environment variable the providerutil.jar and fscontext.jar files extracted from the fscontext1_*.zip file. (Also, use a full pathname for your JAR files.)

In this way, you can deploy a DataSource object by using the following code listings. Specifically, this is the getContext() method:

```
private static Context getContext(String classFactory,
                String providerURL)
   throws javax.naming.NamingException {
   //
   // Set up environment for creating initial context
   //
   Hashtable env = new Hashtable();
   env.put(Context.INITIAL_CONTEXT_FACTORY, classFactory);
   env.put(Context.PROVIDER_URL, providerURL);
   Context context = new InitialContext(env);
   return context;


   throws javax.naming.NamingException {
   //
   // Set up environment for creating initial context
   //
   Hashtable env = new Hashtable();
   env.put(Context.INITIAL_CONTEXT_FACTORY,
      "com.sun.jndi.fscontext.RefFSContextFactory");
   env.put(Context.PROVIDER_URL, "file:" + directoryName);
   Context context = new InitialContext(env);
   return context;
}
```

This is the deployDataSource() method:

```
private static void deployDataSource(Context context,
                String jndiName,
                DataSource ds)
   throws javax.naming.NamingException{
   //
   // register the data source under the jndiName using
   // the provided context
   //
   context.bind(jndiName, ds);
}
```

And this code shows how to deploy/register the DataSource object:

```
// dataSourceName is a unique name to identify the data source.
String jndiDataSourceName = "jdbc/PayrollDataSource";
```

```
// create an Oracle DataSource with
// specific username/password
DataSource ods = createDataSource("oracle",
    "system", "gozal", "scorpian", "thin",
    "tcp", 1521, "localhost");

// now bind it using JNDI
String directoryName = "c:\\jdbcDataSource";
Context context = getFileSystemContext(directoryName);

// register/bind DataSource
deployDataSource(context, jndiDataSourceName, ods);
```

What happens when you deploy a data source using the file system? Under the directory name (c:\jdbcDataSource), it creates a file called .bindings, which has the following content (the content of the .bindings file has been formatted to fit the page):

```
#This file is used by the JNDI FSContext.
#Sun Feb 02 00:20:35 PST 2003
jdbc/MyDataSource/RefAddr/3/Encoding=String
jdbc/MyDataSource/RefAddr/5/Type=databaseName
jdbc/MyDataSource/RefAddr/6/Type=networkProtocol
jdbc/MyDataSource/FactoryName=oracle.jdbc.pool.OracleDataSourceFactory
jdbc/MyDataSource/RefAddr/1/Encoding=String
jdbc/MyDataSource/RefAddr/6/Encoding=String
jdbc/MyDataSource/RefAddr/7/Type=portNumber


jdbc/MyDataSource/RefAddr/5/Content=scorpian
jdbc/MyDataSource/RefAddr/4/Encoding=String
jdbc/MyDataSource/RefAddr/3/Content=thin
jdbc/MyDataSource/RefAddr/1/Content=system
jdbc/MyDataSource/ClassName=oracle.jdbc.pool.OracleDataSource
jdbc/MyDataSource/RefAddr/1/Type=userName
jdbc/MyDataSource/RefAddr/2/Encoding=String
jdbc/MyDataSource/RefAddr/7/Encoding=String
jdbc/MyDataSource/RefAddr/2/Type=passWord
jdbc/MyDataSource/RefAddr/3/Type=driverType
jdbc/MyDataSource/RefAddr/0/Encoding=String
jdbc/MyDataSource/RefAddr/5/Encoding=String
jdbc/MyDataSource/RefAddr/7/Content=1521
jdbc/MyDataSource/RefAddr/4/Type=serverName
jdbc/MyDataSource/RefAddr/4/Content=localhost
jdbc/MyDataSource/RefAddr/2/Content=gozal
jdbc/MyDataSource/RefAddr/0/Content=jdbc\:oracle\:thin\:
    @(DESCRIPTION\=(ADDRESS\=(PROTOCOL\=tcp)(PORT\=1521)
    (HOST\=localhost))(CONNECT_DATA\=(SID\=scorpian)))
```

4-10. What Is the Problem with File-Based DataSource Objects?

The problem with file-based DataSource objects is the compromise on security. Since the password is not encrypted (in any way), this is a security hole; therefore, it is not a viable choice in production systems. In production systems, you should use production-ready "directory-based" products. (In these cases, the password can be protected by groups/roles privileges.) For example, the password in file-based systems can be viewed as clear text if you have access to the file system; see the following password line—no encryption is used at all:

```
#This file is used by the JNDI FSContext.
#Sun Feb 02 00:20:35 PST 2003
jdbc/MyDataSource/RefAddr/3/Encoding=String
jdbc/MyDataSource/RefAddr/5/Type=databaseName
...
jdbc/MyDataSource/RefAddr/2/Type=passWord
...
jdbc/MyDataSource/RefAddr/2/Content=gozal
```

4-11. How Do You Retrieve a Deployed/Registered DataSource?

Assume the registered name of a data source is jdbc/PayrollDataSource. Using JNDI , you can look up (search) a data source with a JNDI naming service. In this way, you can access a DataSource object by using code that looks like this:

```
String dataSourceName = "jdbc/PayrollDataSource";
String user = "dbUser":
String password = "dbPassword";
Context context = new InitialContext();
DataSource ds = (DataSource) context.lookup(dataSourceName);
Connection conn = ds.getConnection(user, password);
//
// or
//
// if a DataSource has been created (before registration)
// with user and password attributes, then you can get the
```

You can use a Java method to accomplish the task:

```
public static DataSource getDataSource(String dataSourceName)
    throws Exception {
    if (dataSourceName == null) {
        return null;
    }
    Context context = new InitialContext();
    DataSource ds = (DataSource) context.lookup(dataSourceName);
    return ds;
}
```

Then you can use the getDataSource() method for getting Connection objects:

```
String dataSourceName = "jdbc/PayrollDataSource";
String user = "dbUser":
String password = "dbPassword";
DataSource ds = null;
try {
    ds = getDataSource(dataSourceName);
}
catch(Exception e) {
    // handle the exception
    // DataSource is not available/registered
}

if (ds != null) {
    Connection conn = ds.getConnection(user, password);
    //
```

```
    // or
    //
    // if a DataSource has been created (before registration)
    // with user and password attributes, then you can get the
    // connection without passing the user/password.
    // Connection conn = ds.getConnection();
}
```

4-12. How Do You Obtain a Connection with the DataSource Without Using JNDI?

A DataSource object provides a portable way for JDBC clients to obtain a DBMS connection. To create a DataSource object, you can use a vendor-specific class (such as OracleDataSource from Oracle or MysqlDataSource from MySQL), and then you can cast it to a DataSource object.

Oracle Example

Using the OracleDataSource class, you can create an instance of a DataSource object like so:

```
String databaseName = "scorpian";
String driverType = "thin";
String networkProtocol = "tcp";
int portNumber = 1521;
String serverName = "localhost";
...


    ods.setDriverType(driverType);
ods.setNetworkProtocol(networkProtocol);
ods.setPortNumber(portNumber);
ods.setServerName(serverName);
DataSource oracleDS = (DataSource) ods;
```

Once you have created an instance of a DataSource object, you can use the getConnection() method:

```
String username = "system";
String password = "gozal";
java.sql.Connection connection = null;
try {
    connection = oracleDS.getConnection(username, password);
}
catch(SQLException e) {
    // database access error occurred
    // handle the exception
    e.printStackTrace();
    ...
}
```

MySQL Example

Using the MysqlDataSource class, you can create an instance of a DataSource object:

```
String databaseName = "tiger";
String networkProtocol = "tcp";
int portNumber = 3306;
String serverName = "localhost";
```

```
...
MysqlDataSource mds = new MysqlDataSource();
mds.setDatabaseName(databaseName);
mds.setNetworkProtocol(networkProtocol);
mds.setPortNumber(portNumber);
mds.setServerName(serverName);
DataSource mysqlDS = (DataSource) mds;
```

Once you have created an instance of a DataSource object, you can use the getConnection() method:

```
String username = "root";
String password = "root";java.sql.Connection connection = null;
try {
    connection = mysqlDS.getConnection(username, password);
}
catch(SQLException e) {
    // database access error occurred
    // handle the exception
    e.printStackTrace();
    ...
}
```

4-13. How Do You Obtain a Connection with the DataSource Using JNDI?

database as follows:

1. Retrieve a javax.sql.DataSource object from the JNDI naming service.

2. Obtain a Connection object from the data source. (If a data source is created with a user-name and password, then you can get a connection without passing a username and password; otherwise, you must pass the username and password.)

3. Using the Connection object (java.sql.Connection), send SQL queries or updates to the database management system.

4. Process the results (returned as ResultSet objects).

Figure 4-2 shows DataSource and JNDI configuration.

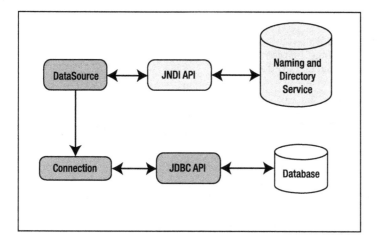

Figure 4-2. DataSource *and JNDI configuration*

DataSource provides two methods for obtaining a java.sql.Connection object:

- Connection getConnection(): Attempts to establish a connection with the data source that this DataSource object represents

-   (,

The following example shows these steps (assuming that the name of the DataSource object is java:comp/env/jdbc/employeeDB):

```
import jcb.util.DatabaseUtil;
...
java.sql.Connection conn = null;
java.sql.Statement stmt = null;
java.sql.ResultSet rs = null;
try {
    // Retrieve a DataSource through the JNDI naming service
    java.util.Properties parms = new java.util.Properties();
    parms.setProperty(Context.INITIAL_CONTEXT_FACTORY,
        "com.ibm.websphere.naming.WsnInitialContextFactory");

    // Create the Initial Naming Context
    javax.naming.Context context = new javax.naming.InitialContext(parms);

    // Look up through the naming service to retrieve a DataSource object
    javax.sql.DataSource ds = (javax.sql.DataSource)
        context.lookup("java:comp/env/jdbc/employeeDB");

    //Obtain a connection from the DataSource; here you
    // are assuming that the DataSource is created with
    // the required username and password.
    conn = ds.getConnection();

    // query the database
    stmt = conn.createStatement();
    rs = stmt.executeQuery("SELECT id, lastname FROM employees");
```

```java
    // process the results
    while (rs.next()) {
        String id = rs.getString("id");
        String lastname = rs.getString("lastname");
        // process and work with results (id, lastname)
    }
}
catch (SQLException e) {
    // handle SQLException
    e.printStackTrace();
}
finally {
    DatabaseUtil.close(rs);
    DatabaseUtil.close(stmt);
    DatabaseUtil.close(conn);
}
```

CHAPTER 5

■ ■ ■

Exploring the ResultSet Interface

The purpose of this chapter is to provide Java snippets, reusable code samples, classes, and methods that deal with the ResultSet interface (defined in java.sql.package). When writing this chapter, I relied on JDK 1.4 and the final release of the JDBC 3.0 specification. This chapter will focus on explaining the ResultSet interface and retrieving data.

5-1. What Is a ResultSet?

The ResultSet interface (not a class) is defined in the java.sql package as java.sql.ResultSet. (In this chapter, I will use ResultSet instead of the full name java.sql.ResultSet.) The ResultSet interface encapsulates the results of a SQL query (such as a select id, name from employees). You might say that the ResultSet and Connection interfaces are the most important objects for getting the result of a SQL query and connecting to relational (SQL-based) databases, respectively.

this package. According to the JDBC 3.0 specification, "the ResultSet interface provides methods for retrieving and manipulating the results of executed queries." A SQL query returns a ResultSet containing the requested data (as a set of rows of data, depending on the submitted SQL query), which is retrieved by type. The ResultSetMetaData interface provides information about a ResultSet.

But what, really, is a ResultSet? What happens when you execute the following query?

```
Connection conn = <get-a-connection-object>;
Statement stmt = conn.createStatement();
String query = "SELECT column_1, column_2 FROM mytable";
ResultSet rs = stmt.executeQuery(query);
```

Does it load the table in random access memory (RAM)? For example, when I do this:

```
String column1 = rs.getString(1)
```

does it give access to the RAM or to the DBMS? All of these answers depend on the type of your JDBC driver (that is, on the JDBC driver's implementation) that you are using. In general, JDBC drivers do not actually execute the statement until next() is called. With each iteration that you call with next(), the next record from the result set is pulled over the network. Some JDBC drivers fetch more than one record at a time to limit network traffic (which can improve your database application's performance). If your JDBC driver supports setting the fetch size, you can modify the number of records fetched with the setFetchSize() method. (Note that all drivers do not support this feature.)

So you can understand ResultSet, I will show how to define a simple table (in MySQL and Oracle), then populate it, and finally retrieve some records from it.

Setting Up the Oracle Database

The following code shows how to set up the Oracle database:

```
SQL> create table employees (
  2      id varchar(10) not null primary key,
  3      name varchar(20) not null,
  4      age int
  5  );

Table created.

SQL> desc employees;
 Name               Null?     Type
 ---------------    --------  ------------
 ID                 NOT NULL  VARCHAR2(10)
 NAME               NOT NULL  VARCHAR2(20)
 AGE                          NUMBER(38)

SQL> insert into employees(id, name, age) values('11', 'Alex Smith', 25);
SQL> insert into employees(id, name, age) values('22', 'Don Knuth', 65);
SQL> insert into employees(id, name, age) values('33', 'Mary Kent', 35);
SQL> insert into employees(id, name, age) values('44', 'Monica Seles', 30);
SQL> insert into employees(id, name) values('99', 'Alex Edison');
SQL> commit;
Commit complete.
```

```
ID         NAME                   AGE
---------  --------------------   ----------
11         Alex Smith             25
22         Don Knuth              65
33         Mary Kent              35
44         Monica Seles           30
99         Alex Edison
```

Setting Up the MySQL Database

The following code shows how to set up the MySQL database:

```
create table employees (
  id varchar(10) not null primary key,
  name varchar(20) not null,
  age int
);

insert into employees(id, name, age) values('11', 'Alex Smith', 25);
insert into employees(id, name, age) values('22', 'Don Knuth', 65);
insert into employees(id, name, age) values('33', 'Mary Kent', 35);
insert into employees(id, name, age) values('44', 'Monica Seles', 30);
insert into employees(id, name) values('99', 'Alex Edison');
mysql> select * from employees;
```

```
+----+--------------+------+
| id | name         | age  |
+----+--------------+------+
| 11 | Alex Smith   |   25 |
| 22 | Don Knuth    |   65 |
| 33 | Mary Kent    |   35 |
| 44 | Monica Seles |   30 |
| 99 | Alex Edison  | NULL |
+----+--------------+------+
Five Rows in a Set (0.00 Sec)
```

Solution

I will now provide a simple Java class to demonstrate how to use ResultSet by querying the employees table and retrieving employee information from a database. Note that the age column can accept null values as well; because of this, after getting the value of age from a ResultSet, you check (by invoking ResultSet.wasNull()) to see if it is a null value.

```java
import java.sql.*;

import jcb.db.VeryBasicConnectionManager;
import jcb.util.DatabaseUtil;

public class DemoResultSet {

    public static void main(String[] args) {


        ResultSet rs = null;
        try {
            System.out.println("--DemoResultSet begin--");
            String dbVendor = args[0]; // { "mysql", "oracle" }
            conn = VeryBasicConnectionManager.getConnection(dbVendor);
            System.out.println("conn="+conn);
            System.out.println("---------------");

            // prepare query
            String query = "select id, name, age from employees";

            // create a statement
            stmt = conn.createStatement();

            // execute query and return result as a ResultSet
            rs = stmt.executeQuery(query);

            // extract data from the ResultSet
            while (rs.next()) {
                String id = rs.getString(1);
                System.out.println("id="+id);
                String name = rs.getString(2);
                System.out.println("name="+name);
                // age might be null (according to schema)
                int age = rs.getInt(3);
                if (rs.wasNull()) {
                    System.out.println("age=null");
                }
```

```
            else {
                System.out.println("age="+age);
            }
            System.out.println("---------------");
        }
        System.out.println("--DemoResultSet end--");
    }
    catch(Exception e){
        e.printStackTrace();
        System.exit(1);
    }
    finally {
        // release database resources
        DatabaseUtil.close(rs);
        DatabaseUtil.close(stmt);
        DatabaseUtil.close(conn);
    }
  }
}
```

The important methods and concepts of this solution are as follows:

- The getConnection() method gets a database connection for the sample Oracle database.
- createStatement() creates a Statement object for sending SQL statements to the database.
- executeQuery() is used for Statement objects that return a ResultSet, which is basically a SELECT statement.

  cursor on the first row; the next() method enables you to iterate through all the records retrieved.
- getString(int columnIndex) retrieves the value of the designated column in the current row of this ResultSet object as a String in the Java programming language. You use getString(1) and getString(2) to get the id and name, respectively. (In the query, id is defined in the first column, and name is defined in the second column.) Note that when using column index, the first column is 1, the second is 2, and so on.
- getInt(int columnIndex) retrieves the value of the designated column in the current row of this ResultSet object as an "int" in the Java programming language. You use getInt(3) to get the age of an employee (note that age is defined in the third column of the query).
- wasNull() reports whether the last column read had a value of SQL NULL.
- The ResultSet object's getXXX() methods (such as getString() and getInt()) retrieve column data. JDBC defines types to match the SQL data types, and there is a getXXX() method for each. You can use the getXXX() method in two ways with the same semantics. (You can retrieve the value of the designated column in the current row of this ResultSet object as an XXX type.)
- getXXX(int columnIndex) is the preferred way of getting data since there is no need to get the column's metadata information.
- getXXX(String columnName) might be a little bit slow because of getting the column's metadata information.

Running the Solution for the Oracle Database

The output of the demo program for Oracle is as follows:

```
$ javac DemoResultSet.java
$ java DemoResultSet oracle
--DemoResultSet begin--
conn=oracle.jdbc.driver.T4CConnection@2ce908
---------------
id=11
name=Alex Smith
age=25
---------------
id=22
name=Don Knuth
age=65
---------------
id=33
name=Mary Kent
age=35
---------------
id=44
name=Monica Seles
age=30
---------------
id=99
name=Alex Edison
age=null
---------------
--DemoResultSet end--
```

The output of the demo program for MySQL is as follows:

```
$ javac DemoResultSet.java
$ java DemoResultSet mysql
--DemoResultSet begin--
conn=com.mysql.jdbc.Connection@1c6f579
---------------
id=11
name=Alex Smith
age=25
---------------
id=22
name=Don Knuth
age=65
---------------
id=33
name=Mary Kent
age=35
---------------
id=44
name=Monica Seles
age=30
---------------
id=99
name=Alex Edison
age=null
---------------
--DemoResultSet end--
```

5-2. What Is the Relationship of ResultSet to Other Classes/Interfaces?

To show the importance of the ResultSet object, Figure 5-1 shows the interactions and relationships between the key classes and interfaces in the java.sql package. The figure also shows the methods involved in creating statements, setting parameters, and retrieving results. (For details, please see the final release of the JDBC 3.0 specification, published by Sun Microsystems.)

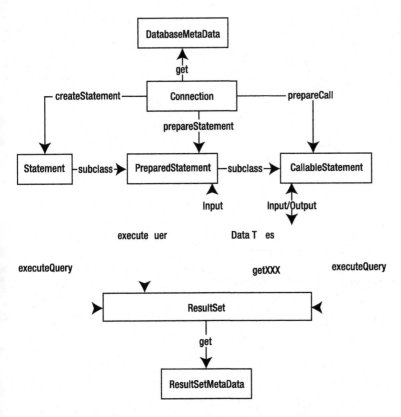

Figure 5-1. *Relationship of* ResultSet *to other classes/interfaces*

As you can observe from the low-level class/interface relationships, to connect to a relational database you use an instance of the Connection object. (To get the Connection object, you need to provide a database URL, username, and password.) Then, to find out the names of the database views, tables, and columns (so-called metadata), you need to get an instance of the DatabaseMetaData object from the Connection object. Next, to issue a SQL query, you compose the SQL query string and use the Connection object to create a Statement object. By executing the statement, you obtain a ResultSet object, and to find out the names of the column rows in that ResultSet, you need to obtain an instance of the ResultSetMetaData object.

5-3. How Does the JDK Define a ResultSet?

The JDK documentation (http://java.sun.com/j2se/1.5.0/docs/api/java/sql/ResultSet.html) defines the ResultSet interface as follows:

> *A table of data representing a database result set, which is usually generated by executing a statement that queries the database. A ResultSet object maintains a cursor pointing to its current row of data. Initially the cursor is positioned before the first row. The next method moves the cursor to the next row, and because it returns false when there are no more rows in the ResultSet object, it can be used in a while loop to iterate through the result set.*

> *A default ResultSet object is not updatable and has a cursor that moves forward only. Thus, you can iterate through it only once and only from the first row to the last row. It is possible to produce ResultSet objects that are scrollable and/or updatable. The following code fragment, in which con is a valid Connection object, illustrates how to make a result set that is scrollable and insensitive to updates by others, and that is updatable. See ResultSet fields for other options.*

```
Statement stmt = conn.createStatement(
                        ResultSet.TYPE_SCROLL_INSENSITIVE,
                        ResultSet.CONCUR_UPDATABLE);
ResultSet rs = stmt.executeQuery("SELECT a, b FROM TABLE2");
```

The ResultSet interface provides getter methods (getBoolean, getLong, and so on) for retrieving column values from the current row. You can retrieve values using either the index number of the column or the name of the column. In general, using the column index will be more efficient. Columns are numbered from 1. For maximum portability, result set columns within each row should be read in left-to-right order, and each column should be read only once. (You may read each column more than once, but this will add more time to your application.)

The numbers, types, and properties of a ResultSet object's columns are provided by the ResulSetMetaData object returned by the ResultSet.getMetaData method.

5-4. What Kinds of ResultSet Objects Exist?

ResultSet objects of a database can have different functionality and characteristics. (Note that in relational database terminology, result sets are called *cursors*.) These characteristics are as follows:

- Result set type.

- Result set concurrency.

- Result set (cursor) holdability, which indicates whether the cursor is closed at the Connection.commit() time. Holdability can control the closing of cursors at the transaction commit time.

What is a result set type? According to the JDBC 3.0 specification, the *type* of a ResultSet object determines the level of its functionality in two main areas: the ways in which the cursor can be manipulated and how concurrent changes made to the underlying data source are reflected by the ResultSet object. (A complete set of rows returned by a SQL statement is known as a *result set*, and the cursor is a *pointer*, which points to one of the records in the result set.)

JDBC defines the following result set types:

- **Forward-only:** Identified by java.sql.ResultSet.TYPE_FORWARD_ONLY, forward-only result sets allow you to move forward, but not backward, through the data. The application can move forward using the next() method. In general, most of the applications work with forward-only result sets.

- **Scroll-insensitive:** Identified by java.sql.ResultSet.TYPE_SCROLL_INSENSITIVE, a scroll-insensitive result set ignores changes that are made while it is open. It provides a static view of the underlying data it contains. The membership, order, and column values of rows are fixed when the result set is created.

- **Scroll sensitive:** Identified by java.sql.ResultSet.TYPE_SCROLL_SENSITIVE, a scroll-sensitive result set provides a dynamic view of the underlying data, reflecting changes that are made while it is open. The membership and ordering of rows in the result set may be fixed, depending on how it is implemented.

You should note that not all JDBC drivers support each of these result set types, and DatabaseMetaData provides methods to determine which ones are supported through its supportsResultSetType() method. The result set's type affects sensitivity only to those changes made by others, and you cannot specify whether a modifiable result set is sensitive to its own changes. This behavior varies from one JDBC driver to the next, but the ownUpdatesAreVisible(), ownInsertsAreVisible(), and ownDeletesAreVisible() methods in DatabaseMetaData are provided so that you can determine what behavior to expect from the driver.

5-5. How Do You Set a ResultSet Type?

Table 5-1. *Connection Methods That Set the* ResultSet *Type*

Method	Description
Statement createStatement()	Creates a Statement object for sending SQL statements to the database. Result sets created using the returned Statement object will by default be type TYPE_FORWARD_ONLY and have a concurrency level of CONCUR_READ_ONLY.
Statement createStatement(int resultSetType, int resultSetConcurrency)	Creates a Statement object that will generate ResultSet objects with the given type and concurrency.
Statement createStatement(int resultSetType, int resultSetConcurrency, int resultSetHoldability)	Creates a Statement object that will generate ResultSet objects with the given type, concurrency, and holdability.

Method	Description
`CallableStatement prepareCall(String sql)`	Creates a `CallableStatement` object for calling database stored procedures. Result sets created using the returned `CallableStatement` object will by default be type `TYPE_FORWARD_ONLY` and have a concurrency level of `CONCUR_READ_ONLY`.

`CallableStatement prepareCall(String sql,`
`                int resultSetType,`
`                int resultSetConcurrency)`
	Creates a `CallableStatement` object that will generate `ResultSet` objects with the given type and concurrency.

`CallableStatement prepareCall(String sql,`
`                int resultSetType,`
`                int resultSetConcurrency,`
`                int resultSetHoldability)`
	Creates a `CallableStatement` object that will generate `ResultSet` objects with the given type and concurrency.

`PreparedStatement prepareStatement(String sql)`	Creates a `PreparedStatement` object for sending returned `PreparedStatement` object will by default be type `TYPE_FORWARD_ONLY` and have a concurrency level of `CONCUR_READ_ONLY`.

`PreparedStatement prepareStatement(String sql,`
`                int resultSetType,`
`                int resultSetConcurrency)`
	Creates a `PreparedStatement` object that will generate `ResultSet` objects with the given type and concurrency.

`PreparedStatement prepareStatement(String sql,`
`                int resultSetType,`
`                int resultSetConcurrency,`
`                int resultSetHoldability)`
	Creates a `PreparedStatement` object that will generate `ResultSet` objects with the given type, concurrency, and holdability.

In all of these methods, the resultSetType parameter can take only one of the following values:

- `java.sql.ResultSet.TYPE_FORWARD_ONLY`: The constant indicating the type for a `ResultSet` object whose cursor may move only forward

- `java.sql.ResultSet.TYPE_SCROLL_INSENSITIVE`: The constant indicating the type for a `ResultSet` object that is scrollable but generally not sensitive to changes made by others

- `java.sql.ResultSet.TYPE_SCROLL_SENSITIVE`: The constant indicating the type for a `ResultSet` object that is scrollable and generally sensitive to changes made by others

5-6. How Do You Get a ResultSet Type?

`ResultSet.getType` returns the type of this result set. Here are the details from JDK 1.4 defined for the `ResultSet` interface:

```
public int getType()
    throws SQLException
```

This retrieves the type of this `ResultSet` object. The type is determined by the `Statement` object that created the result set. It returns one of the following:

```
java.sql.ResultSet.TYPE_FORWARD_ONLY
java.sql.ResultSet.TYPE_SCROLL_INSENSITIVE
java.sql.ResultSet.TYPE_SCROLL_SENSITIVE
```

This throws `SQLException` if a database access error occurs.

Now you can test the program to get the result set type:

```
ResultSet rs = <get-a-result-set>;


    ...
}
else if (rsType == java.sql.ResultSet.TYPE_SCROLL_INSENSITIVE) {
    ...
}
else if (rsType == java.sql.ResultSet.TYPE_SCROLL_SENSITIVE) {
    ...
}
else {
    // it is an error
    ...
}
```

5-7. Which ResultSet Types Are Supported by Databases?

In JDBC, three result set types are defined in the `ResultSet` interface:

- `static int TYPE_FORWARD_ONLY`: The constant indicating the type for a `ResultSet` object whose cursor may move only forward

- `static int TYPE_SCROLL_INSENSITIVE`: The constant indicating the type for a `ResultSet` object that is scrollable but generally not sensitive to changes made by others

- `static int TYPE_SCROLL_SENSITIVE`: The constant indicating the type for a `ResultSet` object that is scrollable and generally sensitive to changes made by others

By using `DatabaseMetaData`, you can find out if a database supports the defined result set types:

```
public boolean supportsResultSetType(int type)
```

This retrieves whether this database supports the given result set type. The parameter is type, which is defined in java.sql.ResultSet. It returns true if the database supports the given result set type; otherwise, it returns false. It throws SQLException if a database access error occurs.

You can use the method getAvailableResultSetTypes() (defined in the class DatabaseMetaDataTool) to find out the result set types supported by your desired vendor. DatabaseMetaDataTool is a user-defined class that provides services for handling database metadata. (You can download this class from the book's Web site, and you can use this class for Oracle, MySQL, and other databases.)

Solution

This solution uses the DatabaseMetaDataTool class, which provides services for handling database metadata. (You can download this class from the book's Web site.) DatabaseMetaDataTool. getAvailableResultSetTypes() returns all available result set types for a given database.

```java
import java.sql.*;

import jcb.db.VeryBasicConnectionManager;
import jcb.meta.DatabaseMetaDataTool;
import jcb.util.DatabaseUtil;

public class TestGetResultSetTypes {

    public static void main(String[] args) {
        Connection conn = null;
        try {
            System.out.println("--TestGetResultSetTypes begin--");


            System.out.println("conn="+conn);
            System.out.println("--------------");

            String resultSetTypes =
                DatabaseMetaDataTool.getAvailableResultSetTypes(conn);
            System.out.println(resultSetTypes);
            System.out.println("--TestGetResultSetTypes end--");
        }
        catch(Exception e){
            e.printStackTrace();
            System.exit(1);
        }
        finally {
            // release database resources
            DatabaseUtil.close(conn);
        }
    }
}
```

Running the Solution for the Oracle Database

This code shows how to run the solution for the Oracle database:

```
$ javac TestGetResultSetTypes.java
$ java TestGetResultSetTypes oracle
--TestGetResultSetTypes_Oracle begin--
conn=oracle.jdbc.driver.OracleConnection@6e70c7
--------------
```

```
<ResultSetTypes>
    <type name="TYPE_FORWARD_ONLY"/>
    <type name="TYPE_SCROLL_INSENSITIVE"/>
    <type name="TYPE_SCROLL_SENSITIVE"/>
</ResultSetTypes>
--TestGetResultSetTypes end--
```

Running the Solution for the MySQL Database

This code shows how to run the solution for the MySQL database:

```
$ javac TestGetResultSetTypes.java
$ java TestGetResultSetTypes mysql
--TestGetResultSetTypes begin--
conn=com.mysql.jdbc.Connection@124bbbf
---------------
<ResultSetTypes>
    <type name="TYPE_SCROLL_INSENSITIVE"/>
</ResultSetTypes>
--TestGetResultSetTypes end--
```

5-8. What Is a ResultSet Concurrency?

Result sets have one of two concurrency types. A *read-only* result set is of type CONCUR_READ_ONLY, and an *updatable* result set is of type CONCUR_UPDATABLE. Therefore, the concurrency mode of a result set refers to the ability to modify the data returned by a result set. JDBC defines the following con-

- *Read-only*: If your application does not need to modify this data, specifying java.sql. ResultSet.CONCUR_READ_ONLY for the concurrency mode parameter will cause the statement to create result sets that are read-only. (The result cannot be modified, updated, or deleted.)

  ```
  java.sql.ResultSet.CONCUR_READ_ONLY
  // The constant indicating the concurrency mode
  // for a ResultSet object that may NOT be updated.
  ```

- *Updatable*: Specifying java.sql.ResultSet.CONCUR_UPDATABLE for the concurrency mode parameter allows your application to make changes to the data in the result set and have those changes stored in the underlying table(s) in the database.

  ```
  java.sql.ResultSet.CONCUR_UPDATABLE
  // The constant indicating the concurrency mode
  // for a ResultSet object that may be updated.
  ```

To further explain, a read-only result set does not allow its contents to be updated. In Java, you can relate this to constants, which are prefixed with public static final or private static final. The read-only result sets can increase the overall level of concurrency between transactions, because multiple read-only locks can be held on a data item simultaneously.

An updatable result set allows its contents to be updated and acts the opposite of read-only result sets. An updatable result set may use database write locks to mediate access to the same data item using different transactions. Because only a single write lock may be held at one time on a data item, updatable result sets can reduce concurrency.

5-9. How Do You Set ResultSet Concurrency?

The java.sql.Connection interface has nine methods that set the result set concurrency; Table 5-1 listed the methods. In all of the methods, the Concurrency parameter can take only one of the following values:

- java.sql.ResultSet.CONCUR_READ_ONLY: The constant indicating the concurrency mode for a ResultSet object that may *not* be updated

- java.sql.ResultSet.CONCUR_UPDATABLE: The constant indicating the concurrency mode for a ResultSet object that may be updated

If the ResultSet Concurrency parameter is not passed explicitly, then it takes the default value (which is CONCUR_READ_ONLY).

5-10. How Do You Get ResultSet Concurrency?

ResultSet.getConcurrency() returns the concurrency of this result set. Here are the details from JDK 1.4 defined for the ResultSet interface:

public int getConcurrency()

This retrieves the concurrency mode of this ResultSet object. The concurrency used is determined by the Statement object that created the result set. This returns the concurrency type, either ResultSet.CONCUR_READ_ONLY or ResultSet.CONCUR_UPDATABLE. It throws SQLException if a database access error occurs.

```
int rsConcurrency = rs.getConcurrency();
if (rsConcurrency == java.sql.ResultSet.CONCUR_READ_ONLY) {
    ...
}
else if (rsConcurrency == java.sql.ResultSet.CONCUR_UPDATABLE) {
    ...
}
else {
    // it is an error
    ...
}
```

5-11. What Is ResultSet Holdability?

JDBC 3.0 adds support for specifying result set (or cursor) holdability. Result set *holdability* is the ability to specify whether cursors (or a result set such as java.sql.ResultSet) should be held open or closed at the end of a transaction. A holdable cursor, or result set, is one that does not automatically close when the transaction that contains the cursor is committed.

You may improve database performance by including the ResultSet holdability. If ResultSet objects are closed when a commit operation is implicitly or explicitly called, this can also improve performance.

5-12. How Do You Set ResultSet Holdability?

You can supply the following constants to the Connection methods createStatement, prepareStatement, and prepareCall:

- java.sql.ResultSet.HOLD_CURSORS_OVER_COMMIT: The constant indicating that ResultSet objects should not be closed when the method Connection.commit is called. ResultSet objects (cursors) are not closed; they are held open when the method commit is called.

- java.sql.ResultSet.CLOSE_CURSORS_AT_COMMIT: The constant indicating that ResultSet objects should be closed when the method Connection.commit is called. ResultSet objects (cursors) are closed when the method commit is called. Closing cursors at commit can result in better performance for some applications.

5-13. How Do You Set ResultSet Holdability Using the Connection Object?

Also, you can set the result set holdability by using the Connection object. This shows how to set holdability to hold the cursor over commit:

```
// changes the holdability of ResultSet objects created
// using this Connection object to the given holdability.
int holdability = java.sql.ResultSet.HOLD_CURSORS_OVER_COMMIT;
Connection conn = ... get a connection object ...
conn.setHoldability(holdability);
```

```
// changes the holdability of ResultSet objects created
// using this Connection object to the given holdability.
int holdability = java.sql.ResultSet.CLOSE_CURSORS_AT_COMMIT;
Connection conn = ... get a connection object ...
conn.setHoldability(holdability);
```

5-14. How Do You Check ResultSet Holdability?

The default holdability of a ResultSet object depends on how the DBMS and driver are implemented. You can call the DatabaseMetaData method supportsResultSetHoldability to see if your desired DBMS supports result set holdability (it retrieves whether this database supports the given result set holdability).

```
Connection conn = ... get a database connection object;
DatabaseMetaData dbMetaData = conn.getDatabaseMetaData();
if (dbMetaData == null) {
    // database metadata is not supported by driver
    ...
}
else {
    if dbMeta.supportsResultSetHoldability(ResultSet.HOLD_CURSORS_OVER_COMMIT) {
        //
        // this database hold cursors over commit
        //
        ...
    }
    if dbMeta.supportsResultSetHoldability(ResultSet.CLOSE_CURSORS_AT_COMMIT) {
        //
        // this database close cursors at commit
```

```
    //
      ...
  }
}
```

5-15. How Do You Get ResultSet Holdability?

The default holdability of a ResultSet object depends on how the DBMS and driver are implemented. You can call the DatabaseMetaData method getResultSetHoldability to get the default holdability for result sets returned by your DBMS and driver.

You can get the result set holdability in three ways.

First, you can use the Statement object:

```
int Statement.getResultSetHoldability()
    // Retrieves the result set holdability for ResultSet
    // objects generated by this Statement object.
```

Second, you can use the DatabaseMetaData object:

```
int DatabaseMetaData.getResultSetHoldability()
    // Retrieves the default holdability of this ResultSet object.
```

Finally, you can use the Connection object:

```
int Connection.getHoldability()
    // Retrieves the current holdability of ResultSet
    // objects created using this Connection object.
```

According to JDK 1.4, the ResultSet object is a table of data representing a database result set, which is usually generated by executing a statement that queries the database. Further, "a ResultSet object maintains a cursor pointing to its current row of data. Initially the cursor is positioned before the first row. The next method moves the cursor to the next row, and because it returns false when there are no more rows in the ResultSet object, it can be used in a while loop to iterate through the result set."

A default ResultSet object (when the result set type is not set explicitly in creating Statement, PreparedStatement, and CallableStatement) is not updatable and has a cursor that moves forward only. Thus, you can iterate through it only once and only from the first row to the last row. It is possible to produce ResultSet objects that are scrollable and/or updatable. The code in the next section illustrates how to make a result set that is scrollable, insensitive to updates by others, and updatable. See the ResultSet fields for other options.

5-17. How Do You Get Rows from a Database Table?

The SQL SELECT statement selects data from a table. The tabular result is stored in a result table (called the *result set*). The following example executes a SQL SELECT query and creates a result set:

```
import java.sql.*;
import jcb.util.Databaseutil;
...
Connection conn = null;
Statement stmt = null;
ResultSet rs = null;
try {
    // first get a valid java.sql.Connection object
    conn = getConnection();
    // Create a result set containing all data from employees table
```

```
    stmt = conn.createStatement();
    rs = stmt.executeQuery("SELECT * FROM employees");
    // now iterate result set object (rs) to get rows
}
catch (SQLException e) {
    // handle exception here
    e.printStackTrace();
    // more statements here for handling the exception
}
finally {
    // close resources
    DatabaseUtil.close(rs);
    DatabaseUtil.close(stmt);
    DatabaseUtil.close(conn);
}
```

To understand this fully, refer to the following examples.

The SQL SELECT statement selects data from a table. The tabular result is stored in a result table (called the *result set*). The general simplified syntax for SQL SELECT is as follows:

```
SELECT column_name(s)
    FROM table_name
```

For example, to select the columns named id and firstname from the employees table, use a SELECT statement like this:

```
SELECT id, firstname
    FROM employees
```

Table 5-2. employees *Table*

id	firstname	lastname	dept
100	Alex	Smith	Sales
200	Mary	Taylor	Software
300	Bob	Stewart	Racing

Table 5-3 shows the result.

Table 5-3. *Result from Database*

id	firstName
100	Alex
200	Mary
300	Bob

To select all columns from the employees table, use * instead of column names, like this:

```
SELECT * FROM employees
```

Note that in real-world applications, if you do not need all the columns, just list the ones required; this can boost the performance of your application. Table 5-4 shows the results.

Table 5-4. *Result from Database*

id	firstName	lastName	dept
100	Alex	Smith	Sales
200	Mary	Taylor	Software
300	Bob	Stewart	Racing

5-18. How Do You Get Data from a ResultSet?

A result set (represented as a ResultSet object) contains the results of a SQL query. (This query can be selected rows from a table, or it can be some data returned by a DatabaseMetaData object.) In general, the results are kept in a set of rows (the number of rows can be zero, one, two, and so on), one of which is designated the current row. A row must be made current before data can be retrieved from it. The result set maintains a reference to the current row called the *cursor*. The cursor is positioned before the first row when a result set is created. When a result set's next() method is called, the cursor moves to the first row of the result set, and that row becomes the current row.

For each column, you have two ways to retrieve the data from the current row. The first method uses a column index starting from 1. The second uses a column name. For example, with the following query:

```
SELECT id, name, address FROM employees
```

you can retrieve the value for the address using a column index of 3 or using the column name address.

The following code shows how to retrieve the value of the address column using the index number:

```
ResultSet rs = null;
Statement stmt = null;
Connection conn = null;
try {
    conn = getConnection(); // get a Connection object
    // create a result set containing all data
    // from your desired table
    stmt = conn.createStatement();
    String query = "SELECT id, name, address FROM employees";
    rs = stmt.executeQuery(query);
    // Fetch each row from the result set
    while (rs.next()) {
        // Get the data from the row using the column name
        // note that using a column index is better than
        // using the column name: using column name might
        // add overhead: there is a need to
        // get column metadata info.
        String employeeAddress = rs.getString(3);
        ...
    }
}
catch (SQLException e) {
    // handle the exception
    ...
}
```

```
finally {
    // close ResultSet, Statement, Connection
}
```

Method 2: Retrieving the Value of the Address Column Using the Column Name

The following code shows how to retrieve the value of the address column using the column name:

```
ResultSet rs = null;
Statement stmt = null;
Connection conn = null;
try {
    conn = getConnection(); // get a Connection object
    // create a result set containing all data
    // from your desired table
    stmt = conn.createStatement();
    String query = "SELECT id, name, address FROM employees";
    rs = stmt.executeQuery(query);
    // Fetch each row from the result set
    while (rs.next()) {
        // Get the data from the row using the column name
        // note that using a column name might add
        // overhead: there is a need to get column metadata info.
        String employeeAddress = rs.getString("address");
        ...
    }
}
    // handle the exception
    ...
}
finally {
    // close ResultSet, Statement, Connection
}
```

For both methods (using the index of the column and using the column name), you invoke an appropriate method to extract the data value of the given column.

5-19. How Do You Get Rows from a Database Table?

You can use a SQL query (by using the SELECT statement or executing a stored procedure, which returns set of rows) to get data from tables/views. The result of the SQL query is called a *result set*. (JDBC represents this as a java.sql.ResultSet object.)

The next example executes a SQL SELECT query (selecting all rows from the table books_table) and creates a result set:

```
ResultSet rs = null;
Statement stmt = null;
Connection conn = null;
try {
    conn = < get-a-database-connection>;
    // Create a result set containing all data from books_table
    stmt = connection.createStatement();
    String query = "SELECT * FROM books_table";
    rs = stmt.executeQuery(query);
    // to get the data from result set (rs),
    // you may iterate by the next() method
```

```
    while (rs.next()) {
      // use getXXX() to extract the data from each row
    }
}
catch (SQLException e) {
  // handle the exception
}
finally {
  // close the ResultSet (rs), connection (conn)
  // and statement (stmt) objects here
}
```

5-20. How Do You Get Data from a ResultSet?

A result set (expressed as a java.sql.ResultSet object) contains the results of a SQL query. The results are kept in a set of rows, one of which is designated the current row.

According to the Java 2 documentation, "a ResultSet object maintains a cursor pointing to its current row of data. Initially the cursor is positioned before the first row. The next method moves the cursor to the next row, and because it returns false when there are no more rows in the ResultSet object, it can be used in a while loop to iterate through the result set." When a ResultSet object's next() method is called, the cursor moves to the first row of the result set, and that row becomes the current row.

Note that a default ResultSet object is not updatable and has a cursor that moves forward only. Thus, you can iterate through it only once and only from the first row to the last row. However, it is possible to produce ResultSet objects that are scrollable and/or updatable (by passing some parameters

- *Case 1*: You know the name (and position) and type of each column. (In this case, you know the SQL query, so you know the name and types of each column. There is no need to discover the names/types of columns at runtime.)

- *Case 2*: You do not know the name/type of columns. (In this case, you need to discover the name and types of columns at runtime.)

You have two ways to retrieve the data from the current row. The first uses a column index starting from 1. The second uses a column name. For example, with the query SELECT employee_id, employee_name FROM employee_table, you can retrieve the value for employee_id using a column index of 1 or using the column name employee_id, and you can retrieve the value for employee_name using a column index of 2 or using the column name employee_name. Note that the order of ResultSet. getXXX(index=1, 2, 3, ...) will not cause any error at all. Therefore, in this example, ResultSet. getString(1) can follow ResultSet.getString(2), or ResultSet.getString(2) can follow ResultSet. getString(1).

The next two sections address these questions in detail.

Case 1: You Know the Name, Position, and Type of Each Column

When you know the name (and position) and type of each column of the result set, you have two options for getting the data:

- Using the column index (starting from 1)

- Using the column names

Using a column index (starting from 1), you can extract the value of columns. In the following class, you select all rows from the employees table and then extract the values using the column index. Before running this solution, you will see the employees table and its contents (using the Oracle 9*i* database).

Solution

The following sample solution extracts data from the ResultSet object by using the column index (1, 2, and so on):

```java
import java.sql.*;

import jcb.util.DatabaseUtil;
import jcb.db.VeryBasicConnectionManager;

public class ExtractResultSetByIndex {
    public static void main(String[] args) {
        Connection conn = null;
        Statement stmt = null;
        ResultSet rs = null;
        try {
            System.out.println("--ExtractResultSetByIndex begin--");
            String dbVendor = args[0];
            conn = VeryBasicConnectionManager.getConnection(dbVendor);
            System.out.println("conn="+conn);
            System.out.println("---------------");

            // create a statement
            stmt = conn.createStatement();

            // execute query and return result as a ResultSet
            rs = stmt.executeQuery(query);

            // extract data from the ResultSet (using the column indexes)
            while (rs.next()) {
                String id = rs.getString(1);     // index 1 = "id" column
                String name = rs.getString(2);   // index 2 = "name" column
                System.out.println("id="+id);
                System.out.println("name="+name);
                // according to table def., age can be null
                int age = rs.getInt(3);          // index 3 = "age" column
                if (rs.wasNull()){
                    System.out.println("age=null");
                }
                else {
                    System.out.println("age="+age);
                }
                System.out.println("---------------");
            }
            System.out.println("--ExtractResultSetByIndex end--");
        }
        catch(Exception e){
            e.printStackTrace();
            System.exit(1);
        }
```

```
        finally {
            // release database resources
            DatabaseUtil.close(rs);
            DatabaseUtil.close(stmt);
            DatabaseUtil.close(conn);
        }
    }
}
```

Setting Up the Oracle Database

This is the code to set up the Oracle database:

```
SQL> desc employees;
 Name                                      Null?    Type
 ----------------------------------------- -------- -------------
 ID                                        NOT NULL VARCHAR2(10)
 NAME                                               VARCHAR2(20)
 AGE                                               NUMBER
SQL> select * from employees;

ID         NAME                 AGE
---------- -------------------- ----------
11         Alex Smith            25
22         Don Knuth             65
33         Mary Kent             35
44         Monica Seles          30


SQL> desc employees;
 Name                                      Null?    Type
 ----------------------------------------- -------- -------------
 ID                                        NOT NULL VARCHAR2(10)
 NAME                                      NOT NULL VARCHAR2(20)
 AGE                                               NUMBER(38)
```

Running the Solution for the Oracle Database

This is how you run the solution for the Oracle database:

```
$ java ExtractResultSetByIndex oracle
--ExtractResultSetByIndex begin--
conn=oracle.jdbc.driver.T4CConnection@341960
---------------
id=11
name=Alex Smith
age=25
---------------
id=22
name=Don Knuth
age=65
---------------
id=33
name=Mary Kent
age=35
```

```
---------------
id=44
name=Monica Seles
age=30
---------------
id=99
name=Alex Edison
age=null
---------------
--ExtractResultSetByIndex end--
```

Setting Up the MySQL Database

This is the code to set up the MySQL database:

```
mysql> select * from employees;
+----+--------------+------+
| id | name         | age  |
+----+--------------+------+
| 88 | Peter Pan    | NULL |
| 77 | Donald Duck  | NULL |
| 33 | Mary Kent    |   35 |
| 44 | Monica Seles |   30 |
+----+--------------+------+
4 rows in set (0.05 sec)
```

```
$ java ExtractResultSetByIndex mysql
--ExtractResultSetByIndex begin--
conn=com.mysql.jdbc.Connection@1dd46f7
---------------
id=88
name=Peter Pan
age=null
---------------
id=77
name=Donald Duck
age=null
---------------
id=33
name=Mary Kent
age=35
---------------
id=44
name=Monica Seles
age=30
---------------
--ExtractResultSetByIndex end--
```

Case 2: You Do Not Know the Name, Position, and Type of Each Column

This solution is identical to ExtractResultSetByIndex with the exception of three lines. Specifically, you need to replace the following lines:

```
String id = rs.getString(1);     // index 1 is the "id" column
String name = rs.getString(2);   // index 2 is the "name" column
int age = rs.getInt(3);          // index 3 is the "age" column
```

with these:

```
String id = rs.getString("id");       // index 1 is the "id" column
String name = rs.getString("name");   // index 2 is the "name" column
int age = rs.getInt("age");           // index 3 is the "age" column
```

5-21. How Do You Determine If a Fetched Value Is NULL?

When a ResultSet.getXXX() method encounters a NULL in the database, it will convert it to a default value (the default value depends on the type of column). For example, if NULL was encountered in a VARCHAR field, ResultSet.getString() will return "". If NULL was encountered in a NUMBER (or INT) field, ResultSet.getInt() will return 0. To determine whether the actual value is a NULL, wasNull() must be called. This method must be called *immediately* after the value is fetched from the result set.

The wasNull() method has the following signature (according to JDK 1.4):

```
public boolean wasNull() throws SQLException
```

This reports whether the last column read had a value of SQL NULL. Note that you must first call one of the getter methods on a column to try to read its value and then call the method wasNull to see if the value read was SQL NULL.

This returns true if the last column value read was SQL NULL. It returns false otherwise.

The following snippet tests a retrieved column value for NULL:

```
String id = rs.getString(1);
if (rs.wasNull()) {
    //
    // then the first column was null
    //
}
else {
    //
    // the first column was not null
    //
}
//...
}
```

5-22. How Do You Get the Column Names in a Result Set?

Given a ResultSet object, it is possible to get the column name, column type, table name (from which table this column came from), and position; all of this is possible by using ResultSetMetaData. (ResultSetMetaData behaves differently for Oracle and MySQL; for the Oracle database, ResultSetMetaData does not provide the correct table name.)

Solution

This is the solution:

```
import java.sql.*;

import jcb.util.DatabaseUtil;
```

```java
import jcb.db.VeryBasicConnectionManager;

public class GetColumnNamesFromResultSet {

    public static String getColumnNames(ResultSet rs)
        throws SQLException {
        if (rs == null) {
            return null;
        }

        // get result set metadata
        ResultSetMetaData rsMetaData = rs.getMetaData();
        int numberOfColumns = rsMetaData.getColumnCount();
        StringBuffer columnNames = new StringBuffer("<columnNames>");

        // get the column names; column indexes start from 1
        for (int i=1; i<numberOfColumns+1; i++) {
            String columnName = rsMetaData.getColumnName(i);
            // Get the name of the column's table name
            String tableName = rsMetaData.getTableName(i);
            columnNames.append("<column name=\""+columnName+
                "\" table=\""+tableName+"\"/>");
        }
        columnNames.append("</columnNames>");
        return columnNames.toString();
    }


        Connection conn = null;
        Statement stmt = null;
        ResultSet rs = null;
        String dbVendor = args[0];  // database vendor
        try {
            System.out.println("--GetColumnNamesFromResultSet begin--");
            conn = VeryBasicConnectionManager.getConnection(dbVendor);
            System.out.println("conn="+conn);
            System.out.println("---------------");

            // prepare query
            String query = "select id, name, age from employees";

            // create a statement
            stmt = conn.createStatement();

            // execute query and return result as a ResultSet
            rs = stmt.executeQuery(query);

            // get the column names from the ResultSet
            String columnNames = getColumnNames(rs);
            System.out.println(columnNames);
            System.out.println("--GetColumnNamesFromResultSet end--");
        }
        catch(Exception e){
            e.printStackTrace();
            System.exit(1);
        }
```

```
        finally {
            // release database resources
            DatabaseUtil.close(rs);
            DatabaseUtil.close(stmt);
            DatabaseUtil.close(conn);
        }
    }
}
```

Running the Solution for the Oracle Database

This shows how to run the solution for the Oracle database:

```
$ javac GetColumnNamesFromResultSet.java
$ java GetColumnNamesFromResultSet oracle
--GetColumnNamesFromResultSet begin--
conn=oracle.jdbc.driver.OracleConnection@11ddcde
---------------
<columnNames>
   <column name="ID" table="">
   <column name="NAME" table="">
   <column name="AGE" table="">
</columnNames>
--GetColumnNamesFromResultSet end--
```

Running the Solution for the MySQL Database

```
$ javac GetColumnNamesFromResultSet.java
$ java GetColumnNamesFromResultSet mysql
--GetColumnNamesFromResultSet begin--
conn=com.mysql.jdbc.Connection@15c7850
---------------
<columnNames>
      <column name="id" table="employees"/>
      <column name="name" table="employees"/>
      <column name="age" table="employees"/>
</columnNames>
--GetColumnNamesFromResultSet end--
```

5-23. How Do You Get the Number of Rows in a Database Table?

To get the number of rows (sometimes database experts use the term *cardinality*) from a table, you need to issue the following SQL query:

```
select count(*) form <table-name>
```

Solution

I provide a complete solution in the CountRows class that you can download from this book's Web site. The following shows only the key method:

```
public static int countRows(Connection conn, String tableName)
  throws SQLException {
    // select the number of rows in the table
    Statement stmt = null;
```

```
        ResultSet rs = null;
        int rowCount = -1;
        try {
            stmt = conn.createStatement();
            rs = stmt.executeQuery("SELECT COUNT(*) FROM "+ tableName);
            // get the number of rows from the result set
            rs.next();
            rowCount = rs.getInt(1);
        }
        finally {
            DatabaseUtil.close(rs);
            DatabaseUtil.close(stmt);
        }
        return rowCount;
}
```

Running the Solution for the Oracle Database

To execute the Oracle solution, use this code:

```
$ javac CountRows.java
$ java CountRows oracle employees
------CountRows begin---------
tableName=employees
conn=oracle.jdbc.driver.OracleConnection@11ddcde
rowCount=4
```

Running the Solution for the MySQL Database

To execute the MySQL solution, use this code:

```
$ javac CountRows.java
$ java CountRows mysql employees
------CountRows_MySQL begin---------
tableName=employees
conn=com.mysql.jdbc.Connection@15c7850
rowCount=4
------CountRows end---------
```

5-24. How Do You Get BLOB Data from a Database Table?

A BLOB is a Binary Large OBject (such as an image, video, document, and so on) in a database. BLOBs can be very large, 2GB or more, depending on the database. A BLOB is a reference to data in a database. There are some restrictions for BLOBs:

- BLOB columns cannot be keys.

- SQL queries cannot group or sort on BLOB.

To get BLOB data from a database table, you create a table with a BLOB column, populate it, and then get the data.

Setting Up the Oracle Database

The Oracle table specification is as follows:

```
$ sqlplus mp/mp2
SQL*Plus: Release 9.2.0.1.0 - Production on Thu Sep 4 13:55:27 2003

SQL> create table my_pictures(
  2      id varchar(10) not null primary key,
  3      photo BLOB
  4  );

Table created.

SQL> desc my_pictures;
 Name            Null?    Type
 -------------- -------- --------------
 ID              NOT NULL VARCHAR2(10)
 PHOTO                    BLOB
```

Next, populate an Oracle table with binary data and verify the population. To accomplish this task, you will learn how to develop a simple Java program (the InsertBLOB_Oracle class) that inserts the desired binary files into the my_pictures table. Figure 5-2 shows the picture (binary files) to be inserted.

Figure 5-2. *Binary files to be inserted into a database*

Viewing the Oracle Database Before Running the Solution

This shows the Oracle database before running the solution:

```
SQL> describe my_pictures;
 Name                            Null?    Type
 ------------------------------ -------- ------------
 ID                              NOT NULL VARCHAR2(10)
 PHOTO                                    BLOB

SQL> select id from my_pictures;
no rows selected
```

Solution: Using the Oracle Database

Using Oracle, when you first insert a new record containing a BLOB data type, you must insert the record with an "empty" BLOB before the BLOB column can be updated with real data. You can insert an empty BLOB with the Oracle EMPTY_BLOB() function. The EMPTY_BLOB() function returns an empty locator of type BLOB (note that EMPTY_BLOB is a proprietary feature of Oracle). The following code shows how to do this:

```java
import java.io.*;
import java.sql.*;
import java.text.*;

import jcb.db.*;
import jcb.meta.*;

import oracle.jdbc.driver.*;
import oracle.sql.BLOB;

public class InsertBLOB_Oracle {
    Connection conn;

    public InsertBLOB_Oracle() throws Exception {
        DriverManager.registerDriver(new oracle.jdbc.driver.OracleDriver());
        conn = DriverManager.getConnection(
          "jdbc:oracle:thin:@localhost:1521:caspian", "mp", "mp2");
    }


        if (args.length != 2) {
            System.out.println("usage: java InsertBLOB_Oracle <id> <binary-file>");
            System.exit(0);
        }

        String id = args[0].trim();
        String binaryFileName = args[1].trim();
        new InsertBLOB_Oracle().process(id, binaryFileName);
    }

    public void process(String id, String binaryFileName)
        throws Exception {
        int              rows      = 0;
        FileInputStream  fin       = null;
        OutputStream     out       = null;
        ResultSet        rs        = null;
        Statement        stmt      = null;
        oracle.sql.BLOB  photo     = null;

        try {
            conn.setAutoCommit(false);
            stmt = conn.createStatement();

            System.out.println("This creates the LOB locators");
            rows = stmt.executeUpdate("insert into my_pictures"+
                "(id, photo ) values ('"+id+"', empty_blob() )");
            System.out.println(rows + " rows inserted");
```

```
      // now retrieve the BLOB locator
      rs = stmt.executeQuery("select photo from  "+
        "my_pictures where id = '"+id+ "' for update nowait");
      rs.next();
      photo = ((OracleResultSet)rs).getBLOB(1);

      // Now, we have the BLOB locator, store the photo
      File binaryFile = new File(binaryFileName);
      fin = new FileInputStream(binaryFile);
      out = photo.getBinaryOutputStream();
      // Get the optimal buffer size from the BLOB
      byte[] buffer = new byte[photo.getBufferSize()];
      int length = 0;
      while ((length = fin.read(buffer)) != -1) {
        out.write(buffer, 0, length);
      }

      // you've got to close the output stream before
      // you commit, or the changes are lost!
      out.close();
      fin.close();
      conn.commit();
  }
  finally {
    DatabaseUtil.close(rs);
    DatabaseUtil.close(stmt);



  protected void finalize() throws Throwable {
      DatabaseUtil.close(conn);
      super.finalize();
  }
}
```

Running the Solution

To execute the Oracle solution, use this code:

```
$ javac InsertBLOB_Oracle.java
$ dir d:\mp\book\images2
Directory of d:\mp\book\images2
05/08/2003   10:13a                36,932 duck1.jpg
05/09/2003   08:50a                20,754 duck2.jpg
05/07/2003   01:45p                18,843 tiger1.jpg
05/09/2003   08:30a                33,097 tiger2.jpg
08/25/2003   03:18p                63,241 tiger3.jpg
08/25/2003   03:21p                79,158 tiger4.jpg
               6 File(s)          252,025 bytes

$ java InsertBLOB_Oracle duck1 d:\mp\book\images2\duck1.jpg
$ java InsertBLOB_Oracle duck2 d:\mp\book\images2\duck2.jpg
$ java InsertBLOB_Oracle tiger1 d:\mp\book\images2\tiger1.jpg
$ java InsertBLOB_Oracle tiger2 d:\mp\book\images2\tiger2.jpg
$ java InsertBLOB_Oracle tiger3 d:\mp\book\images2\tiger3.jpg
$ java InsertBLOB_Oracle tiger4 d:\mp\book\images2\tiger4.jpg
```

Viewing the Oracle Database After Running the Solution

This is the Oracle database after running the solution:

```
SQL> select id from my_pictures;

ID
----------
tiger1
tiger2
tiger3
tiger4
duck1
duck2

6 rows selected.
```

The following example demonstrates how to retrieve bytes from a BLOB:

```
ResultSet rs = null;
Statement stmt = null;
Connection conn = null;
Blob blob = null
InputStream is = null;
try {
     conn = getConnection();
     stmt = conn.createStatement();
     String query = "SELECT col_blob FROM mysql_all_table";


          // Get the BLOB from the result set
          blob = rs.getBlob("col_blob");

          // Get the number bytes in the BLOB
          long blobLength = blob.length();

          // Get bytes from the BLOB in a byte array
          int pos = 1;    // position is 1-based
          int len = 10;
          byte[] bytes = blob.getBytes(pos, len);

          // Get bytes from the BLOB using a stream
          is = blob.getBinaryStream();
          int b = is.read();
     }
}
catch (IOException io) {
     // handle the IOException
}
catch (SQLException se) {
     // handle the SQLException
}
catch (Exception e) {
     // handle the Exception
}
finally {
   // close ResultSet, Statement, Connection
   // close InputStream
}
```

5-25. How Do You Get CLOB Data from a Database Table?

A CLOB is a Character Large OBject. You can use it to store large text data (such as ASCII/text files, PostScript files, and serialized objects). The java.sql.Clob object corresponds to a CLOB LOCATOR in the SQL-99 standard.

 To show how to retrieve data from CLOB columns, I will first provide a general solution and then provide the vendor-specific (MySQL and Oracle) solutions.

General Solution: Retrieving Data from CLOB Columns

Assume that the employees table has two columns: the first column is VARCHAR(10), and the second column is a CLOB data type. The following code snippet shows how to retrieve CLOB values from the ResultSet object using the getClob() method:

```
ResultSet rs = null;
Statement stmt = null;
Connection conn = null;
BufferedReader reader = null;
try {
   // get a Connection object
   conn = getConnection();
   // create a scrollable ResultSet object
   String query = "select emp_id, emp_resume from employees";
   stmt = connection.createStatement(
          ResultSet.TYPE_SCROLL_INSENSITIVE,
          ResultSet.CONCUR_READ_ONLY);


       String id = rs.getString(1);
       Clob resume = rs.getClob(2);
       int clobLength = (int) resume.length();
       // create a buffer to read the stream into a character array
       reader = new BufferedReader(resume.getCharacterStream());
       char[] buffer = new char[ clobLength ];
       reader.read( buffer, 0, clobLength );
   }
}
catch (SQLException e) {
   // handle the exception
}
finally {
   // close database and other resources
   reader.close();
}
```

MySQL/Oracle Solutions: Retrieving Data from CLOB Columns

Using MySQL's driver or Oracle 10 drivers, you can use one of the following methods (which returns the entire CLOB data):

```
ResultSet.getString(clob_column_index)
ResultSet.getString(clob_column_name)
```

5-26. How Do You Match Using Wildcards in a SQL Statement?

SQL provides wildcard matching of text using the LIKE clause. The following is a SQL statement that uses a LIKE clause and a wildcard character. This SQL statement will find all rows with names that start with Pat.

```
SELECT * FROM my_table WHERE name LIKE 'Pat%'
```

Two wildcard characters are available. The underscore (_) matches any character. The percent sign (%) matches zero or more characters.

```
try {
    // Create a statement
    Statement stmt = connection.createStatement();

    // Select the row if col_string contains the word pat
    String sql = "SELECT * FROM my_table WHERE col_string LIKE '%pat%'";

    // Select the row if col_string ends with the word pat
    sql = "SELECT * FROM my_table WHERE col_string LIKE 'pat%'";

    // Select the row if col_string starts with abc and ends with xyz
    sql = "SELECT * FROM my_table WHERE col_string LIKE 'abc%xyz'";

    // Select the row if col_string equals the word pat%
    sql = "SELECT * FROM my_table WHERE col_string LIKE 'pat\\%'";


    sql = "SELECT * FROM my_table WHERE col_string LIKE 'p_t'";

    // Select the row if col_string equals p_t
    sql = "SELECT * FROM my_table WHERE col_string LIKE 'p\\_t'";

    // Execute the query
    ResultSet resultSet = stmt.executeQuery(sql);
}
catch (SQLException e) {
    // handle the exception
}
```

5-27. How Do You Read/Extract Data from a Microsoft Excel Spreadsheet File?

Microsoft Excel is a spreadsheet program that you can use to perform numerical calculations and bookkeeping tasks. Valuable corporate data is often stored in Microsoft Excel spreadsheets. Microsoft refers to Microsoft Excel sheets (so-called tables) as [Sheet1$], [Sheet2$], and so on. (This kind of naming tables is not standard in the relational database industry.) For details, see http://support. microsoft.com/default.aspx?scid=kb;en-us;Q295646.

How It Works

Assume you have created the Microsoft Excel spreadsheet shown in Figure 5-3 in a worksheet called Sheet1 (the default sheet name) and you have saved the file in C:\mp\msAccess\emps.xls.

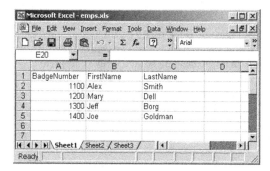

Figure 5-3. *Microsoft Excel spreadsheet*

Since Microsoft Excel comes with an ODBC driver, I will show how to use the JDBC-ODBC bridge driver that comes with Sun Microsystems' JDK to connect to the spreadsheet. In Microsoft Excel, the name of the worksheet is equivalent to the database table name, and the header names found on the first row of the worksheet are equivalent to the table column/field names. Therefore, when accessing Microsoft Excel via JDBC, it is important to place your data with the headers starting at row 1.

To access a Microsoft spreadsheet, you need to create a new ODBC data source using the Microsoft Excel driver.

The first step is to set up an ODBC connection to your data source, which is the Microsoft Excel C:\mp\msAccess\emps.xls spreadsheet file. Follow these steps:

1. Open the Control Panel, select Administrative Tools, and then select ODBC Data Sources.

2. Select System DSN, and then the click the Add button.

3. Select the Microsoft Excel Driver (*.xls) item, as shown in Figure 5-4.

4. Click the Finish button.

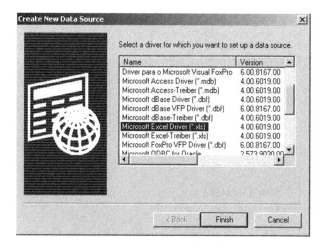

Figure 5-4. *Creating a new data source*

Giving Your Data Source a Name

Give your data source a name; as shown in Figure 5-5, I have used the name excelDB. Next, click the Select Workbook button. Select the name of the Microsoft Excel spreadsheet you want to use (that is, C:\mp\msAccess\emps.xls), and then click OK. Your ODBC Excel data source is now complete.

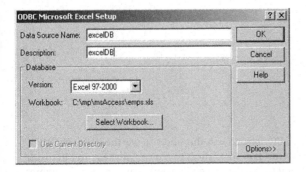

Figure 5-5. *Setting up an ODBC Microsoft Excel data source*

Solution: A JDBC Program to Access/Read Microsoft Excel

The following sample program reads data from Microsoft Excel and prints retrieved data to the standard output:

```java
import java.sql.*;

import jcb.db.*;
import jcb.meta.*;

public class TestAccessExcel {

    public static Connection getConnection() throws Exception {
        String driver = "sun.jdbc.odbc.JdbcOdbcDriver";
        String url = "jdbc:odbc:excelDB";
        String username = "";  // username does not need to be empty.
        String password = "";  // password does not need to be empty.
        Class.forName(driver);  // load JDBC-ODBC driver
        return DriverManager.getConnection(url, username, password);
    }

    public static void main(String args[]) {
        Connection conn=null;
        Statement stmt=null;
        ResultSet rs=null;
        try {
            conn = getConnection();
            stmt = conn.createStatement();
            String excelQuery = "select * from [Sheet1$]";
            rs=stmt.executeQuery(excelQuery);

            while(rs.next()){
                System.out.println(rs.getString("BadgeNumber")+
                    " "+ rs.getString("FirstName")+" "+
```

```
                    rs.getString("LastName"));
            }
        }
        catch (Exception e){
            // handle the exception
            e.printStackTrace();
            System.err.println(e.getMessage());
        }
        finally {
            // release database resources
            DatabaseUtil.close(rs);
            DatabaseUtil.close(stmt);
            DatabaseUtil.close(conn);
        }
    }
}
```

Discussing the JDBC Program to Access Microsoft Excel

To recap, you have done the following:

- You have connected to the Microsoft Excel ODBC data source the same way you would connect to any database server.

- The only significant difference is in the SELECT statement. Although your data is residing in the worksheet called Sheet1, you need to refer to the sheet as Sheet1$ in your SQL statements.

To run the JDBC program to access Microsoft Excel, use this code:

```
$ javac TestAccessExcel.java
$ java TestAccessExcel
1100.0 Alex Smith
1200.0 Mary Dell
1300.0 Jeff Borg
1400.0 Joe Goldman
```

5-28. How Do You Write Data to a Microsoft Excel Spreadsheet File?

The JDBC API allows you to write to Microsoft Excel. Here, I will show how to create new records using Microsoft Excel spreadsheets.

To access a Microsoft Excel spreadsheet, you need to create a new ODBC data source using the Microsoft Excel driver. You will then give it the data source name (DSN) of excelDB and have it point to file C:\mp\msAccess\emps.xls. The next sections show these steps in detail.

Configuring ODBC

The first step is to set up an ODBC connection to your data source, which is the Microsoft Excel C:\mp\msAccess\emps.xls spreadsheet file. To set up Excel as a data source, follow these steps:

1. Open the Control Panel, select Administrative Tools, and then select ODBC Data Sources.

2. Select System DSN, then click the Add button.

3. Select the Microsoft Excel Driver (*.xls) item.

4. Click the Finish button.

Giving Your Data Source a Name

As you did when accessing/reading data from Microsoft Excel, you need to give your data source a name. (This example is using excelDB.) Next, click the Select Workbook button. Select the name of the Excel spreadsheet you want to use (that is, C:\mp\msAccess\emps.xls), and then click OK. Your ODBC Excel data source is now complete.

To be able to write new data (using your JDBC program) to your spreadsheet file, make sure that the Read Only check box is unchecked (not set); if the Read Only check box *is* checked, then you cannot write new data to the file.

Solution: A JDBC Program to Write into Microsoft Excel

This code shows how to write data into Microsoft Excel:

```java
import java.util.*;
import java.io.*;
import java.sql.*;

import jcb.db.*;
import jcb.meta.*;

public class TestWriteExcel {
    public static Connection getConnection() throws Exception {
        String driver = "sun.jdbc.odbc.JdbcOdbcDriver";
        String url = "jdbc:odbc:excelDB";
        String username = "";


        return DriverManager.getConnection(url, username, password);
    }
    public static void main(String args[]) {
        Connection conn=null;
        Statement stmt=null;
        ResultSet rs=null;
        try {
            conn = getConnection();
            stmt = conn.createStatement();
            String excelQuery = "insert into [Sheet1$](BadgeNumber, "+
                "FirstName, LastName) values('9999', 'Al', 'Kent')";
            stmt.executeUpdate(excelQuery);
        }
        catch (Exception e){
            // handle the exception
            e.printStackTrace();
            System.err.println(e.getMessage());
        }
        finally {
            // release database resources
            DatabaseUtil.close(stmt);
            DatabaseUtil.close(conn);
        }
    }
}
```

Discussing the JDBC Program to Access Microsoft Excel

To recap, you have done the following:

- You have connected to the Microsoft Excel ODBC data source the same way you would connect to any database server.

- The only significant difference is in the INSERT statement. Although your data is residing in the worksheet called Sheet1, you have to refer to the sheet as Sheet1$ in your SQL statements. And because the dollar sign symbol is a reserved character in SQL, you have to encapsulate the word Sheet1$ in brackets, as shown in the previous code.

Running the JDBC Program to Write Data into Microsoft Excel

To run the program, use this code:

```
$ javac TestWriteExcel.java
$ java TestWriteExcel
```

Viewing the Content of Microsoft Excel After Inserting New Data

Figure 5-6 shows the Microsoft Excel spreadsheet after inserting the new data.

Figure 5-6. *After inserting new data*

5-29. Which Is the Preferred Collection Class to Use for Storing Database Result Sets?

When retrieving database results, you can use java.util.ArrayList or java.util.LinkedList. (Both of these classes implement the java.util.List interface.) The following is according to Sun Microsystems (http://java.sun.com/developer/JDCTechTips/2002/tt0910.html):

- Appending elements to the end of a list has a fixed, averaged cost for both ArrayList and LinkedList. For ArrayList, appending typically involves setting an internal array location to the element reference but occasionally results in the array being reallocated. For LinkedList, the cost is uniform and involves allocating an internal Entry object.

- Inserting or deleting elements in the middle of an ArrayList implies that the rest of the list must be moved. Inserting or deleting elements in the middle of a LinkedList has a fixed cost.

- A LinkedList does not support efficient random access.

- An ArrayList has space overhead in the form of reserve capacity at the end of the list. A LinkedList has significant space overhead per element.

- Sometimes a Map structure is a better choice than a List.

Adding Database Results to the Rear of the List

Therefore, in retrieving database results, if you are adding objects to the rear (tail) of the list, the best collection implementation to use is the ArrayList. The benefits include the following:

- Retaining the original retrieval order of records
- Quick insertion at the tail

The program structure for retrieving database results is as follows:

```
ResultSet rs = stmt.executeQuery("...");
List list = new ArrayList();
while(rs.next()) {
    list.add(result.getString("column-name"));
}
```

Note that if the result set (the ResultSet object) has multiple columns, you have to combine them into your own data structure for each row.

The following code is proof that ArrayList is faster than LinkedList:

```
import java.util.List;
import java.util.ArrayList;
import java.util.LinkedList;

public class ListDemo {
    // number of objects to add to list
    static final int SIZE = 1000000;


        Object obj = new Object();

        for (int i = 0; i < SIZE; i++) {
            // add object to the rear of the list
            list.add(obj);
        }

        return System.currentTimeMillis() - start;
    }

    public static void main(String args[]) {
        // do timing for LinkedList
        System.out.println("time for LinkedList = " +
            timeList(new LinkedList()));

        // do timing for ArrayList
        System.out.println("time for ArrayList = " +
            timeList(new ArrayList()));
    }
}
```

The following runs the demo:

```
$ javac ListDemo.java
$ java ListDemo
time for LinkedList = 620
time for ArrayList = 210
```

As you can see, adding objects to the end of ArrayList is faster.

Adding Database Results to the Head of the List

In retrieving database results, if you are adding objects to the head (front) of the list, the best collection implementation to use is the LinkedList. The benefits include the following:

- Retaining the reverse of original retrieval order of records

- Quick insertion at the head

The program structure for retrieving database results is as follows:

```
ResultSet rs = stmt.executeQuery("...");
List list = new LinkedList();
while(rs.next()) {
  list.add(0, result.getString("column-name"));
}
```

Note that if the result set (the ResultSet object) has multiple columns, you have to combine them into your own data structure for each row.

The following is proof that LinkedList is faster than ArrayList:

```
import java.util.List;
import java.util.ArrayList;
import java.util.LinkedList;

public class ListDemoHead {
    static final int SIZE = 100000;


        for (int i = 0; i < SIZE; i++) {
            // add object to the head of the list
            list.add(0, obj);
        }

        return System.currentTimeMillis() - start;
    }

    public static void main(String args[]) {
        // do timing for LinkedList
        System.out.println("time for LinkedList = " +
            timeList(new LinkedList()));

        // do timing for ArrayList
        System.out.println("time for ArrayList = " +
            timeList(new ArrayList()));
    }
}
```

The following runs the demo:

```
$ javac ListDemoHead.java
$ java ListDemoHead
time for LinkedList = 80
time for ArrayList = 7011
```

As you can see, adding objects to the head of LinkedList is faster.

5-30. How Do You Retrieve a Whole Row/Record of Data at Once Instead of Calling an Individual ResultSet.getXXX() Method for Each Column?

The ResultSet object is a two-dimensional table of data representing a database result set, which is usually generated by executing a statement that queries the database. A ResultSet object represents data retrieved in table form. The ResultSet interface does not have any method to retrieve a whole row/record of data at once. The ResultSet.getXXX() methods are the only way to retrieve data from a ResultSet object, which means you have to make a method call for each column of a row.

If you need to pass the entire row/record as a single object, then you can do the following: get all the column values and their associated data types, and then create a Row (user-defined object; you have to define this object) using these values. According to Sun Microsystems (http://java.sun.com/products/jdbc/index.jsp), it is unlikely that using ResultSet.getXXX() methods is the cause of any performance problem. Also note that using ResultSet.getXXX(index-number) is usually faster than using ResultSet.getXXX(column-name); using column-name will require additional method calls to the database server for getting metadata information for column names. In general, using ResultSet.getXXX(index-number) is better than using ResultSet.getXXX(column-name) because if the database schema changes (such as renaming column names), then you do not need to modify your JDBC code at all.

CHAPTER 6

■ ■ ■

Working with Scrollable and Updatable ResultSet Objects

The purpose of this chapter is to provide Java snippets, reusable code samples, classes, and methods that deal with the "scrollable" and "updatable" ResultSet objects. When writing this chapter, I relied on JDK 1.4 and the final release of the JDBC 3.0 specification.

6-1. What Is a Scrollable ResultSet?

A ResultSet is scrollable if you have the ability to move its cursor backward as well as forward. The JDBC 2.0 API introduced the scrollable ResultSet concept. The ResultSet object has methods that let you move the cursor to a particular row and check the position of the cursor. Scrollable ResultSet

Before you can use a scrollable ResultSet, you have to create one. The following snippet shows one way to create a scrollable ResultSet object:

```
// assume getConnection() returns a Connection object
Connection conn = getConnection();
...
Statement stmt = conn.createStatement(
                    ResultSet.TYPE_SCROLL_SENSITIVE,
                    ResultSet.CONCUR_READ_ONLY);
String query = "SELECT id, name FROM employees";
ResultSet rs = stmt.executeQuery(query);
```

When creating a Statement object, you need to specify two arguments to the method createStatement(). The first argument indicates the type of a ResultSet object and can be one of three constants:

- ResultSet.TYPE_FORWARD_ONLY: A constant indicating the type for a ResultSet object whose cursor may move only forward (creates a nonscrollable ResultSet object)

- ResultSet.TYPE_SCROLL_INSENSITIVE: A constant indicating the type for a ResultSet object that is scrollable but generally not sensitive to changes made by others

- ResultSet.TYPE_SCROLL_SENSITIVE: A constant indicating the type for a ResultSet object that is scrollable and generally sensitive to changes made by others

The second argument is one of two ResultSet constants for specifying whether a result set is read-only or writable/updatable:

- ResultSet.CONCUR_READ_ONLY: A constant indicating the concurrency mode for a ResultSet object that may *not* be updated

- ResultSet.CONCUR_UPDATABLE: A constant indicating the concurrency mode for a ResultSet object that may be updated

The important point to remember is that if you specify a ResultSet type, you must also specify whether it is read-only or writable/updatable. The following example shows a scrollable ResultSet using a sample program, DemoScrollableResultSet.

Solution

This solution uses the following ResultSet methods:

- next(): Moves the cursor down one row from its current position
- afterLast(): Moves the cursor to the end of this ResultSet object, just after the last row
- previous(): Moves the cursor to the previous row in this ResultSet object

Here's the solution:

```
1 import java.sql.ResultSet;
2 import java.sql.Statement;
3 import java.sql.Connection;


6
7 import jcb.util.DatabaseUtil;
8 import jcb.db.VeryBasicConnectionManager;
9
10 public class DemoScrollableResultSet {
11
12    public static void main(String[] args) {
13       Connection conn = null;
14       Statement stmt = null;
15       ResultSet rs = null;
16       String dbVendor = args[0];   // vendor = {"mysql", "oracle" }
17       try {
18          conn = VeryBasicConnectionManager.getConnection(dbVendor);
19          System.out.println("--DemoScrollableResultSet begin--");
20          System.out.println("conn="+conn);
21          System.out.println("-------");
22
23          // prepare query
24          String query = "select id, name from employees";
25
26          // create a statement
27          stmt = conn.createStatement(ResultSet.TYPE_SCROLL_SENSITIVE,
28                                     ResultSet.CONCUR_READ_ONLY);
29
30          // execute query and return result as a ResultSet
31          rs = stmt.executeQuery(query);
32
```

```
33              // extract data from the ResultSet
34              // scroll from top
35              while (rs.next()) {
36                  String id = rs.getString(1);
37                  String name = rs.getString(2);
38                  System.out.println("id=" + id + "  name=" + name);
39              }
40              System.out.println("---------");
41
42              // scroll from the bottom
43              rs.afterLast();
44              while (rs.previous()) {
45                  String id = rs.getString(1);
46                  String name = rs.getString(2);
47                  System.out.println("id=" + id + "  name=" + name);
48              }
49              System.out.println("---------");
50
51              System.out.println("--DemoScrollableResultSet end--");
52          }
53          catch(Exception e){
54              e.printStackTrace();
55              System.exit(1);
56          }
57          finally {
58              // release database resources

61              DatabaseUtil.close(conn);
62          }
63      }
64 }
```

Running the Solution for the MySQL Database

Here's how to run the solution for the MySQL database:

```
$ javac DemoScrollableResultSet.java
$ java DemoScrollableResultSet  mysql
--DemoScrollableResultSet begin--
conn=com.mysql.jdbc.Connection@19616c7
---------------
id=11  name=Alex Smith
id=22  name=Don Knuth
id=33  name=Mary Kent
id=44  name=Monica Seles
---------------
id=44  name=Monica Seles
id=33  name=Mary Kent
id=22  name=Don Knuth
id=11  name=Alex Smith
---------------
--DemoScrollableResultSet end--
```

6-2. How Do You Determine If a Database Supports Scrollable ResultSets?

A scrollable ResultSet object allows the cursor to be moved to any row in the ResultSet. You can use DatabaseMetaData to determine if a database supports scrollable ResultSet objects.

The following snippet shows how to check whether scrollable ResultSet objects are supported:

```
Connection conn = null;
DatabaseMetaData dbmd = null;
try {
    // assume getConnection() returns a Connection object
    conn = getConnection();
    dbmd = conn.getMetaData();
    if (dbmd == null) {
        // database metadata not supported
        // cannot determine scrollability using DatabaseMetaData
    }
    else {
        if (dbmd.supportsResultSetType(ResultSet.TYPE_SCROLL_INSENSITIVE)) {
            // insensitive scrollable result sets are supported
        }
        if (dbmd.supportsResultSetType(ResultSet.TYPE_SCROLL_SENSITIVE)) {
            // sensitive scrollable result sets are supported
        }
        if (!dbmd.supportsResultSetType(ResultSet.TYPE_SCROLL_INSENSITIVE) &&
            !dbmd.supportsResultSetType(ResultSet.TYPE_SCROLL_SENSITIVE)) {


        }
    }
}
catch (SQLException e) {
    // handle the exception
}
finally {
    // close database resources such as Connection object ...
}
```

6-3. How Do You Create a Scrollable ResultSet?

A scrollable ResultSet object allows the cursor to be moved to any row in the ResultSet.

If a JDBC driver supports ResultSet scrollability, then you can use the JDBC API to create a scrollable ResultSet object. The java.sql.Connection interface has the following methods for creating scrollable ResultSet objects (for details, refer to the JDK documentation):

```
Statement createStatement(int resultSetType,
                          int resultSetConcurrency)
    // Creates a Statement object that will generate ResultSet
    // objects with the given type and concurrency.

Statement createStatement(int resultSetType,
                          int resultSetConcurrency,
                          int resultSetHoldability)
    // Creates a Statement object that will generate ResultSet
    // objects with the given type, concurrency, and holdability.
```

```
PreparedStatement prepareStatement(String sql,
                              int resultSetType,
                              int resultSetConcurrency)
   // Creates a PreparedStatement object that will generate
   // ResultSet objects with the given type and concurrency.

PreparedStatement prepareStatement(String sql,
                              int resultSetType,
                              int resultSetConcurrency,
                              int resultSetHoldability)
   // Creates a PreparedStatement object that will generate
   // ResultSet objects with the given type, concurrency, and holdability.

CallableStatement prepareCall(String sql,
                              int resultSetType,
                              int resultSetConcurrency)
   // Creates a CallableStatement object that will generate
   // ResultSet objects with the given type and concurrency.

CallableStatement prepareCall(String sql,
                              int resultSetType,
                              int resultSetConcurrency,
                              int resultSetHoldability)
   // Creates a CallableStatement object that will generate
   // ResultSet objects with the given type and concurrency.
```

The following shows how to create an insensitive scrollable ResultSet:

```
ResultSet rs = null;
Statement stmt = null;
Connection conn = null;
try {
   // get a Connection object
   conn = getConnection();

   // Create an insensitive scrollable result set
   stmt = connection.createStatement(
      ResultSet.TYPE_SCROLL_INSENSITIVE,
      ResultSet.CONCUR_READ_ONLY);

   // Create the desired scrollable ResultSet object
   String query = "select id, name from employees";
   rs = stmt.executeQuery(query);
}
catch (SQLException e) {
   // handle the exception
}
finally {
   // close resources: ResultSet, Statement, and Connection objects
}
```

Usage: Creating a Sensitive Scrollable ResultSet

The following shows how to create a sensitive scrollable ResultSet:

```
ResultSet rs = null;
Statement stmt = null;
Connection conn = null;
try {
    conn = getConnection(); // get a Connection object

    // Create a sensitive scrollable result set
    stmt = connection.createStatement(
        ResultSet.TYPE_SCROLL_SENSITIVE,
        ResultSet.CONCUR_READ_ONLY);

    // Create the desired scrollable ResultSet object
    String query = "select id, name from employees";
    rs = stmt.executeQuery(query);
}
catch (SQLException e) {
    // handle the exception
}
finally {
    // close resources: ResultSet, Statement, and Connection objects
}
```

6-4. How Do You Determine If a ResultSet Is Scrollable?

Given a ResultSet object, how do you determine whether that ResultSet is scrollable? By using the ResultSet object's getType() method, you can answer this question:

```
if (rs == null) {
    return false;
}

try {
    // get type of the result set
    int type = rs.getType();

    if ((type == ResultSet.TYPE_SCROLL_INSENSITIVE) ||
        (type == ResultSet.TYPE_SCROLL_SENSITIVE)) {
        // Result set is scrollable
        return true;
    }
    else {
        // Result set is not scrollable
        return false;
    }
}
catch (SQLException e) {
    return false;
}
}
```

6-5. How Do You Move the Cursor in a Scrollable ResultSet?

A scrollable ResultSet object has a set of specific methods for moving cursors. Table 6-1 lists the record scrolling methods (for details, see the JDK documentation).

Table 6-1. ResultSet *Object's Scrolling Methods*

Method	Semantics
first()	Moves to the first record
last()	Moves to the last record
next()	Moves to the next record
previous()	Moves to the previous record
beforeFirst()	Moves to immediately before the first record
afterLast()	Moves to immediately after the last record
absolute(int)	Moves to an absolute row number, and takes a positive or negative argument
relative(int)	Moves backward or forward a specified number of rows, and takes a positive or negative argument

The following example demonstrates various methods for moving the cursor in a scrollable ResultSet object:

```
import java.sql.*;
import jcb.util.DatabaseUtil;

ResultSet rs = null;
Statement stmt = null;
Connection conn = null;


    conn = getConnection();

    // Create a scrollable result set
    stmt = connection.createStatement(
        ResultSet.TYPE_SCROLL_INSENSITIVE,
        ResultSet.CONCUR_READ_ONLY);

    // create your desired SQL query
    String query = ""SELECT id, name FROM employees";

    // create scrollable ResultSet object
    rs = stmt.executeQuery(query);

    // Move cursor forward
    while (rs.next()) {
        // Get data at cursor
        String id = rs.getString(1);
        String name = rs.getString(2);
    }

    // Move cursor backward
    while (rs.previous()) {
        // Get data at cursor
        String id = rs.getString(1);
        String name = rs.getString(2);
    }

    // Move cursor to the first row
    rs.first();
```

```
    // Move cursor to the last row
    rs.last();

    // Move cursor to the end, after the last row
    rs.afterLast();

    // Move cursor to the beginning, before the first row.
    // cursor position is 0.
    rs.beforeFirst();

    // Move cursor to the second row
    rs.absolute(2);

    // Move cursor to the last row
    rs.absolute(-1);

    // Move cursor to the second-to-last row
    rs.absolute(-2);

    // Move cursor down 5 rows from the current row. If this moves
    // cursor beyond the last row, cursor is put after the last row
    rs.relative(5);

    // Move cursor up 3 rows from the current row. If this moves
    // cursor beyond the first row, cursor is put before the first row
    rs.relative(-3);


    // handle the exception
}
finally {
    // close database resources
    DatabaseUtil.close(rs);
    DatabaseUtil.close(stmt);
    DatabaseUtil.close(conn);
}
```

6-6. How Do You Get the Cursor Position in a Scrollable Result Set?

The following code shows how to get the cursor position in a given scrollable ResultSet object:

```
import java.sql.*;
import jcb.util.Databaseutil;
...
Connection conn = null;
Statement stmt = null;
ResultSet rs = null;
try {
    get a Connection object
    conn = getConnection();
    // Create a scrollable result set
    stmt = connection.createStatement(
        ResultSet.TYPE_SCROLL_INSENSITIVE,
        ResultSet.CONCUR_READ_ONLY);
    rs = stmt.executeQuery("SELECT * FROM my_table");
```

```
    // Get cursor position
    int pos = rs.getRow();              // 0
    boolean b = rs.isBeforeFirst();     // true

    // Move cursor to the first row
    rs.next();

    // Get cursor position
    pos = rs.getRow();                  // 1
    b = rs.isFirst();                   // true

    // Move cursor to the last row
    rs.last();
    // Get cursor position
    pos = rs.getRow();   // If table has 10 rows, value would be 10
    b = rs.isLast();     // true

    // Move cursor past last row
    rs.afterLast();

    // Get cursor position
    pos = rs.getRow();       // If table has 10 rows, value would be 11
    b = rs.isAfterLast();    // true
}
catch (SQLException e) {
    // handle exception


    DatabaseUtil.close(rs);
    DatabaseUtil.close(stmt);
    DatabaseUtil.close(conn);
}
```

6-7. How Do You Get the Number of Rows in a Table Using a Scrollable ResultSet?

The following example gets the number of rows in a scrollable ResultSet object by moving the cursor to the last row of the ResultSet object and then calling the ResultSet.getRow() method. In general, this method is not a proper way of finding the number of rows; you should use SQL query select count(*) from <table-name> for finding the number of rows in a given table. This example demonstrates the flexibility of scrollable ResultSet objects.

```
ResultSet rs = null;
Statement stmt = null;
Connection conn = null;
try {
    // get a Connection object
    conn = getConnection();

    // create a scrollable ResultSet object
    String query = "select id from employees";

    stmt = connection.createStatement(
        ResultSet.TYPE_SCROLL_INSENSITIVE, ResultSet.CONCUR_READ_ONLY);

    rs = stmt.executeQuery(query);
```

```
    // move to the end of the result set
    rs.last();

    // get the row number of the last row, which is also the row count
    int rowCount = rs.getRow();

    // now you may move the cursor to the front of this ResultSet object,
    // just before the first row
    rs.beforeFirst();
}
catch (SQLException e) {
    // handle the exception
}
finally {
    // close database resources
}
```

I have provided a complete solution, the GetNumberOfRowsScrollableResultSet class, for getting the number of rows from a scrollable ResultSet object; you can download GetNumberOfRowsScrollableResultSet from this book's Web site. To save space, here I will show only how the solution works:

```
$ javac GetNumberOfRowsScrollableResultSet_MySQL.java
$ java GetNumberOfRowsScrollableResultSet_MySQL
------GetNumberOfRowsScrollableResultSet_MySQL begin---------
conn=com.mysql.jdbc.Connection@19616c7
---------------


id=77
id=88
---------------
rowCount=4
------GetNumberOfRowsScrollableResultSet_MySQL end---------
```

6-8. How Do You Determine If a Database Supports Updatable ResultSets?

An updatable ResultSet object allows you to modify data in a table by using the ResultSet methods rather than by sending SQL queries to the database server.

You can use the following snippet to determine if your database supports an updatable ResultSet:

```
import java.sql.*;
import jcb.util.Databaseutil;
...
Connection conn = null;
try {
    get a Connection object
    conn = getConnection();

    DatabaseMetaData dbmd = conn.getMetaData();
    if (dbmd == null) {
        // impossible to make a decision
        // because metadata is not supported
        throw new Exception("DatabaseMetaData not supported");
    }
```

```
        if (dbmd.supportsResultSetConcurrency(ResultSet.TYPE_FORWARD_ONLY,
                                        ResultSet.CONCUR_UPDATABLE)) {
            // Updatable ResultSets are supported
        }
        else {
            // Updatable ResultSets are not supported
        }
    }
}
catch (SQLException e) {
    // handle the exception
}
finally {
    DatabaseUtil.close(conn);
}
```

6-9. How Do You Create an Updatable ResultSet?

An updatable ResultSet object allows you to modify data in a table through the ResultSet.

If the database does not support updatable ResultSet objects, the result sets returned from executeQuery() will be read-only. To get updatable results, the Statement object used to create the result sets must have the concurrency type ResultSet.CONCUR_UPDATABLE. The query of an updatable result set must specify the primary key as one of the selected columns and select from only one table. For some JDBC drivers, the SQL query SELECT * FROM my_table will return a read-only result set, so make sure you specify the column names.

```
import java.sql.*;

...
Connection conn = null;
Statement stmt = null;
ResultSet rs = null;
try {
    conn = getConnection();
    // create a statement that will return
    // updatable result sets
    stmt = conn.createStatement(
            ResultSet.TYPE_SCROLL_SENSITIVE,
            ResultSet.CONCUR_UPDATABLE);
    // Primary key pk_column must be specified
    // so that the result set is updatable
    rs = stmt.executeQuery("SELECT pk_column FROM my_table");
}
catch (SQLException e) {
    // handle exception
}
finally {
    DatabaseUtil.close(rs);
    DatabaseUtil.close(stmt);
    DatabaseUtil.close(conn);
}
```

6-10. How Do You Determine If a ResultSet Is Updatable?

Given a ResultSet object, how do you determine if it is updatable? Using the ResultSet.getConcurrency() method, you can determine the updatability of a given ResultSet object:

```java
import java.sql.*;
import jcb.util.Databaseutil;
...
Connection conn = null;
Statement stmt = null;
ResultSet rs = null;
try {
    // get a Connection object
    conn = getConnection();

    String query = "select id from employees";

    // ...parameters here enable/disable ResultSet updatability...
    stmt = conn.createStatement(...parameters);

    // create a ResultSet object
    rs = stmt.executeQuery(query);

    // get concurrency of the ResultSet object
    int concurrency = resultSet.getConcurrency();

    if (concurrency == ResultSet.CONCUR_UPDATABLE) {
        // ResultSet is updatable
    }
    else {
        // ResultSet is not updatable

}
catch (SQLException e) {
    // handle the exception
}
finally {
    DatabaseUtil.close(rs);
    DatabaseUtil.close(stmt);
    DatabaseUtil.close(conn);
}
```

6-11. How Do You Update a Row in a Database Table Using an Updatable Result Set?

Updating the current row of an updatable result set involves calling the ResultSet.updateXXX() methods followed by a call to updateRow():

```java
import java.sql.*;
import jcb.util.Databaseutil;
...
Connection conn = null;
Statement stmt = null;
ResultSet rs = null;
try {
    // get a Connection object
    conn = getConnection();

    // Create an updatable result set
    stmt = conn.createStatement(
        ResultSet.TYPE_SCROLL_SENSITIVE,
        ResultSet.CONCUR_UPDATABLE);
```

```
        rs = stmt.executeQuery("SELECT * FROM my_table");

        // Move cursor to the row to update
        rs.first();

        // Update the value of column column_1 on that row
        rs.updateString("column_1", "new data");

        // Update the row; if autocommit is enabled,
        // update is committed
        rs.updateRow();
    }
    catch (SQLException e) {
        // handle exception
    }
    finally {
        DatabaseUtil.close(rs);
        DatabaseUtil.close(stmt);
        DatabaseUtil.close(conn);
    }
```

6-12. How Do You Cancel Updates to an Updatable ResultSet?

You can cancel the effects of calling the Result.updateXXX() methods by calling cancelRowUpdates().
Please note that you cannot cancel updates after you have called updateRow().

```
    ...
    Connection conn = null;
    Statement stmt = null;
    ResultSet rs = null;
    try {
        // get a Connection object
        conn = getConnection();

        // Create an updatable result set
        stmt = conn.createStatement(
            ResultSet.TYPE_SCROLL_SENSITIVE,
            ResultSet.CONCUR_UPDATABLE);

        rs = stmt.executeQuery("SELECT * FROM my_table");

        // Move cursor to the row to update
        rs.first();

        // Update the value of column column_1 on that row
        rs.updateString("column_1", "new data");

        // Discard the update to the row
        rs.cancelRowUpdates();
    }
    catch (SQLException e) {
        // handle exception
    }
```

```
finally {
    DatabaseUtil.close(rs);
    DatabaseUtil.close(stmt);
    DatabaseUtil.close(conn);
}
```

6-13. How Do You Insert a Row into a Database Table Using an Updatable ResultSet?

An updatable ResultSet object supports a specific row called the *insert row*. It is a buffer for holding the values of a new row. After you have filled the fields in the insert row, you can insert the new row into the database using the Result.insertRow() method.

How It Works

The following snippet shows how to insert a new row into a table using an updatable ResultSet object:

```
import java.sql.*;
import jcb.util.Databaseutil;
...
Connection conn = null;
Statement stmt = null;
ResultSet rs = null;
try {
    // get a Connection object


    // Create an updatable result set
    stmt = conn.createStatement(
        ResultSet.TYPE_SCROLL_SENSITIVE,
        ResultSet.CONCUR_UPDATABLE);

    String query = "select id, name from employees";

    // Create the desired ResultSet object
    rs = stmt.executeQuery(query);

    // Move cursor to the "insert row"
    rs.moveToInsertRow();

    // Set values for the new row.
    rs.updateString("id", "66");
    rs.updateString("name", "Harrison Ford");

    // Insert the row
    rs.insertRow();
}
catch (SQLException e) {
    // handle exception
}
finally {
    DatabaseUtil.close(rs);
    DatabaseUtil.close(stmt);
    DatabaseUtil.close(conn);
}
```

Solution

Here is the solution:

```
1  import java.sql.*;
2
3  import jcb.util.DatabaseUtil;
4  import jcb.db.VeryBasicConnectionManager;
5
6  public class InsertRowUpdatableResultSet {
7
8      public static void main(String[] args) {
9          Connection conn = null;
10         Statement stmt = null;
11         ResultSet rs = null;
12         try {
13             String dbVendor = args[0];  // vendor = {"mysql", "oracle" }
14             System.out.println("--InsertRowUpdatableResultSet begin--");
15             conn = VeryBasicConnectionManager.getConnection(dbVendor);
16             System.out.println("conn="+conn);
17
18             // prepare query
19             String query = "select id, name from employees";
20
21             // create a statement
22             stmt = conn.createStatement(ResultSet.TYPE_SCROLL_SENSITIVE,
23                                         ResultSet.CONCUR_UPDATABLE);
24
26
27             // extract data from the ResultSet
28             // scroll from top
29             while (rs.next()) {
30                 String id = rs.getString(1);
31                 String name = rs.getString(2);
32                 System.out.println("id=" + id + "  name=" + name);
33             }
34             System.out.println("=======");
35
36             //  Move cursor to the "insert row"
37             rs.moveToInsertRow();
38
39             // Set values for the new row.
40             rs.updateString("id", args[1]);
41             rs.updateString("name", args[2]);
42
43             // Insert the new row
44             rs.insertRow();
45
46             // scroll from the top again
47             rs.beforeFirst();
48             while (rs.next()) {
49                 String id = rs.getString(1);
50                 String name = rs.getString(2);
51                 System.out.println("id=" + id + "  name=" + name);
52             }
53             System.out.println("--InsertRowUpdatableResultSet end--");
54         }
```

```
55          catch(Exception e){
56              e.printStackTrace();
57              System.exit(1);
58          }
59          finally {
60              // release database resources
61              DatabaseUtil.close(rs);
62              DatabaseUtil.close(stmt);
63              DatabaseUtil.close(conn);
64          }
65      }
66 }
```

Discussing the Solution

The following explains the solution:

- *Lines 1–4*: Import the required classes and interfaces.

- *Line 15*: The VeryBasicConnectionManager.getConnection() method returns an instance of a Connection object. You may alter this method to pool your connections for real-world applications.

- *Lines 22–23*: Create a Statement object, which will enable you to create an updatable and scrollable ResultSet object.

- *Lines 25–33*: Create an updatable and scrollable ResultSet object, and then iterate all the rows.

- *Lines 40–41*: Set values for the new row.

- *Line 44*: Insert the new row.

- *Lines 47–52*: Move the cursor to the first row, and then iterate all the rows again.

- *Lines 59–64*: Release database resources.

MySQL Database Before Running the Solution

This is the MySQL database before running the solution:

```
mysql> select * from employees;
+----+--------------+------+
| id | name         | age  |
+----+--------------+------+
| 11 | Alex Smith   |   25 |
| 22 | Don Knuth    |   65 |
| 33 | Mary Kent    |   35 |
| 44 | Monica Seles |   30 |
| 99 | Alex Edison  | NULL |
+----+--------------+------+
5 rows in set (0.01 sec)
```

Running the Solution for the MySQL Database

This is the solution for the MySQL database:

```
$ javac InsertRowUpdatableResultSet.java
$ java InsertRowUpdatableResultSet mysql 777 "Donald Duck"
```

```
--InsertRowUpdatableResultSet begin--
conn=com.mysql.jdbc.Connection@1c6f579
id=11   name=Alex Smith
id=22   name=Don Knuth
id=33   name=Mary Kent
id=44   name=Monica Seles
id=99   name=Alex Edison
=======
id=11   name=Alex Smith
id=22   name=Don Knuth
id=33   name=Mary Kent
id=44   name=Monica Seles
id=99   name=Alex Edison
id=777  name=Donald Duck
--InsertRowUpdatableResultSet end--
```

MySQL Database After Running the Solution

This is the MySQL database after running the solution:

```
mysql> select * from employees;
+-----+--------------+------+
| id  | name         | age  |
+-----+--------------+------+
| 11  | Alex Smith   |   25 |
| 22  | Don Knuth    |   65 |



| 99  | Alex Edison  | NULL |
+-----+--------------+------+
6 rows in set (0.00 sec)
```

Oracle Database Before Running the Solution

This is the Oracle database before running the solution:

```
SQL> select * from employees;
ID          NAME                   AGE
----------  --------------------  ----------
11          Alex Smith             25
22          Don Knuth              65
33          Mary Kent              35
44          Monica Seles           30
99          Alex Edison
```

Running the Solution for the Oracle Database

This shows how to run the solution for the Oracle database:

```
$ java InsertRowUpdatableResultSet oracle 777 "Donald Duck"
--InsertRowUpdatableResultSet begin--
conn=oracle.jdbc.driver.T4CConnection@2ce908
id=11   name=Alex Smith
id=22   name=Don Knuth
id=33   name=Mary Kent
id=44   name=Monica Seles
id=99   name=Alex Edison
```

```
=======
id=11   name=Alex Smith
id=22   name=Don Knuth
id=33   name=Mary Kent
id=44   name=Monica Seles
id=99   name=Alex Edison
--InsertRowUpdatableResultSet end--
```

Oracle Database After Running the Solution

This is the Oracle database after running the solution:

```
SQL> select * from employees;
ID          NAME                      AGE
----------  --------------------  ----------
777         Donald Duck
11          Alex Smith                 25
22          Don Knuth                  65
33          Mary Kent                  35
44          Monica Seles               30
99          Alex Edison

6 rows selected.
```

6-14. How Do You Delete a Row from a Database Table Using an

To delete your desired row from a ResultSet object, create a scrollable and updatable ResultSet object, then point to your desired row, and finally invoke the deleteRow() method.

How It Works

The following snippet demonstrates the required steps for deleting a row:

```java
import java.sql.*;
import jcb.util.Databaseutil;
...
Connection conn = null;
Statement stmt = null;
ResultSet rs = null;
try {
    // get a Connection object
    conn = getConnection();

    // Create an updatable result set
    String query = "select id, name from employees";
    stmt = conn.createStatement(
        ResultSet.TYPE_SCROLL_SENSITIVE,
        ResultSet.CONCUR_UPDATABLE);

    rs = stmt.executeQuery(query);

    // Delete the first row
    rs.first();
    rs.deleteRow();
}
```

```
catch (SQLException e) {
    // handle exception
}
finally {
    DatabaseUtil.close(rs);
    DatabaseUtil.close(stmt);
    DatabaseUtil.close(conn);
}
```

Usage: The Database Before Running the Test Program

This is the database before running the test program:

```
mysql> use octopus;
Database changed
mysql> select * from employees;
+----+--------------+------+
| id | name         | age  |
+----+--------------+------+
| 11 | Alex Smith   |  45  |
| 22 | Don Knuth    |  65  |
| 33 | Mary Kent    |  35  |
| 44 | Monica Seles |  30  |
+----+--------------+------+
4 rows in set (0.00 sec)
```

The following is the script for running the test program (first run):

```
$ javac DeleteRowUpdatableResultSet_MySQL.java
$ java DeleteRowUpdatableResultSet_MySQL
------DeleteRowUpdatableResultSet_MySQL begin---------
conn=com.mysql.jdbc.Connection@19616c7
---------------
id=11   name=Alex Smith
id=22   name=Don Knuth
id=33   name=Mary Kent
id=44   name=Monica Seles
---------------
id=22   name=Don Knuth
id=33   name=Mary Kent
id=44   name=Monica Seles
---------------
------DeleteRowUpdatableResultSet_MySQL end---------
```

Usage: The Database After the First Run

This is the database after the first run:

```
mysql> use octopus;
Database changed
mysql> select * from employees;
```

```
+----+--------------+------+
| id | name         | age  |
+----+--------------+------+
| 22 | Don Knuth    |   65 |
| 33 | Mary Kent    |   35 |
| 44 | Monica Seles |   30 |
+----+--------------+------+
3 rows in set (0.00 sec)

mysql>
```

The Script: Test Program, Second Run

This is how to run the text program for a second time:

```
$ java DeleteRowUpdatableResultSet_MySQL
------DeleteRowUpdatableResultSet_MySQL begin---------
conn=com.mysql.jdbc.Connection@19616c7
---------------
id=22   name=Don Knuth
id=33   name=Mary Kent
id=44   name=Monica Seles
---------------
id=33   name=Mary Kent
id=44   name=Monica Seles
---------------
```

Usage: The Database After the Second Run

This is the database after the second run:

```
mysql> select * from employees;
+----+--------------+------+
| id | name         | age  |
+----+--------------+------+
| 33 | Mary Kent    |   35 |
| 44 | Monica Seles |   30 |
+----+--------------+------+
2 rows in set (0.00 sec)

mysql>
```

Discussing the Solution

The following explains the solution:

- *Lines 1–6*: Import the required classes and interfaces.

- *Lines 10–18*: The getConnection() method returns an instance of a Connection object. You can alter this method to pool your connections for real-world applications.

- *Lines 21–29*: Create a Connection object.

- *Lines 34–40*: Create a Statement object, which will enable you to create an updatable and scrollable ResultSet object.

- *Lines 45–56*: Create an updatable and scrollable ResultSet object, and then iterate all the rows.

- *Lines 61–62*: Point at the first row of the ResultSet object, and then delete it using the deleteRow() method.

- *Lines 67–72*: Move the cursor to the first row, and then iterate all the rows again.

- *Lines 81–86*: Release the database resources.

6-15. How Do You Refresh a Row in an Updatable ResultSet?

The following code shows how to refresh a row in an updatable ResultSet object. ResultSet.refreshRow() does the job. This method refreshes the current row with its most recent value in the database:

```
import java.sql.*;
import jcb.util.Databaseutil;
...
Connection conn = null;
Statement stmt = null;
ResultSet rs = null;
try {
    // get a Connection object
    conn = getConnection();

    // Create an updatable result set
    stmt = conn.createStatement(
        ResultSet.TYPE_SCROLL_SENSITIVE,
        ResultSet.CONCUR_UPDATABLE);



    // Use the result set...

    // Retrieve the current values of the row from the database
    rs.refreshRow();
}
catch (SQLException e) {
    // handle exception
}
finally {
    DatabaseUtil.close(rs);
    DatabaseUtil.close(stmt);
    DatabaseUtil.close(conn);
}
```

■■■

Reading and Writing BLOBs

This chapter shows how to use JDBC's rich data type BLOB. The BLOB type stores/retrieves large binary objects such as PDF files, video clips, JPEG/GIF pictures, and Microsoft Word documents. Today's databases (such as Oracle and MySQL) easily handle BLOBs.

This chapter's focus will be on the following topics:

- How to insert/write a BLOB into a database

- How to retrieve/read a BLOB from a database

- How to update an existing BLOB in a database

- How to delete an existing BLOB in a database

resented as a column object in a database record/row). Database vendors (such as Oracle, MySQL, DB2, and so on) implement BLOBs in different ways, but as long as you use the common interface java.sql.Blob, you should not care about their internal implementations. BLOBs can be large, up to 2GB or more, depending on the database. In general, BLOBs are typically larger than a single block of storage in your database (which might cause performance problems). You should use BLOBs with care and, whenever possible, try to use caching algorithms to improve the overall performance of database applications.

To summarize, a BLOB is any arbitrarily large piece of data that can be treated as autonomous. The JDBC type BLOB represents a SQL3 BLOB. Typically, a JDBC BLOB value is mapped to an instance of the java.sql.Blob interface in the Java programming language. If a driver follows the standard implementation, a Blob object logically points to the BLOB value on the server rather than containing its binary data, greatly improving efficiency. The java.sql.Blob interface provides methods for materializing the BLOB data on the client when that is desired.

Describing the java.sql.Blob Interface

JDBC provides a single interface (java.sql.Blob) for handling large binary objects. According to JDK 1.4.2, java.sql.Blob is defined as follows:

The representation (mapping) in the Java programming language of an SQL BLOB value. An SQL BLOB is a built-in type that stores a Binary Large Object as a column value in a row of a database table. By default drivers implement Blob using an SQL locator (BLOB), which means that a Blob object contains a logical pointer to the SQL BLOB data rather than the data itself. A Blob object is valid for the duration of the transaction in which it was created.

Methods in the interfaces ResultSet, CallableStatement, and PreparedStatement, such as getBlob and setBlob allow a programmer to access an SQL BLOB value. The Blob interface provides methods for getting the length of an SQL BLOB (Binary Large Object) value, for materializing a BLOB value on the client, and for determining the position of a pattern of bytes within a BLOB value. In addition, this interface has methods for updating a BLOB value.

Describing the java.sql.Blob Interface Methods

Table 7-1 lists the java.sql.Blob interface methods (according to JDK 1.4.2).

Table 7-1. *The* java.sql.Blob *Interface Methods*

Return Type	Method	Description
InputStream	getBinaryStream()	Retrieves the BLOB value designated by this Blob instance as a stream
byte[]	getBytes(long pos, int length)	Retrieves all or part of the BLOB value
long	length()	Returns the number of bytes in the BLOB value designated by this Blob object
long	position(Blob pattern, long stat)	Retrieves the byte position in the BLOB value designated by this Blob object at which pattern begins
long	position(byte[] pattern, long start)	Retrieves the byte position at which the specified byte array pattern begins within the BLOB value that this Blob object represents
OutputStream	setBinaryStream(long pos)	Retrieves a stream that can be used to write to the BLOB value that this Blob object represents
int	setBytes(long pos, byte[] bytes)	Writes the given array of bytes to the BLOB value that this Blob object represents, starting at position pos, and returns the number of bytes written
int	setBytes(long pos, byte[] bytes, int offset, int len)	Writes all or part of the given byte array to the BLOB value that this Blob object represents and returns the number of bytes written
void	truncate(long len)	Truncates the BLOB value that this Blob object represents to be len bytes in length

Oracle BLOBs

Oracle has only one type (called BLOB) to support the SQL BLOB data type. The oracle.sql.BLOB class implements the java.sql.Blob interface. Oracle also supports a proprietary BFILE (binary file) data type, implemented by the oracle.sql.BFILE class. (Using BFILE, the binary file is stored as an operating system file, and the reference to that file is kept at the database level.) BFILE is not defined in JDBC but can be accessed by Oracle and JDBC APIs.

MySQL BLOBs

MySQL has four kinds of BLOBs (the JDBC calls are the same for these four types):

- TINYBLOB: A binary object that is stored with its length. This cannot be a key. The maximum length is 255 characters (8 bits).

- BLOB: A binary object that is stored with its length. This cannot be a key. The maximum length is 16,535 characters (16 bits).

- MEDIUMBLOB: A binary object that is stored with its length. This cannot be a key. The maximum length is 16,777,216 characters (24 bits).

- LONGBLOB: A binary object that is stored with its length. This cannot be a key. The range is 4,294,967,295 characters (32 bits).

7-2. How Do You Define a BLOB Data Type in a Table?

Defining the Table: Oracle and MySql

This code defines the table:

```
create table MyPictures (
    id INT PRIMARY KEY,
    name VARCHAR(20),
    photo BLOB
);
```

Creating the Table: Oracle

This code creates a table based on Oracle:

```
$ sqlplus octopus/octopus
SQL*Plus: Release 8.1.7.0.0 - Production on Fri Jun 7 13:37:25 2002

SQL>            create table MyPictures (
  2                         id INT PRIMARY KEY,
  3                         name VARCHAR(20),
  4                         photo BLOB
  5             );

Table created.

SQL> describe MyPictures;
```

Name	Null?	Type
ID	NOT NULL	NUMBER(38)
NAME		VARCHAR2(20)
PHOTO		BLOB

Creating the Table: MySQL

This code creates a table based on MySQL:

```
mysql> use octopus;
Database changed
mysql>          create table MyPictures (
    ->                 id INT PRIMARY KEY,
    ->                 name VARCHAR(20),
    ->                 photo BLOB
    ->          );
Query OK, 0 rows affected (0.04 sec)

mysql> describe MyPictures;
+-----------+-------------+------+-----+---------+-------+
| Field     | Type        | Null | Key | Default | Extra |
+-----------+-------------+------+-----+---------+-------+
| id        | int(11)     |      | PRI | 0       |       |
| name      | varchar(20) | YES  |     | NULL    |       |
| photo     | blob        | YES  |     | NULL    |       |
```

7-3. What Are the Restrictions for Using BLOBs?

Every vendor has some restrictions on using the BLOB data type. Typical restrictions for BLOBs are as follows:

- BLOB columns cannot be keys (primary or foreign).
- You cannot group or sort on a BLOB.

7-4. How Do You Create a java.sql.Blob Object?

You can create a java.sql.Blob object in only one way, and that is by using a ResultSet object's methods. Consider the MyPictures table defined earlier (using a MySql or Oracle database):

```
create table MyPictures (
    id INT PRIMARY KEY,
    name VARCHAR(20),
    photo BLOB
);
```

The ResultSet interface has two methods for creating a java.sql.Blob object:

- getBlob(int columnPosition)
- getBlob(String columnName)

In the following code listings, I will show how to create a java.sql.Blob object by using the overloaded getBlob() methods.

ResultSet.getBlob(int position)

The following shows ResultSet.getBlob(int position):

```
Connection conn = <get-a-valid-connection-object>
Statement stmt = conn.createStatement();
ResultSet rs = stmt.executeQuery("select photo from MyPictures");
while (rs.next()) {
   Blob blob = rs.getBlob(1);
   // now the Blob object is created and you can apply
   // methods defined in the java.sql.Blob interface
   ...
}
```

ResultSet.getBlob(String columnName)

The following shows ResultSet.getBlob(String columnName):

```
Connection conn = <get-a-valid-connection-object>
Statement stmt = conn.createStatement();
ResultSet rs = stmt.executeQuery("select photo from MyPictures");
while (rs.next()) {
   Blob blob = rs.getBlob("photo");
   // now the Blob object is created and you can apply
   // methods defined in the java.sql.Blob interface
   ...
}
```

7-5. How Do You Materialize BLOB Data?

A SQL BLOB maps into a java.sql.Blob object. If you want to operate on the BLOB data, you must first materialize it on the client. The java.sql.Blob interface has two methods for materializing the BLOB data:

- getBinaryStream(): Materializes the BLOB value as an input stream (java.io.InputStream)

- getBytes(): Materializes part or all of the BLOB as an array of bytes

Materializing a BLOB Value As an Input Stream (java.io.InputStream)

This shows how to materialize the BLOB value as an input stream:

```
//
// prints out all bytes in the BLOB
//
byte b;
java.sql.Blob blob = <a-valid-blob>
java.io.InputStream input = blob.getBinaryStream();
while ((b = input.read()) > -1) {
   // process the byte
   System.out.println(b);
}
```

Materializing a BLOB As an Array of Bytes

This shows how to materialize the BLOB as an array of bytes:

```
//
// prints out all bytes in the BLOB
//
long length;
java.sql.Blob blob = <a-valid-blob>
// note that the first byte is at position 1
byte[] blobData = blob.getBytes(1, length);
for (int i=0; i < length; i++) {
    // process the byte
    System.out.println(blobData[i]);
}
```

7-6. How Do You Insert a New Record with a BLOB?

Now that the MyPictures table (which includes a BLOB column) is defined, you should be able to use JDBC to insert new records (which will contain a photo as a BLOB data type). Suppose you want to insert the following data:

id	name	photo filename
1	n1	c:/temp/kournikova/zanna1.jpg
2	n2	c:/temp/kournikova/zanna2.jpg
3	n3	c:/temp/kournikova/zanna3.jpg
4	n4	c:/temp/kournikova/zanna4.jpg
5	n5	c:/temp/kournikova/zanna5.jpg

Your goal is to write a program that will accept an ID, name, and photo (as a filename) and

```
java InsertPictureToMySql <id> <name> <photo>
java InsertPictureToOracle <id> <name> <photo>
```

Therefore, you need to develop two classes (InsertPictureToMySql.java and InsertPictureToOracle.java). To insert the first three records into a MySQL database, execute the following:

```
java InsertPictureToMySql 1  n1 c:/temp/kournikova/zanna1.jpg
java InsertPictureToMySql 2  n2 c:/temp/kournikova/zanna2.jpg
java InsertPictureToMySql 3  n3 c:/temp/kournikova/zanna3.jpg
```

To insert the first three records into an Oracle 9*i* database, execute the following:

```
java InsertPictureToOracle 1  n1 c:/temp/kournikova/zanna1.jpg
java InsertPictureToOracle 2  n2 c:/temp/kournikova/zanna2.jpg
java InsertPictureToOracle 3  n3 c:/temp/kournikova/zanna3.jpg
```

Solution Using MySQL: InsertPictureToMySql.java

Here's the InsertPictureToMySql.java solution:

```
import java.io.*;
import java.sql.*;
import jcb.util.DatabaseUtil;
public class InsertPictureToMySql {
    String INSERT_PICTURE =
      "insert into MyPictures(id, name, photo) values (?, ?, ?)";
    Connection conn = null;

    /**
     * constructor
```

```
    */
    public InsertPictureToMySql() throws SQLException {
        DriverManager.registerDriver(new org.gjt.mm.mysql.Driver());
        conn = DriverManager.getConnection(
            "jdbc:mysql://localhost/octopus", "root", "root");
    }
    public static void main(String[] args)
        throws Exception, IOException, SQLException {
        if ((args == null) || (args.length != 3)) {
            System.err.println("Usage: java InsertPictureToMySql <id> <name> <photo>");
            System.exit(0);
        }
        String id = DatabaseUtil.trimArgument(args[0]);
        String name = DatabaseUtil.trimArgument(args[1]);
        String photo = DatabaseUtil.trimArgument(args[2]);
        new InsertPictureToMySql().insert(id, name, photo);
    }
    public void insert(String id, String name, String photo)
        throws IOException, SQLException {
        FileInputStream fis  = null;
        PreparedStatement ps = null;
        try {
            // begin transaction
            conn.setAutoCommit(false);

            File file = new File(photo);


            ps.setString(1, id);
            ps.setString(2, name);
            ps.setBinaryStream(3, fis,(int)file.length());
            ps.executeUpdate();

            // end transaction
            conn.commit();
        }
        finally {
            DatabaseUtil.close(ps);
            DatabaseUtil.close(fis);
        }
    }
    protected void finalize() throws Throwable {
        DatabaseUtil.close(conn);
        super.finalize();
    }
}
```

As you can see, the code for the MySQL database is straightforward, but that is not the case with the Oracle database.

Solution Using Oracle: InsertPictureToOracle.java

In Oracle, before you can insert a real BLOB, you need to insert an empty BLOB (called empty_blob() in Oracle). empty_blob() is an Oracle function call that creates an empty Blob object. Therefore, in Oracle, you cannot just insert a Blob object into a column. First, create a column with empty_blob(). Second, update that column with the real Blob object.

Here's the InsertPictureToOracle.java solution:

```java
import java.io.*;
import java.sql.*;
import java.text.*;
import jcb.util.DatabaseUtil;

// add these imports for access to the required Oracle classes
import oracle.jdbc.driver.*;
import oracle.sql.BLOB;

public class InsertPictureToOracle {
    Connection conn;

    public InsertPictureToOracle() throws SQLException {
        DriverManager.registerDriver(new oracle.jdbc.driver.OracleDriver());
        conn = DriverManager.getConnection(
            "jdbc:oracle:thin:@mparsian:1521:scorpian", "octopus", "octopus");
    }

    public static void main(String[] args)
        throws Exception, IOException, SQLException {
        if ((args == null) || (args.length != 3)) {
            System.err.println("Usage: java InsertPictureToOracle <id> <name> <photo>");
            System.exit(0);
        }


        new InsertPictureToOracle().insert(id, name, photo);
    }
    public void insert(String id, String name, String photo)
        throws Exception, IOException, SQLException {
        int             rows        = 0;
        FileInputStream fin         = null;
        OutputStream    out         = null;
        ResultSet       result      = null;
        Statement       stmt        = null;
        oracle.sql.BLOB oracleBlob = null;

        try {
            conn.setAutoCommit(false);
            stmt = conn.createStatement();
            result = stmt.executeQuery("select id from MyPictures where id  = "+ id);
            while (result.next()) {
                rows++;
            }

            if (rows > 1) {
                System.err.println("Too many rows!");
                System.exit(1);
            }

            result.close();
            result = null;
```

```
        if (rows == 0) {
            System.out.println("This creates the LOB locators");
            rows = stmt.executeUpdate("insert into MyPictures "+
                "(id, name, photo ) values ("+id+", ""+ name +"", empty_blob() )");
            System.out.println(rows + " rows inserted");
            // Now retrieve the locator
            rows = 0;
            result = stmt.executeQuery("select photo from  MyPictures "+
                        "where   id = "+id+ " for update nowait");
            result.next();
            oracleBlob = ((OracleResultSet)result).getBLOB(1);
            result.close();
            result = null;
        }
        stmt.close();
        stmt = null;
        // Now that you have the locator, store the photo
        File binaryFile = new File(photo);
        fin = new FileInputStream(binaryFile);
        out = oracleBlob.getBinaryOutputStream();
        // Get the optimal buffer size from the BLOB
        byte[] buffer = new byte[oracleBlob.getBufferSize()];
        int length = 0;
        while ((length = fin.read(buffer)) != -1) {
            out.write(buffer, 0, length);
        }


        out.close();
        out = null;
        fin.close();
        fin = null;
        conn.commit();
    }
    finally {
        DatabaseUti.close(result);
        DatabaseUti.close(stmt);
        DatabaseUti.close(out);
        DatabaseUti.close(fin);
    }
}
protected void finalize() throws Throwable {
    DatabaseUti.close(conn);
    super.finalize();
}
}
}
```

Discussing the InsertPictureToOracle Class: Populating a BLOB Column

Note that handling BLOBs in Oracle is different from handling them in MySQL. The preceding example demonstrated how to populate a BLOB column by reading data from a stream. The following steps assume that you have already created your Connection object (called conn) and Statement object (called stmt). MyPictures is the table that was created in the previous sections.

To write a given JPEG file to a BLOB, follow these steps:

1. Begin by using SQL statements to create the BLOB entry in the table. Use Oracle's empty_blob() function to create the BLOB locator.

```
rows = stmt.executeUpdate("insert into MyPictures (id, name, photo ) "+
        "values ("+id+", ""+ name +"", empty_blob() )");
```

2. Get the BLOB locator from the table.

```
result = stmt.executeQuery(
    "select photo from  MyPictures where  id = "+id+ " for update nowait");
result.next();
oracleBlob = ((OracleResultSet)result).getBLOB(1);
```

3. Declare a file handler for the picture file. This value will be used later to ensure that the entire file is read into the BLOB. Next, create a FileInputStream object to read the contents of the JPEG file and an OutputStream object to retrieve the BLOB as a stream.

```
// Now that you have the locator,
// store the photo
File binaryFile = new File(photo);
fin = new FileInputStream(binaryFile);
out = oracleBlob.getBinaryOutputStream();
```

4. Call getBufferSize() to retrieve the ideal buffer size to use in writing to the BLOB, and then create the buffer byte array.

```
byte[] buffer = new byte[oracleBlob.getBufferSize()];
```

```
while ((length = fin.read(buffer)) != -1) {
    out.write(buffer, 0, length);
}
```

7-7. How Do You Select and Display a BLOB in a JFrame?

The following example demonstrates how to retrieve a BLOB data type from the database. In this case, you will retrieve the photo identified by ID (id is the primary key for the MyPictures table) and display it in its own JFrame. Given that the code is lengthy to accomplish this job, the example is split over several pages. First, you perform a query to select the Blob object of interest (by providing the ID) and pull it back to the client (also known as materializing the Blob object). The rest of the code simply creates a JFrame to hold the retrieved image.

Develop the following class:

```
java BlobSelect <db-vendor-mysql> <id>
java BlobSelect <db-vendor-oracle> <id>
```

The BlobSelect class accepts a database vendor (mysql or oracle) and an ID (the primary key to the MyPictures table) and extracts and displays the desired BLOB in a JFrame.

Extracting BLOBs from MySQL

Figure 7-1 shows the BLOB from MySQL by invoking this:

```
$ BlobSelect mysql 3
```

Figure 7-1. *Displaying the* BLOB *from MySQL*

Extracting BLOBs from Oracle

Figure 7-2 shows the BLOB from Oracle by invoking this:

```
$ java BlobSelect oracle 3
```

Figure 7-2. *Displaying the* BLOB *from Oracle*

Solution: BlobSelect.java

The following shows the BlobSelect.java solution:

```
import javax.swing.*;
import java.awt.*;
import java.awt.event.*;
import java.sql.*;
```

```
import jcb.util.DatabaseUtil;
import jcb.db.VeryBasicConnectionManager;

/**
 * This class displays a Blob object in a JFrame
 */
public class BlobSelect extends JPanel {

    // look and feel constants
    public static final String METAL_LOOK_AND_FEEL =
        "javax.swing.plaf.metal.MetalLookAndFeel";

    /**
     * Constructor to display Blob object.
     * @param id the primary key to the MyPictures table
     * @param conn Connection object.
     */
    public BlobSelect(int id, Connection conn) {...}

    /**
     * Extract and return the Blob object.
     * @param id the primary key to the Blob object.
     * @param conn Connection object.
     */
    public static byte[] getBLOB(int id, Connection conn) {...}


        JFrame frame = new JFrame("Blob Demo for MySQL Database");
        frame.addWindowListener(new WindowAdapter() {
            public void windowClosing(WindowEvent e) {
                System.exit(0);
            }
        });

        Connection conn = null;
        String dbVendor = args[0]; // { "mysql", "oracle" }
        int id = Integer.parseInt(args[1]);
        conn = VeryBasicConnectionManager.getConnection(dbVendor);
        frame.setContentPane(new BlobSelect(id, conn)) ;
        frame.pack();
        frame.setVisible(true);
    }
}
```

Solution: getBLOB()

The following shows the getBLOB() solution:

```
/**
 * Extract and return the Blob object.
 * @param id the primary key to the Blob object.
 * @param conn Connection object.
 */
public static byte[] getBLOB(int id, Connection conn)
    throws Exception {
```

```
    ResultSet rs = null;
    PreparedStatement pstmt = null;
    String query = "SELECT photo FROM MyPictures WHERE id = ?" ;
    try {
        pstmt = conn.prepareStatement(query) ;
        pstmt.setInt(1, id);
        rs = pstmt.executeQuery();
        rs.next();
        Blob blob = rs.getBlob("photo");
        // materialize BLOB onto client
        return blob.getBytes(1, (int)blob.length());
    }
    finally {
        DatabaseUtil.close(rs);
        DatabaseUtil.close(pstmt);
        DatabaseUtil.close(conn);
    }
}
```

Solution: Constructor BlobSelect()

The following shows the BlobSelect() solution:

```
/**
 * Constructor to display Blob object.
 * @param id the primary key to the MyPictures table


    throws Exception {
    // materialize BLOB onto client
    ImageIcon icon = new ImageIcon(getBLOB(id, conn)) ;
    JLabel photoLabel = new JLabel(icon) ;
    setLayout(new GridLayout(1, 1));
    add(photoLabel);
}
```

7-8. How Do You Delete an Existing BLOB from the Oracle Database?

The SQL DELETE statement deletes rows in a table. Its simple syntax is as follows:

```
DELETE FROM table_name
    WHERE column_name = some_value
```

Say your goal is to delete an existing database record, which has a BLOB column. To delete the record, you need the primary key for that record (to locate the record). For solving this problem, you will use the MyPictures table. (The ID column is the primary key, and PHOTO is the BLOB column to delete.)

Viewing the Oracle Database Before Deletion

Here is the MyPictures table before the deletion:

```
SQL> desc MyPictures;
 Name                                  Null?    Type
 ------------------------------------- -------- ------------
 ID                                    NOT NULL NUMBER(38)
 NAME                                           VARCHAR2(20)
 PHOTO                                          BLOB

SQL> select id, name from MyPictures;

        ID   NAME
---------- --------------------
        10   goofy-10
        20   goofy-20

SQL>
```

Displaying BLOB Data

Figure 7-3 shows the BLOB from Oracle by invoking this:

```
$ java BlobSelectOracle 10
```

Figure 7-3. *Displaying the* BLOB *from Oracle*

Solution: DeleteOracleBlobRecord

The following is the DeleteOracleBlobRecord solution:

```java
import java.sql.*;
import java.io.*;
import jcb.db.*;

/**
 * This class deletes an Oracle's BLOB record for a given PK.
 */
public class DeleteOracleBlobRecord  {

    private static Connection getConnection() throws Exception {
        String driver = "oracle.jdbc.driver.OracleDriver";
        String url = "jdbc:oracle:thin:@localhost:1521:caspian";
        String username = "scott";
        String password = "tiger";
        Class.forName(driver);  // load Oracle driver
        return DriverManager.getConnection(url, username, password);
    }
```

```
/**
 * deletes an Oracle's BLOB record for a given PK.
 * @param id the primary key to the BLOB record.
 */
private static void deleteBlobRecord(String id) throws Exception {
    Connection conn = null ;
    PreparedStatement pstmt = null;
    String query = "delete from MyPictures where id = ?";
    try {
        conn = getConnection();
        pstmt = conn.prepareStatement(query) ;
        pstmt.setString(1, id);
        pstmt.executeUpdate();
    }
    finally {
        DatabaseUtil.close(pstmt);
        DatabaseUtil.close(conn);
    }
}

public static void main(String args[]) throws Exception {
    if (args.length != 1) {
        System.out.println("usage: java DeleteOracleBlobRecord <id>");
        System.exit(1);
    }
    deleteBlobRecord(args[0]) ;
```

Deleting an Oracle BLOB Record

To delete a BLOB record with a primary key of 10, you issue the following command:

```
$ java  DeleteOracleBlobRecord 10
```

Viewing the Oracle Database After Deletion

This is the database after the deletion:

```
SQL> select id, name from MyPictures;

    ID   NAME
---------- --------------------
    20   goofy-20
```

7-9. How Do You Delete an Existing BLOB from the MySQL Database?

The solution for MySQL is identical to Oracle's solution with the exception of the getConnection() method. The getConnection() for MySQL is as follows. You can download the complete solution (the DeleteMySqlBlobRecord class) for MySQL from this book's Web site.

```
/**
 * Get a MySQL connection object.
 */
public static Connection getConnection() throws Exception {
```

```
String driver = "org.gjt.mm.mysql.Driver";
String url = "jdbc:mysql://localhost/octopus";
String username = "root";
String password = "root";
Class.forName(driver);    // load MySQL driver
return DriverManager.getConnection(url, username, password);
}
```

7-10. How Do You Serialize a Java Object to the Oracle Database?

You could ask this question in another way: how can you save a Java object (that is, an instance of any Java class) to a database for later use? Before serializing Java objects to the Oracle database, you will now look at what Java object serialization is.

Object serialization provides a program with the ability to read or write a whole object to and from a raw byte stream. It allows Java objects and primitives to be encoded into a byte stream suitable for streaming to some type of network or to a file system (or, more generally, to a transmission medium or storage facility); this is according to "The Wonders of Java Object Serialization" by Brian T. Kurotsuchi (http://www.acm.org/crossroads/xrds4-2/serial.html).

Serializing a Java object requires that it meets only one of two criteria. The class either must implement the java.io.Serializable interface, which has no methods (this is a Java marker interface) that you need to write, or must implement the Externalizable interface. (The Externalizable interface gives a client more choices for serialization, which provides a possibility for customizing the serialization process.) The Externalizable interface defines two methods:

- void readExternal(ObjectInput in): The object implements the readExternal method to

- void writeExternal(ObjectOutput out): The object implements the writeExternal method to save its contents by calling the methods of DataOutput for its primitive values or calling the writeObject method of ObjectOutput for objects, strings, and arrays.

In other words, serialization is the storing of a Java object's current state on any permanent/persistent storage media (such as a file system or a database) for later reuse. In the JDK, serialization takes place using three things:

- Implementing the java.io.Serializable interface.
- Using ObjectOutputStream, you write an object to a stream.
- Using ObjectInputStream, you read an object from a stream.

Example: Serializing Java Objects to a File

The following snippet shows how to serialize two Java objects to a file called myFile.ser:

```
FileOutputStream out = new FileOutputStream("myFile.ser");
ObjectOutputStream stream = new ObjectOutputStream(out);
stream.writeObject("my string");
stream.writeObject(new Date());
stream.flush();
```

Example: Unserializing (Deserializing) Java Objects from a File

The following snippet shows how to deserialize Java objects from a file called myFile.ser:

```
FileInputStream in = new FileInputStream("myFile.ser");
ObjectInputStream stream = new ObjectInputStream(in);
String myString = (String) stream.readObject();
Date date = (Date) stream.readObject();
```

Example: Serializing Java Objects to the Oracle Database

As mentioned, *serialization* is the process of converting an entire Java object and all its data and attributes into a serial form: a form that can be transmitted over a stream. Typically, Java objects are serialized and passed around using ObjectInputStream/ObjectOutputStream. The serialization takes place automatically as part of the writeObject() method. Serialized Java objects can be deserialized as well. That is, they can be read from an ObjectInputStream and reconstructed into an exact copy of the object that was serialized. Like serialization, deserialization is transparent, taking place as part of the readObject() method.

Serialized objects can be written to (and read from) files/databases, which is a great way of permanently storing the state of an object for future use or reference.

Preparing the Oracle Database for Serializing Java Objects

The following code shows how to create the table java_objects (to store Java objects) and the sequence java_object_sequence (to be able to create Java object identifiers or primary key values):

```
$ sqlplus octopus/octopus
SQL*Plus: Release 9.2.0.1.0 - Production on Sat Oct 11 23:14:59 2003
SQL> CREATE SEQUENCE java_object_sequence
  2    INCREMENT BY 1


  5    NOCYCLE
  6  ;

Sequence created.

SQL> CREATE TABLE java_objects (
  2    object_id NUMBER,
  3    object_name varchar(128),
  4    object_value BLOB DEFAULT empty_blob(),
  5    primary key (object_id));

Table created.

SQL> desc java_objects;
 Name                 Null?    Type
 ----------------     -------- -------------
 OBJECT_ID            NOT NULL NUMBER
 OBJECT_NAME                   VARCHAR2(128)
 OBJECT_VALUE                  BLOB

SQL> select SEQUENCE_NAME, MIN_VALUE, MAX_VALUE, INCREMENT_BY, LAST_NUMBER
  2    from  user_sequences;

SEQUENCE_NAME         MIN_VALUE  MAX_VALUE INCREMENT_BY LAST_NUMBER
-------------------- ---------- ---------- ------------ -----------
ID_SEQ                        1 1.0000E+27            1          21
JAVA_OBJECT_SEQUENCE          1 1.0000E+27            1           1

SQL> commit;
Commit complete.
```

Serializing/DeSerializing Java Objects

The following class, SerializeJavaObjects_Oracle, performs these tasks:

- Serializes a Java object (as a binary object) to the Oracle database

- Deserializes a Java object from the Oracle database

Here is SerializeJavaObjects_Oracle:

```java
import java.io.*;
import java.sql.*;
import java.util.*;
import oracle.jdbc.driver.*;
import oracle.sql.*;
import jcb.util.DatabaseUtil;

/**
 * The following class provides:
 *    1) how to serialize a Java object to the Oracle database.
 *    2) how to deserialize a Java object from the Oracle database.
 */
class SerializeJavaObjects_Oracle {
    static final String GET_JAVA_OBJECT_SEQUENCE =
        "SELECT java_object_sequence.nextval FROM dual";
    static final String WRITE_OBJECT_SQL =
        "BEGIN   INSERT INTO java_objects(object_id, object_name, object_value) " +
        "VALUES (?, ?, empty_blob())   RETURN object_value INTO ?;   END;";


    /**
     * Create a Connection object.
     */
    public static Connection getConnection() ...

    /**
     * Serialize a Java object: this method writes a Java object
     * to an Oracle database (serialization).
     */
    public static long writeJavaObject(Connection conn, Object object) ...

    /**
     * Deserialize a Java object: this method reads a Java object
     * from an Oracle database (de-serialization).
     */
    public static Object readJavaObject(Connection conn, long id) ...

    /**
     * Create a primary key id for Java objects
     */
    private static long getNextSequenceValue (Connection conn) ...

    private static List buildList() ...

    /**
     * This is the driver method (for testing purposes).
     */
```

```
    public static void main (String args[]) {
       Connection conn = null;
       try {
           // connect to the database
           conn = getConnection();
           System.out.println("conn="+conn);

           // turn off AutoCommit
           conn.setAutoCommit(false);

            List list = buildList();
            System.out.println("[Before Serialization] list="+list);

            // serialize list (as a Java object)
            long objectID = writeJavaObject(conn, list);

            // commit the transaction
            conn.commit();

            System.out.println("Serialized objectID => " + objectID);
            // deserialize a Java object from a given objectID
            List listFromDatabase = (List) readJavaObject(conn, objectID);
            System.out.println("[After De-Serialization] list=" + listFromDatabase);
       }
       catch (Exception e) {
           e.printStackTrace();
       }

           DatabaseUtil.close(conn);
       }
    }
}
```

SerializeJavaObjects_Oracle: getConnection()

The following shows getConnection():

```
/**
 * Create a Connection object.
 */
public static Connection getConnection() throws Exception {
    String driver = "oracle.jdbc.driver.OracleDriver";
    String url = "jdbc:oracle:thin:@localhost:1521:caspian";
    String username = "mp";
    String password = "mp2";
    Class.forName(driver);    // load Oracle driver
    return DriverManager.getConnection(url, username, password);
}
```

SerializeJavaObjects_Oracle: writeJavaObject()

The following shows writeJavaObject():

```
/**
 * Serialize a Java object: this method writes a Java object
 * to an Oracle database (serialization).
 */
```

```
public static long writeJavaObject(Connection conn, Object object)
    throws Exception {
    long id = getNextSequenceValue(conn);
    String className = object.getClass().getName();
    CallableStatement cstmt = conn.prepareCall(WRITE_OBJECT_SQL);
    // set and register input parameters
    cstmt.setLong(1, id);
    cstmt.setString(2, className);

    // register output parameters
    cstmt.registerOutParameter(3, java.sql.Types.BLOB);

    cstmt.executeUpdate();  // exec. stored procedure
    BLOB blob = (BLOB) cstmt.getBlob(3);
    OutputStream os = blob.getBinaryOutputStream();
    ObjectOutputStream stream = new ObjectOutputStream(os);
    stream.writeObject(object);
    stream.flush();
    stream.close();
    os.close();
    DatabaseUtil.close(cstmt);
    System.out.println("writeJavaObject: done serializing: " + className);
    return id;
}
```

SerializeJavaObjects_Oracle: readJavaObject()

```
/**
 * Deserialize a Java object: this method reads a Java object
 * from an Oracle database (deserialization).
 */
public static Object readJavaObject(Connection conn, long id)
    throws Exception {
    Object object = null;
    ResultSet rs = null;
    PreparedStatement pstmt =null;
    try {
        pstmt = conn.prepareStatement(READ_OBJECT_SQL);
        pstmt.setLong(1, id);
        rs = pstmt.executeQuery();
        rs.next();
        InputStream is = rs.getBlob(1).getBinaryStream();
        ObjectInputStream oip = new ObjectInputStream(is);
        object = oip.readObject();
        String className = object.getClass().getName();
        oip.close();
        is.close();
        System.out.println("readJavaObject: done de-serializing: " + className);
    }
    finally {
        DatabaseUtil.close(rs);
        DatabaseUtil.close(pstmt);
    }
    return object;
}
```

SerializeJavaObjects_Oracle: getNextSequenceValue()

The following shows getNextSequenceValue():

```
/**
 * Create a primary key id for Java objects
 */
private static long getNextSequenceValue (Connection conn)
    throws SQLException {
    Statement stmt = null;
    ResultSet rs = null;
    long id = -1; // undefined
    try {
        stmt = conn.createStatement();
        stmt.executeQuery(GET_JAVA_OBJECT_SEQUENCE);
        rs   = stmt.executeQuery(GET_JAVA_OBJECT_SEQUENCE);
        rs.next();
        id = rs.getLong(1);
    finally {
        DatabaseUtil.close(rs);
        DatabaseUtil.close(stmt);
    }
    return id;
}
```

SerializeJavaObjects_Oracle: buildList()

```
private static List buildList() {
    List list = new ArrayList();
        list.add("This is a short string.");
        list.add(new Integer(1234));
        list.add(new java.util.Date());
        return list;
    }
```

Running SerializeJavaObjects_Oracle

The following shows how to run the program:

```
$ javac SerializeJavaObjects_Oracle.java
$ java SerializeJavaObjects_Oracle
conn=oracle.jdbc.driver.OracleConnection@6e70c7
[Before Serialization]
list=[This is a short string., 1234, Sun Oct 12 20:35:54 PDT 2003]
writeJavaObject: done serializing: java.util.ArrayList
Serialized objectID => 1
readJavaObject: done de-serializing: java.util.ArrayList
[After De-Serialization]
list=[This is a short string., 1234, Sun Oct 12 20:35:54 PDT 2003]

$ java SerializeJavaObjects_Oracle
conn=oracle.jdbc.driver.OracleConnection@6e70c7
[Before Serialization]
list=[This is a short string., 1234, Sun Oct 12 20:35:59 PDT 2003]
writeJavaObject: done serializing: java.util.ArrayList
Serialized objectID => 2
```

```
readJavaObject: done de-serializing: java.util.ArrayList
[After De-Serialization]
list=[This is a short string., 1234, Sun Oct 12 20:35:59 PDT 2003]
```

Viewing the Database After Running SerializeJavaObjects_Oracle

This is the database after running the program:

```
SQL> select object_id, object_name from java_objects;

OBJECT_ID    OBJECT_NAME
---------    --------------------
        1    java.util.ArrayList
        2    java.util.ArrayList
```

7-11. How Do You Serialize a Java Object to the MySQL Database?

Serializing Java objects to MySQL is straightforward and much simpler than Oracle: you just use
setObject() and getObject() of a PreparedStatement object.

Preparing the MySQL Database for Serializing Java Objects

Create the table java_objects as follows to store Java objects. The primary key is automatically
generated by using the AUTO_INCREMENT feature of the MySQL database (which is semantically equivalent to using the SEQUENCE concept of Oracle).

```
         object_name varchar(128),
         object_value BLOB,
         primary key (object_id)
    );


Query OK, 0 rows affected (0.09 sec)

mysql> desc java_objects;
```

Field	Type	Null	Key	Default	Extra
object_id	int(11)		PRI	NULL	auto_increment
object_name	varchar(128)	YES		NULL	
object_value	blob	YES		NULL	

```
3 rows in set (0.04 sec)
```

Serializing/DeSerializing Java Objects

The following class, SerializeJavaObjects_MySQL, performs these tasks:

- Serializes a Java object to the MySQL database
- Deserializes a Java object from the MySQL database

Here is SerializeJavaObjects_MySQL:

```java
import java.io.*;
import java.sql.*;
import java.util.*;
import jcb.util.DatabaseUtil;
/**
 * This class provides the following features:
 *    1) how to serialize a Java object to the MySQL database.
 *    2) how to deserialize a Java object from the MySQL database.
 *
 */
class SerializeJavaObjects_MySQL {

    static final String WRITE_OBJECT_SQL =
        "INSERT INTO java_objects(object_name, object_value) VALUES (?, ?)";
    static final String READ_OBJECT_SQL =
        "SELECT object_value FROM java_objects WHERE object_id = ?";

    public static Connection getConnection() ...

    /**
     * Serialize a Java object: this method writes a Java object
     * to a MySQL database (serialization).
     */
    public static long writeJavaObject(Connection conn, Object object) ...

    /**


     */
    public static Object readJavaObject(Connection conn, long id) ...

    private static List buildList() ...

    /**
     * This is the driver method (for testing purposes).
     */
    public static void main (String args[]) {

        Connection conn = null;
        try {
            // connect to the database
            conn = getConnection();
            System.out.println("conn="+conn);

            // turn off AutoCommit
            conn.setAutoCommit(false);

            List list = buildList();
            System.out.println("[Before Serialization] list="+list);

            // serialize list (as a Java object)
            long objectID = writeJavaObject(conn, list);

            // commit the transaction
            conn.commit();
```

```
                    System.out.println("Serialized objectID => " + objectID);
                    // deserialize list a Java object from a given objectID
                    List listFromDatabase = (List) readJavaObject(conn, objectID);
                    System.out.println("[After De-Serialization] list=" + listFromDatabase);
                }
                catch (Exception e) {
                    e.printStackTrace();
                }
                finally {
                    DatabaseUtil.close(conn);
                }
            }
        }
    }
```

SerializeJavaObjects_MySQL: getConnection()

This shows getConnection():

```
    /**
     * Create a MySQL Connection object.
     */
    public static Connection getConnection() throws Exception {
        String driver = "org.gjt.mm.mysql.Driver";
        String url = "jdbc:mysql://localhost/octopus";
        String username = "root";
        String password = "root";
```

SerializeJavaObjects_MySQL: writeJavaObject()

This shows writeJavaObject():

```
/**
 * Serialize a Java object: this method writes a Java object
 * to an Oracle database (serialization).
 */
public static long writeJavaObject(Connection conn, Object object)
    throws Exception {
    ResultSet rs = null;
    PreparedStatement pstmt = null;
    int id = -1; // undefined value
    try {
        String className = object.getClass().getName();
        pstmt = conn.prepareStatement(WRITE_OBJECT_SQL);
        // set input parameters
        pstmt.setString(1, className);
        pstmt.setObject(2, object);
        pstmt.executeUpdate();
        // get the generated key for the object_id
        rs = pstmt.getGeneratedKeys();
        if (rs.next()) {
            id = rs.getInt(1);
        }
        System.out.println("writeJavaObject: done serializing: " + className);
    }
```

```
    finally {
       DatabaseUtil.close(rs);
       DatabaseUtil.close(pstmt);
    }

    return id;
}
```

SerializeJavaObjects_MySQL: readJavaObject()

This shows readJavaObject():

```
/**
 * Deserialize a Java object: this method reads a Java object
 * from a MySQL database (deserialization).
 */
public static Object readJavaObject(Connection conn, long id)
    throws Exception {
    Object object = null;
    ResultSet rs = null;
    PreparedStatement pstmt = null;
    try {
        pstmt = conn.prepareStatement(READ_OBJECT_SQL);
        pstmt.setLong(1, id);
        rs = pstmt.executeQuery();
        rs.next();


    }
    finally {
        DatabaseUtil.close(rs);
        DatabaseUtil.close(pstmt);
    }
    return object;
}
```

SerializeJavaObjects_MySQL: buildList()

This shows buildList():

```
private static List buildList() {
    List list = new ArrayList();
    list.add("This is a short string.");
    list.add(new Integer(1234));
    list.add(new java.util.Date());
    return list;
}
```

Running SerializeJavaObjects_MySQL

This code shows how to run the program:

```
$ javac SerializeJavaObjects_MySQL.java
$ java SerializeJavaObjects_MySQL
conn=com.mysql.jdbc.Connection@cd2c3c
[Before Serialization]
list=[This is a short string., 1234, Sun Oct 12 21:16:20 PDT 2003]
```

```
writeJavaObject: done serializing: java.util.ArrayList
Serialized objectID => 1
readJavaObject: done de-serializing: java.util.ArrayList
[After De-Serialization]
list=[This is a short string., 1234, Sun Oct 12 21:16:20 PDT 2003]

$ java SerializeJavaObjects_MySQL
conn=com.mysql.jdbc.Connection@cd2c3c
[Before Serialization]
list=[This is a short string., 1234, Sun Oct 12 21:16:30 PDT 2003]
writeJavaObject: done serializing: java.util.ArrayList
Serialized objectID => 2
readJavaObject: done de-serializing: java.util.ArrayList
[After De-Serialization]
list=[This is a short string., 1234, Sun Oct 12 21:16:30 PDT 2003]
```

Viewing the Database After Running SerializeJavaObjects_MySQL

This code shows the database after running the program:

```
SQL> select object_id, object_name from java_objects;
mysql> select object_id, object_name from java_objects;
+-----------+----------------------+
| object_id | object_name          |
+-----------+----------------------+
|         1 | java.util.ArrayList  |
```

7-12. Should You Use byte[] or java.sql.Blob? Which Has the Best Performance?

If you have the choice of manipulating binary data (a binary column of a record such as a BLOB data type), should you use byte[] or java.sql.Blob? Which has the best performance?

For better performance, you should use java.sql.Blob, since it does not extract any data from the database until you explicitly ask it to do so (by invoking the getBinaryStream() or getBytes() method). The JDBC data type java.sql.Blob wraps a database locator (which is essentially a pointer to a byte array). That pointer is a rather large number (between 32 and 256 bits in size), but the effort to extract it from the database is insignificant next to extracting the full BLOB content. For insertion into the database, you should use a byte[] since data has not been uploaded to the database yet. Therefore, use the java.sql.Blob object only for data extraction (whenever possible).

When using binary data, you should pay attention to data encoding as well: if your database supports only the Latin character set, and if your client wants to get that data in the ja_JP locale, this will not work—the client will get mostly garbage characters. To handle more than one locale (such as en_US and ja_JP), use UTF-8 encoding for your database. Oracle and MySQL support UTF-8 databases, and MySQL's JDBC driver supports several Connection properties (useUnicode, characterEncoding) for character encoding. For more details on MySQL, refer to http://dev.mysql.com/doc/connector/j/en/index.html.

CHAPTER 8

■ ■ ■

Reading and Writing CLOBs

In this chapter, you will examine all aspects of JDBC's CLOB data type. Specifically, this chapter shows how to use JDBC's rich data type CLOB. This data type stores/retrieves large character/text objects such as large text files or Java/HTML/XML/PostScript source files.

The word *clob* has different meanings; I will use CLOB for the SQL data type and Clob for the java.sql.Clob interface (which represents a SQL CLOB data type).

This chapter's focus is on the following topics:

- How to define a CLOB data type in a database
- How to insert/write a CLOB into a database
- How to retrieve/read a CLOB from a database
- How to update an existing CLOB in a database

You can define, retrieve, store, and update the CLOB data type the same way you do other JDBC data types. You use either the ResultSet.getClob() method or the CallableStatement.getClob() method to retrieve CLOBs, the PreparedStatement.setClob() method to store them, and the ResultSet.updateClob() method to update them.

8-1. What Is a CLOB?

A CLOB is a Character Large OBject in a database. Database vendors (such as Oracle, MySQL, IBM DB2, and so on) implement CLOBs in different ways, but as long as you use the common interface java.sql.Clob, you should not care about the internal implementations. CLOBs can be very large, up to 2GB or more, depending on the database. Use CLOBs with care; whenever possible, try to use caching algorithms to improve the overall performance of database applications. Large character data files can be stored as CLOB types.

JDBC's Support for CLOB

JDBC provides a single interface (java.sql.Clob) for handling large character/text objects. According to J2SE 5.0, java.sql.Clob is defined as follows:

[java.sql.Clob is] the mapping in the Java programming language for the SQL CLOB type. An SQL CLOB is a built-in type that stores a Character Large OBject as a column value in a row of a database table. By default drivers implement a Clob object using an SQL locator (CLOB), which means that a Clob object contains a logical pointer to the SQL CLOB data rather than the data itself. A Clob object is valid for the duration of the transaction in which it was created. The Clob interface provides methods for getting the length of an SQL CLOB (Character Large Object) value, for materializing a CLOB value on the client, and for searching for a substring or CLOB object within a CLOB value. Methods in the interfaces ResultSet, CallableStatement, and PreparedStatement, such as getClob and setClob, allow a programmer to access an SQL CLOB value. In addition, this interface has methods for updating a CLOB value.

Table 8-1 describes the java.sql.Clob interface.

Table 8-1. java.sql.Clob *Interface Description (According to J2SE 5.0)*

Return Type	Method	Description
InputStream	getAsciiStream()	Retrieves the CLOB value designated by this Clob object as an ASCII stream.
Reader	getCharacterStream()	Retrieves the CLOB value designated by this Clob object as a java.io.Reader object (or as
	int length)	substring in the CLOB value designated by this Clob object. Note that Oracle CLOBs can be up to 4GB, which exceeds the maximum "int" limit.
long	length()	Retrieves the number of characters in the CLOB value designated by this Clob object.
long	position(Clob searchstr, long start)	Retrieves the character position at which the specified Clob object searchstr appears in this Clob object.
long	position(String searchstr, long start)	Retrieves the character position at which the specified substring searchstr appears in the SQL CLOB value represented by this Clob object.
OutputStream	setAsciiStream(long pos)	Retrieves a stream to be used to write ASCII characters to the CLOB value that this Clob object represents, starting at position pos.
Writer	setCharacterStream(long pos)	Retrieves a stream to be used to write a stream of Unicode characters to the CLOB value that this Clob object represents, at position pos.
int	setString(long pos, String str)	Writes the given Java String to the CLOB value that this Clob object designates at the position pos.

Return Type	Method	Description
int	setString(long pos, String str, int offset, int len)	Writes len characters of str, starting at the character offset, to the CLOB value that this Clob represents.
void	truncate(long len)	Truncates the CLOB value that this Clob designates to have a length of len characters.

Oracle CLOBs

Oracle has only one type (called CLOB) to support large character/text objects. The oracle.sql.CLOB class is the Oracle JDBC driver's implementation of the standard JDBC java.sql.Clob interface.

MySQL CLOBs

This is according to the MySQL reference manual:

> *The four TEXT types TINYTEXT, TEXT, MEDIUMTEXT, and LONGTEXT correspond to the four CLOB types and have the same maximum lengths and storage requirements. The only difference between BLOB and TEXT types is that sorting and comparison is performed in case-sensitive fashion for BLOB values and case-insensitive fashion for TEXT values. In other words, a TEXT is a case-insensitive BLOB.*

types). Portions of MySQL's CLOB can be indexed.

- TINYTEXT: A character object that is stored with its length. Cannot be a key. The maximum length is 255 characters (8 bits). Takes the (varying per row) length plus 1 byte in the table.

- TEXT: A character object that is stored with its length. Cannot be a key. The maximum length is 16,535 characters (16 bits). Takes the (varying per row) length plus 2 bytes in the table.

- MEDIUMTEXT: A character object that is stored with its length. Cannot be a key. The maximum length is 16,777,216 characters (24 bits). Takes the (varying per row) length plus 3 bytes in the table.

- LONGTEXT: A character object that is stored with its length. Cannot be a key. The range is 4,294,967,295 characters (32 bits). Takes the (varying per row) length plus 4 bytes in the table.

According to MySQL (http://dev.mysql.com/doc/connector/j/en/index.html), "the Clob implementation does not allow in-place modification (they are *copies*, as reported by the DatabaseMetaData.locatorsUpdateCopies() method). Because of this, you should use the PreparedStatement.setClob() method to save changes back to the database."

8-2. How Do You Define a CLOB Data Type in a Table?

Suppose that in your DataFiles table you want to store large text files. Then you might define your table as in the following sections.

Defining the Table: Oracle 9*i*

The following defines a table based on Oracle 9*i*:

```
create table DataFiles (
    id INT PRIMARY KEY,
    fileName VARCHAR(20),
    fileBody CLOB
);
```

Defining the Table: MySQL

The following defines a table based on MySQL:

```
create table DataFiles (
    id INT PRIMARY KEY,
    fileName VARCHAR(20),
    fileBody TEXT
);
```

Creating the Table: Oracle 9i

The following creates the table for Oracle 9i:

```
C:\> sqlplus system/password
SQL*Plus: Release 9.2.0.1.0 - Production on Thu Apr 17 08:40:37 2003
Connected to: Oracle9i Enterprise Edition Release 9.2.0.1.0 - Production

SQL> create table DataFiles
  2  (id INT PRIMARY KEY,
  3    fileName varchar(20),



Table created.
SQL> describe DataFiles;

Name              Null?      Type
---------         ---------  -------------
ID                NOT NULL   NUMBER(38)
FILENAME                     VARCHAR2(20)
FILEBODY                     CLOB
```

Creating the Table: MySQL

The following defines the table for MySQL:

```
mysql>          create table DataFiles (
    ->                  id INT PRIMARY KEY,
    ->                  fileName VARCHAR(20),
    ->                  fileBody TEXT
    ->          );
Query OK, 0 rows affected (0.09 sec)

mysql> describe DataFiles;
+----------+-------------+------+-----+---------+-------+
| Field    | Type        | Null | Key | Default | Extra |
+----------+-------------+------+-----+---------+-------+
| id       | int(11)     |      | PRI | 0       |       |
| fileName | varchar(20) | YES  |     | NULL    |       |
| fileBody | text        | YES  |     | NULL    |       |
+----------+-------------+------+-----+---------+-------+
3 rows in set (0.02 sec)
```

8-3. What Are the Restrictions for Using CLOBs?

For CLOB restrictions (such as indexing and the number of CLOBs that can be used per row), you should consult the database vendor's documentation. In general, restrictions for CLOBs are as follows:

- CLOB columns cannot be keys (primary or foreign).

- One cannot group or sort on CLOB.

The MySQL database allows you to index portions of the CLOB data type. For details, refer to the MySQL reference manual. In the MySQL database, you may also use SQL's LIKE statement for searching keywords and sentences. (You need to understand the performance of SQL's LIKE before using it.)

8-4. How Do You Create a java.sql.Clob Object?

You can create a java.sql.Clob object in only one way, and that is by using a ResultSet object's methods. Consider the DataFiles table defined earlier (using the Oracle database):

```
create table DataFiles(
    id INT PRIMARY KEY,
    fileName varchar(20),
    fileBody CLOB
);
```

The ResultSet interface has two methods for creating a java.sql.Clob object:

- getClob(int columnPosition)

I will show how to create a java.sql.Clob object by using the overloaded getClob() methods.

ResultSet.getClob(int columnPosition)

This shows ResultSet.getClob(int columnPosition):

```
Connection conn = null;
Statement stmt = null;
ResultSet rs = null;
try {
    conn = <get-a-valid-connection-object>
    stmt = conn.createStatement();
    rs = stmt.executeQuery("select fileBody from DataFiles");
    while (rs.next()) {
        java.sql.Clob clob = rs.getClob(1);  // first column
        // now the Clob object is created and you can apply
        // methods defined in the java.sql.Clob interface
        ...
    }
}
catch(SQLException se) {
    // handle database exception
    ...
}
catch(Exception e) {
    // handle other exceptions
    ...
}
finally {
```

```
    // close resources: rs, stmt, conn
    ...
}
```

ResultSet.getClob(String columnName)

This shows ResultSet.getClob(int columnPosition):

```
Connection conn = null;
Statement stmt = null;
ResultSet rs = null;
try {
    conn = <get-a-valid-connection-object>
    stmt = conn.createStatement();
    rs = stmt.executeQuery("select fileBody from DataFiles");
    while (rs.next()) {
        java.sql.Clob clob = rs.getClob("fileBody");
        // now the Clob object is created and you can apply
        // methods defined in the java.sql.Clob interface
        ...
    }
}
catch(SQLException se) {
    // handle database exception
    ...
}


    ...
}
finally {
    // close resources: rs, stmt, conn
    ...
}
```

8-5. How Do You Materialize CLOB Data?

A SQL CLOB maps to a java.sql.Clob object. If you want to operate on CLOB data, you must first materialize it on the client (that is, retrieve the CLOB value's data and put it in memory on the client in the form of a Java object). The java.sql.Clob interface has four methods for materializing CLOB data:

- getAsciiStream(): Materializes the CLOB value as an input stream (java.io.InputStream)
- getCharacterStream(): Materializes the CLOB value as a stream of Unicode characters (java.io.Reader)
- getSubString(): Materializes all of the CLOB as a String object
- getSubString(): Materializes part of the CLOB as a String object

To materialize the CLOB value, assume that there is a Java method that returns a valid java.sql.Clob object:

```
public java.sql.Clob getClob(...)
    throws SQLException {
    ...
}
```

I will use the getClob(...) method in the following snippets.

Materializing the CLOB Value As an Input Stream (java.io.InputStream)

This shows how to materialize the CLOB value as an input stream:

```
import jcb.util.DatabaseUtil;
...//
// prints out all of ASCII bytes in the CLOB
//
byte b; // as an ASCII byte
java.sql.Clob clob = null;
java.io.InputStream input = null;
try {
    clob = getClob(...);
    input = clob.getAsciiStream();
    while ((b = input.read()) > -1) {
        // process the ASCII byte
        System.out.println(b);
    }
}
catch(SQLException se) {
    // handle database exception
    ...
}
catch(Exception e) {
    // handle other exceptions
    ...
}


    DatabaseUtil close(input);
}
```

Materializing the CLOB Value As a Stream of Unicode Characters (java.io.Reader)

This shows how to materialize the CLOB value as a stream of Unicode characters:

```
import jcb.util.DatabaseUtil;
...
    //
    // prints out all of Unicode characters in the CLOB
    //

    // The character read, as an integer
    // in the range 0 to 65535 (0x00-0xffff)
    int aCharacter;
    java.sql.Clob clob = null;
    java.io.Reader input = null;
    try {
        clob = getClob(...);
        input = clob.getCharacterStream();
        while ((aCharacter = input.read()) > -1) {
            // process the unicode character
            System.out.println(aCharacter);
        }
    }
    catch(SQLException se) {
        // handle database exception
        ...
    }
```

```
    catch(Exception e) {
        // handle other exceptions
        ...
    }
    finally {
        // close resources
        DatabaseUtil close(input);
    }
```

Materializing the CLOB As a String Object (Get the Whole CLOB)

This shows how to materialize the CLOB value as a String object:

```
//
// get the whole CLOB as a String object
//
long length;
java.sql.Clob clob = null;
try {
    clob = getClob(...);
    length = clob.length();
    // note that the first character is at position 1
    String wholeClob = clob.getSubString(1, (int) length);
}
catch(SQLException se) {
    // handle database exception
    ...


    // handle other exceptions
    ...
}
```

Materializing the CLOB As a String Object (Get Part of the CLOB)

This shows how to materialize the CLOB value as a String object:

```
//
// get a part of the clob as a String object
// get 25 characters starting from position 10
//
long length = 25;
long startingPosition = 10;
java.sql.Clob clob = null;
String partialClobAsString = null;
try {
    clob = getClob(...);
    partialClobAsString = clob.getSubString(startingPosition, length);
}
catch(SQLException se) {
    // handle database exception
    ...
}
catch(Exception e) {
    // handle other exceptions
    ...
}
```

You can express this as a Java method:

```
/*
 * Get a part of the clob as a String object get "length"
 * characters starting from position "startingPosition"
 *
 * @param clob a CLOB object
 * @param startingPosition  the first character of
 * the substring to be extracted.
 * @param length the number of consecutive characters
 * to be copied
 * @throws SQLException  if there is an error accessing
 * the CLOB value
 *
 */
public static String getPartialClob(java.sql.Clob clob,
                                    long length,
                                    long startingPosition)

    throws SQLException {
    if (clob == null) {
        return null;
    }

    return clob.getSubString(startingPosition, length);
}
```

Consider the DataFiles table (which has a CLOB column):

```
create table DataFiles(
    id INT PRIMARY KEY,
    fileName varchar(20),
    fileBody CLOB
);
```

You should be able to use JDBC to insert new records (which will contain fileBody as a CLOB data type). Suppose you want to insert the following data:

```
id  fileName    fileBody (content of text file)
--  --------    -------------------------------
1   file1.txt   c:/temp/data/file1.txt
2   file2.txt   c:/temp/data/file2.txt
3   file3.txt   c:/temp/data/file3.txt
4   file4.txt   c:/temp/data/file4.txt
```

Your goal is to write a program that will accept id, fileName, and fileBody (the content of the text file, as a full filename) and insert them into the DataFiles table. The client interface is as follows:

```
java InsertTextFileToMySQL <id> <fileName> <fileBody>
java InsertTextFileToOracle <id> <fileName> <fileBody>
```

Therefore, you need to develop two classes (InsertTextFileToMySQL.java and InsertTextFileToOracle.java). To insert the four records into a MySQL database, execute the following:

```
java InsertTextFileToMySQL 1  file1.txt c:/temp/data/file1.txt
java InsertTextFileToMySQL 2  file2.txt c:/temp/data/file2.txt
java InsertTextFileToMySQL 3  file3.txt c:/temp/data/file3.txt
java InsertTextFileToMySQL 4  file4.txt c:/temp/data/file4.txt
```

To insert the first three records into an Oracle 9*i*/10*g* database, execute the following:

```
java InsertTextFileToOracle 1  file1.txt c:/temp/data/file1.txt
java InsertTextFileToOracle 2  file2.txt c:/temp/data/file2.txt
java InsertTextFileToOracle 3  file3.txt c:/temp/data/file3.txt
java InsertTextFileToOracle 4  file4.txt c:/temp/data/file4.txt
```

MySQL Solution: InsertTextFileToMySQL.java

The following shows the InsertTextFileToMySQL.java solution:

```java
import java.io.*;
import java.sql.*;
import jcb.db.DatabaseUtil;

public class InsertTextFileToMySQL {

    private static final String INSERT_TEXT_FILE =
        "insert into DataFiles(id, fileName, fileBody) values (?, ?, ?)";

    private static String trimArgument(String s) {
        if ((s == null) || (s.length() == 0)) {
            return s;
        }
        else {
            return s.trim();
        }
    }


    public static Connection getConnection() throws Exception {
        String driver = "org.gjt.mm.mysql.Driver";
        String url = "jdbc:mysql://localhost/octopus";
        String username = "root";
        String password = "root";
        Class.forName(driver);  // load MySQL driver
        return DriverManager.getConnection(url, username, password);
    }

    public static void main(String[] args) {

        if ((args == null) || (args.length != 3)) {
            System.err.println("Usage: java InsertTextFileToMySQL   ");
            System.exit(0);
        }

        String id = trimArgument(args[0]);
        String name = trimArgument(args[1]);
        String textFile = trimArgument(args[2]);

        FileInputStream fis  = null;
        PreparedStatement pstmt = null;
        Connection conn = null;
        try {
            conn = getConnection();
            conn.setAutoCommit(false);

            File file = new File(textFile);
            fis = new FileInputStream(file);
```

```
            pstmt = conn.prepareStatement(INSERT_TEXT_FILE);
            pstmt.setString(1, id);
            pstmt.setString(2, name);
            pstmt.setAsciiStream(3, fis,(int)file.length());
            pstmt.executeUpdate();
            conn.commit();
        }
        catch (Exception e) {
          System.err.println("Error: " + e.getMessage());
          e.printStackTrace();
        }
        finally {
            DatabaseUtil.close(pstmt);
            DatabaseUtil.close(fis);
            DatabaseUtil.close(conn);
        }
    }
}
```

Testing InsertTextFileToMySQL.java

Testing the solution involves three steps.

Step 1: Prepare Input Text Files

```
$ cat c:/temp/data/file1.txt
this is file1.
hello world.
This is the last line.

$ cat c:/temp/data/file2.txt
import java.util.*;
import java.io.*;
import java.sql.*;

public class TestMySQL {
    public static Connection getConnection() throws Exception {
        String driver = "org.gjt.mm.mysql.Driver";
        String url = "jdbc:mysql://localhost/octopus";
        String username = "root";
        String password = "root";
        Class.forName(driver);     // load MySQL driver
        return DriverManager.getConnection(url, username, password);
    }
}
$
```

Step 2: Compile and Run the Program

Step 2 is to compile and run the program:

```
$ javac InsertTextFileToMySQL.java
$ java InsertTextFileToMySQL 10 file1 c:/temp/data/file1.txt
$ java InsertTextFileToMySQL 20 file2 c:/temp/data/file2.txt
```

Step 3: Check the Database Content

Step 3 is to check the database content. Using MySQL's command line, you can view the inserted CLOB data.

```
mysql> use octopus;
Database changed

mysql> desc DataFiles;
+----------+-------------+------+-----+---------+-------+
| Field    | Type        | Null | Key | Default | Extra |
+----------+-------------+------+-----+---------+-------+
| id       | int(11)     |      | PRI | 0       |       |
| fileName | varchar(20) | YES  |     | NULL    |       |
| fileBody | text        | YES  |     | NULL    |       |
+----------+-------------+------+-----+---------+-------+
3 rows in set (0.00 sec)

mysql> select * from datafiles;
+----+----------+------------------------------------------------------
| id | fileName | fileBody
+----+----------+------------------------------------------------------
| 10 | file1    | this is file1.
|    |          | hello world.
|    |          | This is the last line.
+----+----------+------------------------------------------------------
| 20 | file2    | import java.util.*;
|    |          |
|    |          |
|    |          | public class TestMySQL {
|    |          |     public static Connection getConnection() throws Exception {
|    |          |         String driver = "org.gjt.mm.mysql.Driver";
|    |          |         String url = "jdbc:mysql://localhost/octopus";
|    |          |         String username = "root";
|    |          |         String password = "root";
|    |          |         Class.forName(driver);    // load MySQL driver
|    |          |         return DriverManager.getConnection(url, username, password);
|    |          |     }
|    |          | }
+----+----------+------------------------------------------------------
2 rows in set (0.00 sec)

mysql>
```

Oracle Solution: InsertTextFileToOracle.java

The solution using the Oracle database, the InsertTextFileToOracle class, is identical to the MySQL database solution with the exception of the getConnection() method, shown next. You can download the complete solution from the book's Web site.

```
public static Connection getConnection() throws Exception {
    String driver = "oracle.jdbc.driver.OracleDriver";
    String url = "jdbc:oracle:thin:@localhost:1521:caspian";
    String username = "scott";
    String password = "tiger";
```

```
        Class.forName(driver);  // load Oracle driver
        return DriverManager.getConnection(url, username, password);
}
```

Testing InsertTextFileToOracle.java

Testing the solution involves two steps.

Step 1: Compile and Run the Program

Step 1 is to prepare the input text files:

```
$ cat c:/temp/data/file1.txt
this is file1.
hello world.
This is the last line.
```

```
$ cat c:/temp/data/file2.txt
import java.util.*;
import java.io.*;
import java.sql.*;

public class TestMySQL {
    public static Connection getConnection() throws Exception {
        String driver = "org.gjt.mm.mysql.Driver";
        String url = "jdbc:mysql://localhost/octopus";
        String username = "root";


        return DriverManager.getConnection(url, username, password);
    }
}
$
```

```
$ javac InsertTextFileToOracle.java
$ java InsertTextFileToOracle 100 file1 c:/temp/data/file1.txt
$ java InsertTextFileToOracle 200 file2 c:/temp/data/file2.txt
```

Step 2: Check the Database Content, and View CLOB Data

Step 2 is to check the database content. I have formatted the output so it is easier to read.

```
$ sqlplus scott/tiger
SQL*Plus: Release 10.1.0.2.0 - Production on Thu Jul 22 14:31:43 2004
SQL> desc datafiles;
 Name                                     Null?    Type
 ---------------------------------------- -------- --------------
 ID                                       NOT NULL NUMBER(38)
 FILENAME                                          VARCHAR2(20)
 FILEBODY                                          CLOB

SQL> select * from datafiles;

   ID   FILENAME  FILEBODY
 -----  --------  ----------------------------------------
   100  file1     this is file1.
                  hello world.
                  This is the last line.
```

```
200    file2        import java.util.*;
                     import java.io.*;
                     import java.sql.*;

                     public class TestMySQL...
```

As you can see, using the CLOB data type with the MySQL and Oracle 10g databases is straight-forward, but that is not the case with the Oracle 8 and Oracle 9 databases. In Oracle 8 and Oracle 9, before you can insert a real CLOB, you need to insert an empty CLOB (called empty_clob() in Oracle). empty_clob() is an Oracle function call that creates an empty Clob object. Therefore, in Oracle, you cannot just insert a Clob object into a column. First, you create a column with empty_clob(). Second, you update that column with the real Clob object.

8-7. How Do You Select and Display a CLOB in a JFrame?

The following example demonstrates how to retrieve a CLOB data type from the database. In this case, you retrieve the fileBody (content of the text file) identified by an ID (id is the primary key for the DataFiles table), displaying it in its own JFrame. Given that the code is lengthy to accomplish this job, the example is split over several pages. First, you perform a query to select the CLOB of interest (by providing the ID) and pull it back to the client (also known as materializing the CLOB). The rest of the code simply creates a JFrame to hold the retrieved text.

I have developed two classes: ClobSelectMySQL and ClobSelectOracle. You can invoke these classes by passing the ID of the file:

```
java ClobSelectMySQL <id>
```

DataFiles table) and extract and display the desired CLOB in a JFrame.

Extracting a CLOB from MySQL

Figure 8-1 shows the CLOB from MySQL by invoking this:

```
java ClobSelectMySQL 10
```

Figure 8-1. *Viewing MySQL* CLOB *data using* JFrame

Figure 8-2 shows the CLOB from MySQL by invoking this:

```
java ClobSelectMySQL 20
```

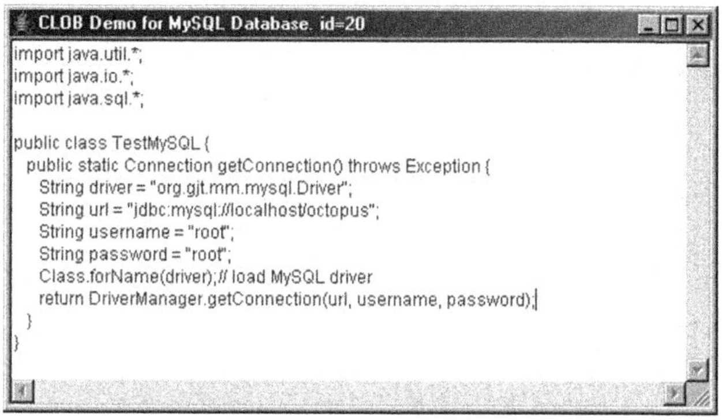

```
CLOB Demo for MySQL Database. id=20                        _ □ ×
import java.util.*;
import java.io.*;
import java.sql.*;

public class TestMySQL {
  public static Connection getConnection() throws Exception {
    String driver = "org.gjt.mm.mysql.Driver";
    String url = "jdbc:mysql://localhost/octopus";
    String username = "root";
    String password = "root";
    Class.forName(driver);// load MySQL driver
    return DriverManager.getConnection(url, username, password);
  }
}
```

Figure 8-2. *Viewing MySQL* CLOB *data using* JFrame

Extracting a CLOB from Oracle

Figure 8-3 shows the CLOB from MySQL by invoking this:

`java ClobSelectMySQL 100`

Figure 8-3. *Viewing Oracle* CLOB *data using* JFrame

Figure 8-4 shows the CLOB from MySQL by invoking this:

`java ClobSelectMySQL 200`

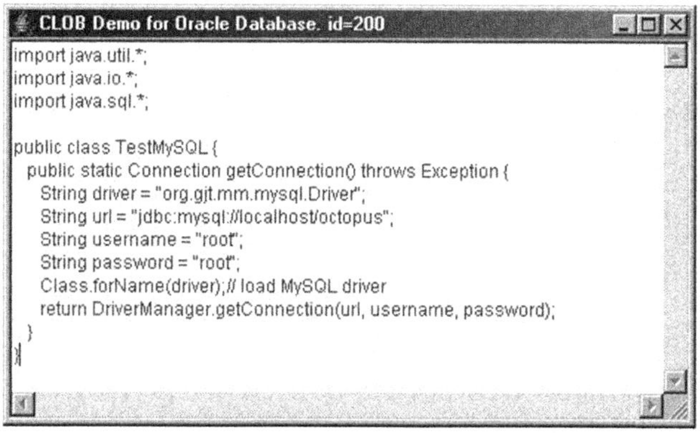

```
CLOB Demo for Oracle Database. id=200                     _ □ ×
import java.util.*;
import java.io.*;
import java.sql.*;

public class TestMySQL {
  public static Connection getConnection() throws Exception {
    String driver = "org.gjt.mm.mysql.Driver";
    String url = "jdbc:mysql://localhost/octopus";
    String username = "root";
    String password = "root";
    Class.forName(driver);// load MySQL driver
    return DriverManager.getConnection(url, username, password);
  }
}
```

Figure 8-4. *Viewing Oracle* CLOB *data using* JFrame

Solution: ClobSelectMySQL.java

The following shows the ClobSelectMySQL.java solution:

```java
import javax.swing.*;
import java.awt.*;
import java.awt.event.*;
import java.sql.*;

import jcb.db.*;

/**
 * This class displays a Clob object in a JFrame
 */
public class ClobSelectMySQL extends JPanel {

    // look and feel constants
    public static final String MOTIF_LOOK_AND_FEEL =
        "com.sun.java.swing.plaf.motif.MotifLookAndFeel";

    public static final String WINDOWS_LOOK_AND_FEEL =
        "com.sun.java.swing.plaf.windows.WindowsLookAndFeel";

    public static final String METAL_LOOK_AND_FEEL =
        "javax.swing.plaf.metal.MetalLookAndFeel";

    /**


    public static Connection getConnection() ...

    /**
     * Extract and return the CLOB object.
     * @param id the primary key to the CLOB object.
     */
    public static String getCLOB(int id) ...

    /**
     * Constructor to display CLOB object.
     * @param id the primary key to the DataFiles table
     */
    public ClobSelectMySQL(int id) ...

    public static void main(String args[]) ...
}
```

getConnection()

The following shows getConnection():

```java
/**
 * Get a connection object.
 */
public static Connection getConnection() throws Exception {
    String driver = "org.gjt.mm.mysql.Driver";
    String url = "jdbc:mysql://localhost/octopus";
    String username = "root";
    String password = "root";
```

```
        Class.forName(driver);  // load MySQL driver
        return  DriverManager.getConnection(url, username, password);
    }
```

getCLOB()

The following shows getCLOB():

```
/**
 * Extract and return the CLOB object as String.
 * @param id the primary key to the CLOB object.
 */
public static String getCLOB(int id) throws Exception {
    Connection conn = null ;
    ResultSet rs = null;
    PreparedStatement pstmt = null;
    String query = "SELECT fileBody FROM DataFiles WHERE id = ?" ;
    try {
        conn = getConnection();
        pstmt = conn.prepareStatement(query) ;
        pstmt.setInt(1, id);
        rs = pstmt.executeQuery();
        rs.next();
        Clob clob = rs.getClob(1);
        // materialize CLOB onto client
        String wholeClob = clob.getSubString(1, (int) clob.length());
        return wholeClob;


        DatabaseUtil.close(rs);
        DatabaseUtil.close(pstmt);
        DatabaseUtil.close(conn);
    }
}
```

constructor ClobSelectMySQL()

The following shows ClobSelectMySQL():

```
/**
 * Constructor to display CLOB object.
 * @param id the primary key to the DataFiles table
 */
 public ClobSelectMySql(int id) throws Exception {
    setLayout(new GridLayout(1, 1));
    add(new TextArea(getCLOB(id), 3, 10));
}
```

main()

The following shows main():

```
public static void main(String args[]) throws Exception {
    int id = Integer.parseInt(args[0]);
    UIManager.setLookAndFeel(METAL_LOOK_AND_FEEL) ;
    JFrame frame = new JFrame("CLOB Demo for MySQL Database. id="+id);
    frame.addWindowListener(new WindowAdapter() {
        public void windowClosing(WindowEvent e) {
```

```
            System.exit(0);
        }
    });
    frame.setContentPane(new ClobSelectMySql(id)) ;
    frame.pack();
    frame.setVisible(true);
}
```

Solution: ClobSelectOracle.java

The Oracle solution is identical to the MySQL solution with the exception of the getConnection()
method, which returns an Oracle Connection object. You can download the complete Oracle solution
from the book's Web site.

This is the Java method getConnection() for the Oracle database:

```
/**
 * Get an Oracle connection object.
 */
public static Connection getConnection() throws Exception {
    String driver = "oracle.jdbc.driver.OracleDriver";
    String url = "jdbc:oracle:thin:@scorpian:1521:caspian";
    String username = "scott";
    String password = "tiger";
    Class.forName(driver);  // load Oracle driver
    return DriverManager.getConnection(url, username, password);
}
```

a Servlet?

I will use the data set up in the previous recipe to show how to select and display an Oracle CLOB
using a servlet.

Viewing Oracle CLOB Data

I have developed a servlet, DisplayOracleClobServlet, that accepts the ID of a file and displays the
associated file. (As you can see from the previous pages, the output has not been formatted, and the
CLOB data has not been altered.) Run the servlet with an ID of 100, as shown in Figure 8-5, and then
run the servlet with an ID of 200, as shown in Figure 8-6. Next, run the servlet with an ID of 300, which
is not in the database. If the file's ID does not exist in the database, then you will get an error, as shown
in Figure 8-7.

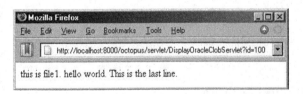

Figure 8-5. *Viewing Oracle* CLOB *data using a servlet* (id=100)

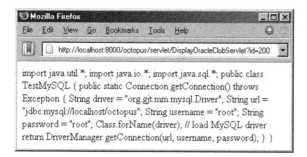

Figure 8-6. *Viewing Oracle* CLOB *data using a servlet (*id=200*)*

Figure 8-7. *Viewing nonexistent Oracle* CLOB *data using a servlet*

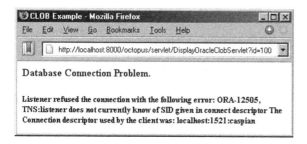

Figure 8-8. *Displaying error message using a servlet*

Displaying a CLOB Using a Servlet: DisplayOracleClobServlet

The following shows the DisplayOracleClobServlet solution:

```
import java.io.*;
import java.sql.*;

import javax.servlet.*;
import javax.servlet.http.*;

import jcb.db.DatabaseUtil;

public class DisplayOracleClobServlet extends HttpServlet {
```

```java
public static Connection getConnection() throws Exception {
    String driver = "oracle.jdbc.driver.OracleDriver";
    String url = "jdbc:oracle:thin:@localhost:1521:caspian";
    String username = "scott";
    String password = "tiger";
    Class.forName(driver);  // load Oracle driver
    return DriverManager.getConnection(url, username, password);
}


public void doGet(HttpServletRequest request,
                  HttpServletResponse response)
    throws IOException, ServletException {

    System.out.println("-- DisplayOracleClobServlet begin --");

    Clob fileAsCLOB = null;
    Connection conn = null;
    Statement stmt = null;
    ResultSet rs = null;

    String id = request.getParameter("id").trim();
    String query = "select fileBody from DataFiles where id = "+id;
    ServletOutputStream out = response.getOutputStream();

    // all responses will be in text/html format


    try {
      conn = getConnection();
    }
    catch(Exception e) {
        out.println("<html><head><title>CLOB Example</title></head>");
        out.println("<body><h4>Database Connection Problem.</h4>");
        out.println("<h5>"+e.getMessage()+"</h5></body></html>");
        return;
    }

    try {
        stmt = conn.createStatement();
        rs = stmt.executeQuery(query);
        if (rs.next()) {
            fileAsCLOB = rs.getClob(1);
        }
        else {
            out.println("<html><head><title>CLOB Example</title></head>");
            out.println("<body><h3>No file found for id="+
                id+"</h3></body></html>");
            return;
        }

        // Materialize the CLOB as a String object (get the whole clob).
        long length = fileAsCLOB.length();
        // note that the first character is at position 1
        String fileAsString = fileAsCLOB.getSubString(1, (int) length);
```

```
                // write it for display
                out.println(fileAsString);
                System.out.println("CLOB writing done.");
            }
            catch (SQLException e) {
                out.println("<html><head><title>Error: CLOB Example</title></head>");
                out.println("<body><h3>Error="+e.getMessage()+"</h3></body></html>");
                return;
            }
            finally {
              DatabaseUtil.close(rs);
              DatabaseUtil.close(stmt);
              DatabaseUtil.close(conn);
            }
            System.out.println("-- DisplayOracleClobServlet end --");
    }

    public void doPost(
        HttpServletRequest request,
        HttpServletResponse response)
        throws IOException, ServletException {
        doGet(request, response);
    }
}
```

MySQL supports CLOB and offers four data types for using it:

```
Type        Format
----------  --------------------------------------------------------
TINYTEXT    A string with a maximum length of 255 characters
TEXT        A string with a maximum length of 65,535 characters
MEDIUMTEXT  A string with a maximum length of 16,777,215 characters
LONGTEXT    A string with a maximum length of 4,294,967,295 characters
```

Setting Up the MySQL Database

This shows how to set up the MySQL database for this example:

```
mysql> use octopus;
Database changed

mysql> desc DataFiles;
+----------+-------------+------+-----+---------+-------+
| Field    | Type        | Null | Key | Default | Extra |
+----------+-------------+------+-----+---------+-------+
| id       | int(11)     |      | PRI | 0       |       |
| fileName | varchar(20) | YES  |     | NULL    |       |
| fileBody | text        | YES  |     | NULL    |       |
+----------+-------------+------+-----+---------+-------+
3 rows in set (0.00 sec)

mysql> select * from datafiles;
```

```
+----+----------+------------------------------------------------------
| id | fileName | fileBody
+----+----------+------------------------------------------------------
| 10 | file1    | this is file1.
|    |          | hello world.
|    |          | This is the last line.
+----+----------+------------------------------------------------------
| 20 | file2    | import java.util.*;
|    |          | import java.io.*;
|    |          | import java.sql.*;
|    |          |
|    |          | public class TestMySQL {
|    |          |     public static Connection getConnection() throws Exception {
|    |          |         String driver = "org.gjt.mm.mysql.Driver";
|    |          |         String url = "jdbc:mysql://localhost/octopus";
|    |          |         String username = "root";
|    |          |         String password = "root";
|    |          |         Class.forName(driver);    // load MySQL driver
|    |          |         return DriverManager.getConnection(url, username, password);
|    |          |     }
|    |          | }
+----+----------+------------------------------------------------------
2 rows in set (0.00 sec)

mysql>
```

I have developed a servlet, DisplayMySqlClobServlet, that accepts the ID of a file and displays the
associated file. (As you can see, the output has not been formatted, and the CLOB data has not been
altered.) Run the servlet with an ID of 10, as shown in Figure 8-9, and then run the servlet with an ID
of 20, as shown in Figure 8-10. Next, run the servlet with an ID of 30 (which is not in the database); if
the data is not in the database, you will see the error shown in Figure 8-11.

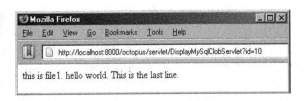

Figure 8-9. *Viewing MySQL* CLOB *data using a servlet* (id=10)

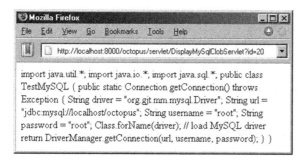

Figure 8-10. *Viewing MySQL* CLOB *data using a servlet (*id=20*)*

Figure 8-11. *Viewing nonexistent Oracle* CLOB *data using a servlet*

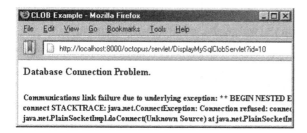

Figure 8-12. *Displaying error message using a servlet*

Displaying a CLOB Using a Servlet: DisplayMySqlClobServlet

The MySQL solution is identical to the Oracle solution with the exception of the getConnection()
method, which returns a MySQL Connection object. You can download the complete MySQL solution from the book's Web site.

This is getConnection() for the MySQL database:

```
public static Connection getConnection() throws Exception {
    String driver = "org.gjt.mm.mysql.Driver";
    String url = "jdbc:mysql://localhost/octopus";
    String username = "root";
```

```
String password = "root";
Class.forName(driver);  // load MySQL driver
return DriverManager.getConnection(url, username, password);
}
```

8-10. How Do You Select and Display an Oracle CLOB (As a URL) Using a Servlet?

If CLOB data (such as an RSS feed, a text résumé, or an HTML blog) is too big (more than a couple of megabytes) and is shared among many users, it is a good idea to retrieve the CLOB from the database, then create a copy of it on the server side, and finally make it URL addressable (to avoid the performance cost).

Here I will provide a solution that displays a CLOB as a URL on the browser; when you click the URL (or open the URL in the browser), then you will view the CLOB. Therefore, a servlet will accept an ID of a CLOB, and then it will store the CLOB on the server as a text file and send an associated URL (of the CLOB) to the browser. To solve this problem effectively, you need to create a directory (on the Web server side) and make it URL addressable; therefore, you need to define the following two parameters (defined inside the servlet):

- CLOB_DIRECTORY, the directory where CLOB data will be placed as files

- CLOB_URL, the CLOB_DIRECTORY as a URL

Setting Up the Database

Solution

I have developed a servlet, DisplayOracleClobAsURLServlet, that accepts the ID of a file and displays the associated file. For example, if id=200, then you will get the screen shown in Figure 8-13.

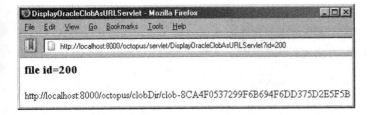

Figure 8-13. *Displaying a generated GUID for a* CLOB *using a servlet*

By opening the CLOB as a URL, you will get the screen shown in Figure 8-14.

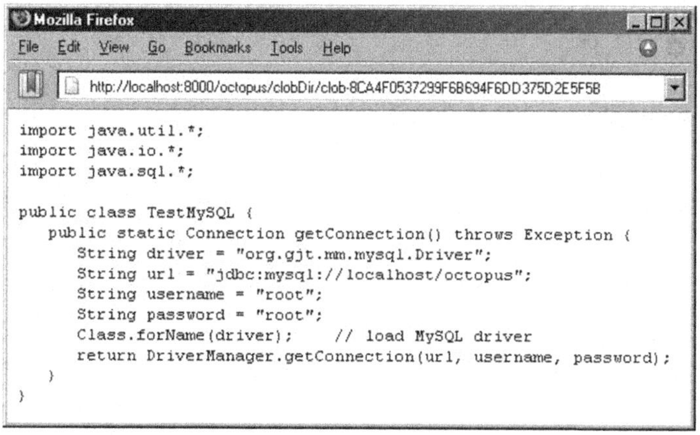

Inside the browser window:

```
import java.util.*;
import java.io.*;
import java.sql.*;

public class TestMySQL {
    public static Connection getConnection() throws Exception {
        String driver = "org.gjt.mm.mysql.Driver";
        String url = "jdbc:mysql://localhost/octopus";
        String username = "root";
        String password = "root";
        Class.forName(driver);    // load MySQL driver
        return DriverManager.getConnection(url, username, password);
    }
}
```

Figure 8-14. *Displaying a* CLOB *using a generated GUID*

If the file's ID does not exist in the database, then you will get the screen shown in Figure 8-15.

Figure 8-15. *Displaying an error for a nonexistent* CLOB *using a servlet*

If the database connection information is not valid (wrong username/password or wrong database URL), then the servlet will display an error message.

Displaying a CLOB Using a Servlet: DisplayOracleClobAsURLServlet

The following shows the DisplayOracleClobAsURLServlet solution:

```
import java.io.*;
import java.sql.*;

import javax.servlet.*;
import javax.servlet.http.*;

import jcb.db.DatabaseUtil;
import jcb.util.IOUtil;
import jcb.util.RandomGUID;

public class DisplayOracleClobAsURLServlet extends HttpServlet {

    // directory where clob data will be placed as files.
    private static final String CLOB_DIRECTORY =
        "c:/tomcat/webapps/octopus/clobDir";
```

```
    // CLOB_DIRECTORY as a URL
    private static final String CLOB_URL =
        "http://localhost:8000/octopus/clobDir";

    private static final String CLOB_FILE_PREFIX = "/clob-";

    public static Connection getConnection() ...
    private static String getClobAsURL(Clob Clob) ...
    public void doGet(...) ...

    public void doPost(
        HttpServletRequest request,
        HttpServletResponse response)
        throws IOException, ServletException {
        doGet(request, response);
    }
}
```

getConnection()

The following shows getConnection():

```
public static Connection getConnection() throws Exception {
    String driver = "oracle.jdbc.driver.OracleDriver";
    String url = "jdbc:oracle:thin:@localhost:1521:caspian";
    String username = "scott";
    String password = "tiger222";



}
```

getClobAsURL()

The following shows getClobAsURL():

```
private static String getClobAsURL(Clob Clob) throws Exception {
    InputStream in = null;
    FileOutputStream out = null;
    try {
        if (Clob == null) {
            return null;
        }

        // get a random GUID for Clob filename
        String guid = RandomGUID.getGUID();
        String ClobFile = CLOB_DIRECTORY + CLOB_FILE_PREFIX + guid;
        in = Clob.getAsciiStream();
        if (in == null) {
            return null;
        }

        out = new FileOutputStream(ClobFile);
        int length = (int) Clob.length();
        int bufferSize = 1024;
        byte[] buffer = new byte[bufferSize];
        while ((length = in.read(buffer)) != -1) {
            out.write(buffer, 0, length);
        }
```

```
          out.flush();
          return CLOB_URL + CLOB_FILE_PREFIX + guid;
      }
      finally {
        IOUtil.close(in);
        IOUtil.close(out);
      }
  }
}
```

doGet()

The following shows doGet():

```
public void doGet(HttpServletRequest request,
                  HttpServletResponse response)
    throws IOException, ServletException {
    Clob clob = null;
    Connection conn = null;
    Statement stmt = null;
    ResultSet rs = null;
    String id = request.getParameter("id").trim();
    String query = "select fileBody from DataFiles where  id = "+id;
    ServletOutputStream out = response.getOutputStream();
    response.setContentType("text/html");
    out.println("<html><head><title>DisplayOracleClobAsURLServlet"+
      "</title></head>");
    try {


    catch(Exception e) {
        out.println("<body><h4>Database Connection Problem.</h4>");
        out.println("<h5>"+e.getMessage()+"</h5></body></html>");
        return;
    }

    try {
      stmt = conn.createStatement();
      rs = stmt.executeQuery(query);
      if (rs.next()) {
        clob = rs.getClob(1);
        out.println("<body><h3>file id="+id+"</h3>"+
                    getClobAsURL(clob)+"</body></html>");
      }
      else {
        out.println("<body><h1>No File found for id="+id+"</h1></body></html>");
        return;
      }
    }
    catch (Exception e) {
        out.println("<body><h1>Error="+e.getMessage()+"</h1></body></html>");
        return;
    }
    finally {
      DatabaseUtil.close(rs);
      DatabaseUtil.close(stmt);
      DatabaseUtil.close(conn);
    }
}
```

8-11. How Do You Select and Display a MySQL CLOB (As a URL) Using a Servlet?

If CLOB data (such as an RSS feed, a text résumé, or an HTML blog) is too big (more than a couple of megabytes) and is shared among many users, it is a good idea to retrieve the CLOB from the database, then create a copy of it on the server side, and finally make it URL addressable (to avoid the performance cost).

Here I provide a solution that displays a CLOB as a URL on the browser; when you click the URL (or open the URL in the browser), then you will view the CLOB. Therefore, a servlet will accept an ID of a CLOB, and then it will store the CLOB on the server as a text file and send an associated URL (of the CLOB) to the browser. To solve this problem effectively, you need to create a directory (on the Web server side) and make it URL addressable; therefore, you need to define the following two parameters (defined inside the servlet):

- CLOB_DIRECTORY, the directory where CLOB data will be placed as files

- CLOB_URL, the CLOB_DIRECTORY as a URL

Solution

I have developed a servlet, DisplayMySqlClobAsURLServlet, that accepts the ID of a file and displays the associated file. For example, if id=10, then you will get the screen shown in Figure 8-16.

Figure 8-16. *Displaying a generated GUID for a* CLOB *using a servlet*

By opening the CLOB as a URL, you will get the screen shown in Figure 8-17.

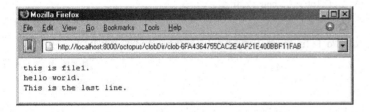

Figure 8-17. *Displaying a* CLOB *using a generated GUID*

If the file's ID does not exist in the database, then you will get the screen shown in Figure 8-18.

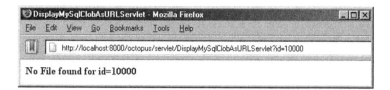

Figure 8-18. *Displaying an error for a nonexistent* CLOB *using a servlet*

If the database connection information is not valid (a wrong username/password or wrong database URL), then you will get an error message.

Setting Up the MySQL Database

To show this example in action, I will use the DataFiles table defined and populated in earlier sections.

Displaying a CLOB Using a Servlet: DisplayMySqlClobAsURLServlet

The MySQL solution is identical to the Oracle solution with the exception of the getConnection() method, which returns a MySQL Connection object. You can download the complete MySQL solution from the book's Web site.

This is getConnection() for the MySQL database:

```
public static Connection getConnection() throws Exception {


    String username = "root";
    String password = "root";
    Class.forName(driver);  // load MySQL driver
    return DriverManager.getConnection(url, username, password);
}
```

8-12. How Do You Insert a CLOB into an Oracle Database Using a Servlet?

The SQL INSERT statement inserts new rows/records into a table. The general syntax is as follows:

```
INSERT INTO table_name (column_name_1, column_name_2, ...)
    VALUES (value_for_column_1, value_for_column_2, ...)
```

To insert a CLOB into an Oracle database using a servlet, you will represent the intended CLOB as a URL (the URL will be pointing to CLOB data, such as a text file). The reason for this is that servlets cannot access the local file system (a client's/browser's local machine). You can also pass the CLOB to the database as a String object. Therefore, you will represent the CLOB as a URL. The following sections will use the DataFiles table defined in the earlier sections.

Setting Up the Oracle Database

Oracle 10 has simplified CLOBs in JDBC. There is no need to use Oracle's proprietary SQL functions, such as empty_clob. Inserting CLOBs is simple; in fact, CLOBs are just long String objects. This shows how to set up the database:

```
$ sqlplus scott/tiger
SQL*Plus: Release 10.1.0.2.0 - Production on Fri Feb 18 16:42:51 2005
Connected to: Oracle Database 10g Enterprise Edition Release 10.1.0.2.0

SQL> desc datafiles;
 Name                            Null?    Type
 ------------------------------- -------- ------------
 ID                              NOT NULL NUMBER(38)
 FILENAME                                 VARCHAR2(20)
 FILEBODY                                 CLOB

SQL> select id, filename from datafiles;

       ID  FILENAME
---------- --------------------
     1000  file1
     2000  file2

SQL> insert into datafiles(id, filename, filebody)
  2  values(4000, 'file4000', 'This is the content of file4000.');

1 row created.

SQL> select id, filename from datafiles;

       ID  FILENAME
     ----  --------
     1000  file1
     2000  file2
```

Creating the Oracle Servlet Interface

The servlet interface is as follows:

```
http://localhost:8000/octopus/servlet/InsertClobToOracleServlet?
    id=<id>&name=<name>&file=<file-as-URL>
```

Therefore, InsertClobToMySqlServlet has three parameters:

- id (the ID of file)

- name (the name of file)

- file (the URL of file, representing the CLOB; the servlet will open the URL, construct a CLOB, and insert it into the CLOB column of the DataFiles table)

Now insert a new record with the following data in the DataFiles table:

- id (500)

- name (file500)

- file (the URL of file: http://www.geocities.com/mparsian/data/file500.txt)

Figure 8-19 shows the content of the URL (http://www.geocities.com/mparsian/data/file500.txt).

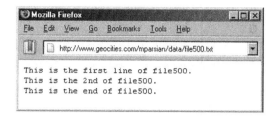

Figure 8-19. *Displaying a file using a servlet*

Therefore, the servlet call is as follows:

```
http://localhost:8000/octopus/servlet/InsertClobToOracleServlet?
id=500&name=file500&file=http://www.geocities.com/mparsian/data/file500.txt
```

Inserting a New CLOB Record

Figure 8-20 shows the result of inserting a new CLOB record using a Java servlet.

Figure 8-20. *Inserting a new CLOB record using a servlet*

Reinserting the Same CLOB Record

Figure 8-21 shows the result of reinserting a new CLOB record using a servlet.

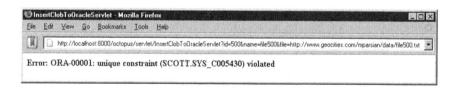

Figure 8-21. *Reinserting the same CLOB record using a servlet*

Viewing the Database Content After Insertion

Using DisplayOracleClobServlet, you can view the CLOB in a Web browser, as shown in Figure 8-22.

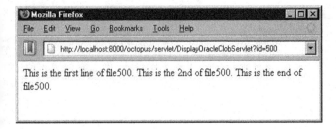

Figure 8-22. *Viewing* CLOB *using a servlet*

Solution: InsertClobToOracleServlet

The following shows the InsertClobToOracleServlet solution:

```java
import java.io.*;
import java.sql.*;

import javax.servlet.*;
import javax.servlet.http.*;

import jcb.db.DatabaseUtil;
import jcb.util.IOUtil;

public class InsertClobToOracleServlet extends HttpServlet {


    public static Connection getConnection() throws Exception {... }
    public void doGet(...) {... }
    public void doPost(...) {...}
    public void insertCLOB(...) {....}
    public static String  getClobsContentAsString(...) {...}
    private static String trimParameter(...) {...}
}
```

getConnection()

The following shows getConnection():

```java
public static Connection getConnection() throws Exception {
    String driver = "oracle.jdbc.driver.OracleDriver";
    String url = "jdbc:oracle:thin:@localhost:1521:caspian";
    String username = "scott";
    String password = "tiger";
    Class.forName(driver);  // load Oracle driver
    return DriverManager.getConnection(url, username, password);
}
```

doGet()

The following shows doGet():

```java
public void doGet(HttpServletRequest request,
                  HttpServletResponse response)
    throws IOException, ServletException {
```

```
    String fileContent = null;
    Connection conn = null;

    String id = trimParameter(request.getParameter("id"));
    String name = trimParameter(request.getParameter("name"));
    String fileAsURL = trimParameter(request.getParameter("file"));
    ServletOutputStream out = response.getOutputStream();

    response.setContentType("text/html");
    out.println("<html><head><title>InsertClobToOracleServlet</title></head>");

    try {
      conn = getConnection();
      fileContent = getClobsContentAsString(fileAsURL);
      insertCLOB(conn, id, name, fileContent);
      out.println("<body><h4>OK: inserted a new record with id="
        +id+"</h4></body></html>");
    }
    catch(Exception e) {
      e.printStackTrace();
      out.println("<body><h4>Error: "+e.getMessage()+"</h4></body></html>");
    }
}
```

insertCLOB()

```
                        String id,
                        String name,
                        String fileContent)
    throws Exception {
    PreparedStatement pstmt = null;
    try {
        pstmt = conn.prepareStatement(INSERT_CLOB);
        pstmt.setString(1, id);
        pstmt.setString(2, name);
        pstmt.setString(3, fileContent);
        pstmt.executeUpdate();
    }
    finally {
        DatabaseUtil.close(pstmt);
    }
}
```

getClobsContentAsString()

The following shows getClobsContentAsString():

```
public static String  getClobsContentAsString(String urlAsString)
    throws Exception {
    InputStream content = null;
    try {
        java.net.URL url = new java.net.URL(urlAsString);
        java.net.URLConnection urlConn = url.openConnection();
        urlConn.connect();
        content = urlConn.getInputStream();
```

```
        return IOUtil.inputStreamToString(content);
    }
    finally {
        IOUtil.close(content);
    }
}
```

trimParameter()

The following shows trimParameter():

```
    private static String trimParameter(String s) {
        if ((s == null) || (s.length() == 0)) {
            return s;
        }
        else {
            return s.trim();
        }
    }
}
```

8-13. How Do You Insert a CLOB into a MySQL Database Using a Servlet?

To insert a CLOB into a MySQL database using a servlet, you will represent the intended CLOB as a URL
                                                                    CLOB

database as a String object. Therefore, you will represent the CLOB as a URL. The following sections
use the DataFiles table defined in the earlier questions.

Setting Up the MySQL Database

Inserting CLOBs in MySQL is simple; in fact, CLOBs are just long String objects. This shows how to set
up the database:

```
mysql> desc datafiles;
+-----------+------------+------+-----+---------+-------+
| Field     | Type       | Null | Key | Default | Extra |
+-----------+------------+------+-----+---------+-------+
| id        | int(11)    |      | PRI | 0       |       |
| fileName  | varchar(6) | YES  |     | NULL    |       |
| fileBody  | text       | YES  |     | NULL    |       |
+-----------+------------+------+-----+---------+-------+
3 rows in set (0.00 sec)

mysql> select id, filename from datafiles;
+----+----------+
| id | filename |
+----+----------+
| 20 | file2    |
+----+----------+
1 row in set (0.00 sec)

mysql> insert into datafiles(id, filename, filebody)
    2  values(4000, 'file4000', 'This is the content of file4000.');
Query OK, 1 row affected, 1 warning (0.00 sec)
```

```
mysql> select id, filename from datafiles;
+------+----------+
| id   | filename |
+------+----------+
| 20   | file2    |
+------+----------+
| 4000 | file4000 |
+------+----------+
2 rows in set (0.00 sec)
```

Creating the Oracle Servlet Interface

The servlet interface is as follows:

```
http://localhost:8000/octopus/servlet/InsertClobToMySqlServlet?
    id=<id>&name=<name>&file=<file-as-URL>
```

Therefore, InsertClobToMySqlServlet has three parameters:

- id (the ID of file)
- name (the name of file)
- file (the URL of file representing the CLOB; the servlet will open the URL, construct a CLOB, and insert it into the CLOB column of the DataFiles table)

Let's insert a new record with the following data in the DataFiles table:

- name
- file (the URL of file: http://www.geocities.com/mparsian/data/file500.txt)

Figure 8-23 shows the content of the URL (http://www.geocities.com/mparsian/data/file500.txt).

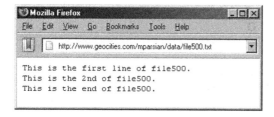

Figure 8-23. *Viewing CLOB using a servlet*

Therefore, the servlet call is as follows:

```
http://localhost:8000/octopus/servlet/InsertClobToMySqlServlet?
    id=500&name=file500&file=http://www.geocities.com/mparsian/data/file500.txt
```

Inserting a New CLOB Record

Figure 8-24 shows the result of inserting a new CLOB record.

OK: inserted a new record with id=500

Figure 8-24. *Inserting a new CLOB record using a servlet*

Viewing the Database Content After Insertion

Using MySQL's command prompt, you can view the inserted record (with id=500):

```
mysql> select id, filename from datafiles;
+------+----------+
| id   | filename |
+------+----------+
| 20   | file2    |
+------+----------+
| 500  | file500  |
+------+----------+
| 4000 | file4000 |
+------+----------+
3 rows in set (0.00 sec)

mysql> select id, filename, filebody from datafiles where id=500;
+-----+----------+-------------------------------------+

+-----+----------+-------------------------------------+
| 500 | file50   | This is the first line of file500.  |
|     |          | This is the 2nd of file500.         |
|     |          | This is the end of file500.         |
+-----+----------+-------------------------------------+

1 row in set (0.00 sec)
```

Using DisplayOracleClobServlet, you can view the CLOB in a Web browser, as shown in Figure 8-25.

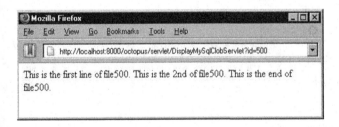

Figure 8-25. *Viewing an inserted CLOB record using a servlet*

Solution: InsertClobToMySqlServlet

The MySQL solution is identical to the Oracle solution with the exception of the getConnection() method, which returns a MySQL Connection object. You can download the complete MySQL solution from the book's Web site.

The following is getConnection() for the MySQL database:

```
public static Connection getConnection() throws Exception {
    String driver = "org.gjt.mm.mysql.Driver";
    String url = "jdbc:mysql://localhost/octopus";
    String username = "root";
    String password = "root";
    Class.forName(driver);  // load MySQL driver
    return DriverManager.getConnection(url, username, password);
}
```

8-14. How Do You Update an Existing CLOB of an Oracle Database Using a Servlet?

The SQL UPDATE statement modifies the existing column's data in a table. The simplified syntax is as follows (which updates a single column):

```
UPDATE table_name
    SET column_name_1 = new_value_1,
        cloumn_name_2 = new_value_2, ...
        WHERE column_name_x = some_value_1 and
              column_name_y = some_value_2 and ...
```

You can update any number of columns using the SQL UPDATE statement. For details, please refer to the following Web site: http://www.w3schools.com/sql/sql_update.asp.

To update a CLOB in an Oracle database using a servlet, you will represent the new value of

pass the new CLOB value to the database as a String object. Therefore, you will represent the new value of a CLOB as a URL. The following sections use the DataFiles table defined in the earlier sections.

Setting Up the Oracle Database

Oracle 10 has simplified CLOBs in JDBC. There is no need to use Oracle's proprietary SQL functions, such as empty_clob. Inserting/updating CLOBs is simple; in fact, CLOBs are just long String objects. This shows how to set up the database:

```
$ sqlplus scott/tiger
SQL*Plus: Release 10.1.0.2.0 - Production on Sat Feb 19 22:38:38 2005
Copyright (c) 1982, 2004, Oracle.  All rights reserved.

SQL> desc datafiles;
 Name                           Null?    Type
 ------------------------------ -------- ----------
 ID                             NOT NULL NUMBER(38)
 FILENAME                                VARCHAR2(20)
 FILEBODY                                CLOB

SQL> select id, filename, filebody from datafiles where id=1000;

ID     FILENAME  FILEBODY
-----  --------  ----------------------------
1000   file1     this is file1. hello world.
```

```
SQL> update datafiles
  2      set filebody='this is a long ... string. aha.'
  3          where id=1000;

1 row updated.

SQL> commit;
Commit complete.

SQL> select id, filename, filebody from datafiles where id=1000;
ID     FILENAME  FILEBODY
-----  --------  ------------------------------
1000   file1     this is a long ... string. aha.
```

Creating the Oracle Servlet Interface

The servlet interface is as follows:

```
http://localhost:8000/octopus/servlet/UpdateOracleClobServlet?
    id=<id>&file=<file-as-URL>
```

Therefore, UpdateOracleClobServlet has two parameters:

- id (the ID of file, which uniquely identifies record)

- file (the URL of file representing the CLOB; the servlet will open the URL, construct a CLOB, and update it into the CLOB column of the DataFiles table)

- id (1000)

- file (the URL of file: http://www.geocities.com/mparsian/data/file500.txt)

Figure 8-26 shows the content of the URL (http://www.geocities.com/mparsian/data/file500.txt).

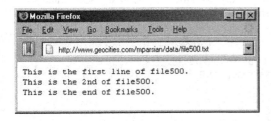

Figure 8-26. *Displaying a file using a servlet*

Therefore, the servlet call is as follows (but all in one line):

```
http://localhost:8000/octopus/servlet/UpdateOracleClobServlet?
    id=1000&file=http://www.geocities.com/mparsian/data/file500.txt
```

Updating an Existing CLOB Record

Figure 8-27 shows the result of updating an existing CLOB record.

Figure 8-27. *Updating a* CLOB *using a servlet*

Database Content After Insertion

The following shows the database after the insertion:

```
SQL> select id, filename, filebody from datafiles where id=1000;

     ID  FILENAME   FILEBODY
   ----  --------   ----------------------------------
   1000  file1      This is the first line of file500.
                    This is the 2nd of file500.
                    This is the end
```

Using DisplayOracleClobServlet, you can view the CLOB in a Web browser, as shown in Figure 8-28.

Figure 8-28. *Viewing an updated* CLOB *using a servlet*

The Solution: UpdateOracleClobServlet

The following shows the UpdateOracleClobServlet solution:

```java
import java.io.*;
import java.sql.*;

import javax.servlet.*;
import javax.servlet.http.*;

import jcb.db.DatabaseUtil;
import jcb.util.IOUtil;

public class UpdateOracleClobServlet extends HttpServlet {
    static final String UPDATE_CLOB =
        "update datafiles set filebody=? where id=?";

    public static Connection getConnection() throws Exception {... }
    public void doGet(...) {... }
    public void doPost(...) {...}
```

```
    public void updateCLOB(...) {....}
    public static String getClobsContentAsString(...) {...}
    private static String trimParameter(...) {...}
}
```

getConnection()

The following shows getConnection():

```
public static Connection getConnection() throws Exception {
    String driver = "oracle.jdbc.driver.OracleDriver";
    String url = "jdbc:oracle:thin:@localhost:1521:caspian";
    String username = "scott";
    String password = "tiger";
    Class.forName(driver);   // load Oracle driver
    return DriverManager.getConnection(url, username, password);
}
```

doGet()

The following shows doGet():

```
public void doGet(HttpServletRequest request,
                  HttpServletResponse response)
    throws IOException, ServletException {
    String fileContent = null;
    Connection conn = null;


    ServletOutputStream out = response.getOutputStream();

    response.setContentType("text/html");
    out.println("<html><head><title>UpdateOracleClobServlet</title></head>");

    try {
      conn = getConnection();
      fileContent = getClobsContentAsString(fileAsURL);
      updateCLOB(conn, id, fileContent);
      out.println("<body><h4>OK: updated an existing "+
          record with id="+id+"</h4></body></html>");
    }
    catch(Exception e) {
      e.printStackTrace();
      out.println("<body><h4>Error: "+e.getMessage()+"</h4></body></html>");
    }
}
```

updateCLOB()

The following shows updateCLOB():

```
public void updateCLOB(Connection conn, String id, String fileContent)
    throws Exception {
    PreparedStatement pstmt = null;
    try {
        pstmt = conn.prepareStatement(UPDATE_CLOB);
        pstmt.setString(1, fileContent);
        pstmt.setString(2, id);
```

```
        pstmt.executeUpdate();
    }
    finally {
        DatabaseUtil.close(pstmt);
    }
}
```

getClobsContentAsString()

The following shows getClobsContentAsString():

```
public static String  getClobsContentAsString(String urlAsString)
    throws Exception {
    InputStream content = null;
    try {
        java.net.URL url = new java.net.URL(urlAsString);
        java.net.URLConnection urlConn = url.openConnection();
        urlConn.connect();
        content = urlConn.getInputStream();
        return IOUtil.inputStreamToString(content);
    }
    finally {
        IOUtil.close(content);
    }
}
```

trimParameter()

```
private static String trimParameter(String s) {
    if ((s == null) || (s.length() == 0)) {
        return s;
    }
    else {
        return s.trim();
    }
}
```

8-15. How Do You Update an Existing CLOB of a MySQL Database Using a Servlet?

The SQL UPDATE statement modifies the existing column's data in a table. The simplified syntax is as follows (which updates a single column):

```
UPDATE table_name
    SET column_name_1 = new_value_1,
        column_name_2 = new_value_2, ...
        WHERE column_name_x = some_value_1 and
            column_name_y = some_value_2 and ...
```

You can update any number of columns using the SQL UPDATE statement. For details, please refer to the following Web site: http://www.w3schools.com/sql/sql_update.asp.

To update a CLOB in a MySQL database using a servlet, you will represent the new value of a CLOB as a URL (the URL will be pointing to a CLOB data, such as a text file). The reason for this is that servlets cannot access the local file system (a client's/browser's local machine). You can also pass the new CLOB value to the database as a String object. Therefore, you will represent the new value of a CLOB as a URL. The following sections use the DataFiles table defined in the earlier questions.

Each database vendor handles BLOB/CLOB updates differently. According to the MySQL documentation (http://dev.mysql.com/doc/connector/j/en/cj-implementation-notes.html), "the Clob implementation does not allow in-place modification (they are *copies*, as reported by the DatabaseMetaData.locatorsUpdateCopies() method). Because of this, you should use the PreparedStatement.setClob() method to save changes back to the database. The JDBC API does not have a ResultSet.updateClob() method." On the other hand, in Oracle, "to write LOB (large objects such as CLOB and BLOB) data, the application must acquire a write lock on the LOB object. One way to accomplish this is through a SELECT FOR UPDATE. Also, disable autocommit mode."

Setting Up the MySQL Database

In MySQL, updating existing CLOBs is simple; in fact, CLOBs are just long String objects. This shows how to set up the database:

```
mysql> use octopus;
Database changed
mysql> desc datafiles;
+----------+------------+------+-----+---------+-------+
| Field    | Type       | Null | Key | Default | Extra |
+----------+------------+------+-----+---------+-------+
| id       | int(11)    |      | PRI | 0       |       |
| fileName | varchar(6) | YES  |     | NULL    |       |
| fileBody | text       | YES  |     | NULL    |       |
+----------+------------+------+-----+---------+-------+
3 rows in set (0.00 sec)


+------+----------+---------------------------------+
| id   | filename | filebody                        |
+------+----------+---------------------------------+
| 4000 | file40   | This is the content of file4000.|
+------+----------+---------------------------------+
1 row in set (0.00 sec)

mysql> update datafiles
    ->       set filebody='My New CLOB Value...!!!'
    ->           where id=4000;
Query OK, 1 row affected (0.00 sec)
Rows matched: 1  Changed: 1  Warnings: 0

mysql> select id, filename, filebody
    ->  from datafiles where id=4000;
+------+----------+------------------------+
| id   | filename | filebody               |
+------+----------+------------------------+
| 4000 | file40   | My New CLOB Value...!!! |
+------+----------+------------------------+
1 row in set (0.00 sec)
```

Creating the MySQL Servlet Interface

The servlet interface is as follows:

```
http://localhost:8000/octopus/servlet/UpdateMySqlClobServlet?
    id=<id>&file=<file-as-URL>
```

Therefore, `InsertClobToMySqlServlet` has two parameters:

- `id` (the ID of file, which uniquely identifies record)
- `file` (the URL of file representing the CLOB; the servlet will open the URL, construct a CLOB, and update it into the CLOB column of the DataFiles table)

Let's update an existing record with the following data in the DataFiles table:

- `id` (4000)
- `file` (the URL of file: `http://www.geocities.com/mparsian/data/file500.txt`)

Figure 8-29 shows the content of the URL (`http://www.geocities.com/mparsian/data/file500.txt`).

Figure 8-29. *Displaying a file using a servlet*

Therefore, the servlet call is as follows (but all in one line):

```
http://localhost:8000/octopus/servlet/UpdateMySqlClobServlet?
    id=4000&file=http://www.geocities.com/mparsian/data/file500.txt
```

Updating an Existing CLOB Record

Figure 8-30 shows the results of updating an existing CLOB record.

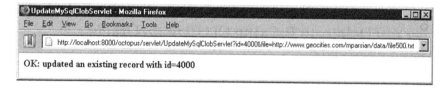

Figure 8-30. *Updating a* CLOB *using a servlet*

Viewing the Database Content After Insertion

This shows the database after the insertion:

```
mysql> select id, filename, filebody from datafiles where id=4000;
+------+----------+-------------------------------------------------- +
| id   | filename | filebody                                          |
+------+----------+--------------------------------------------------+
| 4000 | file40   | This is the first line of file500.                |
|      |          | This is the 2nd of file500.                       |
|      |          | This is the end of file500.                       |
+------+----------+--------------------------------------------------+
1 row in set (0.00 sec)
```

Using DisplayMySqlClobServlet, you can view the CLOB in a Web browser, as shown in Figure 8-31.

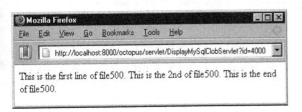

Figure 8-31. *Viewing an updated* CLOB *using a servlet*

Solution: UpdateMySqlClobServlet

The MySQL solution is identical to the Oracle solution with the exception of the getConnection() method, which returns a MySQL Connection object. You can download the complete MySQL solution from the book's Web site.

The following is getConnection() for the MySQL database:

```
public static Connection getConnection() throws Exception {
    String driver = "org.gjt.mm.mysql.Driver";
    String url = "jdbc:mysql://localhost/octopus";
    String username = "root";
    String password = "root";
    Class.forName(driver);   // load MySQL driver
    return DriverManager.getConnection(url, username, password);
}
```

8-16. How Do You Delete an Existing CLOB of an Oracle Database Using a Servlet?

The SQL DELETE statement deletes rows in a table. The simple syntax is as follows:

```
DELETE FROM table_name
    WHERE column_name_1 = some_value_1 and
          Column_name_2 = some_value_2 and ...
```

The goal is to delete an existing database record that has a CLOB column. You can do this by providing the primary key for the desired record (to be deleted). You may also delete the CLOB record using SQL's LIKE statement against the content of the CLOB (the body of the file), but this is not recommended. (Most databases will not allow you to index the CLOBs; for example, MySQL allows you to index portions of CLOBs.) For solving this problem, you will use the DataFiles table (the id column is the primary key, and fileBody is the CLOB column). The servlet interface is as follows:

```
http://localhost:8000/octopus/servlet/DeleteClobFromOracleServlet?id=<id>
```

Therefore, DeleteClobFromMySqlServlet has only one parameter:

- id (the ID of CLOB, which is the primary key that identifies the record)

To delete an existing record with the ID of 500, issue this:

```
http://localhost:8000/octopus/servlet/DeleteClobFromOracleServlet?id=500
```

Viewing the Database Content Before Deletion

This is the database before the deletion:

```
SQL> desc DataFiles;
 Name                    Null?    Type
 --------------------- -------- ------------
 ID                      NOT NULL NUMBER(38)
 FILENAME                         VARCHAR2(20)
 FILEBODY                         CLOB

SQL> select id, filename from dataFiles;

      ID  FILENAME


    1000  file1
    2000  file2
     500  file500
```

Using a Servlet to Delete a Record (with CLOB)

Therefore, the servlet call is as follows:

```
http://localhost:8000/octopus/servlet/DeleteClobFromOracleServlet?id=500
```

Viewing the Actual Servlet Call for Deleting a Record (with CLOB)

Figure 8-32 shows the result of deleting a record.

Figure 8-32. *Deleting a* CLOB *using a servlet*

Viewing the Database Content After Deletion

This shows the database after the deletion:

```
SQL> select id, filename from dataFiles;

      ID  FILENAME
---------- --------------------
    4000  file4000
    1000  file1
    2000  file2
```

Solution: DeleteClobFromOracleServlet

This shows the DeleteClobFromOracleServlet solution:

```java
import java.io.*;
import java.sql.*;

import javax.servlet.*;
import javax.servlet.http.*;

import jcb.db.DatabaseUtil;
import jcb.util.IOUtil;

public class DeleteClobFromOracleServlet extends HttpServlet {

    private static final String DELETE_CLOB_RECORD =
        "delete from DataFiles where id = ?";



}
```

getConnection()

This shows getConnection():

```java
public static Connection getConnection() throws Exception {
    String driver = "oracle.jdbc.driver.OracleDriver";
    String url = "jdbc:oracle:thin:@matrix:1521:caspian";
    String username = "mp";
    String password = "mp2";
    Class.forName(driver);  // load Oracle driver
    return DriverManager.getConnection(url, username, password);
}
```

doGet()

This shows doGet():

```java
public void doGet(HttpServletRequest request,
                  HttpServletResponse response)
    throws IOException, ServletException {

    Connection conn = null;
    PreparedStatement pstmt = null;
    String id = request.getParameter("id").trim();
    ServletOutputStream out = response.getOutputStream();
    response.setContentType("text/html");
    out.println("<html><head><title>Delete CLOB Record</title></head>");
```

```
        try {
            conn = getConnection();
            pstmt = conn.prepareStatement(DELETE_CLOB_RECORD);
            pstmt.setString(1, id);
            pstmt.executeUpdate();
            pstmt.executeUpdate();
            out.println("<body><h4>deleted CLOB record with id="
                +id+"</h4></body></html>");
        }
        catch (Exception e) {
            out.println("<body><h4>Error="+e.getMessage()+"</h4></body></html>");
        }
        finally {
          DatabaseUtil.close(pstmt);
          DatabaseUtil.close(conn);
        }
    }
}
```

doPost()

This shows doPost():

```
public void doPost(
    HttpServletRequest request,
    HttpServletResponse response)
    throws IOException, ServletException {
    doGet(request, response);
}
```

8-17. How Do You Delete an Existing CLOB of an MySQL Database Using a Servlet?

The goal is to delete an existing database record, which has a CLOB column. Basically, you can do this by providing the primary key for the desired record (to be deleted). For solving this problem, you will use the DataFiles table (the id column is the primary key, and fileBody is the CLOB column). The servlet interface is as follows:

```
http://localhost:8000/octopus/servlet/DeleteClobFromMySqlServlet?id=<id>
```

Therefore, DeleteClobFromMySqlServlet has only one parameter:

- id (the ID of CLOB, which is the primary key that identifies the record)

To delete an existing record with the ID of 500, you will issue the following servlet call:

```
http://localhost:8000/octopus/servlet/DeleteClobFromMySqlServlet?id=500
```

Viewing the Database Content Before Deletion

This is the database before the deletion:

```
mysql> use octopus;
Database changed
mysql> desc datafiles;
```

```
+-----------+-------------+------+-----+---------+-------+
| Field     | Type        | Null | Key | Default | Extra |
+-----------+-------------+------+-----+---------+-------+
| id        | int(11)     |      | PRI | 0       |       |
| fileName  | varchar(6)  | YES  |     | NULL    |       |
| fileBody  | text        | YES  |     | NULL    |       |
+-----------+-------------+------+-----+---------+-------+
3 rows in set (0.00 sec)

mysql> select id, filename from datafiles;
+----+----------+
| id | filename |
+----+----------+
| 10 | file1    |
| 20 | file2    |
+----+----------+
2 rows in set (0.05 sec)
```

Using a Servlet to Delete a Record (with CLOB)

Therefore, the servlet call is as follows (deleting an existing record with the ID of 10):

```
http://localhost:8000/octopus/servlet/DeleteClobFromMySqlServlet?id=10
```

Viewing the Actual Servlet Call for Deleting a Record (with CLOB)

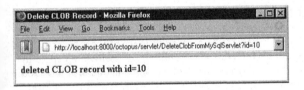

Figure 8-33. *Deleting a CLOB using a servlet*

Viewing the Database Content After Deletion

This is the database after the deletion:

```
mysql> select id, filename from datafiles;
+----+----------+
| id | filename |
+----+----------+
| 20 | file2    |
+----+----------+
1 row in set (0.00 sec)
```

Solution: DeleteClobFromMySqlServlet

The MySQL solution is identical to the Oracle solution with the exception of getConnection(), which returns a MySQL Connection object. You can download the complete MySQL solution from the book's Web site.

The following is getConnection() for the MySQL database:

```
public static Connection getConnection() throws Exception {
    String driver = "org.gjt.mm.mysql.Driver";
    String url = "jdbc:mysql://localhost/octopus";
    String username = "root";
    String password = "root";
    Class.forName(driver);  // load MySQL driver
    return DriverManager.getConnection(url, username, password);
}
```

8-18. Should You Use java.lang.String or java.sql.Clob? Which Has the Best Performance?

If you have the choice of manipulating large text data (a large text column of a record such as the CLOB data type), should you use java.lang.String or java.sql.Clob? Which has the best performance?

For better performance, you should use java.sql.Clob, since it does not extract any data from the database until you explicitly ask it to (by invoking the getAsciiStream() or getCharacterStream() method). The JDBC data type java.sql.Clob wraps a database locator (which is essentially a pointer to char). That pointer is a rather large number (between 32 and 256 bits in size), but the effort to extract it from the database is insignificant next to extracting the full CLOB content. For insertion into the database, you should use java.lang.String since data has not been uploaded to the database yet. Therefore, use the java.sql.Clob object only for data extraction (whenever possible).

CHAPTER 9

■ ■ ■

Working with Date, Time, and Timestamp in JDBC

Date, Time, and Timestamp are important data types in commercial and banking applications. For example, the following are some of their uses:

- Time of airline arrival
- Date of purchase
- Hire date of an employee
- Update date of employee's salary
- Purge date of database

- Account creation date
- Account expiration date

The purpose of this chapter is to provide snippets and code samples that deal with Date, Time, and Timestamp. Please note that most of the solutions are provided as independent static methods (In other words, these methods do not depend on external static data structures and rely only on the passed input arguments; therefore, you can use these methods just as they appear in this chapter.)

The java.sql package provides the following classes that deal with date-related data types (portions of these descriptions were taken from the Java 2 Platform, Standard Edition 1.4.1):

java.sql.Date: Mapping for SQL DATE. The java.sql.Date class extends the java.util.Date class. This is a thin wrapper around a millisecond value that allows JDBC to identify this as a SQL DATE value. A millisecond value represents the number of milliseconds that have passed since January 1, 1970, 00:00:00.000 GMT. To conform with the definition of SQL DATE, the millisecond values wrapped by a java.sql.Date instance must be "normalized" by setting the hours, minutes, seconds, and milliseconds to zero in the particular time zone with which the instance is associated.

java.sql.Time: Mapping for SQL TIME. The java.sql.Time class extends the java.util.Date class. This is a thin wrapper around the java.util.Date class that allows the JDBC API to identify this as a SQL TIME value. The Time class adds formatting and parsing operations to support the JDBC escape syntax for time values. The date components should be set to the "zero epoch" value of January 1, 1970, and should not be accessed.

java.sql.Timestamp: Mapping for SQL TIMESTAMP. The java.sql.Timestamp class extends the java.util.Date class. This is a thin wrapper around java.util.Date that allows the JDBC API to identify this as a SQL TIMESTAMP value. It adds the ability to hold the SQL TIMESTAMP "nanos value" and provides formatting and parsing operations to support the JDBC escape syntax for timestamp values. This type is a composite of a java.util.Date and a separate nanosecond value. Only integral seconds are stored in the java.util.Date component. The fractional seconds—the nanos—are separate. The getTime method will return only integral seconds. If a time value that includes the fractional seconds is desired, you must convert nanos to milliseconds (nanos/1,000,000) and add this to the getTime value. The Timestamp.equals(Object) method never returns true when passed a value of type java.util.Date because the nanos component of a date is unknown. As a result, the Timestamp.equals(Object) method is not symmetric with respect to the java.util.Date.equals(Object) method. Also, the hash code method uses the underlying java.util.Data implementation and therefore does not include nanos in its computation. Because of the differences between the Timestamp class and the java.util.Date class mentioned previously, it is recommended that you check the vendor's implementation of SQL's DATE, TIME, and TIMESTAMP data types. The inheritance relationship between Timestamp and java.util.Date really denotes implementation inheritance, not type inheritance.

Each database vendor provides specific data types for supporting Date, Time, and Timestamp. To fully understand these data types and provide JDBC access to these types, you will see how to use the MySQL and Oracle databases in the examples.

9-1. What Is the Mapping of Date-Related SQL and Java Types?

- The JDBC DATE type (java.sql.Date, which extends java.util.Date) represents a date consisting of the day, month, and year. The corresponding SQL DATE type is defined in SQL-92.

- The JDBC TIME type (java.sql.Time, which extends java.util.Date) represents a time consisting of hours, minutes, and seconds. The corresponding SQL TIME type is defined in SQL-92.

- The JDBC TIMESTAMP type (java.sql.Timestamp, which extends java.util.Date) represents DATE plus TIME plus a nanosecond field. The corresponding SQL TIMESTAMP type is defined in SQL-92.

The DATE type is where most mismatches occur. This is because the java.util.Date class represents both Date and Time, but SQL has the following three types to represent date and time information:

- A SQL DATE type that represents the date only (01/26/88)
- A SQL TIME type that specifies the time only (09:06:56)
- A SQL TIMESTAMP that represents the time value in nanoseconds

Table 9-1 shows the mapping of JDBC types to Java types, which can be mapped back to JDBC types, because this is a one-to-one relationship mapping.

Table 9-1. *JDBC Types Mapped to Java Types*

JDBC Type	Java Type
DATE	java.sql.Date
TIME	java.sql.Time
TIMESTAMP	java.sql.Timestamp

9-2. How Do You Retrieve Date, Time, and Timestamp from a Database?

The ResultSet interface provides the necessary methods for extracting Date, Time, and Timestamp from a database. Table 9-2 lists the ResultSet.getXXX() methods for retrieving data from the Date, Time, and Timestamp types.

Table 9-2. ResultSet *Methods for Retrieving* Date, Time, *and* Timestamp *(According to the JDK)*

Return Type	Method	Description
java.sql.Date	getDate(int columnIndex)	Retrieves the value of the designated column in the current row of this ResultSet object as a java.sql.Date object in the Java programming language.
java.sql.Date	getDate(int columnIndex, Calendar cal)	Retrieves the value of the designated column in the current row of this ResultSet object as a java.sql.Date object in the Java programming language.
java.sql.Date	getDate(String columnName)	Retrieves the value of the designated column in the current row of this ResultSet object as a java.sql.Date object in the Java programming language.
		ResultSet object as a java.sql.Date object in the Java programming language.
java.sql.Time	getTime(int columnIndex)	Retrieves the value of the designated column in the current row of this ResultSet object as a java.sql.Time object in the Java programming language.
java.sql.Time	getTime(int columnIndex, Calendar cal)	Retrieves the value of the designated column in the current row of this ResultSet object as a java.sql.Time object in the Java programming language.
java.sql.Time	getTime(String columnName)	Retrieves the value of the designated column in the current row of this ResultSet object as a java.sql.Time object in the Java programming language.
java.sql.Time	getTime(String columnName, Calendar cal)	Retrieves the value of the designated column in the current row of this ResultSet object as a java.sql.Time object in the Java programming language. This method uses the given calendar to construct an appropriate millisecond value for the time if the underlying database does not store time zone information.

Continued

Table 9-2. (*Continued*)

Return Type	Method	Description
java.sql.Timestamp	getTimestamp(int columnIndex)	Retrieves the value of the designated column in the current row of this ResultSet object as a java.sql.Timestamp object in the Java programming language.
java.sql.Timestamp	getTimestamp(int columnIndex, Calendar cal)	Retrieves the value of the designated column in the current row of this ResultSet object as a java.sql.Timestamp object in the Java programming language.
java.sql.Timestamp	getTimestamp(String columnName)	Retrieves the value of the designated column in the current row of this ResultSet object as a java.sql.Timestamp object.
java.sql.Timestamp	getTimestamp(String columnName, Calendar cal)	Retrieves the value of the designated column in the current row of this ResultSet object as a java.sql.Timestamp object in the Java programming language.

9-3. How Does MySQL Handle Date, Time, and Timestamp?

DATETIME: Use the DATETIME type when you need values that contain both date and time information. MySQL retrieves and displays DATETIME values in YYYY-MM-DD HH:MM:SS format. The supported range is from 1000-01-01 00:00:00 to 9999-12-31 23:59:59. (*Supported* means that although other values might work, there is no guarantee they will.)

DATE: Use the DATE type when you need only a date value without a time part. MySQL retrieves and displays DATE values in YYYY-MM-DD format. The supported range is from 1000-01-01 to 9999-12-31.

TIMESTAMP: The TIMESTAMP column type provides a type that you can use to automatically mark INSERT or UPDATE operations with the current date and time. If you have multiple TIMESTAMP columns, only the first one is updated automatically. For automatic updating of the first TIMESTAMP column, please refer to the MySQL manual.

9-4. How Does Oracle Handle Date, Time, and Timestamp?

The Oracle DATE data type contains both date and time information. The Oracle DATE data type is a complex data type that encapsulates date, time, and timestamp concepts.

Table 9-3 shows the mapping between JDBC data types, Java native data types, and Oracle data types:

Table 9-3. Oracle's Date Types

Standard JDBC Data Types	Java Native Data Types	Oracle Data Types
java.sql.Types.DATE	java.sql.Date	DATE
java.sql.Types.TIME	java.sql.Time	DATE
java.sql.Types.TIMESTAMP	javal.sql.Timestamp	DATE

To understand these three classes, I will show how to define a table that has columns that directly deal with these three classes. Here is the definition of the table:

```
create table TestDates(
    id VARCHAR2(10) NOT NULL Primary Key,
    date_column DATE,
    time_column DATE,
    timestamp_column DATE
);
```

Here is how you create the TestDates table (the output has been formatted):

```
$ sqlplus scott/tiger
SQL*Plus: Release 9.2.0.1.0 - Production on Sun Nov 24 21:47:08 2002

SQL>    create table TestDates(
  2             id VARCHAR2(10) NOT NULL Primary Key,
  3             date_column DATE,
  4             time_column DATE,



Table created.
SQL> commit;
Commit complete.

SQL> describe  TestDates
 Name                     Null?    Type
 --------------------- --------- -------------
 ID                       NOT NULL VARCHAR2(10)
 DATE_COLUMN                       DATE
 TIME_COLUMN                       DATE
 TIMESTAMP_COLUMN                  DATE
```

I will cover the following topics for the TestDates table:

- Inserting a new record

- Retrieving an existing record

- Updating an existing record

- Deleting an existing record

To simplify your work in these examples, you will get a JDBC Connection object from a static method. (In real database applications, you would get the Connection object, java.sql.Connection, from a connection pool manager, which manages a set of JDBC Connection objects.)

Oracle Date and Time Types: Inserting a New Record

The following program creates a new record in the TestDates table (with an ID of "id100"). Here is
the program listing:

```java
import java.sql.*;
import jcb.util.DatabaseUtil;

public class InsertDate {
    public static Connection getConnection() throws Exception {
        String driver = "oracle.jdbc.driver.OracleDriver";
        String url = "jdbc:oracle:thin:@localhost:1521:scorpian";
        Class.forName(driver);
        System.out.println("ok: loaded oracle driver.");
        return DriverManager.getConnection(url, "scott", "tiger");
    }

    public static void main(String args[]) {
        String INSERT_RECORD = "insert into TestDates(id, date_column, "+
            "time_column, timestamp_column) values(?, ?, ?, ?)";
        Connection conn = null;
        PreparedStatement pstmt = null;
        try {
            conn = getConnection();
            pstmt = conn.prepareStatement(INSERT_RECORD);
            pstmt.setString(1, "id100");


            java.sql.Date sqlDate = new java.sql.Date(t);
            java.sql.Time sqlTime = new java.sql.Time(t);
            java.sql.Timestamp sqlTimestamp = new java.sql.Timestamp(t);
            System.out.println("sqlDate="+sqlDate);
            System.out.println("sqlTime="+sqlTime);
            System.out.println("sqlTimestamp="+sqlTimestamp);
            pstmt.setDate(2, sqlDate);
            pstmt.setTime(3, sqlTime);
            pstmt.setTimestamp(4, sqlTimestamp);
            pstmt.executeUpdate();
        }
        catch( Exception e ) {
            e.printStackTrace();
            System.out.println("Failed to insert the record.");
            System.exit(1);
        }
        finally {
            DatabaseUtil.close(pstmt);
            DatabaseUtil.close(conn);
        }
    }
}
```

Testing InsertDate

Running the InsertDate.java program will generate the following output (the values are before
insertion to TestDates):

```
$ javac InsertDate.java
$ java InsertDate
ok: loaded oracle driver.
sqlDate=2002-11-24
sqlTime=23:05:52
sqlTimestamp=2002-11-24 23:05:52.717
```

Oracle Date and Time Types: Retrieving an Existing Record

The following program retrieves an existing record from the TestDates table (with an ID of "id100").
Here is the program listing:

```java
import java.sql.*;
import jcb.util.DatabaseUtil;

public class GetDate {

    public static Connection getConnection() throws Exception {
        String driver = "oracle.jdbc.driver.OracleDriver";
        String url = "jdbc:oracle:thin:@localhost:1521:scorpian";
        Class.forName(driver);
        System.out.println("ok: loaded oracle driver.");
        return DriverManager.getConnection(url, "scott", "tiger");
    }

    public static void main(String args[]) {


        ResultSet rs = null;
        Connection conn = null;
        PreparedStatement pstmt = null;
        try {
            conn = getConnection();
            pstmt = conn.prepareStatement(GET_RECORD);
            pstmt.setString(1, "id100");
            rs = pstmt.executeQuery();
            if (rs.next()) {
                java.sql.Date dbSqlDate = rs.getDate(1);
                java.sql.Time dbSqlTime = rs.getTime(2);
                java.sql.Timestamp dbSqlTimestamp = rs.getTimestamp(3);
                System.out.println("dbSqlDate="+dbSqlDate);
                System.out.println("dbSqlTime="+dbSqlTime);
                System.out.println("dbSqlTimestamp="+dbSqlTimestamp);
            }
        }
        catch( Exception e ) {
            e.printStackTrace();
            System.out.println("Failed to insert the record.");
            System.exit(1);
        }
        finally {
            DatabaseUtil.close(rs);
            DatabaseUtil.close(pstmt);
            DatabaseUtil.close(conn);
        }
    }
}
```

Testing GetDate

Running the GetDate.java program will generate the following output (the values are after retrieval from TestDates):

```
$ javac GetDate.java
$ java GetDate
ok: loaded oracle driver.
dbSqlDate=2002-11-24
dbSqlTime=23:05:52
dbSqlTimestamp=2002-11-24 23:05:52.0
```

As you can observe, whatever values you deposited into the database, you were able to get back correctly (with the exception of Timestamp, which differs in value, so this is negligible).

9-5. How Do You Get the Current Date As a java.util.Date Object?

The class java.util.Date represents a specific instant in time, with millisecond precision. The following method returns the current date as a java.util.Date object:

```
/**
 * Get current date as a java.util.Date object
 * @return current date as a java.util.Date object
 */
public static java.util.Date getJavaUtilDate() {
    java.util.Date date = new java.util.Date();
    return date;
}
```

9-6. How Do You Create a java.sql.Date Object?

The class java.sql.Date descends from the java.util.Date class but uses only the year, month, and day values. The JDK defines java.sql.Date as follows:

```
public class java.sql.Date
    extends java.util.Date
```

Also, the JDK says this about java.sql.Date:

> *A thin wrapper around a millisecond value that allows JDBC to identify this as an SQL DATE value. A milliseconds value represents the number of milliseconds that have passed since January 1, 1970 00:00:00.000 GMT. To conform with the definition of SQL DATE, the millisecond values wrapped by a java.sql.Date instance must be "normalized" by setting the hours, minutes, seconds, and milliseconds to zero in the particular time zone with which the instance is associated.*

You have several ways to create a java.sql.Date object.

Creating java.sql.Date Using java.util.Date

This is how you create a java.sql.Date object using java.util.Date:

```
public static java.sql.Date getJavaSqlDate() {
    java.util.Date today = new java.util.Date();
    return new java.sql.Date(today.getTime());
}
```

Creating java.sql.Date Using java.util.Calendar

The following is according to the JDK:

> *The Calendar class is an abstract class that provides methods for converting between a specific instant in time and a set of calendar fields such as YEAR, MONTH, DAY_OF_MONTH, HOUR, and so on, and for manipulating the calendar fields, such as getting the date of the next week. An instant in time can be represented by a millisecond value that is an offset from the epoch, January 1, 1970, 00:00:00.000 GMT (Gregorian).*

Using the Calendar object, you can set the year, month, and day portions to the desired values. But you must set the hour, minute, second, and millisecond values to zero. At that point, Calendar.getTime().getTime() is invoked to get the java.util.Date in milliseconds. That value is then passed to a java.sql.Date constructor.

```
// get a calendar using the default time zone and locale.
Calendar calendar = Calendar.getInstance();

// set Date portion to January 1, 1970
calendar.set(Calendar.YEAR, 1970 );
calendar.set(Calendar.MONTH, Calendar.JANUARY );
calendar.set(Calendar.DATE, 1 );

// normalize the object
calendar.set(Calendar.HOUR_OF_DAY, 0 );


calendar.set(Calendar.MILLISECOND, 0 );

java.sql.Date javaSqlDate =
   new java.sql.Date( calendar.getTime().getTime() );
```

Creating java.sql.Date Using the java.sql.Date.valueOf() Method

You can use a static method (valueOf()) of the java.sql.Date class. The java.sql.Date object's valueOf() method accepts a String, which must be the date in JDBC time escape format: YYYY-MM-DD. For example, to create a Date object representing November 1, 2000, you would use this:

```
String date = "2000-11-01";
java.sql.Date javaSqlDate = java.sql.Date.valueOf(date);
```

The java.sql.Date.valueOf() method throws an IllegalArgumentException (a runtime exception) if the given date is not in the JDBC date escape format (YYYY-MM-DD).

Creating java.sql.Date Using GregorianCalendar

GregorianCalendar is a concrete subclass of Calendar and provides the standard calendar system used by most of the world. You may use the year, month, and day of month to construct a GregorianCalendar with the given date set in the default time zone with the default locale. For example, to create a Date object representing November 1, 2000, you would use this:

```
// month value is 0-based. e.g., 0 for January.
Calendar calendar = new GregorianCalendar
                         (2000, // year
                          10,   // month
                          1);   // day of month
java.sql.Date date = new java.sql.Date(calendar.getTimeInMillis());
```

9-7. How Do You Get the Current Timestamp As a java.sql.Timestamp Object?

The following methods return a current java.sql.Timestamp object.

Getting a Timestamp Object Using java.util.Date

This shows how to get a Timestamp object using java.util.Date:

```
/**
 * Return a Timestamp for right now
 * @return Timestamp for right now
 */
public static java.sql.Timestamp getJavaSqlTimestamp() {
    java.util.Date today = new java.util.Date();
    return new java.sql.Timestamp(today.getTime());
}
```

Getting a Timestamp Object Using System.currentTimeMillis()

This shows how to get a Timestamp object using System.currentTimeMillis():

```
/**
 * Return a Timestamp for right now
 * @return Timestamp for right now
 */


}
```

9-8. How Do You Get the Current Timestamp As a java.sql.Time Object?

The following method returns a current java.sql.Time object:

```
public static java.sql.Time getJavaSqlTime() {
    java.util.Date today = new java.util.Date();
    return new java.sql.Time(today.getTime());
}
```

9-9. How Do You Convert from a java.util.Date Object to a java.sql.Date Object?

The following code snippet shows how to convert from a java.util.Date object to a java.sql.Date object:

```
java.util.Date utilDate = new java.util.Date();
java.sql.Date sqlDate =  new java.sql.Date(utilDate.getTime());
System.out.println("utilDate:" + utilDate));
System.out.println("sqlDate:" + sqlDate));
```

This shows how to do the preceding as a method:

```
/**
 * Creates a java.sql.Date from a java.util.Date
 * return null if the parameter was null
 * @param utilDate the date to turn into the java.sql.Date object
```

```
 * @return the date or null if the utilDate was null
 */
public static java.sql.Date sqlDate(java.util.Date utilDate) {
  if (utilDate == null) {
     return null;
  }
  else {
     return new java.sql.Date(utilDate.getTime());
  }
}
```

9-10. How Do You Convert a String Date Such As 2003/01/10 into a java.util.Date Object?

When you want to convert a date expressed as a String object, you can use java.text.SimpleDateFormat for formatting purposes, like so:

```
import java.text.SimpleDateFormat;
...
try {
     SimpleDateFormat formatter = new SimpleDateFormat("yyyy/MM/dd");
     String date = "2003/01/10";
     java.util.Date utilDate = formatter.parse(date);
     System.out.println("date:" + date));
     System.out.println("utilDate:" + utilDate));
}


     e.printStackTrace();
}
```

This shows how to do the preceding as a method:

```
import java.text.SimpleDateFormat;
...
/**
 * Make a java.util.Date from a date as a string format of MM/DD/YYYY.
 * @param dateString date as a string of MM/DD/YYYY format.
 * @return a java.util.Date; if input is null return null;
 * @exception throws ParseException if the input is not valid format.
 */
public static java.util.Date makeDate(String dateString)
     throws ParseException {
     if ((dateString == null) || (dateString.length() == 0)) {
        return null;
     }
     SimpleDateFormat formatter = new SimpleDateFormat("MM/dd/yyyy");
     return formatter.parse(dateString);
}
```

9-11. How Do You Create Yesterday's Date from a Date in the String Format of MM/DD/YYYY?

The following code listing creates yesterday's date from a Date in the String format of MM/DD/YYYY:

```
/**
 * Create yesterday's date (as java.util.Date) from a date as a string
 * format of MM/DD/YYYY. If input is 03/01/2000, then it will
```

```
 * return a date with string value of 02/29/2000; and if your input
 * is 03/01/1999, then it will return a date with string value of
 * 02/28/1999.
 * @param dateString date as a string of MM/DD/YYYY format.
 * @return a yesterday's date (as java.util.Date); if input is null
 * return null;
 * @exception throws ParseException if the input is not valid format.
 */
public static java.util.Date makeYesterdayDate(String dateString)
    throws ParseException {

    if ((dateString == null) || (dateString.length() == 0)) {
        return null;
    }

    SimpleDateFormat sdf = new SimpleDateFormat("MM/dd/yyyy");
    GregorianCalendar gc = new GregorianCalendar();
    // the following stmt. will throw a ParseException
    // if dateString does not have a valid format.
    java.util.Date d = sdf.parse(dateString);
    gc.setTime(d);
    System.out.println("Input Date = " + sdf.format(d));
    int dayBefore = gc.get(Calendar.DAY_OF_YEAR);
    gc.roll(Calendar.DAY_OF_YEAR, -1);
    int dayAfter = gc.get(Calendar.DAY_OF_YEAR);
    if(dayAfter > dayBefore) {


    gc.get(Calendar.DATE);
    java.util.Date yesterday = gc.getTime();
    System.out.println("Yesterdays Date = " + sdf.format(yesterday));
    return yesterday;
}
```

9-12. How Do You Create a java.util.Date Object from a Year, Month, Day Format?

The following code listing creates a java.util.Date object from a Year, Month, and Day format:

```
import java.text.SimpleDateFormat;
import java.util.Date;
...
/**
 * Make a java.util.Date from Year, Month, Day.
 * @param year the year
 * @param month the month
 * @param day the day
 * @throws ParseException failed to make a date.
 */
public static Date getJavaUtilDate(int year, int month, int day)
    throws ParseException {

    String date = new String(year) +"/"+ new String(month) +"/"+ new String(day);
    java.util.Date  utilDate = null;
```

```
    try {
            SimpleDateFormat formatter = new SimpleDateFormat("yyyy/MM/dd");
            utilDate  = formatter.parse(date);
            System.out.println("utilDate:" + utilDate));
            return utilDate;
    }
    catch (ParseException e) {
            System.out.println(e.toString());
            e.printStackTrace();
    }
}
```

9-13. How Do You Convert a String Date Such As 2003/01/10 to a java.sql.Date Object?

The following shows how to convert a String date such as 2003/01/10 into a java.sql.Date object:

```
import java.text.SimpleDateFormat;
...
try {
   SimpleDateFormat formatter = new SimpleDateFormat("yyyy/MM/dd");
   String  date  = "2003/01/10";
   java.util.Date utilDate  = formatter.parse(date);
   java.sql.Date  sqlDate = new java.sql.Date(util.getTime());
   System.out.println("date:" + date));
   System.out.println("sqlDate:" + sqlDate));


   System.out.println(e.toString());
   e.printStackTrace();
}
```

This shows how to do the preceding as a method using getJavaSqlDate():

```
import java.text.SimpleDateFormat;
...
/**
 * Make a java.sql.Date from (year, month, day).
 * @param year the year
 * @param month the month
 * @param day the day
 * @throws ParseException failed to make a date.
 */
public static java.sql.Date getJavaSqlDate(int year, int month, int day)
    throws ParseException {
    String date = new String(year) +"/"+ new String(month) +"/"+ new String(day);
    java.sql.Date  sqlDate = null;
    try {
            SimpleDateFormat formatter = new SimpleDateFormat("yyyy/MM/dd");
            java.util.Date utilDate  = formatter.parse(date);
            sqlDate = new java.sql.Date(util.getTime());
            System.out.println("sqlDate:" + sqlDate));
            return sqlDate;
    }
```

```
    catch (ParseException e) {
            System.out.println(e.toString());
            e.printStackTrace();
    }
}
```

9-14. How Do You Get a Timestamp Object?

This shows how to get a Timestamp object:

```
java.sql.Date date = new java.util.Date();
java.sql.Timestamp timestamp = new java.sql.Timestamp(date.getTime());
System.out.println("date: " + date);
System.out.println("Timestamp: " + timestamp);
```

This shows how to get a Timestamp object as a method:

```
import java.sql.Timestamp;
import java.util.Date;
...
/**
 * Creates a java.sql.Timestamp from a java.util.Date or
 * return null if the parameter was null
 * @param utilDate the date to turn into the SQL Timestamp object
 * @return the timestamp or null if the utilDate was null
 */
public static Timestamp getJavaSqlTimestamp(Date utilDate) {


    }
    else {
        return new Timestamp(utilDate.getTime());
    }
}

/**
 * Creates a current java.sql.Timestamp
 * @return the timestamp
 */
public static Timestamp getJavaSqlTimestamp() {
    Date date = new Date();
    return new Timestamp(date.getTime());
}
```

9-15. How Do You Create a java.sql.Time Object?

java.sql.Time descends from java.util.Date but uses only the hour, minute, and second values. The JDK defines java.sql.Time as follows:

```
public class java.sql.Time extends java.util.Date
```

In addition, the JDK says this about java.sql.Time:

A thin wrapper around the java.util.Date class that allows the JDBC API to identify this as an SQL TIME value. The Time class adds formatting and parsing operations to support the JDBC escape syntax for time values. The date components should be set to the "zero epoch" value of January 1, 1970, and should not be accessed.

You have different ways to create a java.sql.Time object, which are presented next.

Creating a java.sql.Time Object from a java.util.Date Object

The following shows how to create a java.sql.Time object from a java.util.Date object:

```
/**
 * Creates a java.sql.Time from a java.util.Date or return null
 * if the parameter was null.
 * @param utilDate the date to turn into the SQL Time object
 * @return the time or null if the utilDate was null
 */
public static java.sql.Time getJavaSqlTime(java.util.Date utilDate) {
  if (utilDate == null) {
      return null;
  }
  else {
      return new java.sql.Time(utilDate.getTime());
  }
}
```

Creating a java.sql.Time Object from a java.util.Calendar Object

You can use a Calendar object by setting the year, month, and day portions to January 1, 1970, which is Java's zero epoch. The millisecond value must also be set to zero. At that point, Calendar.getTime(). getTime() is invoked to get the time in milliseconds. That value is then passed to a java.sql.Time

```
Calendar cal = Calendar.getInstance();

// set Date portion to January 1, 1970
cal.set( Calendar.YEAR, 1970 );
cal.set( Calendar.MONTH, Calendar.JANUARY );
cal.set( Calendar.DATE, 1 );

// set milliseconds portion to 0
cal.set( Calendar.MILLISECOND, 0 );

java.sql.Time javaSqlTime = new java.sql.Time( cal.getTime().getTime() );
```

Creating a java.sql.Time Object Using java.sql.Time.valueOf()

The java.sql.Time object's valueOf() method accepts a String, which must be the time in JDBC time escape format—HH:MM:SS. For example, to create a java.sql.Time object for 9:23 p.m., you can write this:

```
java.sql.Time javaSqlTime = java.sql.Time.valueOf( "21:23:00" );
```

Creating a java.sql.Time Object Using the java.lang.System Class

The following shows how to create a java.sql.Time object using the java.lang.System class:

```
java.sql.Time tm = new java.sql.Time(System.currentTimeMillis());
```

9-16. How Do You Convert the Current Time to a java.sql.Date Object?

The following shows how to convert the current time to a java.sql.Date object:

```
import java.util.Calendar;
import java.sql.Date;
...
Calendar currenttime = Calendar.getInstance();
Date sqldate = new Date((currenttime.getTime()).getTime());
or as a method:

import java.util.Calendar;
import java.sql.Date;
...
public static Date getCurrentJavaSqlDate () {
    Calendar currenttime = Calendar.getInstance();
    return new Date((currenttime.getTime()).getTime());
}
```

9-17. How Do You Determine the Day of the Week from Today's Date?

The answer to this question is to use java.util.Calendar.SUNDAY, java.util.Calendar.MONDAY, and so on:

```
    java.sql.Date date = new java.sql.Date(today.getTime());
    java.util.GregorianCalendar cal = new java.util.GregorianCalendar();
    cal.setTime(date);
    return cal.get(java.util.Calendar.DAY_OF_WEEK);
}
```

9-18. How Do You Determine the Day of the Week from a Given java.util.Date Object?

The answer to this question is to use java.util.Calendar.SUNDAY, java.util.Calendar.MONDAY, and so on:

```
public static int getDayOfWeek(java.util.Date utilDate)
    throws Exception {

    if (utilDate == null) {
        throw new Exception("date can not be null.");
    }
    java.sql.Date d = new java.sql.Date(utilDate.getTime());
    java.util.GregorianCalendar cal = new java.util.GregorianCalendar();
    cal.setTime(d);
    return cal.get(java.util.Calendar.DAY_OF_WEEK);
}
```

9-19. How Do You Convert java.sql.Date to java.util.Date?

The following shows how to convert java.sql.Date to java.util.Date:

```
public java.util.Date convert(java.sql.Date source) {
    if (source == null) {
        return null;
    }
    return new java.util.Date(source.getTime());
}
```

9-20. What Is java.text.SimpleDateFormat?

According to J2SE 5.0, SimpleDateFormat extends the DateFormat class and is defined as follows:

> SimpleDateFormat is a concrete class for formatting and parsing dates in a locale-sensitive manner. It allows for formatting (date -> text), parsing (text -> date), and normalization. SimpleDateFormat allows you to start by choosing any user-defined patterns for date-time formatting. However, you are encouraged to create a date-time formatter with either get-TimeInstance, getDateInstance, or getDateTimeInstance in DateFormat. Each of these class methods can return a date/time formatter initialized with a default format pattern. You may modify the format pattern using the applyPattern methods as desired. For more information on using these methods, see DateFormat.

Table 9-4 lists some useful format strings for java.text.SimpleDateFormat.

Table 9-4. *Sample Format Strings for* SimpleDateFormat

ISO 8160	yyyy-MM-dd'T'H:mm:ss'Z'	Used in EDI/OBI data, and so on
ISO 8610	yyyyMMdd'T'HH:mm:ss	Used in XML-RPC
SQL Date	yyyy.MM.dd	JDBC date format

9-21. How Do You Convert java.util.Date to a Date String in the Format MM/DD/YYYY?

The following shows how to convert java.util.Date to a Date string in the format MM/DD/YYYY:

```
import java.util.Calendar;
import java.util.Date;
...
/**
 * Convert java.util.Date to a date String in the format MM/DD/YYYY
 * @param date the java.util.Date
 * @return a date String in the format MM/DD/YYYY
 * (if input is null, then return null).
 */
public static String toDateString(Date date) {
    if (date == null) {
        return null;
    }

    Calendar calendar = Calendar.getInstance();
    calendar.setTime(date);
    int month = calendar.get(Calendar.MONTH) + 1;
    int day = calendar.get(Calendar.DAY_OF_MONTH);
    int year = calendar.get(Calendar.YEAR);
```

```java
    String monthString;
    if (month < 10) {
        monthString = "0" + month;
    }
    else {
        monthString = "" + month;
    }

    String dayString;
    if (day < 10) {
        dayString = "0" + day;
    }
    else {
        dayString = "" + day;
    }

    String yearString = "" + year;
    return monthString + "/" + dayString + "/" + yearString;
}
```

9-22. How Do You Create a Time String in the Format HH:MM:SS from an Hour, Minute, Second Format?

The following shows how to make a Time string in the format HH:MM:SS from an Hour, Minute, Second format:

```java
 * for hour, minute, and second. If the seconds are 0, then the output
 * is in HH:MM. It is assumed that all of the input arguments will have
 * proper values.
 * @param hour the hours as integer
 * @param minute the minutes as integer
 * @param second the seconds integer
 * @return a time String in the format HH:MM:SS or HH:MM
 */
public static String toTimeString(int hour, int minute, int second) {

    String hourString;
    if (hour < 10) {
        hourString = "0" + hour;
    }
    else {
        hourString = "" + hour;
    }

    String minuteString;
    if (minute < 10) {
        minuteString = "0" + minute;
    }
    else {
        minuteString = "" + minute;
    }
    String secondString;
    if (second < 10) {
        secondString = "0" + second;
    }
```

```
    else {
        secondString = "" + second;
    }

    if (second == 0) {
        return hourString + ":" + minuteString;
    }
    else {
        return hourString + ":" + minuteString + ":" + secondString;
    }
}
```

9-23. How Do You Convert a java.util.Date Object to a Time String in the Format HH:MM:SS?

This method uses the `toTimeString(int hour, int minute, int second)` method defined previously:

```
import java.util.Date;
import java.util.Calendar;
...
/**
 * Convert java.util.Date to a time String in the format HH:MM:SS.
 *   If the seconds are 0, then the output is in HH:MM format.
 * @param date The java.util.Date
 * @return a time String in the format HH:MM:SS or HH:MM
 */


        return null;
    }

    Calendar calendar = Calendar.getInstance();
    calendar.setTime(date);
    return (toTimeString(calendar.get(Calendar.HOUR_OF_DAY),
                         calendar.get(Calendar.MINUTE),
                         calendar.get(Calendar.SECOND)));
}
```

9-24. How Do You Check for a Leap Year?

The following methods check whether a given year is a leap year. A year is a leap year if it is an even multiple of 4; however, years divisible by 100 but not by 400 aren't leap years. For example, 1900 isn't a leap year, but 1600 and 2000 both are. (An alternate definition of a leap year is that a specific year is a leap year if it is either evenly divisible by 400 or evenly divisible by 4 and not evenly divisible by 100.)

  You can check whether a given year is a leap year in one of two ways.

Solution 1: Checking for a Leap Year

This checks for a leap year:

```
/**
 * Checks if a year is a leap year. If input is
 * a negative integer, then it returns false.
```

```
 * @param year The year to check.
 * @return true: the year is a leap year;
 * false: the year is a normal year.
 */
public static boolean isLeapYear(int year) {

    if (year < 0) {
        return false;
    }

    if (year % 400 == 0) {
        return true;
    }
    else if (year % 100 == 0) {
        return false;
    }
    else if (year % 4 == 0) {
        return true;
    }
    else {
        return false;
    }
}
```

Solution 2: Checking for a Leap Year

```
import java.util.GregorianCalendar;
...
/**
 * Determining If a Year Is a Leap Year. If input is
 * a negative integer, then it returns false.
 * @param year The year to check.
 * @return true: the year is a leap year;
 * false: the year is a normal year.
 */
public static boolean isLeapYear(int year) {

    if (year < 0) {
        return false;
    }

    GregorianCalendar gcal = new GregorianCalendar();
    return gcal.isLeapYear(year);
}
```

9-25. How Do You Convert Between Different Java Date Classes?

Table 9-5 shows the conversion of Java Date classes, and Table 9-6 shows the conversion of the Java Date class to Calendar.

Table 9-5. *Conversion of Java* Date *Classes*

From/To...	java.util.Date	java.sql.Date
java.util.Date		to.setTime(from.getTime())
java.sql.Date	to.setTime(from.getTime())	
java.util.Calendar	to = from.getTime()	to.setTime(from.getTime().getTime())
long (milliseconds)	to.setTime(from)	to.setTime(from)

Table 9-6. *Conversion of Java* Date *Classes to* Calendar

From/To	java.util.Calendar	long (Milliseconds)
java.util.Date	to.setTime(from)	to = from.getTime()
java.sql.Date	to.setTimeInMillis(from.getTime())	to = from.getTime()
java.util.Calendar		to = from.getTime().getTime()
long (milliseconds)	to.setTimeInMillis(from)	

9-26. How Do You Add/Subtract Days for a Given Date (Given As a String)?

The following shows how to add/subtract days for a given date (given as a String):

```
import java.text.SimpleDateFormat;
import java.text.ParseException;
...
/**
 * Add/Subtract days for a given date given as a string
 * format of MM/DD/YYYY. If input is 03/01/2000, and delta is -1,
 * then it will return a date with string value of 02/29/2000;
 * and if your input is 03/01/1999, and delta is -1, then it will
 * return a date with string value of 02/28/1999.
 * @param dateString date as a string of MM/DD/YYYY format.
 * @param delta the number of days to add/subtract
 * @return a new date (as java.util.Date) based on delta days; if
 * input is null return null;
 * @exception throws ParseException is the input is not valid format.
 */
public static Date makeDate(String dateString, int delta)
    throws ParseException {

    if ((dateString == null) || (dateString.length() == 0)) {
        return null;
    }

    SimpleDateFormat formatter = new SimpleDateFormat("MM/dd/yyyy");

    // the following stmt. will throw a ParseException
    // if dateString does not have a valid format.
    Date d = formatter.parse(dateString);
    System.out.println("originalDate="+formatter.format(d));
```

```
    if (delta == 0) {
        return d;
    }

    Calendar cal = Calendar.getInstance();
    cal.setTime(d);
    cal.add(Calendar.DATE ,delta);
    Date revisedDate = cal.getTime();
    System.out.println("revisedDate="+formatter.format(revisedDate));
    return revisedDate;
}
```

Testing makeDate()

The following shows how to test makeDate():

```
java.util.Date revisedDate2 = makeDate("03/01/2000", -1);
System.out.println("revisedDate2="+revisedDate2);
System.out.println("---");
java.util.Date revisedDate3 = makeDate("03/01/2000", 10);
System.out.println("revisedDate3="+revisedDate3);
```

Viewing the Output of the Test

The following is the output of the test:

```
revisedDate2=Tue Feb 29 00:00:00 PST 2000
---
originalDate=03/01/2000
revisedDate=03/11/2000
revisedDate3=Sat Mar 11 00:00:00 PST 2000
```

9-27. How Do You Find the Difference Between Two Given Dates?

Let's say that d1 represents 1/10/2000 (as a java.util.Date object) and d2 represents 2/31/2000 (as a java.util.Date object). How do you find the difference of d1 and d2? In other words, how many days apart are these dates from each other? The answer is 52 days. I will provide the solution for finding the difference between two java.util.Date objects as well as for between two java.sql.Date objects. The following solution is a simple class called DateDiff.

Finding the Difference Between Two java.util.Date Objects

The following shows how to find the difference between two java.util.Date objects:

```
java.util.Date   d1 = DateDiff.makeDate("1/10/2000");
java.util.Date   d2 = DateDiff.makeDate("2/31/2000");
int diff = DateDiff.diff( d1, d2 );
System.out.println("d1="+d1);
System.out.println("d2="+d2);
System.out.println("diff="+diff);
output will be:
```

```
d1=Mon Jan 10 00:00:00 PST 2000
d2=Thu Mar 02 00:00:00 PST 2000
diff=52
```

Finding the Difference Between Two java.sql.Date Objects

The following shows how to find the difference between two java.sql.Date objects:

```
java.util.Date utilDate1 = DateDiff.makeDate("12/01/1990");
java.sql.Date sqlDate1 = new java.sql.Date(utilDate1.getTime());
System.out.println("utilDate1:" + utilDate1);
System.out.println("sqlDate1:" + sqlDate1);

java.util.Date utilDate2 = DateDiff.makeDate("1/24/1991");
java.sql.Date sqlDate2 = new java.sql.Date(utilDate2.getTime());
System.out.println("utilDate2:" + utilDate2);
System.out.println("sqlDate2:" + sqlDate2);

int diffSqlDates = diff( sqlDate1, sqlDate2 );
System.out.println("diffSqlDates="+diffSqlDates);
output will be:

utilDate1:Sat Dec 01 00:00:00 PST 1990
sqlDate1:1990-12-01
utilDate2:Thu Jan 24 00:00:00 PST 1991
sqlDate2:1991-01-24
```

Viewing the DateDiff Class

This is the DateDiff class:

```
import java.util.*;
import java.text.*;

public class DateDiff {

    /**
     * Calculate the difference of two dates
     * (in terms of number of days).
     * @param date1 the java.util.Date object
     * @param date2 the java.util.Date object
     */
    public static int diff( Date date1, Date date2 ) {
        Calendar c1 = Calendar.getInstance();
        Calendar c2 = Calendar.getInstance();

        c1.setTime( date1 );
        c2.setTime( date2 );
        int diffDay = 0 ;

        if ( c1.before( c2 ) ) {
            diffDay = countDiffDay ( c1, c2 );
        }
        else {
            diffDay = countDiffDay ( c2, c1 );
        }
```

```java
        return diffDay;
    }

    public DateDiff( Date date1, Date date2 ) {
        int diffDay = diff(date1, date2);
        System.out.println("Different Day : " + diffDay );
    }

    public static int countDiffDay( Calendar c1, Calendar c2 ) {
        int returnInt = 0;
        while ( !c1.after(c2) ) {
            c1.add( Calendar.DAY_OF_MONTH, 1 );
            returnInt ++;
        }

        if ( returnInt > 0 ) {
            returnInt = returnInt - 1;
        }

        return ( returnInt );
    }

    public static Date makeDate(String dateString)
        throws Exception {
        SimpleDateFormat formatter = new SimpleDateFormat("MM/dd/yyyy");
        return formatter.parse(dateString);


    public static void main ( String argv[] ) throws Exception {
        Calendar cc1 = Calendar.getInstance();
        Calendar cc2 = Calendar.getInstance();
        cc1.add( Calendar.DAY_OF_MONTH, 10 );

        DateDiff myDate = new DateDiff( cc1.getTime(), cc2.getTime() );

        java.util.Date   d1 = makeDate("10/10/2000");
        java.util.Date   d2 = makeDate("10/18/2000");
        DateDiff diff12 = new DateDiff( d1, d2 );

        java.util.Date   d3 = makeDate("1/1/2000");
        java.util.Date   d4 = makeDate("12/31/2000");
        int diff34 = diff( d3, d4 );
        System.out.println("diff34="+diff34);

        java.util.Date   d5 = makeDate("1/10/2000");
        java.util.Date   d6 = makeDate("2/31/2000");
        int diff56 = diff( d5, d6 );
        System.out.println("d5="+d5);
        System.out.println("d6="+d6);
        System.out.println("diff56="+diff56);

        java.util.Date utilDate1 = DateDiff.makeDate("12/01/1990");
        java.sql.Date sqlDate1 =  new java.sql.Date(utilDate1.getTime());
        System.out.println("utilDate1:" + utilDate1);
        System.out.println("sqlDate1:" + sqlDate1);
```

```
        java.util.Date utilDate2 = DateDiff.makeDate("1/24/1991");
        java.sql.Date sqlDate2 =  new java.sql.Date(utilDate2.getTime());
        System.out.println("utilDate2:" + utilDate2);
        System.out.println("sqlDate2:" + sqlDate2);

        int diffSqlDates = diff( sqlDate1, sqlDate2 );
        System.out.println("diffSqlDates="+diffSqlDates);
    }
}
```

9-28. How Do You Convert a Timestamp to Month-Day-Year?

In Web/GUI applications, you do not need to display a complete Timestamp object (it is too long and may be unreadable). Some applications may want to display a Timestamp object as a Month-Day-Year string. Here is a class with three methods to accomplish this task:

```
import java.sql.Timestamp;
import java.text.SimpleDateFormat;

/**
 * DateUtil provides some basic methods
 * for formatting Timestamp objects.
 */
public class DateUtil {

    /**


    private static final SimpleDateFormat monthDayYearformatter =
            new SimpleDateFormat("MMMMM dd, yyyy");

    /**
     * SimpleDateFormat object to format Timestamp into "Month-Day" String.
     */
    private static final SimpleDateFormat monthDayformatter =
            new SimpleDateFormat("MMMMM dd");

    /**
     * Return Timestamp object as MMMMM DD, YYYY.
     * @param timestamp a Timestamp object
     * @return Timestamp object as MMMMM DD, YYYY.
     */
    public static String timestampToMonthDayYear(Timestamp timestamp){
        if (timestamp == null) {
            return null;
        }
        else {
            return monthDayYearformatter.format((java.util.Date) timestamp);
        }
    }

    /**
     * Return Timestamp object as MMMMM DD.
     * @param timestamp a Timestamp object
     * @return Timestamp object as MMMMM DD.
     */
```

```java
    public static String timestampToMonthDay(Timestamp timestamp){
        if (timestamp == null) {
            return null;
        }
        else {
            return monthDayformatter.format((java.util.Date) timestamp);
        }
    }

    /**
     * Get the current timestamp.
     * @return the current timestamp.
     */
    public static java.sql.Timestamp getTimestamp() {
        java.util.Date today = new java.util.Date();
        return new java.sql.Timestamp(today.getTime());
    }
}
```

9-29. How Do You Determine the Validity of a Format Pattern for SimpleDateFormat?

A format pattern such as MMMMM DD, YYYY is a valid one, but MMMMM DD, YYYYZZ is not valid. The following method accepts a format pattern and then returns true if it is a valid format pattern; otherwise, it returns false:

```java
 * Tests if the date format pattern specified is valid.
 *
 * @param format The format string to test.
 *
 * @return true if the format parameter contains
 * a valid formatting string; false otherwise.
 */
public static boolean isValidDateFormat(String format) {
    if ((format == null) || ((format.length() == 0)) {
        // not a valid format pattern
        return false;
    }

    java.text.SimpleDateFormat formatter = null;
    try {
        formatter = new java.text.SimpleDateFormat( format );
        formatter.format( new java.util.Date() );
        return true;
    }
    catch(Exception e) {
        // not a valid format pattern
        return false;
    }
}
```

9-30. How Do You Get a Date Label from a java.sql.Timestamp Object?

In GUI database applications, you may need to convert a Timestamp object into a date label such as Today, Yesterday, This Month, and Older Than a Month. By getting a date label, the user can categorize data.

The following method gets a date label for a given Timestamp object:

```
import java.sql.Timestamp;

/**
 * DateLabel provides some basic methods
 * for formatting Date and Timestamp objects.
 */
public class DateLabel {

    private static final long One_Day_In_Milliseconds = 86400000;

    /**
     * This date label represents "Today".
     */
    public static final String DATE_LABEL_TODAY = "Today";

    /**
     * This date label represents "Yesterday".
     */


    /**
     * This date label represents "This Month".
     */
    public static final String DATE_LABEL_THIS_MONTH = "This Month";

    /**
     * This date label represents "Older" (older than a month).
     */
    public static final String DATE_LABEL_OLDER = "Older";

    /**
     * This date label represents "none" (when
     * timestamp is null/undefined).
     */
    public static final String DATE_LABEL_NONE = "";


    /**
     * Get the current timestamp.
     * @return the current timestamp.
     */
    public static java.sql.Timestamp getTimestamp() {
        java.util.Date today = new java.util.Date();
        return new java.sql.Timestamp(today.getTime());
    }

    /**
     * Get the Date Label.
     * @param ts the timestamp you want to get a data label
```

```java
     * @param now the timestamp you want to compare to
     * @return the date label for a given timestamp.
     */
    public static String getDateLabel(java.sql.Timestamp ts,
                                      java.sql.Timestamp now) {
        if (ts == null) {
            return DATE_LABEL_NONE;
        }

        if (now == null) {
            return DATE_LABEL_NONE;
        }

        long tsTime = ts.getTime();
        long nowTime = now.getTime();
        long quotient = (nowTime - tsTime)/One_Day_In_Milliseconds;

        if (quotient < 1) {
            return DATE_LABEL_TODAY;
        }
        else if (quotient < 2) {
            return DATE_LABEL_YESTERDAY;
        }
        else if (quotient < 30) {
            return DATE_LABEL_THIS_MONTH;
        }


    }
}

    public static void main(String[] args) {
        java.sql.Timestamp now = getTimestamp();

        java.sql.Timestamp ts1 = getTimestamp();
        System.out.println(getDateLabel(ts1, now));
        System.out.println(ts1.toString());
        System.out.println("-------------");

        // timestamp in format yyyy-mm-dd hh:mm:ss.fffffffff
        java.sql.Timestamp ts22 =
            java.sql.Timestamp.valueOf("2005-04-06 09:01:10");
        System.out.println(getDateLabel(ts22, now));
        System.out.println(ts22.toString());
        System.out.println("-------------");

        java.sql.Timestamp ts2 =
            java.sql.Timestamp.valueOf("2005-03-26 10:10:10");
        System.out.println(getDateLabel(ts2, now));
        System.out.println(ts2.toString());
        System.out.println("-------------");

        java.sql.Timestamp ts3 =
            java.sql.Timestamp.valueOf("2004-07-18 10:10:10");
        System.out.println(getDateLabel(ts3, now));
        System.out.println(ts3.toString());
        System.out.println("-------------");
```

```
        java.sql.Timestamp ts4 =
            java.sql.Timestamp.valueOf("2004-06-20 10:10:10");
        System.out.println(getDateLabel(ts4, now));
        System.out.println(ts4.toString());
        System.out.println("------------");
    }
}
```

To run the test program, use this:

```
$ javac DateLabel.java
$ java DateLabel
Today
2005-04-07 09:09:47.605
------------
Yesterday
2005-04-06 09:01:10.0
------------
This Month
2005-03-26 10:10:10.0
------------
Older
2004-07-18 10:10:10.0
------------
Older
2004-06-20 10:10:10.0
```

9-31. How Do You Convert a java.sql.Timestamp Object to a java.util.Date Object?

java.sql.Timestamp is a wrapper around java.util.Date that allows the JDBC API to identify it as a SQL TIMESTAMP value. This adds the ability to hold the SQL TIMESTAMP nanos value and provides formatting and parsing operations to support the JDBC escape syntax for timestamp values. The java.sql.Timestamp object stores the fractional part of the time within itself instead of within the Date superclass.

You can use the following to convert a java.sql.Timestamp object to a java.util.Date object:

```
public static java.util.Date toDate(java.sql.Timestamp timestamp) {
    if (timestamp == null) {
        return null;
    }

    long milliseconds  = timestamp.getTime() + (timestamp.getNanos() / 1000000 );
    return new java.util.Date(milliseconds);
}
```

9-32. What Does Normalization Mean for java.sql.Date and java.sql.Time?

To understand normalization, you need to look at the java.sql.Date and java.sql.Time classes. The class java.sql.Date descends from the java.util.Date class but uses only the year, month, and day values. JDK defines java.sql.Date and java.sql.Time as follows:

```
public class java.sql.Date extends java.util.Date
```

The JDK also says this:

A thin wrapper around a millisecond value that allows JDBC to identify this as an SQL DATE value. A milliseconds value represents the number of milliseconds that have passed since January 1, 1970 00:00:00.000 GMT. To conform with the definition of SQL DATE, the millisecond values wrapped by a java.sql.Date instance must be "normalized" by setting the hours, minutes, seconds, and milliseconds to zero in the particular time zone with which the instance is associated.

```
public class java.sql.Time extends java.util.Date
```

A thin wrapper around the java.util.Date class that allows the JDBC API to identify this as an SQL TIME value. The Time class adds formatting and parsing operations to support the JDBC escape syntax for time values. The date components should be set to the "zero epoch" value of January 1, 1970, and should not be accessed.

These classes (`java.sql.Date` and `java.sql.Time`) are thin wrappers that extend the `java.util.Date` class, which has both date and time components. `java.sql.Date` should carry only date information, and a normalized instance has the time information set to zeros. `java.sql.Time` should carry only time information; a normalized instance has the date set to the Java zero epoch (January 1, 1970) and the milliseconds portion set to zero.

The following sections give a complete example for determining the normalization of `java.sql.Time` and `java.sql.Date` objects.

and java.sql.Time Objects?

Normalization depends on the JDBC driver's implementation of the `ResultSet.getDate()` and `ResultSet.getTime()` methods. To determine normalization, you must convert the `java.sql.Date` and `java.sql.Time` objects to an associated `java.util.Date` object.

How It Works

For example, if a `java.sql.Date` object displays 2005-07-01, it's normalized only if its associated `java.util.Date` value is as follows:

```
Fri Jul 01 00:00:00 EDT 2005
```

Further, if a `java.sql.Time` object displays 16:10:12, it's normalized only if its associated `java.util.Date` value is as follows:

```
Thu Jan 01 16:10:12 EST 1970
```

The following solution (the `TestNormalization` class) checks whether the MySQL/Oracle JDBC driver supports normalization for the `java.sql.Date` and `java.sql.Time` objects. Before reviewing this solution, you will see how to set up some database objects.

Setting Up the MySQL Database

This shows how to set up the MySQL database:

```
mysql> create table date_time_table (
    ->  time_col time,
    ->  date_col date,
```

```
    -> date_time_col datetime
    -> );
Query OK, 0 rows affected (0.07 sec)

mysql> desc date_time_table;
+---------------+-----------+------+-----+---------+-------+
| Field         | Type      | Null | Key | Default | Extra |
+---------------+-----------+------+-----+---------+-------+
| time_col      | time      | YES  |     | NULL    |       |
| date_col      | date      | YES  |     | NULL    |       |
| date_time_col | datetime  | YES  |     | NULL    |       |
+---------------+-----------+------+-----+---------+-------+
3 rows in set (0.00 sec)

mysql> insert into date_time_table(time_col, date_col, date_time_col)
values ('10:34:55', '2004-10-23', '2004-10-23 10:34:55');
Query OK, 1 row affected (0.00 sec)

mysql> insert into date_time_table(time_col, date_col, date_time_col)
values ('16:12:50', '2005-07-01', '2005-07-01 16:12:50');
Query OK, 1 row affected (0.00 sec)

mysql> select * from date_time_table;
+----------+------------+---------------------+
| time_col | date_col   | date_time_col       |
+----------+------------+---------------------+


+----------+------------+---------------------+
2 rows in set (0.00 sec)
```

Setting Up the Oracle Database

This shows how to set up the Oracle database:

```
SQL> create table date_time_table (
  2     time_col date,
  3     date_col date,
  4     date_time_col date
  5  );

Table created.

SQL> desc date_time_table;
 Name                    Null?    Type
 --------------------- -------- -------
 TIME_COL                         DATE
 DATE_COL                         DATE
 DATE_TIME_COL                    DATE

SQL> insert into date_time_table(time_col, date_col, date_time_col)
  2  values (sysdate, sysdate, sysdate);

1 row created.

SQL> select * from date_time_table;
```

```
TIME_COL  DATE_COL  DATE_TIME
--------- --------- ---------
01-JUL-05 01-JUL-05 01-JUL-05

SQL> commit;
Commit complete.
```

Solution

This shows the solution:

```java
import java.sql.*;
import jcb.util.DatabaseUtil;
import jcb.db.VeryBasicConnectionManager;

public class TestNormalization {

    public static void main(String args[]) {
        String GET_RECORDS =
            "select time_col, date_col, date_time_col from date_time_table";
        ResultSet rs = null;
        Connection conn = null;
        Statement stmt = null;
        try {
            String dbVendor = args[0];  // {"mysql", "oracle" }
            conn = VeryBasicConnectionManager.getConnection(dbVendor);


            while (rs.next()) {
                java.sql.Time dbSqlTime = rs.getTime(1);
                java.sql.Date dbSqlDate = rs.getDate(2);
                java.sql.Timestamp dbSqlTimestamp = rs.getTimestamp(3);
                System.out.println("dbSqlTime="+dbSqlTime);
                System.out.println("dbSqlDate="+dbSqlDate);
                System.out.println("dbSqlTimestamp="+dbSqlTimestamp);
                System.out.println("-- check for Normalization --");
                java.util.Date dbSqlTimeConverted =
                    new java.util.Date(dbSqlTime.getTime());
                java.util.Date dbSqlDateConverted =
                    new java.util.Date(dbSqlDate.getTime());
                System.out.println("dbSqlTimeConverted="+dbSqlTimeConverted);
                System.out.println("dbSqlDateConverted="+dbSqlDateConverted);
            }
        }
        catch( Exception e ) {
            e.printStackTrace();
            System.out.println("Failed to get the records.");
            System.exit(1);
        }
        finally {
            DatabaseUtil.close(rs);
            DatabaseUtil.close(stmt);
            DatabaseUtil.close(conn);
        }
    }
}
```

Running the Solution for the MySQL Database

As you can see from the following results, the MySQL driver does support normalization for the java.sql.Date and java.sql.Time objects:

```
$ javac TestNormalization.java
$ java TestNormalization mysql
ok: loaded mysql driver.
conn=com.mysql.jdbc.Connection@1e4cbc4
dbSqlTime=10:34:55
dbSqlDate=2004-10-23
dbSqlTimestamp=2004-10-23 10:34:55.0
-- check for Normalization --
dbSqlTimeConverted=Thu Jan 01 10:34:55 PST 1970
dbSqlDateConverted=Sat Oct 23 00:00:00 PDT 2004
dbSqlTime=16:12:50
dbSqlDate=2005-07-01
dbSqlTimestamp=2005-07-01 16:12:50.0
-- check for Normalization --
dbSqlTimeConverted=Thu Jan 01 16:12:50 PST 1970
dbSqlDateConverted=Fri Jul 01 00:00:00 PDT 2005
```

Running Solution for the Oracle Database

As you can see from the following results, the Oracle 10g driver does support normalization for the

```
$ java TestNormalization oracle
ok: loaded oracle driver.
conn=oracle.jdbc.driver.OracleConnection@6e70c7
dbSqlTime=16:15:22
dbSqlDate=2005-07-01
dbSqlTimestamp=2005-07-01 16:15:22.0
-- check for Normalization --
dbSqlTimeConverted=Thu Jan 01 16:15:22 PST 1970
dbSqlDateConverted=Fri Jul 01 00:00:00 PDT 2005
```

9-34. How Do You Make a java.sql.Timestamp Object for a Given Year, Month, Day, Hour, and So On?

Given the year, month, day, hour, minutes, seconds, and milliseconds, the objective of the following code is to create a java.sql.Timestamp object:

```
import java.sql.Timestamp;
import java.util.Calendar;
import java.util.GregorianCalendar;
...
/**
 * Given year, month, day, hour, minutes, seconds, and
 * milliseconds, the objective is to create a Timestamp object.
 * @param year the year
 * @param month the month
 * @param day the day
 * @param hour the hour
```

```
 * @param minute the minute
 * @param second the second
 * @param millisecond the millisecond
 * @return a java.sql.Timestamp object
 */
public static Timestamp makeTimestamp(int year,
                                      int month,
                                      int day,
                                      int hour,
                                      int minute,
                                      int second,
                                      int millisecond) {
   Calendar cal = new GregorianCalendar();
   cal.set(Calendar.YEAR, year);
   cal.set(Calendar.MONTH, month - 1);
   cal.set(Calendar.DATE, day);
   cal.set(Calendar.HOUR_OF_DAY, hour);
   cal.set(Calendar.MINUTE, minute);
   cal.set(Calendar.SECOND, second);
   cal.set(Calendar.MILLISECOND, millisecond);

   // now convert GregorianCalendar object to Timestamp object
   return new Timestamp(cal.getTimeInMillis());
}
```

Los Angeles, California:

```
import java.sql.Date;
import java.sql.ResultSet;
import java.util.Calendar;
import java.util.TimeZone;
...
ResultSet rs = stmt.executeQuery(
   "SELECT date_created FROM products WHERE product_id = 'PRD-123456'");

//creating an instance of Calendar
Calendar cal = Calendar.getInstance();

// get the TimeZone for "America/Los_Angeles"
TimeZone tz = TimeZone.getTimeZone("America/Los_Angeles");
cal.setTimeZone(tz);
if (rs.next()) {
   // the JDBC driver will use the time zone information in
   // Calendar to calculate the date, with the result that
   // the variable dateCreated contains a java.sql.Date object
   // that is accurate for "America/Los_Angeles".
   Date dateCreated = rs.getDate(1, cal);
}
```

CHAPTER 10

■ ■ ■

Handling Exceptions in JDBC

Example isn't another way to teach, it is the only way to teach.

—Albert Einstein

The purpose of this chapter is to provide solutions (expressed as snippets and reusable code samples) that deal with the `java.sql.SQLException` class. You will also examine other JDBC-related exception classes such as `SQLWarning`.

`SQLException`, which extends the `java.lang.Exception` class, is a core JDBC exception class that provides information about database access errors and other errors. Most of the JDBC API methods throw `SQLException`, so client programs must handle it properly. For example, using the `DriverManager`.

This chapter covers the following exception classes used in the JDBC API:

`java.sql.SQLException`: This class extends the `java.lang.Exception` class. This class is an exception that provides information about database access errors and other errors. Also, the `SQLException` class provides information in terms of nested/chained exceptions. Using this class, you can find vendor error codes and messages.

`java.sql.BatchUpdateException`: This exception is thrown when an error occurs during a batch update operation. In addition to the information provided by `SQLException`, a `BatchUpdateException` provides the update counts for all commands that were executed successfully during the batch update (that is, all commands that were executed before the error occurred). The order of elements in an array of update counts corresponds to the order in which commands were added to the batch.

`java.sql.DataTruncation`: This exception reports a `DataTruncation` warning (on reads) or throws a `DataTruncation` exception (on writes) when JDBC unexpectedly truncates a data value.

`java.sql.SQLWarning`: This exception provides information about database access warnings. A warning is silently chained to the object whose method caused the warning to be reported.

In most of the examples in this chapter, I will use the `getConnection(String dbVendor)` method to get a JDBC `Connection` object; you are strongly encouraged to replace it with your desired connection method (such as using a connection pool manager).

10-1. What Is an Exception?

In Java/JDBC programming, a programming *exception* occurs when an error is discovered while running the program. The most commonly known exceptions are divide-by-zero errors and null pointer exceptions (NullPointerException).

According to the second edition of the Java Language Specification (JLS), available at http://java. sun.com/docs/books/jls/, "when a program violates the semantic constraints of the Java programming language, the Java virtual machine signals this error to the program as an exception. An example of such a violation is an attempt to index outside the bounds of an array." Furthermore, the JLS adds that "an exception is said to be thrown from the point where it occurred and is said to be caught at the point to which control is transferred. Programs can also throw exceptions explicitly, using throw statements."

The JLS states that "every exception is represented by an instance of the class Throwable or one of its subclasses; such an object can be used to carry information from the point at which an exception occurs to the handler that catches it. Handlers are established by catch clauses of try statements."

So, to reiterate, an exception occurs when a program is running and something goes wrong. Examples are as follows:

- The program tried to divide by zero.

- The program tried to invoke a method with a nonexistent object.

- The program tried to execute a SQL query, but the database is not available.

- The program tried to insert a new record into a table, but the table does not exist.

- The program tried to open a data file, but the file doesn't exist.

10-2. What Is java.lang.Exception?

The java.lang.Exception class and its subclasses are a form of java.lang.Throwable that indicates conditions that a reasonable application might want to catch.

Consider the following simple Java class Test. (The filename is Test.java; I have added line numbers for discussion purposes.)

```
1   public class Test {
2       public static void main(String[] args) {
3           int x = 1;
4           int y = 0;
5           System.out.println("before division");
6           int z = x/y;    // a division by 0
7           System.out.println("after division");
8       }
9   }
```

Let's compile and run the program:

```
$ javac Test.java
$ java Test
before division
Exception in thread "main" java.lang.ArithmeticException:
/ by zero at Test.main(Test.java:6)
```

The execution of Test stops at line 6; this is caused by the division-by-zero error at x/y; an exception (java.lang.ArithmeticException) has been thrown but has not been handled properly. The exception is thrown to the caller (in this case the operating system is the client/caller) of the main() method. When an exception is thrown but not handled, then the program terminates. As you can see, because of the exception, the program terminated abnormally.

So, how do you handle an exception? To handle an exception, enclose the code that is likely to throw an exception in a try block, and follow it immediately by a catch clause, as follows:

```
public class Test {
    public static void main(String[] args) {
        int x = 1;
        int y = 0;

        System.out.println("try block starts");
        try {
            System.out.println("before division");
            int z = x/y; // division by 0
            System.out.println("after division");
        }
        catch (ArithmeticException ae)  {
            // catch clause below handles the ArithmeticException
            // generated by the division by zero. This exception must be
            // listed before Exception (because it is a subclass of Exception).
            System.out.println("--- attempt to divide by 0: handle exception");
            ae.printStackTrace(); // print the details of exception
            // do whatever here to handle the exception
            System.out.println("--- end to handle the exception");
        }
        catch(Exception e) {


        }
        System.out.println("catch block ends");
    }
}
```

The output of the previous program is as follows:

```
try block starts
before division
--- attempt to divide by 0: handle exception
java.lang.ArithmeticException: / by zero at Test.main(Test.java:9)
--- end to handle the exception
catch block ends
```

As you can see (from the output of the modified program), the statement System.out.println("after division") doesn't execute; once an exception is thrown, the program control moves out of the try block and into the catch block (also called the *exception handling block*). Please note that you don't need to handle all exceptions. You can ignore system errors and can pass responsibility for handling exceptions upward (this must be explicit).

```
public static void main (String[] args)
    throws java.lang.ArithmeticException {
    ...
}
```

When catching exceptions, the try statement defines the scope of its associated exception handlers; you associate exception handlers with a try statement by providing one or more catch blocks directly after the try block.

```
try {
    <code might throw an exception>
}
catch (SomeException1 e1) {
    <code to handle exception e1>
}
catch (SomeException2 e2) {
    <code to handle exception e2>
}
.
.
.
finally {
    <code that is always executed>
}
```

The code within the try block is executed. If an exception is thrown, then execute the code within the matching catch; if no match is found, pass the exception upward and always execute the code on the finally clause (regardless of whether an exception has taken place).

In the preceding example, if SomeException1 is a subclass of SomeException2, then the order of SomeException1 and SomeException2 in the catch block is important. (The order I have listed them is correct—if you list SomeException2 first, then SomeException1 exceptions will never be caught, because all objects of SomeException1 are castable to SomeException2. If the try block throws SomeException1 or SomeException2, then the handler will go to <code to handle exception e1>.) If SomeException1 is not a subclass of SomeException2, then the order of listing exceptions in the catch block is not important. You should note that the order of exception handlers matters! You should list the more

of catch blocks is important.

10-3. What Are the Components of an Exception?

An exception object carries three important pieces of information:

- **The type of exception**: The exception class. If you design your exception classes as fine-grained classes, then the exception classes will give you enough information to react to the type of exception; for example, the java.lang.ArrayIndexOutOfBoundsException exception is a well-defined exception, and it indicates that a client program has accessed an index that does not exist.

- **Where the exception occurred**: The stack trace. The JVM generates a stack trace for you. (A Java *stack trace* is a snapshot of the threads and monitors in a JVM.)

- **Context and explanatory information**: The error message and other state information.

Each item listed previously is relevant to a different party. Software entities care about the exception class; the JVM and the code that calls the throwing method use it to determine how to handle the exception. The other two items are relevant to engineers; an engineer analyzes the stack trace to debug the problem, and a developer examines the error message. Each party must receive the information it needs to effectively deal with the error.

10-4. What Is the Definition of SQLException?

SQLException is an exception that provides information about database access errors or other errors. SQLException is an exception class and is used in most of the JDBC API. When JDBC cannot handle the situation or there is an error in a request or response, then an instance of SQLException is thrown. The SQLException class extends the java.lang.Exception class, and it adds a few extra methods. Since JDK 1.4, SQLExceptions can be chained (by using the setNextException() and getNextException() methods), so a getNextException() has been added that will return another SQLException, if there are anymore. It also has the ability to give you the error message, SQLState, and vendor-specific error codes.

According to the JDK, the SQLException class is defined in the java.sql package as follows (for details, you can look at the SQLException.java source code provided by the JDK src.zip file):

```
package java.sql;

public class SQLException
    extends java.lang.Exception
```

According to the JDK, each SQLException provides several kinds of information:

- A string describing the error. This is used as the Java Exception message, available via the method getMessage().

- A SQLState string, which follows either the XOPEN SQLState conventions or the SQL-99 conventions. The values of the SQLState string are described in the appropriate specification. You can use the DatabaseMetaData method getSQLStateType to discover whether the driver returns the XOPEN type or the SQL-99 type.

- An integer error code that is specific to each vendor. Normally this will be the actual error code returned by the underlying database.

- A chain to the next exception. You can use this to provide additional error information.

The SQLException class has four methods and four constructors, as shown in Table 10-1 and

Table 10-1. java.sql.SQLException *Constructors*

Constructor	Description
SQLException()	Constructs a SQLException object. The reason field defaults to null, the SQLState field defaults to null, and the vendorCode field defaults to 0.
SQLException(String reason, String SQLState)	Constructs a SQLException object with the given reason field and SQLState; the vendorCode field defaults to 0.
SQLException(String reason, String SQLState, int vendorCode)	Constructs a fully specified SQLException object.

Table 10-2. java.sql.SQLException *Methods*

Return Type	Method	Description
int	getErrorCode()	Retrieves the vendor-specific exception code for this SQLException object
SQLException	getNextException()	Retrieves the exception chained to this SQLException object
String	getSQLState()	Retrieves the SQLState for this SQLException object
void	setNextException (SQLException ex)	Adds a SQLException object to the end of the chain

10-5. Is SQLException a "Checked" Exception?

In Java, two kinds of exceptions exist: checked and unchecked. The semantics of these exceptions come from Java compiling. In general, a Java compiler looks for code that does not properly handle checked (explicitly defined) exceptions; any such code causes a compiler error. Any exception for which a lack of proper handling will cause a Java compiler error is called a *checked exception*. Any other kind is an *unchecked exception*.

For example, the following Java code will not compile because java.sql.SQLException is a checked exception (not a runtime exception—all SQLExceptions(s) must be caught explicitly):

```
import java.sql.Connection;
import java.io.DatabaseMetaData;
import java.sql.SQLException;
...
public static DatabaseMetaData getDbMetaData (Connection  conn) {
   if (conn == null) {
      return null;
   }
   // the Connection.getMetaData() can throw SQLException
   DatabaseMetaData dbmd = conn getMetaData();
   return dbmd;
}
```

On the other hand, the following Java code will compile:

```
import java.sql.Connection;
import java.io.DatabaseMetaData;


public static DatabaseMetaData getDbMetaData (Connection  conn)
   throws SQLException {
   if (conn == null) {
      return null;
   }
   // the Connection.getMetaData() can throw SQLException
   DatabaseMetaData dbmd = conn getMetaData();
   return dbmd;
}
```

Some of Java exceptions are unchecked (runtime exceptions), which means the compiler will not complain if your code does not properly handle them. In general, unchecked exceptions indicate conditions that often can't be known during the compilation process.

For example, the following is a valid Java method (it compiles with no problem), even though it will throw a java.lang.ArithmeticException (at runtime) when y=0:

```
public static int divide(int x, int y) {
   return x / y;
}
```

Therefore, in Java, unchecked exceptions are the ones that inherit from java.lang.RuntimeException and java.lang.Error. By following all these Java definitions, java.sql.SQLException is a checked exception, and you must catch it explicitly.

10-6. What Is the Relationship of SQLException to Other Classes?

The Java language supports inheritance among classes and interfaces. The exception classes (those classes involved with exceptions) hold information about the nature of the exception; the three most common exception classes are as follows:

java.lang.Throwable: This is the parent class of all exception-related classes. (The Throwable class is the superclass of all errors and exceptions in the Java language.) Only objects that are instances of this class (or one of its subclasses) are thrown by the JVM or can be thrown by the Java throw statement. Similarly, only this class or one of its subclasses can be the argument type in a catch clause.

java.lang.Error: This is the other subclass of Throwable, but this is reserved for catastrophic errors that can't be normally be handled in a user's program. (An Error is a subclass of Throwable that indicates serious problems that a reasonable application should not try to catch. Most such errors are abnormal conditions. The ThreadDeath error, though a "normal" condition, is also a subclass of Error because most applications should not try to catch it.)

java.lang.Exception: This class is for errors that can be generally handled (most Java applications will subclass the Exception class). The class Exception and its subclasses are a form of Throwable that indicates conditions that a reasonable application might want to catch.

Figure 10-1 shows the relationship of the java.sql.SQLException class to other classes.

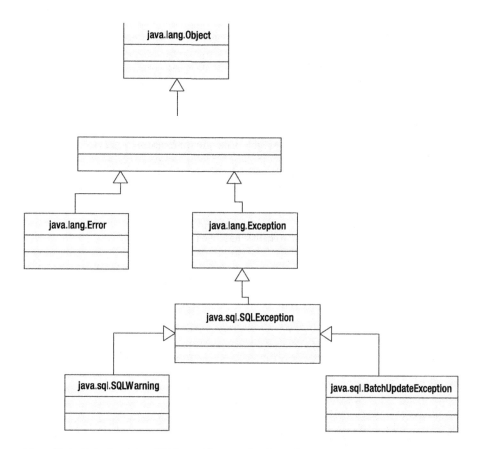

Figure 10-1. *Relationship of* SQLException *to other Java classes*

10-7. What Is an Example of Using SQLException?

In the following sections, I will provide a simple example that shows how to use the SQLException class.

How It Works

In most of the JDBC API, the SQLException class must be caught. For example, if you want to retrieve records from a nonexistent table, then a SQLException will be thrown.

For example, suppose you want to create a new table (called MY_DVDS) in the MySQL database. I will show how to run the solution twice; in the second example, I will provide the "wrong" SQL syntax to force the SQLException.

Solution

Here's the solution:

```java
import java.sql.*;
import jcb.db.VeryBasicConnectionManager;
import jcb.util.DatabaseUtil;

public class CreateTable {

    public static void main(String args[]) {
        Statement stmt = null;
        Connection conn = null;
        String dbVendor = args[0];


            conn = VeryBasicConnectionManager.getConnection(dbVendor);    // 1
            stmt = conn.createStatement();      // 2
            stmt.executeUpdate(createTable);   // 3
            // creation of table was successful.
        }
        catch(SQLException e) {
            // creation of table failed: handle the exception
            // either one of the above statements has been failed
            System.err.println("SQLException: " + e.getMessage());
        }
        catch(Exception e) {
            // other errors: handle the exception
            System.err.println("SQLException: " + e.getMessage());
        }
        finally {
            DatabaseUtil.close(stmt);
            DatabaseUtil.close(conn);
        }
    }
}
```

Running the Solution for the MySQL Database

Here's how to run the solution for the MySQL database:

```
$ javac CreateTable.java
$ java CreateTable mysql "create table MY_DVDS (id INTEGER, title VARCHAR(32))"
$ java CreateTable mysql "create tableZZ MY_DVDS2 (id INTEGER, title VARCHAR(32))"
```

SQLException: You have an error in your SQL syntax; check the manual that corres
ponds to your MySQL server version for the right syntax to use near 'tableZZ MY_
DVDS2 (id INTEGER, title VARCHAR(32))' at line 1

Viewing the MySQL Database After Running the Solution

Here's the MySQL database after running the solution:

```
mysql> desc my_dvds;
+-------+-------------+------+-----+---------+-------+
| Field | Type        | Null | Key | Default | Extra |
+-------+-------------+------+-----+---------+-------+
| id    | int(11)     | YES  |     | NULL    |       |
| title | varchar(32) | YES  |     | NULL    |       |
+-------+-------------+------+-----+---------+-------+
2 rows in set (0.00 sec)
```

Running the Solution for the Oracle Database

Here's how to run the solution for the Oracle database:

```
$ javac CreateTable.java
$ java CreateTable oracle  "create table MY_DVDS (id INTEGER, title VARCHAR(32))"
$ java CreateTable oracle  "create tableZZ MY_DVDS2 (id INTEGER, title VARCHAR(32))"
SQLException: ORA-00901: invalid CREATE command
```

Here's the Oracle database after running the solution:

```
SQL> desc my_dvds;
 Name                            Null?    Type
 ------------------------------- -------- --------------
 ID                                       NUMBER(38)
 TITLE                                    VARCHAR2(32)
```

10-8. How Do You Get the Details of a SQLException?

The SQLException object is comprised of several components. When debugging database-related programs, sometimes you may want to get the details of a SQLException. The following code segment
demonstrates how to retrieve the information in a SQLException:

```
java.sql.Connection conn = null;
try {
    // get the Connection object
    conn = getConnection();

    // Execute SQL statements using Connection object ...JDBC API...
}
catch (SQLException e) {
    while (e != null) {
        // Retrieve a readable message identifying
        // the reason for the exception
        String errorMessage = e.getMessage();
        System.err.println("sql error message:"+errorMessage);
```

```
        // This vendor-independent string contains a code
        // that identifies the reason for the exception.
        // The code follows the Open Group SQL conventions.
        String sqlState = e.getSQLState();
        System.err.println("sql state:"+sqlState);

        // Retrieve a vendor-specific error code
        // identifying the reason for the exception.
        int errorCode = e.getErrorCode();
        System.err.println("error code:"+errorCode);

        // Get driver name: if it is necessary to execute code
        // based on this error code, you should ensure that the
        // expected driver is being used before using the error code.
        String driverName = conn.getMetaData().getDriverName();
        System.err.println("driver name:"+driverName);
        processDetailError(drivername, errorCode);

        // the exception may have been chained;
        // process the next chained exception
        e = e.getNextException();
      }
      finally {
        // close the Connection object
      }
  }
```

processDetailError():

```
    private static void processDetailError(String driverName,
                                           int errorCode) {
        if ((driverName.equals("MySql Driver")) &&
            (errorCode == 121)) {
            // process MySQL error...
        }
        else if ((driverName.equals("Oracle JDBC Driver")) &&
                 (errorCode == 123)) {
            // process Oracle error...
        }
        ...
    }
```

10-9. What Is SQLException Chaining?

Each SQLException provides chain information, and you can use chains to provide additional error information.

A JDBC problem can stem from various problems (such as a driver is not loadable, a database is not available, a table does not exist, and so on). The SQLException class has a method, getNextException(), that returns either the next exception or null when all exceptions have been retrieved. Obtaining multiple exceptions this way is termed *chaining*.

The SQLException class has two methods that provide further information: a method to get (or chain) additional exceptions and a method to set an additional exception.

SQLException.getSQLState() returns a SQLState identifier based on the XOPEN SQL specification. A SQLState string follows either the XOPEN SQLState conventions or the SQL-99 conventions. The values of the SQLState string are described in the appropriate specifications. You can use the

DatabaseMetaData.getSQLStateType() method to discover whether the driver returns the XOPEN type or the SQL-99 type. Your database-specific reference manuals should list some of these.

SQLException.getErrorCode() retrieves the vendor-specific error code. (It retrieves the vendor-specific exception code for this SQLException object.)

SQLException.getNextException() retrieves the next SQLException or null if there are no more exceptions. Many things can go wrong between your client program and the database. This method allows you to track all problems that occur. (Also, the setNextException() method allows the programmer to add a SQLException to the chain.)

Typical catch code would look similar to the following:

```
try {
    // some database/JDBC work
}
catch (SQLException se) {
    //
    // se is the first exception, you may handle this and get
    // the other chained exceptions;
    //
    // in most of the situations, this exception is sufficient and
    // there might not be any need for chained exceptions (this will
    // depend on the requirements of the project)
    //
    while (se != null) {
        // get the next exception from the chain and handle the exception
        System.out.println("SQL Exception:" + se.getMessage());
        System.out.println("SQL State: " + se.getSQLState());


        se = se.getNextException(); // this is chaining
        //
        // handle the se (if necessary)
        //
    }
}
```

10-10. How Do You Get All SQLException Instances?

If you are debugging your database application and you want to be aware of every little thing that goes wrong within the database, you might use a printSQLExceptions() method such as the following one (please note that this method is for debugging purposes only; in a production environment, you would not call such a method):

```
void printSQLExceptions(SQLException e) {
    while (e != null) {
        System.out.println("SQLException: " + e.getMessage());
        System.out.println("SQL State: " + e.getSQLState());
        System.out.println("Vendor specific Error Code: " + e.getErrorCode());
        e = e.getNextException();
    }
}
```

You can then use the printSQLExceptions() method as follows:

```
ResultSet rs = null;
Statement stmt = null;
Connection conn = null;
try {
```

```
    conn = getConnection();
    stmt = conn.createStatement();
    rs = stmt.executeQuery("SELECT id, name FROM EMPLOYEES");
    ...
}
catch(SQLException e) {
    printSQLExceptions(e);
    // handle the exception
}
finally {
    // clean up and close the database/JDBC resources
}
```

10-11. What Is a SQLWarning?

The SQLWarning class is an exception that provides information about database access warnings.

SQLWarning is a class that extends the SQLException class but is not thrown like other exceptions. Warnings are silently chained to the object whose method caused the warning to be reported. To get the SQLWarning exception, the programmer must specifically ask for warnings. SQLWarning indicates that something not exactly right occurred but its effect was not severe enough to end processing.

In general, if SQLException is not caught, it will halt the program, but SQLWarning does not warrant halting the entire program. Warnings may be retrieved from the java.sql.Connection, java.sql.Statement, and java.sql.ResultSet objects. Trying to retrieve a warning on a connection after it has been closed will cause an exception to be thrown. Similarly, trying to retrieve a warning on a statement after it has been closed or on a result set after it has been closed will cause an exception to

- SQLWarning getNextWarning(): Retrieves the warning chained to this SQLWarning object (returns the next SQLException in the chain and returns null if none)

- void setNextWarning(SQLWarning w): Adds a SQLWarning object (denoted by w) to the end of the chain

Table 10-3 lists the java.sql.SQLWarning constructors, and Table 10-4 lists the java.sql.SQLWarning methods.

Table 10-3. java.sql.SQLWarning *Constructors*

Constructor	Description
SQLWarning()	Constructs a default SQLWarning object.
SQLWarning(String reason)	Constructs a SQLWarning object with the given value for a reason. SQLState defaults to null, and vendorCode defaults to 0.
SQLWarning(String reason, String SQLState)	Constructs a SQLWarning object with the given reason field and SQLState. vendorCode defaults to 0.
SQLWarning(String reason, String SQLState, int vendorCode)	Constructs a fully specified SQLWarning object initialized with the given values.

Table 10-4. `java.sql.SQLWarning` *Methods*

Method		Description
SQLWarning	getNextWarning()	Retrieves the warning chained to this SQLWarning object
void	setNextWarning(SQLWarning w)	Adds a SQLWarning object to the end of the chain

10-12. How Do You Get All SQLWarning Instances?

If you are debugging a database application and you want to be aware of every little thing that goes wrong within the database, you might use a `printSQLWarnings()` method such as the following one (please note that this method is for debugging purposes only; in a production environment, you would not call such a method):

```
void printSQLWarnings(SQLWarning w) {
    while (w != null) {
        System.out.println("SQLWarning: " + w.getMessage());
        System.out.println("SQL State: " + w.getSQLState());
        System.out.println("Vendor specific Error Code: " + w.getErrorCode());
        w = w.getNextWarning();
    }
}
```

You can then use the `printSQLWarnings()` method as follows:

```
ResultSet rs = null;


try {
    // get a Connection object
    conn = getConnection();

    stmt = conn.createStatement();
    printSQLWarnings(stmt.getWarnings());

    rs = stmt.executeQuery("SELECT id, name FROM EMPLOYEES");
    printSQLWarnings(rs.getWarnings());
    ...
}
catch(SQLException e) {
    printSQLExceptions(e);
    // handle the exception
}
finally {
    // clean up and close the JDBC data structures
}
```

10-13. How Do You Determine Whether a SQL Warning Has Occurred?

This section shows how to determine whether a SQLWarning has occurred. Some database operations (such as getting a result set from a database query) can cause a warning that is not handled by a SQL exception (that is, SQLException). You must explicitly check for these warnings. An example of a warning is a data truncation error during a read operation. For details, see the java.sql.DataTruncation class; this is an exception that reports a DataTruncation warning (on reads) or throws a DataTruncation exception (on writes) when JDBC unexpectedly truncates a data value.

You can check for a warning in three places:

- The Connection object (java.sql.Connection)
- The Statement object (java.sql.Statement)
- The ResultSet object (java.sql.ResultSet)

For each case, I will provide an example on how to check for a warning.

Checking for a Warning Using a Connection Object

This shows how to check for a warning using a Connection object:

```
// Get warnings on Connection object
Connection conn = null;
try {
    conn = getConnection(); // get a java.sql.Connection object
    SQLWarning warning = conn.getWarnings();
    while (warning != null) {
        // process connection warning
        String message = warning.getMessage();
        String sqlState = warning.getSQLState();
        int errorCode = warning.getErrorCode();
        warning = warning.getNextWarning();
    }
}
catch (SQLException e) {

}
finally {
   // close JDBC resources: ResultSet, Statement, Connection
}
```

Checking for a Warning Using a Statement Object

This shows how to check for a warning using a Statement object:

```
// Get warnings on Statement object
Connection conn = null;
Statement stmt = null;
try {
    conn = getConnection();         // get a java.sql.Connection object
    stmt = conn.createStatement();  // create a statement

    // use the statement...

    // get warnings on Statement object
    warning = stmt.getWarnings();
    if (warning != null) {
        // Process statement warnings...
    }
}
catch (SQLException e) {
    // ignore the exception
}
finally {
   // close JDBC resources: ResultSet, Statement, Connection
}
```

Checking for a Warning Using a ResultSet Object

This shows how to check for a warning using a ResultSet object:

```
// Get warnings on ResultSet object
ResultSet rs = null;
Connection conn = null;
Statement stmt = null;
try {
    conn = getConnection();        // get a java.sql.Connection object
    stmt = conn.createStatement();  // create a statement
    // get a result set
    String sqlQuery = "select id, name from employees"
    rs = stmt.executeQuery(sqlQuery);
    while (rs.next()) {
        // use result set
        // ...
        // get warnings on the current row of the ResultSet object
        warning = rs.getWarnings();
        if (warning != null) {
            // process result set warnings...
        }
    }
}
catch (SQLException e) {
    // ignore the exception
    }


}
```

10-14. How Do You Create and Traverse a Custom SQLWarning Structure?

JDBC allows you to create and traverse a custom SQLWarning.

How It Works

Assume that you are interested in getting the salary of an employee by a badge number (assume that each employee has a unique badge number). Furthermore, assume that the company has a business policy (a so-called business rule) that no employee can make more than $200,000. (For simplicity, you can further assume that all salaries are integers.) Based on this, you want to pass a badge number and get the salary of the employee.

Solution

Here's the solution:

```
import java.sql.*;

public class RasingCustomSqlWarning {

    public static void main(String[] args) {
        if (args.length != 1) {
            System.out.printout("usage: RasingCustomSqlWarning ");
            System.exit(1);
        }
```

```java
        // args[0] denotes the badge number
        String badgeNumber = args[0];
        try {
            // get the salary
            int salary = getEmployeeSalary(badgeNumber);

            // all is OK. we got the salary
            System.out.println("Got all data from database.");
            System.out.println("emp. badge number="+badgeNumber);
            System.out.println("emp. salary="+salary);
        }
        catch(SQLException e) {
            // print out root SQLException
            System.err.println("An SQL exception occurred: " + e);
            e.printStackTrace();

            // get all chained SQLExceptions
            while((e = e.getNextException()) != null) {
               System.err.println("Contained reason: " + e);
            }
        }
    }

    private static int getEmployeeSalary(String badgeNumber)
        throws SQLException {
        // Status flag resulting from database data should be


        int salary = getEmployeeSalaryFromDatabase(badgeNumber);
        if (salary > 200000) {
            somethingWrongHappened = true;
        }

        if(somethingWrongHappened) {
            // Create two custom SQL Warnings
            SQLWarning rootWarning =
              new SQLWarning("Employee Salary Business rules not properly regarded");
            SQLWarning containedWarning =
              new SQLWarning("Salary over $200,000.");

            // Chain the warnings
            rootWarning.setNextWarning(containedWarning);

            // Notify the caller of the warnings
            throw rootWarning;
        }
    }

    private static int getEmployeeSalaryFromDatabase(String badgeNumber)
        throws SQLException {
        // return the salary of employee with
        // the badge number = badgeNumber
    }
}
```

10-15. How Do You Wrap Database Exceptions?

Sometimes you do not want to use JDBC exceptions directly. Instead, you will want to know how to create and use wrapper database exceptions.

How It Works

In real-world database applications, programmers use several types of database exceptions to wrap any SQLException that occurs at runtime. In the database applications that use this framework, you will find it most convenient to make those exceptions runtime exceptions so they bubble up to an exception handler. Some might argue that these exceptions should be declarative so they can be handled as close to the point of error as possible. However, that would make the SQL execution process almost as cumbersome as the original SQLException, something you should try explicitly to avoid.

The following exception class wraps SQLException, which can provide custom error messages. Wrapping database exceptions enables programmers to catch exceptions at a high level (such as with a user-defined DatabaseException) rather than at a low level (such as with a JDBC-defined SQLException).

Solution

Here's the solution:

```
public class DatabaseException extends java.lang.Object {

    SQLException exception = null;  // wrapped SQLException
    int errorCode;                  // error code


    // constructors ...
    public DatabaseException(SQLException e) {
        this.exception = exception;
        ...
    }

    // constructors ...
    public DatabaseException(SQLException e, String extraMessage) {
        this(exception);
        ...
    }

    public String getErrorMessage() {
        return errorMessage;
    }

    public int getErrorCode() {
        return errorCode;
    }

    // and other supporting methods...
}
```

Now you can use DatabaseException rather than use SQLException directly; here is an example:

```
public double getEmployeeSalary(int badgeNumber)
    throws DatabaseException {
    try {
        ...
        // get employee's salary for a given badge number
```

```
    ...
    }
    catch (SQLException e) {
        throw new DatabaseException(e, "could not get the employee's salary");
    }
}
```

10-16. What Are the SQLState Codes Returned by SQL Exception.getSQLState()?

What is a list of the possible SQLState codes returned by SQLException.getSQLState()? To answer this question, you need to look at the details of the SQLException object. Each SQLException object provides several kinds of information:

- A string describing the error. This is used as the Java Exception message, available via the method getMessage().

- A SQLState string of length 5, which follows either the XOPEN SQLState conventions or the SQL-99 conventions. The values of the SQLState string are described in the documents specified by ANSI and XOPEN. You can use the DatabaseMetaData method getSQLStateType() to discover whether the driver returns the XOPEN type or the SQL-99 type.

- An integer error code that is specific to each vendor. Normally this will be the actual error code returned by the underlying database.

- A chain to the next Exception. You can use this to provide additional error information.

edu/~shadow/sql/sql1992.txt), which defines the basic SQLState codes. But note that each database vendor implements its own SQLState codes. (Therefore, a vendor's SQLState codes might differ from the SQL-92 specification.)

What is a SQLState code? In JDBC, the java.sql.SQLException class provides information about database access errors or other errors. For handling the exceptions thrown by JDBC, it is desirable to analyze the error codes, understand them, and take the necessary actions (*handle* the exceptions). You can use SQLException.getSQLState() to get the SQLState code as follows:

```
try {
    ...
}
catch(SQLException e) {
    String sqlStateCode = e.getSQLState();
    ...
}
```

SQLException.getSQLState() returns a SQLState identifier based on the XOPEN SQL or SQL-99 specification. Your database-specific reference manuals should list some or all of these; alternatively, you can refer to your database tool vendor's documentation for information to find SQLState codes.

How Are SQLState Codes Formatted?

Each SQLState code conforms to the following rules (note that the SQLException class does not enforce these rules; it is up to database vendors to follow these standards):

- It is a character string constant of length 5.

- Each character must be a digit from 0 to 9 or a nonaccented uppercase letter (*A* through *Z*).

- It is a two-character class code immediately followed by a three-character subclass code.

- The SQLState class (the first two characters) cannot be 00, since this represents successful completion.

What Is a SQLState Code in Oracle 9*i*?

According to the Oracle documentation (specifically, the Oracle 9*i* JDBC Developer's Guide and Reference), for errors originating in the JDBC driver the getSQLState() method returns no useful information. For errors originating in the Oracle RDBMS, this method returns a five-digit code indicating the SQLState.

In Oracle 9*i*, the SQLException.getErrorCode() method returns better semantics than the SQLException.getSQLState() method. For errors originating in either the JDBC driver or the RDBMS, this method returns the five-digit SQLState code.

Since error codes play an important role in handling database exceptions, the following tables list the error codes for Oracle and MySQL. Specifically, Table 10-5 lists Oracle's predefined class codes, and Table 10-6 lists Oracle's SQLState status codes. This information comes from http://www.lc.leidenuniv.nl/awcourse/oracle/appdev.920/a97269/toc.htm. Further, Table 10-7 lists MySQL's SQLState status codes and messages; this information comes from http://com.mysql.jdbc.SQLError.java.

Table 10-5.

00	Success completion
01	Warning
02	No data
07	Dynamic SQL error
08	Connection exception
0A	Feature not supported
21	Coordinately violation
22	Data exception
23	Integrity constraint violation
24	Invalid cursor state
25	Invalid transaction state
26	Invalid SQL statement name
27	Triggered data change violation
28	Invalid authorization specification
2A	Direct SQL syntax error or access rule violation
2B	Dependent privilege descriptors still exist
2C	Invalid character set name
2D	Invalid transaction termination
2E	Invalid connection name
33	Invalid SQL descriptor name

(Continued)

Table 10-5. *Continued*

Class	Condition
34	Invalid cursor name
35	Invalid condition number
37	Dynamic SQL syntax error or access rule violation
3C	Ambiguous cursor name
3D	Invalid catalog name
3F	Invalid schema name
40	Transaction rollback
42	Syntax error or access rule violation
44	With check option violation
HZ	Remote database access (reserved for conditions defined in ISO/IEC DIS 9579-2, Remote Database Access)

Table 10-6. *Oracle* SQLState *Status Codes*

Code	Condition	Oracle Error(s)
00000	Successful completion	ORA-00000
01000	Warning	
01001	Cursor operation conflict	
01004	String data-right truncation	
01005	Insufficient item descriptor areas	
01006	Privilege not revoked	
01007	Privilege not granted	
01008	Implicit zero-bit padding	
01009	Search condition too long for info schema	
0100A	Query expression too long for info schema	
02000	No data	ORA-01095 and ORA-01403
07000	Dynamic SQL error	
07001	Using clause not matching parameter specs	
07002	Using clause not matching target specs	
07003	Cursor specification cannot be executed	
07004	Using clause required for dynamic parameters	
07005	Prepared statement not a cursor specification	
07006	Restricted data type attribute violation	
07007	Using clause required for result components invalid descriptor count	
07008	Invalid descriptor count	SQL-02126
07009	Invalid descriptor index	
08000	Connection exception	
08001	SQL client unable to establish SQL connection	

Code	Condition	Oracle Error(s)
08002	Connection name in use	
08003	Connection does not exist	SQL-02121
08004	SQL server rejected SQL connection	
08006	Connection failure	
08007	Transaction resolution unknown	
0A000	Feature not supported	ORA-03000..03099
0A001	Multiple server transactions	
21000	Cardinality violation	ORA-01427 and SQL-02112
22000	Data exception	
22001	String data, right truncation	ORA-01406
22002	NULL value, no indicator parameter	SQL-02124
22003	Numeric value out of range	ORA-01426
22005	Error in assignment	
22007	Invalid date/time format	
22008	Date/time field overflow	ORA-01800..01899
22009	Invalid time zone displacement value	
22011	Substring error	
22012	Division by zero	ORA-01476
22019	Invalid escape character	ORA-00911
22021	Character not in repertoire	
22022	Indicator overflow	ORA-01411
22023	Invalid parameter value	ORA-01025 and ORA-04000..04019
22024	Unterminated C string	ORA-01479 and ORA-01480
22025	Invalid escape sequence	ORA-01424 and ORA-01425
22026	String data-length mismatch	ORA-01401
22027	Trim error	
23000	Integrity constraint violation	ORA-02290..02299
24000	Invalid cursor state	ORA-001002, ORA-001003, SQL-02114, and SQL-02117
25000	Invalid transaction state	SQL-02118
26000	Invalid SQL statement name	
27000	Triggered data change violation	
28000	Invalid authorization specification	
2A000	Direct SQL syntax error or access rule violation	
2B000	Dependent privilege descriptors still exist	
2C000	Invalid character set name	
2D000	Invalid transaction termination	
2E000	Invalid connection name	

(Continued)

Table 10-6. *Continued*

Code	Condition	Oracle Error(s)
33000	Invalid SQL descriptor name	
34000	Invalid cursor name	
35000	Invalid condition number	
37000	Dynamic SQL syntax error or access rule violation	
3C000	Ambiguous cursor name	
3D000	Invalid catalog name	
3F000	Invalid schema name	
40000	Transaction rollback	ORA-02091 and ORA-02092
40001	Serialization failure	
40002	Integrity constraint violation	
40003	Statement completion unknown	
42000	Syntax error or access rule violation	ORA-00022, ORA-00251, ORA-00900..00999, ORA-01031, ORA-01490..01493, ORA-01700..01799, ORA-01900..02099, ORA-02140..02289, ORA-02420..02424, ORA-02450..02499, ORA-04070..04099
44000	With check option violation	ORA-01402
60000	System error	ORA-00370..00429, ORA-00600..00899, ORA-06430..06449, ORA-07200..07999, and ORA-09700..09999
61000	Shared server and detached process errors	ORA-00018..00035, ORA-00050..00068, ORA-02376..02399, and ORA-04020..04039
62000	Shared server and detached process errors	ORA-00100..00120 and ORA-00440..00569
63000	Oracle*XA and two-task interface errors	ORA-00150..00159, ORA-02700..02899, ORA-03100..03199, ORA-06200..06249, and SQL-02128
64000	Control file, database file, and redo file errors; archival and media recovery errors	ORA-00200..00369 and ORA-01100..01250
65000	PL/SQL errors	ORA-06500..06599
66000	Oracle Net driver errors	ORA-06000..06149, ORA-06250..06429, ORA-06600..06999, ORA-12100..12299, and ORA-12500..12599

Code	Condition	Oracle Error(s)
67000	Licensing errors	ORA-00430..00439
69000	SQL*Connect errors	ORA-00570..00599 and ORA-07000..07199
72000	SQL execute phase errors	ORA-00001, ORA-01000..01099, ORA-01400..01489, ORA-01495..01499, ORA-01500..01699, ORA-02400..02419, ORA-02425..02449, ORA-04060..04069, ORA-08000..08190, ORA-12000..12019, ORA-12300..12499, and ORA-12700..21999
82100	Out of memory (could not allocate)	SQL-02100
82101	Inconsistent cursor cache (UCE/CUC mismatch)	SQL-02101
82102	Inconsistent cursor cache (no CUC entry for UCE)	SQL-02102
82103	Inconsistent cursor cache (out-or-range CUC ref)	SQL-02103
82104	Inconsistent cursor cache (no CUC available)	SQL-02104
82105	Inconsistent cursor cache (no CUC entry in cache)	SQL-02105
82106	Inconsistent cursor cache (invalid cursor number)	SQL-02106
82108	Invalid descriptor passed to runtime library	SQL-02108
82109	Inconsistent host cache (out-or-range SIT ref)	SQL-02109
82110	Inconsistent host cache (invalid SQL type)	SQL-02110
82111	Heap consistency error	SQL-02111
82113	Code generation internal consistency failed	SQL-02115
82114	Reentrant code generator gave invalid context	SQL-02116
82117	Invalid OPEN or PREPARE for this connection	SQL-02122
82118	Application context not found	SQL-02123
82119	Unable to obtain error message text	SQL-02125
82120	Precompiler/SQLLIB version mismatch	SQL-02127
82121	NCHAR error; fetched number of bytes is odd	SQL-02129
82122	EXEC TOOLS interface not available	SQL-02130
82123	Runtime context in use	SQL-02131
82124	Unable to allocate runtime context	SQL-02132
82125	Unable to initialize process for use with threads	SQL-02133
82126	Invalid runtime context	SQL-02134
HZ000	Remote database access	

Table 10-7. *MySQL* SQLState *Codes and Messages*

Code	Description
01002	Disconnect error
01004	Data truncated
01006	Privilege not revoked
01S00	Invalid connection string attribute
01S01	Error in row
01S03	No rows updated or deleted
01S04	More than one row updated or deleted
07001	Wrong number of parameters
08001	Unable to connect to data source
08002	Connection in use
08003	Connection not open
08004	Data source rejected establishment of connection
08007	Connection failure during transaction
08S01	Communication link failure
21S01	Insert value list does not match column list
22003	Numeric value out of range
22005	Numeric value out of range
28000	Invalid authorization specification
42000	Syntax error or access violation
S0001	Base table or view already exists
S0002	Base table not found
S0011	Index already exists
S0012	Index not found
S0021	Column already exists
S0022	Column not found
S0023	No default for column
S1000	General error
S1001	Memory allocation failure
S1002	Invalid column number
S1009	Invalid argument value
S1C00	Driver not capable
S1T00	Timeout expired

10-17. What Is a BatchUpdateException?

BatchUpdateException is a class that extends the SQLException class and provides information about errors during a batch update operation. This exception is thrown by the Statement.executeBatch() method if one of the SQL commands in the batch fails.

According to the Java documentation, the BatchUpdateException class is defined as follows:

```
package java.sql;

public class BatchUpdateException
    extends SQLException
```

Further, the documentation says this:

An exception thrown when an error occurs during a batch update operation. In addition to the information provided by SQLException, a BatchUpdateException provides the update counts for all commands that were executed successfully during the batch update, that is, all commands that were executed before the error occurred. The order of elements in an array of update counts corresponds to the order in which commands were added to the batch.

After a command in a batch update fails to execute properly and a BatchUpdateException is thrown, the driver may or may not continue to process the remaining commands in the batch. If the driver continues processing after a failure, the array returned by the method BatchUpdateException.getUpdateCounts will have an element for every command in the batch rather than only elements for the commands that executed successfully before the error. In the case where the driver continues processing commands, the array element for any command that failed is Statement.EXECUTE_FAILED.

Table 10-8 lists the BatchUpdateException constructors, and Table 10-9 lists the method.

Constructor	Description
BatchUpdateException()	Constructs a BatchUpdateException object with the reason field, SQLState, and update count initialized to null and the vendor code initialized to 0
BatchUpdateException(int[] updateCounts)	Constructs a BatchUpdateException initialized to null for the reason field and SQLState and 0 for the vendor code
BatchUpdateException(String reason, int[] updateCounts)	Constructs a BatchUpdateException initialized with reason, updateCounts, and null for the SQLState and 0 for the vendor code
BatchUpdateException(String reason, String SQLState, int[] updateCounts)	Constructs a BatchUpdateException initialized with the given arguments (reason, SQLState, and updateCounts) and 0 for the vendor code
BatchUpdateException(String reason, String SQLState, int vendorCode, int[] updateCounts)	Constructs a fully specified BatchUpdateException object, initializing it with the given values

Table 10-9. *Method for* BatchUpdateException

Return Type	Method	Description
int[]	getUpdateCounts()	Retrieves the update count for each update statement in the batch update that executed successfully before this exception occurred

In the following sections, I will provide two complete examples using BatchUpdateException. The first example (the Demo_BatchUpdateException_1 class) uses a batch update and passes all valid/correct SQL statements; the second example (the Demo_BatchUpdateException_2 class) uses a batch update and passes a mix of correct and incorrect SQL statements, which will cause BatchUpdateException to be thrown.

Example 1: Demo_BatchUpdateException_1

The following is Demo_BatchUpdateException_1:

```
import java.util.*;
import java.io.*;
import java.sql.*;

import jcb.util.DatabaseUtil;
import jcb.db.VeryBasicConnectionManager;

public class Demo_BatchUpdateException_1 {

    public static void checkUpdateCounts(int[] updateCounts) {
        for (int i=0; i<updateCounts.length; i++) {
            if (updateCounts[i] >= 0) {
                // Successfully executed;
                // the number represents number of affected rows
                System.out.println("OK: updateCount="+updateCounts[i]);
            }
            else if (updateCounts[i] == Statement.SUCCESS_NO_INFO) {


                System.out.println("OK: updateCount=Statement.SUCCESS_NO_INFO");
            }
            else if (updateCounts[i] == Statement.EXECUTE_FAILED) {
                // Failed to execute
                System.out.println("updateCount=Statement.EXECUTE_FAILED");
            }
        }
    }

    public static void main(String[] args) {
        Connection conn = null;
        Statement stmt = null;
        try {
            System.out.println("-- begin-- dbVendor="+args[0]);
            String dbVendor = args[0];
            conn = VeryBasicConnectionManager.getConnection(dbVendor);
            System.out.println("conn="+conn);

            // Disable autocommit
            conn.setAutoCommit(false);

            // create Statement object
            stmt = conn.createStatement();
            stmt.addBatch("DELETE FROM animals_table");
```

```java
        stmt.addBatch("INSERT INTO animals_table(id, name) "+
            "VALUES(111, 'ginger')");
        stmt.addBatch("INSERT INTO animals_table(id, name) "+
            "VALUES(222, 'lola')");
        stmt.addBatch("INSERT INTO animals_table(id, name) "+
            "VALUES(333, 'freddy')");


        // Execute the batch
        int[] updateCounts = stmt.executeBatch();

        // all statements were successfully executed.
        // updateCounts contains one element for each
        // batched statement. The updateCounts[i] contains
        // the number of rows affected by that statement.
        checkUpdateCounts(updateCounts);

        // since there were no errors, commit
        conn.commit();
        System.out.println("-- end --");
    }
    catch (BatchUpdateException e) {
        // Not all of the statements were successfully executed
        int[] updateCounts = e.getUpdateCounts();

        // Some databases will continue to execute after one fails.


        // of successfully executed statements
        checkUpdateCounts(updateCounts);

        // Either commit the successfully executed statements
        // or roll back the entire batch
        try {
            conn.rollback();
        }
        catch (Exception e2) {
            e.printStackTrace();
            System.exit(1);
        }
    }
    catch (Exception e) {
        e.printStackTrace();
        System.exit(1);
    }
    finally {
        // release database resources
        DatabaseUtil.close(stmt);
        DatabaseUtil.close(conn);
    }
  }
}
```

Viewing the MySQL Database Before Running the Solution

This shows the MySQL database before running the solution:

```
mysql> desc animals_table;
+-------+-------------+------+-----+---------+----------------+
| Field | Type        | Null | Key | Default | Extra          |
+-------+-------------+------+-----+---------+----------------+
| id    | int(11)     |      | PRI | NULL    | auto_increment |
| name  | varchar(10) |      |     |         |                |
+-------+-------------+------+-----+---------+----------------+
2 rows in set (0.00 sec)

mysql> select * from animals_table;
+-----+-------+
| id  | name  |
+-----+-------+
| 22  | puffy |
| 77  | muffy |
+-----+-------+
2 rows in set (0.00 sec)
```

Running the Solution for the MySQL Database

This shows how to run the solution for the MySQL database:

```
$ javac  Demo_BatchUpdateException_1.java


conn=com.mysql.jdbc.Connection@750159
---------------
OK; updateCount=2
OK; updateCount=1
OK; updateCount=1
OK; updateCount=1
-- end --
```

Discussing the Output for the Solution

This is what happened:

- updateCount=2 refers to the fact that the SQL statement DELETE FROM animals_table impacted two rows (that is, two rows were deleted).

- updateCount=1 refers to the fact that the SQL INSERT INTO animals_table(id, name) ... statement impacted one row (that is, one row was inserted).

Viewing the MySQL Database After Running the Solution

This is the MySQL database after running the solution:

```
mysql> select * from animals_table;
+-----+--------+
| id  | name   |
+-----+--------+
| 111 | ginger |
| 222 | lola   |
| 333 | freddy |
+-----+--------+
3 rows in set (0.00 sec)
```

Viewing the Oracle Database Before Running the Solution

This is the Oracle database before running the solution:

```
SQL> create table animals_table(
  2  id int, name varchar2(10));

Table created.

SQL> desc animals_table;
 Name                                      Null?    Type
 ----------------------------------------- -------- --------------
 ID                                                 NUMBER(38)
 NAME                                               VARCHAR2(10)

SQL> insert into animals_table(id, name) values(22, 'puffy');
SQL> insert into animals_table(id, name) values(77, 'muffy');
SQL> commit;
Commit complete.

SQL> select * from animals_table;

        ID  NAME
---------- ----------
        22  puffy
        77  muffy
```

This shows how to run the solution for Oracle:

```
$ javac  Demo_BatchUpdateException_1.java
$ java  Demo_BatchUpdateException_1  oracle
-- begin-- dbVendor=oracle
conn=oracle.jdbc.driver.T4CConnection@6e293a
OK: updateCount=2
OK: updateCount=1
OK: updateCount=1
OK: updateCount=1
-- end --
```

Discussing the Output for the Solution

This is what happened:

- updateCount=2 refers to the fact that the SQL statement DELETE FROM animals_table impacted two rows (that is, two rows were deleted).

- updateCount=1 refers to the fact that the SQL INSERT INTO animals_table(id, name) ... statement impacted one row (that is, one row was inserted).

Viewing the Oracle Database After Running the Solution

This is the Oracle database after running the solution:

```
SQL> select * from animals_table;

       ID   NAME
---------- ----------
      111   ginger
      222   lola
      333   freddy
```

Example 2: Demo_BatchUpdateException_2

This shows Demo_BatchUpdateException_2:

```java
import java.util.*;
import java.io.*;
import java.sql.*;

import jcb.util.DatabaseUtil;
import jcb.db.VeryBasicConnectionManager;

public class Demo_BatchUpdateException_2 {

    public static void checkUpdateCounts(int[] updateCounts) {
        for (int i=0; i<updateCounts.length; i++) {
            if (updateCounts[i] >= 0) {
                // Successfully executed;
                // the number represents number of affected rows



                // Successfully executed; number of affected rows not available
                System.out.println("OK; updateCount=Statement.SUCCESS_NO_INFO");
            }
            else if (updateCounts[i] == Statement.EXECUTE_FAILED) {
                // Failed to execute
                System.out.println("Failure; updateCount=Statement.EXECUTE_FAILED");
            }
        }
    }

    public static void main(String[] args) {
        Connection conn = null;
        Statement stmt = null;
        try {
            System.out.println("-- begin-- dbVendor="+args[0]);
            String dbVendor = args[0];
            conn = VeryBasicConnectionManager.getConnection(dbVendor);
            System.out.println("conn="+conn);

            // Disable autocommit
            conn.setAutoCommit(false);

            // create Statement object
            stmt = conn.createStatement();
            stmt.addBatch("DELETE FROM animals_table");
```

```java
            stmt.addBatch("INSERT INTO animals_table(id, name) "+
                          "VALUES(444, 'ginger')");
            //  we intentionally pass a table name (animals_tableZZ)
            //  that does not exist
            stmt.addBatch("INSERT INTO animals_tableZZ(id, name) "+
                          "VALUES(555, 'lola')");
            stmt.addBatch("INSERT INTO animals_table(id, name) "+
                          "VALUES(666, 'freddy')");


            // Execute the batch
            int[] updateCounts = stmt.executeBatch();

            // all statements were successfully executed.
            // updateCounts contains one element for each
            // batched statement. The updateCounts[i] contains
            // the number of rows affected by that statement.
            checkUpdateCounts(updateCounts);

            // since there were no errors, commit
            conn.commit();
            System.out.println("-- end --");
        }
        catch (BatchUpdateException e) {
            // Not all of the statements were successfully executed
            int[] updateCounts = e.getUpdateCounts();


            // fails. If so, updateCounts.length will equal the
            // number of batched statements. If not, updateCounts.length
            // will equal the number of successfully executed statements
            checkUpdateCounts(updateCounts);

            // Either commit the successfully executed
            // statements or roll back the entire batch
            try {
                conn.rollback();
            }
            catch (Exception e2) {
                e.printStackTrace();
                System.exit(1);
            }
        }
        catch (Exception e) {
            e.printStackTrace();
            System.exit(1);
        }
        finally {
            // release database resources
            DatabaseUtil.close(stmt);
            DatabaseUtil.close(conn);
        }
    }
}
```

Viewing the MySQL Database Before Running the Solution

This is the MySQL database before running the solution:

```
mysql> select * from animals_table;
+-----+--------+
| id  | name   |
+-----+--------+
| 111 | ginger |
| 222 | lola   |
| 333 | freddy |
+-----+--------+
3 rows in set (0.00 sec)
```

Running the Solution for the MySQL Database

For discussion purposes, I have added line numbers to the output:

```
1   $ javac Demo_BatchUpdateException_2.java
2   $ java  Demo_BatchUpdateException_2  mysql
3   -- begin-- dbVendor=mysql
4   conn=com.mysql.jdbc.Connection@1301ed8
5   OK; updateCount=3
6   OK; updateCount=1
7   Failure; updateCount=Statement.EXECUTE_FAILED
8   OK; updateCount=1
```

This is the MySQL database after running the solution:

```
mysql> select * from animals_table;
+-----+--------+
| id  | name   |
+-----+--------+
| 444 | ginger |
| 666 | freddy |
+-----+--------+
2 rows in set (0.01 sec)
```

Discussing the Output of Demo_BatchUpdateException_2

This is what happened:

- *Line 5*: updateCount=3 refers to the fact that the SQL statement DELETE FROM animals_table impacted three rows (that is, three rows were deleted).

- *Line 6*: updateCount=1 refers to the fact that the SQL INSERT INTO animals_table(id, name) ... statement impacted one row (that is, one row was inserted).

- *Line 7*: updateCount=Statement.EXECUTE_FAILED refers to the fact that the SQL INSERT INTO animals_tableZZ(id, name) ... statement failed (because animals_tableZZ is a nonexistent table).

- *Line 8*: updateCount=1 refers to the fact that the SQL INSERT INTO animals_table(id, name) ... statement impacted one row (that is, one row was inserted).

Viewing the Oracle Database Before Running the Solution

This is the Oracle database before running the solution:

```
SQL> select * from animals_table;

        ID  NAME
---------- ----------
       111  ginger
       222  lola
       333  freddy
```

Running the Solution for the Oracle Database

For discussion purposes, I have added line numbers to the output:

```
1   $ javac Demo_BatchUpdateException_2.java
2   $ java  Demo_BatchUpdateException_2  oracle
3   -- begin-- dbVendor=oracle
4   conn=oracle.jdbc.driver.T4CConnection@6e293a
5   OK; updateCount=3
6   OK; updateCount=1
```

Viewing the Oracle Database After Running the Solution

This is the Oracle database after running the solution:

```
        ID  NAME
---------- ----------
       111  ginger
       222  lola
       333  freddy
```

Discussing the Output for the Solution

Because Oracle supports true transactions, none of the inserts was committed (because of the nonexistent table name animals_tableZZ).

10-18. What Is a DataTruncation Class?

DataTruncation is a class that extends the SQLWarning class and provides information about data truncation errors when JDBC unexpectedly truncates a data value (during read/write operations, such as when a column is defined as VARCHAR(10) and you pass more than ten characters during an INSERT/UPDATE operation). Note that no methods in the JDBC API throw the DataTruncation exception explicitly/directly.

You can catch a DataTruncation exception as a SQLWarning or SQLException exception because it is derived from SQLWarning (which is derived from SQLException). When it is caught as a SQLWarning or SQLException, it must be explicitly cast to DataTruncation before you can access the methods of that interface.

For handling and customizing DataTruncation exceptions, MySQL's JDBC driver has a connection property named jdbcCompliantTruncation, which has the following definition (http://72.14.207.104/search?q=cache:9L3ToT2Upx8J:engr.smu.edu/~coyle/cse7346/S12.MySql.Jdbc.pdf+definition+of+jdbcCompliantTruncation&hl=en):

Should the driver throw java.sql.DataTruncation exceptions when data is truncated as is required by the JDBC specification when connected to a server that supports warnings (MySQL 4.1.0 and newer)?

The value of this property can be true/false. You can set this property by either adding it to the database URL or adding it to the java.util.Properties object and then passing it to the DriverManager class. You can use the following three approaches to find out if DataTruncation has occurred:

First approach: To find out if a DataTruncation exception has occurred, you need to catch that exception. MySQL's JDBC driver (Connector/J) throws a DataTruncation exception if you try to write more data than expected (for example, if a column is defined as VARCHAR(10) and you pass more than ten characters). You can use the following snippet:

```
try {
    ...
}
catch(DataTruncation dt) {
    // data truncation has happened.
    //
    // use the DataTruncation methods to
    // handle the exception or ignore it
}
```

Second approach: To find out if a DataTruncation exception has occurred, you need to invoke Statement.getWarnings(), PreparedStatement.getWarnings(), CallableStatement.getWarnings(),

instance of DataTruncation; if it is an instance of DataTruncation, then you must cast the warning object to the DataTruncation object and use its methods accordingly.

Third approach: Finally, you can get the SQLWarning object from Statement, PreparedStatement, CallableStatement, or ResultSet and then check to see if SQLWarning.getSQLState() == "01004". If that is the case, then it means that the SQLWarning object is an instance of DataTruncation. All JDBC-compliant drivers must use 01004 for SQLWarning.getSQLState().

The following examples will demonstrate these concepts.
According to the Java documentation, the DataTruncation class is defined as follows:

```
package java.sql;

public class DataTruncation
    extends SQLWarning
```

The documentation also says this:

An exception that reports a DataTruncation warning (on reads) or throws a DataTruncation exception (on writes) when JDBC unexpectedly truncates a data value. The SQLState for a DataTruncation is 01004.

Table 10-10 shows the DataTruncation constructor.

Table 10-10. DataTruncation *Constructor*

Constructor	Description
DataTruncation(int index, boolean parameter, boolean read, int dataSize, int transferSize)	Creates a DataTruncation object with the SQLState initialized to 01004, the reason field set to data truncation, the vendorCode set to the SQLException default, and the other fields set to the given values

The constructor's parameters are as follows:

- index: The index of the parameter or column value
- parameter: True if a parameter value was truncated
- read: True if a read was truncated
- dataSize: The original size of the data
- transferSize: The size after truncation

Table 10-11 shows the DataTruncation methods.

Table 10-11. DataTruncation *Methods*

Return Type	Method Name	Description
int	getDataSize()	Gets the number of bytes of data that should have been transferred
boolean	getParameter()	Indicates whether the value truncated was a parameter value or a column value
boolean	getRead()	Indicates whether the value was truncated on a read
int	getTransferSize()	Gets the number of bytes of data actually transferred

10-19. How Do You Use DataTruncation?

The following sections explain how to create and use a DataTruncation object.

How It Works

The DataTruncation class has only one constructor, which has five parameters. The following code creates a DataTruncation object with the SQLState initialized to 01004, the reason field set to data truncation, the vendorCode set to the SQLException default, and the other fields set to the given values:

```
// Example of a DataTruncation:
// the index of the parameter or column value
int index = 4;

// true if a parameter value was truncated
boolean parameter = true;

// true if a read was truncated
boolean read = false;

// the original size of the data
int dataSize = 210;
```

```
// the size after truncation
int transferSize = 40;

DataTruncation dt = new DataTruncation(index,
                                       parameter,
                                       read,
                                       dataSize,
                                       transferSize);
```

I will now provide two examples using DataTruncation. The first example uses the instanceof operator to determine if a given SQLWarning object is an instance of the DataTruncation object. The second example uses SQLWarning.getSQLState() and then checks its value against 01004 (the SQLState code for a DataTruncation object is 01004).

Solution

This example (the Demo_DataTruncation_1 class) tries to insert a row with two columns so that one of the columns will be oversized, which will cause DataTruncation to be thrown:

```java
import java.util.*;
import java.io.*;
import java.sql.*;

import jcb.db.*;
import jcb.meta.*;




            if ( dataTruncation != null ) {
                System.out.println("Data truncation error: ");
                System.out.println(dataTruncation.getDataSize() +
                   " bytes should have been ");
                if (dataTruncation.getRead()) {
                    System.out.println("Read (Error:) ");
                }
                else {
                    System.out.println("Written (Error:) ");
                }
                System.out.println(dataTruncation.getTransferSize() +
                   " number of bytes of data actually transferred.");
            }
        }

    public static void displayError(SQLWarning warning) {
        while ( warning != null ) {
            if ( warning instanceof DataTruncation ) {
                displayError((DataTruncation) warning);
            }
            else {
                System.out.println(" Warning: " + warning.getMessage());
            }
            warning = warning.getNextWarning();
        }
    }
}
```

```java
    public static void main(String[] args) {
        Connection conn = null;
        Statement stmt = null;
        try {
            System.out.println("-- Demo_DataTruncation_1 begin --");
            // args[0] = dbVendor = {"mysql", "oracle" }
            conn = VeryBasicConnectionManager.getConnection(args[0]); //
            System.out.println("conn="+conn);
            System.out.println("--------------");

            // create Statement object
            stmt = conn.createStatement();
            stmt.executeUpdate("DELETE FROM animals_table");
            displayError(stmt.getWarnings());
            // try to write more data for the name column.
            stmt.executeUpdate("INSERT INTO animals_table(id, name)"+
                                "VALUES(111, 'ginger123456789')");
            displayError(stmt.getWarnings());

            System.out.println("-- Demo_DataTruncation_1 end --");
        }
        catch (DataTruncation dt) {
            System.out.println("-- got DataTruncation exception --");
            displayError(dt);
            System.out.println("-- printStackTrace --");
            dt.printStackTrace();
        }

        catch (SQLException se) {
            System.out.println("-- got SQLException exception --");
            System.out.println("Database error message: "+se.getMessage());
            System.exit(1);
        }
        catch (Exception e) {
            e.printStackTrace();
            System.exit(1);
        }
        finally {
            // release database resources
            DatabaseUtil.close(stmt);
            DatabaseUtil.close(conn);
        }
    }
}
```

Viewing the MySQL Database Before Running the Solution

This is the MySQL database before running the solution:

```
mysql> desc animals_table;
+-------+-------------+------+-----+---------+----------------+
| Field | Type        | Null | Key | Default | Extra          |
+-------+-------------+------+-----+---------+----------------+
| id    | int(11)     |      | PRI | NULL    | auto_increment |
| name  | varchar(10) |      |     |         |                |
+-------+-------------+------+-----+---------+----------------+
2 rows in set (0.00 sec)
```

```
mysql> select * from animals_table;
+-----+---------+
| id  | name    |
+-----+---------+
| 444 | ginger  |
| 666 | freddy  |
+-----+---------+
2 rows in set (0.00 sec)
```

Running the Solution for the MySQL Database

This shows how to run the solution for the MySQL database:

```
$ javac Demo_DataTruncation_1_MySQL.java
$ java Demo_DataTruncation_1  mysql
-- Demo_DataTruncation_1 begin --
conn=com.mysql.jdbc.Connection@143c8b3
----------------
-- got DataTruncation exception --
Data truncation error: 0 bytes should have been Written (Error:)
0 number of bytes of data actually transferred.
-- printStackTrace --
com.mysql.jdbc.MysqlDataTruncation: Data truncation:
Data truncated for column 'name' at row 1
  at com.mysql.jdbc.SQLError.convertShowWarningsToSQLWarnings(SQLError.java:695)
  at com.mysql.jdbc.MysqlIO.scanForAndThrowDataTruncation(MysqlIO.java:3317)


        at com.mysql.jdbc.Connection.execSQL(Connection.java:2297)
        at com.mysql.jdbc.Statement.executeUpdate(Statement.java:1289)
        at Demo_DataTruncation_1.main(Demo_DataTruncation_1.java:54)
```

Viewing the MySQL Database After Running the Solution

As you can see, this example tried to insert ginger123456789 for the name column; because the size of this data (15) is larger than 10 (the maximum size of a name column), the exception takes place. MySQL's JDBC driver chops the data and inserts only the maximum allowed, as follows:

```
mysql> select * from animals_table;
+-----+------------+
| id  | name       |
+-----+------------+
| 111 | ginger1234 |
+-----+------------+
1 row in set (0.00 sec)
```

Viewing the Oracle Database Before Running the Solution

This is the Oracle database before running the solution:

```
SQL> select id, name from animals_table;
no rows selected
SQL>
```

Running the Solution for the Oracle Database

This shows how to run the solution for the Oracle database:

```
$ javac Demo_DataTruncation_1.java
java Demo_DataTruncation_1 oracle
-- Demo_DataTruncation_1 begin --
conn=oracle.jdbc.driver.T4CConnection@6e293a
---------------
-- got SQLException exception --
Database error message: ORA-12899: value too large for column "SCOTT"."ANIMALS_T
ABLE"."NAME" (actual: 15, maximum: 10)
```

Viewing the Oracle Database After Running the Solution

As you can see, this example tried to insert ginger123456789 for the name column; because the size of this data (15) is larger than 10 (the maximum size of a name column), the exception happens. Oracle's JDBC driver (unlike MySQL) does not insert the record, as follows:

```
SQL> select id, name from animals_table;
no rows selected
SQL>
```

10-20. How Do You Use DataTruncation for ResultSet?

Generating a ResultSet object may throw a DataTruncation exception.

DataTruncation

a DataTruncation, first execute a SQL query, then get a ResultSet object, and finally get a DataTruncation from your ResultSet. The DataTruncation class provides several methods to determine the column or parameter index to which it applies, the actual and expected lengths, and so on. When DataTruncation is chained to a ResultSet object, it can be distinguished from other JDBC warnings based on its SQLState code of 01004.

If data truncation occurs during a read operation (using SQL's SELECT statement) from a ResultSet object, then a DataTruncation object will be added to the ResultSet object's warning list, and the method will return as much data as it was able to read.

The following code snippet shows how to use DataTruncation with the ResultSet object:

```
import java.sql.*;
...
public static final String DATA_TRUNCATION_SQL_STATE = "01004";
...
ResultSet rs = null;
Statement stmt = null;
Connection conn = null;
SQLWarning warning = null;

String sqlQuery = "select ... from ...";  // form your sql query
try {
    conn = getConnection();
    stmt = conn.createStatement();
    rs = stmt.executeQuery(sqlQuery);
    warning = rs.getWarnings();
    while (warning != null) {
        if (warn.getSQLState().equals(DATA_TRUNCATION_SQL_STATE)) {
```

```
            //
            // this means it is a DataTruncation exception
            // and its SQLState is initialized to 01004
            //
            DataTruncation dt = (DataTruncation) warning;
            int columnNumber = dt.getIndex();
            int transferSize = dt.getTransferSize();
            int dataSize = dt.getDataSize();
            // do something useful with this information
            // ...
        }
        else {
            // it is some other SQLWarning
            // handle the exception
        }

        warning = warning.getNextWarning();

    }
}
catch(SQLException se) {
    // handle SQLException
}
catch(Exception e) {
    // handle Exception
}


}
```

CHAPTER 11

■ ■ ■

Exploring the Statement

This chapter describes an important JDBC interface, java.sql.Statement. This interface formulates the SQL statements executed by the database engine. You can use Statement and PreparedStatement to execute SQL queries and statements and return the results (as a ResultSet object or as other data types) to the client. You can use CallableStatement to execute a stored procedure/function and return the result (as a ResultSet object or as other data types) to the client. You can create all three interfaces using a Connection (java.sql.Connection) object. Connection is a factory object for creating other objects (such as Statement, PreparedStatement, and CallableStatement).

By using a Statement object, you can execute static SQL statements. (SQL queries cannot be parameterized with the Statement object; in order to parameterize SQL queries, you must use the PreparedStatement object.) The Statement interface enables you to execute both DDL (such as creating a table or index) and DML (such as retrieving an existing record, inserting a new record, or updating an existing row). The Statement interface provides the following methods for executing SQL requests:

- executeBatch(): Submits a batch of commands to the database for execution and, if all commands execute successfully, returns an array of update counts

- executeQuery(String sql): Executes the given SQL statement, which returns a single ResultSet object

- executeUpdate(String sql): Executes the given SQL statement, which may be an INSERT, UPDATE, or DELETE statement or a SQL statement that returns nothing, such as a SQL DDL statement

11-1. How Do You Represent a SQL Statement Object?

Say you want to send your SQL statements to query the database or create database objects (such as new records/row, tables, and views). How do you do that?

A Statement object is what sends your SQL statement (whether you're creating a table or selecting rows from a table) to the database server. According to the JDK, "the Statement object is used for executing a static SQL statement and returning the results it produces." The Statement interface has about 40 methods.

You simply create a Statement object and then execute it, supplying the appropriate "execute" method with the SQL statement you want to send. For a SELECT statement, the method is executeQuery(). For statements that create or modify tables, the method to use is executeUpdate().

JDK defines the java.sql.Statement as follows:

```
public interface Statement
```

The JDK also says this:

The object used for executing a static SQL statement and returning the results it produces. By default, only one ResultSet object per Statement object can be open at the same time. Therefore, if the reading of one ResultSet object is interleaved with the reading of another, each must have been generated by different Statement objects. All execution methods in the Statement interface implicitly close a statement's current ResultSet object if an open one exists.

If you want to execute a Statement object many times, you can use a PreparedStatement object instead of Statement to reduce execution time. (For details, see Chapter 12.) The main feature of a PreparedStatement object is that, unlike a Statement object, it is given a SQL statement when it is created. The advantage to this is that in most cases this SQL statement will be sent to the database server right away, where it will be compiled. As a result, the PreparedStatement object contains not just a SQL statement but also a SQL statement that has been precompiled. This means that when the PreparedStatement is executed, the database server can just run the PreparedStatement object's SQL statement without having to compile/parse/check semantics first.

When the database "prepares" a Statement object, it creates a *query plan*. A query plan indicates to the database how (using which indexes and other criteria) the SQL query will be executed. Note that Statement prepares and executes the query plan each time, while PreparedStatement prepares the query plan just once and then reuses the query plan. Preparing a statement is also referred to as *precompiling* a statement.

A Statement object executes simple SQL statements with no parameters, and a PreparedStatement object can execute SQL statements with any number of "input" parameters. From the performance

11-2. How Do You Create Statement Objects?

The java.sql.Connection interface has factory methods for creating Statement and PreparedStatement objects. A Statement object is created with the Connection method createStatement(): once a Statement object is created, you may execute any number of SQL queries with that Statement object.

```
Connection conn = null;
Statement stmt = null;
ResultSet rs = null;
try {
    // get a Connection object
    conn = getConnection();

    // create Statement object: once Statement object is
    // created, you can execute queries, send SQL statements
    // to the database, and then get the results back
    stmt = conn.createStatement();

    // create a result set
    String sqlQuery = "SELECT badge_number FROM employee_table";
    rs = stmt.executeQuery(sqlQuery);

    // iterate the result set object, and get all the data
    while (rs.next()) {
        int badgeNumber = rs.getInt(1);
    }
```

```
        // create another result set
        String sqlQuery2 = "SELECT dept_id, dept_name FROM dept_table";
        rs = stmt.executeQuery(sqlQuery2);

        // iterate the result set object, and get all the data
        while (rs.next()) {
            int deptID = rs.getInt(1);
            String deptName = rs.getString(2);
        }
    }
}
catch (SQLException e) {
    // could not create a Statement object, or other
    // problems happened; handle the exception
}
finally {
    // close database/JDBC resources such as
    // ResultSet(s), Statement(s), and Connection(s)
}
```

The JDK defines the Connection.createStatement() method as follows:

```
public Statement createStatement() throws SQLException
```

The JDK also says this:

Creates a Statement object for sending SQL statements to the database. SQL statements with-out parameters are normally executed using Statement objects. If the same SQL statement is

created using the returned Statement object will by default be type TYPE_FORWARD_ONLY and have a concurrency level of CONCUR_READ_ONLY. It returns a new default Statement object. It throws a SQLException if a database access error occurs.

11-3. How Do You Create a Scrollable ResultSet?

You will need to know how to create a scrollable ResultSet so you can iterate your retrieved records forward and backward (that is, move a ResultSet object's cursor backward as well as forward). The default ResultSet object is not scrollable.

When you use Connection.createStatement(), it creates a Statement object that can create result set objects that are scrollable. Therefore, by passing some parameters, you can create scrolla-ble result sets. A scrollable result set allows the cursor to be moved to any row in the result set. This capability is useful for GUI tools that browse result sets.

Creating an Insensitive Scrollable ResultSet Object

The following example shows how to create an insensitive scrollable ResultSet object:

```
Connection conn = null;
Statement stmt = null;
ResultSet rs = null;
try {
    // get a Connection object
    conn = getConnection();

    // create a statement that creates insensitive scrollable result set
    Statement stmt = connection.createStatement(
                    ResultSet.TYPE_SCROLL_INSENSITIVE,
                    ResultSet.CONCUR_READ_ONLY);
```

```
    // create a result set
    rs = stmt.executeQuery("SELECT badge_number FROM employee_table");

    // iterate the result set object, and get all the data
    while (rs.next()) {
        int badgeNumber = rs.getInt(1);
    }
}
catch (SQLException e) {
    // could not create a Statement object, or other problems happened.
    // handle the exception
}
finally {
    // close database/JDBC resources such as
    // ResultSet(s), Statement(s), and Connection(s)
}
```

Creating a Sensitive Scrollable ResultSet Object

The following example shows how to create a sensitive scrollable ResultSet object:

```
Connection conn = null;
Statement stmt = null;
ResultSet rs = null;
try {
    // get a Connection object
    conn = getConnection();



                    ResultSet.TYPE_SCROLL_SENSITIVE,
                    ResultSet.CONCUR_READ_ONLY);

    // create a result set
    rs = stmt.executeQuery("SELECT badge_number FROM employee_table");

    // iterate the result set object, and get all the data
    while (rs.next()) {
        int badgeNumber = rs.getInt(1);
    }
}
catch (SQLException e) {
    // could not create a Statement object, or other problems happened.
    // handle the exception
}
finally {
    // close database/JDBC resources such as
    // ResultSet(s), Statement(s), and Connection(s)
}
```

Before creating scrollable ResultSet(s), you need to determine whether your database supports scrollable ResultSet objects. A scrollable ResultSet object allows the cursor to be moved to any row in the result set. Two types of scrollable result sets exist. An insensitive scrollable result set is one where the values captured in the result set never change (similar to Java's final semantics), even if changes are made to the table from which the data was retrieved. A sensitive scrollable result set is one where the current values in the table are reflected in the result set. So, if a change is made to a row in the table, the result set will show the new data when the cursor moves to that row.

The following code can check whether your database supports scrollable ResultSet objects:

```
Connection conn = null;
try {
    // get a Connection object
    conn = getConnection();

    DatabaseMetaData dbmd = conn.getMetaData();
    if (dbmd.supportsResultSetType(ResultSet.TYPE_SCROLL_INSENSITIVE)) {
        // insensitive scrollable result sets are supported
    }

    if (dbmd.supportsResultSetType(ResultSet.TYPE_SCROLL_SENSITIVE)) {
        // sensitive scrollable result sets are supported
    }

    if (!dbmd.supportsResultSetType(ResultSet.TYPE_SCROLL_INSENSITIVE)
        && !dbmd.supportsResultSetType(ResultSet.TYPE_SCROLL_SENSITIVE)) {
        // updatable result sets are not supported
    }
}
catch (SQLException e) {
    // handle the exception
}
finally {
    // close database/JDBC resources such as
    // ResultSet(s), Statement(s), and Connection(s)
}
```

At some point, you will probably want to create an updatable ResultSet object, which can be saved back in the database, but the default ResultSet object is not updatable.

An updatable result set allows you to modify data in a table through the ResultSet object. If the database does not support updatable result sets, the result sets returned from executeQuery() will be read-only. To get updatable results, the Statement object used to create the result sets must have the concurrency type ResultSet.CONCUR_UPDATABLE. The query of an updatable ResultSet must specify the primary key as one of the selected columns and select from only one table. For some drivers, the "SELECT * FROM <table-name>" SQL query will return a read-only ResultSet, so make sure you specify the column names.

The following code creates a statement that will return an updatable ResultSet object:

```
Connection conn = null;
Statement stmt = null;
ResultSet rs = null;
try {
    // get a Connection object
    conn = getConnection();

    // create a statement that will return updatable result sets
    stmt = connection.createStatement(
                ResultSet.TYPE_SCROLL_SENSITIVE,
                ResultSet.CONCUR_UPDATABLE);

    // the primary key badge_number must be specified
    // so that the result set is updatable
    rs = stmt.executeQuery("SELECT badge_number FROM employee_table");
}
```

```
catch (SQLException e) {
    // handle the exception
}
finally {
    // close database/JDBC resources such as
    // ResultSet(s), Statement(s), and Connection(s)
}
```

Before creating an updatable ResultSet object, you need to determine whether your database supports updatable ResultSet objects. An updatable ResultSet objects allows modification to data in a table through the result set. You may use the following code to determine whether your database supports updatable ResultSet objects:

```
Connection conn = null;
try {
    // get a Connection object
    conn = getConnection();

    DatabaseMetaData dbmd = conn.getMetaData();
    if (dbmd.supportsResultSetConcurrency(
            ResultSet.TYPE_FORWARD_ONLY,
            ResultSet.CONCUR_UPDATABLE)) {
        // Updatable result sets are supported
    }
    else {
        // Updatable result sets are not supported
    }

    // handle the exception
}
finally {
    // close database/JDBC resources such as
    // ResultSet(s), Statement(s), and Connection(s)
}
```

11-5. How Do You Execute SQL Statements Using Statement Objects?

The Statement interface provides sufficient methods for executing SQL statements. For executing SQL statements, you should follow four steps:

1. Get a java.sql.Connection object.

2. Using a Connection object, create a Statement object.

3. Execute your SQL statement using a Statement object and generate ResultSet objects.

■**Note** If a method does not return a ResultSet object explicitly, then you may call the Statement.getResultSet() method to get the desired ResultSet object.

---

4. Extract the values from the generated ResultSet objects.

The Statement interface provides the methods listed in Table 11-1 for executing SQL statements.

Table 11-1. *The* Statement *Object's* execute() *Methods*

Return Type	Method	
boolean	execute(String sql)	Executes the given SQL statement, which may return multiple results
boolean	execute(String sql, int autoGeneratedKeys)	Executes the given SQL statement, which may return multiple results, and signals the driver that any autogenerated keys should be made available for retrieval
boolean	execute(String sql, int[] columnIndexes)	Executes the given SQL statement, which may return multiple results, and signals the driver that the autogenerated keys indicated in the given array should be made available for retrieval
boolean	execute(String sql, String[] columnNames)	Executes the given SQL statement, which may return multiple results, and signals the driver that the autogenerated keys indicated in the given array should be made available for retrieval
int[]	executeBatch()	Submits a batch of commands to the database for execution and, if all commands execute successfully, returns an array of update counts
ResultSet	executeQuery(String sql)	Executes the given SQL statement, which returns a single ResultSet object
int	executeUpdate(String sql)	Executes the given SQL statement, which may be an INSERT, UPDATE, or DELETE statement or a SQL statement that returns nothing, such as
int	executeUpdate(String sql, int autoGeneratedKeys)	Executes the given SQL statement and signals the driver with the given flag about whether the autogenerated keys produced by this Statement object should be made available for retrieval
int	executeUpdate(String sql, int[] columnIndexes)	Executes the given SQL statement and signals the driver that the autogenerated keys indicated in the given array should be made available for retrieval
int	executeUpdate(String sql, String[] columnNames)	Executes the given SQL statement and signals the driver that the autogenerated keys indicated in the given array should be made available for retrieval

11-6. How Do You Create a Database Table Using a Statement?

To create a database table, you need to pass the table definition to the executeUpdate() method of a Statement object. The following example creates a table called employee_table with two columns:

```
Statement stmt = null;
Connection conn = null;
try {
    // get a Connection object and create Statement object
    conn = getConnection();
    stmt = conn.createStatement();

    // create table definition called employee_table
    String tableDefinition = "CREATE TABLE employee_table("+
        "badge_number VARCHAR(10), last_name VARCHAR(64))";
```

```
    stmt.executeUpdate(tableDefinition);
    // table creation was successful
}
catch (SQLException e) {
    // table creation failed.
    // handle the exception
}
finally {
    // close database/JDBC resources such as
    // ResultSet(s), Statement(s), and Connection(s)
}
```

11-7. How Do You Drop a Database Table Using a Statement?

To drop a database table (delete the structure and content of a table), you need to pass drop table
<table-name> to the executeUpdate() method of a Statement object. The following example deletes
a table called employee_table:

```
Statement stmt = null;
Connection conn = null;
String tableName = "employee_table";
try {
    // get a Connection object and create a Statement object
    conn = getConnection();
    stmt = conn.createStatement();
    stmt.executeUpdate("DROP TABLE " + tableName);


catch (SQLException e) {
    // table deletion failed.
    // handle the exception
}
finally {
    // close database/JDBC resources such as
    // ResultSet(s), Statement(s), and Connection(s)
}
```

11-8. How Do You Retrieve Automatically Generated Keys Using a Statement (MySQL)?

Since JDBC 3.0, you can retrieve automatically generated keys using a Statement object. In general,
you want to retrieve automatically generated keys when you use the AUTO_INCREMENT attribute in
MySQL.

How It Works

The MySQL database allows for certain columns to be given automatically generated key values.
When using automatically generated key values, an INSERT statement is not responsible for supply-
ing a value for the column. The database generates a unique value for the column and inserts the
value. You can use this technique for generating unique primary keys.

The MySQL database uses the AUTO_INCREMENT attribute for generating key values. The fol-
lowing example shows how to automatically generate key values before retrieving automatically
generated keys.

Setting Up the MySQL Database

You can use the AUTO_INCREMENT attribute to generate a unique identity for new rows, as shown here:

```
mysql> use octopus;
Database changed
mysql>  CREATE TABLE animals_table (
    ->            id INT NOT NULL AUTO_INCREMENT,
    ->            name VARCHAR(32) NOT NULL,
    ->            PRIMARY KEY (id)
    ->  );
Query OK, 0 rows affected (0.03 sec)

mysql> desc animals_table;
+--------+-------------+------+-----+---------+----------------+
| Field  | Type        | Null | Key | Default | Extra          |
+--------+-------------+------+-----+---------+----------------+
| id     | int(11)     |      | PRI | NULL    | auto_increment |
| name   | varchar(32) |      |     |         |                |
+--------+-------------+------+-----+---------+----------------+
2 rows in set (0.01 sec)

mysql> insert into animals_table(name) values('dog');
mysql> insert into animals_table(name) values('cat');
mysql> insert into animals_table(name) values('rabbit');
mysql> select id, name from animals_table;
+----+--------+

| 1 | dog    |
| 2 | cat    |
| 3 | rabbit |
+----+--------+
3 rows in set (0.00 sec)
```

Solution

The JDBC 3.0 specification proposes a functional Statement interface that provides access to automatically generated key values after an insert. The following code snippet demonstrates how to retrieve AUTO_INCREMENT values using the new JDBC 3.0 method getGeneratedKeys(), which is now the preferred method to use if you need to retrieve AUTO_INCREMENT keys.

```
Connection conn = null;
Statement stmt = null;
ResultSet rs = null;
try {
    conn = getConnection();
    stmt = conn.createStatement();
    // insert a new record into the database
    // notice that the ID column is not accounted for here
    stmt.executeUpdate("insert into animals_table (name) values('tiger')");

    // Retrieve a result set containing all of the autogenerated keys from the
    // last update issued on this statement the specific details of the format
    // of this ResultSet are not clearly specified yet
    rs = stmt.getGeneratedKeys();
}
catch (SQLException e) {
```

```
        // handle the exception
  }
finally {
    // close database/JDBC resources such as
    // ResultSet(s), Statement(s), and Connection(s)
  }
```

The complete solution is as follows. You should note that, for the MySQL database, if a column is an AUTO_INCREMENT, you do not need to pass any value at all (this is different for Oracle).

```java
import java.util.*;
import java.io.*;
import java.sql.*;

import jcb.db.VeryBasicConnectionManager;
import jcb.util.DatabaseUtil;

public class DemoGetGeneratedKeys {

    public static void main(String[] args) {
        ResultSet rs = null;
        Statement stmt = null;
        Connection conn = null;
        try {
            System.out.println("--DemoGetGeneratedKeys begin--");
            String dbVendor = args[0]; // database vendor
            conn = VeryBasicConnectionManager.getConnection(dbVendor);


            // create a statement
            stmt = conn.createStatement();

            // insert a  record into the animals_table
            // note that the SQL INSERT is different for each vendor
            String insert = null;
            if (dbVendor.equalsIgnoreCase("mysql")) {
                insert = "insert into animals_table(name) "+
                        "values('tiger11')";
            }
            else if (dbVendor.equalsIgnoreCase("oracle")) {
                insert = "insert into animals_table(id, name) "+
                        "values(ANIMAL_ID_SEQ.nextval, 'tiger11')";
            }

            stmt.executeUpdate(insert);   // insert the record

            if (dbVendor.equalsIgnoreCase("mysql")) {
                rs = stmt.getGeneratedKeys();
            }
            else if (dbVendor.equalsIgnoreCase("oracle")) {
                rs = stmt.executeQuery("select ANIMAL_ID_SEQ.currval from dual");
            }

            while (rs.next()) {
                ResultSetMetaData rsMetaData = rs.getMetaData();
                int columnCount = rsMetaData.getColumnCount();
                for (int i = 1; i <= columnCount; i++) {
                    String key = rs.getString(i);
```

```
                        System.out.println("key " + i + " is " + key);
                    }
                }
                System.out.println("--DemoGetGeneratedKeys end--");
            }
            catch(Exception e){
                e.printStackTrace();
                System.exit(1);
            }
            finally {
                // release database resources
                DatabaseUtil.close(rs);
                DatabaseUtil.close(stmt);
                DatabaseUtil.close(conn);
            }
        }
    }
}
```

Viewing the MySQL Database Before Running the Solution

This shows the MySQL database before running the solution:

```
mysql> select * from animals_table;
+----+--------+
| id | name   |
+----+--------+
|  1 | dog    |


+----+--------+
3 rows in set (0.00 sec)
```

Running the Solution for the MySQL Database

This shows how to run the solution:

```
$ javac  DemoGetGeneratedKeys.java
$ java DemoGetGeneratedKeys  mysql
-- DemoGetGeneratedKeys_MySQL begin --
conn=com.mysql.jdbc.Connection@15c7850
---------------
key 1 is 4
-- DemoGetGeneratedKeys_MySQL end --
```

Viewing the MySQL Database After Running the Solution

This shows the MySQL database after running the solution:

```
mysql> select * from animals_table;
+----+--------+
| id | name   |
+----+--------+
|  1 | dog    |
|  2 | cat    |
|  3 | rabbit |
|  4 | tiger11 |
+----+--------+
4 rows in set (0.01 sec)
```

11-9. How Do You Retrieve Automatically Generated Keys Using a Statement (Oracle)?

The Oracle database allows for certain columns to be given automatically generated key values. When using automatically generated key values, an insert statement is not responsible for supplying a value for the column. The database generates a unique value for the column and inserts the value. You can use this technique for generating unique primary keys. The Oracle database uses the SEQUENCE objects for generating key values. What is a SEQUENCE object? SEQUENCE is an Oracle database object that does the following:

- Automatically generates unique numbers
- Is a sharable object
- Is typically used to create a primary key value
- Replaces application code
- Speeds up the efficiency of accessing sequence values when cached in memory

Setting Up the Oracle Database

How do you create an Oracle SEQUENCE object? You use the CREATE SEQUENCE statement. The following is a general format for defining a SEQUENCE object to generate sequential numbers automatically:

```
CREATE SEQUENCE sequence-name
    [INCREMENT BY n]
    [START WITH n]


    [{CYCLE | NOCYCLE}]
    [{CACHE n | NOCACHE}];
```

The following example shows how to create a SEQUENCE object:

```
CREATE SEQUENCE ANIMAL_ID_SEQ
    INCREMENT BY 1
    START WITH 1
    MAXVALUE 10000
    NOCACHE
    NOCYCLE;
```

Note that Oracle sequences cannot be accessed directly and can be retrieved only by using the CURRVAL (current value) and NEXTVAL (next value) pseudocolumns. Also, a sequence must be first accessed with NEXTVAL before CURRVAL can be used. For example, if a sequence name is ANIMAL_ID_SEQ (defined in the next section), then ANIMAL_ID_SEQ.NEXTVAL will generate the next sequence number, and ANIMAL_ID_SEQ.CURRVAL will provide the last generated sequence number.

```
$ sqlplus mp/mp2
SQL*Plus: Release 9.2.0.1.0 - Production on Mon Oct 6 16:34:50 2003
Copyright (c) 1982, 2002, Oracle Corporation.  All rights reserved.

SQL>    CREATE SEQUENCE ANIMAL_ID_SEQ
  2              INCREMENT BY 1
  3              START WITH 1
  4              MAXVALUE 10000
  5              NOCACHE
  6              NOCYCLE;

Sequence created.
```

```
SQL> desc user_sequences;
Name                                        Null?     Type
---------------------------------------- -------- -------------
SEQUENCE_NAME                            NOT NULL VARCHAR2(30)
MIN_VALUE                                         NUMBER
MAX_VALUE                                         NUMBER
INCREMENT_BY                             NOT NULL NUMBER
CYCLE_FLAG                                        VARCHAR2(1)
ORDER_FLAG                                        VARCHAR2(1)
CACHE_SIZE                               NOT NULL NUMBER
LAST_NUMBER                              NOT NULL NUMBER

SQL> select SEQUENCE_NAME, MIN_VALUE, MAX_VALUE,
            INCREMENT_BY, LAST_NUMBER
         from  user_sequences;

SEQUENCE_NAME    MIN_VALUE  MAX_VALUE INCREMENT_BY LAST_NUMBER
---------------- ---------- ---------- ------------ -----------
ANIMAL_ID_SEQ            1      10000            1           1
```

Oracle Table Creation and Population with ANIMAL_ID_SEQ

This shows how to create an Oracle table and populate it with ANIMAL_ID_SEQ:

```
$ sqlplus mp/mp2
SQL*Plus: Release 9.2.0.1.0 - Production on Tue Oct 7 11:43:49 2003


  2              id INT NOT NULL,
  3              name VARCHAR(32) NOT NULL,
  4              PRIMARY KEY (id)
  5      );

Table created.

SQL> desc animals_table;
Name            Null?     Type
---------------- -------- -------------
ID              NOT NULL NUMBER(38)
NAME            NOT NULL VARCHAR2(32)

SQL> insert into animals_table(id, name)
       values(ANIMAL_ID_SEQ.nextval, 'dog');

SQL> insert into animals_table(id, name)
        values(ANIMAL_ID_SEQ.nextval, 'cat');

SQL> insert into animals_table(id, name)
        values(ANIMAL_ID_SEQ.nextval, 'rabbit');

SQL> commit;
Commit complete.

SQL> select * from animals_table;
```

```
    ID    NAME
---------  ---------
     1    dog
     2    cat
     3    rabbit
```

Solution

The JDBC 3.0 specification proposes a functional Statement interface that provides access to get automatically generated key values after an insert. The following code examples demonstrate how to retrieve Oracle's sequence values using the new JDBC 3.0 method getGeneratedKeys(), which is now the preferred method to use if you need to retrieve automatically generated keys.

■**Caution** The Oracle JDBC driver does not support access to automatically generated key values after an insert. In other words, the Oracle driver does not implement Statement.getGeneratedKeys());. Instead, you have to use the Statement.executeQuery(); method, as follows:

```
rs = stmt.executeQuery("select ANIMAL_ID_SEQ.currval from dual");
```

Viewing the Oracle Database Before the Running Solution

This is the Oracle database before running the solution:

```
SQL> select * from animals_table;


---------  ----------
     1    dog
     2    cat
     3    rabbit
```

Running the Solution for the Oracle Database

This shows how to run the solution:

```
$ javac DemoGetGeneratedKeys.java
$ java DemoGetGeneratedKeys oracle
--DemoGetGeneratedKeys begin--
conn=oracle.jdbc.driver.OracleConnection@18fb1f7
----------------
key 1 is 4
--DemoGetGeneratedKeysUsingCurrval_Oracle end--
```

Viewing the Oracle Database After Running the Solution

This is the Oracle database after running the solution:

```
SQL> select * from animals_table;

    ID    NAME
---------  ----------
     1    dog
     2    cat
     3    rabbit
     4    tiger11
```

11-10. How Do You Determine Whether a SQL Warning Occurred (Using Statement Objects)?

Some database operations can cause a warning that is not handled by an exception. You must check for these warnings explicitly. An example of such a warning is a data truncation error during a read operation. You should check for warnings in three places: on a Connection object, a Statement object, and a ResultSet object. A SQL Warning (in JDBC defined by the java.sql.SQLWarning class) is an exception that provides information about database access warnings. Warnings are silently chained to the object whose method caused it to be reported.

The following example demonstrates how to check for a warning on a Statement object:

```
Connection conn = null;
SQLWarning warning = null;
try {
    // get a Connection object
    conn = getConnection();

    // Create a statement
    Statement stmt = conn.createStatement();

    // Use the statement...such as selecting some rows from a table

    // Get warnings on Statement object
    warning = stmt.getWarnings();
    while (warning != null) {
        // Process statement warnings...


        int errorCode = warning.getErrorCode();
        warning = warning.getNextWarning();
    }
}
catch (SQLException e) {
    // handle exception...
}
finally {
    // close database/JDBC resources such as
    // ResultSet(s), Statement(s), and Connection(s)
}
```

11-11. How Do You Set the Number of Rows to Prefetch (Using Statement Objects)?

JDBC enables you to set the number of rows to prefetch when executing a SQL query. *Row prefetch* allows the user to specify the number of rows to fetch from the result set (the ResultSet object) in each round-trip to the database. This is one possible way that you can control how many rows are returned. When a SQL query is executed, the number of rows of data that a driver physically copies from the database to the client is called the *fetch size*. If you are performance-tuning a particular query, you might be able to improve the performance by adjusting the fetch size to better match the use of the query.

You can set the fetch size on a Statement object; in this case, all result sets created from that statement will use that fetch size. You can also set the fetch size on a result set at any time. In this case, the next time data needs to be fetched from the database, the driver will copy over as many rows as is specified by the current fetch size.

The following example demonstrates how to set a fetch size using a Statement object:

```
ResultSet rs = null;
Statement stmt = null;
Connection conn = null;
try {
    // get a Connection object
    conn = getConnection();

    // Get the fetch size of a statement
    stmt = conn.createStatement();
    int fetchSize = stmt.getFetchSize();

    // Set the fetch size on the statement
    // each driver might have a different default value for fetch size
    stmt.setFetchSize(200);

    // Create a result set
    rs = stmt.executeQuery("SELECT badge_number FROM employee_table");

    // Change the fetch size on the result set
    rs.setFetchSize(400);
}
catch (SQLException e) {
    // handle the exception
}
finally {


}
```

11-12. How Do You Create a MySQL Table to Store Java Types (Using Statement Objects)?

The following example creates a MySQL table, called mysql_all_types_table, to store Java data types:

```
Statement stmt = null;
Connection conn = null;
try {
    // get a Connection object
    conn = getConnection();

    stmt = conn.createStatement();

    StringBuffer allTypesTable = new StringBuffer("CREATE TABLE mysql_all_types(");
    //                     Column Name          MySQL Type              Java Type
    allTypesTable.append("column_boolean        BOOL, "              // boolean
    allTypesTable.append("column_byte           TINYINT, "           // byte
    allTypesTable.append("column_short          SMALLINT, "          // short
    allTypesTable.append("column_int            INTEGER, "           // int
    allTypesTable.append("column_long           BIGINT, "            // long
    allTypesTable.append("column_float          FLOAT, "             // float
    allTypesTable.append("column_double         DOUBLE PRECISION, "  // double
    allTypesTable.append("column_bigdecimal     DECIMAL(13,0), "     // BigDecimal
    allTypesTable.append("column_string         VARCHAR(254), "      // String
    allTypesTable.append("column_date           DATE, "              // Date
    allTypesTable.append("column_time           TIME, "              // Time
```

```
      allTypesTable.append("column_timestamp     TIMESTAMP, "           // Timestamp
      allTypesTable.append("column_asciistream1  TINYTEXT, "   // Clob (< 2^8 bytes)
      allTypesTable.append("column_asciistream2  TEXT, "       // Clob (< 2^16 bytes)
      allTypesTable.append("column_asciistream3  MEDIUMTEXT, " // Clob (< 2^24 bytes)
      allTypesTable.append("column_asciistream4  LONGTEXT, "   // Clob (< 2^32 bytes)
      allTypesTable.append("column_blob1         TINYBLOB, "   // Blob (< 2^8 bytes)
      allTypesTable.append("column_blob2         BLOB, "       // Blob (< 2^16 bytes)
      allTypesTable.append("column_blob3         MEDIUMBLOB, " // Blob (< 2^24 bytes)
      allTypesTable.append("column_blob4         LONGBLOB)";   // Blob (< 2^32 bytes)

      stmt.executeUpdate(allTypesTable.toString());
      // creation of table ok.
}
catch (SQLException e) {
   // creation of table failed.
   // handle the exception
}
finally {
   // close database/JDBC resources such as
   // ResultSet(s), Statement(s), and Connection(s)
}
```

11-13. How Do You Create an Oracle Table to Store Java Types (Using Statement Objects)?

is converted to F, and true is converted to T. The following example creates an Oracle table called oracle_all_types_table to store Java types. The Oracle database has another restriction for tables: it allows at most one column of the LONG type in a table.

```
Statement stmt = null;
Connection conn = null;
try {
    // get a Connection object
    conn = getConnection();

    stmt = conn.createStatement();

    // Create a VARRAY type
    stmt.execute("CREATE TYPE char_varray AS VARRAY(10) OF VARCHAR(20)");

    // Create an OBJECT type
    stmt.execute ("CREATE TYPE oracle_object AS OBJECT" +
        "(column_string VARCHAR(128), column_integer INTEGER)");

    StringBuffer allTypesTable = new StringBuffer("CREATE TABLE oracle_all_types(");
    //                  Column Name           Oracle Type            Java Type
    allTypesTable.append("column_short        SMALLINT, "            // short
    allTypesTable.append("column_int          INTEGER, "            // int
    allTypesTable.append("column_float        REAL, "               // float
    allTypesTable.append("column_double       DOUBLE PRECISION,"    // double
    allTypesTable.append("column_bigdecimal   DECIMAL(13,0), "      // BigDecimal
    allTypesTable.append("column_string       VARCHAR2(254), "      // String
    allTypesTable.append("column_charStream   LONG, "            // CharacterStream
    allTypesTable.append("column_bytes        RAW(2000), "         // byte[]
```

```
        allTypesTable.append("column_binarystream  RAW(2000), "     // BinaryStream
        allTypesTable.append("column_timestamp      DATE, "          // Timestamp
        allTypesTable.append("column_clob            CLOB, "          // Clob
        allTypesTable.append("column_blob            BLOB, "          // Blob
        allTypesTable.append("column_bfile           BFILE, "         // oracle.sql.BFILE
        allTypesTable.append("column_array           char_varray, "   // oracle.sql.ARRAY
        allTypesTable.append("column_object          oracle_object)"; // oracle.sql.OBJECT

        stmt.executeUpdate(allTypesTable.toString());
        // creation of table ok.
}
catch (SQLException e) {
        // creation of table failed.
        // handle the exception
}
finally {
        // close database/JDBC resources such as
        // ResultSet(s), Statement(s), and Connection(s)
}
```

11-14. How Do You Get Rows from a Database Table Using a Statement?

A SQL SELECT query gets data from a table. The result of the SELECT query is called a *result set* (expressed as a java.sql.ResultSet object). The following example executes a simple SQL SELECT

Setting Up the Database

Here's how to set up the database:

```
$ mysql --user=root --password=root
mysql> use test;
Database changed
mysql> desc employee_table;
+---------------+-------------+------+-----+---------+-------+
| Field         | Type        | Null | Key | Default | Extra |
+---------------+-------------+------+-----+---------+-------+
| badge_number  | int(11)     |      |     | 0       |       |
| last_name     | varchar(32) |      |     |         |       |
+---------------+-------------+------+-----+---------+-------+
2 rows in set (0.00 sec)
```

Solution

Here's the solution:

```
Connection conn = null;
Statement stmt = null;
ResultSet rs = null;
try {
        // get a Connection object
        conn = getConnection();

        // create a Statement object
        stmt = conn.createStatement();
```

```
        // create a result set object
        String query = "SELECT badge_number, last_name FROM employee_table";
        rs = stmt.executeQuery(query);

        // now we may iterate result set object, and get all the rows
        while (rs.next()) {
            int badgeNumber = rs.getInt(1);     // get the badge_number
            String lastName = rs.getString(2); // get the last_name
        }
}
catch (SQLException e) {
    // getting rows failed
    // handle the exception
}
finally {
    // close database/JDBC resources such as
    // ResultSet(s), Statement(s), and Connection(s)
}
```

11-15. How Do You Insert a Row into a Database Table Using a Statement?

The following code shows how to insert a row into a database table using a Statement object:

```
Connection conn = null;
Statement stmt = null;

    stmt = conn.createStatement(); // create a Statement object

    // Prepare a statement to insert a record
    String sql = "INSERT INTO employee_table (badge_number, last_name) " +
                 "VALUES('1122', 'alex smith')";

    // Execute the insert statement
    stmt.executeUpdate(sql);
}
catch (SQLException e) {
    // insert failed
    // handle the exception
}
finally {
    // close database/JDBC resources such as
    // ResultSet(s), Statement(s), and Connection(s)
}
```

11-16. How Do You Update a Row in a Database Table Using a Statement?

The SQL UPDATE statement modifies the data in a table. The basic syntax is as follows:

```
UPDATE table_name
SET column_name = new_value
WHERE column_name = some_value
```

The following example updates a row in a table:

```
Connection conn = null;
Statement stmt = null;
try {
    // get a Connection object
    conn = getConnection();

    stmt = conn.createStatement();

    // Prepare a statement to update a record
    String sql = "UPDATE employee_table "+
      "SET last_name='mary taylor' WHERE badge_number = '5555'";

    // Execute the insert statement
    int updateCount = stmt.executeUpdate(sql);
    // updateCount contains the number of updated rows
}
catch (SQLException e) {
    // update failed
    // handle the exception
}
finally {
    // close database/JDBC resources such as
    // ResultSet(s), Statement(s), and Connection(s)
}
```

You can delete all the rows in a table by using SQL's DELETE statement. This example deletes all the rows from a database table called employee_table:

```
Connection conn = null;
Statement stmt = null;
try {
    // get a Connection object
    conn = getConnection();

    stmt = conn.createStatement();

    // use SQL DELETE
    String tableName = "employee_table";
    String sql = "DELETE FROM " + tableName;

    // Execute deletion
    stmt.executeUpdate(sql);
}
catch (SQLException e) {
    // deletion failed
    // handle the exception
}
finally {
    // close database/JDBC resources such as
    // ResultSet(s), Statement(s), and Connection(s)
}
```

11-18. How Do You Get the Number of Rows for a Database Table Using a Statement?

To count all the rows for a table, you can use the following SQL command:

```
SELECT COUNT(*) from <table-name>
```

This example gets the number of rows in a table using this SQL statement:

```
ResultSet rs = null;
Statement stmt = null;
Connection conn = null;
int rowCount = -1; // nonexistent value
try {
    // get a Connection object
    conn = getConnection();

    // Select the number of rows in the table
    stmt = conn.createStatement();
    rs = stmt.executeQuery("SELECT COUNT(*) FROM employee_table");

    // Get the number of rows from the result set
    if (rs.next()) {
        rowcount = rs.getInt(1);
    }
    else {
       // error: could not get the number of rows


    if (rsCount == -1) {
       // error: could not get the number of rows
    }
}
catch (SQLException e) {
    // counting rows failed
    // handle the exception
}
finally {
    // close database/JDBC resources such as
    // ResultSet(s), Statement(s), and Connection(s)
}
```

11-19. How Do You Insert Binary Data into a Database Table Using a Statement?

It is possible to insert binary data with a Statement object (you can convert your binary data into a stream of String objects and then insert it using a Statement object), but it is much easier (and recommended) to insert binary data using PreparedStatement, which extends the Statement interface.

The following example inserts binary data into a table:

```
ResultSet rs = null;
Statement stmt = null;
Connection conn = null;
try {
    // get a Connection object
    conn = getConnection();
```

```java
    // prepare a statement to insert binary data
    String sql = "INSERT INTO mysql_all_table (col_binarystream) VALUES(?)";
    PreparedStatement pstmt = conn.prepareStatement(sql);

    // create some binary data
    String myData = "some string data ...";
    byte[] binaryData = myData.getBytes();

    // set value for the prepared statement
    pstmt.setBytes(1, binaryData);

    // insert the data
    pstmt.executeUpdate();

    // insert was successful
}
catch (SQLException e) {
    // insert failed
    // handle the exception
}
finally {
    // close database/JDBC resources such as
    // ResultSet(s), Statement(s), and Connection(s)
}
```

```java
ResultSet rs = null;
Statement stmt = null;
Connection conn = null;
try {
    // get a Connection object
    conn = getConnection();

    // select records from the table
    stmt = conn.createStatement();
    String query = "SELECT col_binarystream FROM mysql_all_table";
    rs = stmt.executeQuery(query);
    while (rs.next()) {
        // get data from the binary column
        byte[] bytes = rs.getBytes(1);
        // process bytes
    }
}
catch (SQLException e) {
    // retrieving binary data failed
    // handle the exception
}
finally {
    // close database/JDBC resources such as
    // ResultSet(s), Statement(s), and Connection(s)
}
```

11-21. How Do You Execute a Batch of SQL Statements in a Database Using a Statement?

The java.sql package provides the ability to send multiple updates (such as updating records or creating new records) to the database server for execution as a batch. The Statement.addBatch() method enables you to accomplish this task, which might improve the performance of the entire transaction. You can reduce the amount of time it takes to perform repetitive inserts and updates if you batch them using the Statement object's addBatch() method.

The signature of addBatch() is as follows:

```
public void addBatch(String sql)
    throws SQLException
```

This adds the given SQL command to the current list of commands for this Statement object. The commands in this list can be executed as a batch by calling the method executeBatch. Its parameter is sql; typically this is a static SQL INSERT or UPDATE statement. This throws SQLException if a database access error occurs.

Both the Oracle and MySQL drivers support the Statement.addBatch() and PreparedStatement. addBatch() methods, which send multiple updates to the database server. With batch updating, a set of SQL statements is assembled and then sent altogether to the database server for execution. Batch updating can improve performance. Using the batch functionality involves two methods (the descriptions of the methods are from the JDK documentation):

> addBatch(String sql): Adds the given SQL command to the current list of commands for this Statement object. The commands in this list can be executed as a batch by calling the method

.

execute successfully, returns an array of update counts. The int elements of the returned array are ordered to correspond to the commands in the batch, which are ordered according to how they were added to the batch. The elements in the array returned by the method executeBatch may be one of the following:

- *A number greater than or equal to zero*: Indicates that the command was processed successfully and is an update count giving the number of rows in the database that were affected by the command's execution.

- *A value of* SUCCESS_NO_INFO: Indicates that the command was processed successfully but that the number of rows affected is unknown. If one of the commands in a batch update fails to execute properly, this method throws a BatchUpdateException, and a JDBC driver may or may not continue to process the remaining commands in the batch. However, the driver's behavior must be consistent with a particular DBMS, either always continuing to process commands or never continuing to process commands. If the driver continues processing after a failure, the array returned by the method BatchUpdateException. getUpdateCounts will contain as many elements as there are commands in the batch, and at least one of the elements will be a value of EXECUTE_FAILED, which indicates that the command failed to execute successfully and occurs only if a driver continues to process commands after a command fails.

This example creates a batch of insert statements. Note that autocommit is disabled, so you have the choice of committing or not committing in the event of an exception.

```
Statement stmt = null;
Connection conn = null;
```

```java
try {
    // get a Connection object
    conn = getConnection();

    // disable autocommit
    conn.setAutoCommit(false);

    // the number of statements that can be batched depends on a specific drive
    stmt = conn.createStatement();
    stmt.addBatch("DELETE FROM animals_table");
    stmt.addBatch("INSERT INTO animals_table(id, name) VALUES(111, 'ginger')");
    stmt.addBatch("INSERT INTO animals_table(id, name) VALUES(222, 'lola')");
    stmt.addBatch("INSERT INTO animals_table(id, name) VALUES(333, 'freddy')");

    // Execute the batch
    int[] updateCounts = stmt.executeBatch();

    // All statements were successfully executed.
    // updateCounts array contains one element for
    // each batched statement; updateCounts[i] contains
    // the number of rows affected by that statement.
    checkUpdateCounts(updateCounts);

    // Since there were no errors, commit
    conn.commit();
}


    int[] updateCounts = e.getUpdateCounts();

    // Some databases will continue to execute after one fails.
    // If so, updateCounts.length will equal the number of
    // batched statements.  If not, updateCounts.length will
    // equal the number of successfully executed statements
    checkUpdateCounts(updateCounts);

    // Either commit the successfully executed statements
    // or roll back the entire batch
    conn.rollback();
}
catch (SQLException e) {
    // handle the exception
}
finally {
    // close database/JDBC resources such as
    // ResultSet(s), Statement(s), and Connection(s)
}

    ...

public static void checkUpdateCounts(int[] updateCounts) {
    for (int i=0; i < updateCounts.length; i++) {
        if (updateCounts[i] >= 0) {
            // Successfully executed; the number represents number of affected rows
            System.out.println("Succ. executed; updateCount="+updateCounts[i]);
        }
        else if (updateCounts[i] == Statement.SUCCESS_NO_INFO) {
```

```
                    // Successfully executed; number of affected rows not available
                    System.out.println("Succ. executed; "+
                        "updateCount=Statement.SUCCESS_NO_INFO");
            }
            else if (updateCounts[i] == Statement.EXECUTE_FAILED) {
                    // Failed to execute
                    System.out.println("Failed to execute; "+
                        updateCount=Statement.EXECUTE_FAILED");
            }
        }
    }
}
```

Setting Up the Oracle Database

This example will use the animals_table table defined earlier in this chapter.

```
SQL>    CREATE TABLE animals_table (
  2                 id INT NOT NULL,
  3                 name VARCHAR(32) NOT NULL,
  4                 PRIMARY KEY (id)
  5      );
Table created.
SQL> desc animals_table;
 Name                Null?    Type
 ---------------- -------- ------------
 ID                  NOT NULL NUMBER(38)
```

Solution

This class will delete all the existing records from the animals_table table and then insert the records
(111, 'ginger'), (222, 'lola'), and (333, 'freddy') into the animals_table table using the
Statement.addBatch() method:

```java
import java.util.*;
import java.io.*;
import java.sql.*;

import jcb.db.VeryBasicConnectionManager;
import jcb.util.DatabaseUtil;

public class Demo_Statement_AddBatch {

    public static void checkUpdateCounts(int[] updateCounts) {
        for (int i=0; i<updateCounts.length; i++) {
            if (updateCounts[i] >= 0) {
                // Successfully executed; the number
                // represents number of affected rows
                System.out.println("OK; updateCount="+updateCounts[i]);
            }
            else if (updateCounts[i] == Statement.SUCCESS_NO_INFO) {
                // Successfully executed; number of
                // affected rows not available
                System.out.println("OK; updateCount=Statement.SUCCESS_NO_INFO");
            }
            else if (updateCounts[i] == Statement.EXECUTE_FAILED) {
                // Failed to execute
                System.out.println("Failure; updateCount=Statement.EXECUTE_FAILED");
```

```java
                }
            }
        }

        public static void main(String[] args) {
            Connection conn = null;
            Statement stmt = null;
            String dbVendor = args[0];
            try {
                System.out.println("--Demo_Statement_AddBatch begin--");
                conn = VeryBasicConnectionManager.getConnection(dbVendor);
                System.out.println("conn="+conn);

                // Disable autocommit
                conn.setAutoCommit(false);

                // create Statement object
                stmt = conn.createStatement();
                stmt.addBatch("DELETE FROM animals_table");
                stmt.addBatch("INSERT INTO animals_table(id, name) "+
                        "VALUES(111, 'ginger')");
                stmt.addBatch("INSERT INTO animals_table(id, name) "+
                        "VALUES(222, 'lola')");
                stmt.addBatch("INSERT INTO animals_table(id, name) "+
                        "VALUES(333, 'freddy')");


                int[] updateCounts = stmt.executeBatch();

                // all statements were successfully executed.
                // updateCounts contains one element for each
                // batched statement. The updateCounts[i] contains
                // the number of rows affected by that statement.
                checkUpdateCounts(updateCounts);

                // since there were no errors, commit
                conn.commit();
            }
            catch (BatchUpdateException e) {
                // Not all of the statements were successfully executed
                int[] updateCounts = e.getUpdateCounts();

                // Some databases will continue to execute after one
                // fails. If so, updateCounts.length will equal the
                // number of batched statements. If not, updateCounts.length
                // will equal the number of successfully executed statements
                checkUpdateCounts(updateCounts);

                // Either commit the successfully executed
                // statements or roll back the entire batch
                try {
                    conn.rollback();
                }
                catch (Exception e2) {
                    e.printStackTrace();
                    System.exit(1);
```

```
                }
            }
        catch (Exception e) {
            e.printStackTrace();
            System.exit(1);
        }
        finally {
            // release database resources
            DatabaseUtil.close(stmt);
            DatabaseUtil.close(conn);
        }
    }
}
```

Running the Solution for the Oracle Database

This shows how to run the solution (Oracle):

```
$ javac  Demo_Statement_AddBatch.java
$ java  Demo_Statement_AddBatch  oracle
--Demo_Statement_AddBatch begin--
conn=oracle.jdbc.driver.T4CConnection@6e293a
----------------
Successfully executed; updateCount=5
Successfully executed; updateCount=1
Successfully executed; updateCount=1
Successfully executed; updateCount=1
```

This shows the Oracle database after running the solution:

```
SQL> select * from animals_table;

        ID    NAME
        ---   -------
        111   ginger
        222   lola
        333   freddy
```

Setting Up the MySQL Database

This example will use the animals_table table defined earlier in this chapter:

```
mysql>  CREATE TABLE animals_table (
    ->          id INT NOT NULL AUTO_INCREMENT,
    ->          name VARCHAR(32) NOT NULL,
    ->          PRIMARY KEY (id)
    ->  );
Query OK, 0 rows affected (0.03 sec)

mysql> desc animals_table;
+-------+-------------+------+-----+---------+----------------+
| Field | Type        | Null | Key | Default | Extra          |
+-------+-------------+------+-----+---------+----------------+
| id    | int(11)     |      | PRI | NULL    | auto_increment |
| name  | varchar(32) |      |     |         |                |
+-------+-------------+------+-----+---------+----------------+
2 rows in set (0.01 sec)
```

Viewing the Program to Use Statement.addBatch()

This class will delete all the existing records from the animals_table table and then insert the records (111, 'ginger'), (222, 'lola'), and (333, 'freddy') into the animals_table table using the addBatch() method.

Running the Solution for the MySQL Database

This shows how to run the solution (MySQL):

```
$ javac  Demo_Statement_AddBatch.java
$ java  Demo_Statement_AddBatch  mysql
--Demo_Statement_AddBatch begin--
conn=com.mysql.jdbc.Connection@1546e25
---------------
Successfully executed; updateCount=2
Successfully executed; updateCount=1
Successfully executed; updateCount=1
Successfully executed; updateCount=1
```

Viewing the MySQL Database After Running the Solution

This shows the MySQL database after running the solution:

```
mysql> select * from animals_table;
+-----+--------+
| id  | name   |
+-----+--------+

| 222 | lola   |
| 333 | freddy |
+-----+--------+
3 rows in set (0.03 sec)
```

11-22. How Do You Create an OBJECT Type in an Oracle Database?

In the Oracle database, you can create a user-defined composite data structure called an OBJECT. (This is a proprietary feature of Oracle database and should not be confused with the java.lang.Object class.) The OBJECT structure consists of one or more basic types. For example, you could define an object called EMPLOYEE_TYPE with a name (VARCHAR2) and a badge_number (NUMBER). An OBJECT can also contain other OBJECT structures. The following example creates an EMPLOYEE_TYPE as an Oracle OBJECT and then creates an employee table using the EMPLOYEE_TYPE (as a data type for the first column).

Creating an Oracle OBJECT Using Oracle's SQL*Plus

This shows how to create the OBJECT structure using SQL*Plus:

```
$ sqlplus mp/mp2
SQL*Plus: Release 9.2.0.1.0 - Production on Mon Nov 17 13:17:01 2003

SQL> CREATE OR REPLACE TYPE employee_type IS OBJECT
  2  (name VARCHAR2(32),
  3  badge_number NUMBER);
  4  /

Type created.
```

```
SQL> desc employee_type;
 Name                      Null?     Type
 ---------------------     --------  ------------
 NAME                                VARCHAR2(32)
 BADGE_NUMBER                        NUMBER

SQL> create table employee (
  2  emp employee_type,
  3  age NUMBER );

Table created.

SQL> desc employee;
 Name                      Null?     Type
 ----------------          --------  ----------------
 EMP                                 EMPLOYEE_TYPE
 AGE                                 NUMBER

SQL> insert into employee(emp, age)
  2      values ( EMPLOYEE_TYPE('alex', 1234), 24);

SQL> insert into employee(emp, age)
  2      values ( EMPLOYEE_TYPE('david', 7777), 35);

SQL> commit;
Commit complete.
```

```
EMP(NAME, BADGE_NUMBER)        AGE
---------------------------    ---
EMPLOYEE_TYPE('alex', 1234)    24
EMPLOYEE_TYPE('david', 7777)   35
```

Creating an Oracle OBJECT Using JDBC

This shows how to create the OBJECT structure using JDBC:

```
Connection conn = null;
Statement stmt = null;
try {
    // create Connection object
    conn = getConnection();
    System.out.println("conn="+conn);

    // create Statement object
    stmt = conn.createStatement();

    // Create the EMPLOYEE_TYPE  OBJECT
    stmt.execute("CREATE TYPE employee_type IS "+
        "OBJECT (name VARCHAR2(32), badge_number NUMBER)");

    // Create a table with a column to hold a new employee_type OBJECT
    stmt.execute("create table employee(emp employee_type, age NUMBER)");
}
catch (SQLException e) {
```

```
    // handle the exception
}
finally {
    // close and clean up database/JDBC resources
}
```

11-23. How Do You Insert an OBJECT Value into an Oracle Table?

You can insert Oracle's OBJECT (which is a proprietary feature of the Oracle database and should not be confused with the java.lang.Object class) into an Oracle table using Oracle's SQL*Plus and JDBC. The following sections show examples.

Inserting an OBJECT Value into an Oracle Table Using SQL*Plus

This shows how to insert the OBJECT value using SQL*Plus:

```
SQL> select * from employee;

no rows selected

SQL> insert into employee(emp, age)
  2      values ( EMPLOYEE_TYPE('alex smith', 1122), 45);

SQL> insert into employee(emp, age)
  2      values ( EMPLOYEE_TYPE('bob taylor', 1155), 26);



SQL> select * from employee;

EMP(NAME, BADGE_NUMBER)                 AGE
-----------------------------------     ---
EMPLOYEE_TYPE('alex smith', 1122)       45
EMPLOYEE_TYPE('bob taylor', 1155)       26
```

Inserting an OBJECT Value into an Oracle Table Using JDBC

This example inserts two rows into a table with a column that contains an OBJECT type (that is, employee_type OBJECT). The example uses the employee table defined earlier.

```
Connection conn = null;
Statement stmt = null;
try {
    // create Connection object
    conn = getConnection();
    System.out.println("conn="+conn);

    // create Statement object
    stmt = conn.createStatement();

    // Create the EMPLOYEE_TYPE  OBJECT
    // stmt.execute("CREATE TYPE employee_type IS OBJECT " +
    //      "(name VARCHAR2(32), badge_number NUMBER)");

    // Create a table with a column to hold a new employee_type OBJECT
    // stmt.execute("create table employee(emp employee_type, age NUMBER)");
```

```
        // insert the two new records:
        stmt.execute("insert into employee(emp, age) values "+
                "( EMPLOYEE_TYPE('alex smith', 1122), 45)");
        stmt.execute("insert into employee(emp, age) values "+
                "( EMPLOYEE_TYPE('bob taylor', 1155), 26)");
    }
catch (SQLException e) {
        // handle the exception
    }
finally {
        // clean up
    }
```

11-24. How Do You Get an Oracle's OBJECT Value from an Oracle Table?

Suppose you want to retrieve values contained in an Oracle OBJECT type. The following examples show how to retrieve (using SQL*Plus and JDBC) all the records from employee_table.

Setting Up the Oracle Database

This shows how to set up the Oracle database:

```
SQL> desc employee_type;
 Name            Null?    Type
 --------------- -------- -------------



SQL>
SQL> create table employee (
  2  emp employee_type,
  3  age NUMBER );

Table created.

SQL> desc employee;
 Name            Null?    Type
 --------------- -------- --------------
 EMP                      EMPLOYEE_TYPE
 AGE                      NUMBER

SQL> insert into employee(emp, age)
  2     values ( EMPLOYEE_TYPE('alex smith', 1122), 45);

SQL> insert into employee(emp, age)
  2     values ( EMPLOYEE_TYPE('bob taylor', 1155), 26);

SQL> commit;
Commit complete.

SQL> select * from employee;

EMP(NAME, BADGE_NUMBER)             AGE
--------------------------------    ---
EMPLOYEE_TYPE('alex smith', 1122)   45
EMPLOYEE_TYPE('bob taylor', 1155)   26
```

Solution

The Demo_Statement_GetObjectValues_Oracle class retrieves OBJECT values. Note that Oracle's JDBC implementation maps NUMBER types to the java.math.BigDecimal objects.

```java
import java.util.*;
import java.io.*;
import java.sql.*;

import jcb.db.*;
import jcb.meta.*;

public class Demo_Statement_GetObjectValues_Oracle {

    public static Connection getConnection() throws Exception {
        String driver = "oracle.jdbc.driver.OracleDriver";
        String url = "jdbc:oracle:thin:@localhost:1521:caspian";
        String username = "mp";
        String password = "mp2";
        Class.forName(driver);   // load Oracle driver
        return DriverManager.getConnection(url, username, password);
    }

    public static void main(String[] args) {
        Connection conn = null;
        Statement stmt = null;
        ResultSet rs = null;


            conn = getConnection();
            System.out.println("conn="+conn);
            System.out.println("---------------");

            // create Statement object
            stmt = conn.createStatement();

            // Select rows from the employee table
            // note that emp is an EMPLOYEE_TYPE object
            rs = stmt.executeQuery("SELECT emp, age FROM employee");

            // Get the OBJECT values from each row
              while (rs.next()) {
                  // Handle the first column:
                  // Get the EMPLOYEE_TYPE value from the first column emp
                  oracle.sql.STRUCT emp = (oracle.sql.STRUCT) rs.getObject(1);

                  // Get the emp values from each row
                  Object[] empValues = emp.getAttributes();

                  // Get the  values of emp
                  String name = (String) empValues[0];
                  java.math.BigDecimal badgeNumber =
                          (java.math.BigDecimal) empValues[1];

                  // Handle the second column:
                  // Get the age from the second column employee of the row
                  int age = rs.getInt(2);
```

```
                    System.out.println("name="+name);
                    System.out.println("badgeNumber="+badgeNumber);
                    System.out.println("age="+age);
                    System.out.println("--------------------");
                }
            }
            catch (Exception e) {
                e.printStackTrace();
                System.exit(1);
            }
            finally {
                // release database resources
                DatabaseUtil.close(rs);
                DatabaseUtil.close(stmt);
                DatabaseUtil.close(conn);
            }
        }
    }
}
```

To run the solution for an Oracle database, use this code:

```
$ javac Demo_Statement_GetObjectValues_Oracle.java
$ java Demo_Statement_GetObjectValues_Oracle
--Demo_Statement_GetObjectValues_Oracle begin--
conn=oracle.jdbc.driver.OracleConnection@860d49
---------------
name=alex smith


---------------------
name=bob taylor
badgeNumber=1155
age=26
---------------------
```

11-25. How Do You Delete an OBJECT Type from an Oracle Table?

The following example deletes the Oracle OBJECT structures and tables created in the earlier sections.

```
Connection conn = null;
Statement stmt = null;
try {
    // create Connection object
    conn = getConnection();
    System.out.println("conn="+conn);

    // create Statement object
    stmt = conn.createStatement();

    // drop table employee and type employee_type
    // Oracle's FORCE means ignore referential integrity
    stmt.execute("DROP TABLE employee");
    stmt.execute("DROP TYPE employee_type FORCE");
}
catch (SQLException e) {
    // handle the exception
}
```

```
finally {
    // clean up
}
```

11-26. How Does JDBC Support Batch Updates?

In relational databases, some applications require multiple updates/inserts for certain operations (*batch updates*). For example, mapping a tree data structure to a relational model is one of them. For details on mapping trees to SQL, see *Joe Celko's Trees and Hierarchies in SQL for Smarties* (Morgan Kaufmann, 2004). A tree data structure has lots of uses, such as representing a hierarchy of employees and folders (such as file and directory systems). Trees in SQL require multiple SQL operations (such as adding a new node, deleting an existing node, or deleting a subtree) that are good candidates for the Statement.batchUpdate() operation. With several examples (working with a tree structure in SQL), I will demonstrate how to use the Statement.batchUpdate() properly.

Both the Oracle and MySQL databases support the Statement.addBatch() and Statement.batchUpdate() methods, which send multiple updates to the database server. With batch updating, a set of SQL statements is assembled and then sent altogether to the database server for execution. Batch updating can improve performance.

By using the Statement.batchUpdate() method, you can reduce the number of round-trips to the database, thereby improving database application performance. This allows you to group multiple SQL UPDATE, SQL DELETE, or SQL INSERT statements into a single batch and have the whole batch sent to the database and processed in one trip. In high-volume database applications, whenever possible, you should batch update to avoid multiple trips (over the network) to database servers.

How does JDBC support batch operations? The java.sql package provides the ability to send which might improve the performance of the entire transaction. You can reduce the amount of time it takes to perform repetitive inserts and updates if you batch them using the Statement object's addBatch() method.

Using the batch functionality involves two methods (the description of the methods are from the JDK 1.4 documentation): Statement.addBatch() and Statement.executeBatch() are used together to support SQL batch operations. The signature of Statement.addBatch() is as follows:

```
public void addBatch(String sql)
        throws SQLException
```

This adds the given SQL command to the current list of commands for this Statement object. The commands in this list can be executed as a batch by calling the method executeBatch.

The parameter is sql, which is typically a static SQL INSERT or UPDATE statement.

This throws SQLException if a database access error occurs.

The signature of Statement.executeBatch() is as follows:

```
public int[] executeBatch()
        throws SQLException
```

This submits a batch of commands to the database for execution and, if all commands execute successfully, returns an array of update counts. The int elements of the returned array are ordered to correspond to the commands in the batch, which are ordered according to how they were added to the batch. The elements in the array returned by the method executeBatch can be one of the following:

A number greater than or equal to zero: Indicates that the command was processed successfully and is an update count giving the number of rows in the database that were affected by the command's execution.

A value of SUCCESS_NO_INFO: Indicates that the command was processed successfully but that the number of rows affected is unknown. If one of the commands in a batch update fails to execute properly, this method throws a BatchUpdateException, and a JDBC driver may or may not continue to process the remaining commands in the batch. However, the driver's behavior must be consistent with a particular DBMS, either always continuing to process commands or never continuing to process commands. If the driver continues processing after a failure, the array returned by the method BatchUpdateException.getUpdateCounts will contain as many elements as there are commands in the batch, and at least one of the elements will be a value of EXECUTE_FAILED, which indicates that the command failed to execute successfully and occurs only if a driver continues to process commands after a command fails.

A driver is not required to implement this method. The possible implementations and return values have been modified in version 1.3 of the Java 2 SDK, Standard Edition, to accommodate the option of continuing to process commands in a batch update after a BatchUpdateException object has been thrown.

Statement.executeBatch() returns an array of update counts containing one element for each command in the batch. The elements of the array are ordered according to the order in which commands were added to the batch.

This throws SQLException if a database access error occurs or the driver does not support batch statements. This throws BatchUpdateException (a subclass of SQLException) if one of the commands sent to the database fails to execute properly or attempts to return a result set.

11-27. How Do You Map Trees into SQL Using Batch Updates?

jhtml). Two major approaches exist: the adjacency list model and the modified preorder tree traversal algorithm. Just like Joe Celko, I will show a preorder tree traversal algorithm (also known as a *nested set*). Here I will focus on three specific tree operations:

- Inserting a new node (InsertNode.java)
- Deleting an existing node (DeleteNode.java)
- Deleting an existing subtree (DeleteSubtree.java)

Suppose you want to map the tree shown in Figure 11-1 to a relational model. (For a moment, ignore the numbers next to the names; you will use these numbers to define and implement the tree using nested sets later in this chapter.)

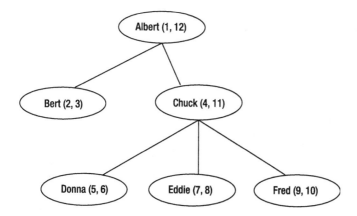

Figure 11-1. *Mapping tree to relational model*

Setting Up the Database

You can prepare the database in such a way to map trees into SQL using nested sets. Using nested sets, you need the following database schema and elements. Note that the root node's parent (that is, Albert's parent) is null.

```
$ mysql --user=root --password=root --default-character-set=utf8
mysql> use snipit;
Database changed
mysql> drop table folders;

mysql> create table folders (
    ->     id   varchar(10),
    ->     parent varchar(10),
    ->     lft int, -- left_pointer
    ->     rgt int  -- right_pointer
    -> );

mysql> insert into folders(id, parent, lft, rgt) values('Albert', null, 1, 12);
mysql> insert into folders(id, parent, lft, rgt) values('Bert', 'Albert', 2, 3);
mysql> insert into folders(id, parent, lft, rgt) values('Chuck', 'Albert', 4, 11);
mysql> insert into folders(id, parent, lft, rgt) values('Donna', 'Chuck', 5, 6);
mysql> insert into folders(id, parent, lft, rgt) values('Eddie', 'Chuck', 7, 8);
mysql> insert into folders(id, parent, lft, rgt) values('Fred', 'Chuck', 9, 10);

mysql> desc folders;
+--------+-------------+------+-----+---------+-------+
| id     | varchar(10) | YES  |     | NULL    |       |
| parent | varchar(10) | YES  |     | NULL    |       |
| lft    | int(11)     | YES  |     | NULL    |       |
| rgt    | int(11)     | YES  |     | NULL    |       |
+--------+-------------+------+-----+---------+-------+
4 rows in set (0.00 sec)

mysql> select * from folders;
+--------+--------+------+------+
| id     | parent | lft  | rgt  |
+--------+--------+------+------+
| Albert | NULL   |    1 |   12 |
| Bert   | Albert |    2 |    3 |
| Chuck  | Albert |    4 |   11 |
| Donna  | Chuck  |    5 |    6 |
| Eddie  | Chuck  |    7 |    8 |
| Fred   | Chuck  |    9 |   10 |
+--------+--------+------+------+
6 rows in set (0.00 sec)
```

Inserting a New Node (InsertNode.java)

The objective of the InsertNode class is to insert a new node for an existing tree (identified by the folders table). To insert a new node, you need to supply the parent. Therefore, you need two pieces of information for inserting a new node: the node to be inserted and the parent (where it's to be inserted). So, the InsertNode class's main() method will accept two arguments: the parentID and ID, where ID is the new node to be inserted and parentID is the ID of the parent for the new node.

To insert Mike under Bert, use this code:

```
C:\mp\sql-trees>java InsertNode Bert Mike
------InsertNode begin---------
conn=com.mysql.jdbc.Connection@750159
parentID=Bert
ID=Mike
------InsertNode end---------

mysql> select * from folders;
+---------+--------+------+------+
| id      | parent | lft  | rgt  |
+---------+--------+------+------+
| Albert  | NULL   |    1 |   14 |
| Bert    | Albert |    2 |    5 |
| Chuck   | Albert |    6 |   13 |
| Donna   | Chuck  |    7 |    8 |
| Eddie   | Chuck  |    9 |   10 |
| Fred    | Chuck  |   11 |   12 |
| Mike    | Bert   |    3 |    4 |
+---------+--------+------+------+
7 rows in set (0.00 sec)
```

To insert Mary under Bert, use this code:

```
$ java InsertNode Bert Mary
------InsertNode begin---------
conn=com.mysql.jdbc.Connection@750159


------InsertNode end---------

mysql> select * from folders;
+---------+--------+------+------+
| id      | parent | lft  | rgt  |
+---------+--------+------+------+
| Albert  | NULL   |    1 |   16 |
| Bert    | Albert |    2 |    7 |
| Chuck   | Albert |    8 |   15 |
| Donna   | Chuck  |    9 |   10 |
| Eddie   | Chuck  |   11 |   12 |
| Fred    | Chuck  |   13 |   14 |
| Mike    | Bert   |    5 |    6 |
| Mary    | Bert   |    3 |    4 |
+---------+--------+------+------+
8 rows in set (0.00 sec)
```

To insert Jeff under Albert, use this code:

```
$ java InsertNode Albert Jeff
------InsertNode begin---------
conn=com.mysql.jdbc.Connection@750159
parentID=Albert
ID=Jeff
------InsertNode end---------

mysql> select * from folders;
```

```
+---------+--------+------+------+
| id      | parent | lft  | rgt  |
+---------+--------+------+------+
| Albert  | NULL   |    1 |   18 |
| Bert    | Albert |    4 |    9 |
| Chuck   | Albert |   10 |   17 |
| Donna   | Chuck  |   11 |   12 |
| Eddie   | Chuck  |   13 |   14 |
| Fred    | Chuck  |   15 |   16 |
| Mike    | Bert   |    7 |    8 |
| Mary    | Bert   |    5 |    6 |
| Jeff    | Albert |    2 |    3 |
+---------+--------+------+------+
9 rows in set (0.00 sec)
```

InsertNode.java

This shows InsertNode.java:

```java
1    import java.sql.Connection;
2    import java.sql.Statement;
3    import java.sql.PreparedStatement;
4    import java.sql.ResultSet;
5    import java.sql.DriverManager;
6    import java.sql.BatchUpdateException;
7    import java.sql.SQLException;


10
11       public static Connection getConnection() throws Exception {
12           String driver = "org.gjt.mm.mysql.Driver";
13           String url = "jdbc:mysql://localhost/snipit";
14           String username = "root";
15           String password = "root";
16           Class.forName(driver);   // load MySQL driver
17           return DriverManager.getConnection(url, username, password);
19       }
20
21       public static void main(String[] args) {
23           Connection conn = null;
24           ResultSet rs = null;
25           Statement stmt = null;
26           PreparedStatement pstmt = null;
27           try {
28               System.out.println("------InsertNode begin---------");
29
30               if (args.length != 2) {
31                   System.out.println("usage: InsertNode  ");
32                   System.exit(1);
33               }
34
35               conn = getConnection();
36               System.out.println("conn="+conn);
37
38               String parentID = args[0];
39               String ID = args[1]; // node with value of ID will be inserted
40
```

```
41              System.out.println("parentID="+parentID);
42              System.out.println("ID="+ID);
43
44              String getParentLeftRight =
45              "select lft, rgt from folders where id = ?";
                pstmt = conn.prepareStatement(getParentLeftRight);
46              pstmt.setString(1, parentID);
47              rs = pstmt.executeQuery();
48              rs.next();
49              int pLeft = rs.getInt(1);
50              int pRight = rs.getInt(2);
51              int pLeftPlus1 = pLeft + 1;
52              int pLeftPlus2 = pLeft + 2;
53              String update1 =
54                 "update folders set rgt = rgt + 2 where rgt > "+ pLeft;
55              String update2 =
56                 "update folders set lft = lft + 2 where lft > "+ pLeft;
57              String insert = "insert into folders (id, parent, lft, rgt)"+
58                 "values ('"+ID +"', '"+ parentID +"', 0, 0)";
59              String update3 = "update folders set lft = "+pLeftPlus1+
                   ", rgt = "+pLeftPlus2+ " where id = '"+ID+"'";
                // start transaction for batch updates
60              conn.setAutoCommit(false);
61              stmt = conn.createStatement();
62
63              // create a set of batch operations


66              stmt.addBatch(insert);
67              stmt.addBatch(update3);
68
69              // send batch operations to the database server
70              int[] batchUpdateCounts = stmt.executeBatch();
71
72              // commit transaction for batch updates
73              conn.commit();
74              conn.setAutoCommit(true);
75              System.out.println("------InsertNode end---------");
76          }
77      catch(BatchUpdateException be) {
78          System.err.println("--- caught BatchUpdateException ---");
79          System.err.println("SQLState:  " + be.getSQLState());
80          System.err.println("Message:   " + be.getMessage());
81          System.err.println("Vendor:    " + be.getErrorCode());
82          System.err.print("Update counts are:  ");
83          int[] batchUpdateCounts = be.getUpdateCounts();
84          for (int i = 0; i < batchUpdateCounts.length; i++) {
85              System.err.print(batchUpdateCounts[i] + " ");
86          }
87          System.err.println("");
88      }
89      catch(SQLException se) {
90          System.err.println("--- caught SQLException ---");
91          System.err.println("SQLState:  " + se.getSQLState());
92          System.err.println("Message:   " + se.getMessage());
93          System.err.println("Vendor:    " + se.getErrorCode());
94      }
```

```
 95              catch (Exception e) {
 96                  // other exceptions
 97                  e.printStackTrace();
 98                  System.exit(1);
 99              }
100              finally {
101                  // release database resources
102                  DatabaseUtil.close(rs);
103                  DatabaseUtil.close(pstmt);
104                  DatabaseUtil.close(stmt);
105                  DatabaseUtil.close(conn);
106              }
107          }
108      }
```

Discussing InsertNode.java

The following explains how the program works:

Lines 1–9: You import the required classes and interfaces.

Lines 11–19: The getConnection() method returns a java.sql.Connection object.

Lines 38–42: These lines get the command-line arguments parentID and ID (which is the node ID to be inserted).

Lines 44–50: Here, you retrieve the left and right of the parentID. These values will be used for

Line 60: This lines starts the transaction for batch updates. No SQL operation will be committed until you invoke the conn.commit() statement.

Line 61: Creates a generic Statement object to be used for batch updates.

Lines 64–67: Create a set of batch operations. The order of these batch operations is important, and the batch works as a queue (first-in, first-out).

Line 69: Sends batch operations to the database server (operations are not committed yet!).

Line 73: Commits transaction for batch updates (either all succeed or all fail—no partial success).

Lines 100–106: Release database resources (to free up memory and data structures used by the JDBC driver and database server).

Deleting an Existing Node (DeleteNode.java)

The objective of the DeleteNode class is to delete an existing node from a tree (identified by the folders table). To delete an existing node, you need to supply the ID of the node being deleted. Also, you need to indicate whether to promote the subtree of the deleted node; you pass this argument as a boolean (true/false). So, the DeleteNode class's main() method will accept two arguments: the ID of the node to be deleted and a boolean (true/false) to indicate the promotion of the subtree of the deleted node.

If a node is a leaf node, it is easy to delete it, because it has no impact on other nodes. But if a node to be deleted is an inner node (a nonleaf node, which has at least one child), then the deletion process is complex. When a node is deleted from the tree, you have to preserve the integrity of the tree if the node has any subnodes. You have two approaches:

The first approach is to promote one of the deleted node's children (a subnode) to take over the position of the deleted node. The remaining subnodes of the deleted node become subnodes to the promoted node. To understand this, take a look at the following figures: assume that the original tree is Figure 11-2, and you want to delete node B. Using the promotion approach, the resultant tree will become Figure 11-3.

The second approach is to promote the entire subtree (all the children) of the deleted node so that all the subnodes of the deleted node become the subnodes of the deleted node's parent node. Assume that the original tree is Tree-1, and you want to delete node B. Using the promotion of the entire subtree approach, the resultant tree will become Figure 11-4.

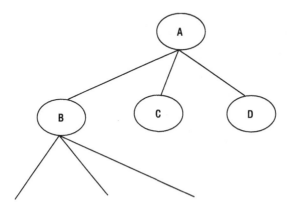

Figure 11-2. *Mapping tree to relational model: original tree*

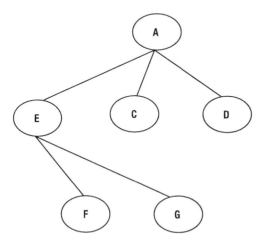

Figure 11-3. *Deleting node B by promoting one of the deleted node's children*

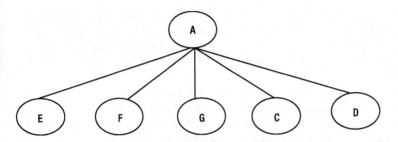

Figure 11-4. *Deleting node B by promoting the entire subtree*

Viewing the Tree Structure Before the Deletion

This is the tree structure before the deletion:

```
mysql> select * from folders;
+--------+--------+------+------+
| id     | parent | lft  | rgt  |
+--------+--------+------+------+
| Albert | NULL   |    1 |   18 |
| Bert   | Albert |    4 |    9 |
| Chuck  | Albert |   10 |   17 |
| Donna  | Chuck  |   11 |   12 |
| Eddie  | Chuck  |   13 |   14 |
| Fred   | Chuck  |   15 |   16 |

| Jeff   | Albert |    2 |    3 |
+--------+--------+------+------+
```

To delete Jeff (under Albert), use this code:

```
$ java DeleteNode Jeff false
------DeleteNode begin---------
conn=com.mysql.jdbc.Connection@750159
ID=Jeff
promoteSubtreeAsString=false
------DeleteNode end---------

mysql> select * from folders;
+--------+--------+------+------+
| id     | parent | lft  | rgt  |
+--------+--------+------+------+
| Albert | NULL   |    1 |   16 |
| Bert   | Albert |    2 |    7 |
| Chuck  | Albert |    8 |   15 |
| Donna  | Chuck  |    9 |   10 |
| Eddie  | Chuck  |   11 |   12 |
| Fred   | Chuck  |   13 |   14 |
| Mike   | Bert   |    5 |    6 |
| Mary   | Bert   |    3 |    4 |
+--------+--------+------+------+
8 rows in set (0.01 sec)
```

To delete Chuck (under Albert), use this code:

```
$ java DeleteNode Chuck true
```

```
------DeleteNode begin---------
conn=com.mysql.jdbc.Connection@750159
ID=Chuck
promoteSubtreeAsString=true
------DeleteNode end---------

mysql> select * from folders;
+--------+--------+------+------+
| id     | parent | lft  | rgt  |
+--------+--------+------+------+
| Albert | NULL   |    1 |   14 |
| Bert   | Albert |    2 |    7 |
| Donna  | Albert |    8 |    9 |
| Eddie  | Albert |   10 |   11 |
| Fred   | Albert |   12 |   13 |
| Mike   | Bert   |    5 |    6 |
| Mary   | Bert   |    3 |    4 |
+--------+--------+------+------+
7 rows in set (0.00 sec)
```

To delete Bert (under Albert), use this code:

```
$ java DeleteNode Bert false
------DeleteNode begin---------
conn=com.mysql.jdbc.Connection@750159
ID=Bert
promoteSubtreeAsString=false


delLeft=2
delRight=7
newParentID=Mary
------DeleteNode end---------

C:\mp\sql-trees>

mysql> select * from folders;
+--------+--------+------+------+
| id     | parent | lft  | rgt  |
+--------+--------+------+------+
| Albert | NULL   |    1 |   12 |
| Donna  | Albert |    6 |    7 |
| Eddie  | Albert |    8 |    9 |
| Fred   | Albert |   10 |   11 |
| Mike   | Mary   |    3 |    4 |
| Mary   | Albert |    2 |    5 |
+--------+--------+------+------+
6 rows in set (0.00 sec)
```

DeleteNode.java

This shows DeleteNode.java:

```
1    import java.util.*;
2    import java.io.*;
3    import java.sql.*;
4
5    public class DeleteNode {
6
```

```
7       public static Connection getConnection() throws Exception {
8           String driver = "org.gjt.mm.mysql.Driver";
9           String url = "jdbc:mysql://localhost/snipit";
10          String username = "root";
11          String password = "root";
12          Class.forName(driver);  // load MySQL driver
13          return DriverManager.getConnection(url, username, password);
15      }
16
17      public static void usage() {
18          System.out.println("usage: DeleteNode    ");
19          System.out.println("Example-1: DeleteNode  Bob true");
20          System.out.println("Example-2: DeleteNode  Bob false");
21          System.exit(1);
22      }
23
24      public static void main(String[] args) {
25          Connection conn = null;
26          PreparedStatement pstmt = null;
27          try {
28              System.out.println("------DeleteNode begin---------");
29
30              if (args.length != 2) {
31                  usage();
32              }
33


36
37              String ID = args[0]; // node with value of ID will be deleted
38              String promoteSubtreeAsString = args[1];
39
40              System.out.println("ID="+ID);
41              System.out.println("promoteSubtree="+promoteSubtreeAsString);
42
43              if ((promoteSubtreeAsString == null) ||
44                  (promoteSubtreeAsString.length() == 0)) {
45                  usage();
46              }
47
48              boolean promoteSubtree = false;
49              if (promoteSubtreeAsString.equals("true")) {
50                  promoteSubtree = true;
51              }
52              else if (promoteSubtreeAsString.equals("false")) {
53                  promoteSubtree = false;
54              }
55              else {
56                  usage();
57              }
58              String getLeftRight =
59                  "select parent, lft, rgt from folders where id = ?";
60              pstmt = conn.prepareStatement(getLeftRight);
61              pstmt.setString(1, ID);
62              ResultSet rs = pstmt.executeQuery();
63              rs.next();
64              String parentID = rs.getString(1);
65              int delLeft = rs.getInt(2);
```

```
66              int delRight = rs.getInt(3);
67              System.out.println("ID="+ID);
68              System.out.println("parentID="+parentID);
69              System.out.println("delLeft="+delLeft);
70              System.out.println("delRight="+delRight);
71
72              if(promoteSubtree) {
73                  // promote the subtree
74                  promoteTheSubTree(conn, ID, parentID, delLeft, delRight);
75              }
76              else {
77                  // promote the leftmost sibling to the new parent
78                  promoteSibling(conn, ID, parentID, delLeft, delRight);
79              }
80
81
82              System.out.println("------DeleteNode end---------");
83          }
84      catch (Exception e) {
85          e.printStackTrace();
86          System.exit(1);
87      }
88      finally {
89          // release database resources
90      }
91  }


94  public static void promoteTheSubTree(Connection conn,
95                                      String ID,
96                                      String parentID,
97                                      int delLeft,
98                                      int delRight)
99      throws SQLException, BatchUpdateException {
100
101     // start transaction for batch updates
102     conn.setAutoCommit(false);
103     Statement stmt = conn.createStatement();
104
105     String deleteID = "delete from folders where ID = '"+ID+"'";
106     String update1 = "update folders set lft = lft - 1, "+
            "rgt = rgt - 1 where lft between "+delLeft+" and "+delRight;
107     String update2 = "update folders set rgt = rgt - 2 "+
            "where rgt > "+delRight;
108     String update3 = "update folders set lft = lft - 2 "+
            "where lft > "+delRight;
109     String update4 = "update folders set parent = '"+parentID+
            "' where parent='"+ID+"'";
110     stmt.addBatch(deleteID);
111     stmt.addBatch(update1);
112     stmt.addBatch(update2);
113     stmt.addBatch(update3);
114     stmt.addBatch(update4);
115
116     // send batch operations to the database server
117     int[] batchUpdateCounts = stmt.executeBatch();
118
119     // commit transaction for batch updates
```

```
120            conn.commit();
121            conn.setAutoCommit(true);
122        }
123
124        public static void promoteSibling(Connection conn,
125                                          String ID,
126                                          String parentID,
127                                          int delLeft,
128                                          int delRight)
129            throws SQLException, BatchUpdateException {
130
131            // promote the leftmost sibling to the new parent
132            // find the new parent's ID (which is the new promoted node ID)
133            // then set the parent of siblings to the found id
134            int delLeftPlus1 = delLeft + 1;
135            String findID = "select id from folders where lft = "+delLeftPlus1;
136            Statement findStmt = conn.createStatement();
137            ResultSet rs = findStmt.executeQuery(findID);
138            rs.next();
139            String newParentID = rs.getString(1);
140            rs.close();
141            System.out.println("newParentID="+newParentID);
142
143            // start transaction for batch updates
144            conn.setAutoCommit(false);
145            Statement stmt = conn.createStatement();


148            String updateParents = "update folders set parent = '"+
                 newParentID+"' where lft > "+delLeft+" and rgt < "+delRight;
149            String update1 = "update folders set lft = lft - 1, "+
                 "rgt = "+delRight+", parent= '"+parentID+
                 "' where lft = "+delLeftPlus1;
150            String update2 = "update folders set rgt = rgt - 2 "+
                 " where rgt > "+delLeft;
151            String update3 = "update folders set lft = lft - 2 "+
                 "where lft > "+delLeft;
152            String deleteID = "delete from folders where ID = '"+ID+"'";
153            stmt.addBatch(updateParents);
154            stmt.addBatch(update1);
155            stmt.addBatch(update2);
156            stmt.addBatch(update3);
157            stmt.addBatch(deleteID);
158
159            // send batch operations to the database server
160            int[] batchUpdateCounts = stmt.executeBatch();
161
162            // commit transaction for batch updates
163            conn.commit();
164            conn.setAutoCommit(true);
165        }
166    }
```

Discussing DeleteNode.java

The following explains the program:

> *Lines 1–3*: Import the required classes and interfaces.
>
> *Lines 7–15*: The getConnection() method returns a java.sql.Connection object.
>
> *Lines 30–57*: Get the command-line argument ID (which is the node ID to be deleted) and a boolean to indicate how to promote subnodes of the deleted node (identified by ID).
>
> *Lines 59–70*: Here, you retrieve the parent, left, and right of the ID. These values will be used for further processing.
>
> *Lines 72–79*: If the second argument is true, then you must promote the entire subtree.
>
> *Line 74*: Promotes the subtree. If the second argument is false, then you must promote only the leftmost sibling, and the other nodes will not be affected at all.
>
> *Line 78*: Promotes the leftmost sibling to the new parent.
>
> *Lines 94–122*: Start the transaction for batch updates. No SQL operation will be committed until you invoke the conn.commit() statement.
>
> *Lines 110–114*: Create a set of batch operations. The order of these batch operations is important, and the batch works as a queue (first-in, first-out).
>
> *Lines 124–165*: Start the transaction for batch updates. No SQL operation will be committed until you invoke the conn.commit() statement.
>
> *Lines 153–157*: Create a set of batch operations. The order of these batch operations is important,

Deleting an Existing Subtree (DeleteSubtree.java)

The objective of the DeleteSubtree class is for a given node to delete an existing subtree from a tree. To delete an existing subtree, you need to supply the root ID of the subtree being deleted. To understand DeleteSubtree, refer to Figure 11-5; assume that the original tree is Tree-41, and you want to delete subtree with the root node of B. The resultant tree will become Tree-42.

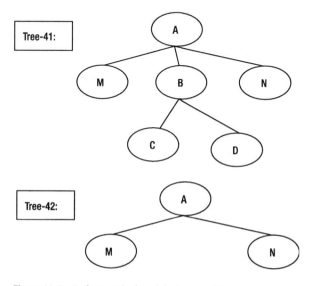

Figure 11-5. *Before and after deleting a subtree*

Setting Up the Database

The tree structure before the deletion of a subtree is as follows:

```
mysql> select * from folders;
+--------+--------+------+------+
| id     | parent | lft  | rgt  |
+--------+--------+------+------+
| Albert | NULL   |    1 |   18 |
| Bert   | Albert |    4 |    9 |
| Chuck  | Albert |   10 |   17 |
| Donna  | Chuck  |   11 |   12 |
| Eddie  | Chuck  |   13 |   14 |
| Fred   | Chuck  |   15 |   16 |
| Mike   | Bert   |    7 |    8 |
| Mary   | Bert   |    5 |    6 |
| Jeff   | Albert |    2 |    3 |
+--------+--------+------+------+
9 rows in set (0.00 sec)
```

To delete the subtree rooted by Bert, use this code:

```
$ java DeleteSubtree Bert
------DeleteSubtree begin---------
conn=com.mysql.jdbc.Connection@750159
ID=Bert
------DeleteSubtree end---------
```

```
| id     | parent | lft  | rgt  |
+--------+--------+------+------+
| Albert | NULL   |    1 |   12 |
| Chuck  | Albert |    4 |   11 |
| Donna  | Chuck  |    5 |    6 |
| Eddie  | Chuck  |    7 |    8 |
| Fred   | Chuck  |    9 |   10 |
| Jeff   | Albert |    2 |    3 |
+--------+--------+------+------+
6 rows in set (0.00 sec)
```

DeleteSubtree.java

This shows DeleteSubtree.java:

```
1    import java.util.*;
2    import java.io.*;
3    import java.sql.*;
4
5    public class DeleteSubtree {
6
7        public static Connection getConnection() throws Exception {
8            String driver = "org.gjt.mm.mysql.Driver";
9            String url = "jdbc:mysql://localhost/snipit";
10           String username = "root";
11           String password = "root";
12           Class.forName(driver);  // load MySQL driver
13           return DriverManager.getConnection(url, username, password);
15       }
16
```

```
17      public static void usage() {
18          System.out.println("usage: DeleteSubtree    ");
19          System.out.println("Example-1: DeleteSubtree  Bob");
20          System.exit(1);
21      }
22
23      public static void main(String[] args) {
24          Connection conn = null;
25          PreparedStatement pstmt = null;
26          Statement stmt = null;
27          try {
28              System.out.println("------DeleteSubtree begin---------");
29
30              if (args.length != 1) {
31                  usage();
32              }
33
34              conn = getConnection();
35              System.out.println("conn="+conn);
36
37              // subtree/node with value of ID will be deleted
38              String ID = args[0];
39              System.out.println("ID="+ID);
40              String getLeftRight =
41                  "select lft, rgt from folders where id = ?";
42              pstmt = conn.prepareStatement(getLeftRight);


45              rs.next();
46              int delLeft = rs.getInt(1);
47              int delRight = rs.getInt(2);
48              int delta = delRight - delLeft + 1;
49
50              // start transaction for batch updates
51              conn.setAutoCommit(false);
52              stmt = conn.createStatement();
53
54              String deleteID = "delete from folders "+
                    "where lft between "+delLeft+" and "+delRight;
55              String update1 = "update folders set lft = lft - "+delta+
                    "  where lft > "+delLeft;
56              String update2 = "update folders set rgt = rgt - "+delta+
                    "  where rgt > "+delRight;
57              stmt.addBatch(deleteID);
58              stmt.addBatch(update1);
59              stmt.addBatch(update2);
60
61              // send batch operations to the database server
62              int[] batchUpdateCounts = stmt.executeBatch();
63
64              // commit transaction for batch updates
65              conn.commit();
66              conn.setAutoCommit(true);
67              System.out.println("------DeleteSubtree end---------");
68          }
69          catch (Exception e) {
70              e.printStackTrace();
```

```
71                System.exit(1);
72            }
73            finally {
74                // release database resources
75            }
76        }
77    }
```

Discussing DeleteSubtree.java

The following explains the program:

Lines 1–3: Import the required classes and interfaces.

Lines 7–14: The getConnection() method returns a java.sql.Connection object.

Lines 41–48: Here, you retrieve the left and right of the root node to be deleted. These values will be used for further processing.

Lines 54–57: These lines prepare SQL queries for batch updates.

Line 51: Starts the transaction for batch updates. No SQL operation will be committed until you invoke the conn.commit() statement.

Line 52: Creates a generic Statement object to be used for batch updates.

Lines 54–59: Create a set of batch operations. The order of these batch operations is important, and the batch works as a queue (first-in, first-out).

success).

Lines 73–75: Release database resources (to free up memory and data structures used by the JDBC driver and database server).

CHAPTER 12

■■■

Working with the PreparedStatement

This chapter describes one of the most important interfaces from the java.sql package, java.sql. PreparedStatement (which inherits from java.sql.Statement). The java.sql.PreparedStatement interface formulates the dynamic statements executed by the database engine.

Statement and PreparedStatement objects can execute SQL statements and return the results (as a ResultSet object or another type) to the client. CallableStatement can execute a stored procedure/function and return the results (as a ResultSet object or another type) to the client. You can create all three interfaces using a Connection (java.sql.Connection) object. Connection is a factory object for creating other JDBC objects (such as Statement, PreparedStatement, and CallableStatement).

When the database "prepares" your SQL statement, it creates two query plans: physical and logical (see Figure 12-1). The DBMS engine reads your SQL query, and then the DBMS parser creates a logical query plan. Finally, the DBMS Query Optimizer receives the logical query plan and creates the physical query plan. The main job of the Query Optimizer is to choose the most efficient

Database Systems, Eighth Edition (Addison-Wesley, 2003) and Jeffrey Ullman's website at http:// www-db.stanford.edu/~ullman/dbsi/win99-346/query1.txt.

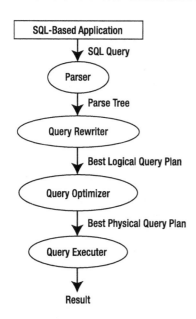

Figure 12-1. *DBMS query plans*

The main difference between Statement and PreparedStatement is this: Statement prepares and executes the query plan each time, while PreparedStatement prepares the query plan once and then just reuses it. (Preparing a statement is also referred to as *precompiling* a SQL statement.) So, use PreparedStatement objects when you are going to repeat a SQL query/update often.

For example, if you are going to retrieve books from a database (using the table books_table) based on the name of the author, then you might write this:

```
Connection conn = getConnection();  // get a database Connection object
// here "author" column is parameterized
String query = "select isbn, title, price from books_table where author=?";
PreparedStatement pstmt = conn.prepareStatement(query);
```

Then you can use pstmt (a PreparedStatement object) as many times as necessary with different author information. You can consider the PreparedStatement object to be an independent static Java method: the result depends on the parameters passed (in this case, the parameter is the name of the author).

Here is how you can pass different authors to get your results from the database:

```
pstmt.setString(1, "don knuth");        // author is Don Knuth
ResultSet rs1 = pstmt.executeQuery();   // create a result set
// now iterate result set rs1
while (rs1.next()) {
    ...
}

pstmt.setString(1, "niklus wirth");     // author is Niklus Wirth
ResultSet rs2 = pstmt.executeQuery();   // create a result set


    ...
}
```

The main point is that you can use a single PreparedStatement object many times to query/update the database. If you are going to use a PreparedStatement object only once or twice, then it has greater initial overhead from precompiling the SQL statement (that is, creating an optimized query plan) than a Statement object. But if you are going to use a PreparedStatement object many times, then it has better performance than a Statement object in future executions.

By using a PreparedStatement object, you can execute SQL statements and pass input parameters to your statement. Like the Statement interface (since PreparedStatement inherits from java.sql.Statement), PreparedStatement enables you to execute both DDL (such as creating a table or index) and DML (such as inserting a new record, deleting an existing record, or updating an existing record). (In typical database applications, most DDLs are executed by SQL scripts.) The PreparedStatement interface provides the following methods for executing SQL requests:

- execute(): Executes the SQL statement in this PreparedStatement object, which may be any kind of SQL statement (such as DDL and DML).

- executeQuery(): Executes the SQL query in this PreparedStatement object and returns the ResultSet object generated by the query.

- executeUpdate(): Executes the SQL statement in this PreparedStatement object (which must be a SQL INSERT, UPDATE, or DELETE statement) or a SQL statement that returns nothing, such as a DDL statement (for creating a table).

- addBatch(String sql): Adds the given SQL command to the current list of commands for this PreparedStatement object. The commands in this list can be executed as a batch by calling the method executeBatch.

- excteBatch(): Submits a batch of commands to the database for execution and, if all commands execute successfully, returns an array of update counts.

Passing input values of different data types to the PreparedStatement object is discussed in detail in Chapter 13.

12-1. What Is a PreparedStatement Object?

When your SQL query is parameterized, you should use a PreparedStatement object. A PreparedStatement object is what sends your dynamic SQL statement (for creating tables, selecting rows from a table, or inserting new records) to the database server. A PreparedStatement object enables you to pass input parameters to the SQL statement before sending it to the database server for execution.

You simply create a PreparedStatement object, pass your input parameters, and then execute it, supplying the appropriate execute method with the SQL statement you want to send. For a SELECT statement, the method to use is executeQuery(). For statements that create or modify tables, the method to use is executeUpdate().

JDK 1.5 defines the PreparedStatement as follows:

```
public interface PreparedStatement extends Statement
```

An object that represents a precompiled SQL statement. A SQL statement is precompiled and stored in a PreparedStatement object. This object can then be used to efficiently execute this statement multiple times. Note: The setter methods (setShort, setString, and so on) for setting IN parameter values must specify types that are compatible with the defined SQL type of the input parameter. For instance, if the IN parameter has SQL type INTEGER, then the method setInt should be used. If arbitrary parameter type conversions are required, the method setObject should be used with a target SQL type. In the following example of setting a parameter, conn represents an active connection:

```
PreparedStatement pstmt = conn.prepareStatement(
    "UPDATE EMPLOYEES SET SALARY = ? WHERE ID = ?");
pstmt.setBigDecimal(1, 153833.00); // set parameter 1 (SALARY)
pstmt.setInt(2, 110592);           // set parameter 2 (ID)
```

12-2. How Do You Create a PreparedStatement Object?

The following sections show you how to create a PreparedStatement object and then use it to execute SQL queries and updates.

How It Works

The java.sql.Connection object is a factory for creating PreparedStatement objects. The Connection interface has six methods for creating PreparedStatement objects, as shown in Table 12-1.

Table 12-1. *The* Connection *Interface's Methods for Creating* PreparedStatement

Return Type	Method	Description
PreparedStatement	prepareStatement(String sql)	Creates a PreparedStatement object for sending parameterized SQL statements to the database
PreparedStatement	prepareStatement(String sql, int autoGeneratedKeys)	Creates a default PreparedStatement object that has the capability to retrieve autogenerated keys
PreparedStatement	prepareStatement (String sql, int[] columnIndexes)	Creates a default PreparedStatement object capable of returning the autogenerated keys designated by the given array
PreparedStatement	prepareStatement(String sql, int resultSetType, int resultSetConcurrency)	Creates a PreparedStatement object that will generate ResultSet objects with the given type and concurrency
PreparedStatement	prepareStatement(String sql, int resultSetType, int resultSetConcurrency, int resultSetHoldability)	Creates a PreparedStatement object that will generate ResultSet objects with the given type, concurrency, and holdability
PreparedStatement	prepareStatement(String sql, String[] columnNames)	Creates a default PreparedStatement object capable of returning the autogenerated keys designated by the given array

The JDK defines the Connection.prepareStatement() method as follows:

```
public PreparedStatement prepareStatement(String sql)
    throws SQLException
```

This creates a PreparedStatement object for sending parameterized SQL statements to the database. A SQL statement with or without IN (input) parameters can be precompiled and stored in a PreparedStatement object. You can then use this object to efficiently execute this statement multiple times.

Note that this method is optimized for handling parameterized SQL statements that benefit from precompilation. If the driver supports precompilation, the method prepareStatement will send the statement to the database for precompilation. Some drivers may not support precompilation. In this case, the statement may not be sent to the database until the PreparedStatement object is executed. This has no direct effect on users; however, it does affect which methods throw certain SQLException objects.

Result sets created using the returned PreparedStatement object will by default be type TYPE_FORWARD_ONLY and have a concurrency level of CONCUR_READ_ONLY.

The parameter to this method is sql, which is a SQL statement that may contain one or more ? IN parameter placeholders.

This method returns a new default PreparedStatement object containing the precompiled SQL statement.

It throws SQLException if a database access error occurs.

Solution

In the following sections, I will provide several examples for creating PreparedStatement objects. To illustrate how to create PreparedStatement objects, I will use the following table definition:

```
create table books_table (
    isbn VARCHAR(12) not null PRIMARY KEY,
    author VARCHAR(64) not null,
    publisher VARCHAR(64)
);
```

The java.sql.Connection interface has factory methods for creating Statement and PreparedStatement objects. You can create a PreparedStatement object using the Connection method prepareStatement(). I will provide three examples in the next sections:

- Example 1: Creating a PreparedStatement object with one parameter marker
- Example 2: Creating a PreparedStatement object with two parameter markers
- Example 3: Creating a PreparedStatement object with no parameter markers

As you will notice in the following examples, you can use a PreparedStatement object any number of times after you create it (in all of the next three examples, I will show the PreparedStatement objects being used twice).

Example 1: Creating a PreparedStatement Object with One Parameter Marker

This shows how to create a PreparedStatement object with one parameter marker:

```
import jcb.util.DatabaseUtil;
...
ResultSet rs = null;
Connection conn = null;


try {
    conn = getConnection(); // get a Connection object
    // create query object: this query has only one
    // parameter marker, which denotes an ISBN
    query = "select author, publisher from books_table where isbn = ?";

    // create PreparedStatement object
    pstmt = conn.prepareStatement(query);

    // this query has only one parameter marker;
    // we have to "pass in" the values for parameters
    pstmt.setString(1, "111222333");

    // execute the query, and create a result set
    rs = pstmt.executeQuery();

    // iterate the ResultSet object, and get all the data
    while (rs.next()) {
        String author = rs.getString(1);
        String publisher = rs.getString(2);
    }

    // now we can use the same PreparedStatement object
    // (i.e., pstmt) to execute another SQL query:
    // this query has only one parameter marker;
    // we have to "pass in" the values for parameters
    pstmt.setString(1, "1112224444");
```

```
    // execute the query, and create a result set
    rs = pstmt.executeQuery();

    // iterate the ResultSet object, and get all the data
    while (rs.next()) {
        String author = rs.getString(1);
        String publisher = rs.getString(2);
    }
}
catch (SQLException e) {
    // could not create a PreparedStatement object,
    // or other problems happened.
    // handle the exception
}
finally {
    // close ResultSet, PreparedStatement, and Connection objects
    DatabaseUtil.close(rs);
    DatabaseUtil.close(pstmt);
    DatabaseUtil.close(conn);
}
```

Example 2: Creating a PreparedStatement Object with Two Parameter Markers

This shows how to create a PreparedStatement object with two parameter markers:

```
import jcb.util.DatabaseUtil;
...


PreparedStatement pstmt = null;
String query = null;
try {
    conn = getConnection(); // get a Connection object
    // create query object: this query has only one
    // parameter marker, which denotes an ISBN
    query = "select publisher from books_table where isbn = ? and author = ?";

    // create PreparedStatement object
    pstmt = conn.prepareStatement(query);

    // this query has only two parameter markers;
    // we have to "pass in" the values for both parameters
    pstmt.setString(1, "111222333"); // sets the isbn
    pstmt.setString(2, "knuth"); // sets the author

    // execute the query, and create a result set
    rs = pstmt.executeQuery();

    // iterate the ResultSet object, and get all the data
    while (rs.next()) {
        String publisher = rs.getString(2);
    }

    // now we can use the same PreparedStatement object
    // (i.e., pstmt) to execute another SQL query:
    // this query has two parameter markers;
    // we have to "pass in" the values for parameters
```

```
        pstmt.setString(1, "111555666"); // sets the isbn
        pstmt.setString(2, "don knuth"); // sets the author

        // execute the query, and create a result set
        rs = pstmt.executeQuery();

        // iterate the ResultSet object, and get all the data
        while (rs.next()) {
            String publisher = rs.getString(2);
        }
    }
}
catch (SQLException e) {
    // could not create a PreparedStatement object,
    // or other problems happened; handle the exception
}
finally {
    // close ResultSet, PreparedStatement, and Connection objects
    DatabaseUtil.close(rs);
    DatabaseUtil.close(pstmt);
    DatabaseUtil.close(conn);
}
```

Example 3: Creating a PreparedStatement Object with No Parameter Markers

When your SQL query does not have any parameters, you should use a Statement instead of a PreparedStatement object (unless you are going to use it many times), as shown here:

```
...
ResultSet rs = null;
Connection conn = null;
PreparedStatement pstmt = null;
String query = null;
try {
    conn = getConnection(); // get a Connection object
    // create query object: this query has no parameter marker
    query = "select isbn, author, publisher from books_table";

    // create PreparedStatement object
    pstmt = conn.prepareStatement(query);

    // this query has no parameter marker;
    // no need to "pass in" any parameters

    // execute the query, and create a result set
    rs = pstmt.executeQuery();

    // iterate the ResultSet object, and get all the data
    while (rs.next()) {
        String isbn = rs.getString(1);
        String author = rs.getString(2);
        String publisher = rs.getString(3);
    }

    // now we can use the same PreparedStatement object
    // (i.e., pstmt) to execute another SQL query:
```

```
        // execute the query, and create a result set
        rs = pstmt.executeQuery();

        // iterate the ResultSet object, and get all the data
        while (rs.next()) {
            String isbn = rs.getString(1);
            String author = rs.getString(2);
            String publisher = rs.getString(3);
        }
    }
    catch (SQLException e) {
        // could not create a PreparedStatement object,
        // or other problems happened; handle the exception
    }
    finally {
        // close ResultSet, PreparedStatement, and Connection objects
        DatabaseUtil.close(rs);
        DatabaseUtil.close(pstmt);
        DatabaseUtil.close(conn);
    }
```

12-3. What Are the Differences Between Statement and PreparedStatement?

You can use both Statement and PreparedStatement objects to execute SQL statements. A Statement

SQL statement is executed many times, it may be more efficient to use a PreparedStatement object. (You can create a single PreparedStatement object and use it any number of times by setting different input parameter values.)

When a database server parses your SQL query/statement for execution, it creates an optimized query plan (how to execute your SQL statement). When the database prepares a statement, it creates a query plan. Statement prepares and executes the query plan each time, while PreparedStatement prepares the query plan once and then reuses the same query plan. This is the main difference between Statement and PreparedStatement.

The database optimizer's job is to determine the most efficient method of accessing the data and passing on this information for the execution of the query. The query plan is the set of information/steps/APIs of how to execute the query, which is produced by the database optimizer. Therefore, the query plan contains a series of specific instructions on how to most efficiently retrieve the required data from the tables/views/indexes.

So, the PreparedStatement object differs from the Statement object in two ways:

The precompiled statement: Instances of PreparedStatement contain a SQL statement that has already been compiled (it has a determined and prepared query plan). This is what makes a statement "prepared."

The input parameters: The SQL statement contained in a PreparedStatement object may have one or more IN (input) parameters. An IN parameter is a parameter whose value is not specified when the SQL statement is created. Instead, the statement has a question mark (?) as a placeholder for each IN parameter. The ? is also known as a *parameter marker* or *parameter placeholder*. A client application must set a value for each parameter marker in a PreparedStatement before executing the prepared statement.

12-4. What Type Conversions Are Supported by MySQL?

MySQL Connector/J is an implementation of Sun's JDBC 3.0 API for the MySQL relational database server. It strives to conform as much as possible to the JDBC API. This is according to the MySQL Connector/J documentation (`http://www.mysql.com/documentation/connector-j/index.html`):

> *MySQL Connector/J is flexible in the way it handles conversions between MySQL data types and Java data types. In general, any MySQL data type can be converted to a java.lang.String, and any numerical type can be converted to any of the Java numerical types, although round-off, overflow, or loss of precision may occur.*

According to the documentation, the conversions listed in Table 12-2 are guaranteed to work.

Table 12-2. *MySQL Conversion Table*

These MySQL Data Types...	Can Always be Converted to These Java Types...
CHAR, VARCHAR, BLOB, TEXT, ENUM, and SET	java.lang.String, java.io.InputStream, java.io.Reader, java.sql.Blob, and java.sql.Clob
FLOAT, REAL, DOUBLE PRECISION, NUMERIC, DECIMAL, TINYINT, SMALLINT, MEDIUMINT, INTEGER, and BIGINT	java.lang.String, java.lang.Short, .lang.Integer, java.lang.Long, java.lang.Double, and java.math.BigDecimal (Note: Round-off, overflow, or loss of precision may occur if you choose a Java numeric data type that has less precision or capacity than the MySQL data type you are converting to/from.)

12-5. What Type Conversions Are Supported by Oracle?

The Oracle JDBC drivers support standard JDBC 1.0 and 2.0 types as well as Oracle-specific (that is, proprietary) BFILE and ROWID data types and types of the REF CURSOR category. This section documents standard and Oracle-specific SQL-Java default type mappings.

Table 12-3 shows the default mappings between SQL data types, JDBC type codes, standard Java types, and Oracle extended types. (This information comes from the Oracle 9*i* JDBC Developer's Guide and Reference, Release 2.) Specifically, note the following about the table:

- The SQL Data Types column lists the SQL types that exist in the Oracle database.

- The JDBC Type Codes column lists the data type codes supported by the JDBC standard and defined in the java.sql.Types class or defined by Oracle in the oracle.jdbc.OracleTypes class. For standard type codes, the codes are identical in these two classes.

- The Standard Java Types column lists standard types defined in the Java language.

- The Oracle Extension Java Types column lists the oracle.sql.* Java types that correspond to each SQL data type in the database.

2-3. *Oracle's Default Mappings Between SQL Types and Java Types*

ata Types	JDBC Type Codes	Standard Java Types	Oracle Extension Java Types
ard JDBC 1.0 Types			
	java.sql.Types.CHAR	java.lang.String	oracle.sql.CHAR
AR2	java.sql.Types.VARCHAR	java.lang.String	oracle.sql.CHAR
	java.sql.Types.LONGVARCHAR	java.lang.String	oracle.sql.CHAR
R	java.sql.Types.NUMERIC	java.math.BigDecimal	oracle.sql.NUMBER
R	java.sql.Types.DECIMAL	java.math.BigDecimal	oracle.sql.NUMBER
R	java.sql.Types.BIT	boolean	oracle.sql.NUMBER
R	java.sql.Types.TINYINT	byte	oracle.sql.NUMBER
R	java.sql.Types.SMALLINT	short	oracle.sql.NUMBER
R	java.sql.Types.INTEGER	int	oracle.sql.NUMBER
R	java.sql.Types.BIGINT	long	oracle.sql.NUMBER
R	java.sql.Types.REAL	float	oracle.sql.NUMBER
R	java.sql.Types.FLOAT	double	oracle.sql.NUMBER
R	java.sql.Types.DOUBLE	double	oracle.sql.NUMBER
	java.sql.Types.BINARY	byte[]	oracle.sql.RAW
	java.sql.Types.VARBINARY	byte[]	oracle.sql.RAW
RAW	java.sql.Types.LONGVARBINARY	byte[]	oracle.sql.RAW
	java.sql.Types.TIMESTAMP	javal.sql.Timestamp	oracle.sql.DATE
ard JDBC 2.0 Types			
	java.sql.Types.BLOB	java.sql.Blob	oracle.sql.BLOB
	java.sql.Types.CLOB	java.sql.Clob	oracle.sql.CLOB
defined t	java.sql.Types.STRUCT	java.sql.Struct	oracle.sql.STRUCT
defined ence	java.sql.Types.REF	java.sql.Ref	oracle.sql.REF
defined ction	java.sql.Types.ARRAY	java.sql.Array	oracle.sql.ARRAY
e Extensions			
	oracle.jdbc.OracleTypes.BFILE		oracle.sql.BFILE
	oracle.jdbc.OracleTypes.ROWID		oracle.sql.ROWID
URSOR	oracle.jdbc.OracleTypes.CURSOR	java.sql.ResultSet	oracle.jdbc.OracleResultSet
	oracle.jdbc.OracleTypes.TIMESTAMP		oracle.sql.TIMESTAMP
	oracle.jdbc.OracleTypes.TIMESTAMPTZ		oracle.sql.TIMESTAMPTZ
	oracle.jdbc.OracleTypes.TIMESTAMPLTZ		oracle.sql.TIMESTAMPLTZ

12-6. How Do You Use Batch Multiple Updates with Prepared-Statement?

The following sections show how to execute a set of SQL statements as a batch multiple update using a PreparedStatement object.

How It Works

The java.sql package provides the ability to send multiple updates (for updating records or creating new records) to the database server for execution as a batch. The PreparedStatement.addbatch() method enables you to accomplish this task, which might improve the performance of the entire transaction. You can reduce the amount of time it takes to perform repetitive inserts and updates if you batch them using the PreparedStatement object's addBatch() method.

Both the Oracle and MySQL databases support the PreparedStatement.addBatch() method, which sends multiple updates to the database server. The signature of addBatch() is as follows:

```
public void addBatch() throws SQLException
```

This adds a set of parameters to the PreparedStatement object's batch of commands. This throws a SQLException if a database access error occurs.

Setting Up the Oracle Database

This shows how to set up the Oracle database:

```
SQL> desc add_batch_table;
 Name                    Null?    Type
 ---------------         --------  ---------------
 STRING_COLUMN                    VARCHAR2(10)
 INT_COLUMN                       NUMBER

SQL> insert into add_batch_table(string_column,int_column) values('id-55', 55);
SQL> insert into add_batch_table(string_column,int_column) values('id-66', 66);
SQL> commit;
Commit complete.

SQL> select * from add_batch_table;

STRING_COLUMN   INT_COLUMN
-------------   ----------
id-55                   55
id-66                   66
```

Solution

This solution (the Demo_PreparedStatement_AddBatch class) will insert three records—('id-1', 100), ('id-2', 200), and ('id-3', 300)—into the add_batch_table using the addBatch() method. It is important to note that you can call addBatch() any number of times without any parameter changes or without even calling the setXXX( ) methods before calling addBatch(). If your batch statements violate database integrity rules (such as having duplicate keys), then you will get a run-time exception.

```java
import java.util.*;
import java.io.*;
import java.sql.*;

import jcb.util.DatabaseUtil;
import jcb.db.VeryBasicConnectionManager;

public class Demo_PreparedStatement_AddBatch {

    public static void checkUpdateCounts(int[] updateCounts) {
        for (int i=0; i<updateCounts.length; i++) {
            if (updateCounts[i] >= 0) {
                // Successfully executed; the number
                // represents number of affected rows
                System.out.println("OK; updateCount="+updateCounts[i]);
            }
            else if (updateCounts[i] == Statement.SUCCESS_NO_INFO) {
                // Successfully executed; number of
                // affected rows not available
                System.out.println("OK; updateCount=Statement.SUCCESS_NO_INFO");
            }
            else if (updateCounts[i] == Statement.EXECUTE_FAILED) {
                // Failed to execute


            }
        }
    }

    public static void main(String[] args) {
        Connection conn = null;
        PreparedStatement pstmt = null;
        try {
            System.out.println("--Demo_PreparedStatement_AddBatch begin--");
            String dbVendor = args[0];
            conn = VeryBasicConnectionManager.getConnection(dbVendor);
            System.out.println("conn="+conn);
            System.out.println("---------------");

            // Disable autocommit
            conn.setAutoCommit(false);

            // prepare query
            String query = "insert into add_batch_table"+
                " (string_column, int_column) values(?, ?)";

            // create PreparedStatement object
            pstmt = conn.prepareStatement(query);

            // add the first batch
            pstmt.setString(1, "id-1");
            pstmt.setInt(2, 100);
            pstmt.addBatch();
```

```java
        // add the second batch
        pstmt.setString(1, "id-2");
        pstmt.setInt(2, 200);
        pstmt.addBatch();

        // add the third batch
        pstmt.setString(1, "id-3");
        pstmt.setInt(2, 300);
        pstmt.addBatch();

        // execute the batch
        int[] updateCounts = pstmt.executeBatch();

        // all statements were successfully executed.
        // updateCounts contains one element for each
        // batched statement. The updateCounts[i] contains
        // the number of rows affected by that statement.
        checkUpdateCounts(updateCounts);

        // since there were no errors, commit
        conn.commit();
    }
    catch (BatchUpdateException e) {
        // Not all of the statements were successfully executed
        int[] updateCounts = e.getUpdateCounts();


        // number of batched statements. If not, updateCounts.length
        // will equal the number of successfully executed statements
        checkUpdateCounts(updateCounts);

        // Either commit the successfully executed statements
        // or roll back the entire batch
        try {
            conn.rollback();
        }
        catch (Exception e2) {
            e.printStackTrace();
            System.exit(1);
        }
    }
    catch (Exception e) {
        e.printStackTrace();
        System.exit(1);
    }
    finally {
        // release database resources
        DatabaseUtil.close(pstmt);
        DatabaseUtil.close(conn);
    }
  }
}
```

Running the Solution for the Oracle Database

This shows how to run the solution for the Oracle database:

```
$ javac  Demo_PreparedStatement_AddBatch.java
$ java  Demo_PreparedStatement_AddBatch  oracle
--Demo_PreparedStatement_AddBatch begin--
conn=oracle.jdbc.driver.OracleConnection@6e70c7
----------------
Successfully executed; updateCount=Statement.SUCCESS_NO_INFO
Successfully executed; updateCount=Statement.SUCCESS_NO_INFO
Successfully executed; updateCount=Statement.SUCCESS_NO_INFO
$
```

Viewing the Oracle Database After Running the Program

This shows the Oracle database after running the program:

```
SQL> select * from add_batch_table;

STRING_COLUMN    INT_COLUMN
-------------    ----------
id-55                    55
id-66                    66
id-1                    100
id-2                    200
id-3                    300
```

This shows how to set up the MySQL database:

```
mysql> create table add_batch_table (
    -> string_column varchar(10),
    -> int_column integer );

mysql> desc add_batch_table;
+---------------+-------------+------+-----+---------+-------+
| Field         | Type        | Null | Key | Default | Extra |
+---------------+-------------+------+-----+---------+-------+
| string_column | varchar(10) | YES  |     | NULL    |       |
| int_column    | int(11)     | YES  |     | NULL    |       |
+---------------+-------------+------+-----+---------+-------+
2 rows in set (0.03 sec)

mysql> insert into add_batch_table(string_column,int_column) values('id-55', 55);
mysql> insert into add_batch_table(string_column,int_column) values('id-66', 66);
mysql> select * from add_batch_table;
+---------------+------------+
| string_column | int_column |
+---------------+------------+
| id-55         |         55 |
| id-66         |         66 |
+---------------+------------+
2 rows in set (0.00 sec)
```

Running the Solution for the MySQL Database

This shows how to run the solution for the MySQL database:

```
$ javac  Demo_PreparedStatement_AddBatch.java
$ java  Demo_PreparedStatement_AddBatch  mysql
--Demo_PreparedStatement_AddBatch begin--
conn=com.mysql.jdbc.Connection@1e4cbc4
---------------
Successfully executed; updateCount=1
Successfully executed; updateCount=1
Successfully executed; updateCount=1
```

Viewing the MySQL Database After Running the Program

This shows the MySQL database after running the program:

```
mysql> select * from add_batch_table;
+---------------+------------+
| string_column | int_column |
+---------------+------------+
| id-55         |         55 |
| id-66         |         66 |
| id-1          |        100 |
| id-2          |        200 |
| id-3          |        300 |
+---------------+------------+
```

12-7. How Do You Execute a SQL Statement Using a Prepared-Statement Object?

The following sections show you how to execute SQL queries and statements using a PreparedStatement object.

How It Works

The PreparedStatement (a parameterized SQL statement) is derived from the interface Statement. When you pass input parameter values to your SQL query, then it becomes more convenient and efficient to use a PreparedStatement object for sending SQL statements to the database.

When to Use a PreparedStatement Object

If you want to execute a SQL query many times, you can usually reduce the execution time by using a PreparedStatement object instead. The Statement object is compiled for each execution, while the PreparedStatement object is compiled only once. In general, compiling SQL queries is expensive. SQL query compilation involves checking that the database user has access to the database objects (such as tables, views, and columns) used in the query. Before the compilation is completed, the query is optimized. The compiler needs to find the optimal search path for queries and statements.

Creating a PreparedStatement Object

You can create a PreparedStatement object using a Connection factory object. For example, if you have a SQL query with two input parameters, you might write the following (note that ? is a place-holder for an input parameter, and the following example has two input parameters):

```
Connection conn = getConnection();  // get a Connection object
String insertQuery = "INSERT into cats_tricks(name, trick) values(?, ?)";
PreparedStatement pstmt = conn.prepareStatement(insertQuery);

// at this point the PreparedStatement object (i.e., pstmt)
// is precompiled and can be used any number of times to create
// new records for the cats_tricks table; you just need to pass two
// parameter values: value for name and value for trick.
```

Supplying Values for PreparedStatement Parameters

To execute your PreparedStatement object, you need to supply values to be used instead of the ?
placeholders before you can execute a PreparedStatement object. PreparedStatement.setXXX()
methods enable you to supply values for PreparedStatement input parameters. For example, if the
value you want to substitute for a ? is a Java int, you call the method setInt(). If the value you want
to substitute for a question mark is a Java String, you call the method setString(). There is
a setXXX() method for each type in the Java programming language. Continuing with the preceding
example, you can supply values for input parameters like so:

```
Connection conn = getConnection();  // get a Connection object
String insertQuery = "INSERT into cats_tricks(name, trick) values(?, ?)";
PreparedStatement pstmt = conn.prepareStatement(insertQuery);

// at this point the PreparedStatement object (i.e., pstmt)
// is compiled and can be used any number of times to create
// new records for the cats_tricks table.


// Supplying Values for PreparedStatement Parameters
pstmt.setString(1, "mono");       // value for "name" column
pstmt.setString(2, "rollover");   // value for "trick" column
// create the record (update the database)
pstmt.executeUpdate():

// create second record with values ("ginger", "jump")
// Supplying Values for PreparedStatement Parameters
pstmt.setString(1, "ginger");  // value for "name" column
pstmt.setString(2, "jump");    // value for "trick" column
// create the record (update the database)
pstmt .executeUpdate():
```

Using the PreparedStatement object pstmt, the following line of code sets the first ? placeholder
to a Java String with a value of "mono":

```
pstmt.setString(1, "mono");      // value for "name" column
```

Using the PreparedStatement object pstmt, the following line of code sets the ? placeholder to
a Java String with a value of "rollover":

```
pstmt.setString(2, "rollover");      // value for "trick" column
```

Using a Loop to Set Values

You can make coding easier by using a for loop or a while loop to set values for the
PreparedStatement object's input parameters. The following example demonstrates how to use
a loop to set values:

```
Connection conn = getConnection();  // get a Connection object
String insertQuery = "INSERT into cats_tricks(name, trick) values(?, ?)";
PreparedStatement pstmt = conn.prepareStatement(insertQuery);

// at this point the PreparedStatement object (i.e., pstmt)
// is compiled and can be used any number of times to create
// new records for the cats_tricks table.

// create two arrays: cats and tricks (will be used as input parameters)
String[] cats = {"mono", "mono", "ginger", "lola", "pishi", "pishi"};
String[] tricks = {"jump", "rollover", "sleep", "talk", "hop", "jump"};

// now loop and create 6 records (cats[i] is associated
// with the tricks[i] (i=0, 1, ..., 5)
for (int i = 0; i < cats.length; i++) {
    pstmt.setString(1, cats[i]);     // value for "name" column
    pstmt.setString(2, tricks[i]);   // value for "trick" column
    // create the record (update the database)
    updateSales.executeUpdate()
}
```

Executing SQL Queries and Statements Using PreparedStatement

The PreparedStatement interface provides sufficient methods for executing SQL statements. To execute SQL statements, follow these steps:

3. Create a PreparedStatement object by using Connection.prepareStatement(your-SQL-query).

4. Set all input parameters by using the PreparedStatement.setXXX() method.

5. Execute your SQL statement using a PreparedStatement object, and generate ResultSet objects. (Note that if a method does not return a ResultSet object explicitly, then you can call the PreparedStatement.getResultSet() method to get the desired ResultSet object.)

6. Extract the values from the generated ResultSet objects.

The PreparedStatement interface provides the following methods for executing SQL statements (note that PreparedStatement extends Statement, which inherits all the methods from the Statement interface):

- boolean execute(): Executes the SQL statement in this PreparedStatement object, which may be any kind of SQL statement

- ResultSet executeQuery(): Executes the SQL query in this PreparedStatement object and returns the ResultSet object generated by the query

- int executeUpdate(): Executes the SQL statement in this PreparedStatement object (which must be a SQL INSERT, UPDATE, or DELETE statement) or a SQL statement that returns nothing, such as a DDL statement

- int[] executeBatch(): Submits a batch of commands to the database for execution and, if all commands execute successfully, returns an array of update counts

12-8. How Do You Retrieve Automatically Generated Keys Using PreparedStatement (MySQL)?

The following sections show how to retrieve automatically generated keys using the PreparedStatement object. In general, you want to retrieve automatically generated keys when you use the AUTO_INCREMENT attribute (in MySQL) for table columns.

How It Works

The Oracle and MySQL databases allow for certain columns to be given automatically generated key values. When using automatically generated key values, an insert statement is responsible for supplying a value for the column. The database generates a unique value for the column and inserts the value. You can use this technique for generating unique primary keys.

The MySQL database uses the AUTO_INCREMENT attribute for generating key values; on the other hand, an Oracle database uses a SEQUENCE concept for generating key values. In the following sections, you will look at these two databases for automatically generating key values before retrieving them.

Setting Up the MySQL Database

Consider the following table definition; you can use the AUTO_INCREMENT attribute to generate a unique identity for new rows:

```
mysql> use octopus;
Database changed


    ->              name VARCHAR(32) NOT NULL,
    ->              PRIMARY KEY (id) );
Query OK, 0 rows affected (0.03 sec)

mysql> desc animals_table;
+-------+-------------+------+-----+---------+----------------+
| Field | Type        | Null | Key | Default | Extra          |
+-------+-------------+------+-----+---------+----------------+
| id    | int(11)     |      | PRI | NULL    | auto_increment |
| name  | varchar(32) |      |     |         |                |
+-------+-------------+------+-----+---------+----------------+
2 rows in set (0.01 sec)

mysql> insert into animals_table(name) values('dog');
mysql> insert into animals_table(name) values('cat');
mysql> insert into animals_table(name) values('rabbit');
mysql> select id, name from animals_table;
+----+--------+
| id | name   |
+----+--------+
|  1 | dog    |
|  2 | cat    |
|  3 | rabbit |
+----+--------+
3 rows in set (0.00 sec)
```

Solution

The JDBC 3.0 specification proposes a functional Statement interface that provides access to auto-matically generated key values after an insert. The following solution demonstrates how to retrieve AUTO_INCREMENT values using the new JDBC 3.0 method getGeneratedKeys(), which is now the pre-ferred method to use if you need to retrieve AUTO_INCREMENT keys. Oracle's JDBC driver does not support getGeneratedKeys(), so you have to use the select <sequence-name>.currval from dual query to access automatically generated key values after an insert.

The following is the complete solution. You should note that, for the MySQL database, if a col-umn is an AUTO_INCREMENT, you do not need to pass any value; however, for the Oracle database, you need to pass <sequence-name>.nextval (which gives you the next value of <sequence-name>).

```java
import java.util.*;
import java.io.*;
import java.sql.*;

import jcb.db.VeryBasicConnectionManager;
import jcb.util.DatabaseUtil;

public class GetGeneratedKeys {
    public static void main(String[] args) {
        ResultSet rs = null;
        Connection conn = null;
        PreparedStatement pstmt = null;
        try {
            System.out.println("--GetGeneratedKeys begin--");


            conn = VeryBasicConnectionManager.getConnection(dbVendor);
            System.out.println("conn="+conn);

            // insert a  record into the animals_table using PreparedStatement
            // note that the SQL INSERT is different for each vendor
            String insert = null;
            if (dbVendor.equalsIgnoreCase("mysql")) {
                insert = "insert into animals_table(name) values(?)";
            }
            else if (dbVendor.equalsIgnoreCase("oracle")) {
                insert = "insert into animals_table(id, name) "+
                        "values(ANIMAL_ID_SEQ.nextval, ?)";
            }

            pstmt = conn.prepareStatement(insert);   // create a PreparedStatement
            pstmt.setString(1, name);                // set input values
            pstmt.executeUpdate();                   // insert the record

            if (dbVendor.equalsIgnoreCase("mysql")) {
                rs = stmt.getGeneratedKeys();
            }
            else if (dbVendor.equalsIgnoreCase("oracle")) {
                rs = stmt.executeQuery("select ANIMAL_ID_SEQ.currval from dual");
            }

            while (rs.next()) {
                ResultSetMetaData rsMetaData = rs.getMetaData();
                int columnCount = rsMetaData.getColumnCount();
```

```
                for (int i = 1; i <= columnCount; i++) {
                    String key = rs.getString(i);
                    System.out.println("key " + i + " is " + key);
                }
            }
            System.out.println("--GetGeneratedKeys end--");
        }
        catch(Exception e){
            e.printStackTrace();
            System.exit(1);
        }
        finally {
            // release database resources
            DatabaseUtil.close(rs);
            DatabaseUtil.close(pstmt);
            DatabaseUtil.close(conn);
        }
    }
}
```

Viewing the MySQL Database Before Running the Solution

This is the MySQL database before running the solution:

```
mysql> select * from animals_table;
+----+--------+
| id | name   |

| 2 | cat     |
| 3 | rabbit |
+----+--------+
3 rows in set (0.00 sec)
```

Running the Solution for the MySQL Database

This shows how to run the solution (MySQL):

```
$ javac  GetGeneratedKeys.java
$ java GetGeneratedKeys  mysql duck
-- GetGeneratedKeys begin --
conn=com.mysql.jdbc.Connection@15c7855
---------------
key 1 is 4
-- GetGeneratedKeys end --
```

Viewing the MySQL Database After Running the Solution

This is the MySQL database after running the solution:

```
mysql> select * from animals_table;
+----+---------+
| id | name    |
+----+---------+
| 1 | dog      |
| 2 | cat      |
| 3 | rabbit  |
| 4 | duck     |
+----+---------+
4 rows in set (0.01 sec)
```

12-9. How Do You Retrieve Automatically Generated Keys Using PreparedStatement (Oracle)?

The following sections show how to retrieve automatically generated keys using a PreparedStatement object.

How It Works

The Oracle and MySQL databases allow certain columns to be given automatically generated key values. When using automatically generated key values, an insert statement is not responsible for supplying a value for the column. The database generates a unique value for the column and inserts the value. You can use this technique for generating unique primary keys. The Oracle database uses the SEQUENCE objects for generating key values. What is a SEQUENCE? SEQUENCE is a Oracle database object that does the following:

- Automatically generates unique numbers
- Is a sharable object
- Is typically used to create a primary key value
- Replaces application code
- Speeds up the efficiency of accessing sequence values when cached in memory

Setting Up the Oracle Database

```
CREATE SEQUENCE sequence-name
    [INCREMENT BY n]
    [START WITH n]
    [{MAXVALUE n | NOMAXVALUE}]
    [{MINVALUE n | NOMINVALUE}]
    [{CYCLE | NOCYCLE}]
    [{CACHE n | NOCACHE}];
```

This is an example of creating a SEQUENCE:

```
CREATE SEQUENCE ANIMAL_ID_SEQ
    INCREMENT BY 1
    START WITH 1
    MAXVALUE 10000
    NOCACHE
    NOCYCLE;
```

Note that Oracle SEQUENCE objects cannot be accessed directly and can be retrieved only using the CURRVAL (current value) and NEXTVAL (next value) pseudocolumns. Also, you must first access a SEQUENCE with NEXTVAL before using CURRVAL. For example, if a sequence name is ANIMAL_ID_SEQ (defined in the next section), then ANIMAL_ID_SEQ.NEXTVAL will generate the next sequence number and ANIMAL_ID_SEQ.CURRVAL will provide the last generated sequence number.

```
SQL>    CREATE SEQUENCE ANIMAL_ID_SEQ
  2              INCREMENT BY 1
  3              START WITH 1
  4              MAXVALUE 10000
  5              NOCACHE
  6              NOCYCLE;
```

```
Sequence created.

SQL> desc user_sequences;
 Name                                         Null?    Type
 -------------------------------------------- -------- --------------
 SEQUENCE_NAME                                NOT NULL VARCHAR2(30)
 MIN_VALUE                                             NUMBER
 MAX_VALUE                                             NUMBER
 INCREMENT_BY                                 NOT NULL NUMBER
 CYCLE_FLAG                                            VARCHAR2(1)
 ORDER_FLAG                                            VARCHAR2(1)
 CACHE_SIZE                                   NOT NULL NUMBER
 LAST_NUMBER                                  NOT NULL NUMBER

SQL> select SEQUENCE_NAME, MIN_VALUE, MAX_VALUE,
            INCREMENT_BY, LAST_NUMBER
          from  user_sequences;

SEQUENCE_NAME     MIN_VALUE  MAX_VALUE INCREMENT_BY LAST_NUMBER
---------------- ---------- ---------- ------------ -----------
ANIMAL_ID_SEQ             1      10000            1           1
```

To create an Oracle table and populate it with `ANIMAL_ID_SEQ`, use this code:

```
SQL>    CREATE TABLE animals_table (
  2              id INT NOT NULL,
  3              name VARCHAR(32) NOT NULL,


Table created.

SQL> desc animals_table;
 Name              Null?    Type
 ----------------- -------- ------------
 ID                NOT NULL NUMBER(38)
 NAME              NOT NULL VARCHAR2(32)

SQL> insert into animals_table(id, name)
       values(ANIMAL_ID_SEQ.nextval, 'dog');
SQL> insert into animals_table(id, name)
       values(ANIMAL_ID_SEQ.nextval, 'cat');
SQL> insert into animals_table(id, name)
       values(ANIMAL_ID_SEQ.nextval, 'rabbit');
SQL> commit;
Commit complete.

SQL> select * from animals_table;

        ID  NAME
---------- ---------
         1  dog
         2  cat
         3  rabbit
```

Solution

The JDBC 3.0 specification proposes a functional Statement interface that provides access to auto-matically generated key values after an insert. The following sections demonstrate how to retrieve

Oracle's SEQUENCE values using the new JDBC 3.0 method getGeneratedKeys(), which is now the preferred method to use if you need to retrieve automatically generated keys.

Caution The Oracle JDBC driver does not support access to automatically generated key values after an insert; that is, Oracle's driver does not implement Statement.getGeneratedKeys();. Instead, you have to use the Statement.executeQuery(); method as follows:

```
rs = stmt.executeQuery("select ANIMAL_ID_SEQ.currval from dual");
```

Viewing the Oracle Database Before Running the Solution

This is the Oracle database before running the solution:

```
SQL> select * from animals_table;

        ID   NAME
---------- ----------
         1   dog
         2   cat
         3   rabbit
```

Running the Solution for the Oracle Database

This shows how to run the solution for the Oracle database:

```
--GetGeneratedKeys begin--
conn=oracle.jdbc.driver.OracleConnection@18fb2f7
---------------
key 1 is 4
--GetGeneratedKeys end--
```

Viewing the Oracle Database After Running the Solution

This is the Oracle database after running the solution:

```
SQL> select * from animals_table;

        ID   NAME
---------- -----------
         1   dog
         2   cat
         3   rabbit
         4   duck
```

12-10. How Do You Check for a SQL Warning Using PreparedStatement?

SQLWarning is an exception that provides information about database access warnings. This section shows you how to use a PreparedStatement object to learn whether a SQL warning has occurred.

Some database operations (such as SQL's SELECT, INSERT, and UPDATE) can cause a warning that is not handled by an exception. You must explicitly check for these warnings. An example of a warning is a data truncation error during a read operation. You should check for a warning in three places: on a Connection object, a PreparedStatement object, and a ResultSet object. A SQL Warning (in JDBC defined by the java.sql.SQLWarning class) is an exception that provides information about database access warnings. Warnings are silently chained to the object whose method caused it to be reported.

The following example demonstrates how to check for a warning on a PreparedStatement object:

```
ResultSet rs = null;
Connection conn = null;
SQLWarning warning = null;
PreparedStatement pstmt = null;
try {
    conn = getConnection();  // get a Connection object

    // Create a PreparedStatement object
    String query = "select column1, column2 from table_x where column3 = ?";
    pstmt = conn.prepareStatement(query);
    pstmt.setString(1, "some-value");
    // Use the pstmt...such as selecting
    // some rows from a table
    rs = pstmt.executeQuery();

    // ...more JDBC operations

    // Get warnings on PreparedStatement object
    warning = pstmt.getWarnings();


        String message = warning.getMessage();
        String sqlState = warning.getSQLState();
        int errorCode = warning.getErrorCode();
        warning = warning.getNextWarning();
    }
}
catch (SQLException e) {
    // handle exception...
}
finally {
    // close JDBC/Database resources such as
    // ResultSet, ...
}
```

12-11. How Does PreparedStatement Support Scrollable ResultSets?

java.sql.PreparedStatement has two methods that support scrollable result sets. The signature of the PreparedStatement.prepareStatement() method that supports scrollability and updatability is as follows:

```
Signature:
    PreparedStatement prepareStatement(String sql,
                                int resultSetType,
                                int resultSetConcurrency)
                                throws SQLException
```

Description:
Creates a PreparedStatement object that will generate ResultSet
objects with the given type and concurrency. This method is the
same as the prepareStatement method above, but it allows the
default result set type and concurrency to be overridden.

Parameters:
sql - a String object that is the SQL statement to be sent to the
database; may contain one or more ? IN parameters

resultSetType - a result set type; one of
ResultSet.TYPE_FORWARD_ONLY,
ResultSet.TYPE_SCROLL_INSENSITIVE, or
ResultSet.TYPE_SCROLL_SENSITIVE

resultSetConcurrency - a concurrency type; one of
ResultSet.CONCUR_READ_ONLY or
ResultSet.CONCUR_UPDATABLE

Returns:
a new PreparedStatement object containing the pre-compiled
SQL statement that will produce ResultSet objects with the
given type and concurrency

Throws:
SQLException - if a database access error occurs or the

The signature of the PreparedStatement.prepareStatement() method that supports scrollability, updatability, and holdability is as follows:

Signature:
PreparedStatement prepareStatement(String sql,
                                   int resultSetType,
                                   int resultSetConcurrency,
                                   int resultSetHoldability)
                                   throws SQLException

Description:
Creates a PreparedStatement object that will generate ResultSet
objects with the given type, concurrency, and holdability. This
method is the same as the prepareStatement method above, but it
allows the default result set type, concurrency, and holdability
to be overridden.

Parameters:
sql - a String object that is the SQL statement to be sent to the
database; may contain one or more ? IN parameters

resultSetType - one of the following ResultSet constants:
ResultSet.TYPE_FORWARD_ONLY,
ResultSet.TYPE_SCROLL_INSENSITIVE, or
ResultSet.TYPE_SCROLL_SENSITIVE

resultSetConcurrency - one of the following ResultSet constants:
ResultSet.CONCUR_READ_ONLY or
ResultSet.CONCUR_UPDATABLE

```
resultSetHoldability - one of the following ResultSet constants:
        ResultSet.HOLD_CURSORS_OVER_COMMIT or
        ResultSet.CLOSE_CURSORS_AT_COMMIT
```

Returns:
        a new PreparedStatement object, containing the pre-compiled SQL
        statement, that will generate ResultSet objects with the given
        type, concurrency, and holdability

Throws:
        SQLException - if a database access error occurs or the given
        parameters are not ResultSet constants indicating type,
        concurrency, and holdability

12-12. What Are Updatability, Scrollability, and Holdability for ResultSet Objects?

The following sections define updatability, scrollability, and holdability in relation to ResultSet objects in JDBC applications.

How It Works

In most JDBC applications, using the ResultSet object, you move forward one row at a time (until you visit all of the rows returned). In addition to moving forward one row at a time through a ResultSet

- Go directly to a specific row
- Update rows of a ResultSet
- Delete rows of a ResultSet
- Leave the ResultSet open after a database commit operation

Defining Updatability, Scrollability, and Holdability

The following database terms describe the characteristics of a ResultSet object:

- *Scrollability*: Whether the cursor can move forward, can move backward, or can move to a specific row
- *Updatability*: Whether the cursor can be used to update or delete rows
- *Holdability*: Whether the cursor stays open after a database commit operation

The ResultSet type values are defined in the ResultSet interface as static integers:

- ResultSet.TYPE_FORWARD_ONLY: The constant indicating the type for a ResultSet object whose cursor may move only forward
- ResultSet.TYPE_SCROLL_INSENSITIVE: The constant indicating the type for a ResultSet object that is scrollable but generally not sensitive to changes made by others
- ResultSet.TYPE_SCROLL_SENSITIVE: The constant indicating the type for a ResultSet object that is scrollable and generally sensitive to changes made by others

The ResultSet concurrency values are defined in the ResultSet interface as static integers:

- ResultSet.CONCUR_READ_ONLY: The constant indicating the concurrency mode for a ResultSet object that may *not* be updated

- ResultSet.CONCUR_UPDATABLE: The constant indicating the concurrency mode for a ResultSet object that may be updated

The ResultSet holdability values are defined in the ResultSet interface as static integers. ResultSet holdability has two possible values: HOLD_CURSORS_OVER_COMMIT and CLOSE_CURSORS_AT_COMMIT. You can specify either of these values with any valid combination of ResultSet concurrency and ResultSet holdability. The value that you set overrides the default holdability for the connection.

- ResultSet.CLOSE_CURSORS_AT_COMMIT: The constant indicating that ResultSet objects should be closed when the method Connection.commit is called

- ResultSet.HOLD_CURSORS_OVER_COMMIT: The constant indicating that ResultSet objects should not be closed when the method Connection.commit is called

Table 12-4 lists the valid combinations of ResultSet type and ResultSet concurrency for scrollable ResultSet objects.

Table 12-4. *Valid Combinations of Scrollable* ResultSet *Type/Concurrency*

ResultSet Type Value	ResultSet Concurrency Value
TYPE_SCROLL_INSENSITIVE	CONCUR_READ_ONLY
TYPE_SCROLL_SENSITIVE	CONCUR_READ_ONLY
TYPE_SCROLL_SENSITIVE	CONCUR_UPDATABLE

12-13. How Do You Create a Scrollable and Updatable ResultSet Object?

The following sections show how to create a scrollable and updatable ResultSet using a PreparedStatement object.

How It Works

This is according to Sun's JDBC tutorial (http://java.sun.com/docs/books/tutorial/jdbc/jdbc2dot0/cursor.html):

> One of the new features in the JDBC 2.0 API is the ability to move a result set's cursor backward as well as forward. There are also methods that let you move the cursor to a particular row and check the position of the cursor. Scrollable result sets make it possible to create a GUI (graphical user interface) tool for browsing result sets, which will probably be one of the main uses for this feature. Another use is moving to a row in order to update it.

Table 12-5 lists the ResultSet methods for positioning a scrollable cursor, according to Sun.

Table 12-5. ResultSet *Methods for Scrolling*

Method	Positions the Cursor...
first()	On the first row of the ResultSet.
last()	On the last row of the ResultSet.
next()	On the next row of the ResultSet.
previous()	On the previous row of the ResultSet.
absolute(int n)	If n>0, on row n of the ResultSet. If n<0 and m is the number of rows in the ResultSet, on row m+n+1 of the ResultSet.
relative(int n)	If n>0, on the row that is n rows after the current row. If n<0, on the row that is n rows before the current row. If n=0, on the current row.
afterLast()	After the last row in the ResultSet.
beforeFirst()	Before the first row in the ResultSet.

Solution

The following code shows how to create a scrollable and updatable ResultSet object using PreparedStatement:

```
ResultSet rs = null;
Connection conn = null;
PreparedStatement pstmt = null;
String authorLastName = "Knuth";
try {

    ...
    // prepare SQL query
    String query = "select isbn from books_table where author = ?";

    // create a PreparedStatement object for
    // a scrollable, updatable ResultSet
    pstmt = conn.prepareStatement(query,
                          ResultSet.TYPE_SCROLL_SENSITIVE,
                          ResultSet.CONCUR_UPDATABLE);

    // fill in input parameters
    pstmt.setString(1, authorLastName);

    // execute query, and create the ResultSet
    rs = pstmt.executeQuery();

    // position the cursor at the end of the ResultSet
    rs.afterLast();

    // Position the cursor backward
    while (rs.previous()) {
        String bookISBN = rs.getString(1);
        System.out.println("bookISBN= " + bookISBN);
        // Look for isbn 1122334455
        if (bookISBN.equals("1122334455")) {
            updateBookTitle("1122334455","new title");
            updateTheRow();
        }
    }
}
```

```
    }
catch(SQLException e) {
    // handle the exception
    e.printStacktrace();
    ...
}
finally {
    // cleanup time
    // close ResultSet, Statement, and Connection objects
}
```

12-14. How Do You Create a Scrollable ResultSet Object?

The following sections show how to create a scrollable ResultSet using a PreparedStatement object.

How It Works

When you use Connection.prepareStatement(), it creates a PreparedStatement object, which can create result set objects that are scrollable. By passing some parameters, you can create scrollable result sets. A scrollable result set allows the cursor to be moved to any row in the result set. This capability is useful for GUI tools for browsing result sets.

Solution

The following example shows how to create an insensitive scrollable ResultSet:

```
Connection conn = null;
PreparedStatement pstmt = null;
try {
    conn = getConnection(); // get-a-connection-object
    // create a statement that creates
    // insensitive scrollable result set
    String query = "SELECT last_name FROM employee_table where first_name = ?";
    pstmt = conn.prepareStatement(
                    query,
                    ResultSet.TYPE_SCROLL_INSENSITIVE,
                    ResultSet.CONCUR_READ_ONLY);

    // fill in all input parameters
    pstmt.setString(1, "alex");

    // create a result set
    rs = pstmt.executeQuery();

    // iterate the ResultSet object and get all of the data
    while (rs.next()) {
        String lastName = rs.getString(1);
    }
}
catch (SQLException e) {
    // could not create a PreparedStatement object,
    // or other problems happened.
    // handle the exception
}
```

```
finally {
    // cleanup time
    // close Connection object
    // close PreparedStatement object
    // close ResultSet object
}
```

The following example shows how to create a sensitive scrollable ResultSet:

```
ResultSet rs = null;
Connection conn = null;
PreparedStatement pstmt = null;
try {
    conn = getConnection(); // get-a-connection-object
    // create a statement that creates
    // a sensitive scrollable result set
    String query = "SELECT last_name FROM employee_table where first_name = ?";
    pstmt = conn.prepareStatement(
                query,
                ResultSet.TYPE_SCROLL_SENSITIVE,
                ResultSet.CONCUR_READ_ONLY);

    // fill in all input parameters
    pstmt.setString(1, "alex");

    // create a result set
    rs = stmt.executeQuery();


    while (rs.next()) {
        String lastName = rs.getString(1);
    }
}
catch (SQLException e) {
    // could not create a PreparedStatement object,
    // or other problems happened.
    // handle the exception
}
finally {
    // cleanup time
    // close Connection object
    // close PreparedStatement object
    // close ResultSet object
}
```

Discussion

Before creating scrollable ResultSet objects, you need to determine whether your database supports them. A scrollable ResultSet allows the cursor to move to any row in the result set. Two types
of scrollable result sets exist. An *insensitive scrollable* result set is one where the values captured in
the result set never change, even if changes are made to the table from which the data was
retrieved. A *sensitive scrollable* result set is one where the current values in the table are reflected in
the result set. So, if a change is made to a row in the table, the result set will show the new data when
the cursor is moved to that row.

The following code can check whether your database supports scrollable ResultSet objects:

```
Connection conn = null;
try {
conn = getConnection(); // get-a-connection-object
    DatabaseMetaData dbmd = conn.getMetaData();
    if (dbmd == null) {
        //  database metadata NOT supported...
        // you should throw an exception or...stop here
    }

    if (dbmd.supportsResultSetType(ResultSet.TYPE_SCROLL_INSENSITIVE)) {
        // insensitive scrollable result sets are supported
    }

    if (dbmd.supportsResultSetType(ResultSet.TYPE_SCROLL_SENSITIVE)) {
        // Sensitive scrollable result sets are supported
    }

    if (!dbmd.supportsResultSetType(ResultSet.TYPE_SCROLL_INSENSITIVE)
        && !dbmd.supportsResultSetType(ResultSet.TYPE_SCROLL_SENSITIVE)) {
        // updatable result sets are not supported
    }
}
catch (SQLException e) {
    // handle the exception
}


    // close Connection object
    }
```

12-15. How Do You Create an Updatable ResultSet Object?

The following sections show how to create an updatable ResultSet using a PreparedStatement object.

How It Works

An updatable result set allows you to modify data in a table through the ResultSet object. If the database does not support updatable result sets, the result sets returned from executeQuery() will be read-only. To get updatable results, the PreparedStatement object used to create the result sets must have the concurrency type of ResultSet.CONCUR_UPDATABLE. The query of an updatable ResultSet must specify the primary key as one of the selected columns and select from only one table. For some drivers, the following query will return a read-only ResultSet:

```
SELECT * FROM  <table-name>
```

Therefore, make sure you specify the column names.

According to the J2SE documentation, you can use the ResultSet object's updater methods in two ways:

To update a column value in the current row: In a scrollable ResultSet object, the cursor can move backward and forward, to an absolute position, or to a position relative to the current row. The following code fragment updates the NAME column in the fifth row of the ResultSet object rs and then uses the method updateRow to update the data source table from which rs was derived.

```
rs.absolute(5); // moves the cursor to the fifth row of rs
rs.updateString("NAME", "AINSWORTH"); // updates the
    // NAME column of row 5 to be AINSWORTH
rs.updateRow(); // updates the row in the data source
```

To insert column values into the insert row: An updatable ResultSet object has a special row associated with it that serves as a staging area for building a row. The following code fragment moves the cursor to the insert row, builds a three-column row, and inserts it into rs and into the data source table using the method insertRow:

```
rs.moveToInsertRow(); // moves cursor to the insert row
rs.updateString(1, "AINSWORTH"); // updates the
    // first column of the insert row to be AINSWORTH
rs.updateInt(2,35); // updates the second column to be 35
rs.updateBoolean(3, true); // updates the third column to true
rs.insertRow();
rs.moveToCurrentRow();
```

Setting Up the MySQL Database

This shows how to set up the MySQL database:

```
mysql> use octopus;
Database changed
mysql> select * from employees;
+-----+--------------+------+
| id  | name         | age  |
+-----+--------------+------+
| 22  | Don Knuth    |  65  |
| 33  | Mary Kent    |  35  |
| 44  | Monica Seles |  30  |
| 777 | Donald Duck  | NULL |
| 99  | Alex Edison  | NULL |
+-----+--------------+------+
6 rows in set (0.00 sec)
```

Running the Solution for MySQL Database

This shows how to run the solution for the MySQL database:

```
$ javac DemoUpdatableResultSet.java
$ java DemoUpdatableResultSet mysql 20
--DemoUpdatableResultset begin--
conn=com.mysql.jdbc.Connection@1c6f579
ageLimit=20
--DemoUpdatableResultset end--
```

MySQL Database After Running the Solution

This shows the MySQL database after running the solution:

```
mysql> select * from employees;
```

```
+------+------------------+------+
| id   | name             | age  |
+------+------------------+------+
| 11   | Alex Smith       |   25 |
| 22   | NEW-NAME         |   65 |
| 33   | Mary Kent        |   35 |
| 44   | Monica Seles     |   30 |
| 5000 | NEW-NAME-IS-HERE |   99 |
| 777  | Donald Duck      | NULL |
| 99   | Alex Edison      | NULL |
+------+------------------+------+
7 rows in set (0.00 sec)
```

Setting Up the Oracle 10*g* Database

This shows how to set up the Oracle 10g database:

```
SQL> select * from employees;

ID          NAME                     AGE
----------  --------------------  ----------
777         Donald Duck
11          Alex Smith                25
22          Don Knuth                 65
33          Mary Kent                 35
44          Monica Seles              30
99          Alex Edison
```

Running the Solution for the Oracle 10*g* Database

This shows how to run the solution for the Oracle 10g database:

```
$ javac DemoUpdatableResultSet.java
$ java DemoUpdatableResultSet oracle 20
--DemoUpdatableResultset begin--
conn=oracle.jdbc.driver.T4CConnection@2ce908
ageLimit=20
--DemoUpdatableResultset end--
```

Viewing the Oracle 10*g* Database After Running the Solution

This shows the Oracle 10g database after running the solution:

```
SQL> select * from employees;

ID          NAME                     AGE
----------  --------------------  ----------
5000        NEW-NAME-IS-HERE          99
777         Donald Duck
11          Alex Smith                25
22          NEW-NAME                  65
33          Mary Kent                 35
44          Monica Seles              30
99          Alex Edison

7 rows selected.
```

Solution

The following code creates a PreparedStatement object that will return updatable ResultSet objects:

```java
import java.util.*;
import java.io.*;
import java.sql.*;

import jcb.db.VeryBasicConnectionManager;
import jcb.util.DatabaseUtil;

public class DemoUpdatableResultSet {
    public static void main(String[] args) {
        ResultSet rs = null;
        Connection conn = null;
        PreparedStatement pstmt = null;
        try {
            System.out.println("--DemoUpdatableResultset begin--");
            // read command line arguments
            String dbVendor = args[0]; // database vendor
            int ageLimit = Integer.parseInt(args[1]); // age limit

            conn = VeryBasicConnectionManager.getConnection(dbVendor);
            System.out.println("conn="+conn);
            System.out.println("ageLimit="+ageLimit);
            String query = "select id, name, age from employees where age > ?";


            pstmt = conn.prepareStatement(query,
                        ResultSet.TYPE_SCROLL_SENSITIVE,
                        ResultSet.CONCUR_UPDATABLE);
            pstmt.setInt(1, ageLimit);  // set input values
            rs = pstmt.executeQuery();  // create an updatable ResultSet

            //
            // update a column value in the current row.
            //
            // moves the cursor to the 2nd row of rs
            rs.absolute(2);
            // updates the NAME column of row 2 to be NEW-NAME
            rs.updateString("NAME", "NEW-NAME");
            // updates the row in the data source
            rs.updateRow();

            //
            // insert column values into the insert row.
            //
            rs.moveToInsertRow(); // moves cursor to the insert row
            rs.updateInt(1, 5000); // 1st column id=5000
            rs.updateString(2, "NEW-NAME-IS-HERE"); // updates the 2nd column
            rs.updateInt(3, 99); // updates the 3rd column to 99
            rs.insertRow();
            rs.moveToCurrentRow();

            System.out.println("--DemoUpdatableResultset end--");
        }
        catch(Exception e){
```

```
            e.printStackTrace();
            System.exit(1);
        }
        finally {
            // release database resources
            DatabaseUtil.close(rs);
            DatabaseUtil.close(pstmt);
            DatabaseUtil.close(conn);
        }
    }
}
```

Discussion

Before creating an updatable ResultSet object, you need to determine whether your database supports updatable ResultSet objects. An updatable ResultSet object allows you to modify data in a table through the result set.

You can use the following code to determine whether your database supports updatable ResultSet objects:

```
Connection conn = null;
try {
    conn = getConnection(); // get-a-connection-object
    DatabaseMetaData dbmd = conn.getMetaData();
    if (dbmd == null) {
        //  database metadata NOT supported...



    if (dbmd.supportsResultSetConcurrency(
            ResultSet.TYPE_FORWARD_ONLY,
            ResultSet.CONCUR_UPDATABLE)) {
        // Updatable result sets are supported
    }
    else {
        // Updatable result sets are not supported
    }
}
catch (SQLException e) {
    // handle the exception
}
finally {
    // cleanup time
    // close Connection object
}
```

12-16. How Do You Create a Table Using PreparedStatement?

The following sections show how to create a table using a PreparedStatement object.

How It Works

Although you can create a database table by using the PreparedStatement object, this is not recommended. Instead, you should use a Statement object to create a database table. (Using PreparedStatement objects are ideal if you are going to use the same object many times, not just once for creating a table.) To create a database table, you need to pass the table definition to the executeUpdate() method of a Statement object.

Solution

The following example creates a table called employee_table with two columns:

```
import jcb.util.DatabaseUtil;
...
Connection conn = null;
PreparedStatement pstmt = null;
try {
    conn = getConnection(); // get-a-valid-connection;

    // define your table: employee_table
    String tableDefinition = "CREATE TABLE employee_table" +
           " (badge_number VARCHAR(10), last_name VARCHAR(64))";
    pstmt = conn.prepareStatement(tableDefinition);
    pstmt.executeUpdate();
    // table creation was successful
}
catch (SQLException e) {
    // table creation failed.
    // handle the exception
}
finally {

    DatabaseUtil.close(conn);
}
```

12-17. How Do You Drop a Table Using PreparedStatement?

The following sections show how to drop a table using a PreparedStatement object.

How It Works

Even though you can drop a database table by using a PreparedStatement object (that is, delete a table's structure and contents), this is not recommended. Instead, you should use a Statement object to delete a database table. (Using PreparedStatement objects are ideal if you are going to use the same object many times—not just once for deleting a table.) To delete a database table, you need to pass the table name to the executeUpdate() method of a Statement object. You might ask, if I want to drop couple of tables, can I use the SQL query drop table and then pass the table name as a parameter (using a loop) to a PreparedStatement object? The answer is no. When you pass a parameter to a PreparedStatement object, it automatically surrounds it with a single quote, and the database server will not understand the SQL command:

```
drop table 'table-name'
```

In addition, it will complain that the table name table-name is not found.

Solution

The following example drops/deletes a given table:

```
import jcb.util.DatabaseUtil;
...
public static void deleteTable(Connection conn, String tableName)
    throws SQLException {
    if (conn == null) {
      return;
    }

    PreparedStatement pstmt = null;
    try {
       // create table definition called employee_table
       String tableDeletion = "DROP TABLE "+ tableName;
       pstmt = conn.prepareStatement(tableDeletion);
       pstmt.executeUpdate();
       // table deletion was successful
    }
    finally {
       // cleanup time
       DatabaseUtil.close(pstmt);
    }
}
```

12-18. How Do You Set the Number of Rows to Prefetch Using PreparedStatement?

How It Works

JDBC enables you to set the number of rows to prefetch when executing a SQL query. This is a way to control how many rows are returned. When a SQL query is executed, the number of rows of data that a driver physically copies from the database to the client is called the *fetch size*. If you are performance-tuning a particular query, you might be able to improve performance by adjusting the fetch size to better match the query.

You can set the fetch size on a PreparedStatement object, in which case all result sets created from that statement will use that fetch size. You can also set the fetch size on a result set at any time. In this case, the next time data needs to be fetched from the database, the driver will copy over as many rows as specified by the current fetch size.

Solution

The following example demonstrates how to set a fetch size using a PreparedStatement object:

```
ResultSet rs = null;
Connection conn = null;
PreparedStatement pstmt = null;
try {
    conn = getConnection(); // get-a-valid-connection;
    String query = "select id from my_table where id > ?";
    // Get the fetch size of a statement
    pstmt = conn.prepareStatement(query);
    pstmt.setInt(1, 1200);
    int fetchSize = pstmt.getFetchSize();
```

```
    // Set the fetch size on the statement
    pstmt.setFetchSize(200);

    // Create a result set
    rs = pstmt.executeQuery();

    // Change the fetch size on the result set
    rs.setFetchSize(400);
}
catch (SQLException e) {
    // handle the exception
    ...
}
finally {
    // cleanup time
    // close result set, statement, and Connection objects
}
```

12-19. How Do You Create a MySQL Table to Store Java Types Using PreparedStatement?

The following sections show how to create a MySQL table to store Java data types using a
PreparedStatement object.

time use of SQL statements.

Solution

The following example creates a MySQL table called mysql_all_types to store Java types:

```
import java.util.*;
import java.io.*;
import java.sql.*;

import jcb.util.DatabaseUtil;
import jcb.db.VeryBasicConnectionManager;

public class Demo_Create_Table_All_Types_MySQL {

    public static void main(String[] args) {
        String dbVendor = args[0]; // { "mysql", "oracle" }
        Connection conn = null;
        PreparedStatement pstmt = null;
        try {
            System.out.println("--Create_Table_All_Types_MySQL begin--");
            StringBuffer buffer = new StringBuffer();
            buffer.append("CREATE TABLE mysql_all_types(");
            //                    Column Name    MySQL Type           Java Type
            buffer.append("column_boolean        BOOL, ");         // boolean
            buffer.append("column_byte           TINYINT, ");      // byte
            buffer.append("column_short          SMALLINT, ");     // short
            allTypesTable.append("column_int     INTEGER, ");      // int
            buffer.append("column_long           BIGINT, ");       // long
```

```
                buffer.append("column_float          FLOAT, ");            // float
                buffer.append("column_double         DOUBLE PRECISION, ");  // double
                buffer.append("column_bigdecimal     DECIMAL(13,0), ");     // BigDecimal
                buffer.append("column_string         VARCHAR(254), ");      // String
                buffer.append("column_date           DATE, ");              // Date
                buffer.append("column_time           TIME, ");              // Time
                buffer.append("column_timestamp      TIMESTAMP, ");         // Timestamp
                buffer.append("column_clob1  TINYTEXT, ");    // Clob (< 2^8 bytes)
                buffer.append("column_clob2  TEXT, ");        // Clob (< 2^16 bytes)
                buffer.append("column_clob3  MEDIUMTEXT, ");  // Clob (< 2^24 bytes)
                buffer.append("column_clob4  LONGTEXT, ");    // Clob (< 2^32 bytes)
                buffer.append("column_blob1  TINYBLOB, ");    // Blob (< 2^8 bytes)
                buffer.append("column_blob2  BLOB, ");        // Blob (< 2^16 bytes)
                buffer.append("column_blob3  MEDIUMBLOB, ");  // Blob (< 2^24 bytes)
                buffer.append("column_blob4  LONGBLOB)");     // Blob (< 2^32 bytes)

                conn = VeryBasicConnectionManager.getConnection(dbVendor);
                pstmt = conn.prepareStatement(buffer.toString());
                pstmt.executeUpdate();
                // creation of table ok.
                System.out.println("Create_Table_All_Types_MySQL(): end");
            }
            catch (Exception e) {
                // creation of table failed.
                // handle the exception
                e.printStackTrace();


                DatabaseUtil.close(pstmt);
                DatabaseUtil.close(conn);
            }
        }
    }
}
```

Running the Solution for the MySQL Database

This shows how to run the solution for the MySQL database:

```
$ javac Create_Table_All_Types_MySQL.java
$ java Create_Table_All_Types_MySQL mysql
Create_Table_All_Types_MySQL(): begin
Create_Table_All_Types_MySQL(): end
```

Viewing the MySQL Database After Running the Solution

This shows the MySQL database after running the solution:

```
mysql> desc mysql_all_types;
```

Field	Type	Null	Key	Default	Extra
column_boolean	tinyint(1)	YES		NULL	
column_byte	tinyint(4)	YES		NULL	
column_short	smallint(6)	YES		NULL	
column_int	int(11)	YES		NULL	
column_long	bigint(20)	YES		NULL	
column_float	float	YES		NULL	
column_double	double	YES		NULL	

```
| column_bigdecimal | decimal(13,0) | YES |   | NULL |   |   |
| column_string     | varchar(254)  | YES |   | NULL |   |   |
| column_date       | date          | YES |   | NULL |   |   |
| column_time       | time          | YES |   | NULL |   |   |
| column_timestamp  | timestamp     | YES |   | NULL |   |   |
| column_clob1      | tinytext      | YES |   | NULL |   |   |
| column_clob2      | text          | YES |   | NULL |   |   |
| column_clob3      | mediumtext    | YES |   | NULL |   |   |
| column_clob4      | longtext      | YES |   | NULL |   |   |
| column_blob1      | tinyblob      | YES |   | NULL |   |   |
| column_blob2      | blob          | YES |   | NULL |   |   |
| column_blob3      | mediumblob    | YES |   | NULL |   |   |
| column_blob4      | longblob      | YES |   | NULL |   |   |
+-------------------+---------------+-----+-----+--------+-------+
20 rows in set (0.13 sec)
```

12-20. How Do You Create an Oracle Table to Store Java Types Using PreparedStatement?

The following sections show how to create an Oracle table to store Java data types using a PreparedStatement object.

How It Works

In general, you should use a Statement object instead of a PreparedStatement object for the one-

Solution

The following example creates an Oracle table called oracle_all_types to store Java types:

```java
import java.util.*;
import java.io.*;
import java.sql.*;

import jcb.util.DatabaseUtil;
import jcb.db.VeryBasicConnectionManager;

public class Demo_Create_Table_All_Types_Oracle {

    public static void main(String[] args) {
        String dbVendor = args[0]; // { "mysql", "oracle" }
        Connection conn = null;
        PreparedStatement pstmt = null;
        try {
            System.out.println("--Create_Table_All_Types_Oracle begin--");
            conn = VeryBasicConnectionManager.getConnection(dbVendor);

            // create an varray type
            pstmt = conn.prepareStatement("CREATE TYPE varray_type is " +
                        "VARRAY(5) OF VARCHAR(10)");
            pstmt.executeUpdate();

            // create an OBJECT type
            pstmt = conn.prepareStatement("CREATE TYPE oracle_object is " +
                "OBJECT(column_string VARCHAR(128), column_integer INTEGER)");
            pstmt.executeUpdate();
```

```
        StringBuffer buffer = new StringBuffer();
        buffer.append("CREATE TABLE oracle_all_types(");
        //              Column Name          Oracle Type            Java Type
        buffer.append("column_short          SMALLINT, ");          // short
        buffer.append("column_int            INTEGER, ");           // int
        buffer.append("column_float          REAL, ");              // float
        buffer.append("column_double         DOUBLE PRECISION, ");  // double
        buffer.append("column_bigdecimal  DECIMAL(13,0), ");        // BigDecimal
        buffer.append("column_string   VARCHAR2(254), ");       // String
        buffer.append("column_characterstream LONG, ");         // CharacterStream
        buffer.append("column_bytes            RAW(2000), ");   // byte[];
        buffer.append("column_binarystream     RAW(2000), ");   // BinaryStream
        buffer.append("column_timestamp        DATE, ");        // Timestamp
        buffer.append("column_clob             CLOB, ");        // Clob
        buffer.append("column_blob             BLOB, ");         // Blob or BFILE
        buffer.append("column_bfile            BFILE, ");     // oracle.sql.BFILE
        buffer.append("column_array      varray_type, ");     // oracle.sql.ARRAY
        buffer.append("column_object    oracle_object)");     // oracle.sql.OBJECT
        pstmt.executeUpdate(buffer.toString());
        // when you are at this point, creation of table ok.
        System.out.println("Create_Table_All_Types_Oracle(): end");
    }
    catch (Exception e) {
        // creation of table failed.
        // handle the exception
        e.printStackTrace();


        DatabaseUtil.close(pstmt);
        DatabaseUtil.close(conn);
    }
  }
}
```

Running Solution for the Oracle Database

This shows how to run the solution for the Oracle database:

```
$ javac Create_Table_All_Types_Oracle.java
$ java Create_Table_All_Types_Oracle oracle
Create_Table_All_Types_Oracle(): begin
Create_Table_All_Types_Oracle(): end
```

Viewing the Oracle Database After Running the Solution

This shows the Oracle database after running the solution:

```
SQL> desc varray_type;
 varray_type VARRAY(5) OF VARCHAR2(10)

SQL> desc oracle_object;
 Name                             Null?   Type
 -------------------------------- ------- -------------
 COLUMN_STRING                            VARCHAR2(128)
 COLUMN_INTEGER                           NUMBER(38)
```

```
SQL> desc oracle_all_types;
 Name                            Null?    Type
 -------------------------------- -------- ----------------
 COLUMN_SHORT                              NUMBER(38)
 COLUMN_INT                                NUMBER(38)
 COLUMN_FLOAT                              FLOAT(63)
 COLUMN_DOUBLE                             FLOAT(126)
 COLUMN_BIGDECIMAL                         NUMBER(13)
 COLUMN_STRING                             VARCHAR2(254)
 COLUMN_CHARACTERSTREAM                    LONG
 COLUMN_BYTES                              RAW(2000)
 COLUMN_BINARYSTREAM                       RAW(2000)
 COLUMN_TIMESTAMP                          DATE
 COLUMN_CLOB                               CLOB
 COLUMN_BLOB                               BLOB
 COLUMN_BFILE                              BINARY FILE LOB
 COLUMN_ARRAY                              VARRAY_TYPE
 COLUMN_OBJECT                             ORACLE_OBJECT
```

12-21. How Do You Get Rows/Records from a Table Using PreparedStatement?

The following sections show how to retrieve selected rows/records from a table using a PreparedStatement object.

The following example creates a PreparedStatement object to retrieve selected records from the dept table. A SQL SELECT query gets data from a table. The result of the SELECT query is called a *result set*. This example executes a SQL SELECT query using PreparedStatement.executeQuery() and creates a ResultSet object. (Once a ResultSet object is created, then you can iterate on it by using the ResultSet.next() method.)

Solution

Here's the solution:

```
import java.util.*;
import java.io.*;
import java.sql.*;

import jcb.util.DatabaseUtil;
import jcb.db.VeryBasicConnectionManager;

public class Select_Records_Using_PreparedStatement {

    public static void main(String[] args) {
        String dbVendor = args[0]; // { "mysql", "oracle" }
        int deptNumber = Integer.parseInt(args[1]);

        ResultSet rs = null;
        Connection conn = null;
        PreparedStatement pstmt = null;
        try {
            System.out.println("--Select_Records_... begin--");
```

```
            conn = VeryBasicConnectionManager.getConnection(dbVendor);
            System.out.println("conn="+conn);
            System.out.println("deptNumber="+ deptNumber);
            System.out.println("---------------");

            // prepare query
            String query = "select DEPT_NUM, DEPT_NAME, DEPT_LOC " +
                    "from DEPT where DEPT_NUM > ?";

            pstmt = conn.prepareStatement(query); // create a statement
            pstmt.setInt(1, deptNumber); // set input parameter
            // execute query and return result as a ResultSet
            rs = pstmt.executeQuery();

            // extract data from the ResultSet
            while (rs.next()) {
                int dbDeptNumber = rs.getInt(1);
                String dbDeptName = rs.getString(2);
                String dbDeptLocation = rs.getString(3);
                System.out.println(dbDeptNumber +"\t"+ dbDeptName +
                    "\t"+ dbDeptLocation);
            }
            System.out.println("---------------");
            System.out.println("--Select_Records_... end--");
        }
        catch(Exception e){


        }
        finally {
            // release database resources
            DatabaseUtil.close(rs);
            DatabaseUtil.close(pstmt);
            DatabaseUtil.close(conn);
        }
    }
}
```

Setting Up the Oracle Database

This shows how to set up the Oracle database:

```
SQL> desc dept;
 Name                   Null?      Type
 -------------------    --------   --------------
 DEPT_NUM               NOT NULL   NUMBER(2)
 DEPT_NAME                         VARCHAR2(14)
 DEPT_LOC                          VARCHAR2(13)

SQL> select * from dept;

 DEPT_NUM   DEPT_NAME       DEPT_LOC
 ---------- --------------  ---------
       10   ACCOUNTING      NEW YORK
       20   RESEARCH        DALLAS
       30   SALES           CHICAGO
       40   OPERATIONS      BOSTON
```

```
SQL> select DEPT_NUM, DEPT_NAME, DEPT_LOC from dept where DEPT_NUM > 20;

  DEPT_NUM  DEPT_NAME        DEPT_LOC
---------- --------------- ----------
        30  SALES            CHICAGO
        40  OPERATIONS       BOSTON
```

Running the Solution for the Oracle Database

This shows how to run the solution for the Oracle database:

```
$ javac Select_Records_Using_PreparedStatement.java
$ java Select_Records_Using_PreparedStatement oracle 10
--Select_Records_... begin--
conn=oracle.jdbc.driver.OracleConnection@edc3a2
deptNumber=10
----------------
20       RESEARCH        DALLAS
30       SALES           CHICAGO
40       OPERATIONS      BOSTON
----------------
--Select_Records_... end--

$ java Select_Records_Using_PreparedStatement oracle 20
--Select_Records_... begin--
conn=oracle.jdbc.driver.OracleConnection@edc3a2


30       SALES           CHICAGO
40       OPERATIONS      BOSTON
----------------
--Select_Records_... end--
```

Setting Up the MySQL Database

This shows how to set up the MySQL database:

```
mysql> desc dept;
+-----------+-------------+------+-----+---------+-------+
| Field     | Type        | Null | Key | Default | Extra |
+-----------+-------------+------+-----+---------+-------+
| dept_num  | int(11)     |      | PRI | 0       |       |
| dept_name | varchar(14) | YES  |     | NULL    |       |
| dept_loc  | varchar(14) | YES  |     | NULL    |       |
+-----------+-------------+------+-----+---------+-------+
3 rows in set (0.00 sec)

mysql> select * from dept;
+----------+------------+----------+
| dept_num | dept_name  | dept_loc |
+----------+------------+----------+
|       10 | Accounting | New York |
|       20 | Research   | Dallas   |
|       30 | Sales      | Chicago  |
|       40 | Operations | Boston   |
+----------+------------+----------+
4 rows in set (0.00 sec)
```

Running the Solution for the MySQL Database

This shows how to run the solution for the MySQL database:

```
$ javac Select_Records_Using_PreparedStatement.java
$ java Select_Records_Using_PreparedStatement mysql 10
--Select_Records_... begin--
conn=com.mysql.jdbc.Connection@8fce95
deptNumber=10
---------------
20      Research        Dallas
30      Sales           Chicago
40      Operations      Boston
---------------
--Select_Records_... end--
$ java Select_Records_Using_PreparedStatement mysql 20
--Select_Records_... begin--
conn=com.mysql.jdbc.Connection@8fce95
deptNumber=10
---------------
30      Sales           Chicago
40      Operations      Boston
---------------
--Select_Records_... end--
```

12-22. What Are the Steps for Inserting a New Record Using Pre-

The following sections show the specific steps for inserting a new record into an existing table using a PreparedStatement object.

How It Works

To insert/add new rows/records into a database table, you need to prepare a SQL INSERT statement. If you have a SQL INSERT statement that needs to be executed many times but with different values, you can use a PreparedStatement object to improve performance. (Also, you can use the same PreparedStatement object to insert any number of records.) A PreparedStatement object is a pre-compiled SQL statement, and using it saves the database from repeatedly having to compile the SQL statement each time it is executed. A SQL query (such as INSERT or SELECT) in a PreparedStatement contains placeholders (represented by the ? character) instead of explicit values. You set values for these placeholders and then execute them by invoking the PreparedStatement.executeUpdate() method.

The following steps are required for inserting a new row/record into an existing database table:

- Step 1: Creating a PreparedStatement object
- Step 2: Supplying values for PreparedStatement parameters
- Step 3: Executing the PreparedStatement object

Step 1: Creating a PreparedStatement Object

You create PreparedStatement objects with a Connection object. You might write code such as the following to create a PreparedStatement object that takes two input parameters:

```
java.sql.Connection conn = null;
java.sql.PreparedStatement pstmt = null;
```

```
try {
    // get a database connection
    conn = getConnection();

    // prepare your SQL insert query
    String insertStatement =
        "insert into my_table(id, name) values(?, ?)";

    // create PreparedStatement object
    pstmt = conn.prepareStatement(insertStatement);

    // at this point your PreparedStatement object is ready
    // to be used for inserting records into my_table.

    // insert new records...
}
catch(Exception e) {
    // could not create a PreparedStatement object
    // handle the exception
}
finally {
    // cleanup time
// close prepared statement and Connection objects
}
```

into my_table(id, name) values(?, ?), which has been sent to the DBMS and precompiled. Before you can insert records into the database table (in this case my_table), you need to supply values to be used in place of the question mark placeholders, if there are any, before you can execute a PreparedStatement object. You do this by calling one of the PreparedStatement.setXXX() methods (XXX refers to the data type of columns for a given table). If the value you want to substitute for a question mark is a Java int, you call the method setInt(columnsPosition, integerValue). If the value you want to substitute for a question mark is a Java String, you call the method setString(columnsPosition, columnsStringValue), and so on. The PreparedStatement interface provides a setXXX() method for each type in the Java programming language.

The following example shows the revised code that supplies values for placeholders. This shows how to prepare the table my_table:

```
mysql> create table my_table(id int, name varchar(20));
Query OK, 0 rows affected (0.02 sec)
mysql> desc my_table;
+-------+-------------+------+-----+---------+-------+
| Field | Type        | Null | Key | Default | Extra |
+-------+-------------+------+-----+---------+-------+
| id    | int(11)     | YES  |     | NULL    |       |
| name  | varchar(20) | YES  |     | NULL    |       |
+-------+-------------+------+-----+---------+-------+
2 rows in set (0.00 sec)

mysql> insert into my_table(id, name) values(100, 'alex');
mysql> insert into my_table(id, name) values(200, 'mary');
mysql> commit;
mysql> select * from my_table;
```

```
+------+------+
| id   | name |
+------+------+
|  100 | alex |
|  200 | mary |
+------+------+
2 rows in set (0.00 sec)
```

Using the PreparedStatement object pstmt from the previous example, the following code sets the first question mark placeholder to a Java int with a value of 300 and the second question mark placeholder to a Java String with value of "joe":

```
pstmt.setInt(1, 300);
pstmt.setString(2, "joe");
```

After you have set these values for the two input parameters, the SQL statement in pstmt will be equivalent to the SQL statement in the String object insertStatement that was used in the previous update example. Therefore, the next code fragment:

```
String insertStatement = "insert into my_table(id, name) values(300, 'joe')";
pstmt = conn.prepareStatement(insertStatement);
pstmt.executeUpdate();
```

accomplishes the same thing as the following one (note that the method PreparedStatement. executeUpdate() executes the PreparedStatement pstmt object):

```
String insertStatement = "insert into my_table(id, name) values(?, ?)";
pstmt = conn.prepareStatement(insertStatement);
```

Step 3: Executing the PreparedStatement Object

If your SQL statement is SELECT, then you use executeQuery(), which returns a ResultSet object. However, if your SQL statement is INSERT, UPDATE, or DELETE, then you use executeUpdate(), which returns an integer. (This number indicates how many rows were affected by your update statement.)

12-23. How Do You Insert a New Record into a Table Using PreparedStatement?

The following sections show how to insert a new record into an existing table using a PreparedStatement object.

How It Works

The following example creates a PreparedStatement object to insert a new record into the dept table. You can use a SQL INSERT statement to insert a new record into an existing dept table.

Solution

Here's the solution:

```
import java.util.*;
import java.io.*;
import java.sql.*;
```

```java
import jcb.util.DatabaseUtil;
import jcb.db.VeryBasicConnectionManager;

public class Insert_Records_Using_PreparedStatement {

    public static void main(String[] args) {
        String dbVendor = args[0]; // { "mysql", "oracle" }
        int deptNumber = Integer.parseInt(args[1]);
        String deptName = args[2];
        String deptLocation = args[3];

        Connection conn = null;
        PreparedStatement pstmt = null;
        try {
            System.out.println("--Insert_Records_... begin--");
            conn = VeryBasicConnectionManager.getConnection(dbVendor);
            System.out.println("conn="+conn);
            System.out.println("deptNumber= "+ deptNumber);
            System.out.println("deptName= "+ deptName);
            System.out.println("deptLocation= "+ deptLocation);

            // prepare query
            String query = "insert into dept(DEPT_NUM, DEPT_NAME, DEPT_LOC) " +
                    "values(?, ?, ?)";

            pstmt = conn.prepareStatement(query); // create a statement


            pstmt.setString(3, deptLocation);     // set input parameter 3
            pstmt.executeUpdate();                // execute insert statement
            System.out.println("--Insert_Records_... end--");
        }
        catch(Exception e){
            e.printStackTrace();
            System.exit(1);
        }
        finally {
            // release database resources
            DatabaseUtil.close(pstmt);
            DatabaseUtil.close(conn);
        }
    }
}
```

Setting Up the Oracle Database

This shows how to set up the Oracle database:

```
SQL> desc dept;
 Name                 Null?    Type
 -------------------- -------- --------------
 DEPT_NUM             NOT NULL NUMBER(2)
 DEPT_NAME                     VARCHAR2(14)
 DEPT_LOC                      VARCHAR2(13)

SQL> select * from dept;
```

```
DEPT_NUM  DEPT_NAME        DEPT_LOC
--------- --------------   ---------
       10  ACCOUNTING       NEW YORK
       20  RESEARCH         DALLAS
       30  SALES            CHICAGO
       40  OPERATIONS       BOSTON
```

Running the Solution for the Oracle Database

This shows how to run the solution for the Oracle database:

```
$ javac Insert_Records_Using_PreparedStatement.java
$ java Insert_Records_Using_PreparedStatement oracle 60 Marketing "Los Gatos"
--Insert_Records_... begin--
conn=oracle.jdbc.driver.OracleConnection@edc3a2
deptNumber= 60
deptName= Marketing
deptLocation= Los Gatos
--Insert_Records_... end--

$ java Insert_Records_Using_PreparedStatement oracle 70 Sports Cupertino
--Insert_Records_... begin--
conn=oracle.jdbc.driver.OracleConnection@edc3a2
deptNumber= 70
deptName= Sports
deptLocation= Cupertino
```

Viewing the Oracle Database After Running the Solution

This shows the Oracle database after running the solution:

```
SQL> select * from dept;

DEPT_NUM  DEPT_NAME        DEPT_LOC
--------- --------------   ---------
       10  ACCOUNTING       NEW YORK
       20  RESEARCH         DALLAS
       30  SALES            CHICAGO
       40  OPERATIONS       BOSTON
       60  Marketing        Los Gatos
       70  Sports           Cupertino
```

Setting Up the MySQL Database

This shows how to set up the MySQL database:

```
mysql> desc dept;
+-----------+-------------+------+-----+---------+-------+
| Field     | Type        | Null | Key | Default | Extra |
+-----------+-------------+------+-----+---------+-------+
| dept_num  | int(11)     |      | PRI | 0       |       |
| dept_name | varchar(14) | YES  |     | NULL    |       |
| dept_loc  | varchar(14) | YES  |     | NULL    |       |
+-----------+-------------+------+-----+---------+-------+
3 rows in set (0.00 sec)
```

```
mysql> select * from dept;
+----------+------------+----------+
| dept_num | dept_name  | dept_loc |
+----------+------------+----------+
|       10 | Accounting | New York |
|       20 | Research   | Dallas   |
|       30 | Sales      | Chicago  |
|       40 | Operations | Boston   |
+----------+------------+----------+
4 rows in set (0.00 sec)
```

Running the Solution for the MySQL Database

This shows how to run the solution for the MySQL database:

```
$ javac Insert_Records_Using_PreparedStatement.java
$ java Insert_Records_Using_PreparedStatement mysql 60 Marketing "Los Gatos"
--Select_Records_... begin--
conn=com.mysql.jdbc.Connection@8fce99
deptNumber= 60
deptName= Marketing
deptLocation= Los Gatos
--Select_Records_... end--

$ java Insert_Records_Using_PreparedStatement mysql 70 Sports Cupertino
--Select_Records_... begin--


deptName= Sports
deptLocation= Cupertino
```

12-23. How Do You Update an Existing Record Using Prepared-Statement?

The following sections show how to update an existing record of a table using a PreparedStatement object.

How It Works

The following example creates a PreparedStatement object to update an existing record of the dept table (this program updates department locations for a given department number). The example uses a SQL UPDATE statement to update data for a table.

Solution

Here's the solution:

```java
import java.util.*;
import java.io.*;
import java.sql.*;

import jcb.util.DatabaseUtil;
import jcb.db.VeryBasicConnectionManager;

public class Update_Records_Using_PreparedStatement {
```

```java
    public static void main(String[] args) {
        String dbVendor = args[0]; // { "mysql", "oracle" }
        int deptNumber = Integer.parseInt(args[1]);
        String deptLocation = args[2];

        Connection conn = null;
        PreparedStatement pstmt = null;
        try {
            System.out.println("--Update_Records_... begin--");
            conn = VeryBasicConnectionManager.getConnection(dbVendor);
            System.out.println("conn="+conn);
            System.out.println("deptNumber= "+ deptNumber);
            System.out.println("deptLocation= "+ deptLocation);

            // prepare query
            String query = "update dept set DEPT_LOC = ? where DEPT_NUM = ? ";
            pstmt = conn.prepareStatement(query); // create a statement
            pstmt.setString(1, deptLocation);    // set input parameter 1
            pstmt.setInt(2, deptNumber);         // set input parameter 2
            pstmt.executeUpdate();               // execute update statement
            System.out.println("--Update_Records_... end--");
        }
        catch(Exception e){
            e.printStackTrace();
            System.exit(1);
        }


        DatabaseUtil.close(pstmt);
        DatabaseUtil.close(conn);
        }
    }
}
```

Setting Up the Oracle Database

This shows how to set up the Oracle database:

```
SQL> select * from dept;
```

DEPT_NUM	DEPT_NAME	DEPT_LOC
10	ACCOUNTING	NEW YORK
20	RESEARCH	DALLAS
30	SALES	CHICAGO
40	OPERATIONS	BOSTON

Running the Solution for the Oracle Database

This shows how to run the solution for the Oracle database:

```
$ javac Update_Records_Using_PreparedStatement.java
$ java Insert_Records_Using_PreparedStatement oracle 30 "Los Angeles"
--Update_Records_... begin--
conn=oracle.jdbc.driver.OracleConnection@edc3a2
deptNumber= 40
deptLocation= Los Angeles
--Update_Records_... end--
```

```
$ java Update_Records_Using_PreparedStatement oracle 40 Saratoga
--Select_Records_... begin--
conn=oracle.jdbc.driver.OracleConnection@edc3a2
deptNumber= 40
deptLocation= Saratoga
--Update_Records_... end--
```

Viewing the Oracle Database After Running the Solution

This shows the Oracle database after running the solution:

```
SQL> select * from dept;

  DEPT_NUM  DEPT_NAME        DEPT_LOC
  --------- ---------------  ---------
        10  ACCOUNTING       NEW YORK
        20  RESEARCH         DALLAS
        30  SALES            Los Angeles
        40  OPERATIONS       Saratoga
```

Setting Up the MySQL Database

This shows how to set up the MySQL database:

```
mysql> select * from dept;
+----------+------------+----------+
| dept_num | dept_name  | dept_loc |
+----------+------------+----------+

|       20 | Research   | Dallas   |
|       30 | Sales      | Chicago  |
|       40 | Operations | Boston   |
+----------+------------+----------+
4 rows in set (0.00 sec)
```

Running the Solution for the MySQL Database

This shows how to run the solution for the MySQL database:

```
$ javac Update_Records_Using_PreparedStatement.java
$ java Insert_Records_Using_PreparedStatement mysql 30 "Los Angeles"
--Update_Records_... begin--
conn=com.mysql.jdbc.Connection@8fce99
deptNumber= 40
deptLocation= Los Angeles
--Update_Records_... end--

$ java Update_Records_Using_PreparedStatement mysql 40 Saratoga
--Select_Records_... begin--
conn=com.mysql.jdbc.Connection@8fce99
deptNumber= 40
deptLocation= Saratoga
--Update_Records_... end--
```

Viewing the MySQL Database After Running the Solution

This shows the MySQL database after running the solution:

```
mysql> select * from dept;
+----------+-------------+-------------+
| dept_num | dept_name   | dept_loc    |
+----------+-------------+-------------+
|       10 | Accounting  | New York    |
|       20 | Research    | Dallas      |
|       30 | Sales       | Los Angeles |
|       40 | Operations  | Saratoga    |
+----------+-------------+-------------+
4 rows in set (0.00 sec)
```

12-24. How Do You Delete All Rows from a Table Using PreparedStatement?

The following sections show how to delete all existing records of a table (that is, how to delete all of a table's data but not the table's structure) using a PreparedStatement object.

How It Works

The following example creates a PreparedStatement object to delete all rows from a database table (called the dept table). The example uses a SQL DELETE query (DELETE FROM my_dept) to delete all rows from the

<table-name> statement. In the MySQL and Oracle databases, you can use an alternative command to delete all rows from a table:

```
TRUNCATE TABLE <table-name>
```

This is according to Oracle 9*i* SQL Reference, Release 2:

> Use the TRUNCATE statement to remove all rows from a table or cluster. By default, Oracle
> also deallocates all space used by the removed rows except that specified by the MINEXTENTS
> storage parameter and sets the NEXT storage parameter to the size of the last extent removed
> from the segment by the truncation process. Removing rows with the TRUNCATE statement
> can be more efficient than dropping and re-creating a table. Dropping and re-creating a table
> invalidates the table's dependent objects, requires you to regrant object privileges on the
> table, and requires you to re-create the table's indexes, integrity constraints, and triggers and
> respecify its storage parameters. Truncating has none of these effects. You cannot roll back
> a TRUNCATE statement.

Solution

Here's the solution:

```
import java.util.*;
import java.io.*;
import java.sql.*;
```

```java
import jcb.util.DatabaseUtil;
import jcb.db.VeryBasicConnectionManager;

public class Delete_Records_Using_PreparedStatement {

    public static void main(String[] args) {
        String dbVendor = args[0]; // { "mysql", "oracle" }
        String tableName = args[1]; // table to be deleted
        Connection conn = null;
        PreparedStatement pstmt = null;
        try {
            System.out.println("--Delete_Records_... begin--");
            conn = VeryBasicConnectionManager.getConnection(dbVendor);
            System.out.println("conn="+conn);

            // prepare query
            String query = "delete from" + tableName;
            pstmt = conn.prepareStatement(query); // create a statement
            pstmt.executeUpdate();                 // execute delete statement
            System.out.println("--Delete_Records_... end--");
        }
        catch(Exception e){
            e.printStackTrace();
            System.exit(1);
        }
        finally {

            DatabaseUtil.close(conn);
        }
    }
}
```

Setting Up the Oracle Database

This shows how to set up the Oracle database:

```
SQL> select * from dept;

  DEPT_NUM  DEPT_NAME       DEPT_LOC
---------- --------------- ---------
        10  ACCOUNTING      NEW YORK
        20  RESEARCH        DALLAS
        30  SALES           CHICAGO
        40  OPERATIONS      BOSTON
```

Running the Solution for the Oracle Database

This shows how to run the solution for the Oracle database:

```
$ javac Delete_Records_Using_PreparedStatement.java
$ java Delete_Records_Using_PreparedStatement oracle dept
--Delete_Records_... begin--
conn=oracle.jdbc.driver.OracleConnection@edc3a2
--Delete_Records_... end--
```

Viewing the Oracle Database After Running the Solution

This shows the Oracle database after running the solution:

```
SQL> select * from dept;
no rows selected
```

Setting Up the MySQL Database

This shows how to set up the MySQL database:

```
mysql> select * from dept;
+----------+------------+----------+
| dept_num | dept_name  | dept_loc |
+----------+------------+----------+
|       10 | Accounting | New York |
|       20 | Research   | Dallas   |
|       30 | Sales      | Chicago  |
|       40 | Operations | Boston   |
+----------+------------+----------+
4 rows in set (0.00 sec)
```

Running the Solution for the MySQL Database

This shows how to run the solution for the MySQL database:

```
$ javac Delete_Records_Using_PreparedStatement.java


--Delete_Records_... end--
```

Viewing the MySQL Database After Running the Solution

This shows the MySQL database after running the solution:

```
mysql> select * from dept;
Empty set (0.00 sec)
```

12-25. How Do You Get the Number of Rows for a Table Using PreparedStatement?

The following sections show how to get the total number of records for an existing table using a PreparedStatement object.

How It Works

To get the number of rows/records for a database table, you should use the Statement object rather than a PreparedStatement object. (For queries that will be executed more than once with different arguments, PreparedStatement can work better.) However, this solution uses the PreparedStatement object.

The following example gets the number of rows in a table using the SQL statement SELECT COUNT(*). In the MySQL and Oracle databases, you can use the following SQL statement to get the number of rows/records in a database table:

```
SELECT COUNT(*) from <table-name>
```

Solution

Here's the solution:

```java
import java.util.*;
import java.io.*;
import java.sql.*;

import jcb.util.DatabaseUtil;
import jcb.db.VeryBasicConnectionManager;

public class Count_Records_Using_PreparedStatement {

    public static void main(String[] args) {
        String dbVendor = args[0];  // { "mysql", "oracle" }
        String tableName = args[1]; // table to be counted

        ResultSet rs = null;
        Connection conn = null;
        PreparedStatement pstmt = null;
        try {
            System.out.println("--Count_Records_... begin--");
            conn = VeryBasicConnectionManager.getConnection(dbVendor);
            System.out.println("conn="+conn);

            // prepare query
            String query = "select count(*) from " + tableName;


            // get the number of rows from result set
            if (rs.next()) {
                int numberOfRows = rs.getInt(1);
                System.out.println("numberOfRows= "+numberOfRows);
            }
            else {
                System.out.println("error: could not get the record counts");
                System.exit(1);
            }

            System.out.println("--Count_Records_... end--");
        }
        catch(Exception e){
            e.printStackTrace();
            System.exit(1);
        }
        finally {
            // release database resources
            DatabaseUtil.close(rs);
            DatabaseUtil.close(pstmt);
            DatabaseUtil.close(conn);
        }
    }
}
```

Setting Up the Oracle Database

This shows how to set up the Oracle database:

```
SQL> select count(*) from dept;
  COUNT(*)
----------
        6

SQL> select count(*) from emp;
  COUNT(*)
----------
       14
```

Running the Solution for the Oracle Database

This shows how to run the solution for the Oracle database:

```
$ javac Count_Records_Using_PreparedStatement.java
$ java Count_Records_Using_PreparedStatement oracle dept
--Count_Records_... begin--
conn=oracle.jdbc.driver.OracleConnection@edc3a2
numOfRecords=6
--Count_Records_... end--
$ java Count_Records_Using_PreparedStatement oracle emp
--Count_Records_... begin--
conn=oracle.jdbc.driver.OracleConnection@edc3a2
```

Viewing the Oracle Database After Running the Solution

There are no changes in the Oracle database after running the solution.

Setting Up the MySQL Database

This shows how to set up the MySQL database:

```
mysql> select count(*) from dsns;
+----------+
| count(*) |
+----------+
|       30 |
+----------+
1 row in set (0.00 sec)

mysql> select count(*) from connectors;
+----------+
| count(*) |
+----------+
|        7 |
+----------+
1 row in set (0.00 sec)
```

Running the Solution for the MySQL Database

This shows how to run the solution for the MySQL database:

```
$ javac Count_Records_Using_PreparedStatement.java
$ java Count_Records_Using_PreparedStatement mysql dsns
--Count_Records_... begin--
conn=com.mysql.jdbc.Connection@8fce76
numOfRecords=30
--Count_Records_... end--
$ java Count_Records_Using_PreparedStatement mysql connectors
--Count_Records_... begin--
conn=com.mysql.jdbc.Connection@8fce76
numOfRecords=7
--Count_Records_... end--
```

Viewing the MySQL Database After Running the Solution

There are no changes in the MySQL database after running the solution.

12-26. What Is the Caching of PreparedStatement Objects?

In general, caching PreparedStatement objects improves the performance of database applications. The following sections show how to cache PreparedStatement objects.

How It Works

PreparedStatement object over a range of input data, then you have cached your PreparedStatement object. The next two examples show how to use PreparedStatement with and without a cache.

Using PreparedStatement Without Caching

In this example, a PreparedStatement object is created for every iteration of the loop. JDBC will create 100 PreparedStatement objects.

```
Connection conn = getConnection();
...
for(int num = 0; num < 100; num++) {
    PreparedStatement ps =
        conn.prepareStatement("select x from t where c = " + num);
    ResultSet rs = ps.executeQuery();
    // process result set
    rs.close();
    ps.close();
}
```

Using PreparedStatement with Caching

In this example, a PreparedStatement object is created for the entire loop. JDBC will create only one PreparedStatement object.

```
Connection conn = ...;
...
PreparedStatement ps =
        conn.prepareStatement("select x from t where c = ?");
for(int num = 0; num < 100; num++) {
```

```
    ps.setInt(num);
    ResultSet rs = ps.executeQuery();
    // process result set
    rs.close();
}
ps.close();
```

12-27. What Is the Pooling of PreparedStatement Objects?

In general, pooling PreparedStatement objects improves performance of database applications. The following sections show how to pool PreparedStatement objects.

How It Works

Connection object pooling improves the performance of database applications, so this is another way to improve the performance of user queries. By pooling objects, you do not need to create and delete them for every request. The object pool is a container, which not only allows objects to be borrowed from and returned but also creates them on the fly, whenever you want to draw more objects than you have at the pool. Typically, *object pools* are used to manage the sharing of objects between multiple clients.

The main reason for creating a PreparedStatement object is to improve the performance of SQL statements that will be executed many times between multiple clients. You can enhance the performance of database applications using JDBC by pooling PreparedStatement objects, which the JDBC 3.0 specification makes possible. When a PreparedStatement object is pooled, it is not

This is according to the JDBC API Tutorial and Reference:

> *From the developer's viewpoint, using a PreparedStatement object that is pooled is exactly the same as using one that is not pooled. An application creates a PreparedStatement object, sets its parameters (if any), executes it, and closes it in exactly the same way. This means that after a PreparedStatement object is closed, even if it is being pooled, it must be created again for the next use. The only difference is that there should be an improvement in efficiency when a pooled statement is used multiple times.*

A JDBC application can check (see the following code segment) to see if the driver supports statement pooling by calling the DatabaseMetaData method supportsStatementPooling. If the return value is true, the application can use PreparedStatement objects armed with that knowledge.

Solution

Here's the solution:

```
import java.sql.*;
import jcb.util.DatabaseUtil;
import jcb.db.VeryBasicConnectionManager;

public class CheckStatementPooling {
    public static boolean supportsStatementPooling(Connection conn)
        throws SQLException {
        if ((conn == null) || (conn.isClosed())) {
            return false;
        }
```

```
        DatabaseMetaData dbmd = conn.getMetaData();
        if (dbmd == null) {
            // database metadata NOT supported...
            // you should throw an exception or...stop here
            System.out.println("can not determine if statement "+
                "pooling is supported or not.");
            return false;
        }

        if (dbmd.supportsStatementPooling ()) {
            // statement pooling is supported
            return true;
        }
        else {
            // statement pooling is NOT supported
            return false;
        }
    }

    public static void main(String[] args) {
        String dbVendor = args[0];  // { "mysql", "oracle" }
        Connection conn = null;
        try {
            System.out.println("--CheckStatementPooling begin--");
            conn = VeryBasicConnectionManager.getConnection(dbVendor);
            System.out.println("supportsStatementPooling="+


        }
        catch(Exception e){
            e.printStackTrace();
            System.exit(1);
        }
        finally {
            // release database resources
            DatabaseUtil.close(conn);
        }
    }
}
```

Running the Solution for the Oracle Database

This shows how to run the solution for the Oracle database:

```
$ javac CheckStatementPooling.java
$ java CheckStatementPooling oracle
--CheckStatementPooling begin--
supportsStatementPooling=true
--CheckStatementPooling end--
```

As you can see, Oracle's JDBC driver supports the pooling of PreparedStatement objects, and it supports implicit and explicit statement caching. For details, see the Oracle Database JDBC Developer's Guide and Reference 10g.

Running the Solution for the MySQL Database

This shows how to run the solution for the MySQL database:

```
$ javac CheckStatementPooling.java
$ java CheckStatementPooling mysql
--CheckStatementPooling begin--
supportsStatementPooling=false
--CheckStatementPooling end--
```

As you can see, MySQL's JDBC driver does not support the pooling of PreparedStatement objects.

Discussion

You should note that the pooling of PreparedStatement objects takes place behind the scenes and is available only if connection pooling is available.

Table 12-6 has been adapted from the JDBC API Tutorial and Reference; it shows the standard properties that a ConnectionPoolDataSource implementation may set for a PooledConnection object.

Table 12-6. *Standard Connection Pool Properties*

Property	Type	Description
maxStatements	int	The total number of statements the pool should keep open. 0 (zero) indicates that caching of statements is disabled.
initialPoolSize	int	The number of physical connections the pool should contain
maxPoolSize	int	The maximum number of physical connections the pool should contain. 0 (zero) indicates no maximum size.
maxIdleTime	int	The number of seconds that a physical connection should remain unused in the pool before it is closed. 0 (zero) indicates no time limit.
propertyCycle	int	The interval, in seconds, that the pool should wait before enforcing the policy defined by the values currently assigned to these connection pool properties.

The JDBC API Tutorial and Reference also says this:

> *An application server that is managing a pool of PooledConnection objects uses these properties to determine how to manage the pool. Because the getter and setter methods for properties are defined in ConnectionPoolDataSource implementations and are not part of the JDBC API, they are not available to clients. If there is a need to access the properties, such as, for example, when a tool is generating a list of them, they can be obtained through introspection.*

For example, if a vendor XXX wrote a class that implemented the ConnectionPoolDataSource interface, the code for creating the ConnectionPoolDataSource object and setting its properties might look like this:

```
XXXConnectionPoolDataSource connPDS = new XXXConnectionPoolDataSource ();
connPDS.setMaxStatements(10);
connPDS.setInitialPoolSize(5);
connPDS.setMinPoolSize(1);
connPDS.setMaxPoolSize(0); // no upper limit on pool size
connPDS.setMaxIdleTime(0); // no limit
   connPDS.setPropertyCycle(300);
```

If a PreparedStatement is a pooled statement, then PreparedStatement.close() will return the object to the pool rather than actually close the object (this is called a *soft close*).

■ ■ ■

Passing Input Parameters to PreparedStatement

By using a PreparedStatement object, you can execute dynamic parameterized SQL statements and pass input parameters at runtime to your statements. This chapter will show you how to pass input values of different data types (such as Timestamp, CLOB, BLOB, URL, String, InputStream, and so on) to a PreparedStatement object.

13-1. How Do You Pass Input Parameters to a PreparedStatement Object?

You can pass many different data types (such as String, Blob, Clob, Float, and so on) to a

A PreparedStatement object can have zero, one, or more parameter markers. Before sending a SQL statement for execution, you must set all the parameter markers to the appropriate values (depending on the data type of the parameters, represented by ?, a question mark). If a PreparedStatement object has zero parameter markers, then you don't have to set any input parameters. You set parameters by calling the appropriate setter method (PreparedStatement.setXXX()) for the type of the value being set, such as setString(), setClob(), setString(), and so on.

The PreparedStatement.setXXX() method has the following signature:

```
void setXXX(int parameterIndex, XXX value)
```

where parameterIndex is the *ordinal position* of the parameter. (Possible ordinal position values are 1, 2, 3, and so on.) The second parameter is the value of the parameter. Note that the order of the input parameters is not important. For example, if you have two input parameters, then the following two statements (where pstmt is a PreparedStatement object):

```
pstmt.setXXX(1, value-1);
pstmt.setXXX(2, value-2);
```

are semantically equivalent to the following two statements:

```
pstmt.setXXX(2, value-2);
pstmt.setXXX(1, value-1);
```

PreparedStatement enables you to have input parameters of almost any data type. For example, if the parameter is of type double in the Java programming language, the setter method to use is setDouble(). If the parameter is of type String in the Java programming language, the setter method to use is setString().

Table 13-1 lists the signatures of the PreparedStatement.setXXX() methods.

Table 13-1. `PreparedStatement.setXXX()` *Method Summary*

Return Type		Method
void	setArray(int i, Array x)	Sets the designated parameter to the given Array object.
void	setAsciiStream (int parameterIndex, InputStream x, int length)	Sets the designated parameter to the given input stream, which will have the specified number of bytes. (By using the int data type for length, the JDBC API assumes that the stream will be up to 2GB.)
void	setBigDecimal (int parameterIndex,BigDecimal x)	Sets the designated parameter to the given java.math.BigDecimal value.
void	setBinaryStream (int parameterIndex, InputStream x, int length)	Sets the designated parameter to the given input stream, which will have the specified number of bytes. (By using the int data type for length, the JDBC API assumes that the stream will be up to 2GB.)
void	setBlob(int i, Blob x)	Sets the designated parameter to the given Blob object.
void	setBoolean (int parameterIndex, boolean x)	Sets the designated parameter to the given Java boolean value.
void	setByte (int parameterIndex, byte x)	Sets the designated parameter to the given Java byte value.
void	setBytes	Sets the designated parameter to the given
	(int parameterIndex, Reader reader, int length)	Reader object, which is the given number of characters long.
void	setClob(int i, Clob x)	Sets the designated parameter to the given Clob object.
void	setDate (int parameterIndex, Date x)	Sets the designated parameter to the given java.sql.Date value.
void	setDate(int parameterIndex, Date x, Calendar cal)	Sets the designated parameter to the given java.sql.Date value, using the given Calendar object.
void	setDouble (int parameterIndex, double x)	Sets the designated parameter to the given Java double value.
void	setFloat (int parameterIndex, float x)	Sets the designated parameter to the given Java float value.
void	setInt (int parameterIndex, int x)	Sets the designated parameter to the given Java int value.
void	setLong (int parameterIndex, long x)	Sets the designated parameter to the given Java long value.
void	setNull (int parameterIndex, int sqlType)	Sets the designated parameter to SQL NULL.
void	setNull(int paramIndex, int sqlType, String typeName)	Sets the designated parameter to SQL NULL.
void	setObject(int parameterIndex, Object x)	Sets the value of the designated parameter using the given object.
void	setObject(int parameterIndex, Object x, int targetSqlType)	Sets the value of the designated parameter with the given object.

Table 13-1. `PreparedStatement.setXXX()` *Method Summary*

Return Type		Method
void	setObject(int parameterIndex, Object x, int targetSqlType, int scale)	Sets the value of the designated parameter with the given object.
void	setRef(int i, Ref x)	Sets the designated parameter to the given REF(<structured-type>) value.
void	setShort(int parameterIndex, short x)	Sets the designated parameter to the given Java short value.
void	setString(int parameterIndex, String x)	Sets the designated parameter to the given Java String value.
void	setTime(int parameterIndex, Time x)	Sets the designated parameter to the given java.sql.Time value.
void	setTime(int parameterIndex, Time x, Calendar cal)	Sets the designated parameter to the given java.sql.Time value, using the given Calendar object.
void	setTimestamp(int parameterIndex, Timestamp x)	Sets the designated parameter to the given java.sql.Timestamp value.
void	setTimestamp(int parameterIndex, Timestamp x, Calendar cal)	Sets the designated parameter to the given java.sql.Timestamp value, using the given Calendar object.
void	setURL(int parameterIndex, URL x)	Sets the designated parameter to the given java.net.URL value.

13-2. How Do You Use PreparedStatement.setArray()?

The following sections show how to pass a java.sql.Array object (as an input parameter) to a PreparedStatement object.

How It Works

The signature of PreparedStatement.setArray() is as follows:

```
void setArray(int parameterIndex, java.sql.Array array)
    throws SQLException
```

This sets the designated parameter to the given Array object. The driver converts this to a SQL ARRAY value when it sends it to the database.

The parameters are as follows:

- parameterIndex: The first parameter is 1, the second is 2, and so on.

- array: This is a java.sql.Array object, which must be implemented by a class.

What is java.sql.Array? This is the mapping in the Java programming language for the SQL type ARRAY. By default, an Array value is a transaction-duration reference to a SQL ARRAY value. By default, an Array object is implemented using a SQL LOCATOR (array) internally, which means that an Array object contains a logical pointer to the data in the SQL ARRAY value rather than containing the ARRAY value's data.

The Array interface provides methods for bringing a SQL ARRAY value's data to the client as either an array or a ResultSet object. If the elements of the SQL ARRAY are a user-defined type, they may be custom mapped. To create a custom mapping, follow these steps:

1. Create a class that implements the SQLData interface for the user-defined type to be custom mapped.

2. Make an entry in a type map that contains the following:

   - The fully qualified SQL type name of the user-defined type
   - The Class object for the class that implements SQLData

When a type map with an entry for the base type is supplied to the methods getArray and getResultSet, the mapping it contains will map the elements of the ARRAY value. If no type map is supplied, which will typically be the case, the connection's type map is used by default. If the connection's type map, or a type map supplied to a method, has no entry for the base type, the elements are mapped according to the standard mapping.

The Oracle database supports the ARRAY feature, but the MySQL database does not. (The feature is not implemented in the MySQL database.) The java.sql.Array implementation is provided by the driver.

In the following sections, I will provide an example of using PreparedStatement.setArray() for an Oracle database. To complete this example, first you need to set up some Oracle database objects, as shown in the next section.

Setting Up the Oracle Database

Using Oracle, you can define type objects such as the VARRAY type, which is an array of data types. The following defines a new type, CHAR_ARRAY, which is an array of CHAR(2). In this example, array element types are CHAR(2), but these can be any valid data type. Therefore, you can use CHAR_ARRAY

```
  2  /

Type created.

SQL> desc CHAR_ARRAY;
 CHAR_ARRAY VARRAY(10) OF CHAR(2)
```

Now, create a table that uses the VARRAY type in the Oracle database. Using Oracle, you can define a table that has columns of VARRAY type, as shown here:

```
SQL>  create table CHAR_ARRAY_TABLE(id varchar(10), array CHAR_ARRAY);
Table created.

SQL> desc CHAR_ARRAY_TABLE;
 Name           Null?     Type
 -----------   --------  ------------
 ID                       VARCHAR2(10)
 ARRAY                    CHAR_ARRAY

SQL> insert into CHAR_ARRAY_TABLE(id, array)
  2    values('id100', CHAR_ARRAY('aa', 'bb', 'cc'));

SQL> insert into CHAR_ARRAY_TABLE(id, array)
  2    values('id100', CHAR_ARRAY('aa', 'dd', 'pp'));

SQL> commit;
Commit complete.
```

```
SQL>
SQL> select * from CHAR_ARRAY_TABLE;

ID      ARRAY
-----   ------------------------------
id100   CHAR_ARRAY('aa', 'bb', 'cc')
id100   CHAR_ARRAY('aa', 'dd', 'pp')
```

Solution

The following program demonstrates how to use PreparedStatement.setArray(). This is according to Oracle (the JDBC Developer's Guide and Reference, Release 2):

> An ArrayDescriptor is an object of the oracle.sql.ArrayDescriptor class and describes the SQL type of an array. Only one array descriptor is necessary for any one SQL type. The driver caches ArrayDescriptor objects to avoid re-creating them if the SQL type has already been encountered. You can reuse the same descriptor object to create multiple instances of an oracle.sql.ARRAY object for the same array type.

Here's the solution:

```java
import java.util.*;
import java.io.*;
import java.sql.*;



import jcb.db.VeryBasicConnectionManager;

public class Demo_PreparedStatement_SetArray {

    public static void main(String[] args) {
        String dbVendor = args[0]; // { "mysql", "oracle" }
        Connection conn = null;
        PreparedStatement pstmt = null;
        java.sql.Array sqlArray = null;
        try {
            System.out.println("--Demo_PreparedStatement_SetArray begin--");

            conn = VeryBasicConnectionManager.getConnection(dbVendor);
            System.out.println("conn="+conn);
            System.out.println("---------------");

            // For oracle you need an array descriptor specifying
            // the type of the array and a connection to the database
            // the first parameter must match with the SQL ARRAY type created
            ArrayDescriptor arrayDescriptor =
                ArrayDescriptor.createDescriptor("CHAR_ARRAY", conn);
            // then obtain an Array filled with the content below
            String[] content = { "v1", "v2", "v3", "v4" };
            sqlArray= new oracle.sql.ARRAY(arrayDescriptor, conn, content);

            // prepare query
            String query = "insert into CHAR_ARRAY_TABLE(id, array) values(?, ?)";
```

```
                // create PrepareStatement object
                pstmt = conn.prepareStatement(query);
                // set input parameters to PreparedStatement object
                // the order of setting input parameters is not important
                pstmt.setString(1, "id300");
                pstmt.setArray(2, sqlArray);

                // execute query, and return number of rows created
                int rowCount = pstmt.executeUpdate();
                System.out.println("rowCount="+rowCount);
                System.out.println("--Demo_PreparedStatement_SetArray end--");
            }
        catch(Exception e){
                e.printStackTrace();
                System.exit(1);
            }
        finally {
                // release database resources
                DatabaseUtil.close(pstmt);
                DatabaseUtil.close(conn);
            }
        }
    }
}
```

Running the Solution for the Oracle Database

```
$ java  Demo_PreparedStatement_SetArray  oracle
--Demo_PreparedStatement_SetArray begin--
conn=oracle.jdbc.driver.OracleConnection@1edc073
---------------
rowCount=1
--Demo_PreparedStatement_SetArray end--
```

Viewing the Oracle Database After Running the Solution

This shows the Oracle database after running the solution:

```
SQL>  select * from CHAR_ARRAY_TABLE;
ID          ARRAY
--------    -------------------------------------
id100       CHAR_ARRAY('aa', 'bb', 'cc')
id100       CHAR_ARRAY('aa', 'dd', 'pp')
id300       CHAR_ARRAY('v1', 'v2', 'v3', 'v4')
```

13-3. How Do You Use PreparedStatement.setAsciiStream()?

The following sections show you how to pass an InputStream object (as an input parameter) to a PreparedStatement object.

How It Works

You can use setAsciiStream() on both the Oracle and MySQL databases. In Oracle, when a column data type is LONG, VARCHAR, or CLOB, then you can use setAsciiStream(). In MySQL, when a column data type is TINYTEXT, TEXT, MEDIUMTEXT, or LONGTEXT, then you can use setAsciiStream().

The signature of `PreparedStatement.setAsciiStream()` is as follows:

```
public void setAsciiStream(int parameterIndex,
                           InputStream stream,
                           int length)
    throws SQLException
```

This sets the designated parameter to the given input stream, which will have the specified number of bytes. When a very large ASCII value is input to a LONGVARCHAR parameter, it may be more practical to send it via `java.io.InputStream`. Data will be read from the stream as needed until reaching the end of the file. The JDBC driver will do any necessary conversion from ASCII to the database char format.

This stream object can either be a standard Java stream object or be your own subclass that implements the standard interface.

The parameters are as follows:

- `parameterIndex`: The first parameter is 1, the second is 2, and so on.

- `stream`: The Java input stream that contains the ASCII parameter value.

- `length`: The number of bytes in the stream.

This throws a `SQLException` if a database access error occurs.

Solution

The following solution uses `PreparedStatement.setAsciiStream()` to solve the problem. This class

```java
import java.util.*;
import java.io.*;
import java.sql.*;

import jcb.util.DatabaseUtil;
import jcb.db.VeryBasicConnectionManager;

public class Demo_PreparedStatement_SetAsciiStream {

    public static void main(String[] args) {
        String dbVendor = args[0]; // { "mysql", "oracle" }
        String fileName = args[1];
        Connection conn = null;
        PreparedStatement pstmt = null;
        String query = null;
        try {
            System.out.println("--Demo_PreparedStatement_setAsciiStream begin--");
            conn = VeryBasicConnectionManager.getConnection(dbVendor);
            System.out.println("conn="+conn);
            System.out.println("---------------");

            // prepare text stream
            File file = new File(fileName);
            int fileLength = (int) file.length();
            InputStream stream = (InputStream) new FileInputStream(file);

            // prepare SQL query
            query = "insert into  LONG_VARCHAR_TABLE(id, stream) values(?, ?)";
```

```
            // create PrepareStatement object
            pstmt = conn.prepareStatement(query);
            pstmt.setString(1, fileName);
            pstmt.setAsciiStream(2, stream, fileLength);

            // execute query, and return number of rows created
            int rowCount = pstmt.executeUpdate();
            System.out.println("rowCount="+rowCount);
            System.out.println("--Demo_PreparedStatement_setAsciiStream end--");
        }
        catch(Exception e){
            e.printStackTrace();
            System.exit(1);
        }
        finally {
            // release database resources
            DatabaseUtil.close(pstmt);
            DatabaseUtil.close(conn);
        }
    }
}
```

Setting Up the Oracle Database

Using Oracle, define a table that has a column of the LONG VARCHAR type (up to 2.14GB), as shown here:

```
SQL> desc LONG_VARCHAR_TABLE;
 Name           Null?    Type
 -----------    --------  ------------
 ID                       VARCHAR2(12)
 STREAM                   LONG
```

Setting Up the Data File

Use the following text file as input to the program:

```
$ cat file1.txt
this is line 1.
this is line two.
This is the last line.
```

Running the Solution for the Oracle Database

This shows how to run the solution for the Oracle database:

```
$ javac  Demo_PreparedStatement_SetAsciiStream.java
$ java  Demo_PreparedStatement_SetAsciiStream  oracle  file1.txt
--Demo_PreparedStatement_setAsciiStream begin--
conn=oracle.jdbc.driver.OracleConnection@d251a3
---------------
rowCount=1
--Demo_PreparedStatement_setAsciiStream end--
```

Viewing the Oracle Database After Running the Solution

This shows the Oracle database after running the solution:

```
SQL> select * from LONG_VARCHAR_TABLE;
ID                STREAM
---------         -----------------------
file1.txt         this is line 1.
                  this is line two.
                  This is the last line.
```

Setting Up the MySQL Database

Using MySQL, define a table that has a column of the TEXT type, up to a maximum length of 65,535 (2^{16} - 1) characters.

```
mysql> create table LONG_VARCHAR_TABLE (id VARCHAR(12), stream TEXT);
Query OK, 0 rows affected (0.10 sec)

mysql> desc LONG_VARCHAR_TABLE;
+--------+-------------+------+-----+---------+-------+
| Field  | Type        | Null | Key | Default | Extra |
+--------+-------------+------+-----+---------+-------+
| id     | varchar(12) | YES  |     | NULL    |       |
| stream | text        | YES  |     | NULL    |       |
+--------+-------------+------+-----+---------+-------+
2 rows in set (0.01 sec)
```

Use the following text file as input to the program:

```
$ cat  file1.txt
this is line 1.
this is line two.
This is the last line.
```

Running the Solution for the MySQL Database

This shows how to run the solution for the MySQL database:

```
$ jvac  Demo_PreparedStatement_SetAsciiStream.java
$ java  Demo_PreparedStatement_SetAsciiStream  mysql  file1.txt
--Demo_PreparedStatement_setAsciiStream begin--
conn=com.mysql.jdbc.Connection@15c7850
---------------
rowCount=1
--Demo_PreparedStatement_setAsciiStream end--
```

Viewing the MySQL Database After Running the Solution

This shows the MySQL database after running the solution:

```
mysql> select * from LONG_VARCHAR_TABLE;
+-----------+----------------------------------+
| id        | stream                           |
+-----------+----------------------------------+
| file1.txt | this is line 1.                  |
|           | this is line two.                |
|           | This is the last line.           |
+-----------+----------------------------------+
1 row in set (0.02 sec)
```

13-4. How Do You Use PreparedStatement.setBigDecimal()?

The following sections show how to pass a BigDecimal object (as an input parameter) to a PreparedStatement object.

How It Works

You can use setBigDecimal() on both the Oracle and MySQL databases. In Oracle, when a column data type is NUMBER, then you can use setBigDecimal(). In MySQL, when a column data type is FLOAT, REAL, DOUBLE PRECISION, NUMERIC, DECIMAL, TINYINT, SMALLINT, MEDIUMINT, INTEGER, or BIGINT, then you can use setBigDecimal().

The signature of PreparedStatement.setBigDecimal() is as follows:

```
                       java.math.BigDecimal bigDecimal)
     throws SQLException
```

This sets the designated parameter to the given java.math.BigDecimal value (immutable, arbitrary-precision, signed decimal numbers; a BigDecimal consists of an arbitrary-precision integer that is an unscaled value and a non-negative 32-bit integer scale, which represents the number of digits to the right of the decimal point. The driver converts this to a SQL NUMERIC value when it sends it to the database.

These are the parameters:

- parameterIndex: The first parameter is 1, the second is 2, and so on.

- bigDecimal: The parameter value.

This throws SQLException if a database access error occurs.

Solution

The main() method of this class will read three values (dbVendor, id, and a big decimal number) and then insert a new record by using PreparedStatement.setBigDecimal():

```
import java.util.*;
import java.io.*;
import java.sql.*;

import jcb.util.DatabaseUtil;
import jcb.db.VeryBasicConnectionManager;

public class Demo_PreparedStatement_SetBigDecimal {
```

```
    public static void main(String[] args) {
        String dbVendor = args[0]; // { "mysql", "oracle" }
        String id = args[1];
        java.math.BigDecimal bigDecimal = new java.math.BigDecimal(args[2]);
        Connection conn = null;
        PreparedStatement pstmt = null;
        String query = null;
        try {
            System.out.println("--Demo_PreparedStatement_setBigDecimal begin--");

            conn = VeryBasicConnectionManager.getConnection(dbVendor);
            System.out.println("conn="+conn);
            System.out.println("---------------");

            // prepare SQL query
            query = "insert into  BIG_DECIMAL_TABLE(id, big_decimal) values(?, ?)";

            // create PrepareStatement object
            pstmt = conn.prepareStatement(query);
            pstmt.setString(1, id);
            pstmt.setBigDecimal(2, bigDecimal);

            // execute query, and return number of rows created
            int rowCount = pstmt.executeUpdate();
            System.out.println("rowCount="+rowCount);
            System.out.println("--Demo_PreparedStatement_setBigDecimal end--");


            e.printStackTrace();
            System.exit(1);
        }
        finally {
            // release database resources
            DatabaseUtil.close(pstmt);
            DatabaseUtil.close(conn);
        }
    }
}
```

Setting Up the Oracle Database

Using Oracle, define a table that has a column of the NUMBER type, as shown next. Oracle's data type NUMBER(p, s) denotes a number having the precision p and scale s. The precision p can range from 1 to 38, and the scale s can range from -84 to 127.

```
SQL>  create table BIG_DECIMAL_TABLE(id VARCHAR(12), big_decimal NUMBER(16, 5));

Table created.

SQL> desc BIG_DECIMAL_TABLE;
 Name                  Null?    Type
 ----------------- -------- -------------
 ID                          VARCHAR2(12)
 BIG_DECIMAL                 NUMBER(16,5)
```

```
SQL> insert into BIG_DECIMAL_TABLE(id, big_decimal)
     values ('id-1', 1234567.123456);
SQL> insert into BIG_DECIMAL_TABLE(id, big_decimal)
     values ('id-2', 99994567.778899);
SQL> insert into BIG_DECIMAL_TABLE(id, big_decimal)
     values ('id-3', 123.4455);
SQL> insert into BIG_DECIMAL_TABLE(id, big_decimal)
     values ('id-4', 12.123456789);
SQL> commit;
SQL> select * from BIG_DECIMAL_TABLE;

ID            BIG_DECIMAL
---------     -----------
id-1          1234567.12
id-2          99994567.8
id-3            123.4455
id-4            12.12346
```

Running the Solution for the Oracle Database

This shows how to run the solution for the Oracle database:

```
$ javac Demo_PreparedStatement_SetBigDecimal.java
$ java Demo_PreparedStatement_SetBigDecimal oracle id-44 98765.1234
--Demo_PreparedStatement_setBigDecimal begin--
conn=oracle.jdbc.driver.OracleConnection@1edc073
---------------

--Demo_PreparedStatement_setBigDecimal end--
```

Viewing the Oracle Database After Running the Solution

This shows the Oracle database after running the solution:

```
SQL> select * from BIG_DECIMAL_TABLE;

ID            BIG_DECIMAL
---------     -----------
id-1          1234567.12
id-2          99994567.8
id-3            123.4455
id-4            12.12346
id-44         98765.1234
```

Setting Up the MySQL Database

Using MySQL, define a table that has a column of the DECIMAL type, as shown next. For example, using DECIMAL(5, 2), the precision (5) represents the number of significant decimal digits that will be stored for values, and the scale (2) represents the number of digits that will be stored following the decimal point. In this case, therefore, the range of values that can be stored in this column is from -99.99 to 99.99.

```
mysql> create table big_decimal_table(id varchar(12), big_decimal decimal(15, 5));
Query OK, 0 rows affected (0.04 sec)
```

```
mysql> desc big_decimal_table;
+-------------+---------------+------+-----+---------+-------+
| Field       | Type          | Null | Key | Default | Extra |
+-------------+---------------+------+-----+---------+-------+
| id          | varchar(12)   | YES  |     | NULL    |       |
| big_decimal | decimal(15,5) | YES  |     | NULL    |       |
+-------------+---------------+------+-----+---------+-------+
2 rows in set (0.00 sec)

mysql> insert into big_decimal_table(id, big_decimal)
    values('id-1', 123456789.12345);
mysql> insert into big_decimal_table(id, big_decimal)
    values('id-2', 123456789.12345678);
mysql> insert into big_decimal_table(id, big_decimal)
    values('id-3', 1234567890123.12345);
mysql> insert into big_decimal_table(id, big_decimal)
    values('id-4', 123.123456789);

mysql> select * from big_decimal_table;
+------+-------------------+
| id   | big_decimal       |
+------+-------------------+
| id-1 |     123456789.12345 |
| id-2 |     123456789.12346 |
| id-3 | 99999999999.99999 |
| id-4 |           123.12346 |
+------+-------------------+
```

Running the Solution for the MySQL Database

This shows how to run the solution for the MySQL database:

```
$ javac  Demo_PreparedStatement_SetBigDecimal.java
$ java  Demo_PreparedStatement_SetBigDecimal  mysql  id-99  5678.1234
--Demo_PreparedStatement_setBigDecimal begin--
conn=com.mysql.jdbc.Connection@1ded0fd
---------------
rowCount=1
--Demo_PreparedStatement_setBigDecimal end--
```

Viewing the MySQL Database After Running the Solution

This shows the MySQL database after running the solution:

```
mysql> select * from big_decimal_table;
+-------+-------------------+
| id    | big_decimal       |
+-------+-------------------+
| id-3  | 99999999999.99999 |
| id-2  |     123456789.12346 |
| id-1  |     123456789.12345 |
| id-4  |           123.12346 |
| id-99 |         5678.12340 |
+-------+-------------------+
5 rows in set (0.00 sec)
```

13-5. How Do You Use PreparedStatement.setBinaryStream()?

The following sections show how to pass a binary stream (InputStream represents binary data as an input parameter) to a PreparedStatement object.

How It Works

You can use PreparedStatement.setBinaryStream() on both the Oracle and MySQL databases.

In Oracle, when a column data type is RAW or LONG RAW, then you can use setBinaryStream(). Oracle's RAW(length) represents raw binary data of length bytes. The maximum size is 2,000 bytes. You must specify a size for a RAW value; Oracle's LONG RAW represents raw binary data of a variable length up to 2GB.

In MySQL, when a column data type is TINYBLOB, BLOB, MEDIUMBLOB, or LONGBLOB, then you can use setBinaryStream().

The signature of setBinaryStream() is as follows:

```
public void setBinaryStream(int parameterIndex,
                            InputStream stream,
                            int length)  throws SQLException
```

This sets the designated parameter to the given input stream, which will have the specified number of bytes. When a large binary value is input to a LONGVARBINARY parameter, it may be more practical to send it via a java.io.InputStream object. The data will be read from the stream as needed until the end of the file is reached. This stream object can be either a standard Java stream object or your own subclass that implements the standard interface.

The parameters are as follows:

- stream: The Java input stream that contains the binary parameter value.

- length: The number of bytes in the stream.

This throws a SQLException if a database access error occurs.

Setting Up the Oracle Database

Using Oracle, define a table that has the RAW and LONG RAW types, as shown next:

```
SQL> create table binary_table(
  2    id VARCHAR(12),
  3    raw_column RAW(2000),
  4    long_raw_column LONG RAW);
Table created.

SQL> desc binary_table;
 Name                    Null?    Type
 ----------------------  -------- -------------
 ID                               VARCHAR2(12)
 RAW_COLUMN                       RAW(2000)
 LONG_RAW_COLUMN                  LONG RAW
```

Solution

This solution uses PreparedStatement.setBinaryStream() and inserts a new record into binary_table:

```java
import java.util.*;
import java.io.*;
import java.sql.*;

import jcb.util.DatabaseUtil;
import jcb.db.VeryBasicConnectionManager;

public class Demo_PreparedStatement_SetBinaryStream {

    public static void main(String[] args) {
        // set up input parameters from command line:
        String dbVendor = args[0]; // { "mysql", "oracle" }
        String id = args[1];
        String smallFileName = args[2];
        String largeFileName = args[3];
        Connection conn = null;
        PreparedStatement pstmt = null;
        try {
            System.out.println("--Demo_PreparedStatement_setBinaryStream begin--");
            // get a database Connection object
            conn = VeryBasicConnectionManager.getConnection(dbVendor);
            System.out.println("conn="+conn);
            System.out.println("---------------");

            // prepare small binary stream
            File smallFile = new File(smallFileName);



            // prepare large binary stream
            File largeFile = new File(largeFileName);
            int largeFileLength = (int) largeFile.length();
            InputStream largeStream = (InputStream) new FileInputStream(largeFile);

            // prepare SQL query
            String query = "insert into binary_table" +
                "(id, raw_column, long_raw_column) values(?, ?, ?)";

            // begin transaction
            conn.setAutoCommit(false);

            // create PrepareStatement object
            pstmt = conn.prepareStatement(query);
            pstmt.setString(1, id);
            pstmt.setBinaryStream(2, smallStream, smallFileLength);
            pstmt.setBinaryStream(3, largeStream, largeFileLength);

            // execute query, and return number of rows created
            int rowCount = pstmt.executeUpdate();
            System.out.println("rowCount="+rowCount);

            // end transaction
            conn.commit();
            System.out.println("--Demo_PreparedStatement_setBinaryStream end--");
        }
```

```
        catch(Exception e){
            e.printStackTrace();
            System.exit(1);
        }
        finally {
            // release database resources
            DatabaseUtil.close(pstmt);
            DatabaseUtil.close(conn);
        }
    }
}
```

Setting Up the Data File

I will use the binary tomcat_logo.gif file (1,934 bytes) and the binary tomcat_f14.gif file (37,454 bytes) as inputs to the program. Figure 13-1 shows the file thumbnails, and Figure 13-2 shows the files and their associated sizes.

Figure 13-1. *Binary files to be inserted as a binary stream*

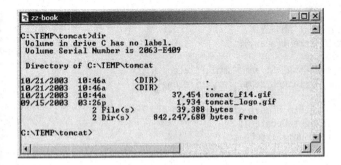

Figure 13-2. *Binary files and their associated sizes*

Running the Solution for the Oracle Database

This shows how to run the solution for the Oracle database:

```
$ javac  Demo_PreparedStatement_SetBinaryStream.java
$ java  Demo_PreparedStatement_SetBinaryStream  oracle id-100 \
  c:/temp/tomcat/tomcat_logo.gif  c:/temp/tomcat/tomcat_f14.gif
--Demo_PreparedStatement_setBinaryStream begin--
conn=oracle.jdbc.driver.OracleConnection@d251a3
---------------
rowCount=1
--Demo_PreparedStatement_setBinaryStream_Oracle end--
```

Viewing the Oracle Database After Running the Solution

To verify that you have inserted the binary data correctly, use a small Java program to display the binary data inserted:

```
java  DemoDisplayBinary  oracle  id-100
```

Running the program generates the image shown in Figure 13-3.

Figure 13-3. *Retrieving the binary data from the database*

Here is a program to display binary data:

```java
import javax.swing.*;
import java.awt.*;
import java.awt.event.*;
import java.util.*;
import java.io.*;
import java.sql.*;

import jcb.util.DatabaseUtil;
import jcb.db.VeryBasicConnectionManager;

/**
 * This class displays binary objects in a JFrame
 */
public class DemoDisplayBinary extends JPanel {
    /**
     * Constructor to display BLOB object.
     * @param dbVendor database vendor.
```

```java
 * @param id the primary key to the MyPictures table
 */
public DemoDisplayBinary(String dbVendor, String id) throws Exception {
    // materialize BLOB onto client
    Object[] binaryData = getBinaryData(dbVendor, id);
    setLayout(new GridLayout(1, 2));
    ImageIcon icon1 = new ImageIcon((byte[])binaryData[0]) ;
    JLabel photoLabel1 = new JLabel(icon1) ;
    add(photoLabel1);
    ImageIcon icon2 = new ImageIcon((byte[])binaryData[1]) ;
    JLabel photoLabel2 = new JLabel(icon2) ;
    add(photoLabel2);
}


/**
 * Extract and return the BLOB object.
 * @param dbVendor database vendor.
 * @param id the primary key to the BLOB object.
 */
public static Object[] getBinaryData(String dbVendor, String id)
    throws Exception {
    Connection conn = null ;
    ResultSet rs = null;
    PreparedStatement pstmt = null;
    String query = "SELECT raw_column, long_raw_column "+
                    "FROM binary_table WHERE id = ?";


        Object[] results = new Object[2];
        pstmt = conn.prepareStatement(query) ;
        pstmt.setString(1, id);
        rs = pstmt.executeQuery();
        rs.next();
        // materialize binary data onto client
        results[0] = rs.getBytes("RAW_COLUMN");
        results[1] = rs.getBytes("LONG_RAW_COLUMN");
        return results;
    }
    finally {
        DatabaseUtil.close(rs);
        DatabaseUtil.close(pstmt);
        DatabaseUtil.close(conn);
    }
}

public static void main(String args[]) throws Exception {
    String dbVendor = args[0]; // { "mysql", "oracle" }
    String id = args[1];
    UIManager.setLookAndFeel("javax.swing.plaf.metal.MetalLookAndFeel") ;
    JFrame frame = new JFrame("Binary Demo for" + dbVendor + " Database");
    frame.addWindowListener(new WindowAdapter() {
        public void windowClosing(WindowEvent e) {
            System.exit(0);
        }
    });
```

```
        frame.setContentPane(new DemoDisplayBinary(dbVendor, id)) ;
        frame.pack();
        frame.setVisible(true);
    }
}
```

Setting Up the MySQL Database

Using MySQL, define a table that has BLOB and MEDIUMBLOB types, as shown next. A BLOB column can hold a maximum length of 65,535 (2^{16} - 1) characters, and a MEDIUMBLOB column can hold a maximum length of 16,777,215 (2^{24} - 1) characters.

```
mysql>  create table binary_table(
    -> id VARCHAR(12),
    -> raw_column BLOB,
    -> long_raw_column MEDIUMBLOB);
Query OK, 0 rows affected (0.04 sec)

mysql> desc binary_table;
+-----------------+-------------+------+-----+---------+-------+
| Field           | Type        | Null | Key | Default | Extra |
+-----------------+-------------+------+-----+---------+-------+
| id              | varchar(12) | YES  |     | NULL    |       |
| raw_column      | blob        | YES  |     | NULL    |       |
| long_raw_column | mediumblob  | YES  |     | NULL    |       |
+-----------------+-------------+------+-----+---------+-------+
```

Setting Up the Data File

I will use the binary files anna-1.jpg (5,789 bytes) and anna-2.jpg (112,375 bytes) as input to the program. Figure 13-4 shows the file thumbnails, and Figure 13-5 shows the files and their associated sizes.

Figure 13-4. *Binary files to be inserted as a binary stream*

```
zz-book                                                        _ □ ×
C:\TEMP\anna>dir
 Volume in drive C has no label.
 Volume Serial Number is 2063-E409

 Directory of C:\TEMP\anna

10/22/2003  11:28a      <DIR>        .
10/22/2003  11:28a      <DIR>        ..
04/24/2002  01:35p              5,789 anna-1.jpg
05/21/2002  04:53p            112,375 anna-2.jpg
                2 File(s)        118,164 bytes
                2 Dir(s)     637,624,320 bytes free

C:\TEMP\anna>
```

Figure 13-5. *Binary files and their associated sizes*

Running the Solution for the MySQL Database

This shows how to run the solution for the MySQL database:

```
$ javac  Demo_PreparedStatement_SetBinaryStream.java
$ java  Demo_PreparedStatement_SetBinaryStream  mysql  id-100
c:/temp/anna/anna-1.jpg  c:/temp/anna/anna-2.jpg
--Demo_PreparedStatement_setBinaryStream_MySQL begin--
conn=com.mysql.jdbc.Connection@15c7850
---------------
rowCount=1
```

Viewing the MySQL Database After Running the Solution

To verify that you have inserted the binary data correctly, you can use a small Java program to display the binary data inserted:

```
java DemoDisplayBinary  mysql  id-100
```

This generates the image shown in Figure 13-6 (I have made the image smaller to fit the page).

Figure 13-6. *Retrieving binary data from the database*

13-6. How Do You Use PreparedStatement.setBlob()?

In RDBMS systems, BLOB is a Binary Large OBject. java.sql.Blob is the mapping in the Java programming language of a SQL BLOB value. The following sections show how to pass a java.sql.Blob object to a PreparedStatement object.

How It Works

You can use PreparedStatement.setBlob() on both the Oracle and MySQL databases. Using the Oracle database, when a column data type is BLOB, then you can use setBlob(). Oracle's BLOB represents raw binary data of a variable length up to 2GB. Using the MySQL database, when a column data type is TINYBLOB with a maximum length of 255 (2^8 - 1) characters, BLOB with a maximum length of 65,535 (2^{16} - 1) characters, MEDIUMBLOB with a maximum length of 16,777,215 (2^{24} - 1) characters, or LONGBLOB with a maximum length of 4,294,967,295 or 4G (2^{32} - 1) characters, then you can use setBlob().
The signature of setBlob() is as follows:

```
public void setBlob(int parameterIndex, java.sql.Blob blob)
    throws SQLException
```

This sets the designated parameter to the given Blob object. The driver converts this to a SQL BLOB value when it sends it to the database.
The parameters are as follows:

- parameterIndex: The first parameter is 1, the second is 2, and so on.

- blob: A Blob object that maps a SQL BLOB value.

Solution

The following program uses PreparedStatement.setBlob() and inserts a new record into binary_table. Note that in the JDBC API, there is no constructor to build a java.sql.Blob object directly; therefore, to use the setBlob() method, you need to create a ResultSet object, extract a Blob object, and then pass it to the PreparedStatement.setBlob() method. I will show how to extract a Blob from binary_table and then insert it into the blob_table table using the PreparedStatement.setBlob() method.

```
import java.util.*;
import java.io.*;
import java.sql.*;

import jcb.util.DatabaseUtil;
import jcb.db.VeryBasicConnectionManager;

public class Demo_PreparedStatement_SetBlob {

    public static void main(String[] args) {
        // set up input parameters from command line:
        String dbVendor = args[0]; // { "mysql", "oracle" }
        String id = args[1];

        Connection conn = null;
        PreparedStatement pstmt = null;
        ResultSet rs = null;
        java.sql.Blob blob = null;
        try {
            System.out.println("--Demo_PreparedStatement_SetBlob begin--");
```

```
        // get a database Connection object
        conn = VeryBasicConnectionManager.getConnection(dbVendor);
        System.out.println("conn="+conn);
        System.out.println("---------------");

        // prepare blob object from an existing binary column
        String query1 = "select photo from my_pictures where id = ?";
        pstmt = conn.prepareStatement(query1);
        pstmt.setString(1, id);
        rs = pstmt.executeQuery();
        rs.next();
        blob = rs.getBlob(1);

        // prepare SQL query for inserting a new row using setBlob()
        String query = "insert into blob_table(id, blob_column) values(?, ?)";

        // begin transaction
        conn.setAutoCommit(false);

        // create PrepareStatement object
        pstmt = conn.prepareStatement(query);
        pstmt.setString(1, id);
        pstmt.setBlob(2, blob);

        // execute query, and return number of rows created
        int rowCount = pstmt.executeUpdate();


        // end transaction
        conn.commit();
        System.out.println("--Demo_PreparedStatement_SetBlob end--");
    }
    catch(Exception e){
        e.printStackTrace();
        System.exit(1);
    }
    finally {
        // release database resources
        DatabaseUtil.close(rs);
        DatabaseUtil.close(pstmt);
        DatabaseUtil.close(conn);
    }
  }
}
```

Setting Up the Oracle Database

Using Oracle, define a table that has a BLOB type, as shown here:

```
SQL> create table blob_table (
  2  id VARCHAR(12) NOT NULL PRIMARY KEY,
  3  blob_column BLOB default empty_blob()
  4  );

Table created.
```

```
SQL> desc blob_table;
 Name                       Null?    Type
 ----------------------     -------- -------------
 ID                         NOT NULL VARCHAR2(12)
 BLOB_COLUMN                         BLOB
```

Running the Solution for the Oracle Database

This shows how to run the solution for the Oracle database:

```
$ javac  Demo_PreparedStatement_SetBlob.java
$ java  Demo_PreparedStatement_SetBlob  oracle  tiger1
--Demo_PreparedStatement_SetBlob begin--
conn=oracle.jdbc.driver.OracleConnection@d251a3
---------------
rowCount=1
--Demo_PreparedStatement_SetBlob end--
```

Viewing the Oracle Database After Running the Solution

To verify that you have inserted the binary data correctly, you can use a small Java program to display the binary data inserted:

```
java DemoDisplayBlob oracle tiger1
```

Running this program generates the image shown in Figure 13-7.

Figure 13-7. *Retrieving binary data from an Oracle database*

Here is a Java program to display Blob data:

```
import javax.swing.*;
import java.awt.*;
import java.awt.event.*;
import java.util.*;
import java.io.*;
import java.sql.*;

import jcb.util.DatabaseUtil;
import jcb.db.VeryBasicConnectionManager;
```

```java
/**
 * This class displays blob objects in a JFrame
 */
public class DemoDisplayBlob extends JPanel {
    /**
     * Constructor to display BLOB object.
     * @param dbVendor database vendor
     * @param id the primary key to the MyPictures table
     */
    public DemoDisplayBlob(String dbVendor, String id) throws Exception {
        // materialize BLOB onto client
        java.sql.Blob blob = getBlob(dbVendor, id);
        byte[] data = blob.getBytes(1, (int)blob.length());

        // add blob to frame
        setLayout(new GridLayout(1, 1));
        JLabel label = new JLabel(new ImageIcon(data)) ;
        add(label);
    }

    /**
     * Extract and return the BLOB object.
     * @param dbVendor database vendor
     * @param id the primary key to the BLOB object.
     */
    public static java.sql.Blob getBlob(String dbVendor, String id)


        ResultSet rs = null;
        PreparedStatement pstmt = null;
        String query = "SELECT blob_column FROM blob_table WHERE id = ?";

        try {
            conn = VeryBasicConnectionManager.getConnection(dbVendor);
            pstmt = conn.prepareStatement(query) ;
            pstmt.setString(1, id);
            rs = pstmt.executeQuery();
            rs.next();
            // materialize binary data onto client
            java.sql.Blob blob = rs.getBlob(1);
            return blob;
        }
        finally {
            DatabaseUtil.close(rs);
            DatabaseUtil.close(pstmt);
            DatabaseUtil.close(conn);
        }
    }

    public static void main(String args[]) throws Exception {
        UIManager.setLookAndFeel("javax.swing.plaf.metal.MetalLookAndFeel") ;
        JFrame frame = new JFrame("Blob Demo for Oracle Database");
        frame.addWindowListener(new WindowAdapter() {
            public void windowClosing(WindowEvent e) {
                System.exit(0);
            }
        });
```

```
        String dbVendor = args[0]; // { "mysql", "oracle" }
        String id = args[1];
        frame.setContentPane(new DemoDisplayBlob(dbVendir, id)) ;
        frame.pack();
        frame.setVisible(true);
    }
}
```

Setting Up the MySQL Database

Using MySQL, define a table that has the BLOB and MEDIUMBLOB types, as shown next. A BLOB column can hold a maximum length of 65,535 (2^16 - 1) characters, and a MEDIUMBLOB column can hold a maximum length of 16,777,215 (2^24 - 1) characters.

```
mysql> create table blob_table (
    -> id VARCHAR(12) NOT NULL PRIMARY KEY,
    -> blob_column BLOB
    -> );
Query OK, 0 rows affected (0.10 sec)

mysql> desc blob_table;
+-------------+-------------+------+-----+---------+-------+
| Field       | Type        | Null | Key | Default | Extra |
+-------------+-------------+------+-----+---------+-------+
| id          | varchar(12) |      | PRI |         |       |
| blob_column | blob        | YES  |     | NULL    |       |
```

I will show how to use existing binary data in a database to create a java.sql.Blob object. To do this, I will use the binary column shown in Figure 13-8 to create a java.sql.Blob object and then insert it into blob_table table using the PreparedStatement.setBlob() method.

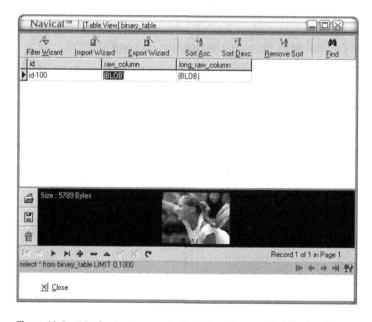

Figure 13-8. *Displaying* java.sql.Blob *data from a MySQL database*

Running the Solution for the MySQL Database

This shows how to run the solution for the MySQL database:

```
$ javac Demo_PreparedStatement_SetBlob.java
$ java Demo_PreparedStatement_SetBlob mysql id-100
--Demo_PreparedStatement_SetBlob begin--
conn=com.mysql.jdbc.Connection@15c7850
---------------
rowCount=1
--Demo_PreparedStatement_SetBlob end--
```

Viewing the MySQL Database Content After Running the Solution (First Method)

Running the solution will create Figure 13-9.

Figure 13-9. *Displaying binary data (`java.sql.Blob`) from a MySQL database*

Viewing the MySQL Database Content After Running the Solution (Second Method)

To verify that you have inserted the binary data correctly, you can use a small Java program to display the binary data inserted:

```
java DemoDisplayBlob mysql id-100
```

Running this program generates the image shown in Figure 13-10 (I have made this image smaller to fit the page).

Figure 13-10. *Displaying binary data from a MySQL database (second method)*

13-7. How Do You Use PreparedStatement.setBoolean()?

The following sections show how to pass a boolean value (a Java primitive data type representing true and false) to a PreparedStatement object.

How It Works

You can use setBoolean() on both the Oracle and MySQL databases. Oracle does not have a built-in boolean data type; in Oracle, when a column data type is NUMBER, then you can use the setBoolean() method. A TINYINT is the usual type to use when storing a boolean in MySQL. You can use the ResultSet.get and setBoolean(int, boolean) methods when using TINYINT. PreparedStatement. setBoolean() will use 1/0 for values if your MySQL version is greater than or equal to 3.21.23.

The signature of setBoolean() is as follows:

```
public void setBoolean(int parameterIndex,
                       boolean bool)
    throws SQLException
```

This sets the designated parameter to the given Java boolean value. The driver converts this to a SQL BIT value when it sends it to the database.

The following are the parameters:

- parameterIndex: The first parameter is 1, the second is 2, and so on.

- bool: The parameter value.

This throws a SQLException if a database access error occurs.

Solution

Here's the solution:

```
import java.util.*;
import java.io.*;
import java.sql.*;

import jcb.util.DatabaseUtil;
import jcb.db.VeryBasicConnectionManager;

public class Demo_PreparedStatement_SetBoolean {

    public static void main(String[] args) {
        String dbVendor = args[0]; // values are: { "mysql", "oracle" }
        String idValue = args[1];
        boolean booleanValue;
        if (args[2].equals("0")) {
            booleanValue = false;
        }
        else {
            booleanValue = true;
        }

        Connection conn = null;
        PreparedStatement pstmt = null;
        try {
            System.out.println("--Demo_PreparedStatement_setBoolean begin--");
            conn = VeryBasicConnectionManager.getConnection(dbVendor);
```

```
                System.out.println("conn="+conn);
                System.out.println("---------------");

                // prepare query
                String query =
                    "insert into boolean_table(id, boolean_column) values(?, ?)";

                // create PrepareStatement object
                pstmt = conn.prepareStatement(query);
                pstmt.setString(1, idValue);
                pstmt.setBoolean(2, booleanValue);

                // execute query, and return number of rows created
                int rowCount = pstmt.executeUpdate();
                System.out.println("rowCount="+rowCount);
                System.out.println("--Demo_PreparedStatement_setBoolean end--");
        }
        catch(Exception e){
                e.printStackTrace();
                System.exit(1);
        }
        finally {
                // release database resources
                DatabaseUtil.close(pstmt);
                DatabaseUtil.close(conn);
        }
```

Setting Up the Oracle Database

Using Oracle, define a table that has a column of the NUMBER type, as shown next. Oracle's data type NUMBER(p, s) denotes a number having the precision p and scale s. The precision p can range from 1 to 38, and the scale s can range from -84 to 127.

```
SQL> create table boolean_table(id varchar(12), boolean_column NUMBER(1));

Table created.

SQL> desc boolean_table;
 Name                                    Null?    Type
 --------------------------------------- -------- --------------
 ID                                               VARCHAR2(12)
 BOOLEAN_COLUMN                                   NUMBER(1)

SQL> insert into boolean_table(id, boolean_column) values('id-1', 1);
SQL> insert into boolean_table(id, boolean_column) values('id-2', 0);
SQL> commit;

SQL> select * from boolean_table;

ID              BOOLEAN_COLUMN
------------    --------------
id-1                         1
id-2                         0
```

Running the Solution for the Oracle Database

This shows how to run the solution for the Oracle database:

```
$ javac Demo_PreparedStatement_SetBoolean.java
$ java Demo_PreparedStatement_SetBoolean oracle id-200 0
--Demo_PreparedStatement_setBoolean begin--
conn=oracle.jdbc.driver.OracleConnection@ece65
---------------
rowCount=1
--Demo_PreparedStatement_setBoolean end--

$ java Demo_PreparedStatement_SetBoolean oracle id-400 1
--Demo_PreparedStatement_setBoolean begin--
conn=oracle.jdbc.driver.OracleConnection@ece65
---------------
rowCount=1
--Demo_PreparedStatement_setBoolean_Oracle end--
```

Viewing the Oracle Database After Running the Program

This shows the Oracle database after running the program:

```
SQL> select * from boolean_table;

ID              BOOLEAN_COLUMN
---------       --------------


id-200                  0
id-400                  1
```

Setting Up the MySQL Database

Using MySQL 4.1.7, define a table that has a column of the BOOLEAN (or TINYINT) type, as shown here:

```
mysql> use octopus;
Database changed
mysql> create table boolean_table(id varchar(12), boolean_column BOOLEAN);
Query OK, 0 rows affected (0.09 sec)

mysql> desc boolean_table;
+----------------+-------------+------+-----+---------+-------+
| Field          | Type        | Null | Key | Default | Extra |
+----------------+-------------+------+-----+---------+-------+
| id             | varchar(12) | YES  |     | NULL    |       |
| boolean_column | tinyint(1)  | YES  |     | NULL    |       |
+----------------+-------------+------+-----+---------+-------+
2 rows in set (0.00 sec)
```

Running the Solution for the MySQL Database

This shows how to run the solution for the MySQL database:

```
$ java Demo_PreparedStatement_SetBoolean mysql id-100 0
--Demo_PreparedStatement_setBoolean begin--
conn=com.mysql.jdbc.Connection@8fce95
---------------
```

```
rowCount=1
--Demo_PreparedStatement_setBoolean end--

$ java Demo_PreparedStatement_SetBoolean mysql id-400 1
--Demo_PreparedStatement_setBoolean begin--
conn=com.mysql.jdbc.Connection@8fce95
---------------
rowCount=1
--Demo_PreparedStatement_setBoolean end--
```

Viewing the MySQL Database After Running the Solution

This shows the MySQL database after running the solution:

```
mysql> use octopus;
Database changed
mysql> select * from boolean_table;
+---------+----------------+
| id      | boolean_column |
+---------+----------------+
| id-100  |              0 |
| id-400  |              1 |
+---------+----------------+
2 rows in set (0.01 sec)
```

The following sections show how to pass an integer value (which includes the Java primitive data types byte, short, int, and long) to a PreparedStatement object.

How It Works

Here I will show how to use the PreparedStatement object's setByte(), setShort(), setInt(), and setLong() methods. The signatures of these methods are as follows:

```
public void setByte(int parameterIndex, byte x) throws SQLException
public void setShort(int parameterIndex, short x) throws SQLException
public void setInt(int parameterIndex, int x) throws SQLException
public void setLong(int parameterIndex, long x) throws SQLException
```

This sets the designated parameter to the given Java primitive value (byte, short, int, or long). The driver converts byte to SQL TINYINT, short to SQL SMALLINT, int to SQL INTEGER, and long to SQL BIGINT when it sends it to the database.

The parameters are as follows:

- parameterIndex: The first parameter is 1, the second is 2, and so on.

- x: The parameter value.

This throws a SQLException if a database access error occurs.

You can use all four methods (setByte(), setShort(), setInt(), and setLong()) on both the Oracle and MySQL databases.

The Oracle data types CHAR, VARCHAR2, LONG, NUMBER, RAW, and LONG RAW can be materialized as a Java primitive type byte, short, int, or long. In practice, it makes sense to map Oracle's SQL NUMBER type to a Java primitive type byte, short, int, or long, and then you can use setByte(), setShort(), setInt(), or setLong() accordingly to set the proper value. Note that you can use Oracle's NUMBER to support most of the Java primitive data types.

In MySQL, when a column data type is TINYINT, SMALLINT, MEDIUMINT, INT, BIGINT, CHAR, or VARCHAR, then you can use the setByte() method. In practice, it makes sense to map MySQL's TINYINT to the Java primitive type byte, MySQL's SMALLINT to the Java primitive type short, MySQL's INT to the Java primitive type int, MySQL's BIGINT to the Java primitive type long and then use the setByte(), setShort(), setInt(), or setLong() method accordingly to set the proper value.

Solution

This class will read an ID followed by four numbers (byte, short, int, and long) and then insert these values as a record of integer_table:

```java
import java.util.*;
import java.io.*;
import java.sql.*;

import jcb.util.DatabaseUtil;
import jcb.db.VeryBasicConnectionManager;

public class Demo_PreparedStatement_SetIntegers {

    public static void main(String[] args) {
        String dbVendor = args[0]; // {"mysql", "oracle" }
        String id = args[1];
        byte byteValue = Byte.parseByte(args[2]);


        long longValue = Long.parseLong(args[5]);

        Connection conn = null;
        PreparedStatement pstmt = null;
        try {
            System.out.println("--Demo_PreparedStatement_SetIntegers begin--");
            conn = VeryBasicConnectionManager.getConnection(dbVendor);
            System.out.println("conn="+conn);
            System.out.println("---------------");

            // prepare query
            String query = "insert into integer_table(id, byte_column, " +
                "short_column, int_column, long_column) values(?, ?, ?, ?, ?)";

            // create PrepareStatement object
            pstmt = conn.prepareStatement(query);
            pstmt.setString(1, id);
            pstmt.setByte(2, byteValue);
            pstmt.setShort(3, shortValue);
            pstmt.setInt(4, intValue);
            pstmt.setLong(5, longValue);

            // execute query, and return number of rows created
            int rowCount = pstmt.executeUpdate();
            System.out.println("rowCount="+rowCount);
            System.out.println("--Demo_PreparedStatement_SetIntegers end--");
        }
```

```
        catch(Exception e){
            e.printStackTrace();
            System.exit(1);
        }
        finally {
            // release database resources
            DatabaseUtil.close(pstmt);
            DatabaseUtil.close(conn);
        }
    }
}
```

Setting Up the Oracle Database

Using Oracle, define a table that has a column of the NUMBER type, as shown next. Oracle's data type NUMBER(p, s) denotes a number having the precision p and scale s. The precision p can range from 1 to 38, and the scale s can range from -84 to 127.

```
SQL> create table integer_table(
  2       id varchar(12),
  3       byte_column NUMBER,
  4       short_column NUMBER,
  5       int_column NUMBER,
  6       long_column NUMBER
  7  );
```

```
SQL> desc integer_table;
 Name                Null?    Type
 -------------       -------- ------------
 ID                           VARCHAR2(12)
 BYTE_COLUMN                  NUMBER
 SHORT_COLUMN                 NUMBER
 INT_COLUMN                   NUMBER
 LONG_COLUMN                  NUMBER
```

```
SQL> insert into integer_table
  2   (id, byte_column, short_column, int_column, long_column)
  3  values('id-1', 12, 1234, 1234567890, 12345678901234567890);
```

```
SQL> insert into integer_table
  2   (id, byte_column, short_column, int_column, long_column)
  3  values('id-2', 12, 1234, 1234567890, 1234567890123456);
```

```
SQL> commit;
Commit complete.
```

```
SQL> set numwidth 25;
SQL> select * from integer_table;
ID    BYTE_COLUMN  SHORT_COLUMN  INT_COLUMN  LONG_COLUMN
----  -----------  ------------  ----------  --------------------
id-1  12           1234          1234567890  12345678901234567890
id-2  12           1234          1234567890  1234567890123456
```

Running the Solution for the Oracle Database

This shows how to run the solution for the Oracle database:

```
$ javac Demo_PreparedStatement_SetIntegers.java
$ java Demo_PreparedStatement_SetIntegers oracle \
    id-33 44 4455 44556677 2233445566778899
--Demo_PreparedStatement_SetIntegers begin--
conn=oracle.jdbc.driver.OracleConnection@860d49
--------------
rowCount=1
--Demo_PreparedStatement_SetIntegers end--
```

Viewing the Oracle Database After Running the Solution

This shows the Oracle database after running the solution:

```
SQL> select * from integer_table;
ID     BYTE_COLUMN  SHORT_COLUMN  INT_COLUMN   LONG_COLUMN
----   -----------  ------------  ----------   --------------------
id-1   12           1234          1234567890   12345678901234567890
id-2   12           1234          1234567890   1234567890123456
id-33  44           4455          44556677     2233445566778899
```

Setting Up the MySQL Database

Using MySQL, define a table that has the following columns: TINYINT (maps to byte), SMALLINT

```
    -> id varchar(12),
    -> byte_column TINYINT,
    -> short_column SMALLINT,
    -> int_column INT,
    -> long_column BIGINT
    -> );
Query OK, 0 rows affected (0.25 sec)

mysql> desc integer_table;
+--------------+-------------+------+-----+---------+-------+
| Field        | Type        | Null | Key | Default | Extra |
+--------------+-------------+------+-----+---------+-------+
| id           | varchar(12) | YES  |     | NULL    |       |
| byte_column  | tinyint(4)  | YES  |     | NULL    |       |
| short_column | smallint(6) | YES  |     | NULL    |       |
| int_column   | int(11)     | YES  |     | NULL    |       |
| long_column  | bigint(20)  | YES  |     | NULL    |       |
+--------------+-------------+------+-----+---------+-------+
5 rows in set (0.03 sec)

mysql> insert into integer_table
    -> (id, byte_column, short_column, int_column, long_column)
    -> values('id-1', 12, 1234, 1234567890, 12345678901234567890);

mysql> insert into integer_table
    -> (id, byte_column, short_column, int_column, long_column)
    -> values('id-2', 12, 1234, 1234567890, 12345678901234567);
```

```
mysql> commit;
mysql> select * from integer_table;
+-------+-------------+--------------+------------+----------------------+
| id    | byte_column | short_column | int_column | long_column          |
+-------+-------------+--------------+------------+----------------------+
| id-1  |          12 |         1234 | 1234567890 | -6101065172474983726 |
| id-2  |          12 |         1234 | 1234567890 |    12345678901234567 |
+-------+-------------+--------------+------------+----------------------+
2 rows in set (0.02 sec)
```

Running the Solution for the MySQL Database

This shows how to run the solution for the MySQL database:

```
$ javac Demo_PreparedStatement_SetIntegers.java
$ java Demo_PreparedStatement_SetIntegers mysql \
    id-22 34 34567 1222333444 1222333444555
Exception in thread "main" java.lang.NumberFormatException:
Value out of range. Value:"34567" Radix:10
        at java.lang.Short.parseShort(Short.java:122)
        at java.lang.Short.parseShort(Short.java:78)
        at Demo_PreparedStatement_SetIntegers.main
        (Demo_PreparedStatement_SetIntegers.java:14)

$ java Demo_PreparedStatement_SetIntegers mysql \
    id-22 34 3456 1222333444 1222333444555



--------------
rowCount=1
--Demo_PreparedStatement_SetIntegers end--
```

Viewing the MySQL Database After Running the Solution

This shows the MySQL database after running the solution:

```
mysql> select * from integer_table;
+-------+-------------+--------------+------------+----------------------+
| id    | byte_column | short_column | int_column | long_column          |
+-------+-------------+--------------+------------+----------------------+
| id-1  |          12 |         1234 | 1234567890 | -6101065172474983726 |
| id-2  |          12 |         1234 | 1234567890 |    12345678901234567 |
| id-22 |          34 |         3456 | 1222333444 |       1222333444555  |
+-------+-------------+--------------+------------+----------------------+
3 rows in set (0.00 sec)
```

13-9. How Do You Use PreparedStatement.setBytes()?

The following sections show how to pass an array of bytes (representing binary data) to a
PreparedStatement object.

How It Works

The Oracle and MySQL databases both support PreparedStatement.setBytes(). In general, the
method setBytes() is capable of sending unlimited amounts of data. But each database driver can
set limitations on the maximum number of bytes sent. For example, in the Oracle database, there
is a limit on the maximum size of the array that can be bound using the PreparedStatement class's

setBytes() method. In Oracle 8 and higher, the maximum size for setBytes() is 2,000 bytes (in Oracle 7, the maximum size is 255).

The signature of setBytes() is as follows:

```
void setBytes(int parameterIndex,
              byte[] x) throws SQLException
```

This sets the designated parameter to the given Java array of bytes. The driver converts this to a SQL VARBINARY or LONGVARBINARY (depending on the argument's size relative to the driver's limits on VARBINARY values) when it sends it to the database.

The parameters are as follows:

- parameterIndex: The first parameter is 1, the second is 2, and so on.

- x: The parameter value (as an array of byte).

This throws a SQLException if a database access error occurs.

Solution

Here's the solution:

```java
import java.util.*;
import java.io.*;
import java.sql.*;

import jcb.util.DatabaseUtil;
import jcb.db.VeryBasicConnectionManager;


    public static void main(String[] args) {
        // read inputs from command line
        String dbVendor = args[0]; // {"mysql", "oracle" }
        String id = args[1];
        byte[] shortData = args[2].getBytes();
        byte[] longData = args[3].getBytes();

        Connection conn = null;
        PreparedStatement pstmt = null;
        try {
            System.out.println("--Demo_PreparedStatement_SetBytes begin--");
            conn = VeryBasicConnectionManager.getConnection(dbVendor);
            System.out.println("conn="+conn);
            System.out.println("--------------");

            // prepare query
            String query = "insert into bytes_table" +
                " (id, short_data, long_data) values(?, ?, ?)";

            // create PrepareStatement object
            pstmt = conn.prepareStatement(query);
            pstmt.setString(1, id);
            pstmt.setBytes(2, shortData);
            pstmt.setBytes(3, longData);
```

```
            // execute query, and return number of rows created
            int rowCount = pstmt.executeUpdate();
            System.out.println("rowCount="+rowCount);
            System.out.println("--Demo_PreparedStatement_SetBytes end--");
        }
        catch(Exception e){
            e.printStackTrace();
            System.exit(1);
        }
        finally {
            // release database resources
            DatabaseUtil.close(pstmt);
            DatabaseUtil.close(conn);
        }
    }
}
```

Setting Up the Oracle Database

This example uses a table that has columns of the RAW and LONG RAW data types. The maximum size for the RAW data type is 2,000 bytes, and you must specify a size for a RAW value. The maximum size for the LONG RAW data type is up to 2GB.

```
SQL> create table bytes_table(
  2    id varchar2(10),
  3    short_data RAW(1000),



Table created.

SQL> desc bytes_table;
 Name              Null?      Type
 ------------      --------   --------------

 ID                           VARCHAR2(10)
 SHORT_DATA                   RAW(1000)
 LONG_DATA                    LONG RAW
```

Running the Solution for the Oracle Database

This shows how to run the solution for the Oracle database:

```
$ javac Demo_PreparedStatement_SetBytes.java
$ java Demo_PreparedStatement_SetBytes oracle id11 "abcd" "longrawdata"
--Demo_PreparedStatement_SetBytes begin--
conn=oracle.jdbc.driver.OracleConnection@1a125f0
---------------
rowCount=1
--Demo_PreparedStatement_SetBytes end--

$ java Demo_PreparedStatement_SetBytes oracle id22 "abcdef" "longrawdata2222"
--Demo_PreparedStatement_SetBytes begin--
conn=oracle.jdbc.driver.OracleConnection@1a125f0
---------------
rowCount=1
--Demo_PreparedStatement_SetBytes end--
```

Viewing the Oracle Database After Running the Solution

This shows the Oracle database after running the solution:

```
SQL> select id, short_data from bytes_table;

ID      SHORT_DATA
----    -----------
id11    61626364
id22    616263646566
```

Setting Up the MySQL Database

Using MySQL database, you can use PreparedStatement.setBytes() for the VARCHAR BINARY, TINYBLOB, BLOB, MEDIUMBLOB, and LONGBLOB data types. For this example, use a table that has columns of the VARCHAR BINARY and TINYBLOB data types. The maximum size for the TINYBLOB data type is 255 bytes.

```
mysql> create table bytes_table(
    -> id varchar(10),
    -> short_data VARCHAR(16) BINARY,
    -> long_data TINYBLOB
    -> );
Query OK, 0 rows affected (0.16 sec)

mysql> desc bytes_table;
+----------------+---------------------+------+-----+---------+-------+
| id             | varchar(10)         | YES  |     | NULL    |       |
| short_data     | varchar(16) binary  | YES  |     | NULL    |       |
| long_data      | tinyblob            | YES  |     | NULL    |       |
+----------------+---------------------+------+-----+---------+-------+
3 rows in set (0.04 sec)
```

Running the Solution for the MySQL Database

This shows how to run the solution for the MySQL database:

```
$ javac Demo_PreparedStatement_SetBytes.java
$ java Demo_PreparedStatement_SetBytes mysql id22 "abcd" "abcd1122"
--Demo_PreparedStatement_SetBytes begin--
conn=com.mysql.jdbc.Connection@14ed9ff
---------------
rowCount=1
--Demo_PreparedStatement_SetBytes end--

$ java Demo_PreparedStatement_SetBytes mysql id44 "abcdef" "abcd11223344"
--Demo_PreparedStatement_SetBytes begin--
conn=com.mysql.jdbc.Connection@14ed9ff
---------------
rowCount=1
--Demo_PreparedStatement_SetBytes end--
```

MySQL Database after Running Solution

This shows the MySQL database after running the solution:

```
mysql> select * from binary_table;
+------+------------+--------------+
| id   | short_data | long_data    |
+------+------------+--------------+
| id22 | abcd       | abcd1122     |
| id44 | abcdef     | abcd11223344 |
+------+------------+--------------+
2 rows in set (0.02 sec)
```

13-10. How Do You Use PreparedStatement.setCharacterStream()?

The following sections show how to pass a character stream (represented as a java.io.Reader) to a PreparedStatement object.

How It Works

You can use PreparedStatement.setCharacterStream() on both the Oracle and MySQL databases.

In the Oracle database, when a column data type is LONG (character large object), then you can use setCharacterStream(). Oracle's LONG represents character data of a variable length up to 2GB. Oracle's LONG maps to java.sql.Types.LONGVARCHAR, which maps to java.lang.String.

In the MySQL database, when a column data type is TINYTEXT with a maximum length of 255 (2^8 - 1) characters, TEXT with a maximum length of 65,535 (2^{16} - 1) characters, MEDIUMTEXT with a maximum length of 16,777,215 (2^{24} - 1) characters, or LONGTEXT with a maximum length of 4,294,967,295 or 4G (2^{32} - 1) characters, then you can use setCharacterStream().

setCharacterStream() is as follows:

```
java.io.Reader reader,
int length)
throws SQLException
```

This sets the designated parameter to the given Reader object, which is the given number of characters long. When a large Unicode value is input to a LONGVARCHAR parameter, it may be more practical to send it via a java.io.Reader object. The data will be read from the stream as needed until reaching the end of the file. The JDBC driver will do any necessary conversion from Unicode to the database char format.

This stream object can either be a standard Java stream object or be your own subclass that implements the standard interface.

The parameters are as follows:

- parameterIndex: The first parameter is 1, the second is 2, and so on.
- reader: The java.io.Reader object that contains the Unicode data.
- length: The number of characters in the stream.

This throws a SQLException if a database access error occurs.

Solution

This solution will read a text file and then insert its name (as an ID) and content (as a char_stream_column) into the char_stream_table:

```
import java.util.*;
import java.io.*;
import java.sql.*;
```

```java
import jcb.util.DatabaseUtil;
import jcb.db.VeryBasicConnectionManager;

public class Demo_PreparedStatement_SetCharacterStream {

    public static void main(String[] args) {
        System.out.println("--Demo_PreparedStatement_SetCharacterStream begin--");
         // read inputs from command line
        String dbVendor = args[0];
        String fileName = args[1];
        Reader fileReader = null;
        long fileLength = 0;
        try {
            File file = new File(fileName);
            fileLength = file.length();
            fileReader = (Reader) new BufferedReader(new FileReader(file));
            System.out.println("fileName="+fileName);
            System.out.println("fileLength="+fileLength);
        }
        catch(Exception e) {
            e.printStackTrace();
            System.exit(1);
        }

        Connection conn = null;
        PreparedStatement pstmt = null;


            conn = VeryBasicConnectionManager.getConnection(dbVendor);
            System.out.println("conn="+conn);
            System.out.println("---------------");

            // begin transaction
            conn.setAutoCommit(false);

            // prepare SQL query for inserting a new row using SetCharacterStream()
            String query = "insert into char_stream_table" +
                " (id, char_stream_column) values(?, ?)";

            // create PrepareStatement object
            pstmt = conn.prepareStatement(query);
            pstmt.setString(1, fileName);
            pstmt.setCharacterStream(2, fileReader, (int)fileLength);

            // execute query, and return number of rows created
            int rowCount = pstmt.executeUpdate();
            System.out.println("rowCount="+rowCount);

            // end transaction
            conn.commit();
            System.out.println("--Demo_PreparedStatement_SetCharacterStream end--");
        }
        catch(Exception e){
            e.printStackTrace();
            System.exit(1);
        }
        finally {
            // release database resources
```

```
            DatabaseUtil.close(pstmt);
            DatabaseUtil.close(conn);
        }
    }
}
```

Setting Up the Oracle Database

This shows how to set up the Oracle database:

```
$ sqlplus octopus/octopus
SQL> create table char_stream_table (
  2   id VARCHAR(16) NOT NULL PRIMARY KEY,
  3   char_stream_column LONG
  4  );

Table created.

SQL> desc char_stream_table;
 Name                    Null?     Type
 ----------------        --------  -----------
 ID                      NOT NULL  VARCHAR2(16)
 CHAR_STREAM_COLUMN                LONG

SQL> insert into char_stream_table(id, char_stream_column)
  2      values('id-1', 'abcdef');



SQL> commit;
Commit complete.

SQL> select * from char_stream_table;

ID      CHAR_STREAM_COLUMN
----    ------------------
id-1    abcdef
id-2    0123456789
```

Running the Solution for the Oracle Database

This shows how to run the solution for the Oracle database:

```
$ cat sample.txt
this is line1.
this is the last line.

$ javac Demo_PreparedStatement_SetCharacterStream.java
$ java Demo_PreparedStatement_SetCharacterStream oracle sample.txt
--Demo_PreparedStatement_SetCharacterStream begin--
fileName=sample.txt
fileLength=38
conn=oracle.jdbc.driver.OracleConnection@ae506e
---------------
rowCount=1
--Demo_PreparedStatement_SetCharacterStream end--
```

Viewing the Oracle Database After Running the Program

This shows the Oracle database after running the program:

```
SQL> select * from char_stream_table;

ID          CHAR_STREAM_COLUMN
----        ------------------
id-1        abcdef
id-2        0123456789
sample.txt  this is line1.
            this is the last line.
```

Setting Up the MySQL Database

Using MySQL, define a table that has a TEXT data type, as shown next. A TEXT data type is semantically equivalent to a SQL CLOB data type and can hold a maximum length of 65,535 (2^{16} - 1) characters.

```
mysql> use tiger;
Database changed

mysql> create table char_stream_table(
    -> id VARCHAR(16) NOT NULL PRIMARY KEY,
    -> char_stream_column TEXT
    -> );
Query OK, 0 rows affected (0.07 sec)
```

Field	Type	Null	Key	Default	Extra
id	varchar(16)		PRI		
char_stream_column	text	YES		NULL	

```
2 rows in set (0.02 sec)

mysql> insert into char_stream_table(id, char_stream_column)
    -> values('id-1', 'abcde1234');

mysql> insert into char_stream_table(id, char_stream_column)
    -> values('id-2', 'zzzzzzz1234');

mysql> select * from char_stream_table;
```

id	char_stream_column
id-1	abcde1234
id-2	zzzzzzz1234

```
2 rows in set (1.45 sec)
```

Running the Solution for the MySQL Database

This shows how to run the solution for the MySQL database:

```
$ javac Demo_PreparedStatement_SetCharacterStream.java
$ java Demo_PreparedStatement_SetCharacterStream mysql sample.txt
--Demo_PreparedStatement_SetCharacterStream begin--
```

```
fileName=sample.txt
fileLength=38
conn=com.mysql.jdbc.Connection@1fdc96c
----------------
rowCount=1
--Demo_PreparedStatement_SetCharacterStream end--
```

MySQL Database after Running Solution

This shows the MySQL database after running the solution:

```
mysql> select * from char_stream_table;
+-------------+------------------------------------------+
| id          | char_stream_column                       |
+-------------+------------------------------------------+
| id-1        | abcde1234                                |
+-------------+------------------------------------------+
| id-2        | zzzzzzz1234                               |
+-------------+------------------------------------------+
| sample.txt  | this is line1.                           |
|             | this is the last line.                   |
+-------------+------------------------------------------+
3 rows in set (0.00 sec)
```

13-11. How Do You Use PreparedStatement.setClob()?

How It Works

java.sql.Clob is the mapping in the Java programming language for the SQL CLOB type. A SQL CLOB is a built-in type that stores a character large object as a column value in a row of a database table. You can use PreparedStatement.setClob() on both the Oracle and MySQL databases.

In Oracle, when a column data type is CLOB, then you can use setClob(). Oracle's CLOB represents character data of a variable length up to 2GB.

In MySQL, when a column data type is TINYTEXT with a maximum length of 255 (2^8 - 1) characters, TEXT with a maximum length of 65,535 (2^{16} - 1) characters, MEDIUMTEXT with a maximum length of 16,777,215 (2^{24} - 1) characters, or LONGTEXT with a maximum length of 4,294,967,295 or 4G (2^{32} - 1) characters, then you can use setClob().

The signature of setClob() is as follows:

```
public void setClob(int parameterIndex,
                    java.sql.Clob clob)  throws SQLException
```

This sets the designated parameter to the given Clob object. The driver converts this to a SQL CLOB value when it sends it to the database.

The parameters are as follows:

- parameterIndex: The first parameter is 1, the second is 2, and so on.

- clob: A java.sql.Clob object that maps a SQL CLOB value.

This throws a SQLException if a database access error occurs.

Setting Up the Oracle Database

This shows how to set up the Oracle database:

```
SQL> create table clob_table (
  2  id VARCHAR(12) NOT NULL PRIMARY KEY,
  3  clob_column CLOB default empty_clob()
  4  );

Table created.

SQL> desc clob_table;
 Name                Null?    Type
 ---------------- -------- ------------
 ID                 NOT NULL VARCHAR2(12)
 CLOB_COLUMN                 CLOB

SQL> insert into clob_table(id, clob_column)
        values('id-1', 'value-111111');

SQL> insert into clob_table(id, clob_column)
        values('id-2', 'value-22222222222');

SQL> commit;
SQL> select * from clob_table;

ID     CLOB_COLUMN


id-2    value-22222222222
```

Solution

This class uses PreparedStatement.setClob() to insert a new record into a SQL CLOB column:

```java
import java.util.*;
import java.io.*;
import java.sql.*;

import jcb.util.DatabaseUtil;
import jcb.db.VeryBasicConnectionManager;

public class Demo_PreparedStatement_SetClob {

    public static void main(String[] args) {
        System.out.println("--Demo_PreparedStatement_SetCharacterStream begin--");
        // read inputs from command line
        String dbVendor = args[0]; // {"mysql", "oracle" }
        String id = args[1];
        String newID = args[2];

        ResultSet rs = null;
        Connection conn = null;
        PreparedStatement pstmt = null;
        try {
            System.out.println("--Demo_PreparedStatement_SetClob begin--");
```

```
            // get a database connection object
            conn = VeryBasicConnectionManager.getConnection(dbVendor);
            System.out.println("conn="+conn);
            System.out.println("---------------");

            // begin transaction
            conn.setAutoCommit(false);

            // prepare blob object from an existing binary column
            String query1 = "select clob_column from clob_table where id = ?";
            pstmt = conn.prepareStatement(query1);
            pstmt.setString(1, id);
            rs = pstmt.executeQuery();
            rs.next();
            java.sql.Clob clob = (java.sql.Clob) rs.getObject(1);
            // prepare SQL query for inserting a new row using setClob()
            String query = "insert into clob_table(id, clob_column) values(?, ?)";

            // create PrepareStatement object
            pstmt = conn.prepareStatement(query);
            pstmt.setString(1, newID);
            pstmt.setClob(2, clob);

            // execute query, and return number of rows created
            int rowCount = pstmt.executeUpdate();
            System.out.println("rowCount="+rowCount);


            conn.commit();
            System.out.println("--Demo_PreparedStatement_SetClob end--");
        }
        catch(Exception e){
            e.printStackTrace();
            System.exit(1);
        }
        finally {
            // release database resources
            DatabaseUtil.close(rs);
            DatabaseUtil.close(pstmt);
            DatabaseUtil.close(conn);
        }
    }
}
```

Running the Solution for the Oracle Database

This shows how to run the solution for the Oracle database:

```
$ javac Demo_PreparedStatement_SetClob.java
$ java Demo_PreparedStatement_SetClob  oracle id-1 id-111
--Demo_PreparedStatement_SetClob_Oracle begin--
conn=oracle.jdbc.driver.OracleConnection@6e70c7
---------------
rowCount=1
--Demo_PreparedStatement_SetClob end--
```

Viewing the Oracle Database After Running the Solution

This shows the Oracle database after running the solution:

```
SQL> select * from clob_table;

ID      CLOB_COLUMN
----    ----------------
id-1    value-111111
id-2    value-22222222222
id-111  value-111111
```

Setting Up the MySQL Database

Using MySQL, define a table that has a TEXT data type, as shown next. A TEXT data type is semantically equivalent to a SQL CLOB data type and can hold a maximum length of 65,535 (2^16 - 1) characters.

```
mysql> create table clob_table (
    -> id VARCHAR(12) NOT NULL PRIMARY KEY,
    -> clob_column TEXT);

mysql> desc clob_table;
+-------------+-------------+------+-----+---------+-------+
| Field       | Type        | Null | Key | Default | Extra |
+-------------+-------------+------+-----+---------+-------+
| id          | varchar(12) |      | PRI |         |       |
| clob_column | text        | YES  |     | NULL    |       |
+-------------+-------------+------+-----+---------+-------+


mysql> insert into clob_table(id, clob_column)
    -> values('id-1', '123abc');

mysql> insert into clob_table(id, clob_column)
    -> values('id-2', '444zzzzz');

mysql> select * from clob_table;
+------+-------------+
| id   | clob_column |
+------+-------------+
| id-1 | 123abc      |
| id-2 | 444zzzzz    |
+------+-------------+
2 rows in set (0.00 sec)
```

Running the Solution for the MySQL Database

In the JDBC API, there is no constructor to build a java.sql.Clob object directly; therefore, to use the setClob() method, you need to create a ResultSet object, extract a Clob object, and then pass it to the PreparedStatement.setClob() method. I will show how to extract a Clob from clob_table and then insert it into clob_table using the PreparedStatement.setClob() method.

```
$ javac Demo_PreparedStatement_SetClob.java
$ java Demo_PreparedStatement_SetClob mysql id-1 id-1000
--Demo_PreparedStatement_SetClob begin--
conn=com.mysql.jdbc.Connection@1e4cbc4
--------------
```

```
clob.length()=6
rowCount=1
--Demo_PreparedStatement_SetClob end--
```

Viewing the MySQL Database After Running the Solution

This shows the MySQL database after running the solution:

```
mysql> select * from clob_table;
+---------+-------------+
| id      | clob_column |
+---------+-------------+
| id-1    | 123abc      |
| id-2    | 444zzzzz    |
| id-1000 | 123abc      |
+---------+-------------+
3 rows in set (0.00 sec)
```

13-12. How Do You Use PreparedStatement.setDate()?

Java.sql.Date is a thin wrapper around a millisecond value that allows JDBC to identify it as a SQL DATE value. You want to pass a java.sql.Date (character large object) object to a PreparedStatement object.

How It Works

is DATE, then you can use the setDate() method. Note that in Oracle the DATE data type can represent three distinct data types: Date, Time, and Timestamp. In MySQL, when a column data type is DATE, then you can use the setDate() method.

The signature of setDate() is as follows:

```
public void setDate(int parameterIndex,
                    java.sql.Date date)   throws SQLException
```

This sets the designated parameter to the given java.sql.Date value. The driver converts this to a SQL DATE value when it sends it to the database.

The parameters are as follows:

- parameterIndex: The first parameter is 1, the second is 2, and so on.

- date: The parameter value.

This throws a SQLException if a database access error occurs.

Solution

This solution will use the PreparedStatement.setDate() method:

```
import java.util.*;
import java.io.*;
import java.sql.*;

import jcb.util.DatabaseUtil;
import jcb.db.VeryBasicConnectionManager;

public class Demo_PreparedStatement_SetDate {
    public static java.sql.Date getCurrentJavaSqlDate() {
```

```
        java.util.Date today = new java.util.Date();
        return new java.sql.Date(today.getTime());
    }
    public static void main(String[] args) {
        System.out.println("--Demo_PreparedStatement_SetDate begin--");
         // read inputs from command line
        String dbVendor = args[0];
        String id = args[1];
        Connection conn = null;
        PreparedStatement pstmt = null;
        try {
            conn = VeryBasicConnectionManager.getConnection(dbVendor);
            System.out.println("conn="+conn);
            System.out.println("---------------");

            // prepare query
            String query = "insert into date_table(id, date_column) values(?, ?)";

            // create PrepareStatement object
            pstmt = conn.prepareStatement(query);
            pstmt.setString(1, id);
            java.sql.Date date = getCurrentJavaSqlDate();
            pstmt.setDate(2, date);

            // execute query, and return number of rows created
            int rowCount = pstmt.executeUpdate();


        }
        catch(Exception e){
            e.printStackTrace();
            System.exit(1);
        }
        finally {
            // release database resources
            DatabaseUtil.close(pstmt);
            DatabaseUtil.close(conn);
        }
    }
}
```

Setting Up the Oracle Database

This shows how to set up the Oracle database:

```
SQL> create table date_table(id VARCHAR(12), date_column DATE);
Table created.
SQL> desc date_table;
 Name                                      Null?    Type
 ----------------------------------------- -------- ------------
 ID                                                 VARCHAR2(12)
 DATE_COLUMN                                        DATE

SQL> insert into date_table(id, date_column) values('id-1', '12-JUN-2003');
SQL> insert into date_table(id, date_column) values('id-2', '12-DEC-2003');
SQL> commit;
SQL> select * from date_table;
```

```
ID            DATE_COLUMN
--------      ---------------
id-1          12-JUN-03
id-2          12-DEC-03
```

Running the Solution for the Oracle Database

This shows how to run the solution for the Oracle database:

```
$ javac Demo_PreparedStatement_SetDate.java
$ java Demo_PreparedStatement_SetDate oracle id-200
--Demo_PreparedStatement_SetDate begin--
conn=oracle.jdbc.driver.OracleConnection@6e70c7
----------------
rowCount=1
--Demo_PreparedStatement_SetDate end--

$ java Demo_PreparedStatement_SetDate oracle id-400
--Demo_PreparedStatement_SetDate begin--
conn=oracle.jdbc.driver.OracleConnection@6e70c7
----------------
rowCount=1
--Demo_PreparedStatement_SetDate end--
```

Viewing the Oracle Database After Running the Solution

```
ID            DATE_COLU
--------      ---------
id-1          12-JUN-03
id-2          12-DEC-03
id-200        07-NOV-03
id-400        07-NOV-03
```

Setting Up the MySQL Database

Using Oracle, define a table that has a column of the DATE type, as shown next. The Oracle database accepts dates in the dd-MMM-yyyy format, while the MySQL database accepts dates in the yyyy-mm-dd format.

```
mysql> create table date_table(id VARCHAR(12), date_column DATE);
Query OK, 0 rows affected (0.14 sec)

mysql> desc date_table;
+-------------+-------------+------+-----+---------+-------+
| Field       | Type        | Null | Key | Default | Extra |
+-------------+-------------+------+-----+---------+-------+
| id          | varchar(12) | YES  |     | NULL    |       |
| date_column | date        | YES  |     | NULL    |       |
+-------------+-------------+------+-----+---------+-------+
2 rows in set (0.06 sec)

mysql> insert into date_table(id, date_column) values('id-1', '12-JUN-2003');
Query OK, 1 row affected (0.01 sec)

mysql> insert into date_table(id, date_column) values('id-2', '12-DEC-2003');
```

```
Query OK, 1 row affected (0.00 sec)

mysql> select * from date_table;
+------+-------------+
| id   | date_column |
+------+-------------+
| id-1 | 0000-00-00  |
| id-2 | 0000-00-00  |
+------+-------------+
2 rows in set (0.13 sec)

mysql> insert into date_table(id, date_column) values('id-3', '2003-06-12');
mysql> insert into date_table(id, date_column) values('id-3', '2003-12-12');
mysql> select * from date_table;
+------+-------------+
| id   | date_column |
+------+-------------+
| id-1 | 0000-00-00  |
| id-2 | 0000-00-00  |
| id-3 | 2003-06-12  |
| id-4 | 2003-12-12  |
+------+-------------+
4 rows in set (0.00 sec)
```

Running the Solution for the MySQL Database

```
$ java Demo_PreparedStatement_SetDate mysql id-300
--Demo_PreparedStatement_SetDate begin--
conn=com.mysql.jdbc.Connection@cd2c3c
---------------
rowCount=1
--Demo_PreparedStatement_SetDate_MySQL end--

$ java Demo_PreparedStatement_SetDate mysql id-500
--Demo_PreparedStatement_SetDate begin--
conn=com.mysql.jdbc.Connection@cd2c3c
---------------
rowCount=1
--Demo_PreparedStatement_SetDate_MySQL end--
```

Viewing the MySQL Database After Running the Solution

This shows the MySQL database after running the solution:

```
mysql> select * from date_table;
+--------+-------------+
| id     | date_column |
+--------+-------------+
| id-1   | 0000-00-00  |
| id-2   | 0000-00-00  |
| id-3   | 2003-06-12  |
| id-4   | 2003-12-12  |
| id-300 | 2003-11-07  |
| id-500 | 2003-11-07  |
+--------+-------------+
6 rows in set (0.00 sec)
```

13-13. How Do You Use PreparedStatement's setFloat() and setDouble()?

The following sections show how to pass a floating-point value (the Java primitive data types float and double) to a PreparedStatement object.

How It Works

You can use the PreparedStatement object's setFloat() and setDouble() methods on both the Oracle and MySQL databases. In Oracle, when a column data type is NUMBER, then you can use setFloat() and setDouble(). Oracle uses the NUMBER type for integers and floating-point numbers. In MySQL, when a column data type is FLOAT, REAL, DOUBLE PRECISION, NUMERIC, or DECIMAL, then you can use setFloat() and setDouble().

The signature of setDouble() is as follows:

```
public void setDouble(int parameterIndex,
                      double x)  throws SQLException
```

This sets the designated parameter to the given Java double value. The driver converts this to a SQL DOUBLE value when it sends it to the database.

The parameters are as follows:

- parameterIndex: The first parameter is 1, the second is 2, and so on.

- x: The parameter value.

This throws a   if a database access error occurs.

```
public void setFloat(int parameterIndex,
                     float x)  throws SQLException
```

This sets the designated parameter to the given Java float value. The driver converts this to a SQL FLOAT value when it sends it to the database.

The parameters are as follows:

- parameterIndex: The first parameter is 1, the second is 2, and so on.

- x: The parameter value.

This throws a SQLException if a database access error occurs.

Solution

Here's the solution:

```
import java.util.*;
import java.io.*;
import java.sql.*;

import jcb.util.DatabaseUtil;
import jcb.db.VeryBasicConnectionManager;

public class Demo_PreparedStatement_SetFloatAndDouble {
    public static void main(String[] args) {
        System.out.println("--Demo_PreparedStatement_SetFloatAndDouble begin--");
        // read inputs from command line
        String dbVendor = args[0];
        String stringValue = args[1];
```

```
        float floatValue = Float.parseFloat(args[2]);
        double doubleValue = Double.parseDouble(args[3]);
        Connection conn = null;
        PreparedStatement pstmt = null;
        try {
            conn = VeryBasicConnectionManager.getConnection(dbVendor);
            System.out.println("conn="+conn);
            System.out.println("--------------");

            // prepare query
            String query = "insert into double_table( " +
                "id, float_column, double_column) values(?, ?, ?)";
            // create PrepareStatement object
            pstmt = conn.prepareStatement(query);
            pstmt.setString(1, stringValue);
            pstmt.setFloat(2, floatValue);
            pstmt.setDouble(3, doubleValue);

            // execute query, and return number of rows created
            int rowCount = pstmt.executeUpdate();
            System.out.println("rowCount="+rowCount);
            System.out.println("--Demo_PreparedStatement_SetFloatAndDouble end--");
        }
        catch(Exception e){
            e.printStackTrace();
            System.exit(1);


            // release database resources
            DatabaseUtil.close(pstmt);
            DatabaseUtil.close(conn);
        }
    }
}
```

Setting Up the Oracle Database

Using Oracle, define a table that has a column of the NUMBER type, as shown next. Oracle's data type NUMBER(p, s) denotes a number having the precision p and scale s. The precision p can range from 1 to 38, and the scale s can range from -84 to 127.

```
$ sqlplus octopus/octopus
SQL> create table double_table (
  2      id VARCHAR(4),
  3      float_column NUMBER(6, 2),
  4      double_column NUMBER(16, 4) );

Table created.

SQL> desc double_table;
 Name                                      Null?    Type
 ----------------------------------------- -------- ------------
 ID                                                 VARCHAR2(4)
 FLOAT_COLUMN                                       NUMBER(6,2)
 DOUBLE_COLUMN                                      NUMBER(16,4)
```

```
SQL> insert into double_table(id, float_column, double_column)
values('id-1', 123.34, 12.123);
SQL> insert into double_table(id, float_column, double_column)
values('id-2', 555.1, 89.1122);
sql> commit;
SQL> select * from double_table;
ID    FLOAT_COLUMN    DOUBLE_COLUMN
----  ------------    -------------
id-1         123.34          12.123
id-2          555.1         89.1122
```

Running the Solution for the Oracle Database

This shows how to run the solution for the Oracle database:

```
$ javac Demo_PreparedStatement_SetDouble.java
$ java Demo_PreparedStatement_SetFloatAndDouble oracle id-5 22.34 224455.678
--Demo_PreparedStatement_SetFloatAndDouble begin--
conn=oracle.jdbc.driver.OracleConnection@228a02
----------------
rowCount=1
--Demo_PreparedStatement_SetFloatAndDouble end--
```

Viewing the Oracle Database After Running the Solution

This shows the Oracle database after running the solution:

```
----  ------------    -------------
id-1         123.34          12.123
id-2          555.1         89.1122
id-5          22.34      224455.678
```

Setting Up the MySQL Database

Using MySQL, you can use the FLOAT and DOUBLE data types to store Java's float and double primitive data type values. This shows how to set up the MySQL database:

```
mysql> use tiger;
Database changed
mysql> create table double_table (
    ->   id varchar(4),
    ->   float_column FLOAT,
    ->   double_column DOUBLE );

mysql> desc double_table;
+---------------+------------+------+-----+---------+-------+
| Field         | Type       | Null | Key | Default | Extra |
+---------------+------------+------+-----+---------+-------+
| id            | varchar(4) | YES  |     | NULL    |       |
| float_column  | float      | YES  |     | NULL    |       |
| double_column | double     | YES  |     | NULL    |       |
+---------------+------------+------+-----+---------+-------+
```

```
mysql> insert into double_table(id, float_column, double_column)
> values('id-1', 123.45, 123.45);
mysql> insert into double_table(id, float_column, double_column)
> values('id-2', 1.2345, 1.2345);
mysql> select * from double_table;
+------+--------------+--------------+
| id   | float_column |double_column |
+------+--------------+--------------+
| id-1 |       123.45 |       123.45 |
| id-2 |       1.2345 |       1.2345 |
+------+--------------+--------------+
2 rows in set (0.01 sec)
```

Running the Solution for the MySQL Database

This shows how to run the solution for the MySQL database:

```
$ javac Demo_PreparedStatement_SetFloatAndDouble.java
$ java Demo_PreparedStatement_SetFloatAndDouble mysql id-7 11.22 1122334455.66
--Demo_PreparedStatement_SetFloatAndDouble begin--
conn=com.mysql.jdbc.Connection@b2fd8f
---------------
rowCount=1
--Demo_PreparedStatement_SetFloatAndDouble end--
```

Viewing the MySQL Database After Running the Solution

```
mysql> select * from double_table;
+------+--------------+---------------+
| id   | float_column | double_column |
+------+--------------+---------------+
| id-1 |       123.45 |        123.45 |
| id-2 |       1.2345 |        1.2345 |
| id-7 |        11.22 | 1122334455.66 |
+------+--------------+---------------+
3 rows in set (0.00 sec)
```

13-14. How Do You Use PreparedStatement.setNull()?

How do you set the designated parameter to SQL NULL? The following sections explain how to do this.

How It Works

Both the Oracle and MySQL databases support the PreparedStatement.setNull() method, which sets the designated parameter to SQL NULL. The signature of setNull() is as follows:

```
public void setNull(int parameterIndex,
                    int sqlType)  throws SQLException
```

This sets the designated parameter to SQL NULL. You must specify the parameter's SQL type. The parameters are as follows:

- parameterIndex: The first parameter is 1, the second is 2, and so on.

- sqlType: The SQL type code defined in java.sql.Types.

This throws a SQLException if a database access error occurs.

Solution

This solution inserts a record with SQL NULL values:

```java
import java.util.*;
import java.io.*;
import java.sql.*;

import jcb.util.DatabaseUtil;
import jcb.db.VeryBasicConnectionManager;

public class Demo_PreparedStatement_SetNull {
    public static void main(String[] args) {
        System.out.println("--Demo_PreparedStatement_SetNull begin--");
        // read inputs from command line
        String dbVendor = args[0];
        String idValue = args[1];
        Connection conn = null;
        PreparedStatement pstmt = null;
        try {
            conn = VeryBasicConnectionManager.getConnection(dbVendor);
            System.out.println("conn="+conn);
            System.out.println("---------------");

            // prepare query
            String query = "insert into nullable_table(id, " +
                "string_column, int_column) values(?, ?, ?)";


            pstmt = conn.prepareStatement(query);
            pstmt.setString(1, idValue);
            pstmt.setNull(2, java.sql.Types.VARCHAR);
            pstmt.setNull(3, java.sql.Types.INTEGER);

            // execute query, and return number of rows created
            int rowCount = pstmt.executeUpdate();
            System.out.println("rowCount="+rowCount);
            System.out.println("--Demo_PreparedStatement_SetNull end--");
        }
        catch(Exception e){
            e.printStackTrace();
            System.exit(1);
        }
        finally {
            // release database resources
            DatabaseUtil.close(pstmt);
            DatabaseUtil.close(conn);
        }
    }
}
```

Setting Up the Oracle Database

This shows how to set up the Oracle database:

```
SQL> create table nullable_table(
  2   id varchar(4),
  3   string_column VARCHAR(10),
```

```
   4  int_column NUMBER
   5  );
```

Table created.

```
SQL> desc nullable_table;
 Name                    Null?    Type
 ----------------        -------- -------------
 ID                               VARCHAR2(4)
 STRING_COLUMN                    VARCHAR2(10)
 INT_COLUMN                       NUMBER

SQL> insert into set_null_table(id, string_column, int_column)
  2  values('id-1', 'abcde', 123);

SQL> insert into set_null_table(id, string_column, int_column)
  2  values('id-2', 'zzzzzzz', 777);

SQL> commit;
Commit complete.

SQL> select * from set_null_table;

ID    STRING_COLUMN  INT_COLUMN
----  -------------  ----------
id-1  abcde                 123
```

Running the Solution for the Oracle Database

This shows how to run the solution for the Oracle database:

```
$ javac Demo_PreparedStatement_SetNull.java
$ java Demo_PreparedStatement_SetNull oracle id-3
--Demo_PreparedStatement_SetNull begin--
conn=oracle.jdbc.driver.OracleConnection@6e70c7
---------------
rowCount=1
--Demo_PreparedStatement_SetNull end--

$ java Demo_PreparedStatement_SetNull oracle id-4
--Demo_PreparedStatement_SetNull begin--
conn=oracle.jdbc.driver.OracleConnection@6e70c7
---------------
rowCount=1
--Demo_PreparedStatement_SetNull end--
```

Viewing the Oracle Database After Running the Solution

This shows the Oracle database after running the solution:

```
SQL> select * from nullable_table;
ID    STRING_COL  INT_COLUMN
----  ----------  ----------
id-1  abcde              123
id-2  zzzzzzz            777
id-3
id-4
```

Setting Up the MySQL Database

This shows how to set up the MySQL database:

```
create table nullable_table(
    id varchar(4),
    string_column VARCHAR(10),
    int_column INTEGER,
);
```

Running the Solution for the MySQL Database

This shows how to run the solution for the MySQL database:

```
$ javac Demo_PreparedStatement_SetNull.java
$ java Demo_PreparedStatement_SetNull mysql id-3
--Demo_PreparedStatement_SetNull begin--
conn=com.mysql.jdbc.Connection@1e4cbc4
---------------

rowCount=1
--Demo_PreparedStatement_SetNull end--

$ java Demo_PreparedStatement_SetNull mysql id-4
--Demo_PreparedStatement_SetNull begin--
conn=com.mysql.jdbc.Connection@1e4cbc4
---------------

rowCount=1
```

Viewing the MySQL Database After Running the Program

This shows the MySQL database after running the solution:

```
mysql> select * from set_null_table;
+------+---------------+------------+
| id   | string_column | int_column |
+------+---------------+------------+
| id-3 | NULL          |       NULL |
| id-4 | NULL          |       NULL |
+------+---------------+------------+
2 rows in set (0.00 sec)
```

13-15. How Do You Use PreparedStatement.setObject()?

The following sections show how to pass a Java Object (an instance of java.lang.Object) to a PreparedStatement object.

How It Works

Both the Oracle and MySQL databases support the PreparedStatement.setObject() method, which sets the designated parameter to SQL's data types. (The target data types can be different depending on the database vendor.) The PreparedStatement.setObject() method uses reflection to figure out a Java object's type at runtime before converting it to an appropriate SQL data type. The setObject() method converts Java types to SQL types using a standard JDBC map. If no match is found on the map, the method throws a SQLException.

The signature of setObject() is as follows:

```
void setObject(int parameterIndex,
               Object x)
               throws SQLException
```

This sets the value of the designated parameter using the given object. The second parameter must be of type Object; therefore, you should use the java.lang equivalent objects for built-in types.

The JDBC specification specifies a standard mapping from Java Object types to SQL types. The given argument will be converted to the corresponding SQL type before being sent to the database.

You can use this method to pass database-specific abstract data types by using a driver-specific Java type. If the object is of a class implementing the interface SQLData, the JDBC driver should call the method SQLData.writeSQL to write it to the SQL data stream. If, on the other hand, the object is of a class implementing Ref, Blob, Clob, Struct, or Array, the driver should pass it to the database as a value of the corresponding SQL type.

This method throws an exception if there is an ambiguity, for example, if the object is of a class implementing more than one of the interfaces named previously.

The parameters are as follows:

- parameterIndex: The first parameter is 1, the second is 2, and so on.

- x: The object containing the input parameter value.

This throws a SQLException if a database access error occurs or the type of the given object is ambiguous.

```
void setObject(int parameterIndex,
               Object x,
               int targetSqlType)
```

This sets the value of the designated parameter with the given object. This method is like the method setObject, except that it assumes a scale of zero.

The parameters are as follows:

- parameterIndex: The first parameter is 1, the second is 2, and so on.

- x: The object containing the input parameter value.

- targetSqlType: The SQL type (as defined in java.sql.Types) to be sent to the database.

This throws a SQLException if a database access error occurs.

```
void setObject(int parameterIndex,
               Object x,
               int targetSqlType,
               int scale)
               throws SQLException
```

This sets the value of the designated parameter with the given object. The second argument must be an object type; for integral values, you should use the java.lang equivalent objects.

The given Java object will be converted to the given targetSqlType before being sent to the database. If the object has a custom mapping (is of a class implementing the interface SQLData), the JDBC driver should call the method SQLData.writeSQL to write it to the SQL data stream. If, on the other hand, the object is of a class implementing Ref, Blob, Clob, Struct, or Array, the driver should pass it to the database as a value of the corresponding SQL type.

Note that you can use this method to pass database-specific abstract data types.

The parameters are as follows:

- parameterIndex: The first parameter is 1, the second is 2, and so on.

- x: The object containing the input parameter value.

- targetSqlType: The SQL type (as defined in java.sql.Types) to be sent to the database. The scale argument may further qualify this type.

- scale: For java.sql.Types.DECIMAL or java.sql.Types.NUMERIC types, this is the number of digits after the decimal point. For all other types, this value will be ignored.

This throws a SQLException if a database access error occurs.

Setting Up the MySQL Database

This shows how to set up the MySQL database:

```
mysql> use octopus;
Database changed
mysql> CREATE TABLE resume (
    ->    id              BIGINT(20) PRIMARY KEY,
    ->    name            VARCHAR(255),
    ->    content         TEXT,   -- CLOB data type
    ->    date_created DATETIME
    -> );
Query OK, 0 rows affected (0.23 sec)

mysql> desc resume;
+--------------+--------------+------+-----+---------+-------+
| Field        | Type         | Null | Key | Default | Extra |
+--------------+--------------+------+-----+---------+-------+
| id           | bigint(20)   |      | PRI | 0       |       |

| date_created | datetime     | YES  |     | NULL    |       |
+--------------+--------------+------+-----+---------+-------+
4 rows in set (0.01 sec)
```

Setting Up the Oracle Database

This shows how to set up the Oracle database:

```
$ sqlplus scott/tiger
SQL*Plus: Release 10.1.0.2.0 - Production on Mon Jul 11 14:14:13 2005
SQL> CREATE TABLE resume (
  2    id              NUMBER(20) PRIMARY KEY,
  3    name            VARCHAR2(255),
  4    content         CLOB,
  5    date_created DATE
  6  );

Table created.

SQL> desc resume;
 Name                                      Null?    Type
 ----------------------------------------- -------- -------------

 ID                                        NOT NULL NUMBER(20)
 NAME                                               VARCHAR2(255)
 CONTENT                                            CLOB
 DATE_CREATED                                       DATE
```

Solution

Here's the solution:

```java
import java.util.*;
import java.io.*;
import java.sql.*;

import jcb.util.DatabaseUtil;
import jcb.db.VeryBasicConnectionManager;

/**
 * @author: Mahmoud Parsian
 */
public class Demo_PreparedStatement_SetObject {

    public static void main(String[] args) {

        System.out.println("-- Demo_PreparedStatement_SetObject begin--");
        ResultSet rs = null;
        Connection conn = null;
        PreparedStatement pstmt = null;
        PreparedStatement pstmt2 = null;
        try {
            String dbVendor = args[0]; // { "mysql", "oracle" }
            conn = VeryBasicConnectionManager.getConnection(dbVendor);
            System.out.println("conn="+conn);


            // table column names
            String [] columnNames = {"id", "name", "content", "date_created"};

            // inputValues contains the data to put in the database
            Object [] inputValues = new Object[columnNames.length];


            // fill input values
            inputValues[0] = new java.math.BigDecimal(100);
            inputValues[1] = new String("Alex Taylor");
            inputValues[2] = new String("This is my resume.");
            inputValues[3] = new Timestamp ( (new java.util.Date()).getTime() );

            // prepare blob object from an existing binary column
            String insert =  "insert into resume (id, name, content, date_created)"+
                             "values(?, ?, ?, ?)";
            pstmt = conn.prepareStatement(insert);

            // set input parameter values
            pstmt.setObject(1, inputValues[0]);
            pstmt.setObject(2, inputValues[1]);
            pstmt.setObject(3, inputValues[2]);
            pstmt.setObject(4, inputValues[3]);

            // execute SQL INSERT statement
            pstmt.executeUpdate();
```

```java
            // now retrieve the inserted record from db
            String query =
               "select id, name, content, date_created from resume where id=?";

            // create PrepareStatement object
            pstmt2 = conn.prepareStatement(query);
            pstmt2.setObject(1, inputValues[0]);
            rs = pstmt2.executeQuery();
            Object [] outputValues = new Object[columnNames.length];
            if (rs.next()) {
                // outputValues contains the data retrieved from the database
                for ( int i = 0; i < columnNames.length; i++) {
                    outputValues[i] = rs.getObject(i+1);
                }
            }


            //
            // display retrieved data
            //
            if (dbVendor.equalsIgnoreCase("oracle")) {
                System.out.println("id="+
                    ((java.math.BigDecimal) outputValues[0]).toString());
                System.out.println("name="+ ((String) outputValues[1]));
                System.out.println("content="+
                    ((Clob) outputValues[2]));


            }
            else if (dbVendor.equalsIgnoreCase("mysql")) {
                System.out.println("id="+ ((Long) outputValues[0]).toString());
                System.out.println("name="+ ((String) outputValues[1]));
                System.out.println("content="+
                    ((String) outputValues[2]));
                System.out.println("date_created="+
                    ((java.sql.Timestamp) outputValues[3]).toString());
            }

            System.out.println("---------------");
            System.out.println("-- Demo_PreparedStatement_SetObject end--");
        }
        catch(Exception e){
            e.printStackTrace();
            System.exit(1);
        }
        finally {
            // release database resources
            DatabaseUtil.close(rs);
            DatabaseUtil.close(pstmt);
            DatabaseUtil.close(pstmt2);
            DatabaseUtil.close(conn);
        }
    }
}
```

Running the Solution for the Oracle Database

This shows how to run the solution for the Oracle database:

```
$ java Demo_PreparedStatement_SetObject oracle
-- Demo_PreparedStatement_SetObject begin--
conn=oracle.jdbc.driver.T4CConnection@341960
---------------
id=100
name=Alex Taylor
content=oracle.sql.CLOB@ccc588
date_created=2005-07-11
---------------
-- Demo_PreparedStatement_SetObject end--
```

Viewing the Oracle Database After Running the Solution

This shows the Oracle database after running the solution:

```
SQL> select * from resume;
        ID   NAME          CONTENT              DATE_CREATED
       100   Alex Taylor   This is my resume.   11-JUL-05
SQL>
```

Running the Solution for the MySQL Database

This shows how to run the solution for the MySQL database:

```
conn=com.mysql.jdbc.Connection@1dd46f7
---------------
id=100
name=Alex Taylor
content=This is my resume.
date_created=2005-07-11 14:44:29.0
---------------
-- Demo_PreparedStatement_SetObject end--
```

Viewing the MySQL Database After Running the Program

This shows the MySQL database after running the solution:

```
mysql> select * from resume;
+-----+-------------+--------------------+---------------------+
| id  | name        | content            | date_created        |
+-----+-------------+--------------------+---------------------+
| 100 | Alex Taylor | This is my resume. | 2005-07-11 13:56:55 |
+-----+-------------+--------------------+---------------------+
1 row in set (0.00 sec)
```

13-16. How Do You Use PreparedStatement.setRef()?

A REF CURSOR is a ResultSet object that represents the result of a SQL query (such as select last_name, badge_number from employee) returned one row at a time. The following sections show how to pass a java.sql.Ref (a REF CURSOR) object to a PreparedStatement object.

How It Works

The Oracle database supports the REF data type, and you can use the setRef() method on Oracle databases. The MySQL database does not support the setRef() method. setRef() is not implemented in the MySQL server, according to the MySQL Connector/J documentation. In fact, the following methods in the MySQL driver have not been implemented yet. They rely on functionality that is not currently present in the MySQL server.

```
PreparedStatement.setRef()
ResultSet.getRef(int)
ResultSet.getRef(String)
ResultSet.updateRef(int, Ref)
ResultSet.updateRef(String, Ref)
```

The signature of setRef() is as follows:

```
public void setRef(int index,
                   java.sql.Ref ref)  throws SQLException
```

This sets the designated parameter to the given REF(<structured-type>) value. The driver converts this to a SQL REF value when it sends it to the database.

The parameters are as follows:

- index: The first parameter is 1, the second is 2, and so on.

- ref: A SQL REF value.

This throws a SQLException if a database access error occurs.

```
public interface Ref
```

This is according to the JDK:

The mapping in the Java programming language of a SQL REF value, which is a reference to a SQL structured type value in the database. SQL REF values are stored in a table that contains instances of a referenceable SQL structured type, and each REF value is a unique identifier for one instance in that table. A SQL REF value may be used in place of the SQL structured type it references, either as a column value in a table or an attribute value in a structured type.

Because a SQL REF value is a logical pointer to a SQL structured type, a Ref object is by default also a logical pointer. Thus, retrieving a SQL REF value as a Ref object does not materialize the attributes of the structured type on the client. A Ref object (see Table 13-2) can be stored in the database using the PreparedStatement.setRef method.

Table 13-2. *Method Summary for* java.sql.Ref *Interface*

Return Type	Method	
String	getBaseTypeName()	Retrieves the fully qualified SQL name of the SQL structured type that this Ref object references
Object	getObject()	Retrieves the SQL structured type instance referenced by this Ref object
Object	getObject(Map map)	Retrieves the referenced object and maps it to a Java type using the given type map
void	setObject(Object value)	Sets the structured type value that this Ref object references to the given instance of Object

Solution

This class will read a REF (a reference of a manager column) from dept_table and then use that REF to create a new dept_table record:

```java
import java.util.*;
import java.io.*;
import java.sql.*;

import jcb.util.DatabaseUtil;
import jcb.db.VeryBasicConnectionManager;

public class Demo_PreparedStatement_SetRef {
    public static void main(String[] args) {
        System.out.println("--Demo_PreparedStatement_SetRef begin--");
        // read database vendor
        String dbVendor = args[0];
        // prepare arguments for dept_table
        String deptName = args[0];
        String newDeptName = args[1];

        ResultSet rs = null;
        Connection conn = null;
        PreparedStatement pstmt = null;
        PreparedStatement pstmt2 = null;
        try {
            conn = VeryBasicConnectionManager.getConnection(dbVendor);


            // prepare query for getting a REF object and PrepareStatement object
            String refQuery = "select manager from dept_table where dept_name=?";
            pstmt = conn.prepareStatement(refQuery);
            pstmt.setString(1, deptName);
            rs = pstmt.executeQuery();
            java.sql.Ref ref = null;
            if (rs.next()) {
                ref = rs.getRef(1);
            }

            if (ref == null) {
                System.out.println("error: could not get a reference for manager.");
                System.exit(1);
            }

            // prepare query and create PrepareStatement object
            String query = "INSERT INTO dept_table(dept_name, manager) "+
                "values(?, ?)";
            pstmt2 = conn.prepareStatement(query);
            pstmt2.setString(1, newDeptName);
            pstmt2.setRef(2, ref);

            // execute query, and return number of rows created
            int rowCount = pstmt2.executeUpdate();
            System.out.println("rowCount="+rowCount);
            System.out.println("--Demo_PreparedStatement_setRef end--");
        }
```

```
        catch(Exception e){
            e.printStackTrace();
            System.exit(1);
        }
        finally {
            // release database resources
            DatabaseUtil.close(pstmt);
            DatabaseUtil.close(pstmt2);
            DatabaseUtil.close(conn);
        }
    }
}
```

Setting Up the Oracle Database

Using Oracle, define a table that has a column of the REF type, as shown next:

```
SQL> desc employee_type;
 Name                    Null?    Type
 ----------------        -------- ------------
 NAME                             VARCHAR2(32)
 BADGE_NUMBER                     NUMBER

SQL> CREATE TABLE employee_table OF employee_type
  2   (primary key (badge_number));



 ----------------        -------- ------------
 NAME                             VARCHAR2(32)
 BADGE_NUMBER            NOT NULL NUMBER

SQL> CREATE TABLE dept_table
  2   (dept_name varchar2(10),
  3    manager REF employee_type SCOPE IS employee_table);

SQL> desc dept_table;
 Name                    Null?    Type
 --------------------    -------- --------------------
 DEPT_NAME                        VARCHAR2(10)
 MANAGER                          REF OF EMPLOYEE_TYPE
    NAME                          VARCHAR2(32)
     BADGE_NUMBER                 NUMBER

SQL> INSERT INTO employee_table(name, badge_number) VALUES ('alex', '111');
SQL> INSERT INTO employee_table(name, badge_number) VALUES ('jane', '222');
SQL> INSERT INTO employee_table(name, badge_number) VALUES ('mary', '333');
SQL> select * from employee_table;

NAME            BADGE_NUMBER
---------       ------------
alex                     111
jane                     222
mary                     333

SQL> INSERT INTO dept_table
  2 select 'software', REF(e) FROM employee_table e
```

```
  3      where badge_number='111';

SQL> select * from dept_table;

DEPT_NAME   MANAGER
---------   ------------------------------------------------------------------------
software    00002202089C70D37E33D943BEABDB84570C8588E4679E191E70DE4A00B8F64B3FA2FF8389

SQL> select dept_name, DEREF(manager) from dept_table;

DEPT_NAME   DEREF(MANAGER)(NAME, BADGE_NUMBER)
---------   ----------------------------------
software    EMPLOYEE_TYPE('alex', 111)


SQL>  INSERT INTO dept_table
  2 select 'marketing', REF(e) FROM employee_table e
  3      where badge_number='222';

SQL>  select * from dept_table;

DEPT_NAME   MANAGER
---------   ------------------------------------------------------------------------
software    00002202089C70D37E33D943BEABDB84570C8588E4679E191E70DE4A00B8F64B3FA2FF8389
marketing   0000220208AE8D0652916243378F27890BA1937A40679E191E70DE4A00B8F64B3FA2FF8389


DEPT_NAME   DEREF(MANAGER)(NAME, BADGE_NUMBER)
---------   ----------------------------------
software    EMPLOYEE_TYPE('alex', 111)
marketing   EMPLOYEE_TYPE('jane', 222)

SQL> commit;
Commit complete.
```

Running the Solution for the Oracle Database

This shows how to run the solution for the Oracle database:

```
$ javac Demo_PreparedStatement_SetRef.java
$ java Demo_PreparedStatement_SetRef oracle software sales
--Demo_PreparedStatement_setRef begin--
conn=oracle.jdbc.driver.OracleConnection@860d49
---------------
rowCount=1
--Demo_PreparedStatement_setRef end--
```

Viewing the Oracle Database After Running the Solution

This shows the Oracle database after running the solution:

```
SQL> select dept_name, DEREF(manager) from dept_table;
DEPT_NAME   DEREF(MANAGER)(NAME, BADGE_NUMBER)
---------   ----------------------------------
software    EMPLOYEE_TYPE('alex', 111)
marketing   EMPLOYEE_TYPE('jane', 222)
sales       EMPLOYEE_TYPE('alex', 111)
```

13-17. How Do You Use PreparedStatement.setString()?

The String class in Java is the most commonly used class in most database applications. The following sections show how to pass a String object to a PreparedStatement object.

How It Works

The setString() method is the most commonly used method in PreparedStatement. You can use setString() in both the Oracle and MySQL databases. In Oracle, when a column data type is VARCHAR or VARCHAR2, then you can use setString(). In MySQL, when a column data type is VARCHAR, TINYTEXT, TEXT, MEDIUMTEXT, or LONGTEXT, then you can use setString().

The signature of setString() is as follows:

```
public void setString(int parameterIndex,
                      java.lang.String x)  throws SQLException
```

This sets the designated parameter to the given Java String value. The driver converts this to a SQL VARCHAR or LONGVARCHAR value (depending on the argument's size relative to the driver's limits on VARCHAR values) when it sends it to the database.

The parameters are as follows:

- parameterIndex: The first parameter is 1, the second is 2, and so on.

- x: The parameter value.

This throws a SQLException if a database access error occurs.

Here's the solution:

```
import java.util.*;
import java.io.*;
import java.sql.*;

import jcb.util.DatabaseUtil;
import jcb.db.VeryBasicConnectionManager;

public class Demo_PreparedStatement_SetString {
    public static void main(String[] args) {
        System.out.println("--Demo_PreparedStatement_SetString begin--");
        String dbVendor = args[0];  // database vendor = { "mysql", "oracle" }
        String stringValue = args[1];  // value to be inserted
        Connection conn = null;
        PreparedStatement pstmt = null;
        try {
            conn = VeryBasicConnectionManager.getConnection(dbVendor);
            System.out.println("conn="+conn);
            System.out.println("---------------");
            // prepare query
            String query = "insert into string_table(string_column) values(?)";

            // create PrepareStatement object
            pstmt = conn.prepareStatement(query);
            pstmt.setString(1, stringValue);
```

```
            // execute query, and return number of rows created
            int rowCount = pstmt.executeUpdate();
            System.out.println("rowCount="+rowCount);
            System.out.println("--Demo_PreparedStatement_SetString end--");
        }
        catch(Exception e){
            e.printStackTrace();
            System.exit(1);
        }
        finally {
            // release database resources
            DatabaseUtil.close(pstmt);
            DatabaseUtil.close(conn);
        }
    }
}
```

Setting Up the Oracle Database

This shows how to set up the Oracle database:

```
SQL> create table string_table(
  2   string_column VARCHAR(300)
  3  );

SQL> desc string_table;




SQL> insert into string_table(string_column) values('abc');
SQL> insert into string_table(string_column) values('1234567890');
SQL> commit;
Commit complete.
SQL> select * from string_table;
STRING_COLUMN
--------------------
abc
1234567890
```

Running the Solution for the Oracle Database

This show how to run the solution for the Oracle database:

```
$ javac Demo_PreparedStatement_SetString.java
$ java Demo_PreparedStatement_SetString oracle "hello friend!"
--Demo_PreparedStatement_SetString begin--
conn=oracle.jdbc.driver.OracleConnection@6e70c7
---------------
rowCount=1
--Demo_PreparedStatement_setString_Oracle end--
$ java Demo_PreparedStatement_SetString oracle "hello oracle world."
--Demo_PreparedStatement_SetString begin--
conn=oracle.jdbc.driver.OracleConnection@6e70c7
---------------
rowCount=1
--Demo_PreparedStatement_SetString end--
```

Viewing the Oracle Database After Running the Solution

This shows the Oracle database after running the program:

```
SQL> select * from string_table;

STRING_COLUMN
-------------------------------------
abc
1234567890
hello friend!
hello oracle world.
```

Setting Up the MySQL Database

Using MySQL, define a table that has a single column of the VARCHAR type. (In MySQL, the VARCHAR data type has a limitation size of 255 characters: see the following error from the MySQL server.)

```
mysql> create table string_table(
    -> string_column VARCHAR(255)
    -> );

mysql> desc string_table;
+---------------+--------------+------+-----+---------+-------+
| Field         | Type         | Null | Key | Default | Extra |
+---------------+--------------+------+-----+---------+-------+
| string_column | varchar(255) | YES  |     | NULL    |       |
+---------------+--------------+------+-----+---------+-------+


mysql> insert into string_table(string_column) values('abcdef');
mysql> insert into string_table(string_column) values('hello MySQL!');
mysql> commit;
mysql> select * from string_table;
+------------------+
| string_column    |
+------------------+
| abcdef           |
| hello MySQL!     |
+------------------+
2 rows in set (0.02 sec)
```

Running the Solution for the MySQL Database

This shows how to run the solution for the MySQL database:

```
$ javac Demo_PreparedStatement_SetString.java
$ java Demo_PreparedStatement_SetString mysql "this is it."
--Demo_PreparedStatement_SetString begin--
conn=com.mysql.jdbc.Connection@124bbbf
---------------
rowCount=1
--Demo_PreparedStatement_SetString end--

$ java Demo_PreparedStatement_SetString mysql "hello MySQL!!!"
--Demo_PreparedStatement_SetString begin--
conn=com.mysql.jdbc.Connection@124bbbf
---------------
rowCount=1
--Demo_PreparedStatement_SetString end--
```

Viewing the MySQL Database After Running the Program

This shows the MySQL database after running the program:

```
mysql> select * from string_table;
+------------------+
| string_column    |
+------------------+
| abcdef           |
| hello MySQL!     |
| this is it.      |
| hello MySQL!!!   |
+------------------+
4 rows in set (0.00 sec)
```

13-18. How Do You Use PreparedStatement's setTime() and setTimestamp()?

The following sections show how to pass time-related objects (java.sql.Time and java.sql.Timestamp) to a PreparedStatement object.

How It Works

You can use the setTime() and setTimestamp() methods on both the Oracle and MySQL databases. In Oracle, when a column data type is DATE, then you can use the setTime() and setTimestamp() methods. Note that in Oracle the DATE data type can represent three distinct data types: Date, Time, and Timestamp.

The signatures of setTime() is as follows:

```
public void setTimestamp(int parameterIndex,
                         java.sql.Timestamp x)  throws SQLException
```

This sets the designated parameter to the given java.sql.Timestamp value. The driver converts this to a SQL TIMESTAMP value when it sends it to the database.

The parameters are as follows:

- parameterIndex: The first parameter is 1, the second is 2, and so on.

- x: The parameter value.

This throws a SQLException if a database access error occurs.
The signature of setTimestamp() is as follows:

```
public void setTime(int parameterIndex,
                    java.sql.Time x)  throws SQLException
```

This sets the designated parameter to the given java.sql.Time value. The driver converts this to a SQL TIME value when it sends it to the database.

The parameters are as follows:

- parameterIndex: The first parameter is 1, the second is 2, and so on.

- x: The parameter value.

This throws a SQLException if a database access error occurs.

Solution

Here's the solution:

```java
import java.util.*;
import java.io.*;
import java.sql.*;

import jcb.util.DatabaseUtil;
import jcb.db.VeryBasicConnectionManager;

public class Demo_PreparedStatement_SetTimeAndTimestamp {
    public static java.sql.Timestamp getCurrentJavaSqlTimestamp() {
        java.util.Date date = new java.util.Date();
        return new java.sql.Timestamp(date.getTime());
    }
    public static java.sql.Time getCurrentJavaSqlTime() {
        java.util.Date date = new java.util.Date();
        return new java.sql.Time(date.getTime());
    }
    public static void main(String[] args) {
        System.out.println("--SetTimeAndTimestamp begin--");
        String dbVendor = args[0]; // database vendor = { "mysql", "oracle" }
        String id = args[1];
        Connection conn = null;
        PreparedStatement pstmt = null;
        try {


            // prepare query
            String query = "insert into time_table(id, "+
                "time_column, timestamp_column) values(?, ?, ?)";

            // create PrepareStatement object
            pstmt = conn.prepareStatement(query);
            pstmt.setString(1, id);
            java.sql.Time time = getCurrentJavaSqlTime();
            System.out.println("time="+time);
            pstmt.setTime(2, time);
            java.sql.Timestamp timestamp = getCurrentJavaSqlTimestamp();
            System.out.println("timestamp="+timestamp);
            pstmt.setTimestamp(3, timestamp);

            // execute query, and return number of rows created
            int rowCount = pstmt.executeUpdate();
            System.out.println("rowCount="+rowCount);
            System.out.println("--SetTimeAndTimestamp end--");
        }
        catch(Exception e){
            e.printStackTrace();
            System.exit(1);
        }
        finally {
            // release database resources
            DatabaseUtil.close(pstmt);
            DatabaseUtil.close(conn);
        }
    }
}
```

Setting Up the Oracle Database

This shows how to set up the Oracle database:

```
SQL> create table time_table(
        id VARCHAR(12), time_column DATE, timestamp_column DATE);
SQL> insert into time_table(id, time_column, timestamp_column)
     values('id-1', '12-JUN-2003', '12-JUN-2003');
SQL> insert into time_table(id, time_column, timestamp_column)
     values('id-2', '01-JAN-2001',
              to_date('01/01/2001 09:30:00','dd/mm/yyyy hh24:mi:ss'));

SQL> select * from time_table;
ID          TIME_COLUMN  TIMESTAMP_COLUMN
--------    -----------  ----------------
id-1        12-JUN-03    12-JUN-03
id-2        01-JAN-01    01-JAN-01

SQL> select id , to_char(time_column,'HH24:MI:SS') as time,
to_char(timestamp_column,'DD-MM-YYYY HH24:MI:SS') as timestamp from time_table;
ID       TIME        TIMESTAMP
--------  --------    -------------------
id-1      00:00:00    12-06-2003 00:00:00
id-2      09:30:00    01-01-2001 09:30:00
SQL> commit;
Commit complete.
```

This shows how to run the solution for the Oracle database:

```
$ javac Demo_PreparedStatement_SetTimeAndTimestamp.java
$ java Demo_PreparedStatement_SetTimeAndTimestamp oracle id-999
--SetTimeAndTimestamp begin--
conn=oracle.jdbc.driver.OracleConnection@860d49
---------------
time=09:57:42
timestamp=Wed Nov 12 09:57:42 PST 2003
rowCount=1
--SetTimeAndTimestamp end--
```

Viewing the Oracle Database After Running the Solution

This shows the Oracle database after running the solution:

```
SQL> select id, to_char(time_column,'HH24:MI:SS') as time,
to_char(timestamp_column,'DD-MM-YYYY HH24:MI:SS') as timestamp
from time_table;
ID       TIME        TIMESTAMP
-------   ---------   -------------------
id-1      00:00:00    12-06-2003 00:00:00
id-2      09:30:00    01-01-2001 09:30:00
id-999    09:57:42    11-12-2003 09:57:42
```

Setting Up the MySQL Database

Using MySQL, define a table that has a column of the TIME and TIMESTAMP types, as shown next. The MySQL database accepts times in the HH:MM:SS format.

```
mysql> create table time_table(id VARCHAR(12),
          time_column TIME, timestamp_column TIMESTAMP);
mysql> desc time_table;
+------------------+---------------+------+-----+---------+-------+
| Field            | Type          | Null | Key | Default | Extra |
+------------------+---------------+------+-----+---------+-------+
| id               | varchar(12)   | YES  |     | NULL    |       |
| time_column      | time          | YES  |     | NULL    |       |
| timestamp_column | timestamp(14) | YES  |     | NULL    |       |
+------------------+---------------+------+-----+---------+-------+
3 rows in set (0.03 sec)

mysql> insert into time_table(id, time_column, timestamp_column)
          values('id-1', '10:23:45', '2002-10-25 10:23:45');
mysql> insert into time_table(id, time_column, timestamp_column)
          values('id-2', '23:10:55', '2004-10-25 10:23:45');
mysql> select * from time_table;
+------+-------------+-------------------+
| id   | time_column | timestamp_column  |
+------+-------------+-------------------+
| id-1 | 10:23:45    | 20021025102345    |
| id-2 | 23:10:55    | 20041025102345    |
+------+-------------+-------------------+
```

Running the Solution for the MySQL Database

This shows how to run the solution for the MySQL database:

```
$ javac Demo_PreparedStatement_SetTimeAndTimestamp.java
$ java Demo_PreparedStatement_SetTimeAndTimestamp mysql id-5
--SetTimeAndTimestamp begin--
conn=com.mysql.jdbc.Connection@1546e25
----------------
time=11:11:10
timestamp=Wed Nov 12 11:11:10 PST 2003
rowCount=1
--SetTimeAndTimestamp end--
```

Viewing the MySQL Database After Running the Solution

This shows the MySQL database after running the solution:

```
mysql> select * from time_table;
+------+-------------+-------------------+
| id   | time_column | timestamp_column  |
+------+-------------+-------------------+
| id-1 | 10:23:45    | 20021025102345    |
| id-2 | 23:10:55    | 20041025102345    |
| id-5 | 11:11:10    | 20031112111110    |
+------+-------------+-------------------+
3 rows in set (0.03 sec)
```

13-19. How Do You Use PreparedStatement.setURL()?

A URL is a reference (an address) to a resource on the Internet. The following sections show how to pass a URL (a java.net.URL object) to a PreparedStatement object.

How It Works

You cannot use setURL() on the Oracle database because it is an unsupported feature, as I will illustrate with an example. In MySQL, when a column data type is VARCHAR, then you can use setURL(). MySQL does not have a URL data type, but when you pass a java.net.URL object, the driver converts it to a String object.

The signature of setURL() is as follows:

```
public void setURL(int parameterIndex,
                java.net.URL url)  throws SQLException
```

This sets the designated parameter to the given java.net.URL value. The driver converts this to a SQL DATALINK value when it sends it to the database.

The parameters are as follows:

- parameterIndex: The first parameter is 1, the second is 2, and so on.

- url: The java.net.URL object to be set.

This throws a SQLException if a database access error occurs.

Solution

values:

```
import java.util.*;
import java.io.*;
import java.sql.*;

import jcb.util.DatabaseUtil;
import jcb.db.VeryBasicConnectionManager;

public class Demo_PreparedStatement_SetURL {
    public static void main(String[] args) {
        System.out.println("--SetURL begin--");
        String dbVendor = args[0];  // database vendor = { "mysql", "oracle" }
        String idValue = args[1];
        String urlValue = args[2];
        Connection conn = null;
        PreparedStatement pstmt = null;
        try {
            System.out.println("--SetURL begin--");
            conn = VeryBasicConnectionManager.getConnection(dbVendor);
            System.out.println("conn="+conn);
            System.out.println("--------------");

            // prepare query
            String query = "insert into url_table(id, url) values(?, ?)";

            // create PrepareStatement object
            pstmt = conn.prepareStatement(query);
            pstmt.setString(1, idValue);
            pstmt.setURL(2, new java.net.URL(urlValue));
```

```
            // execute query, and return number of rows created
            int rowCount = pstmt.executeUpdate();
            System.out.println("rowCount="+rowCount);
            System.out.println("--SetURL end--");
        }
        catch(Exception e){
            System.out.println("ERROR: "+ e.getMessage());
            System.exit(1);
        }
        finally {
            // release database resources
            DatabaseUtil.close(pstmt);
            DatabaseUtil.close(conn);
        }
    }
}
}
```

Setting Up the Oracle Database

This shows how to set up the Oracle database:

```
SQL> create table url_table(id varchar(10), url varchar(255));
SQL> desc url_table;
 Name                 Null?    Type
 ---------------- -------- ----------------
 ID                        VARCHAR2(10)


SQL> insert into url_table(id, url) values('IBM', 'http://www.ibm.com');
SQL> commit;
Commit complete.
SQL> select * from url_table;
ID        URL
-------   ---------------------------
ASKJ      http://www.askjeeves.com
IBM       http://www.ibm.com
```

Running the Solution for the Oracle Database

This shows that setURL() is unsupported:

```
$ javac Demo_PreparedStatement_SetURL.java
$ java Demo_PreparedStatement_SetURL oracle SUNW "http://www.sun.com"
--SetURL begin--
conn=oracle.jdbc.driver.OracleConnection@6e70c7
---------------
ERROR: java.sql.SQLException: Unsupported feature
```

Viewing the Oracle Database After Running the Solution

The Oracle database has no changes, because setURL() is unsupported.

Setting Up the MySQL Database

The MySQL database does not have a URL data type; however, if you pass a java.net.URL object, the driver converts it to a String object. Using MySQL, define a table that has a column of the VARCHAR type, as shown next:

```
mysql> create table url_table (
    -> id varchar(10),
    -> url varchar(255) );
mysql> desc url_table;
+-------+--------------+------+-----+---------+-------+
| Field | Type         | Null | Key | Default | Extra |
+-------+--------------+------+-----+---------+-------+
| id    | varchar(10)  | YES  |     | NULL    |       |
| url   | varchar(255) | YES  |     | NULL    |       |
+-------+--------------+------+-----+---------+-------+
2 rows in set (0.02 sec)

mysql> insert into url_table(id, url) values('ASKJ', 'http://www.askjeeves.com');
mysql> insert into url_table(id, url) values('IBM', 'http://www.ibm.com');
mysql> commit;
mysql> select * from url_table;
+------+--------------------------+
| id   | url                      |
+------+--------------------------+
| ASKJ | http://www.askjeeves.com |
| IBM  | http://www.ibm.com       |
+------+--------------------------+
```

Running the Solution for the MySQL Database

This shows how to run the solution for the MySQL database:

```
$ javac Demo_PreparedStatement_SetURL.java
$ java Demo_PreparedStatement_SetURL mysql SUNW "http://www.sun.com"
--SetURL begin--
conn=com.mysql.jdbc.Connection@124bbbf
---------------
rowCount=1
--SetURL end--
```

Viewing the MySQL Database After Running the Solution

This shows the MySQL database after running the solution:

```
mysql> select * from url_table;
+------+--------------------------+
| id   | url                      |
+------+--------------------------+
| ASKJ | http://www.askjeeves.com |
| IBM  | http://www.ibm.com       |
| SUNW | http://www.sun.com       |
+------+--------------------------+
3 rows in set (0.00 sec)
```

■ ■ ■

Exploring JDBC Utilities

What is a JDBC *utility*? A JDBC utility is a small Java component (such as a package, class, interface, or method) that does something useful and should have the following characteristics:

- It has small, clean, and fast code.
- It is commonly used by most of the JDBC application programs.
- Is a safe call (has no possibility for resource leaks).
- It improves the readability and maintenance of the code.
- It is portable across databases as well as operating systems (as much as possible).
- It avoids repetition and improves reliability.

data structures and values), and should be defined inside a helper/utility class. For example, javax.imageio.ImageIO is a utility class; it contains static convenience methods for locating ImageReader and ImageWriter objects and performing simple encoding and decoding. Another example is the DbUtils package from Apache (http://jakarta.apache.org/commons/dbutils/); it contains a small set of classes designed to make working with JDBC easier.

14-1. What Are JDBC Utilities?

JDBC utilities are useful, fast, independent, small, and well-tested classes/methods that are used in most JDBC applications and are the commonly used methods in many classes. The JDBC classes/methods make working with JDBC easier. For example, closing a Connection object and closing a ResultSet object are considered utility tasks. (These actions will occur in most of the JDBC classes/methods.) Another example is getting a current date as a java.sql.Date object. You need to organize the utilities (in a helper package/class) and then use them in a consistent fashion in your application or framework.

14-2. How Do You Close a java.sql.Connection Object?

java.sql.Connection represents a database Connection object. In general, you should close a database connection after its usage (in order to release database and JDBC resources, such as memory and data structures, to other users). If you obtain a connection from a connection pool, then you must return it to the pool; otherwise, you have to properly close it. In the following sections, I will show you several solutions for closing a Connection object.

Soft Closing a Connection (Using a Connection Pool Manager)

This shows how to soft close a connection:

```
/**
 * Soft close a connection;
 * return the connection to the pool manager.
 * @param conn a java.sql.Connection object.
 */
public static void closeQuietly(java.sql.Connection conn) {
    if (conn == null) {
        return;
    }

    // "soft" close of a Connection object; instead of actual closing
    // a Connection object, it is returned to the pool for reuse.
    // you may replace ConnectionPoolManager with your desired connection
    // pool manager class.
    ConnectionPoolManager.close(conn);
}
```

Closing a Connection and Not Reporting Exceptions

This shows how to close a connection and not report exceptions:

```
/**
 * Close a connection; avoid closing if null, and


 */
public static void closeQuietly(java.sql.Connection conn) {
    if (conn == null) {
        return;
    }

    try {
        if(!conn.isClosed()) {
            // releases this Connection object's database and
            // JDBC resources immediately instead of waiting
            // for them to be automatically released.
            conn.close();
        }
    }
    catch (Exception e) {
        // ignore exceptions
        e.printStackTrace();
    }
}
```

Closing a Connection and Logging Exceptions

This shows how to close a connection and log exceptions:

```
/**
 * Close a connection; avoid closing if null, and
 * hide any SQLExceptions that occur.
 * @param conn a java.sql.Connection object.
 * @param logger a Logger object is used to log messages
```

```
    */
    public static void closeQuietly(java.sql.Connection conn,
                                java.util.logging.Logger logger) {
        if (conn == null) {
            return;
        }

        try {
            if(!conn.isClosed()) {
                // releases this Connection object's database and
                // JDBC resources immediately instead of waiting
                // for them to be automatically released.
                conn.close();
            }
        }
        catch (Exception e) {
            // handle the exception and log it
            e.printStackTrace();
            if (logger != null) {
                logger.warning("closeQuietly: could not close connection object");
            }
        }
    }
}
```

Closing a Connection and Reporting Exceptions

```
/**
 * Close a connection; avoid closing if null, and
 * report any SQLExceptions that occur.
 * @param conn a java.sql.Connection object.
 * @throws SQLException failed to close the connection
 */
public static void close(java.sql.Connection conn)
        throws java.sql.SQLException {

    if (conn == null) {
        return;
    }

    if(!conn.isClosed()) {
        // releases this Connection object's database and
        // JDBC resources immediately instead of waiting
        // for them to be automatically released.
        conn.close();
    }
}
```

14-3. How Do You Commit and Close a Connection Object?

In general, you should close a database connection after its usage. If you obtain a connection from a connection pool, then you must return it to the pool; otherwise, you have to properly close it. In the following sections, I will show you several solutions for closing a Connection object.

Committing and Closing a Connection and Not Reporting Exceptions

This shows how to commit and close a connection and not report exceptions:

```java
/**
 * Commit and close a connection; avoid closing if
 * null and hide any SQLExceptions that occur.
 * @param conn a java.sql.Connection object.
 */
public static void commitAndCloseQuietly(java.sql.Connection conn) {
    if (conn == null) {
        return;
    }

    if(conn.isClosed()) {
        return;
    }

    try {
        conn.commit();
        conn.close();
        // hint the "garbage collector"
        conn = null;
    }
    catch (SQLException e) {
        // ignore the exception
    }
```

Committing and Closing a Connection and Logging Exceptions

This shows how to commit and close a connection and log exceptions:

```java
/**
 * Commit and close a connection; avoid closing
 * if null, and hide any SQLExceptions that occur.
 * @param conn a java.sql.Connection object.
 * @param logger a Logger object is used to log messages.
 */
public static void commitAndCloseQuietly(java.sql.Connection conn,
                                 java.util.logging.Logger logger) {
    if(conn == null) {
        return;
    }

    if(conn.isClosed()) {
        return;
    }

    try {
        conn.commit();
        conn.close();
        // hint the "garbage collector"
        conn = null;
    }
    catch( SQLException e ) {
        // handle the exception and log it
        e.printStackTrace();
```

```
            if (logger != null) {
                logger.warning("commitAndCloseQuietly: "+e.getMessage());
            }
        }
    }
}
```

Committing and Closing Connection and Reporting Exceptions

This shows how to commit and close a connection and report exceptions:

```
/**
 * Commit and close a connection; avoid closing if null, and
 * report any SQLExceptions that occur.
 * @param conn a java.sql.Connection object.
 * @throws SQLException failed to commit and close the connection
 */
public static void commitAndClose(java.sql.Connection conn)
    throws java.sql.SQLException {

    if( conn == null ) {
        return;
    }

    if( conn.isClosed()) {
        throw new SQLException("Connection closed.");
    }


        conn.close();
        // hint the "garbage collector"
        conn = null;
    }
    catch( SQLException e ) {
        e.printStackTrace();
        throw e;
    }
}
```

14-4. How Do You Roll Back and Close a Connection Object?

In general, you should close database connections after their usage. If you obtain a connection from a connection pool, then you must return it to the pool; otherwise, you have to properly close it. In the following sections, I will show you several solutions for closing a Connection object.

The Connection.rollback() statement in SQL cancels the proposed changes in a pending database transaction. According to the JDK, Connection.rollback() undoes all changes made in the current transaction and releases any database locks currently held by this Connection object. You should use this method only when autocommit mode has been disabled.

Rolling Back and Closing a Connection and Not Reporting Exceptions

This shows how to roll back and close a connection and not report exceptions:

```
/**
 * Roll back and close a connection; avoid closing
 * if null, and hide any SQLExceptions that occur.
```

```
 * @param conn a java.sql.Connection object.
 */
public static void rollbackAndCloseQuietly(java.sql.Connection conn) {
    try {
        if(conn == null) {
            return;
        }

        if(conn.isClosed()) {
            return;
        }

        conn.rollback();
        conn.close();
        // hint the "garbage collector"
        conn = null;
    }
    catch(SQLException e) {
        // ignore
    }
}
```

Rolling Back and Closing a Connection and Logging Exceptions

This shows how to roll back and close a connection and log exceptions:

```
/**

 * if null, and hide any SQLExceptions that occur.
 * @param conn a java.sql.Connection object.
 * @param logger a Logger object is used to log messages.
 */
public static void rollbackAndCloseQuietly(java.sql.Connection conn,
                                java.util.logging.Logger logger) {
    try {
        if(conn == null) {
            return;
        }

        if(conn.isClosed()) {
            return;
        }

        conn.rollback();
        conn.close();
        // hint the "garbage collector"
        conn = null;
    }
    catch(SQLException e) {
        // handle the exception and log it
        e.printStackTrace();
        if (logger != null) {
            logger.warning("rollbackAndCloseQuietly: "+e.getMessage());
        }
    }
}
```

Rolling Back and Closing Connection and Reporting Exceptions

This shows how to roll back and close a connection and report exceptions:

```
/**
 * Roll back and close a connection; avoid closing if null, and
 * report any SQLExceptions that occur.
 * @param conn a java.sql.Connection object.
 * @throws SQLException failed to roll back and close the connection
 */
public static void rollbackAndClose(java.sql.Connection conn)
    throws SQLException {
    try {
        if(conn == null) {
            return;
        }

        if(conn.isClosed()) {
            throw new SQLException("connection is closed.");
        }

        conne.rollback();
        conn.close();
        // hint the "garbage collector"
        conn = null;
    }
    catch(SQLException e) {


    }
}
```

14-5. How Do You Close a ResultSet Object?

ResultSet.close() releases the ResultSet object's database and JDBC resources immediately instead of waiting for this to happen automatically when it is closed.

Closing a ResultSet and Not Reporting Exceptions

This shows how to close a ResultSet and not report exceptions:

```
/**
 * Close a ResultSet; avoid closing if null, and
 * hide any SQLExceptions that occur.
 * @param rs a java.sql.ResultSet object.
 */
public static void closeQuietly(java.sql.ResultSet rs) {
    if (rs == null) {
        return;
    }

    try {
        // releases this ResultSet object's database and
        // JDBC resources immediately instead of waiting
        // for this to happen when it is automatically closed.
        rs.close();
    }
```

```
    catch (Exception e) {
        //ignore
        e.printStackTrace();
    }
}
```

Closing a ResultSet and Logging Exceptions

This shows how to close a ResultSet and log exceptions:

```
/**
 * Close a ResultSet; avoid closing if null, and
 * hide any SQLExceptions that occur.
 * @param rs a java.sql.ResultSet object.
 * @param logger a Logger object is used to log messages.
 */
public static void closeQuietly(java.sql.ResultSet rs,
                                java.util.logging.Logger logger) {
    if (rs == null) {
        return;
    }

    try {
        rs.close();
    }
    catch (Exception e) {


        logger.warning("closeQuietly: "+e.getMessage());
    }
}
}
```

Closing ResultSet and Reporting Exceptions

This shows how to close a ResultSet and report exceptions:

```
/**
 * Close a ResultSet; avoid closing if null, and
 * report any SQLExceptions that occur.
 * @param rs a java.sql.ResultSet object.
 * @throws SQLException failed to close the ResultSet
 */
public static void close(java.sql.ResultSet rs)
    throws java.sql.SQLException {
    if (rs != null) {
        rs.close();
    }
}
```

14-6. How Do You Close a Statement Object?

Statement.close() releases the Statement object's database and JDBC resources immediately instead of waiting for this to happen automatically when it is closed.

Closing a Statement and Not Reporting Exceptions

This shows how to close a Statement and not report exceptions:

```
/**
 * Close a Statement; avoid closing if null, and
 * hide any SQLExceptions that occur.
 * @param stmt a java.sql.Statement object.
 */
public static void closeQuietly(java.sql.Statement stmt) {

    if (stmt == null) {
        return;
    }

    try {
        // releases this Statement object's database and
        // JDBC resources immediately instead of waiting
        // for this to happen when it is automatically closed.
        stmt.close();
    }
    catch (Exception e) {
        //ignore
        e.printStackTrace();
    }
}
```

This shows how to close a Statement and log exceptions:

```
/**
 * Close a Statement; avoid closing if null,
 * and hide any SQLExceptions that occur.
 * @param stmt a java.sql.Statement object.
 * @param logger a Logger object is used to log messages.
 */
public static void closeQuietly(java.sql.Statement stmt,
                            java.util.logging.Logger logger) {
    if (stmt == null) {
        return;
    }

    try {
        stmt.close();
    }
    catch (Exception e) {
        //ignore
        // handle the exception and log it
        e.printStackTrace();
        if (logger != null) {
            logger.warning("closeQuietly: "+e.getMessage());
        }
    }
}
```

Closing a Statement and Reporting Exceptions

This shows how to close a Statement and report exceptions:

```
/**
 * Close a Statement; avoid closing if null,
 * and report any SQLExceptions that occur.
 * @param stmt a java.sql.Statement object.
 * @throws SQLException failed to close the Statement
 */
public static void close(java.sql.Statement stmt)
    throws java.sql.SQLException {
    if (stmt != null) {
        stmt.close();
    }
}
```

14-7. How Do You Close a PreparedStatement Object?

PreparedStatement.close() releases the PreparedStatement object's database and JDBC resources immediately instead of waiting for this to happen automatically when it is closed.

Closing a PreparedStatement and Not Reporting Exceptions

This shows how to close a PreparedStatement and not report exceptions:

```
/**

 * @param pstmt a java.sql.PreparedStatement object.
 */
public static void closeQuietly(java.sql.PreparedStatement pstmt) {
    try {
        if (pstmt != null) {
            pstmt.close();
        }
    }
    catch (Exception e) {
        //ignore
        e.printStackTrace();
    }
}
```

Closing a PreparedStatement and Logging Exceptions

This shows how to close a PreparedStatement and log exceptions:

```
/**
 * Close a PreparedStatement; avoid closing if null, and
 * hide any SQLExceptions that occur.
 * @param pstmt a java.sql.PreparedStatement object.
 * @param logger a Logger object is used to log messages .
 */
public static void closeQuietly(java.sql.PreparedStatement pstmt,
                                java.util.logging.Logger logger) {
    try {
        if (pstmt != null) {
```

```
            pstmt.close();
        }
    }
    catch (Exception e) {
        // handle the exception and log it
        e.printStackTrace();
        if (logger != null) {
            logger.warning("closeQuietly: "+e.getMessage());
        }
    }
}
```

Closing PreparedStatement and Reporting Exceptions

This shows how to close a PreparedStatement and report exceptions:

```
/**
 * Close a PreparedStatement; avoid closing if null, and
 * report any SQLExceptions that occur.
 * @param pstmt a java.sql.PreparedStatement object.
 * @throws SQLException failed to close the PreparedStatement
 */
public static void close(java.sql.PreparedStatement pstmt)
    throws java.sql.SQLException {
    if (pstmt != null) {
        pstmt.close();
```

14-8. How Do You Close Statement and Connection Objects Together?

The following utility method closes a Statement object and a Connection object where Statement is derived from the Connection object.

Closing Statement and Connection Objects and Ignoring Exceptions

This shows how to close Statement and Connection objects and ignore exceptions:

```
/**
 * Close a statement and connection.
 * @param stmt a Statement object (derived from conn object)
 * @param conn a Connection object
 */
public static void closeQuietly(Statement stmt, Connection conn) {
    if (stmt != null) {
        try {
            // close the statement
            stmt.close();
        }
        catch (Exception ignored1) {
        }
    }

    if (conn != null) {
        try {
```

```
                // close the connection
                if (!conn.isClosed()) {
                    conn.close();
                }
            }
            catch (Exception ignored2) {
            }
        }
    }
}
```

Closing Statement and Connection Objects and Reporting Exceptions

This shows how to close Statement and Connection objects and report exceptions:

```
/**
 * Close a statement and connection.
 * @param stmt a Statement object (derived from conn object)
 * @param conn a Connection object
 * @throws SQLException failed to close statement and connection.
 */
public static void close(Statement stmt, Connection conn)
        throws SQLException {

    if (stmt != null) {
        // close the statement
        stmt.close();


        // close the connection
        if (!conn.isClosed()) {
            conn.close();
        }
    }
}
```

14-9. How Do You Close ResultSet, Statement, and Connection Objects Together?

The following utility method closes ResultSet, Statement, and Connection objects where Statement is derived from the Connection object and ResultSet is derived from the Statement object.

Closing ResultSet, Statement, and Connection Objects and Ignoring Exceptions

This shows how to close ResultSet, Statement, and Connection objects and ignore exceptions:

```
/**
 * Close ResultSet, Statement, and Connection objects.
 * @param rs a ResultSet object (derived from stmt object)
 * @param stmt a Statement object (derived from conn object)
 * @param conn a Connection object
 */
public static void closeQuietly(ResultSet rs, Statement stmt, Connection conn) {

    if (rs != null) {
        try {
```

```
                // close the statement
                rs.close();
            }
            catch (Exception ignored1) {
            }
        }

    if (stmt != null) {
        try {
            // close the statement
            stmt.close();
        }
        catch (Exception ignored2) {
        }
    }
    if (conn != null) {
        try {
            // close the connection
            if (!conn.isClosed()) {
                conn.close();
            }
        }
        catch (Exception ignored3) {
        }
    }
}
```

This shows how to close ResultSet, Statement, and Connection objects and report exceptions:

```
/**
 * Close ResultSet, Statement, and Connection objects.
 * @param rs a ResultSet object (derived from stmt object)
 * @param stmt a Statement object (derived from conn object)
 * @param conn a Connection object
 * @throws SQLException failed to close statement and connection.
 */
public static void close(ResultSet rs, Statement stmt, Connection conn)
    throws SQLException {

    if (rs != null) {
        // close the result set
        rs.close();
    }

    if (stmt != null) {
        // close the statement
        stmt.close();
    }

    if (conn != null) {
        // close the connection
        if (!conn.isClosed()) {
            conn.close();
        }
    }
}
```

14-10. How Do You Return a Long Text Column/Field from a Database?

The following utility can apply to a long column/field such as a CLOB or LongVarChar data type.

Returning a Larger Text Column/Field Using a Column Index

This shows how to return a larger text column/field using a column index:

```
/**
 * Return a larger text field from the database.
 * @param rs a ResultSet object
 * @param columnIndex index column of a long column/field
 * @return a larger text field from the database.
 * @throws SQLException failed to get a long string field/column.
 */
public static String getLargerString(ResultSet rs, int columnIndex)
        throws SQLException {
    if ((rs == null) || (columnIndex < 1)) {
        return null;
    }

    // buffer size when reading long strings
    InputStream in = null;
    int BUFFER_SIZE = 1024;
    try {


        // ASCII characters. The value can then be read in chunks
        // from the stream. This method is particularly suitable
        // for retrieving large LONGVARCHAR values. The JDBC driver
        // will do any necessary conversion from the database
        // format into ASCII
        in = rs.getAsciiStream(columnIndex);
        if (in == null) {
            return "";
        }

        byte[] arr = new byte[BUFFER_SIZE];
        StringBuffer buffer = new StringBuffer();
        int numRead = in.read(arr);
        while (numRead != -1) {
            buffer.append(new String(arr, 0, numRead));
            numRead = in.read(arr);
        }
        return buffer.toString();
    }
    catch (Exception e) {
        e.printStackTrace();
        throw new SQLException(e.getMessage());
    }
}
```

Returning a Larger Text Column/Field Using a Column Name

This shows how to return a larger text column/field using a column name:

```
/**
 * Return a larger text field from the database.
 * @param rs a ResultSet object
 * @param columnName name of column a long column/field
 * @return a long text field from the database.
 * @throws SQLException failed to get a long string field/column.
 */
public static String getLargerString(ResultSet rs, String columnName)
        throws SQLException {
    if ((rs == null) || (columnName == null)) {
        return null;
    }

    // buffer size when reading long strings
    InputStream stream = null;
    int BUFFER_SIZE = 1024;
    try {
    // retrieves the value of the designated column in the
    // current row of this ResultSet object as a stream of
    // ASCII characters. The value can then be read in chunks
    // from the stream. This method is particularly suitable
    // for retrieving large LONGVARCHAR values. The JDBC driver
    // will do any necessary conversion from the database
    // format into ASCII
        stream = rs.getAsciiStream(columnName);
        if (stream == null) {



            byte[] arr = new byte[BUFFER_SIZE];
            StringBuffer buffer = new StringBuffer();
            int numRead = stream.read(arr);
            while (numRead != -1) {
                buffer.append(new String(arr, 0, numRead));
                numRead = stream.read(arr);
            }
            return buffer.toString();
        }
    catch (Exception e) {
        e.printStackTrace();
        throw new SQLException(e.getMessage());
    }
}
```

14-11. How Do You Store a Long Text Field in a Database?

This utility stores a long text field in a database:

```
/**
 * Store a long text field in the database. For some strings,
 * for example, a message's text will be quite long and cannot
 * be stored using JDBC's setString() method.
 *
 * @param pstmt a PreparedStatement object.
 * @param parameterIndex the first parameter is 1, the second is 2, ...
 * @param data string to be set
 * @throws Exception failed to Store a long text field in the database.
```

```
*/
public static void setLongString(PreparedStatement pstmt,
                                 int parameterIndex,
                                 String data) throws Exception {
    if (pstmt == null) {
        return;
    }

    if (data == null) {
        // sets the designated parameter to SQL NULL.
        pstmt.setNull(parameterIndex, java.sql.Types.LONGVARCHAR);
    }
    else if (data.length() > 0) {
            // possibly a long string
            pstmt.setAsciiStream(
                    parameterIndex,
                    new ByteArrayInputStream(data.getBytes()),
                    data.length());
    }
    else {
            // empty string
            pstmt.setString(parameterIndex, "");
    }
}
```

Viewing the Constants Required

These are the constants required:

```
final static String TABLE_NAME = "TABLE_NAME";
final static String TABLE_SCHEMA = "TABLE_SCHEM";
final static String[] TABLE_TYPES = {"TABLE"};
final static String[] VIEW_TYPES = {"VIEW"};
final static String[] TABLE_AND_VIEW_TYPES = {"TABLE","VIEW"};
```

Getting Table Names from a Database

This shows how to get the table names from a database:

```
public java.util.Map getTables(Connection conn) throws Exception {
    if ( (conn == null) || (conn.isClosed()) ) {
        return null;
    }

    DatabaseMetaData dbmd = conn.getMetaData();
    if (dbmd == null) {
        throw new Exception("metadata not supported by vendor");
    }
    java.util.Map result = new HashMap();
    ResultSet tables = dbmd.getTables(null,null,null,TABLE_TYPES);
    while(tables.next()){
        result.put(tables.getString(TABLE_NAME),
```

```
                    tables.getString(TABLE_SCHEMA));
    }
    closeQuietly(tables);
    return result;
}
```

In general, if you know the catalog or schema of your database, you should pass these—instead of passing null—in the getTables() method, which can improve the performance of your query (for getting table names).

14-13. How Do You Get View Names from a Database?

The following utility returns view names from a database:

Viewing the Constants Required

These are the constants required:

```
final static String TABLE_NAME = "TABLE_NAME";
final static String TABLE_SCHEMA = "TABLE_SCHEM";
final static String[] TABLE_TYPES = {"TABLE"};
final static String[] VIEW_TYPES = {"VIEW"};
final static String[] TABLE_AND_VIEW_TYPES = {"TABLE","VIEW"};
```

Getting View Names from a Database

```
public java.util.Map getViews(Connection conn) throws Exception {
    if ( (conn == null) || (conn.isClosed()) ) {
        return null;
    }

    DatabaseMetaData dbmd = conn.getMetaData();
    if (dbmd == null) {
        throw new Exception("metadata not supported by vendor");
    }
    java.util.Map result = new HashMap();
    ResultSet views = dbmd.getTables(null,null,null,VIEW_TYPES);
    while(views.next()){
        result.put(views.getString(TABLE_NAME),
                   views.getString(TABLE_SCHEMA));
    }

    closeQuietly(views);
    return result;
}
```

In general, if you know the catalog or schema of your database, you should pass these—instead of passing null—in the getTables() method, which can improve the performance of your query (for getting table names).

14-14. How Do You Get Table and View Names from a Database?

The following utility returns table and view names from a database.

Viewing the Constants Required

These are the constants required:

```
final static String TABLE_NAME = "TABLE_NAME";
final static String TABLE_SCHEMA = "TABLE_SCHEM";
final static String[] TABLE_TYPES = {"TABLE"};
final static String[] VIEW_TYPES = {"VIEW"};
final static String[] TABLE_AND_VIEW_TYPES = {"TABLE","VIEW"};
```

Getting Table and View Names from a Database

This shows how to get table and view names from a database:

```
public java.util.Map getTablesAndViews(Connection conn) throws Exception {
    if ( (conn == null) || (conn.isClosed()) ) {
        return null;
    }

    DatabaseMetaData dbmd = conn.getMetaData();
    if (dbmd == null) {
        throw new Exception("metadata not supported by vendor");
    }
    java.util.Map result = new HashMap();


    while(rs.next()){
        result.put(rs.getString(TABLE_NAME), rs.getString(TABLE_SCHEMA));
    }

    closeQuietly(rs);
    return result;
}
```

In general, if you know the catalog or schema of your database, you should pass these—instead of passing null—in the getTables() method, which can improve the performance of your query (for getting table names).

14-15 How Do You Convert an InputStream Object to a Byte Array?

This utility reads the entire input stream provided (as an InputStream object) and returns its content as a byte array:

```
/**
 * Read the entire input stream provided and
 * return its content as a byte array.
 *
 * @param input the InputStream from
 *    which a result is being retrieved.
 * @return a byte array containing the content of the input stream
 * @throws Exception Failed to read the entire input stream provided
 */
public static byte[] getByteArray(InputStream input) throws Exception {
    if (input == null) {
        return null;
    }
```

```
        byte[] result = null;
        try {
            int length = in.available();
            result = new byte[length];
            in.read(result, 0, length);
            return result;
        }
        catch (Exception e) {
            throw new Exception("could not read InputStream: "+e.getMessage());
        }
}
```

14-16. How Do You Get a Current java.sql.Date Object?

This is how you get a current java.sql.Date:

```
public static java.sql.Date getJavaSqlDate() {
    java.util.Date date = new java.util.Date();
    return new java.sql.Date(date.getTime());
}
```

14-17. How Do You Get a Trimmed String from a Database Column?

When creating a new table, when you use a CHAR(n) instead of a VARCHAR(n), then the database server will pad your data with spaces. You can use the following method to get rid of redundant spaces:

```
 * Get a trimmed string from a database column.
 * @param rs a ResultSet object.
 * @param index column's index
 * @throws SQLException failed to get a trimmed string
 * from a database column.
 */
public static String getTrimmedString(ResultSet rs, int index)
    throws SQLException {
    String value = rs.getString(index);

    if (value != null) {
    value = value.trim();
    }

    return value;
}


/**
 * Get a trimmed string from a database column.
 * @param rs a ResultSet object.
 * @param columnName   column's name
 * @throws SQLException failed to get a trimmed string
 * from a database column.
 */
public static String getTrimmedString(ResultSet rs , String columnName)
    throws SQLException {
    String value = rs.getString(columnName);
```

```
    if (value != null) {
        value = value.trim();
    }

    return value;
}
```

14-18. How Do You Load a JDBC Driver?

This shows how to load a JDBC driver:

```
/**
 * Loads and registers a database driver class. If this
 * succeeds, it returns true, else it returns false.
 *
 * @param driverClassName name of JDBC driver
 *
 * @return true if driver is loaded successfully,
 * otherwise return false.
 */
public static boolean loadDriver(java.lang.String driverClassName)
    try {
    Class.forName(driverClassName);
        //
        // loaded driver successfully
        //


    catch(Exception e) {
        //
        // could not load a driver.
        //
        return false;
    }
}
```

14-19. How Do You Format a String?

You can format a String in three ways, as shown in the following sections.

First Solution: Using String Concatenation

This solution will generate lots of unneeded String objects (and is not an efficient solution):

```
/**
 * Format a string and return it with the desired length.
 * @param str input string
 * @param finalLength final length desired
 * @return a formatted string with the desired length
 * @throws Exception failed to format a string
 */
public static String format(String str, int finalLength) throws Exception {
    if (str == null) {
        return null;
    }
```

```
  String result=null;
  if (finalLength <= str.length()){
    result = str.substring(0, finalLength);
  }
  else {
    result = str;
    for (int i = str.length(); i < finalLength; i++) {
      // pad with spaces
      result = result + " ";
    }
  }
  return (result);
}
```

Second Solution: Using StringBuffer's append()

This solution is an efficient solution and will not generate lots of unneeded String objects:

```
/**
 * Format a string and return it with the desired length.
 * @param str input string
 * @param finalLength final length desired
 * @return a formatted string with the desired length
 * @throws Exception failed to format a string
 */
public static String format(String str, int finalLength) throws Exception {



  String result=null;
  if (finalLength <= str.length()){
    result = str.substring(0, finalLength);
    return result;
  }
  else {
    StringBuffer buffer = new StringBuffer(str);
    for (int i = str.length(); i < finalLength; i++) {
      // pad with spaces
      buffer.append(" ");
    }
    return buffer.toString();
  }
}
```

Third Solution: Using the java.lang.StringBuilder Class

You can use the StringBuilder class (since JDK 1.5) to efficiently format String objects. This solution is an efficient solution and will not generate lots of unneeded String objects:

```
/**
 * Format a string and return it with the desired length.
 * @param str input string
 * @param finalLength final length desired
 * @return a formatted string with the desired length
 * @throws Exception failed to format a string
 */
```

```
public static String format(String str, int finalLength) throws Exception {
    if (str == null) {
        return null;
    }

    String result=null;
    if (finalLength <= str.length()){
        result = str.substring(0, finalLength);
        return result;
    }
    else {
        StringBuilder buffer = new StringBuilder(str);
        for (int i = str.length(); i < finalLength; i++) {
            // pad with spaces
            buffer.append(" ");
        }
        return buffer.toString();
    }
}
```

14-20. How Do You Format an Integer (int Data Type)?

You can format an integer in two ways, as shown in the next sections.

First Solution: Using String Concatenation

```
/**
 * Format an integer and return it with the desired length.
 * @param intData an integer input
 * @param finalLength final length desired
 * @return a formatted integer with the desired length
 * @throws Exception failed to format an integer
 */
public static String format(int intData, int finalLength) throws Exception {
    String strData = String.valueOf(intData);
    String result=null;
    if (finalLength <= strData.length()) {
        result = strData.substring(0, finalLength);
    }
    else {
        result = "";
        for (int i = 0; i < finalLength - strData.length(); i++) {
            result = result + " ";
        }
        result = result + strData;
    }
    return (result);
}
```

Second Solution: Using StringBuffer's append()

This solution is an efficient solution and will not generate lots of unneeded String objects:

```
/**
 * Format an integer and return it with the desired length.
 * @param intData an integer input
 * @param finalLength final length desired
 * @return a formatted integer with the desired length
 * @throws Exception failed to format an integer
 */
public static String format(int intData, int finalLength) throws Exception {
    String strData = String.valueOf(intData);
    String result=null;
    if (finalLength <= strData.length()) {
      result = strData.substring(0, finalLength);
      return result;
    }
    else {
      StringBuffer result = new StringBuffer("");
      for (int i = 0; i < finalLength - strData.length(); i++) {
        result.append(" ");
      }
      result.append(strData);
      return (result.toString());
    }
}
```

14-21. How Do You Format an Integer Object?

```
/**
 * Format an Integer object to a desired length.
 * @param integerData an integer input
 * @param finalLength final length desired
 * @return a formatted integer with the desired length
 * @throws Exception failed to format an integer
 */
*public static String format(Integer integerData, int finalLength)
    throws Exception {
    if (integerData == null) {
      return null;
    }

    return format(integerData.intValue(), finalLength);
}
```

14-22. How Do You Format a Double Data Type?

You can format a Double data type in two ways, as shown in the following sections.

First Solution: Using String

This solution will generate lots of unneeded String objects:

```
/**
  * Format a double and return it with the desired precision and scale.
  * @param doubleData a double input
  * @param precision the desired precision
```

```
 * @param scale the desired scale
 * @return a formatted double with the desired length
 * @throws Exception failed to format a double
 */
public static String format(double doubleData, int precision, int scale)
   throws Exception {
   java.math.BigDecimal bigDecimal = new java.math.BigDecimal(doubleData);
   bigDecimal = bigDecimal.setScale(scale, BigDecimal.ROUND_HALF_EVEN);
   String strData = big.toString();

   // prepare the final string
   int finalLength = precision + 1;
   String result=null;
   if (finalLen <= strData.length()) {
     result = strData.substring(0, finalLength);
   }
   else {
     result = "";
     for (int i = 0; i < finalLen - strData.length(); i++){
       result = result + " ";
     }
     result = result + strData;
   }

   return result;
}
```

This solution is an efficient solution and will not generate lots of unneeded String objects:

```
/**
 * Format a double, and return it with the desired precision and scale.
 * @param doubleData a double input
 * @param precision the desired precision
 * @param scale the desired scale
 * @return a formatted double with the desired length
 * @throws Exception failed to format a double
 */
public static String format(double doubleData, int precision, int scale)
     throws Exception {
     java.math.BigDecimal bigDecimal = new java.math.BigDecimal(doubleData);
     bigDecimal = bigDecimal.setScale(scale, BigDecimal.ROUND_HALF_EVEN);
     String strData = big.toString();

     // prepare the final string
     int finalLength = precision + 1;
     String result=null;
     if (finalLen <= strData.length()) {
       result = strData.substring(0, finalLength);
       return result;
     }
     else {
       StringBuffer result = new StringBuffer("");
       for (int i = 0; i < finalLength - strData.length(); i++){
         result.append(" ");
       }
```

```
        result.append(strData);
        return result.toString();
    }
}
```

14-23. How Do You Format a java.math.BigDecimal Object?

You can format a java.math.BigDecimal object in two ways, as shown in the following sections.

First Solution: Using String

This solution will generate lots of unneeded String objects:

```
/**
 * Format a double and return it with the desired precision and scale.
 * @param bigDecimal a java.math.BigDecimal object
 * @param precision the desired precision
 * @param scale the desired scale
 * @return a formatted "big decimal" with the desired length
 * @throws Exception failed to format a "big decimal"
 */
public static String format(java.math.BigDecimal bigDecimal,
                            int precision,
                            int scale)  throws Exception {
  if (bigDecimal == null) {
      return null;


  bigDecimal = bigDecimal.setScale(scale,
                          java.math.BigDecimal.ROUND_HALF_EVEN);
  String strData = bigDecimal.toString();

  // prepare the final string
  int finalLength = precision + 1;

  // use a utility method defied earlier (code reuse)
  return format(strData, finalLength);

}
```

Second Solution: Use StringBuffer

This solution is an efficient solution and will not generate lots of unneeded String objects:

```
/**
 * Format a double and return it with the desired precision and scale.
 * @param bigDecimal a java.math.BigDecimal object
 * @param precision the desired precision
 * @param scale the desired scale
 * @return a formatted "big decimal" with the desired length
 * @throws Exception failed to format a "big decimal"
 */
public static String format(java.math.BigDecimal bigDecimal,
                            int precision,
                            int scale) throws Exception {
```

```
if (bigDecimal == null) {
    return null;
}

bigDecimal = bigDecimal.setScale(scale, java.math.BigDecimal.ROUND_HALF_EVEN);
String strData = bigDecimal.toString();

// prepare the final string
int finalLength = precision + 1;

// use a utility method defined earlier (code reuse)
return format(strData, finalLength);

}
```

14-24. How Do You Format a Double Object?

This shows how to format a Double object:

```
/**
 * Format a double and return it with the desired precision and scale.
 * @param doubleData a Double object
 * @param precision the desired precision
 * @param scale the desired scale
 */
public static String format(Double doubleData, int precision, int scale)
  throws Exception {


    return null;
  }

  return format(doubleData.doubleValue(), precision, scale);
}
```

14-25. How Do You Build a URL in the Format Needed by the JDBC Drivers?

The JDBC specification has a standard for database URLs, but each vendor has its own format. In general, each database has a unique URL format.

Viewing the JDBC URL Format for MySQL

The JDBC URL format for MySQL Connector/J is as follows, with items in square brackets ([,]) being optional (note that the JDBC URL is a single line):

```
jdbc:mysql://[host][,failoverhost...][:port]/[database]
[?propertyName1][=propertyValue1][&propertyName2][=propertyValue2]...
```

If the hostname is not specified, it defaults to 127.0.0.1. If the port is not specified, it defaults to 3306, which is the default port number for MySQL servers.

Viewing the JDBC URL Format for Oracle

The Oracle URL format is as follows:

```
jdbc:oracle:thin:@[hostName]:[portNumber]:[databaseName]
```

The following example connects the user scott with a password of tiger to a database with INSTANCE_NAME orcl through port number 1521 of host myhost by using the Thin driver:

```
String dbURL = "jdbc:oracle:thin:@myhost:1521:orcl";
Connection conn = DriverManager.getConnection(dbURL, "scott", "tiger");
```

The following method, makeURL(), accepts required parameters and then builds a database URL for MySQL and Oracle:

```
// default port numbers
public static final int DEFAULT_PORT_NUMBER_MYSQL = 3306;
public static final int DEFAULT_PORT_NUMBER_ORACLE = 1521;

// database vendors
public static final String DATABASE_VENDOR_MYSQL = "mysql";
public static final String DATABASE_VENDOR_ORACLE = "oracle";

/**
 * Build a URL in the format needed by the JDBC drivers.
 * @param hostname of the host
 * @param dbName name of the database
 * @param vendor name of the vendor
 * @return a URL in the format needed by the JDBC drivers.
 * @throws Exception failed to build a database URL.
 */
public static String makeURL(String host,
                             String dbName,



             DEFAULT_PORT_NUMBER_ORACLE+":" + dbName);
    }
    else if (vendor.equalsIgnoreCase(DATABASE_VENDOR_MYSQL)) {
        return("jdbc:mysql://" + host + ":"+
               DEFAULT_PORT_NUMBER_MYSQL+"/" + dbName);
    }
    else {
        throw new Exception("makeURL: database vendor undefined.")
    }
}


/**
 * Build a URL in the format needed by the JDBC drivers.
 * @param host name of the host
 * @param dbName name of the database
 * @param vendor name of the vendor
 * @param properties additional database URL properties
 * @return a URL in the format needed by the JDBC drivers.
 * @throws Exception failed to build a database URL.
 */
public static String makeURL(String host,
                             String dbName,
                             String vendor,
                             java.util.Map properties) throws Exception {
    if ((properties == null) || (properties.size() == 0)) {
        return makeURL(host, dbName, vendor);
    }
```

```
        if (vendor.equalsIgnoreCase(DATABASE_VENDOR_ORACLE)) {
            return("jdbc:oracle:thin:@" + host + ":"+
                   DEFAULT_PORT_NUMBER_ORACLE+":" + dbName);
        }
        else if (vendor.equalsIgnoreCase(DATABASE_VENDOR_MYSQL)) {
            StringBuffer buffer = new StringBuffer("jdbc:mysql://");
            buffer.append(host);
            buffer.append(":");
            buffer.append(DEFAULT_PORT_NUMBER_MYSQL);
            buffer.append("/");
            buffer.append(dbName);
            Iterator iter = properties.iterator();
            while (iter.hasNext()) {
                String propertyName = (String) iter.next();
                String propertyValue = (String) properties.get(propertyName);
                buffer.append("?");
                buffer.append(propertyName);
                buffer.append("=");
                buffer.append(propertyValue);
            }
            return buffer.toString();
        }
        else {
            throw new Exception("makeURL: database vendor undefined.")
        }
}


/**
 * Build a URL in the format needed by the JDBC drivers.
 * @param host name of the host
 * @param dbName name of the database
 * @param vendor name of the vendor
 * @param port the port number
 * @return a URL in the format needed by the JDBC drivers.
 * @throws Exception failed to build a database URL.
 */
public static String makeURL(String host,
                             String dbName,
                             String vendor,
                             int port) throws Exception {
    if (vendor.equalsIgnoreCase(DATABASE_VENDOR_ORACLE)) {
        return("jdbc:oracle:thin:@" + host + ":"+port+":" + dbName);
    }
    else if (vendor.equalsIgnoreCase(DATABASE_VENDOR_MYSQL)) {
        return("jdbc:mysql://" + host + ":"+port+"/" + dbName);
    }
    else {
        throw new Exception("makeURL: database vendor undefined.")
    }
}


/**
 * Build a URL in the format needed by the JDBC drivers.
 * @param host name of the host
 * @param dbName name of the database
```

```
 * @param vendor name of the vendor
 * @param port the port number
 * @param properties additional database URL properties
 * @return a URL in the format needed by the JDBC drivers.
 * @throws Exception failed to build a database URL.
 */
public static String makeURL(String host,
                            String dbName,
                            String vendor,
                            int port,
                            java.util.Map properties) throws Exception {
    if ((properties == null) || (properties.size() == 0)) {
        return makeURL(host, dbName, vendor, port);
    }
    if (vendor.equalsIgnoreCase(DATABASE_VENDOR_ORACLE)) {
        return("jdbc:oracle:thin:@" + host + ":"+port+":" + dbName);
    }
    else if (vendor.equalsIgnoreCase(DATABASE_VENDOR_MYSQL)) {
        StringBuffer buffer = new StringBuffer("jdbc:mysql://");
        buffer.append(host);
        buffer.append(":");
        buffer.append(port);
        buffer.append("/");
        buffer.append(dbName);
        Iterator iter = properties.iterator();
        while (iter.hasNext()) {


            buffer.append("?");
            buffer.append(propertyName);
            buffer.append("=");
            buffer.append(propertyValue);
        }
        return buffer.toString();
    }
    else {
        throw new Exception("makeURL: database vendor undefined.")
    }
}
```

14-26. How Do You Get the Version Number of a JDBC Driver?

DatabaseMetaData.getDriverVersion() retrieves the version number of a JDBC driver as a String:

```
public static String getDriverVersion(Connection conn)
    throws SQLException {

    if ((conn == null) || (conn.isClosed())) {
        return null;
    }

    DatabaseMetaData meta = conn.getMetaData();
    if (meta == null) {
        return null;
    }

    return meta.getDriverVersion();
}
```

14-27. What Is a JDBC Utility Component (DbUtils)?

DbUtils is a subproject of Apache Jakarta project. It is a small set of classes designed to make working with JDBC easier. Writing JDBC resource cleanup code is a mundane, error-prone task, so these classes abstract all the cleanup tasks from your code. This leaves you with what you really want to do with JDBC in the first place: query and update data. DbUtils is available from the Apache Software Foundation as a free download.

DbUtils Pointers

Here are some helpful DbUtils links:

- *Home page*: http://jakarta.apache.org/commons/dbutils/
- *Java docs*: http://jakarta.apache.org/commons/dbutils/apidocs/index.html
- *Examples*: http://jakarta.apache.org/commons/dbutils/examples.html

DbUtils Design Goals

DbUtils is designed to be the following:

- *Small*: You should be able to understand the whole package in a short amount of time.
- *Transparent*: DbUtils doesn't do any magic behind the scenes. You give it a query, and then it executes the query and cleans up for you.
- *Fast*: You don't need to create a million temporary objects to work with DbUtils.

DbUtils (DbUtils 1.1-dev) has three packages:

- org.apache.commons.dbutils
- org.apache.commons.dbutils.handlers
- org.apache.commons.dbutils.wrappers

DbUtils Core Classes/Interfaces

The core classes/interfaces in DbUtils are QueryRunner and ResultSetHandler. You don't need to know about any other DbUtils classes to benefit from using the library. The following example demonstrates how you use these classes together.

- org.apache.commons.dbutils.DbUtils: DbUtils is a class that provides utility methods to do routine tasks such as closing connections and loading JDBC drivers. DbUtils is collection of JDBC helper methods. This class is thread-safe, and all the methods are static.
- org.apache.commons.dbutils.QueryRunner: This class executes SQL queries with pluggable strategies for handling ResultSet objects. This class is thread-safe.
- org.apache.commons.dbutils.ResultSetHandler: Implementations of this interface convert ResultSet objects into other objects.

Using the DbUtils Package (Example 1)

In these examples, you will use some of the core classes and interfaces from the DbUtils package. You will issue a query to read the entire animals_table table and convert every row to a JavaBean object (called AnimalBean).

Step 1: Preparing the Database (Example 1)

For these examples, you will use a table called animals_table (which is a simple table with two columns):

```
mysql> use octopus;
Database changed
mysql> desc animals_table;
+-------+-------------+------+-----+---------+----------------+
| Field | Type        | Null | Key | Default | Extra          |
+-------+-------------+------+-----+---------+----------------+
| id    | int(11)     |      | PRI | NULL    | auto_increment |
| name  | varchar(10) |      |     |         |                |
+-------+-------------+------+-----+---------+----------------+
2 rows in set (0.00 sec)

mysql> select * from animals_table;
+-----+--------+
| id  | name   |
+-----+--------+
| 111 | ginger |
| 222 | lola   |
| 333 | freddy |
+-----+--------+
3 rows in set (0.01 sec)
```

specify the bean class to be AnimalBean, as shown next. The DbUtils package's ResultSetHandler class converts a ResultSet into a java.util.List of beans.

```
public class AnimalBean {

    private int id;
    private String name;

    public AnimalBean() {
    }

    public void setName(String name) {
        this.name = name;
    }

    public String getName() {
        return this.name;
    }

    public void setId(int id) {
        this.id = id;
    }

    public int getId() {
        return this.id;
    }
}
```

Step 3: Using BeanListHandler (Example 1)

This shows how to use BeanListHandler:

```
1    import org.apache.commons.dbutils.DbUtils;
2    import org.apache.commons.dbutils.QueryRunner;
3    import org.apache.commons.dbutils.handlers.BeanListHandler;
4
5    import java.sql.Connection;
6    import java.sql.DriverManager;
7    import java.sql.SQLException;
8
9    import java.util.List;
10
11   public class DbUtils_UseBean_MySQL {
12
13       public static void main(String[] args) {
14
15           Connection conn = null;
16           String jdbcURL = "jdbc:mysql://localhost/octopus";
17           String jdbcDriver = "com.mysql.jdbc.Driver";
18           String user = "root";
19           String password = "root";
20
21           try {
22               DbUtils.loadDriver(jdbcDriver);
23               conn = DriverManager.getConnection(jdbcURL, user, password);


26               System.out.println("MySQL: begin using BeanListHandler...");
27
28               List beans = (List) qRunner.query(conn,
29                   "select id, name from animals_table",
30                   new BeanListHandler(AnimalBean.class));
31
32               for (int i = 0; i < beans.size(); i++) {
33                   AnimalBean bean = (AnimalBean) beans.get(i);
34                   bean.print();
35               }
36               System.out.println("DbUtils_UseBean_MySQL: end.");
37
38           }
39           catch (SQLException e) {
40               // handle the exception
41               e.printStackTrace();
42           }
43           finally {
44               DbUtils.closeQuietly(conn);
45           }
46       }
47   }
```

Step 4: Running the Test Program (Example 1)

Before you run the test program, you have to add the MySQL driver's .jar file and the DbUtils package's .jar file to your CLASSPATH, as shown here:

```
$ javac  DbUtils_UseBean_MySQL.java
$ java DbUtils_UseBean_MySQL
begin using BeanListHandler...
id=111 name=ginger
id=222 name=lola
id=333 name=freddy
DbUtils_UseBean_MySQL: end.
```

Discussing DbUtils_UseBean_MySQL (Example 1)

This breaks down the program:

- *Lines 1–9*: Import the required Java classes and interfaces.

- *Lines 15–23*: Load the JDBC driver class, and get a database Connection object using the DriverManager class.

- *Lines 25–25*: Instantiate the QueryRunner class. (QueryRunner executes SQL queries with plug-gable strategies for handling ResultSet objects. This class is thread-safe.)

- *Lines 28–30*: Here you use the QueryRunner to execute a SQL query. You pass the BeanListHandler object (as a parameter), which is a ResultSetHandler that can convert the ResultSet into a List of a specific bean. (The bean class will be AnimalBean.)

- *Lines 32–35*: You iterate through the List of beans retrieved and invoke AnimalBean.print() on each bean.

In the following examples, you will use some of the core classes and interfaces from the DbUtils package. You will issue a query to read the entire animals_table table and convert every row to a java.util.Map object.

Step 1: Preparing the Database (Example 2)

Use a table called animals_table (which is a simple table with two columns):

```
mysql> use octopus;
Database changed
mysql> desc animals_table;
+-------+-------------+------+-----+---------+----------------+
| Field | Type        | Null | Key | Default | Extra          |
+-------+-------------+------+-----+---------+----------------+
| id    | int(11)     |      | PRI | NULL    | auto_increment |
| name  | varchar(10) |      |     |         |                |
+-------+-------------+------+-----+---------+----------------+
2 rows in set (0.00 sec)

mysql> select * from animals_table;
+-----+--------+
| id  | name   |
+-----+--------+
| 111 | ginger |
| 222 | lola   |
| 333 | freddy |
+-----+--------+
3 rows in set (0.01 sec)
```

Step 2: Using MapListHandler (Example 2)

The MapListHandler class implements ResultSetHandler, which is defined as follows (for details, see http://jakarta.apache.org/commons/dbutils/):

```
package org.apache.commons.dbutils;
public interface ResultSetHandler {
   // Implementations of this interface convert
   // ResultSets into other objects.
   ...
}

package org.apache.commons.dbutils.handlers;
public class MapListHandler
   extends java.lang.Object
   implements ResultSetHandler {
   // ResultSetHandler implementation that converts a ResultSet
   // object into a List of Maps. This class is thread-safe.
   ...
}
```

The following example show how to use a MapListHandler object:

```
1    import org.apache.commons.dbutils.DbUtils;
2    import org.apache.commons.dbutils.QueryRunner;
3    import org.apache.commons.dbutils.handlers.MapListHandler;
4
5    import java.sql.Connection;


8
9    import java.util.Map;
10   import java.util.List;
11
12   public class DbUtils_UseMap_MySQL {
13
14       public static void main(String[] args) {
15
16           Connection conn = null;
17           String jdbcURL = "jdbc:mysql://localhost/octopus";
18           String jdbcDriver = "com.mysql.jdbc.Driver";
19           String user = "root";
20           String password = "root";
21
22           try {
23               DbUtils.loadDriver(jdbcDriver);
24               conn = DriverManager.getConnection(jdbcURL, user, password);
25
26               QueryRunner qRunner = new QueryRunner();
27               System.out.println("begin using MapListHandler...");
28
29               List mapList = (List) qRunner.query(conn,
30                   "select id, name from animals_table",
31                   new MapListHandler());
32
33               for (int i = 0; i < mapList.size(); i++) {
34                   Map map = (Map) mapList.get(i);
35                   System.out.println("id=" + map.get("id"));
```

```
36                          System.out.println("name=" + map.get("name"));
37                          System.out.println("----------------");
38                      }
39
40                  System.out.println("DbUtils_UseMap_MySQL: end.");
41
42          }
43          catch (SQLException e) {
44              // handle the exception
45              e.printStackTrace();
46          }
47          finally {
48              DbUtils.closeQuietly(conn);
49          }
50      }
51  }
```

Step 3: Running the Test Program (Example 2)

Before you run the test program, you have to add the MySQL driver's .jar file and the DbUtils package's .jar file to your CLASSPATH, as shown here:

```
$ javac DbUtils_UseMap_MySQL.java
$ java DbUtils_UseMap_MySQL
begin using MapListHandler...
id=111



name=lola
----------------
id=333
name=freddy
----------------
DbUtils_UseMap_MySQL: end.
```

Discussing DbUtils_UseMap_MySQL (Example 2)

This breaks down the program:

- *Lines 1–10*: Import the required Java classes and interfaces.

- *Lines 16–24*: Load the JDBC driver class, and get a database Connection object using the DriverManager class.

- *Lines 25–25*: Instantiate the QueryRunner class. (QueryRunner executes SQL queries with pluggable strategies for handling ResultSet objects. This class is thread-safe.)

- *Lines 29–31*: Here you use the QueryRunner to execute a SQL query. You pass the MapListHandler object (as a parameter), which is a ResultSetHandler that can convert the ResultSet into a List of Map objects (each result row is represented as a java.util.Map object).

- *Lines 33–38*: You iterate through the List of Map objects retrieved.

DbUtils Generic Example from the Apache Software Foundation

The following examples are from the Web site at http://jakarta.apache.org/commons/dbutils/examples.html:

```
// Create a ResultSetHandler implementation to
// convert the first row into an Object[].
ResultSetHandler h = new ResultSetHandler() {
    public Object handle(ResultSet rs) throws SQLException {
        if (!rs.next()) {
            return null;
        }

        ResultSetMetaData meta = rs.getMetaData();
        int cols = meta.getColumnCount();
        Object[] result = new Object[cols];

        for (int i = 0; i < cols; i++) {
            result[i] = rs.getObject(i + 1);
        }

        return result;
    }
};

// Create a QueryRunner that will use connections
// from the given DataSource
QueryRunner run = new QueryRunner(dataSource);

// Execute the query and get the results back from the handler
Object[] result = (Object[]) run.query(
```

a DataSource. Notice that you are responsible for closing the Connection in this example.

```
ResultSetHandler h = ... // Define a handler the same as the previous example

// No DataSource, so you must handle Connections manually
QueryRunner run = new QueryRunner();

Connection conn = ... // open a connection
try{
    Object[] result = (Object[]) run.query(
        conn, "SELECT * FROM Person WHERE name=?", "John Doe", h);
    // do something with the result

}
finally {
    // Use this helper method, so you do not have to check for null
    DbUtils.close(conn);
}
```

In the previous examples, you implemented the ResultSetHandler interface to turn the first row of the ResultSet into an Object[]. This is a fairly generic implementation that can be reused across many projects. In recognition of this, DbUtils provides a set of ResultSetHandler implementations in the org.apache.commons.dbutils.handlers package that perform common transformations into arrays, Map objects, and JavaBeans. Each implementation has a version that converts just the first row and another that converts all rows in the ResultSet.

```
QueryRunner run = new QueryRunner(dataSource);
```

14-28. How Do You Debug/Display a SQLException Object?

Sometimes during application development, you might get a SQLException that you are not familiar with. In this case, you can use the following method to get some detailed information:

```
/**
 * This method checks for sql exceptions and displays
 * error information; note that multiple exception
 * objects could be chained together.
 * @param e The SQLException object.
 */
public static printSQLExceptions(SQLException e) {
    if (e == null) {
        System.out.println("printSQLExceptions: exception is null.");
        return;
    }

    System.out.println("--- printSQLExceptions: SQLException caught ---");
    while (e != null) {
        System.out.println("printSQLExceptions: SQLState: " + e.getSQLState());
        System.out.println("printSQLExceptions: Message:  " + e.getMessage());
        System.out.println("printSQLExceptions: Vendor:   " + e.getErrorCode());
        System.out.println("");
        e = e.getNextException();
    }
}


 * This method checks for sql exceptions and displays
 * error information; note that multiple exception
 * objects could be chained together.
 * @param methodName The name of a method.
 * @param e The SQLException object.
 */
public static printSQLExceptions(SQLException e, String methodName) {
    if (e == null) {
        System.out.println("printSQLExceptions: exception is null.");
        return;
    }

    System.out.println("--- SQLException caught in method "+methodName);
    while (e != null) {
        System.out.println("printSQLExceptions: SQLState: " + e.getSQLState());
        System.out.println("printSQLExceptions: Message:  " + e.getMessage());
        System.out.println("printSQLExceptions: Vendor:   " + e.getErrorCode());
        System.out.println("");
        e = e.getNextException();
    }
}
```

14-29. How Do You Debug/Display a SQLWarning Object?

Sometimes during application development, you might get a SQLWarning that you are not familiar with. In that case, you can use the following method to get some detailed information:

```
/**
 * This method checks for sql warnings and displays
 * error information; note that multiple exception
 * objects could be chained together.
 * @param w The SQLWarning object.
 */
public static printSQLWarnings(SQLWarning w) {

    if (w == null) {
        System.out.println("printSQLWarnings: warning is null.");
        return;
    }

    System.out.println("--- printSQLWarnings: Warning  ---");
    while (w != null) {
        System.out.println("printSQLWarnings: SQLState: " + w.getSQLState());
        System.out.println("printSQLWarnings: Message:  " + w.getMessage());
        System.out.println("printSQLWarnings: Vendor:   " + w.getErrorCode());
        System.out.println("");
        w = w.getNextWarning();
    }
}
```

14-30. How Do You Debug/Display a ResultSet Object?

When debugging ResultSet objects, you may use the following two methods to print the content of

displayResultSet()

This is displayResultSet():

```
/**
 * This method displays the content of a given ResultSet object,
 * which contains all rows and columns in the given result set.
 * @param rs  The result set to be displayed/debugged.
 * @return  None.
 * @exception SQLException, failed to display the result set object.
 */
public static void displayResultSet(ResultSet rs)
    throws SQLException {
    if (rs == null) {
        System.out.print("displayResultSet: result set is null.");
        return;
    }

    // get the ResultSetMetaData, which will
    // be used for the column headings
    ResultSetMetaData metaData = rs.getMetaData();
    if (metaData == null) {
        System.out.print("displayResultSet: metadata for result set is null.");
        return;
    }

    // get the number of columns for the given ResultSet object
    int numberOfColumns = metaData.getColumnCount();
```

```java
        // display column headings
        for (int i = 1; i <= numberOfColumns; i++) {
            if (i > 1) {
                System.out.print(",");
            }
            System.out.print(metaData.getColumnLabel(i));
        }
        System.out.println("\n-------------------------------------");

        //
        // display data, iterate the ResultSet object,
        // fetching until end of the result set
        //
        while (rs.next())  {
            // loop through each column, getting
            // the column data and displaying
            for (int i = 1; i <= numberOfColumns; i++)  {
                if (i > 1) {
                    System.out.print(",");
                }
                System.out.print(rs.getString(i));
            }
            System.out.println("");
        }
    }
}
```

This is resultSetAsTable():

```java
/**
 * Provide a readable view of a JDBC ResultSet object.
 *
 * Here is sample output, showing two data rows and the column names.
 *
 * [
 *    [column-name-1, column-name-2, ...],
 *    [data-1, data-2, ...],
 *    [data-1, data-2, ...]
 *    ...
 * ]
 *
 * @param rs   The result set to be displayed/debugged.
 * @return A string representation that looks like a List of Lists.
 * @throws SQLException failed to display result set object.
 */
public static java.util.List resultSetAsTable(ResultSet rs)
    throws SQLException {
    if (rs == null) {
        return null;
    }

    java.util.List rows = new java.util.ArrayList();
    ResultSetMetaData rsMetaData = rs.getMetaData();
    if (rsMetaData == null) {
        // JDBC driver does not support metadata
        return null;
    }
```

```
    int columnCount = rsMetaData.getColumnCount();
    java.util.List columnNames = new java.util.ArrayList();

    // add column names
    for (int i = 1; i <= columnCount; i++) {
        String columnName = rsMetaData.getColumnName(i);
        columnNames.add(columnName);
    }

    rows.add(columnNames);

    // add actual data
    while (rs.next()) {
        java.util.List rowData = new java.util.ArrayList();
        for (int i = 1; i <= columnCount; i++) {
            Object columnData = rs.getObject(i);
            rowData.add(columnData);
        }
        rows.add(rowData);
    }

    return rows;
}
```

14-31. What Is the Best Way to Generate a Random GUID?

```
create table employee_table (
    internal_id varchar(32),
    ...
);
```

where internal_id is a GUID. But how do you create these GUIDs at runtime (when you want to create a new record of employee_table)? In the multitude of Java GUID generators, I found one that guarantees the randomness of the GUID generated. The GUID generator is from http://www. JavaExchange.com and is open-source.

Producing a Random GUID Generator

This shows how to code the random GUID generator:

```
/*
 * RandomGUID from http://www.javaexchange.com/aboutRandomGUID.html
 * @version 1.2.1 11/05/02
 * @author Marc A. Mnich
 *
 * From www.JavaExchange.com, Open Software licensing
 *
 * 11/05/02 -- Performance enhancement from Mike Dubman.
 *             Moved InetAddr.getLocal to static block. Mike has measured
 *             a tenfold improvement in runtime.
 * 01/29/02 -- Bug fix: Improper seeding of nonsecure Random object
 *             caused duplicate GUIDs to be produced. Random object
 *             is now created only once per JVM.
 * 01/19/02 -- Modified random seeding and added new constructor
```

```
*               to allow secure random feature.
* 01/14/02 -- Added random function seeding with JVM runtime
*
* NOTE:
*
* 06/24/2004 -- adopted by Mahmoud Parsian.
*/

import java.net.InetAddress;
import java.net.UnknownHostException;
import java.security.MessageDigest;
import java.security.NoSuchAlgorithmException;
import java.security.SecureRandom;
import java.util.Random;
/*
 * In the multitude of java GUID generators, I found none that
 * guaranteed randomness. GUIDs are guaranteed to be globally unique
 * by using Ethernet MACs, IP addresses, time elements, and sequential
 * numbers. GUIDs are not expected to be random and most often are
 * easy/possible to guess given a sample from a given generator.
 * SQL Server, for example, generates GUID that are unique but
 * sequential within a given instance.
 *
 * GUIDs can be used as security devices to hide things such as
 * files within a file system where listings are unavailable (e.g., files
 * that are served up from a Web server with indexing turned off).


 * Another example is using GUIDs for primary keys in a database
 * where you want to ensure that the keys are secret. Random GUIDs can
 * then be used in a URL to prevent hackers (or users) from accessing
 * records by guessing or simply by incrementing sequential numbers.
 *
 * There are many other possibilities of using GUIDs in the realm of
 * security and encryption where the element of randomness is important.
 * This class was written for these purposes but can also be used as a
 * general-purpose GUID generator as well.
 *
 * RandomGUID generates truly random GUIDs by using the system's
 * IP address (name/IP), system time in milliseconds (as an integer),
 * and a very large random number joined together in a single String
 * that is passed through an MD5 hash. The IP address and system time
 * make the MD5 seed globally unique, and the random number guarantees
 * that the generated GUIDs will have no discernable pattern and
 * cannot be guessed given any number of previously generated GUIDs.
 * It is generally not possible to access the seed information (IP, time,
 * random number) from the resulting GUIDs, as the MD5 hash algorithm
 * provides one-way encryption.
 *
 * ----> Security of RandomGUID: <-----
 * RandomGUID can be called one of two ways -- with the basic java Random
 * number generator or a cryptographically strong random generator
 * (SecureRandom). The choice is offered because the secure random
 * generator takes about 3.5 times longer to generate its random numbers,
 * and this performance hit may not be worth the added security
 * especially considering the basic generator is seeded with a
 * cryptographically strong random seed.
 *
```

```
 * Seeding the basic generator in this way effectively decouples
 * the random numbers from the time component, making it virtually impossible
 * to predict the random number component even if one had absolute knowledge
 * of the System time. Thanks to Ashutosh Narhari for the suggestion
 * of using the static method to prime the basic random generator.
 *
 * Using the secure random option, this class complies with the statistical
 * random number generator tests specified in FIPS 140-2, Security
 * Requirements for Cryptographic Modules, section 4.9.1.
 *
 * I converted all the pieces of the seed to a String before handing
 * it over to the MD5 hash so that you could print it out to make
 * sure it contains the data you expect to see and to give a nice
 * warm fuzzy. If you need better performance, you may want to stick
 * to byte[] arrays.
 *
 * I believe that it is important that the algorithm for
 * generating random GUIDs be open for inspection and modification.
 * This class is free for all uses.
 *
 *
 * - Marc
 */
public class RandomGUID extends Object {

    public String valueBeforeMD5 = "";


    private static SecureRandom mySecureRand;

    private static String s_id;

    /*
     * Static block to take care of one time secureRandom seed.
     * It takes a few seconds to initialize SecureRandom.  You might
     * want to consider removing this static block or replacing
     * it with a "time since first loaded" seed to reduce this time.
     * This block will run only once per JVM instance.
     */

    static {
        mySecureRand = new SecureRandom();
        long secureInitializer = mySecureRand.nextLong();
        myRand = new Random(secureInitializer);
        try {
            s_id = InetAddress.getLocalHost().toString();
        } catch (UnknownHostException e) {
            e.printStackTrace();
        }

    }


    /*
     * Default constructor. With no specification of security option,
     * this constructor defaults to lower security, higher performance.
     */
```

```java
public RandomGUID() {
    getRandomGUID(false);
}

/*
 * Constructor with security option. Setting secure true
 * enables each random number generated to be cryptographically
 * strong. Secure false defaults to the standard Random function seeded
 * with a single cryptographically strong random number.
 */
public RandomGUID(boolean secure) {
    getRandomGUID(secure);
}

/*
 * Method to generate the random GUID
 */
private void getRandomGUID(boolean secure) {
    MessageDigest md5 = null;
    StringBuffer sbValueBeforeMD5 = new StringBuffer();

    try {
        md5 = MessageDigest.getInstance("MD5");
    } catch (NoSuchAlgorithmException e) {
        System.out.println("Error: " + e);
    }


        long time = System.currentTimeMillis();
        long rand = 0;

        if (secure) {
            rand = mySecureRand.nextLong();
        } else {
            rand = myRand.nextLong();
        }

        // This StringBuffer can be as long as you need; the MD5
        // hash will always return 128 bits. You can change
        // the seed to include anything you want here.
        // You could even stream a file through the MD5, making
        // the odds of guessing it at least as great as that
        // of guessing the contents of the file!
        sbValueBeforeMD5.append(s_id);
        sbValueBeforeMD5.append(":");
        sbValueBeforeMD5.append(Long.toString(time));
        sbValueBeforeMD5.append(":");
        sbValueBeforeMD5.append(Long.toString(rand));

        valueBeforeMD5 = sbValueBeforeMD5.toString();
        md5.update(valueBeforeMD5.getBytes());

        byte[] array = md5.digest();
        StringBuffer sb = new StringBuffer();
        for (int j = 0; j < array.length; ++j) {
            int b = array[j] & 0xFF;
            if (b < 0x10) sb.append('0');
```

```java
                sb.append(Integer.toHexString(b));
        }

        valueAfterMD5 = sb.toString();

    } catch (Exception e) {
        System.out.println("Error:" + e);
    }
}


/*
 * Convert to the standard format for GUID
 * (Useful for SQL Server UniqueIdentifiers, etc.)
 * Example: C2FEEEAC-CFCD-11D1-8B05-00600806D9B6
 */
public String toString() {
    String raw = valueAfterMD5.toUpperCase();
    StringBuffer sb = new StringBuffer();
    sb.append(raw.substring(0, 8));
    sb.append("-");
    sb.append(raw.substring(8, 12));
    sb.append("-");
    sb.append(raw.substring(12, 16));
    sb.append("-");
    sb.append(raw.substring(16, 20));


    return sb.toString();
}

/**
 * Return a random GUID.
 */
public static String getGUID() {
    RandomGUID myGUID = new RandomGUID();
    return myGUID.valueAfterMD5;
}

/*
 * For Debugging purposes only.
 * Demonstraton and self-test of class.
 */
public static void main(String args[]) {
    // 64A4DD34-78C2-FB3C-7075-5198CB9C7868
    // 64a4dd3478c2fb3c70755198cb9c7868
    long  start = System.currentTimeMillis();
    for (int i=0; i< 10; i++) {
        RandomGUID myGUID = new RandomGUID();
        //System.out.println("Seeding String=" + myGUID.valueBeforeMD5);
        System.out.println("rawGUID=" + myGUID.valueAfterMD5);
        //System.out.println("RandomGUID=" + myGUID.toString());
    }
    long  end = System.currentTimeMillis();
    long time = end - start;
    System.out.println("time="+time);
```

```
        //String oneMoreGUID = RandomGUID.getGUID();
        //System.out.println("oneMoreGUID=" + oneMoreGUID);

    }
}
```

Testing the Random GUID Generator

This tests the random GUID generator:

```
$ javac RandomGUID.java
$ java RandomGUID
rawGUID=bdc8f9750d2c7dd06670082019a6d7fd
rawGUID=a5ad65c353abc36a28e689465ac7c1c4
rawGUID=c7be28ef811efa14704f0f7bfd455e22
rawGUID=1e2ddf6453ac6ce65333cc52b8dc9910
rawGUID=36a7903c45fabb3f1ce398effc102594
rawGUID=4aec56173827af462050e8f88979ce3b
rawGUID=fc0c91bddd4ef325d5a842fd10a1e2fd
rawGUID=60ae4f6d558d3d9db5a01f7e618c67dc
rawGUID=c668c167b6d79e14d0e36374b524b736
rawGUID=d6141ddb58b96a75d94ceac49bf98b51
time=20
```

As you can see, RandomGUID is fast: it created ten GUIDs in twenty milliseconds.

Index

forums.apress.com

JOIN THE APRESS FORUMS AND BE PART OF OUR COMMUNITY. You'll find discussions that cover topics of interest to IT professionals, programmers, and enthusiasts just like you. If you post a query to one of our forums, you can expect that some of the best minds in the business—especially Apress authors, who all write with *The Expert's Voice*™—will chime in to help you. Why not aim to become one of our most valuable participants (MVPs) and win cool stuff? Here's a sampling of what you'll find:

DATABASES

Data drives everything.

Share information, exchange ideas, and discuss any database programming or administration issues.

PROGRAMMING/BUSINESS

Unfortunately, it is.

Talk about the Apress line of books that cover software methodology, best practices, and how programmers interact with the "suits."

INTERNET TECHNOLOGIES AND NETWORKING

Try living without plumbing (and eventually IPv6).

Talk about networking topics including protocols, design, administration, wireless, wired, storage, backup, certifications, trends, and new technologies.

WEB DEVELOPMENT/DESIGN

Ugly doesn't cut it anymore, and CGI is absurd.

Help is in sight for your site. Find design solutions for your projects and get ideas for building an interactive Web site.

Hang out and discuss Java in whatever flavor you choose: J2SE, J2EE, J2ME, Jakarta, and so on.

Discuss computer and network security issues here. Just don't let anyone else know the answers!

MAC OS X

All about the Zen of OS X.

OS X is both the present and the future for Mac apps. Make suggestions, offer up ideas, or boast about your new hardware.

TECHNOLOGY IN ACTION

Cool things. Fun things.

It's after hours. It's time to play. Whether you're into LEGO® MINDSTORMS™ or turning an old PC into a DVR, this is where technology turns into fun.

OPEN SOURCE

Source code is good; understanding (open) source is better.

Discuss open source technologies and related topics such as PHP, MySQL, Linux, Perl, Apache, Python, and more.

WINDOWS

No defenestration here.

Ask questions about all aspects of Windows programming, get help on Microsoft technologies covered in Apress books, or provide feedback on any Apress Windows book.

HOW TO PARTICIPATE:

Go to the Apress Forums site at **http://forums.apress.com/**.
Click the New User link.